FREE FRANCE'S LION

FREE FRANCE'S LION

*The Life of Philippe Leclerc,
de Gaulle's Greatest General*

WILLIAM MORTIMER MOORE

CASEMATE
Philadelphia & Newbury

Published in the United States of America and Great Britain in 2011 by
CASEMATE PUBLISHERS
908 Darby Road, Havertown, PA 19083
and
17 Cheap Street, Newbury RG14 5DD

ISBN 978-1-61200-068-8
Digital Edition: ISBN 978-1-61200-080-0

Cataloging-in-publication data is available from the Library of Congress
and the British Library.

10 9 8 7 6 5 4 3 2 1

Printed and bound in the United States of America.

For a complete list of Casemate titles please contact:

CASEMATE PUBLISHERS (US)
Telephone (610) 853-9131, Fax (610) 853-9146
E-mail: casemate@casematepublishing.com

CASEMATE PUBLISHERS (UK)
Telephone (01635) 231091, Fax (01635) 41619
E-mail: casemate-uk@casematepublishing.co.uk

MIX
Paper from
responsible sources
FSC® C011935
FSC
www.fsc.org

CONTENTS

*In memory of my great uncle, Geoffrey Bles, 1886–1957,
publisher of CS Lewis, Vicki Baum, Maria von Trapp and many others.*

FOREWORD

One of the central and most tragic consequences of France's defeat, surrender and occupation in 1940 was the range of practical and moral choices that confronted French soldiers of equal patriotism. The constantly changing complexities of real life seldom offer clearcut moments of decision between courses of action with predictable, black-or-white consequences. The continuum of French politico-military history between 1940 and 1962 shows many examples of individuals choosing–under the practical and emotional pressures of the moment, and often for uncynical motives – paths that would lead them into unanticipated positions. The malign consequences of these choices could spoil (or even end) lives, and created spirals of hatred that lasted for more than the next generation.

In the English language there are few accounts of that period that are thorough enough to carry us back beyond the easy conclusions of hindsight, and thus to correct any hasty tendency to judge the men who shaped it in simplistic terms. This book is one of them–although it must be said at once that one of the author's advantages, and the reader's pleasures, is that its subject was as unambiguously admirable as any of the leading figures in French affairs during the 1940s. Philippe de Hautcloque, remembered by his *nom-de-guerre* of Leclerc, was not only an honourable and skillful soldier, but also an attractive personality.

Wounded during the Battle of France in spring 1940, he twice escaped German captivity by exercising nerve and physical daring. He was of exactly the class and *milieu* to which Marshal Pétain's Vichy regime, established in late June, should have had its strongest appeal—indeed, the extended de Hautcloque family was itself divided in its loyalites; yet when he was told of General De Gaulle's broadcast from London, Leclerc unhesitatingly decided to risk everthing for the splendid but then-tiny flag of Free France. By August 1940 he was leading half-a-dozen men on a 'James Bond' mission in French West Africa, and by the end of that year he was organizing the first raids against the Italians in southern Libya, in co-operation with the British Long Range Desert Group. For the next two years, drawing upon his early experience of colonial soldiering in southern Morocco, he pursued the often frustrating task of building up a multi-national Free French brigade in this remote and fly-blown pre-Saharan backwater, and sending it into battle in realistic increments. It was a task that demanded, and revealed, all his energy and intelligence, and the charismatic powers of leadership that enabled him to forge an effective group of subordinates from a wide spectrum of backgrounds, from Catholic aristocrats like himself to brawlers like the future paratroop general Jacques Massu.

When, in January 1943, Leclerc led his brigade northwards to join British Eighth Army in Tripolitania, this proud Frenchman even managed to cement a tolerably good relationship with the blindly undiplomatic General Montgomery. He was unshaken in his loyalty to De Gaulle during the intensely difficult period following the Anglo-American landings in French Morocco and Algeria, which led to bitter hostility between the 'Gaullists of the first hour' and Vichy's French African Army. In August 1944 it was Leclerc's 2nd Armoured Division that was given the honour of liberating central Paris, and by VE-Day his prestige among the Fighting French was unrivalled, despite the more senior command held by Jean de Lattre at the head of troops who had mostly only got back into the war on the right side in early 1943.

While Leclerc was as decisive as any successful officer must be, one of his rarer qualities was the ability to change his opinions when they were contradicted by experience on the ground. He displayed this quality most strikingly during his senior command in French Indochina in 1946. Unlike

General De Gaulle, his experience of soldiering in co-operation with the British and Americans in World War II had not left Leclerc with the former's often paranoid suspicion of the 'Anglo-Saxons', and he was able to work constructively with Admiral Mounbatten in 1945. Nevertheless, he was at first unable to share British scepticism about the recreation of the pre-war white colonial empires in Asia, and he landed in Saigon determined to achieve as much as he could for De Gaulle. He achieved a good deal, despite his inadequate military resources; but he also proved himself open to arguments and analysis from a number of quarters, both French and Indochinese.

It takes a most unusual soldier to move beyond the aggressively patriotic instincts that have served him well in the past, and to develop a clear-eyed, long-term view of the political dimensions of his theatre of operations—and this, while men under his command are actually fighting and dying. That Leclerc's heartfelt advice to his successor Emile Bollaert—'Negotiate; above all, negotiate'—was in the end to come to nothing condemned France (and after her, the United States) to decades of costly sacrifices, for no eventual reward. Leclerc's premature death in late 1947 robbed France of an intelligent, faithful and upright servant, whose prestige might have given weight to advice that a succession of weak governments would sorely need during the 1950s.

The author's research into a life lived among the movers and shakers of a period of great complexity has been admirably deep and wide, and he presents his clear, fair-minded and balanced conclusions in an extremely readable text, full of insights into the characters and relationships that shaped the events that he unfolds. This book is the work of a fine historian and a fine writer.

MARTIN WINDROW
Author of *The Last Valley: Dien Bien Phu
and the French Defeat in Vietnam*

MAPS

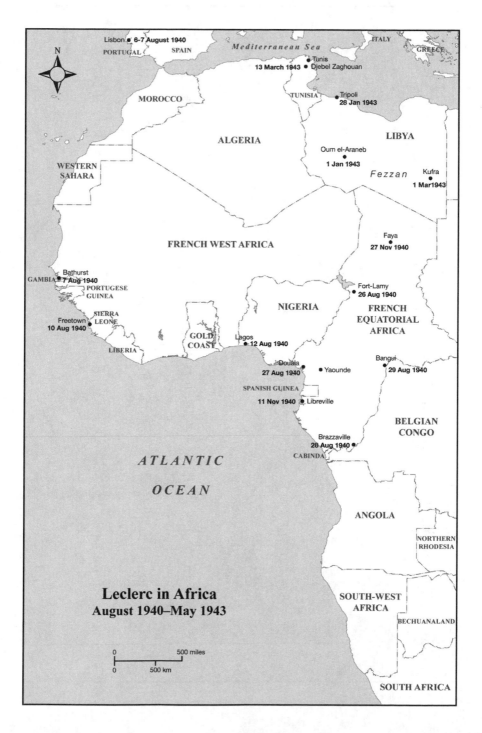

Leclerc in Africa
August 1940–May 1943

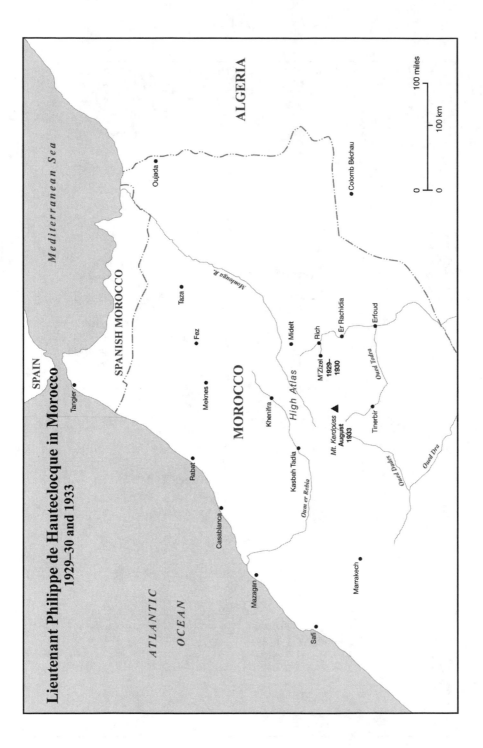

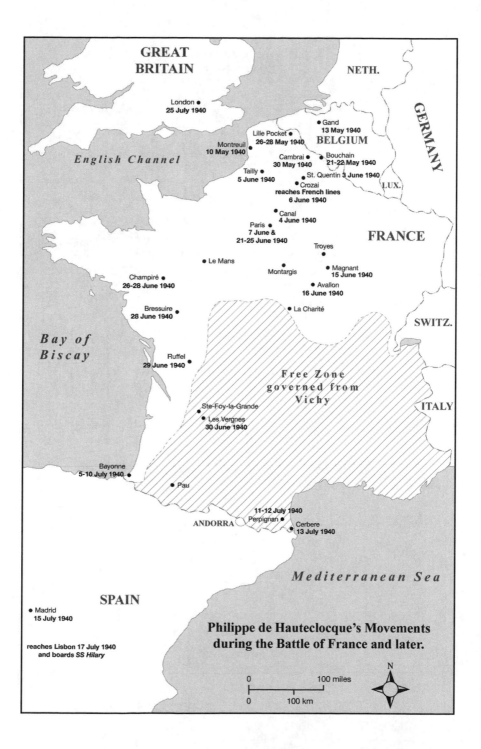

Philippe de Hauteclocque's Movements during the Battle of France and later.

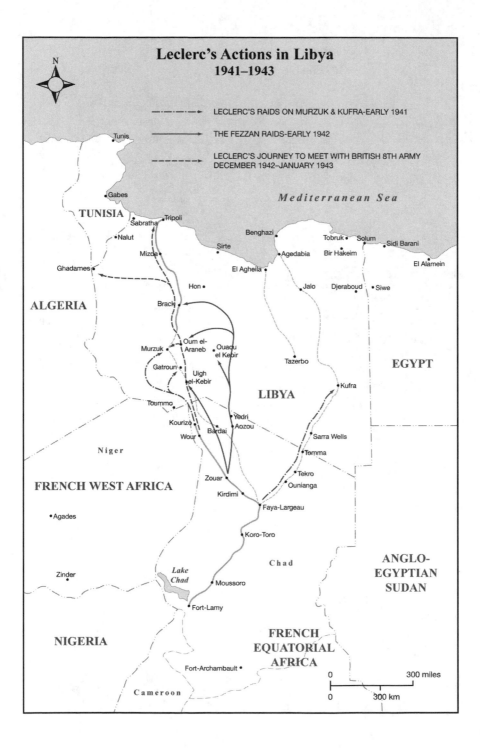

Leclerc's Actions in Libya
1941–1943

N

– · – · – · –→ LECLERC'S RAIDS ON MURZUK & KUFRA–EARLY 1941

————→ THE FEZZAN RAIDS–EARLY 1942

– – – – –→ LECLERC'S JOURNEY TO MEET WITH BRITISH 8TH ARMY
DECEMBER 1942–JANUARY 1943

Mediterranean Sea

Tunis

Gabes

TUNISIA

Sabratha   Tripoli

Nalut

Mizde   Sirte   Benghazi   Tobruk   Solum

Sidi Barani

Agedabia   Bir Hakeim

Ghadames   El Agheila   El Alamein

Hon

ALGERIA   Brack   Jalo   Djeraboud   Siwe

Oum el-
Araneb   Ouaou
el Kebir

Murzuk   Tazerbo   **EGYPT**

Gatroun   Uigh
el-Kebir

Toummo   **LIBYA**   Kufra

Kourizo   Yedri
Bardai   Aozou

Wour   Sarra Wells

Niger   Temma

FRENCH WEST AFRICA   Zouar   Tekro

Kirdimi   Ounianga

Faya-Largeau

Agades   Koro-Toro

**ANGLO-
EGYPTIAN
SUDAN**

Zinder   *Lake
Chad*   *Chad*

Moussoro

Fort-Lamy

NIGERIA   **FRENCH
EQUATORIAL
AFRICA**

Fort-Archambault

0   300 miles

0   300 km

Cameroon

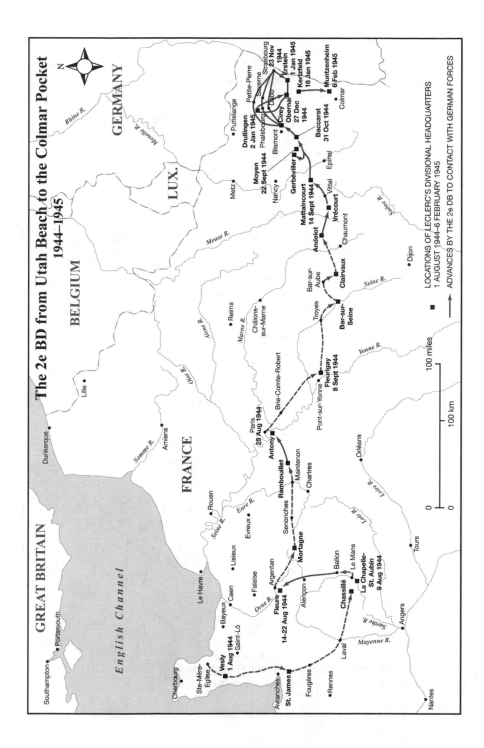

The 2e BD from Utah Beach to the Colmar Pocket
1944-1945

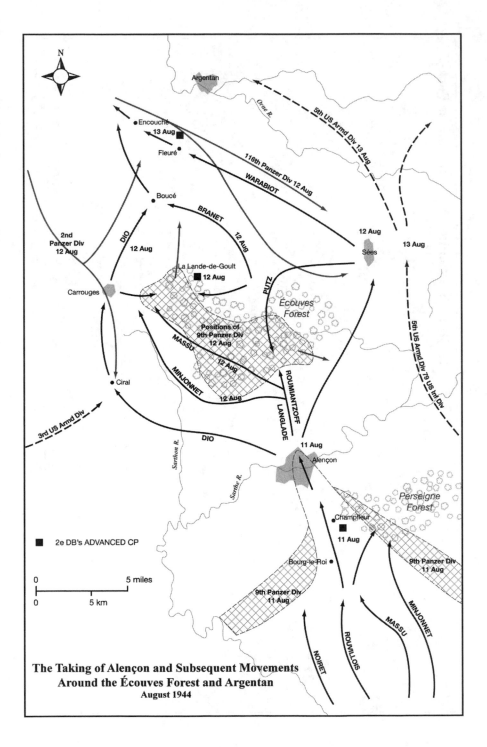

**The Taking of Alençon and Subsequent Movements
Around the Écouves Forest and Argentan**
August 1944

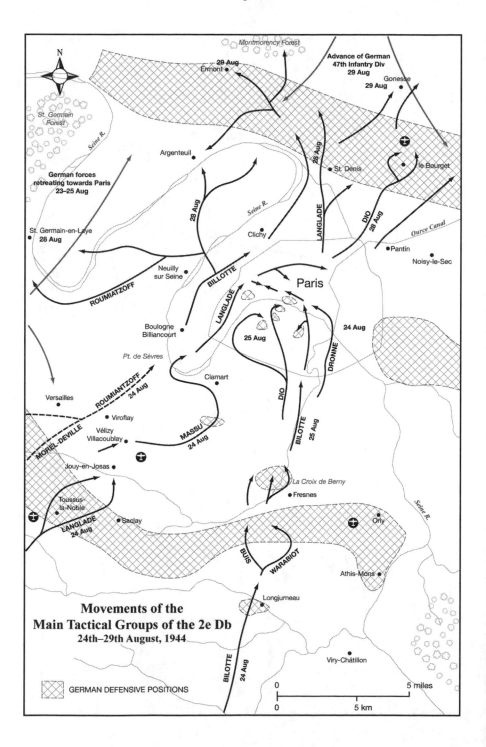

Montmorency Forest

Advance of German
47th Infantry Div
29 Aug

28 Aug
Ermont

Gonesse
29 Aug

St. Germain
Forest

Seine R.

German forces
retreating towards Paris
23–25 Aug

Argenteuil

28 Aug

St. Denis

le Bourget

28 Aug

LANGLADE

DIO
28 Aug

Ource Canal

St. Germain-en-Laye
28 Aug

Seine R.

Clichy

Pantin

Noisy-le-Sec

ROUMIATZOFF

Neuilly
sur Seine

BILLOTTE

Paris

Pt. de Sèvres

Boulogne
Billiancourt

LANGLADE

24 Aug

25 Aug

DRONNE

ROUMIANTZOFF
24 Aug

Clamart

Versailles

Viroflay

DIO

Vélizy
Villacoublay

MASSU
24 Aug

BILLOTTE
25 Aug

MOREL-DEVILLE

Jouy-en-Josas

La Croix de Berny

Fresnes

Seine R.

Toussus-
la-Noble

Saclay

Orly

LANGLADE
24 Aug

BUIS

WARABIOT

Athis-Mons

**Movements of the
Main Tactical Groups of the 2e Db**
24th–29th August, 1944

Longjumeau

BILLOTTE
24 Aug

Viry-Châtillon

0   5 miles

0   5 km

GERMAN DEFENSIVE POSITIONS

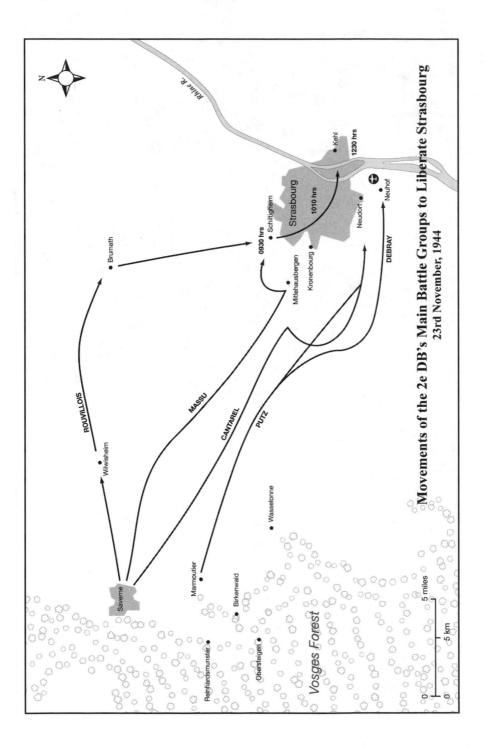

Movements of the 2e DB's Main Battle Groups to Liberate Strasbourg
23rd November, 1944

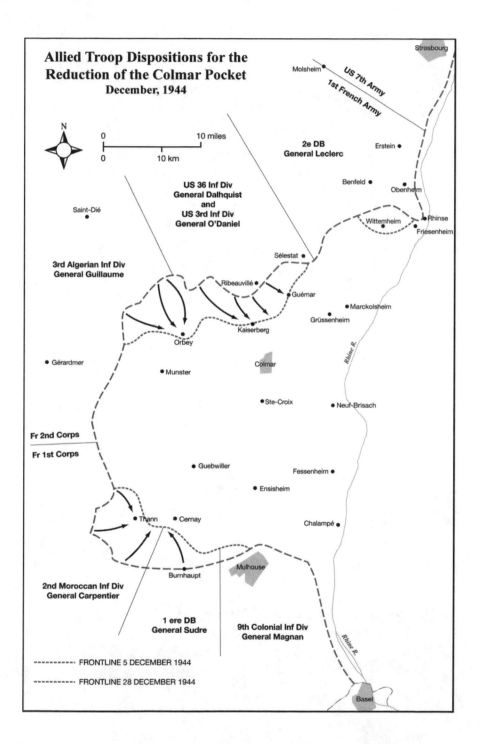

**Allied Troop Dispositions for the
Reduction of the Colmar Pocket**
December, 1944

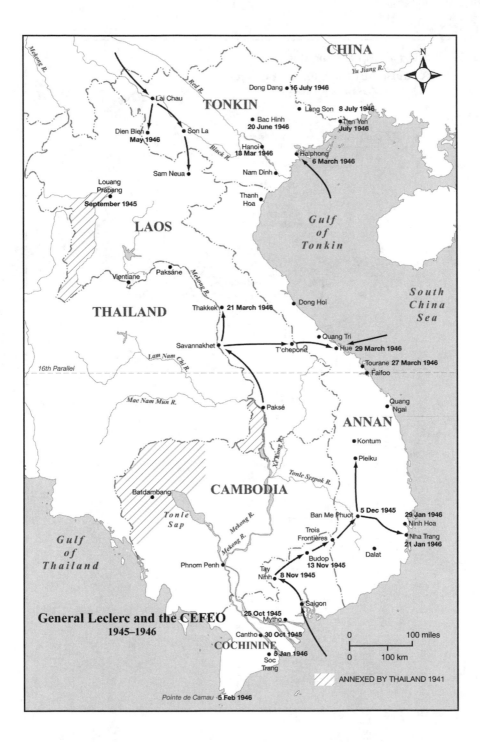

CHINA

Yu Jiang R.

Dong Dang ● **15 July 1946**

TONKIN

Lang Son ● **8 July 1946**

● Bac Hinh
20 June 1946

Tien Yen ●
July 1946

Lai Chau ●

Dien Bien ●   ● Son La
May 1946

Hanoi ●
18 Mar 1946

● Haiphong
6 March 1946

Sam Neua ●

Nam Dinh ●

Thanh
Hoa ●

*Gulf
of
Tonkin*

Louang
Prabang ●
September 1945

LAOS

Vientiane ●   ● Paksane

Mekong R.

THAILAND

Thakkek ● **21 March 1946**

● Dong Hoi

*South
China
Sea*

Lam Nam Chi R.

Savannakhet ●   T'chepone ●   ● Quang Tri
                              Hue ● **29 March 1946**

16th Parallel   Tourane ● **27 March 1946**
                              ● Faifoo

Mae Nam Mun R.

Paksé ●

Quang
Ngai ●

ANNAN

● Kontum

● Pleiku

CAMBODIA

Tonle Srepok R.

Batdambang ●

*Tonle
Sap*

Ban Me Phuot ● **5 Dec 1945**   **29 Jan 1946**
                              ● Ninh Hoa
Trois
Frontières ●   Nha Trang
                              21 Jan 1946
          Budop
          13 Nov 1945   ● Dalat

*Gulf
of
Thailand*

Phnom Penh ●

Tay
Ninh ●   **8 Nov 1945**

Mekong R.

● Saigon

**General Leclerc and the CEFEO
1945–1946**

25 Oct 1945
Mytho ●
Cantho ● **30 Oct 1945**

COCHININE

● **5 Jan 1946**
Soc
Trang

0 ——————— 100 miles

0 ——————— 100 km

▨ ANNEXED BY THAILAND 1941

Pointe de Camau **5 Feb 1946**

DEATH IN THE DESERT

Madame la Générale Thérèse Leclerc de Hauteclocque knew her husband was wilting with exhaustion. It had been almost nine years since he last spent Christmas at home; nine years during which he never stopped at the business of war and she barely saw him. Now, in late November 1947, with France falling into the grip of the worst winter on record and his health worn down by recurrent malaria, Leclerc was off again. This time it was a tour of Algeria following his appointment a few months earlier as inspector of armed forces in French North Africa. But Thérèse let him sleep late the morning he was due to leave; Leclerc had his own aircraft which could hardly take off without him.

"I was ill, wasn't I?" he asked, wakening.

"Yes," replied Thérèse.

"No longer any good to my country."

"But," teased Thérèse, using an Aquinas-style metaphor, "it is when the sieve is well used that grace flows through best."

"You're right," said the general looking at his wife gently.[1]

Within an hour, having sung the *Magnificat* together, she was seeing her husband, uniformed and breakfasted, to the door of their Avenue Kléber apartment. The general's Horch motor car (booty from Hitler's mountain retreat two years earlier) waited outside. Once soldier-servant

Louis Loustalot had loaded his luggage, Thérèse kissed her husband *adieu* and waved him off into the morning darkness.

At Villacoublay military airport where his personal aircraft, a converted B-25 Mitchell bomber, was waiting, Leclerc was joined by some of his team: three artillery colonels, Théodore Fieschi, Charles Clementin, and Louis du Garreau de la Mécherie. From the navy came Captain Georges Frichement; and from the air force came Commandant Michel Meyrand, a veteran of the "Free French" *Bretagne* bomber group. Last and youngest was Leclerc's new *aide de camp*, Lieutenant Robert Miron de l'Espinay.

The morning began badly. Freezing conditions had solidified the lubricant in the starboard motor, preventing take-off until almost noon. Leclerc was used to such hiccups, but many thought he seemed less cheerful than usual.[2] Following his liberation of Paris on the Feast of St. Louis three years earlier, fame weighed heavily on him. Post-war France, disillusioned and paralysed by strikes, was back to its old emnities. The Parisian *beau monde* hoped Leclerc would retake command of his division, the famous 2e DB (2nd Armoured) and push General de Gaulle back into government, like the grenadiers had pushed Napoleon Bonaparte into power during *Brumaire* 1799. But de Gaulle would never have retaken office in such a way.[3] Nor, unless "*l'interet générale*," (the general interest) forced him to act in politically charged situations, was Leclerc a politician. Unsurprisingly he found the patriotism of soldiers purer. Perhaps seeing old faces would do him good.

Once airborne, the flight to Oran was uneventful. Manoeuvres were already underway with "blue" forces invading "red" territory, simulating an insurgency around the coastal towns of La Marta, Port-aux-Poules and Arzew. Trite stuff compared to the guerrilla war facing France in Indo-China, but soldiers have to be trained. After casting a weary eye over these proceedings for a day and a half, Leclerc gathered the officers around him.

"I know very well that in the present circumstances, unrest and incidents can take a toll of your spirits. For those in Indo-China the situation is clear: it's war. One fights or one prepares for combat. For you it's different; it isn't war, it isn't peace either, and one has to await grave developments at a time that no one can foresee. . . . One simply has to hold on, to keep making an effort with no let-up. I can confirm to you that the army is in the process of retaking the position it ought to have and refinding in the nation the respect that it should never have lost."[4]

Two years after the Second World War, and with two decolonisation wars escalating inexorably, France's humiliation of 1940 was burnt into Leclerc's soul. But what was the "nation"? France was as bitterly divided as she had been during the 1930s. The latest wave of strikes had even crossed the Mediterranean.

"Would the army be available to keep railways running in French North Africa?" the Prefect of the Oranais asked him.

"Naturally, if ordered."[5]

Remaining in Arzew till mid-morning to drape General Conne with the ribbon of the Companion of the Légion d'Honneur, it was nearly 10am before Leclerc reached La Sénia airfield south of Oran. The town of Colomb-Béchar, two hours flight to the southwest, was next stop for a parade, followed by distribution of couscous to combat veterans.

Leclerc originally intended to take General Olleris to Colomb-Béchar with him, but amid the growing unrest Olleris did not want to be too far from Algiers. Leclerc's aircraft therefore had a free seat. Seeing Colonel Paul Fouchet on La Sénia's little concourse, Leclerc hailed him.

"You are the only person who knows the southern territories. Come with us, you'll be useful."

Fouchet, a veteran *méhariste* (camel soldier), who age now confined to attaché appointments, accepted gladly.[6]

The crew of Leclerc's aircraft, pilot Lieutenant Francois Delluc, navigator Lieutenant André Pilleboue, mechanic Warrant Officer Jean Guillou and radioman Staff-Sergeant Eugene Lamotte, were lined up to welcome him. General Olleris watched as Leclerc approached his aircraft. A cold, circling wind was whipping grit into a light sandstorm.

"What's the weather information?" asked Leclerc.

"Windspeed at forty to fifty kilometres and quickening. Sandstorm on all routes," said Delluc matter of factly.

Leclerc looked him in the eye. Delluc was an experienced pilot with a solid "Free French" career behind him flying Halifax bombers with the RAF.

"Even so, we're going," insisted Leclerc, who was not used to letting the weather stop him.

Perhaps it was weakness. Perhaps Delluc did not want to countermand

Leclerc in front of others. Perhaps his personality was not strong enough to face down someone as strong-willed as Leclerc.

"Yes, *mon général*," replied Delluc, in a manner which seemed to General Olleris lacking in enthusiasm.[7] Yet earlier Delluc had told Lt. Paul Burlet (pilot of a war booty Junkers-52 also at La Sénia that morning), "We're going to Colomb-Béchar to take a look. If we can't land we'll come back."[8]

Leclerc's B-25, named *Tailly II* after his home in Picardy, took off at 10.15am just as the wind whipped the fine sand of the Grand Erg Occidental into a soup of grit swirling high above western Algeria.

Sandstorm or no, on Colomb-Béchar's camel square the area's *gratin*—upper crust—were gathering for the parade. Leclerc's arrival would be biggest thing since the inauguration of the Mediterranean-Niger railway in 1941, and Colonel Quénard, the military district commander, wanted to make a splash for Leclerc's visit. A camel patrol was coming in from Maghzen and a *goum* from Abadla, along with two Saharan companies and two platoons of the Foreign Legion.

The manpower of the Legion had changed dramatically in seven years. Whereas the majority of Foreign Legionaires who served Free France were Spanish Republicans dedicated to defeating fascism, those now waiting to greet Leclerc were ninety percent Germans who preferred serving France to prisoner of war camps from which repatriation was slow.

Little is known of events aboard *Tailly II* just prior to the tragedy. There were no black box recorders in 1947. Perhaps Delluc got lost; the crash site is twenty-five kilometres east of the usual air route from Oran to Béchar. Ten minutes before their arrival time Delluc radioed, "All well on board, are six minutes from landing at Colomb-Béchar." Shortly afterwards a crisis must have occurred aboard the plane. In such situations it is common practice for pilots making forced landings in the desert to seek a road, track or railway for the very good reason that, even if they survive the landing they may not survive the thirsty wait to be picked up. Sensibly, Delluc tried to land *Tailly II* by the Mediterranean-Niger railway, but as the aircraft slowed for impact it exploded, throwing debris and human remains 100 metres around. A railway employee working nearby ran for help.

At Colomb-Béchar, the crowd waiting to greet "Leclerc the liberator" grew anxious. Ten minutes became twenty, twenty minutes became an hour. Some speculated idly that Leclerc had made a detour or stopped off. But once news of the crash came through, a shocked silence fell across the camel square. Lieutenant Coutin told his mainly German Legionaires to remount their trucks and head out along the railway. They were soon followed by Colonel Quénard, his adjutant, an ambulance and a salvage truck.

After reaching Menhaba railway station, Coutin's platoon were guided to the crash site. Seeing debris of all sizes, including the carcasses of two Wright radial engines blown thirty metres apart, it was clear that no one could have survived. High-octane aviation fuel makes a good explosive, and *Tailly II*'s tanks had been nearly full. Both Coutin and his company commander, Captain Schalk, were deeply affected by what they saw. Schalk had been at Saint-Cyr during the 1930s when Leclerc, or Captain de Hauteclocque as he then was, had been an instructor. Coutin had been with the Free French. Unscientifically, and with little regard for the methodology of modern crash investigation, German Legionaires began gathering France's dead, laying each victim on a tarpaulin.

Wehrmacht veteran Sergeant Horst Slesiona thought himself pretty hardened. Every corpse was badly calcinated and headless. Some were limbless as well.[9] Slesiona found Leclerc's trunk; recognisable thanks to his tunic remaining largely intact. His wallet contained identification papers, pictures of Thérèse, the family, and a dog. His left hand was recognisable thanks to his *chevalière* (signet ring), worn continental style on the left middle finger. Others were unrecognisably charred. Even veterans, however, can only take so much and eventually Slesiona asked for time alone.[10]

The news reached Paris quickly. It was a cold, foggy day in the French capital with an attempt at snow. Prime Minister Robert Schumann was among the first to be informed. "*Encore cela!*" he remarked, already vexed by the resignation of his Minister of Works, Daniel Mayer. At once, French President Vincent Auriol ordered his military secretary, General Grossin, to visit Thérèse Leclerc.

But it was Colonel Adolphe Vézinet and Captain Langlois de Bazillac, both *anciens* (veterans) of the 2e DB, who first called at 26 Avenue Kléber. Greeted by faithful Sergeant Loustalot, they were told that Thérèse was organising a charity sale at the 2e DB club. Without telling Loustalot the grim tidings, Vézinet and Langlois told him not to answer the door or telephone to anyone but *Madame la générale* or themselves before they set off to find Thérèse before anyone else did. Uncomprehendingly, Loustalot obeyed. But French reporters, not known for their tact, were soon clamouring outside and Louis Loustalot soon knew his general was dead.

"Loustalot, what's happening?" asked Jeanne, Leclerc's eldest daughter, from the doorway of her room.

Then Thérèse arrived, brushing past the ratpack to get into her home. She knew. Calmly she called Jeanne and her young son Bénédicte to her. They kneeled and prayed.

France Soir was the first to publish, altering its last edition to carry the story. Leclerc's second son, Hubert, learned the news on the Métro, reading the paper's front page over another passenger's shoulder, while Michel, still a schoolboy, discovered from a newsstand as he walked home.[11]

In the early evening, veteran Gaullist and "Free Frenchman" René Pleven arrived. As executor of Leclerc's will, Pleven assured Thérèse he would always be available to help her and the children. Next came General Grossin, offering the condolences of the state.

General Charles de Gaulle, the leader of Free France from 1940 to 1944—to whom Leclerc owed his short but brilliant career—had just returned from Paris with Madame de Gaulle and *aide* Claude Guy, an air force officer who joined him in the spring of 1944 after being wounded. Snow was falling when they arrived at La Boisserie in Colombey-les-deux-Églises. Getting out of the car, de Gaulle and his wife made a game of following their maids' footprints through the snow to their front door where they were welcomed by their cook, Philomène.

"Commandant de Bonneval telephoned," Philomène told Guy. "He wants you to call him back immediately."

Guy ensconced himself in the telephone booth under the stairs, which, in spite of La Boisserie's recent renovation, was also the log cupboard.

"We haven't yet got the final details," said Bonneval. "But everything leads us to conclude that General Leclerc was killed this afternoon in an aircraft accident."

The news had been confirmed by Leclerc's staff at Les Invalides. Seeing Guy's ashen face the *grand Charles* knew something was terribly wrong.

"Commandant de Bonneval asked me to tell you, *Mon general*. It seems that Leclerc has perished in an aircraft accident."

"What do you mean 'it seems that'?" de Gaulle snapped.

Guy repeated Bonneval's exact words. It was "ninety-nine percent certain that Leclerc was on that plane."

De Gaulle threw up his massive arms in one of his enormous gestures, then let them fall to his sides in an absolute expression of sadness.

"If it's true, it will be lamentable," he said, shuffling disconsolately into his library. For a while de Gaulle stared at the floor, absolutely downcast, before saying "It's a national catastrophe." Then he went to the phone booth himself where Bonneval was still on the line. "Are you there Bonneval?" Thinking aloud, he asked Bonneval to go with Gaston Palewski to pass on his condolences to Thérèse Leclerc. Instinctively, de Gaulle knew that both President Auriol and Schumann's government would want to give Leclerc a state funeral. If that was the case, de Gaulle, as France's only "political" general, would have to stay out of it.

A few moments later, de Gaulle asked Guy in an extraordinarily soft voice if Leclerc's aircraft was a Mitchell. Then, as he stood with one of Leclerc's last letters in his hand, de Gaulle speculated that there might have been an *"attentat,"* as assassinations are called in French and German. Then he read Leclerc's last letter aloud, which warned that it was only a matter of time before Communists began "operations" in French North Africa, and briefly the idea made sense.[12]

By the end of the day all Paris knew. Rumour-mongers claimed the crash was sabotage, comparable to the death of General Sikorski, suggesting that Communists had somehow put sugar in *Tailly II*'s fuel tanks. British novelist Nancy Mitford said as much in a letter to her sister Diana Mosley: "The whole population of Paris is certain it was sabotage and it's done the Communists a lot of harm."[13]

British Ambassador Duff Cooper knew as early as January 1944 that Leclerc was "the most popular man in France after de Gaulle."[14] He first met Leclerc the following April during arrangements to ship the 2e DB to England in time for the Normandy campaign, writing "a dapper little soldier exactly like an English officer, quiet and giving one the impression of competence. I told Leclerc and Vanier [Canadian ambassador to France] that I understood that it was almost certain that his division would go to England to take part in the invasion. He was naturally delighted to hear it."[15] Three and a half years later Cooper wrote, "During dinner came the

shocking news that Leclerc had been killed in an aircrash. It is a great loss
to France. I had known him very little until that recent day in the Black
Forest when we were shooting together. I had then liked him so much. He
was only 44."[16] In fact, Leclerc celebrated his 45th birthday six days before
his death.

Back in the south Oranais, the clean-up operation continued. By 8pm
Schalk's Legionaires had gathered every human remain they could and
delivered them to the mortuary of Colomb-Béchar's Quémeneur Hospital.
With little forensic experience, two military doctors, Captains Ardeber and
Rondreux, assisted by 2nd Lieutenant Dauphin of the Foreign Legion,
worked their way through fragments of bodies and clothes to piece together
the bodies of Leclerc and the other victims of the crash.

Being furthest from the fuel tanks when *Tailly II* exploded, the passengers were easiest to identify: Leclerc, Fouchet, du Garreau, Clementin,
Frichement and the mechanic Guillou were identified from personal
papers. Meyrand, Miron de l'Espinay and Fieschi were recognised from
their uniforms. The remains of aircrew Delluc, Pilleboue and Lamotte were
the most calcinated and, by the time the Legion's doctors had finished sort-
ing out twelve sets of remains for burial, there still seemed to be enough
body parts left for a thirteenth.[17] The following day, medical Colonel
Dudézert signed thirteen death certificates, the last for an unidentified victim. But an emergency order had already been placed in Algiers for only
twelve lead-lined coffins. To the annoyance of the White Fathers, the
hospital cloisters became an impromptu chapel where the coffins were laid
out for *colons* and military to pay their respects.[18]

At 11am in Colombey-les-Deux-Églises, Charles de Gaulle, sat down
somberly at his bureau. After more than three years at his side, Claude Guy
still had not learned to read de Gaulle's moods. Suddenly the night's
thoughts flowed out of him. "Leclerc's death is an incalculable loss for the
country," announced de Gaulle. "I loved him. Oh, he was headstrong
("*cabochard*") certainly. One can't be among the greats without being a bit
headstrong. But, you see, I will always remember *this* about him; he had
something that others don't often have—no sentiment in him, no thought,
no word, no gesture that was ever vulgar or mediocre. A year ago I asked
him to go to Africa. It was only reluctantly that he agreed. He was one of
the only ones, perhaps the only one, who would go on right to the end

over there without second thoughts." Looking down at his feet, de Gaulle murmured, "It's lamentable." Then, with a voice of resignation, "In the end, it's just too bad."

Removing a large sheet atlas from a bookshelf, de Gaulle laid it on Claude Guy's writing table, opened to northern Algeria.

"Yesterday evening," de Gaulle continued, "I thought it might be an assassination. But, on reflection, I do not think that is possible. If it had happened taking off from Oran, then yes. But why would such a tragedy happen out in the open so near their destination? No, I don't think so."

Returning to Leclerc's funeral, "Whatever the funeral arrangements," de Gaulle remarked to Guy, "they are going to be impressive, don't doubt it. In any case, Teitgen and other scatterbrains will have decided at once to put him in Les Invalides.

In which case I will be unable to take part in any ceremony."

"And if he is buried on his home ground?" asked Guy.

De Gaulle reflected: "In that case members of the government will still be there. Therefore I won't be able to go until the following day."

It was one of those moments when Claude Guy found de Gaulle infathomable. "That does not matter!" the *aide* protested. "The Companions of the Liberation will remain [loyal to] you; that would mean that they too appear the day after to associate themselves with your gesture . . ."[19]

"Oh, that's not certain," de Gaulle told Claude Guy, letting out a sigh of bitterness. "There's nothing to stop them turning up the day before me as well. You'll see them taking the train like everyone else."

Claude Guy protested further.

"In the end we will have to wait and see what's decided," de Gaulle said.[20]

Having resigned the French leadership in early 1946, hoping for reassurance from the French people that they still loved and needed him—a reassurance that did not come for another eleven years—de Gaulle thought it best to distance himself from matters of state. Perhaps he also thought Parisians should have their last day with their liberator free from political controversy. Yet de Gaulle's story was thoroughly entwined with that of Leclerc, the Picardian aristocrat who arrived at 4 Carlton Gardens with a bandaged head on 25th July 1940. Of all those Frenchmen who, like de Gaulle, refused to accept defeat after Marshal Pétain's Armistice, few encapsulated their uncompromising commitment like Philippe Leclerc.

Though normally immensely controlled, de Gaulle was capable of expressing deep feelings. Writing to Thérèse of his "immense pain," he continued with words rehearsed earlier: "I loved your husband; he was not only the companion of the worst and greatest days, but a dependable friend, incapable of any feeling, any action, any gesture, any word that betrayed the slightest mediocrity." Some thought such unusual effusiveness might have been the result of de Gaulle's emotions being in overdrive; his disabled daughter Anne's health was beginning to fail. (She died quite suddenly after catching double pneumonia in early 1948, another victim of that terrible winter.) In truth, he loved those whose support in the bleak days of 1940 had been reflexive and unconditional; not just Leclerc but men like Thierry d'Argenlieu, Pierre Billotte and his son-in-law Alain de Boissieu, who joined him as soon as they could without a second thought or moment's hesitation; even if such men could not always love each other.[21] It was partly comradeship, partly their commitment to his higher idea of France. On this Leclerc had been as one with de Gaulle. In person they also differed. It was not in Leclerc's nature to be rude or bloodyminded for the sake of it. Nor did Leclerc share de Gaulle's intense aversion to showing gratitude, or, if he did, he was tactful enough not to show it.

Before leaving Colomb-Béchar, a service of blessing was given for the dead men by White Fathers Bronner and Duvollet.[22] Another early member of "Free France," Bronner was present when Leclerc captured the Italian fort at Kufra in March 1941. Since French military law requires members of holy orders to bear arms at times of national danger, Bronner took his turn standing guard over "Free France's" first acquisition. Six years later, at the expense of making himself tiresome, Bronner ensured that the *colons* paid their respects to his former chief.

Fittingly, the steam engine taking the bodies to Algiers was called "Charles de Foucauld" after the religious mystic murdered at Tamanrasset in 1916, who had been an inspiration to Leclerc. For a man who had only been a staff captain seven years earlier, the itinerary north resembled the whistle-stop journey taken by President Roosevelt's body to Washington after his death at Warm Springs in April 1945. For two days the train halted at small towns and garrisons so *colons* could wave and clap. Happily or otherwise, Algeria still regarded itself as French at this time, and patriotic

Frenchmen needed something to be proud of. From 1940 until his death, Leclerc had provided that. Finally, on the evening of 2nd December, the "Charles de Foucauld" slid into Algiers railway station.[23]

As the press grappled over the mystery of the "thirteenth man," and rumours persisted of an assassination, the twelve coffins were laid out in the Salle Pierre Bordes, guarded by Companions of the Liberation, for the *gratin* of Algiers to file past. The following day, twelve White halftracks carried each coffin to the quayside where the cruiser *Émile Bertin* waited. After a eulogy from Governor-General Chataigneau and a blessing by the Archbishop of Algiers, the coffins were taken aboard. On the evening of 3rd December the *Émile Bertin* slipped its moorings to cross a raging Mediterranean Sea.[24]

After two days of heavy seas they reached Toulon to be welcomed by a picket of *Fusiliers Marins*, French marines, commanded by Ensign Philippe de Gaulle. To avoid using railways paralysed by industrial action (and sabotage which could be taken to murderous lengths), the coffins were driven to Paris in lorries under military escort, accompanied by a smart American limousine carrying Leclerc's eldest son, Henri Leclerc de Haute-clocque, and Colonel Fieschi's widow. Henri had just returned from Brazzaville, where General de Gaulle's son-in-law, Alain de Boissieu, and his family were also stationed. Flying in stages, a letter written by General Delange, one of his father's former officers, had finally caught up with him at Impfodo.[25] Throughout Metropolitan France the *Tricolore* was at half-mast; French armed forces would be officially in mourning until 12th December. As in Algeria, the French, both rich and poor, left and right wing, turned out along the route to watch the mortal remains of "Free" France's greatest soldier pass, until black ice forced them to halt for the night at Auxerre. Even strikers had doffed their caps.[26]

By early afternoon next day, the coffins reached the industrial town of Antony south of Paris, through which the 2e DB had entered the French capital three and a half years earlier. Welcomed by the Prefect of the Seine, the Military Governor of Paris, the Prefect of Police, the cortege was now escorted by a detachment of the famous Chad Regiment, the 2e DB's divisional infantry. President Auriol, due to lead the cortege from there, was delayed by government matters—coping with continuous resignations being a hallmark of his time in office—finally arriving at 6pm, long after dusk. Continuing along the route the 2e DB took on 25th August 1944, the cortege passed through the Porte d'Orléans moving on to the Place Denfert-Rochereau, where Leclerc had met up with General Jacques Chaban-Delmas, de Gaulle's delegate to the Paris resistance; then Boulevard Montparnasse and, finally, Les Invalides.

In this, de Gaulle's instincts, as aired to Claude Guy, had been correct. It had indeed been decided that Leclerc would be lain to rest alongside such men as Marshal Foch, Turenne and Vauban. Welcomed onto the front esplanade by floodlights, the coffins were greeted by armed forces minister Pierre-Henri Teitgen, his deputies and the post-liberation president of the Municipal Council, Pierre de Gaulle—brother of the general, whose presence signified the end of the old guard that had governed Paris through the 1930s and the Vichy era. Led by Sergeant Loustalot, who carried the 2e DB insignia decorated with the presidential citation, six veterans from the division carried Leclerc's coffin, now with a five-starred képi and his favourite walking stick "Baraka" lain over the *Tricolore*, into the choir of Saint-Louis des Invalides. The other eleven victims followed, attended by their families.[27]

De Gaulle had visited Thérèse five days earlier, on the evening of 2nd December. Departing, he became so emotional that he asked his wife, Yvonne, for support as he descended the front steps while wiping his eyes. Apart from praying at the foot of Leclerc's coffin, as planned, he played a small part in the proceedings despite a prompt from Prime Minister Schumann which the great man regarded as inappropriate. Claude Guy found him crying on several occasions following the tragedy. Leclerc's death had another effect on him; having been a lifelong chain smoker and reeking of tobacco all through the war, from 28th November 1947 de Gaulle never touched a cigarette again.[28]

"All Leclerc's boys are pouring into town," Nancy Mitford wrote to her sister, Diana. "It is like mobilisation. There will be 2,000 of them in Notre Dame."

Indeed it was like mobilisation. But Mitford underestimated; according to Leclerc's former operations officer, André Gribius, it was more like 10,000, two-thirds the 2e DB's strength.[29] Leclerc's Sherman command tank, *Tailly*, was polished and turned out along with the *Romilly*, one of three Sherman tanks that Lt. Michard, another soldier-priest, led into Paris on the evening of 24th August 1944. These would lead the parade, with Leclerc's coffin borne on the self-propelled gun *Alsace*, also from the 2e DB.

On Sunday, 7th December, Leclerc and the other victims left Les Invalides for the Champs Élysées, escorted by officers of the 2e DB. At the *rond-point* the cortege met up with "Leclerc's boys," some uniformed, some in a mix of uniform and mufti, but usually in a beret or forage cap, chests covered in medals. Formed up by regiment, they slow-marched their *chef* to the Arc de Triomphe. There, close to the Unknown Soldier, *Alsace* remained for eight hours while the French paid their respects and consoled with his family. Thérèse, dressed in black, looking washed out and forlorn, was supported by her children; the eldest, Henri, in uniform with the anchor badge of *La Coloniale* on his képi.

The day of the actual funeral, the 8th December, was set aside as a day of national mourning. Leading the foreign diplomats, British Ambassador Duff Cooper thought the presence of the other crash victims detracted from Leclerc's funeral and that each should have had his own ceremony. A valid viewpoint. However, despite the best efforts of surgeon captains Ardeber and Rondreux in Colomb-Béchar, and in the absence of DNA testing, it is inevitable that some body parts would have been mixed up. The French arrangement was more appropriate than Cooper realised.[30]

With every seat in Notre Dame taken, the coffins were welcomed into the great cathedral by the Archbishop of Paris, the same Cardinal Suhard that de Gaulle had barred from conducting the liberation service on 26th August 1944, believing him too tainted with collaboration. Behind Suhard were standard bearers with the forty colours for veterans' associations, and the regiments making up the 2e DB: the Chad Regiment (*Régiment de marche du Tchad*–RMT); the tank regiments 501e RCC, 12e Cuirassiers, 12e Chasseurs d'Afrique, the Spahis Marocains; the division's reconnaissance regiment; and, most extraordinary of all, the shipless sailors of the RBFM. Leclerc's anti-tank regiment had come from *La Royale*, the French Navy.

The passing of monarchy and the secularity of the French state meant that the great medieval cathedral of Notre Dame had little formal place in the political life of the nation any more. State funerals tended to be reserved only for presidents who died in office like the assassinated Sadi Carnot, stabbed to death by an Italian anarchist in 1894. But it would very much depend on the place a man held in the nation's heart. Rightly, de Gaulle regarded the state funeral given the collaborationist rabble rouser Philippe Henriot during the spring of 1944 as an aberration that Cardinal Suhard should never have allowed. However much "Free France" might have thought it deserved a turn, de Gaulle, being out of power, had little influence over such matters. Even so, a soldier normally had to be a Marshal of France like Foch or Joffre to merit a state funeral on such a scale. When he died, Leclerc was still a young general. But there was never any doubt among the mourners that day that Leclerc was immensely special to France and its history during the Second World War.

Following the Mass for the Dead, Leclerc, surrounded once again by veterans of the 2e DB, was carried out of the cathedral. Separated from his fellow crash victims, he was now on his own, as veterans, generals, clergy, students from Saint-Cyr and the Polytechnique fell into line to escort him on his last earthly journey to Les Invalides. Once the cortege had advanced onto the esplanade the great gates closed. Only Leclerc's family followed to the graveside. The following day *les cheminots*—the railwaymen—returned to work and the press turned their attention to the Paris-Arras train crash, which had claimed twenty lives five days earlier.

CHAPTER ONE

A TRUE SON OF FRANCE

For a man whose death united all classes in grief, Leclerc had begun life in the privileged upper stratum that typified "Old France." He officially adopted the name Leclerc in 1945 from the *nom de guerre* he had used since 1940, but he always stayed true to the traditional values of his up-bringing.

Born on 22 November 1902, he was christened Philippe Francois Marie de Hauteclocque, and was the fifth child and second son of Count and Countess Adrien de Hauteclocque of Chateau Belloy Saint Leonard in Picardy. His father, an aristocratic patriarch, ruled the locality, setting a traditional tone both for his family and the village he dominated. For Count Adrien the Third Republic, which followed Prussia's defeat of Napoleon III, was not good enough for *la belle France*. Yet, even in the days of monarchy, the Hauteclocque family usually preferred its own patch to hanging around court at Versailles or cavorting in Paris—a stance which attracted the nickname "*gentilhomme fesses-lièvres*" ("gentleman hare-buttocks") from flashier branches of the French aristocracy.

Even with industrial Amiens nearby, life at Belloy Saint Leonard was self-contained, time-warped and exclusive. The estate pack of hounds, the "Rallye Scarbon," attracted glamorous and influential guests including "Bendor,' the Duke of Westminster who courted Coco Chanel,[1] while

Count Adrien's love of deer and boar stalking often made him drive his Bugatti or Lancia to distant forests in eastern Europe.

More serious and reflective than his older brother, Philippe was educated at home until the age of thirteen. Count Adrien himself gave his younger son competent Latin lessons and, supported by a solid grounding in Catholic morals from the Countess and German from his Alsatian governess, Philippe rose to the top of his first year when he was sent to the Jesuit-run École de la Providence in Amiens. This Catholic education, so similar to de Gaulle's, was to be one of the most formative influences on Philippe's character.

The Hauteclocques were Papal counts, ennobled by Pius IX in 1857 for their longstanding support of Catholic interests. The title carried social prestige but no political rights, and eclipsed the rank of chevalier (the French equivalent of a baronet or hereditary knight), which had been bestowed on earlier branches of the family. When the Revolution of 1789 erupted, the Hauteclocques, having been *seigneurs* in Picardy for eight centuries, were undoubtedly at risk. Fortunately, Robespierre's Committee of Public Safety were after larger fish, and the family's only brush with "the Terror" was borne by Chevalier Francois Louis de Hauteclocque, who was imprisoned but not guillotined.

Of Chevalier de Hauteclocque's five sons, three served Napoleon: Stanislas, the eldest, fought at Essling and Saragossa; César, the second son, also fought in Prussia and Spain before serving the restored Bourbons until 1830; and Constantin, the third son, suffered such severe frostbite in his toes during the infamous retreat from Moscow that he was forced to resign his commission. Constantin, raised to *chevalier* by Louis XVIII and made Papal Count in 1857,[2] had two sons: Alfred Francois Marie (1822–1902) who died childless, and Gustave Francois Marie Joseph (1829–1914). In 1859 Gustave married Marie-Henriette de Morgan-Frondeville, producing three sons: Henry (1862–1914), Adrien (1864–1945) and Wallerand (1866–1914). Marie-Henriette, a strong and lively character, was also an heiress who brought a considerable fortune to the Hauteclocques, including the chateau of Belloy Saint Leonard.[3] Count Adrien's wife, Marie-Therese Van der Cruisse de Waziers (1870–1956), was also descended from a family of Papal counts, and sufficiently beautiful for her portrait to be exhibited at the Paris Salon of 1908.

Steeped in the traditions of France's Catholic aristocracy, it was naturally impossible for Philippe de Hauteclocque to conceive of a France where Catholic belief was not central to daily life. Religious practice was carried out with an intensity few outside holy orders would now recognise. Count Adrien's chateau was a place of *pries-dieux*, mantillas, crucifixes, and frequent prayer, where the encyclicals of nineteenth-century Catholicism were followed to the letter. When the new Third Republic attempted to sever the historic ties between church and state, families like the Hauteclocques felt compelled to express their quasi-medieval patriotism through Christian democracy. Bow as he must to political changes, the staunchly monarchist Count Adrien never allowed Bastille Day celebrations at Belloy, and increasingly adhered to the right wing views of Charles Maurras.

Maurras first made his name as an *anti-Dreyfusard* when a Jewish officer was falsely accused of spying for Germany. Like Maurras, the Hauteclocques were horrified that the predominantly Catholic and aristocratic officer corps should be attacked over the fate of a single officer, even if he was innocent! Following the success of his pamphlet *Enquete sur la monarchie*, Maurras launched the right-wing journal *Action Française* in 1908. *Action Française* quickly evolved into a highly influential movement, especially in the countryside. For the next thirty years, sons of the landed and business classes (*Camelots du Roi*, or "Peddlers of the King"), brandishing hawkers' licences issued by the *Gendarmerie*, sold the journal after Sunday Mass. Regarding itself as the standard bearer of "Old France" and taking the royal *fleur de lys* as its emblem, *Action Française* advocated restoration of the monachy, mystical devotion to *la Patrie*, and Christianity (preferably Catholicism), the recovery of the lost provinces of Alsace and Lorraine, and it also included a hefty dose of social—as distinct from murderous—anti-Semitism.[4] The Hauteclocques were early subscribers to the journal, as was Henri de Gaulle, the future leader's father. But *Action Française* also had an inherent flaw: Maurras himself was not a Christian but saw "Frenchness" in almost racial terms. This factor made little difference unless, or until, French patriotism required a moral—and necessarily Christian—core in order to reinvent itself.

The Hauteclocques in all other respects saw themselves as any other European aristocratic family—well armed with common sense and more than a little "gung-ho." Anecdotes of Count Adrien's nonchalance towards hunting injuries were inevitably absorbed by Philippe. One story relates how Count Adrien, after being decked and gored in the thigh by a wild boar, got to his feet expecting to continue the hunt, and only allowed a doctor to examine him when he was almost fainting from blood loss. Another anecdote concerns uncle Wallerand, who broke both legs when his horse bucked during a parade at Belfort. Wallerand insisted on handing the parade to another officer before being taken to hospital. Yet typically, when fighting Samory in the Soudan, Wallerand's letters home were more concerned with *la chasse*: "The first day I didn't feel too well, but since then I have regularly been king of the hunt. . . . The day before yesterday I shot a bustard which I offered straight away to Lieutenant Cambaceres. . . . A little while ago I managed to put a bullet into a large cayman by the river bank. This pleased me a lot as we hadn't managed to bag anything for four days. We have also discharged our guns at a lot of monkeys!"[5]

So far, however, the family's military tradition was neither unbroken nor especially distinguished. France's defeat by Prussia in 1870 reinvigorated the Hauteclocque family's martial instincts that had lain dormant since Napoleon. But while the French Army commissioned his brothers, Adrien was declared unfit because his chest was too small. But then the Great War changed everything.[6] On 5th August 1914, Adrien pretended he was going into Amiens to run a few errands but went instead to the recruitment office. That evening he told his wife that he could not live with himself while others fought, saying God had given him a chance to prove himself. A few days later he jumped on a tram in Amiens and went off to war, making a good-bye gesture with his helmet, while his wife, who thought the war purifying, waved him *au revoir* with a newspaper.[7] Though pushing fifty years of age, he enlisted in the 11e Cuirassiers where his eldest son Guy was already a cornet. Relishing life as an ordinary cavalryman, Adrien astonished everyone with his toughness. However, during the very first month of the war, both his brothers Henri and Wallerand and his nephew Bernard were killed. Trooper Adrien thus became Count de Hauteclocque.

After a spell in the ranks, Count Adrien was commissioned. He won his first *Croix de Guerre* in May 1917 during the disastrous Nivelle offensive: "Showing great endurance and selflessness, he showed a remarkable disregard for danger in leading his troop into the attack under heavy fire."

Later that same summer Count Adrien carried the ensign at the Bastille Day parade in Paris, despite his monarchist views and the tradition that colours are usually entrusted to younger officers. His second *Croix de Guerre* came the following year: "Finding himself at his colonel's command post at a time when it was severely menaced by an outflanking movement by the enemy, he took command of a hastily formed detachment made up of whoever was available, and advanced resolutely to contact with the enemy over open ground . . . he fought all day at the head of his detachment with great courage and coolness, succeeding in halting the German advance."[8]

When the 11e Cuirassiers were ordered to fight as infantry Count Adrien was offered a transfer to a mounted regiment but chose to stay with the men. Trench life did not curtail his indulgence in *la chasse*, and he even managed to keep his dog with him. "The game seemed impervious to the dangers," he wrote joyfully in his diary.[9]

On leave, Count Adrien gave his younger son as much time as possible. If leave dates did not coincide with Philippe's exeats, the Jesuits were flexible in allowing Philippe to make his own way back to Amiens even if it meant walking through snow.[10] The École de la Providence provided a comprehensive classical and religious education combined with physical fitness. Philippe's older brother Guy, Count Adrien and his uncles had also attended, though his grandfather, Gustave, was educated in Belgium since the Jesuits were then still banned from running schools in France.

Amiens' proximity to the trenches meant classes were often conducted amid the sound of not so very distant cannon fire. Following the failure of Nivelle's 1917 offensive, the school moved temporarily to Abbeville. The German spring offensive of 1918 then forced the school to evacuate to Poitiers until the war's end.[11] Any joy the Armistice held for Philippe was eclipsed by the death of his eldest sister, Françoise, who was also his godmother, a usual practice in such families.

Despite the continuous stress that all pupils shared with their fathers and brothers in the front line, Philippe did well academically and was popular enough for his class to vote him a prize for good behaviour. They also called him the "aristo" due to his cool shyness. Unless obliged to tell someone exactly what he thought of them, Philippe always had perfect manners. His strong Christian faith was also always remarked upon, both by those who had known him as a young man and by officers who later built their careers with him. École de la Providence's Father Villaret would write:

> You must understand that it is difficult for me to give you concrete details and circumstances of his spiritual life; his actions speak for themselves. But I can note, as a particular character trait, his intense devotion for the Holy Eucharist and for the Sacred Virgin. He consecrated himself to her in the Marist congregation at Amiens, Poitiers, and at Versailles, in the fullest possible meaning of the term, that is to say by a total and absolute gift of himself. This exquisite devotion is the source of the marvellous purity which struck everybody; even the most indifferent and distracted, without being able to explain it even to themselves, submitted to his charm.[12]

It is hard to imagine anyone writing such things in our more secularised age. Yet Philippe studied Catholicism extensively while at Amiens. Surviving library entries show that he withdrew titles such as *La communion fréquente et quotidienne* ("Frequent and Daily Communion") and *De la chasteté* ("On Chastity"), both written for young Christians.[13] Even so Philippe was no paragon; Father Villaret spotted his talent for teasing and noted that being "very sharp, he seized quickly on the essential aspect that was comic in things, people, even masters, guying them openly . . . "[14] Philippe, even then, was quick to recognise another's weaknesses.

In 1920, shortly before his eighteenth birthday, Philippe de Hauteclocque arrived at École Sainte-Geneviève at Versailles. Recognised by France's Society of Preparatory Schools, this college was also run on strict Jesuit lines, and taught officer candidates their science baccalaureat. Called "Ginette" by former pupils to this day, the school's present website suggests a relaxed, easy and informal atmosphere, with religious staff dressed in mufti, belying its militaristic past and the strong patriotic sense of duty which it instilled into the war generations.[15] It had only been seven years at its Versailles venue where it had taken over the Grand Montreuil. This fine building retained its grand chapel and cloistered courtyard, though was augmented with laboratories and had its park laid out to sports fields. The walls of Philippe's spartan room were soon decorated with pictures of

Belloy, family and dogs. Yet trips into 1920s Paris often included punch-ups with students from similar academies, which would be unthinkable today.[16]

Each year the top student was awarded a sabre blessed in front of the statue of Joan of Arc. General de Maud'huy[17] presented this in Philippe's year, with the words:

"Never draw this sabre without reason, never return it to its scabbard until you have accomplished the task for which it was drawn. When I look back on the last forty-five years, I remember around me the same faces, the same names and the same families who seem to have the monopoly on furnishing the officers of France. As Napoleon said, it's always the same ones who get killed.

"You receive scruffy peasants without cohesion and you turn them into handsome soldiers; guys without discipline, working class revolutionaries, and you turn them into soldiers, patriots, men who will obey your slightest sign, ready to die for their country. Isn't that wonderful? An officer must be a reservoir of energy and conscience. . . . It's up to us, after the terrible losses of young Saint-Cyriens, many brave officers, very brave, but who cannot now go higher and become our great chiefs. The men lack instruction. You have a gap of ten years to make good in front of you."

Nor did religious instruction subside at any point; the Catholic aspect of French patriotism was continually reinforced. On Remembrance Day, Father Pouquet demanded in the name of Sainte Geneviève that France should possess "a strong core of Christian officers, fit to be chosen by God as instruments to appear as timely saviours in the hour of danger. God watch over our Country." At the *Procession et la Fête des Anciens*—a veterans' festival—which was attended by the Papal Nuncio Monsignor Ceretti, the congregation gave hommage to Raoul de Manoir, who fell at the battle of Castelfidardo defending the Papal States against Garibaldi's Redshirts in 1860. Father de Maupeou called this "a glorious beginning of which we are proud. It is in the service of the Pope that the first member of this school to die on the field of honour shed his blood."[18]

By today's standards Ginette's patriotic fervour might seem risible. But, coming from a family that lost three men in August 1914, and with the *génération de feu*—as the Great War generation were called in France—all around him, Philippe would have found nothing strange in such unrelenting reference to self-sacrifice. He enjoyed his time at Ginette, excelling in science and history, and would no doubt have enjoyed it more with a bigger allowance from his father. Trips with *petits-cos* to the races at Longchamp or Auteil were simply not worth it without thirty francs in one's pocket.[19] He passed into Saint-Cyr as the second of Ginette's entries and fifth overall. Father de Maupeou thought Philippe might have done better had he interviewed more confidently, but nevertheless regarded him as head and shoulders above the rest.[20]

The military academy of Saint-Cyr had changed since the Second Empire. By the 1920s, being Catholic and royalist no longer necessarily went together. After Pope Leo XIII ordered French Catholics to accept their country's political status quo, senior officers like General de Castelnau, once known as a "capucin in boots," led a sea-change in the officer corps' social outlook. At Saint-Cyr there was *l'Amicale* ("the Club"), an inner core of officers and cadets who supported Leo XIII's directive, from which Philippe de Hauteclocque was excluded. Imperceptibly perhaps, *Action Française*, though fiercely loyal throughout the Great War, was losing its influence and was having to compete with new right-wing groups whose outlook was often more populist.[21] In the company of other aristocratic cadets, Philippe may possibly not have noticed.

At Saint-Cyr he made lifelong friends like Marc Rouvillois, Jean Fanneau de la Horie and Jean Lecomte. (During the 1940s these were among the few men Philippe forgave for following Vichy.) Like any military academy there was hardship—shouting by sergeant majors and hazing by senior cadets. Newcomers were called *bazars* ("stuff") and had to kneel while seniors stood. Whereas in 1873 the first class of the *revanchiste* period was called "Alsace-Lorraine," the class of 1923 was called "Metz et Strasbourg" after the cities recovered from Imperial Germany in 1919, continuously reinforcing the enmity between France and its powerful neighbour. And, just like at Ginette, there was constant emphasis on *les tombés*—the fallen of the Great War.

In his first year Hauteclocque had to pass his science *baccalaureat* part one, for which Ginette had well prepared him. Sons of career officers had usually been prepared at the less cosmopolitan but more traditional Prytanée Militaire de La Flèche, while the rest came from other big private *lycées*. Many were destined for *La Coloniale*—colonial regiments—where life was cheaper. A huge proportion would go into the artillery and engineers, which had become pre-eminent during the Great War, while the social élite, including Hauteclocque, opted for the cavalry.

Saint-Cyr's cavalry cadets were known collectively as *la basane*, "the dark skinned," on account of their black tunics, while the infantry were called *les biffes*. Then there was the choice of serving in France's mainland—known as *Métropolitan* —regiments, or serving in the colonial branch of the French Army which, in their turn, were divided between *La Coloniale*, who served throughout the French Empire, and the *Armée d'Afrique* (Army of Africa) which was recruited exclusively from the inhabitants of Morocco, Algeria and Tunisia, and considered somewhat smarter than *La Coloniale*. Having chosen Arabic as his first language choice (Saint-Cyriens have to learn languages) Hauteclocque was looking for adventure in a cavalry regiment of *L'Armée d'Afrique*, Spahis or Chasseurs d'Afrique, after a spell in a *Métropolitan* cavalry regiment.

The Saint-Cyr timetable was split between physical training and military theory. Hauteclocque was good at both, although many were too exhausted by the physical régime to concentrate much in the lecture halls. Wearing the Great War's *horizon bleu* uniform with its baggy coats, rough brown *brodequins* (boots) and puttees, the cadets exercised around the parks of Versailles and the camp at Satory. Weapons were the standard Lebel rifle with its incredibly long spike bayonet, the 1915 Chatellerault machine gun (similar to the British Lewis gun), the Hotchkiss heavy machine gun, light artillery pieces such as the 37mm cannon and the 81mm mortar. As yet, motorised warfare was not on the curriculum, so cadets trained with small arms and horses.[22]

However, end of year manoeuvres were marked by the introduction of the Renault F5 tanks. Later, the inauguration of the new *Armée de l'Air* at Villacoublay demonstrated the inexorable encroachment of modern warfare. But the cadets of "Metz et Strasbourg" were more concerned with promotions to corporal and sergeant or, if cavalry, sergeant-farrier and quarter-master-farrier—appointments which would help them to reach their chosen regiment.

The attraction of the cavalry was obvious, with the extra riding lessons and its innate obsession with horses. For its blue-blooded officers the lifestyle was inevitably more expensive than the infantry, and promotion was often slower. For less financially secure cavalry officers, service in a colonial cavalry regiment was often the only viable option.

Captain Peillon, ex Ginette, and commander of "Metz et Strasbourg's" cavalry squadron, wrote these notes on Hauteclocque:

> *Intellectual value:* Remarkably intelligent. *Moral value and military spirit:* Perfect; a soldier to his soul. *Physical Courage and aptitude in the field:* Very good, never stops. *Military value (Aptitude for command):* Very apt. *Qualities as instructor:* Will make a very good instructor. *Theoretical instruction:* Perfect. *Practical instruction and tactical sense:* Very good, very sound judgement. Accurate and quick. *Aptitude to specialities:* No remarks. *Character:* Perfect, energetic, rigorously correct. *Conduct:* Perfect. *Attitude and turn-out:* Perfect. *Education:* Perfect. *Diverse Particularities:* None. "*Overall Appreciation:* Outstanding pupil, combining the best qualities of intelligence and of heart with a high understanding of his military duties. Head and shoulders above his contemporaries. Irreproachable in conduct and turn-out, strong character, passionate in everything he does, devoting himself body and soul to his profession. His energy and willpower will make him a decent cavalryman, depending on one's point of view. Has in him the makings of an officer of high calibre.[23]

This opinion was echoed by General Decarpentry, head of cavalry training and a big name in 1920s French equitation. Hauteclocque's marks were higher than those awarded Charles de Gaulle twelve years earlier.

On 1st October 1924, the cadets of "Metz et Strasbourg" passed out of Saint-Cyr as "*Sous Lieutenants*" (Second Lieutenants). While the infantrymen went directly to their regiments, the newly commissioned cavalry officers still had a further hurdle to overcome: Saumur.

Before arriving at the Loire's city of the horse, new officers were accepted by their regiments and received their uniforms and a mount. Having registered with the 24th Dragoons, Hauteclocque installed himself at 16 Rue de Lorraine, one of the private residences set aside for officer-pupils. Following the traditions of a squire's finishing school, Saumur's instructors set out to instill "self possession," especially in the presence of *la cadre rose*—

the wives and daughters of the garrison. In such an environment one could almost believe the 1789 Revolution never happened. Officers divided themselves between the "black cadre," the sons of gentleman farmers and professional classes; or the "blue cadre," the nobly bred. The first worked and read; the others talked endlessly. On occasions, the *cadre bleu* would take off into a local town, accompanied by *demi-mondaines* (whose presence was well known) to have a good time.

Philippe de Hauteclocque, though good company, stood back from such jaunts. Having decided early in life that it was his Christian duty to found a family, Philippe cut out the usual string of girlfriends and went straight for the virgin bride. Following his older brother Guy's marriage to Madeleine de Gargan, Philippe found himself welcome at the Gargans' home, 2 Rue Mansart, and thrown into the company of younger daughters Marie and Thérèse. Preferring Thérèse's seriousness to Marie's unrestrained taste for comedy, Philippe was soon in love.[24] During his year at Ginette they had met on Sundays at Versailles, and the steady rhythm of this demurely conducted romance lasted through Saint-Cyr until its point of decision during his Saumur year.

A girl of steady character, Thérèse did not distract her boyfriend from his training. After eleven months at Saumur, Philippe qualified as a troop commander, capable of training and leading thirty cavalrymen. Though tactics were still reminiscent of the age of Napoleon, training with Hotchkiss machine guns was included along with greater emphasis on infantry tactics. Nevertheless, French cavalry officers were trained to assimilate a particular sequence of tactical reasoning: "situation, mission, intention, decision, orders." "Intention" meant the foreseeing of how situations could develop while the orders given had to be short and simple.[25]

Passing out of Saumur at the top of his class on 8th August 1925, Philippe de Hauteclocque received a glowing report from Colonel Lafond declaring that he was excellent officer material, strong charactered, well turned out, had made himself tough in spite of not really being a tough type, knew the rules and how to apply them, was decisive, authoritative and clear thinking. He got on with other cadets and knew how to get the best out of a horse.[26]

Philippe was glad to complete the course "without having cheated or licked anyone's boots."[27] He was fast establishing a reputation for having a frank, open character and a quick temper demonstrated by blasts of fruity language. The terms *salopard* (creep) and *bâtard* often appeared in his future reports and letters.

Three days later he married Thérèse in the church of newly beatified Saint Joan of Arc. Though Baroness de Gargan was surprised that Philippe should chose Thérèse over her jollier sister, both mothers thought the union a good idea. Musical as well as serious, Thérèse once considered becoming a Carmelite nun but, after much soul-searching with her confessor, convinced herself she was "destined for the world" to build a Christian family with an officer of her own class. Traditionally conservative, the Gargans also subscribed to *Action Française*. In their *milieu* giving books on Catholic theology was a mark of extreme affection. The baroness sent Philippe a copy of "*L'Ame de tous apostolat*" ("The soul of all Apostles"). Although he had already read it, Philippe wrote to his mother that it was a handsome gift, which, along with the prospect of his suitable bride, made him feel "truly spoilt." "With her it would never be hard to walk on the right road."[28]

In "Old France" tradition, Count Adrien asked Baron de Gargan for Thérèse's hand before sending a telegram to Philippe at Saumur: "*Gargan tu as.*"[29] Once a certificate of the bride's good character had been obtained from the Versailles *gendarmerie*, the wedding went ahead.[30] Philippe, with trim moustache and hair *en brosse*, cut a dapper figure in summer walking-out uniform while his bride wore a white lace gown, cut calf-length in the fashion of 1920s Paris to reveal high-heeled satin shoes. Count Adrien then gave the couple the chateau of Tailly near Belloy as a wedding present, and Lieutenant de Hauteclocque became a very well set up young man at a time when many French officers took jobs on the side to make ends meet.[31]

There is little doubt that Philippe loved Thérèse absolutely, nor can one find the slightest hint of an infidelity on either side throughout their separation from July 1940 until the liberation of Paris in August 1944. Aged 23 and 22 years old respectively, it could not have escaped Philippe's awareness that officers marrying too young is frowned on in any army. Thérèse, however, was the perfect army wife, taking an enthusiastic part in garrison social events, accommodating her husband's career, accepting the inevitable absences and recognising that France came first.

Their shared reading matter was nevertheless more likely to be *Action Française* than a tome of Catholic theology. But as acute social unrest afflicted Europe, the Papacy became wary of the French Right using religion as a political weapon, and officially discouraged French Catholics from reading Maurras's journal. Stunned, Philippe wrote to his sister Yvonne, "What do you think of Rome raving about *Action Française*? When one judges things coolly and from the beginning, one cannot really share their concerns because, from the outset, their condemnations are based on errors, omissions, false interpretations, deliberate or involuntary, and in the development of the affair, the Pope has either not accepted or not received other information or advice. Moreover, since on his own side there are eminent priests compelled to keep quiet, one cannot have scruples. How sad to think that it is not impossible to see us one day excommunicated!"[32]

At first Philippe regarded the Papal interdiction as something of a joke, and was nonplussed when brother officer Maurice Catoire took it seriously. Arrogantly perhaps, even after Thérèse was refused absolution in the confessional, the couple continued to subscribe.

Derived from Napoleon's élite breastplated cavalry, the 5e Regiment des Cuirassiers was based at Trier as part of France's occupation force in the Rhineland. With Germany exhausted by the Great War and unwilling to pay the hefty reparations demanded under the Versailles Treaty, the exasperated French government sent troops into the Ruhr. In the meantime, for somewhere to start military and married life, the 5e Cuir' was quite a family regiment. During the Great War, Count Adrien had served under the 5e Cuir's Colonel de Penfentinyo, whose son-in-law was now Philippe's squadron commander. The 5e Cuir' was smart, and officers were allowed to quarter horses for personal use. With his lifelong friend Jean la Horie posted nearby, the newly married couple settled in quickly. Philippe grew vegetables and had chickens in the garden attached to their billet, and they spent the evenings listening to concerts from all over Europe on the powerful radio he bought. Soon, however, Thérèse was expecting their first child, and avoided large gatherings like the big Sunday church service and social events organised for officers' families. After she returned home for her confinement, Philippe was left to cook his own meals, the frustration of having to mix his own béchamel sauce merely adding to the *ennui* of occupation duties.[33]

Cadet life behind him, Philippe now found himself encountering officers barely five years older with chests full of Great War medals. To look
them in the eye he also needed medals, and the only place to earn them
was France's overseas empire. To help speed his way to a posting *outremer*,
Colonel Penfentinyo wrote glowingly of Philippe's smartness, punctuality,
skill at training men and potential for high command. General Brécard
was not so impressed. "Has real qualities, but knows it too well—has been
spoilt. Too sure of himself. Needs advice and doesn't take it willingly."
When Brécard became Inspector General of cavalry shortly afterwards, he
was able to comment further on Hauteclocque to his new commander:
"This is a young officer who is head and shoulders above others; he is
young and needs advice. He has a temper and a strong personality; he needs
to be commanded with tact. I wanted to warn you."[34]

The word "spahi" is descended from the Asian *cipahi* from which
"sepoy" is also derived, before evolving into the *Armée d'Afrique*'s flowingly
dressed cavalry.[35] The 8e Régiment des Spahis Algériens based at Taza in
Morocco had eight vacancies for junior officers seeking adventure in the
Maghreb, and Philippe got his way. Gazetted as First Lieutenant on 1st
October 1926, Philippe set about perfecting his skills as a troop leader as
soon as he arrived, taking his men on week-long flag-waving patrols to
demonstrate French strength and beneficence after the defeat of Abd el
Krim's rebellion and his attempt to form a breakaway province six months
earlier.

Philippe and Thérèse had plain but comfortable quarters in upper Taza,
where the bedroom was reached by a ladder. Their first son, Henri, had
been born at Versailles; their second son, Hubert, was on the way; and
Action Française lay defiantly on the sofa table. Glad to find Hauteclocque
getting settled in, Colonel Prioux noted that the young officer was cheerful
and good humoured, flexible in his approach to colonial soldiering,
and had a good eye for ground. On a personal level, Prioux thought
Hauteclocque shy, which "could be taken for smugness, but one must hope
this minor failing will disappear with the experience of years."[36] But Taza
was a small, sleepy town, hardly propitious for a newly married officer
wanting to develop his career. Again Philippe asked for something more
interesting.

Remarking upon Philippe's abilities as an instructor, Colonel Prioux had him appointed to the École de Dar el-Beida at Meknes. Set in the old fort of Sidi Mohammed Ben Abdallah, this school attempted to recreate a Saint-Cyr style education for the sons of families *des grandes tentes*—from big tents—the Arab equivalent of aristocracy. Given French losses in the Great War, indigenous officers were needed, even though their promotional ceiling was captain (which fueled bitter resentment by the 1940s). Accompanied at first by Thérèse, who now had Hubert as well as Henri to look after, returning home at the day's end was Philippe's greatest joy. To get to know his pupils, whom he wisely regarded as comrades rather than second-class citizens, Philippe improved his Arabic and also learned Berber, enabling him to meet many cadets' families in their houses or tents. In return, star pupils were invited to Tailly during the long summer holiday. Indigenous teachers such as Moulay Kebir ben Zidane advised pupils that Hauteclocque could be trusted for his common sense and, when necessary, plain speaking. On one occasion he bluntly told a high-living cadet that the army would never lead him to wealth, and to choose another career while he still had time. When teaching horse riding, he expected the same determination from his pupils as he expected from himself, and excuses regarding restive animals were not allowed. At Meknes he first formed the habit of saying, "Don't tell me it's impossible." He was also immensely skilled at explaining the essentials of a problem and making a clear yet flexible plan. When explaining Marshal Joffre's victory at the Battle of the Marne in 1914, Philippe demonstrated the simplicity and ingeniousness of Joffre's strategy with just a few deft phrases.

At Meknes, Philippe first met one of his most important comrades of future years. Eight years older, Paul de Langlade was a Great War veteran now serving with a Spahi regiment. Despite not knowing each other particularly well, Philippe left a strong enough impression for Langlade to reintroduce himself in an Algiers restaurant in 1943.[37] Presciently, Dar el Beida's commandant, Lt. Colonel Tarrit, thought Philippe's abilities as an instructor so great that he must nurture a burning desire to raise original units. But to gain experience in the field, Hauteclocque needed a combat posting. Despite the defeat of Abd el Krim, Morocco remained a deeply troubled country, with rebel gunfire sometimes audible in Meknes. Aircraft reconnaissance usually warned French garrisons of any large raiding parties, or *razzias,* gathering in the desert, while lesser groupings were dealt with in the usual way by *Groupes Nomades*—camel soldiers making sweeps across the sands.[38]

In the summer of 1929, having packed off Thérèse and their three sons (Charles had arrived by then) back to Tailly, Philippe got himself attached to the *38e Goum Mixte Marocains* at M'Zizel, which had recently lost several men in the Ouled Yacoub affair. *Goums* were recruited on a pre-colonial model dating from the old Moroccan Sultan's army. A rough equivalent would be the British Indian Army's Scouts of the North West Frontier. *Goums* were part-police, part-soldiers recruited for service in French North Africa only. "*Goum*" was the name of the unit, roughly the size of a company, about 120 men called "*goumiers*" commanded by two or three French officers. They had no barrack lifestyle, living instead in walled communities that housed their entire families, including the sick and elderly as well as livestock. Their womenfolk cleaned rifles and weapons alongside their pots and pans. During the Great War, *goums* were used to police Morocco, thereby releasing other forces to fight in France. After the Armistice, as French power in North Africa reached its zenith, *goums* were used to pacify the High Atlas Mountains, and increasingly recruited from Berbers instead of Arabs.[39] Hence, Hauteclocque's ability to speak both languages was useful.

Arriving at M'Zizel, 3000m up in the High Atlas, Philippe found that the only other officer was Jean Lecomte, *petit-co* from both Ginette and Saint-Cyr, who had attended shooting parties back home. The local population were friendly enough, and the *goum*, being "*mixte,*" had both horse and foot *goumiers* working in unison. Being an infantryman, Lecomte had been gazetted to his first regiment a year before Hauteclocque, making him notionally senior. But the *goum*'s communal lifestyle made the formal exercise of authority somewhat difficult, and demanded a more intellectual, special forces style of leadership. At first both officers found this situation awkward; not helped by Philippe desperately missing his loved ones and constantly playing *Mon coeur soupire la nuit et le jour* on his portable gramophone. But the two men soon got used to each other, mucking in and sharing the lives of the *goumiers*' families. Philippe even got Thérèse to send out campfire friendly recipes, and soon the *goumiers* nicknamed him "Lieut'nant Haclocque."[40] Lecomte recognised Hauteclocque's moral and spiritual side (Philippe always kept a portrait photo of Charles de

Foucauld and prayed on his knees before a little alter laid out on the sand), while Hauteclocque profited from Lecomte's greater experience in the field. In any case, as the only French officers for miles around, they eventually knew each other well enough to have no secrets.[41]

Goumiers were recruited individually, their enlistment often taking the form of a simple, almost casual agreement to follow the individual officer or sergeant who originally negotiated his service. It was an arrangement based on trust. If he brought a horse with him the *goumier* received an extra 1.25FF a day to look after it. In recognition of their loyalty, by the 1920s the French were increasingly content to allow them modern rifles and a few machine guns. Their most distinctive item of uniform, insofar as anything was uniform, was the *djellebah*, a coarse woollen cape with a hood and sleeves resembling a monk's habit, but woven in stripes of black, brown and grey which varied from *goum* to *goum* like Scottish clan tartans. They also wore a *rezzah*, which was similar to a turban.[42]

Discipline, which was not easily enforced outside formal barracks, usually took the form of docking pay; a serious penalty in communities so poor that womenfolk sometimes resorted to prostitution. Not wishing men to sink too low materially, and with no available lock-up facilities, Lecomte and Hauteclocque brought miscreants into line with a *bastonnade*, a traditional punishment involving beating the soles of the feet with a cane. Strictly speaking this was forbidden, but in an era that took corporal punishment for granted, it was common sense that a brief bout of pain caused less overall hardship than loss of pay. However, a denouncement was made, and both officers were reprimanded. Lecomte was jailed for fifteen days and Hauteclocque for eight.[43]

Orders concerning dissident tribes emanated from the faraway Colonial Office in Paris, and were often restrained, much to the annoyance of both officers. Lecomte believed in spreading French influence by winning "hearts and minds," a tactic the French call *la tache d'huile* ("the oil stain"). Hauteclocque, on the other hand, believed rebels should be pursued off limits wherever it was practicable to do so.

Despite the defeat of Abd el Krim, by 1930 a new tribal leader called Hammou, a Grand Caid of great cruelty, began attacking French outposts in the southern High Atlas. French reaction was to create a new command under Colonel (later General) Henri Giraud covering the area between

Colomb-Béchar in western Algeria and southern Morocco. Giraud planned to drive the rebels westwards into the mountains where they would come up against a line of French outposts along the whole Atlas range. Assisted by reconnaissance aircraft, *goumiers* would then envelop the rebels from the southeast.[44] Knowing their ground but with insufficient modern weapons, Hammou's rebels pursued the classic tactic of 1930s North African warfare by feigning an attack, then retreating after seeming to have second thoughts. European forces then pursued them and were drawn into an ambush. In Libya, Senoussi guerrillas led by elderly teacher Omar Mukhtar were irking the Italians in the same way.

Hauteclocque and Lecomte first came across Hammou in April after his men murdered fifty of the Ait Aissa tribe at Kerrando. Sent into the hills after him, the *38e Goum Mixte* played cat and mouse in the mountains for four days before an exhausting march back to M'Zizel with no water in their canteens. It might have been worse if undercover French officers disguised as Arabs had not warned them of an ambush on their return route.[45]

The onset of summer heat temporarily stopped everything, but Hammou was active again in July. By then much of the *38e Goum Mixte* was recruited by Hauteclocque. He led patrols through hostile territory without mishap, later describing the experience to his mother as "sportive."[46] Then, at 10.25 am on the 13th July the whole *goum* and a *fezza* of loyal tribesmen were ordered to the hill of Timezdarine to rendez-vous with the 14e Régiment des Tirailleurs Algériens from Taguendoust. A little later a second telephone call advised Lecomte that the garrison at Amougueur had been attacked at dawn by five hundred Hammou tribesmen, suffering heavy losses including their commanding officer. By 10.45am the *38e Goum Mixte* were on their way to the rescue with Lecomte at the head of twenty mounted partisans followed by Hauteclocque and the cavalry of half the *goum*.

Arriving at the Mouabane hills an hour later, they dismounted to cover the Tirailleurs Algériens following behind. They covered 12 kilometres in a little over an hour without encountering any resistance. After their arrival, Hauteclocque ordered an advance to contact towards a hill called Timesjaline, followed by a squad of mounted *goumiers* at the trot. Other squads trotted up behind at spaces of 200 to 400 hundred metres, soon coming under intense fire from Hammou's tribesmen. After ordering the first two troops to dismount and take up firing positions from a pair of unoccupied ridges, Hauteclocque saw that Hammou's men were manoeuvring to envelop the French force, and managed to get more men onto another ridge behind his position to maintain their line of retreat. As the fighting raged, Hauteclocque's horse collapsed under him, but luckily a *goumier* quickly found another mount. Adjutant Touzain was not so lucky, and it took little imagination to guess how Hammou's tribesmen would treat the unrecovered body of a French NCO. Drawing his sabre, Hauteclocque rallied his men and ordered an advance.

"One hundred douros to the man who brings back the adjutant," he shouted as his *goumiers* fought their way up the slopes under rebel fire. After twenty minutes Hammou's men withdrew. Though proud of his men's performance, Hauteclocque also found himself respecting Hammou's Chleuh tribesmen, who "attacked like regulars," firing non-stop.

As they regrouped, Hauteclocque saw more Hammou riflemen attempting to infiltrate the French flank. Acting decisively to protect his men from encirclement, he drew his sabre again, leading a charge of eighteen mounted *goumiers*. Lack of fitness, however, meant eighteen horses soon became six, but the charge had the desired effect. Alerted to French reinforcements by smoke signals, Hammou staged a fighting withdrawal, but without fresh horses, Hauteclocque was unable to pursue. After an action lasting two and a half hours, the adjutant's body was recovered and a reconnaissance aircraft dropped yellow smoke flares to signal that their return route seemed clear of enemy.

Although the fort was relieved, it was hard to tell who, if anyone, had won the day. *Goumiers* were not great respecters of enemy corpses either, so Hammou removed his dead, making his losses uncountable. Four French, including the adjutant, had been killed, and seventeen French, *goumiers* and partisans injured. As for horses, once dismounted they made easy targets; fourteen were killed (two under Hauteclocque) and eight injured in terrain where injuries were merely delayed fatalities. But infantry without horses could never move quickly enough to protect themselves.

This was Hauteclocque's first real action. He had shown he could lead men under fire both on foot and horseback. When he gave the order to "draw sabres," his *goumiers* were galvanised, though facing a skilful enemy combining accurate fire with manoeuvre.[47]

His first action behind him, Hauteclocque was posted to the 1e Chasseurs d'Afrique in Rabat. This was the *Armée d'Afrique's* senior cavalry regiment dating from 1831. Recruited from European personnel and considered exceedingly smart, most senior cavalry officers served in it at some stage of their careers.[48] Life in Rabat could also be fairly sophisticated. French officers coming into contact with the Moroccan nobility would enjoy their urbanity mixed with a particular brand of religious nationalism. However, without the prospect of action, Philippe decided it was not worth being so far from Thérèse. In February 1931, on the strength of his record at Meknes, he returned to Saint-Cyr as an instructor, which allowed him to pick up the reins of family life again. Thérèse was soon expecting their fourth child.

It was a joy to walk the avenues and boulevards of Versailles again with his young family, but the interwar Métropolitan French Army was not in the habit of rewarding initiative and strength of character. Philippe was torn between the needs of his family and the urge to prove himself professionally in an army where men a mere five years older than himself had "done" the Great War. While making clear to Thérèse that he was not pursuing a Moroccan career for its own sake, he stressed that only action in Africa would "satisfy honour for a young officer."[49]

In April 1931, during Saint-Cyr's spring break, Hauteclocque returned to Rabat at his own expense. Having passed the train journey through Spain hoping there would be something exciting to do when he arrived, he found himself sent back to Saint-Cyr with nothing but the army's appreciation of his willingness. Complaining to Thérèse that few opportunities remained for real horse soldiering, he immersed himself afresh in training cavalry cadets for a role few would ever play.

For two years he commanded a troop in Captain Marion's squadron, establishing a name among promotions "Bournazel" to "Tafilalet" (1930–1933) for being a *seigneur* and finicky over details. Some cadets thought he delighted in catching them out, while others, destined for the infantry, got the impression he discriminated against *les Biffes*. In truth "Monsieur Clo-clo," as he was sometimes nicknamed, would not tolerate any breach of rules that he believed existed for a reason. In some ways he felt that Saint-Cyr had gone to pot since his own cadet days. In a letter to Lecomte he proudly described his reproaching ten cadets for long hair. Ruling with a rod of iron and sometimes sounding disconcertingly like a sergeant major, Hauteclocque chewed out his squadron at every opportunity. When they left their quarters desultorily during a fire drill he called them a "gaggle of sheep." On another occasion, while inspecting walking-out dress before his cadets caught the "Crampton," the Saturday evening train to Paris, he was confronted with Cadet Terras mistakenly attired in full parade dress including sabre and carbine. Hauteclocque did not punish him but commented sarcastically, "Well done, Terras, you're a good fellow as we can see from your walking out dress. Without the aid of your comrades you're passed to go out this evening."[50] For Hauteclocque, turnout was not essential for its own sake, as later photographs from the desert would show.

His intolerance while an instructor at Saint-Cyr was simply due to his short temper, exacerbated by the malaria he had contracted in Morocco. On the other hand, there is little doubt that, given his experiences in the High Atlas and his first rate horsemanship, his cadets admired him. From 1931 until 1937, two and a half thousand future officers passed through his hands, each remembering him for the surname of a known aristocratic family, his elegant turnout, and of course his taste for going off to Morocco during the holidays in hope of seeing action.

In the meantime, France at this time was in dire economic straits. The old and newly rich were out of kilter, while the industrial working classes were turning to communism as a solution to their woes. Believing conservative principles were best, Hauteclocque still read *Action Française*, yet sometimes, when walking home from Saint-Cyr, he stopped to read Communist tracts from *L'Humanité* pasted on walls. But if he could not be in Morocco, his favourite place was Tailly, where he enjoyed the life of a squire. His life with Thérèse was simple. They kept pretty much to themselves, living frugally, true to the traditions of lesser aristocracy (of *gentilhommes fesses-lièvres*) and their wives.[51]

Lecomte kept him informed what was happening in Morocco. Hammou was still at large in the High Atlas, with insurrection threatening to spread to Berber rebels elsewhere or fuel religious nationalism among youths in the big cities. While army chiefs in Paris became increasingly concerned over the rise of Hitler, the last thing they needed was unrest in North Africa. General Henri Giraud, the army commander in Morocco, favoured force in dealing with rebels, while General Georges Catroux, commander in Algeria, preferred negotiation. Incapable of compromise at this stage of his life, Hauteclocque supported Giraud's viewpoint, regarding him as a soldier's soldier—a view echoed by Franklin D. Roosevelt ten years later.[52] By contrast Catroux, even then, was thought of as a more political general. He was also a longstanding friend of Charles de Gaulle and, ironically, in years to come, it was Catroux rather than Giraud who would become a *Gaulliste de la première heure* along with Hauteclocque.

Fully supported by Thérèse, Hauteclocque's desire for more action was insatiable. By relentless use of connections ("*piston*" as the French call it) Philippe opened the necessary doors. But first he had to obtain the support of Saint-Cyr's commandant, General Frère. Having done his own junior officer years in French North Africa, Frère was sympathetic, content to turn a blind eye to one of his instructors using the *grandes vacances* for real soldiering, providing he came back in one piece. Nevertheless, Hautclocque wrote to Lecomte that he still needed his help in pulling off *cette petite folie*. Flying out from Toulouse at his own expense, carrying only a small suitcase containing such things as the *Essaies de Montaigne*, Hauteclocque arrived in Rabat on 11th July 1933.[53] From there he hitched a four-day lorry ride through the Atlas' most inhospitable territory to Giraud's command post at Midelt.

While wanting to reward Hauteclocque's persistence, Giraud was in two minds as to what to do with him. If a valued Saint-Cyr instructor got himself killed when he was meant to be on vacation it could lead to tiresome paperwork. Later in the mess tent, however, Hauteclocque overheard Giraud saying, "When an opportunity to do something presents itself, one should take it, as it may not happen again." Cheekily, Hauteclocque caught up with Giraud afterwards and repeated those words back to him. Giraud's force disposed of seven groups, each consisting of a hundred-man *goum* and a hundred and fifty partisans supported by machine guns, artillery and air reconnaissance.[54] Each needed a liaison officer to keep Giraud in touch with outlying formations. Hauteclocque got the job. In one area, Tinerhir, Hauteclocque felt one group commander was not really up to his task so he simply created his own band and put it at Giraud's disposal.

Facing Giraud were the Ait Morrhad with over a thousand modern rifles dug into the heights of the Kerdouss massif. As dangerous as the Ait Hammou, not least because they hated the French, they knew their home territory well. On 2nd August Hauteclocque was called to see Colonel Trinquet, a popular officer with a deeply autocratic command style. "Ah, you're the chap who wants to do something," said Trinquet. Within two days Hauteclocque was under Trinquet's orders, riding a horse borrowed from the Spahis and dressed once again in a *goumier's* djellabah and bonnet and with two *goumiers* as servants: a scruffy Zemmour called Hammadi, and a somewhat smarter Chleuh called Tahar.[55]

Two days later he was on operations, a night march, tasked with taking a mountain called the Akerjioun. Surveying its slopes, he reckoned twenty gunmen could pin down ten times their number for hours unless he got there first. He offered a "roast lamb feast," or *méchouis*, and ten douros to the first man who reached the top. After an hour and a half's hot climbing they reached the summit unopposed. Then shots rang out from a neighbouring crest. As they pushed up the second crest, the bandits withdrew while firing accurately enough to kill two *goumiers* and wound several others.

Watching from the valley below, Colonel Trinquet admired the work of repetitive attrition as they cleared one crest after another until, by the end of the day, control was established. Reflecting on his *goum's* performance over canned food and a drink of kessera, Hauteclocque thought *some* had been very brave, and about twenty to thirty reasonable. But half had huddled behind rocks and, if someone was injured, as many as possible took the opportunity to leave: six to carry him, two to carry his rifle and two more his belongings! Hauteclocque learnt a valuable lesson about irregular operations, the comparative qualities of regular and irregular troops, and the attitudes of opposing troops. Both rebels and *goumiers* could be from the same tribes. During exchanges of rifle fire they often talked to each other, firing at an opponent one second and next asking him if he had been hit, "No, I'm all right," and then "Why fight for the French? Why be a Christian's dog?" and so on. When rebels and indigenous troops captured each other they would talk as comrades.[56] Future actions between Free French and Vichy troops between 1940 and 1942 sometimes had a similar ring.

In the days that followed, more mountains, crests and ridges were taken the same way by *groupement Trinquet*, closing down the last resistance to French rule in Morocco until after World War II. From the main peak in the Djebel Amdoun range, Hauteclocque could see the hinterlands between the mountains and the sea, with Meknes and Marrakech in the blue distance beyond. As if to bring home to him the childlike way the rebels saw their fight, on 9th August Hauteclocque captured a hill from which Chleuh marksmen had given harrassing fire. Arriving at the crest he found their positions empty. Walking on, revolver in hand, he found them sitting in a circle. It was midday and they were drinking mint tea. War was a game to them.

On 11th August, as Hauteclocque was sitting in circle with his *goumiers*, Giraud and Trinquet arrived. They said that the ravines and caves of Amdoun hill, from which the range is named, were hiding anything up to a thousand gunmen who still refused to recognise the beneficence of French rule. Somehow, anyhow, it had to be taken. Hauteclocque suggested an advance up the hill's blank face so that rebel-occupied caves and ravines could be outflanked and cleared with hand grenades. "Do what you want to do, " General Giraud told him.

With six *goumiers* carrying as many hand grenades as they could, supported by partisans, Hauteclocque set off across sand and shale towards the foot of the mountain. Once the rebels opened fire, the *goumiers* doubled forward, taking cover among the mountain's lower rocks. From there they started to climb, jumping across ravines and cave entrances as Hauteclocque sought the extreme flank of their position. By early afternoon, rebel fire reached a crescendo. *Goumiers* and partisans took cover, exchanging shot for shot. Being better equipped, the French fire lasted longer until, after half an hour, the rebels pulled back and the remainder raised a white flag. By 3pm the *goumiers* could stand up and walk about. It was over. After a long drink of water, Hauteclocque reported to Colonel Trinquet, who congratulated him warmly. That night, as Philippe lay on a bed made from a *burnous* and *djellabah* by his servant Hammadi, he listened to the captured Ait Morrhad singing heroic folk poems in the darkness.

Two days later, Hauteclocque came down from the hills to hear that Colonel Trinquet had recommended him for a *Croix de Guerre*. Having won the recognition he had sought for so long, Hauteclocque telegrammed Thérèse at Tailly, saying Providence had repaid her sacrifice and he would soon be home. To Lecomte he wrote, "The game and the *salopards* surpassed his hopes." However, on returning to civilisation, he looked back at the mountains with a pang of regret that the old life of the North African tribes was over forever.

Having won his medal, Philippe returned to France for a brief holiday at Tailly before resuming his post at Saint-Cyr. France's North African emergencies during this period would, in English military parlance, be described as "low intensity operations." From 1933 onwards, France faced the much harder question of how to defend herself from German aggression yet again, but this time with an exhausted economy and severely depleted manpower.

In 1918 the Western Allies were ultimately successful against Germany, but the losses among French adult males had not adequately been recovered by the 1930s. The strategic dangers of France's low population were openly admitted under the term *dénatalité*, and the military establishment shared the widely held viewpoint that Frenchmen were becoming an endangered species. They simply could not afford a battle like Verdun again, however much young officers like Philippe de Hauteclocque admired Verdun generals such as Mangin, the "butcher."

The Pyrrhic victory of Verdun had convinced the French top brass that a system of fortifications, properly manned and gunned, could withstand an enemy indefinitely. By contrast, German military planners looked upon the almost successful "Blitzkieg" of 1918—the Ludendorff offensive, also called the *Kaiserschlacht* ("Kaiser's Battle")—for new inspiration. While the French replaced trenches and the forts of Verdun with the heavily fortified Maginot Line, stretching along its German frontier between Belgium and Switzerland, the Germans replaced the lumbering tanks of 1918 with a new range of up-to-date tanks, better than anything possessed by the British or French. British and French tanks were not entirely useless, but British tanks were undergunned and slow, while French tank design consistently placed the tank commander in a one man turret where he had to load, aim and fire the gun as well as give directions. Any advantages gained from moving *en masse* were negated by the lack of radios.

By 1935 French Army recruitment began to hit the "hollow classes" caused by the lowered birth rate during the Great War. There were nowhere near enough young men aged between twenty and twenty-five. France had to raise a larger army from the colonies to have any hope of making up this deficiency. But neither French North Africa, Senegal, the Levant, Madagascar nor Indochina were entirely stable.

Another problem was that army morale was low. The vicissitudes of France's economy meant that her soldiers received roughly a third of the pay "enjoyed" by the British Army. Lieutenant de Hauteclocque might have been happy to father a large family while still a junior officer, but then he was one of the few who could afford to.

It was not only French tanks that were inferior to those of the Germans. While there was some good artillery borne on tracked vehicles, most was still horse-drawn. Basic French infantry equipment was old fashioned and much of it was shared with the cavalry. The Hotchkiss machine gun's ammunition came on clips looking like hair combs, while the new German MG32 was belt-fed, capable of firing up to 1,200 rounds per minute. The standard rifle was the short and handy MAS36, a good enough weapon. But many regiments still had the old Lebel rifle with its exceptionally long bayonet; fine if one stood a reasonable chance of getting close to the enemy, but not much use if attacking infantry were raked with overwhelming machine gun fire before leaving their start line.

Uniforms were also desperately old fashioned. The heavy coat with its button-back skirts combined with lace-up leather leggings made the ordinary *poilu* look like a governess on a cold winter's day. Only a few regiments received more up-to-date uniforms, but mainly mountain troops. Although a new cotton summer uniform resembling US-style combat clothing was designed in 1938, few regiments had received it by the spring of 1940.

In terms of moral and social preparations for war, France, along with her chief ally, Great Britain, was in a lamentable state. Despite several revolutions since 1789, France during the 1930s was just as socially divided between Catholics and atheists, rich and poor, employers and workers as Spain before the civil war. Some members of the French right preferred the idea of being ruled by Hitler to French Communists. For their part the French left thought it futile to fight another costly war to protect the rich, daubing posters with the phrase "*pour qui et pourquoi?*"

Action Française by then had a circulation of about one hundred thousand. The Papal ban had cost it some, but not all, of its readers. Its editor, Charles Maurras, was not the same angry young man of the right he had been during the Dreyfus affair, and some *Action Française* writers, including

Robert Brasillach, left to form a new right-wing journal called *Je Suis Partout*. In the meantime the older publication was increasingly called *Inaction Française*.[57] Furthermore, being right-wing and patriotic were not the same thing, as Philippe de Hauteclocque would eventually discover. The right-wing movements of 1930s France—whether *Action Française*, the *Croix de Feu*, led by Colonel Count François de La Rocque, or the *Jeunesses Patriotes* founded by industrialist and champagne house owner Pierre Taittinger—had much in common with those in other European countries. Self-invented flags and uniforms abounded, yet the desire to defeat the left and, at the same time, maintain a higher ideal of *La France* commanding her own destiny at any price did not always coincide.

If Philippe was not reading moral warnings on the rise of Nazism from his favourite journal, he certainly got them from closer to home. Xavier de Hauteclocque, the younger son of his uncle Wallerand, who was killed in 1914, left the army after the Armistice to become an investigative journalist. During the 1920s Xavier wrote first for *La Liberté*, then the *Petit Journal* where his competence in English and German put him on the foreign desk. He was almost a French Peter Fleming, with a taste for exotic expeditions. In 1929 Xavier was a herring fisherman off Greenland. The following year he followed Moslem pilgrims making the Haj from Tunisia to Mecca. In 1931 he covered the war in Libya between the Italians and Senoussi rebels. Then in 1932 he followed British gunrunners to the Arctic to arm Russian outlaws so they could rescue their brothers from Soviet concentration camps. Unsurprisingly, this expedition failed and Xavier had to escape on foot across summertime Lapland's insect-infested swamps to safety across the Finnish frontier.[58]

Xavier also enjoyed the low life. He wrote about armed robbers, Parisian loan sharks, high-flying swindlers, white slave traders, drug dealers, forgers, murderers and the antics of British and German secret agents. Fellow writers liked him. He was on the level, kind, fun and into everything. But there was little point in being a Hauteclocque just to write about lowlifes. Like the rest of his family he was on the Catholic conservative right and read *Action Française* (though he was not on the payroll), and particularly followed the military page, which the journal ran twice a month from 1928, on which older officers lamented the passing of the horse from the military armoury.[59] Xavier was passionately patriotic, complaining that France's dwindling whaling fleet was a symptom of national malaise rather than shifting market conditions, and he was farsighted enough to see the importance of petroleum in the Sahara.[60]

Most importantly, Xavier warned about the rise of Hitler. During 1932 he stayed with various Prussian landowners who regarded Nazism as a bulwark against socialism and anarchy. He described these families in his book *Aigles de Prusse* ("Eagles of Prussia"). His next book, *A l'ombre de la croix gamée* ("In the shadow of the swastika") won the Gringoire prize and tells of meetings with various senior Nazis, a visit to a concentration camp, and a stormtrooper *beerfest*. Xavier only found out about his prize by telegram because once again he was in Berlin covering the passing of the Enabling Act in the Reichstag whereby Hitler became dictator. In *La Tragédie brune* ("The brown tragedy") he describes watching Hitler giving one of his speeches:

> Listen to this! Never did he make the slightest attempt to appeal to the reason of his audience. Instead he relied on heavy and ringing phrases like the blows of a hammer to evoke the most rudimentary sentiments and reactions: pride, hate, the wish to live, the need to dominate. I heard him speaking a few days ago on May Day at Tempelhof. That time he discussed more, he sought to convince. This time he just gave orders.

However, while he had not done anything very different compared to other foreign journalists like William Shirer, Xavier de Hauteclocque had made himself a marked man. In the spring of 1933 he was welcome everywhere, but by the autumn, doors were slamming against him. Good investigative journalists like to cause embarrassment, and Xavier had been turning up at concentration camps like Dachau asking to see interned Catholic priests and touting for information on conditions inside. He also collected stories about political murders, and was turning his spotlight on the systematic persecution of Jews.[61]

In 1934 Xavier spent six weeks in Berlin covering the murder of Ernst Röhm 's Brownshirts in the Night of the Long Knives, going around nightclubs and restaurants interviewing witnesses. Seeing the process of *gleichschaltung* (coordination) whereby the Nazis extended their grip over every aspect of German life, Xavier was horrified to find that people who had once been more than happy to speak to him were now afraid to. This fear became the subject of his last book, *Police politique Hitlérienne.* After a last trip to Germany in the spring of 1935 to cover the Saar plebiscite, he returned to France sick and dying, believing he had been poisoned by the Germans in a restaurant.[62]

Philippe and Thérèse last saw Xavier when they bumped into him at Amiens' railway station shortly before his death on April 3rd. "*Je suis grillé.*" Xavier said. "The swines have got me." Though he was only 37, there was no autopsy to ascertain the actual cause of death. His funeral at the Church of Saint Ferdinand des Ternes was well attended by the great and good. Distinguished soldiers were present, including Marshal Franchet d'Espéry and General Weygand. The right-wing press circles were represented by Charles Maurras and Maurice Pujo, while Corsican deputy Horace de Carbuccia, who was also editor of *Gringoire* and a friend of Xavier's, gave the valedictory: ". . . one of the first, he had the courage to give the French a precious introduction . . . He has awakened France to the danger that menaces it . . . We his comrades, whether from the front during the Great War, or from the continuing struggle during peacetime, will piously guard his memory."[63]

Even if service life meant Philippe had not seen much of his cousin, it is quite clear that Xavier was the Hauteclocque most in the public eye during the 1930s. Philippe would have been aware of his work and its content. Indeed, one of Xavier's earlier works had been prefaced by Marshal Lyautey. In 1934 the aging Marshal, who shared Xavier's misgivings, had appeared at the Conseil Supérieur de la Guerre for the first time since 1925 on the pretext of a meeting with Pétain, but in fact to give them a copy of Hitler's *Mein Kampf,* saying "All France should read this book."[64] Whether or not the Nazis killed Xavier de Hauteclocque, they certainly knew all about him. When France was occupied five years later they raided Xavier's former home in Picardy and banned his books.[65]

With growing misgivings about the international situation, Philippe wrote in January 1936 to Maurice Catoire, then an attaché in Rome, complaining of Europeans' willingness to kill each other again. He also took a dim view of the unproductive wave of Anglophobia sweeping the country and, among religious circles, extreme pacifism, none of which he believed would get France anywhere.[66]

The ideological and colonial wars of the 1930s gave French Army officers a strange cocktail of viewpoints. French policy in Africa meant they had little right to criticise the Italian invasion of Ethiopia, while officers such as Henri Giraud were naturally interested in Italian use of air power against the Senoussi in Libya. In Spain they wanted Franco to defeat the "reds" who had been murdering priests. It was not in France's interest for the Spanish nationalists to be defeated by a Soviet-backed adversary. Yet the *Front Populaire* government had renewed the old anti-German alliance with the Soviet Union in 1935.

Such confusion blighted French thinking over who represented their true enemy. This continued through the early years of the war, manifesting itself in fruitless escapades and deaths, whether sending aid to Finland less than a year before Marshal Mannerheim allied with Germany, or useless naval actions against the British during the Vichy period.

To this day the fall of France is subject to continuous reanalysis by French historians. At first there was little during the interwar years to distinguish Philippe de Hauteclocque from officers who, a few short years later, would obey Pétainist orders to fire on the British and Free French in Syria or Madagascar, or upon the American landings of November 1942. By background, religion and politics Philippe could so easily have been one of them. But in 1940 he made a choice whereas most did not, including many future comrades in the 2e DB. Like an obscure captain from the Wehrmacht's 17th Cavalry Regiment, Claus von Stauffenberg, who later attempted to assassinate Hitler, Philippe's religious upbringing gave him the ability to identify true evil.

In Philippe's case, this ability was enhanced by studying religious thinkers, in particular Charles de Foucauld, the flamboyant Chasseurs d'Afrique officer turned religious mystic, who founded the order of the Little Fathers in Algeria and strove to bring Christianity to impoverished tribesmen in the western Sahara until he was murdered in 1916. Philippe de Hauteclocque always carried a photograph of Foucauld with the credo "*se commander à soi meme*"—"to demand the same even of oneself" (as Christ).

All he needed was the opportunity, when faced with the unacceptable, to say "no."

From the summer of 1933 until the outbreak of war, the question of mechanising the French cavalry was a matter of continuous interest for Philippe. In September he began the instructor's course at Saumur. Being only thirty years old, many discussions that took place among the army's tank men were above Philippe's pay grade. Since 1931 the new director of cavalry was General Flavigny, who had been advocating mechanisation since the 1920s. There were two divergent concepts for the use of tanks: in the first, tanks were to be used for infantry support at the infantry's pace; in the second, tanks would move *en masse* to punch large holes in enemy formations, supported by aircraft and followed up by motorised infantry to hold the ground taken. In German hands the second philosophy evolved as *Blitzkrieg*.

In 1925 renewed trust between France and Germany, following Briand and Stresemann's conference at Locarno, meant that new military ideas were put on the backburner.[67] But growing wariness of the Nazis during the early 1930s coincided with André Maginot's appointment as secretary of state for defence, and heralded a disastrous return to defensive thinking. The Maginot Line was so expensive that there was no money left over to bring the rest of the army up to date, let alone the air force. Yet, surprisingly, during this time France gave herself a powerful and modern navy.

Nevertheless, General Flavigny and officers such as Captain Leyer did what they could to develop France's tank force. The first units to benefit were the *Divisions Légères Méchaniques*—mechanised light divisions. But these were conceived for rapid intervention, not as main attack forces.

The head of cavalry squadrons at Saumur was Commandant Touzet du Vigier, a few years older than Hauteclocque, but already an apostle of armoured warfare. In 1914 he had conducted a successful mounted reconnaissance behind the German lines and gathered important intelligence prior to the Battle of the Marne. In 1920 he was a French military observer during the Russo-Polish War along with Captain Charles de Gaulle. Although this generation of officers would become important, the substance of armoured training at Saumur was farcical. Lack of money meant armoured exercises were conducted using pennants to signify tanks in action. There was not even enough cash to pay for wooden tank mock-ups as seen in so many photographs of the renascent Wehrmacht.

In the meantime, Philippe learnt to be the perfect instructor in horsemanship, with excellent reports for dressage. Returning to Saint-Cyr the following year, he was soon promoted to captain. Although a year older than most of his contemporaries from the *Metz et Strasbourg,* promotion to captain by the age of thirty-two in the large, slow-changing French Army represented a considerable acceleration up the chain of command. The careers of *Fantassins*, infantrymen, tended to move faster, but only Le Puloch was to beat him to the third *galon* (bar) on his cuff. Most cavalry-men from Philippe's year had to wait until 1936; nineteen were still waiting in 1937; and Prince Kourakine, a white Russian serving with the Foreign Legion Cavalry Regiment, was still waiting in 1938.[68]

Back at Saint-Cyr, Philippe commanded a cavalry squadron of thirty second-year cadets split into two troops, instilling in them the cavalry's sense of superiority: "Doubtless there are those of you arriving in the cav-alry squadron who aren't up to it and who haven't thought it through. The cavalry does not tolerate mediocrity. You will be dourly put to the test… you will have a hard time. Some won't find their feet. Never mind, they can go back to the infantry."[69] No one fell out. His command style then and later was to tell his men the worst, what was expected and why. If he criticised a soldier he could be severe but never wounding. Invariably he left the impression of being tough but fair.

In 1936 Philippe suffered two mishaps. First, reminiscent of his uncle Wallerand, he broke his leg when his horse slipped during a parade and he fell off. Like Wallerand, Philippe also waited until relieved of his duties before allowing himself to be stretchered away. Next, at summer camp at Sissonne, he lost his way during an exercise and found himself stuck in an area cordoned off with barbed wire. "Gentlemen, when one has done something bloody stupid (*"somptueuse bêtise"*), it's best to say so," he told his pupils with utmost honesty.

However severe he may have been on his cadets, Captain de Haute-clocque, and Lieutenants de Courtils and de Royere, knew how to take the pressure off with breaks at a tavern in Pontchartrain on the way back to Saint-Cyr from exercises. On Saturday afternoons they went cross-country, riding in the Forest of Marly for frenzied galloping and jumping obstacles as large as Grand National fences.[70]

In 1936, German troops reoccupied the west bank of the Rhineland. Many French officers thought that this was the time to stop the Nazis before they grew any more powerful. But the weakness of both the French and British governments meant the opportunity was allowed to slip. The following year General Franco's Nationalists established control over most of Spain, aided by Germany's Condor Legion. Desperate for help, the Republican government turned to Soviet Russia for aid, while Europe's trade unionists and intellectuals formed the International Brigades under the direction of Frenchman André Marty. Yet, while the French right preferred to see a Nationalist victory, Philippe de Hauteclocque maintained a distaste for Franco's Nationalists, disliking Franco's obvious personal ambition, and he regarded Spain as inferior to France in any case.

In the spring of 1938 Hauteclocque was appointed to the École Supérieure de Guerre (ESG), France's equivalent of the British Staff College at Warminster, founded in 1876. Wallerand de Hauteclocque had attended in 1913 in the same class as General Weygand. De Gaulle had been there during the early 1920s. Although his time at ESG would be overshadowed by the Munich crisis, Philippe's days were taken up with studying reviews from each branch of the army, including infantry, cavalry, artillery and logisitics. An important course book was General Descoins' *Étude synthétique des principales campagnes modernes*. This *magnum opus* came in two thick volumes and charted the development of warfare from Louis XIV until 1914. Descoins' book, while out of date regarding modern weaponry, nevertheless made points that are eternal. Wars are not simply won on battlefields but with the politics, diplomacy and economy of every nation involved. But, stopping at 1914, the book failed to mention Great War developments such as machine guns, tanks and aircraft, and many pupils, including Philippe, pencilled questions in its margins "What about the motor engine?"

Even in 1938, the ESG trained officers to observe and reconnoitre from horseback rather than cars, armoured cars or motorbikes. This astonishing oversight was only offset slightly by the availability of Potez 25 reconnaissance aircraft, in which Hauteclocque managed to run up twenty hours practice in aerial reconnaissance, aerial photography and target shooting. A member of ESG's 60th promotion, Philippe was not the first member of "Metz et Strasbourg" to reach ESG. Three old friends had been on ESG's 58th promotion and left before his arrival, while La Horie and Jobert were in the 59th class, often bumping into him in the corridors. Still living off the prestige of victory in the Great War, however close-run, the ESG had foreign students from countries with less military establishment: eastern European nations like Poland, Greece and Romania as well as Latin American countries. Militarily, France still believed she had much to teach.

The mobilisation exercises precipitated by the Munich crisis—during which Philippe served on the staff of the 52nd Infantry Division—demonstrated alarming deficiencies. For a start there were simply not enough men. The Great War's manpower losses were felt in French industry as well. Skilled labour was at a premium, and union collective bargaining had pushed through a forty-hour week, useless if France was to close the productivity gap with Germany. So even the partial mobilisation of the Métropolitan army brought everything to a grinding halt. Then, after the sell-out of Czechoslovakia, which outraged the left's previously pacifist politicians, the army desultorily returned to barracks and the reservists to their factories. With a sigh of relief, France went back to normal. Most Frenchmen believed it was a victory.

At least Hauteclocque came out of it with good reports. Living between Tailly and an apartment on the Avenue de Breteuil near Les Invalides, the family spent the last year of peace living the way military upper class families always do. Their youngest child, Bénédicte, had just arrived. The others were at Hattemer, a select private school for which they had been prepared with the assistance of an Austrian governess, Anne-Marie Lang. In order to improve their children's command of German, Philippe, Thérèse and Anne-Marie spoke the language in front of them at home, little knowing how soon they would need it. Though only 37, Philippe was a traditional father just like Count Adrien had been, old world and puritanical, not wanting his children to see their mother in bathing costume on seaside holidays, severe with naughtiness, firm but fair, and rewarding good conduct with small, well chosen gifts.[71]

ESG's 60th promotion would not have a second year. In March 1939 Hitler took over the remaining Czech provinces, Bohemia and Moravia, which had never even been German. Then it was Poland's turn. Germany resented the "corridor" which gave Poland a Baltic coastline through former old Prussia. Faked border incidents raised the tension along the Polish border all summer.

Philippe de Hauteclocque spent the last days of peace at Tailly, getting in the harvest and preparing his elder children, Henri, Hubert, Charles, Jeanne and Michel, for the new academic year. As summer turned to autumn, diplomatic events punctuated the countdown to war. On 23rd August 1939, German Foreign Minister Joachim von Ribbentrop signed the non-aggression pact with his Soviet opposite number, Molotov. In eastern Europe, Poland was isolated; her historic friendship with Hungary had no diplomatic or military value whatsoever. Only the alliance with France and Great Britain could help her. French reservists were called up. Six days later, Germany invaded Poland. The following day, Britain and France declared a general mobilisation, and on 3rd September Europe was at war.

Philippe's orders were not to return to ESG but instead to report to General Musse's 4th Infantry Division as chief of staff. Musse had been military attaché at the French Embassy in Warsaw, getting out via Romania when the Germans invaded. A local reserve formation which included men Philippe knew personally, the 4e DI consisted of three infantry regiments, the 45e, 72e and 124e, along with the 12e cavalry reconnaissance group, the 29e artillery regiment and the 229e heavy artillery regiment. As soon as each regiment was fully formed it took its place in the line facing the Belgian frontier around Hirson near the Ardennes forest. The Maginot Line was being extended northwards to the sea, and the division was ordered to send working parties into the Ardennes to improve defences, though many reassured themselves that the forest was impassable.

France and Great Britain were still mobilising while Hitler's Wehrmacht and the Soviet Union carved up Poland between them. Then they sat in their positions to await events for a period known as the "Phoney War" to the British, the "*drôle de guerre*" to the French, and the *Sitzkrieg* to the Germans. A French foray into the Saarland during the autumn, known as the Saar offensive, withdrew to its start line, accomplishing nothing and meeting little German resistance. Once the 4e DI arrived in the area, some WWI-style night patrolling took place in no-man's land. Hauteclocque usually followed this from the divisional CP (command post), but sometimes his daring-do temperament got the better of him and he went out also, face blacked, with an Adrian helmet on his head and carrying a Lebel revolver.

That winter was a hard one. The Channel froze at Boulogne, and work extending the Maginot Line slowed to a standstill, since earth was rock hard and concrete impossible to pour or lay. With nothing to do but watch the frontier in bitter cold, drunkenness became widespread. Conscription meant that most men had taken a steep cut in wages. With poor army pay and the national labour shortage more acute than ever, many soldiers became obsessed with leave, hoping to make extra wages either at their old job, if their home was not too far to travel, or doing whatever they could find.

On 7th January 1940, the 4e DI was sent to Montreuil near Abbeville for rest and reorganisation. Though reasonably near Tailly, Philippe did not go home often, spending his time on divisional matters with General Lafontaine instead. While he enjoyed this responsible position, Philippe most preferred being among the officers and men of the 12e cavalry reconnaissance regiment. Here he was in his *métier*. When the division's operations' chief was sent with the French mission to Romania, Hauteclocque took his place, a position he held until the 28th May.

The 4e DI had another four months of *Sitzkrieg* to sit through.

CHAPTER TWO

LA CHUTE—THE FALL OF FRANCE

On 10th May 1940, Philippe's parents' golden wedding anniversary was cancelled when Germany attacked Holland and Belgium. In a massive aerial campaign, paratroops secured Holland's Rhine delta bridges while glider-borne combat engineers took out the Belgian fortress of Eben Emael. This was the "matador's cloak" intended to draw British and French forces into the Low Countries. The Dutch, untouched by war since Napoleon, were completely taken by surprise and surrendered. Supported by the best troops of the British Expeditionary Force and French Army, the Belgians lasted a little longer.

On 13th May an article in *The New York Journal* said the Germans seemed uninterested in France this time.[1] In fact, knowing there was little point in attacking the Maginot Line directly, Lieutenant-General Erich von Manstein had been working furiously on an alternative plan. Seeing the Maginot Line's northern end as a hinge on which French and British operations must pivot, and anxious to avoid repeating the horrors of the Great War's trenches, Manstein concluded that success in the West depended on annihilating Allied forces in northern France and the Low Countries. The Allies' solar plexus was at Sedan, where the Prussians defeated Napoleon III, ending the French Second Empire. Now France had neglected this area, believing it impassable due to the surrounding

Ardennes forest. Desultory efforts had been made to patch up infantry defences with pillboxes, not least by personnel from General Musse's 4e DI, but nothing was finished.

Facing Sedan was General Corap's Ninth Army. Though reckoned a soldier's soldier, well liked by his men, Corap had spent his career almost entirely with the *Armée d'Afrique*, its high point being the capture of Abd-el-Krim. His tactical thinking was *passé*, and he lacked any theoretical knowledge of armoured warfare, let alone experience.

Opposite Corap was the German tank expert Heinz Guderian, commanding a vast armoured phalanx run by young, energetic subordinates. One of these was up-and-coming Major-General Erwin Rommel, whose 7th Panzer Division reached the Meuse's east bank by dawn on 13th May, immediately drawing accurate artillery and small arms fire from the French. Rommel rapidly called down suppressing fire from artillery and tanks while his combat engineers set about building pontoon bridges under fire. French counterattacks cost many German casualties but were never pressed home strongly enough. In the meantime, Rommel's officers scoured the banks of the Meuse for a crossing place solid enough to support tanks, settling on an old weir.

Man for man, French soldiers fought well, but logistics and communications behind their lines were sluggish, an atrophy going right to the top. Information reached General Gamelin's HQ at Vincennes via motorcycle dispatch riders rather than radio; orders arrived at the front the same way. Such time delays were crucial, and by 14th May Rommel and Guderian had both consolidated bridgeheads over the Meuse. The next day their Panzers broke out into northern France. Corap's army, consisting of many fine colonial units, but lacking modern transport and adequate artillery, collapsed under further blows, now supported by the full weight of German air power as well. By the 16th, the French High Command was in panic. The German Luftwaffe was asserting its technical superiority over lesser French aircraft, and the Allies' most advanced fighter planes, British Spitfires, were being kept in reserve in southern England.

Musse's 4e DI was ordered to hold the banks of the River Sambre. Amid steadily mounting casualties, Hauteclocque found himself commanding three battalions of infantry, taking position along the river with the Forest of Mormal behind them. Hauteclocque, along with his men, was in a resolute mood, but being on the north side of the German breakthrough, they soon detected German infiltration in the forest behind them. Among French senior commanders the fever of retreat was spreading rapidly, and Musse felt he had no option but to pull the 4e DI back behind the Escaut canal, something Hauteclocque accepted with difficulty.

Manstein's plan was taking shape with startling speed. After breaking through on the Meuse in a sickle-shaped movement (the plan was code-named "*Sichelschnitt*") German forces swung northwest towards the English Channel, trapping France's northern armies and the British Expeditionary Force around the ports of the Pas de Calais. Roads quickly became clogged with refugees carrying all their possessions on wagons and hand-carts, intermittently strafed by German aircraft. Even at night, incessant machine-gun fire kept pressure on these columns of human misery, whose most vulnerable were the elderly and very young. Death from dehydration and exhaustion became commonplace.

As the German Panzer corridor deepened, the 4e DI was forced to retreat northwards, finding itself in peaceful, totally untouched woodland just inside Belgium. Throughout this time, Hauteclocque, maintaining an aura of dutiful indefatigability, had to draft the 4e DI's retreat orders. Regrouped behind the Éscaut, the division had three days' respite as the Wehrmacht's *Schwerpunkt* passed them by. On the 21st May, Guderian's Panzers reached the Channel, cutting off Blanchard's First Army and the BEF from the rest of the reeling French Army. As the Germans began wearing down the pocket, the 4e and 25e DIs held out around Mastaing. By now General Musse had sustained a nasty head injury, and many command functions were falling upon Hauteclocque. When a counterattack at Arras by British tanks failed, the situation became even more desperate. By the 25th May the 4e DI was being pressed northwards into Armentières and Lille, where the compounding chaos of exhausted refugees and dishevelled *poilus* could only spell defeat. Continuous German pressure from the south quickly turned Lille into a witches' cauldron. Although the 4e DI's artillery and some infantry fought to keep the line from Lille to the coast open through the night of 27th–28th May, by morning these exhausted troops and remnants of other divisions were forced back into the town.

By 8am Lille was completely cut off from the coastal pocket around Dunkirk, as well as from the rest of France. With little hope of resupply, ammunition was running low and Musse's division was disintegrating into a mob of hungry, scruffy, desperate men. There were traffic jams everywhere; only one bridge remained intact, and Lille was being pummelled by German aircraft.

"What next?" Hauteclocque asked a colonel.

"Wait and see," came the reply.

Surveying the sea of dishevelled soldiery, and recognising that only prison camps awaited them, Philippe presented himself to the wounded General Musse. "Sir," he began. "I do not want to be taken prisoner. My role as a staff officer without troops has become useless. May I have your permission to take my chance?"

"*Entendu* [agreed]," said Musse. "I wish I could go too, but I must stay with the men." With that, the bandaged general offered a warm handshake to the determined young captain. Hauteclocque returned the salute and turned about.

Hauteclocque headed out of Lille's Douai gate, walking quietly through the wreckage of France's worst-ever defeat. Unshaven *poilus* were scavenging for any food and drink they could find. Terrified and hungry horses roamed loose. Abandoned vehicles littered the streets, intact but lacking petrol following the breakdown of logistics. Famished and exhausted, Hauteclocque found a baguette in an abandoned field bakery van, and then used an abandoned bicycle to ride to the southern outskirts and await nightfall. After dark he headed south to Faches et Vendeville. Emerging from the village, he heard a German Panzer column rolling towards Wattignies and hid quickly in a field of rye. The sound of distant gunfire indicated street fighting. Lying in the tall rye he contemplated the extraordinary way German machine-guns fired without cease compared to French ones.[2]

When the firing died down he continued southwards across the German corridor until he found his path blocked again by a column of Wehrmacht vehicles between Ennetières and Fretin. He lay down in a field for a while to watch them before continuing. Sometimes German patrols would shout out "*Wer da?*" ("Who goes there?"), but always too late as the thirty-seven year old French captain slipped away into the darkness. The following day he lay up in a copse near a squadron of parked German tanks whose crews were eating, drinking, singing and playing guitars and accordions. Nightfall again, with clouds hiding the Pole star, he oriented himself as best he could with neither map nor compass and headed in the direction of Orchies. Avoiding any village that seemed German-occupied, Hauteclocque walked for three hours until he came to a hamlet where dogs still barked, suggesting some French inhabitants had remained. Knocking on a door Philippe learnt he was in Ostricourt, but when he asked for civilian clothes the owner refused, asking him to disappear. This area had been occupied during the Great War and the locals knew about going with the tide. Approaching another house, once again he was asked to scram—this time with the additional threat of denunciation. Sickened and furious, Hauteclocque pushed past the man, grabbed a coat and hat off a clothes peg, and turned away into the night.

As the sun rose he came across a couple of teenage lads who directed him towards an abandoned house. He approached cautiously, taking in the atmosphere of despair and the evidence of sudden departure. Inside he found an old jacket that just about fit him, and a bicycle in an outshed. Philippe dumped as much uniform as he could in a field, changed, mounted the bicycle and peddled away as fast as he could.

Virtually the whole population of northwest France was displaced by the rapid German attack which pushed almost eight million people onto the roads as refugees. It was now less risky for Philippe to travel by day. Putting abandoned goods on the bicycle, he mingled in, following the tide of human despair to the Scarpe river at Lallaing. There French workers were mucking in cheerfully with the Wehrmacht engineers repairing the bridge, all saying how they hoped "all this" would soon be over.

Heading on towards Cambrai, scene of the Great War's first tank battle, Hauteclocque noticed that German bombers had taken over a landing strip with all the logistical back-up needed for an airfield, while nearby the road was lined with abandoned French artillery. Every so often a German staff car or *kubelwagen* would hoot its horn at refugees, squeezing past down the road to the south. Reaching Cambrai at night, Philippe slept in an abandoned house, helping himself to more civilian clothing.

The following day, 31st May, the Lille pocket surrendered. On the coast the British Expeditionary Force was taking to the fleet of little boats rounded up by the Royal Navy in Operation Dynamo. As the "miracle of Dunkirk" unfolded, a rearguard, including elements of the French First Army, fought doggedly to hold the Germans back.

Leaving Cambrai for St. Quentin, Philippe found the flow of refugees had ebbed away. Instead there was the traffic and marching of German infantry divisions, young soldiers fresh from their barracks and training areas, radiating confidence. Occasionally a tank would come along from the north, churning up the dirt and coating everyone with a fine film of dust. The debris of battle blotched the countryside and lined the roads, including burnt out Somua, Hotchkiss and Char B tanks, and French Army lorries often in good working order but lacking petrol.

Then Philippe's luck ran out. A Wehrmacht lieutenant armed with a Schmeisser submachine gun asked to see his papers and travel permit. Having neither, he was taken to a battalion headquarters and presented to senior lieutenant Wengler. Subjected to a full search, including shoes and socks, Philippe pleaded that his wife and children were in St. Quentin. Hoping there were no papers left identifying him, his spirits sank as Wengler emptied his wallet. In an inner pocket lurked an old salary slip from ESG made out to "Captain de Hauteclocque." Wengler solemnly declared, "Monsieur, you are a prisoner of war. If you try to escape our sentries will shoot you."

Shut in a barn on his own, Philippe peered morosely through the shutters of its only window at the passing traffic of German victors. For twenty-four hours he noted passing German staff cars, large Mercedes carrying smiling senior officers in uniforms with the red piping and *lampassen* of the general staff. At about midday he was joined by three young French soldiers, remnants of General Didelet's 9e Mechanised Infantry Division. Hoping to rejoin French forces in the south, they had disguised themselves as workers and succeeded in evading capture for six days before being betrayed by the owner of a house where they had rested.

Notwithstanding their POW status, the Germans treated the Frenchmen properly. They were given a substantial rice and vegetable soup with some locally slaughtered meat. As the Frenchmen ate, a German officer was delighted to inform Hauteclocque that the Lille pocket had surrendered and the British were scurrying into little boats at Dunkirk. The German then confidently declared the war would be over in a month. Through a crack in the barn doors they noticed the German soldiers holding a small parade, shouting "Heil Hitler," and cheering Lille's fall.

On the afternoon of 1st June the Frenchmen were loaded into a lorry, guarded by two soldiers armed with Mauser rifles, bayonets attached. Wengler had thrown in a box containing their personal effects taken during questioning the previous day. But the German guards were intermittently nodding off, tired out after the exhausting pace of their advance. Philippe seized the chance to rummage in his wallet and remove the incriminating ESG wage slip.

On reaching the German divisional command post, Hauteclocque found himself interrogated by a dour colonel and repeated the same story; his family were in St. Quentin and they needed him. But he embellished it further, saying he had been injured fighting in Morocco, suffered from malaria, and was unfit for military service. Then, acting a bit simple, he said, "I've got six children!" The colonel, ignorant of the missing wage slip, turned to a subordinate, exclaiming in German "What do you think of a nation where a man is exempted from defending his country because he has six children?" Then, not knowing that Hauteclocque understood German, the colonel barked, "If you find anything that shows he's militarily unfit, let him go. We've had enough." There was a brief attempt at another search, which Philippe protested, still pretending to be simple. "Get out!" said the German colonel. For a moment Philippe mumbled a request for a German travel permit. "Push off, or we'll arrest you again." With that he was thrown onto the streets of Bohain.

Anxious to make up for lost time, Hauteclocque walked all through the night of 1st and 2nd June towards the southwest. By daybreak he was within sight of Saint Quentin Cathedral, whose spire he could see over the trees. Approaching the town he noticed another column of marching German soldiers led by officers on horseback. The ordinary divisions of the Wehrmacht seemed no more modern than most of the French Army. Thousands of Germans marched past him into Saint Quentin, hobnailed jackboots pounding the macadam. There was plenty of horse drawn artillery and a military band with their black and white striped birdsnest epaulets, trumpets, fifes and glockenspiels, thumping out traditional German marching songs. The townsfolk of Saint Quentin looked on stunned with tears in their eyes, their humiliation momentarily lifted by the sight of a German aircraft going down in flames outside the town.

The following night was clear enough for Philippe to use the Pole star as he threaded his way through occupied villages amid the crump of

artillery fire. German horsed transport was going in all directions. For
much of the following day he was held up by the proximity of a German
checkpoint which could not fail to detect him if he emerged from a wood.
That night, the 4th, he reached the Crozat Canal northwest of Jussy. In
spite of a couple of close shaves with German patrols, he stripped to the
waist and swam across. Reaching the opposite bank at 5am on the morning
of 5th June, he was stopped by a French patrol and declared himself. After
eight days Philippe had reached the main French lines.

The Crozat Canal was held by General Jeannel's fresh 23e DI, which
barely four weeks earlier had been part of General Gamelin's Supreme
Headquarters Reserve (*Réserve du Grand Quartier Général*). After a good
cleanup and a meal, the commander of the 107e RI's signal company,
Captain Précheur, found Philippe a new uniform, artillery officer's garb
being the nearest he could find to cavalry officer's elegance. Later that
morning Philippe reported his experiences to Captain Paoli of the 23e
Infantry Division's *2e bureau*.[3]

Philippe was sent to Seventh Army HQ at Chantilly. Seventh Army
was now commanded by the former commandant of Saint-Cyr, General
Frère, whom he knew reasonably well. The French supreme commander
was now General Weygand, who had been recalled from Syria to replace
Gamelin after the latter's collapse following the failure at Sedan. Hauteclocque gave Frère an account of German movements during his eight days
behind German lines. Impressed by the former cavalry instructor, Frère
was happy to inform de Hauteclocque that his home Tailly was still behind
French lines in a sector held by the 3e DLC (*Division légère e de cavalerie*)
commanded by General Pettiet. 3e DLC had been badly mauled by German armour whilst supporting General de Gaulle's armoured counterattack
a few days earlier, but Frère lent Philippe a car so that he could visit his
family.

He drove as fast as he dared. The Picardy countryside was already
regarded as a battlefield, and looters were already at work stealing from
those who had shut up their houses. Philippe's mind was a storm of worry.[4]
First he went to Belloy to see his parents. As mayor, Count Adrien could
not dream of leaving his people. At Tailly, he discovered his wife and children had already left for Sainte-Foy-La-Grande in the southwest, an estate
belonging to relations where they were sure of being put up. For a few

moments, he wandered around his home, speaking to servants and retainers he had known all his life. The sun shone brightly but no one enjoyed it. All the younger men had gone to the war, and there was no news of them. He gave a few last instructions, got back in the car and returned to the front. The following day, 5th June, there was another breakthrough by Rommel and, by 4.30pm, Tailly was behind German lines.

On 7th June Philippe was ordered by Frère to report on his escape through the German corridor to Supreme Headquarters. He took the opportunity to buy a new uniform in Paris. Philippe was not the only future Free French officer to do this. In all this military chaos even Charles de Gaulle, newly promoted to brigadier-general, had found time for his tailor a few days earlier!

Smartened up, Hauteclocque received a new appointment to the hastily cobbled together *2eme groupement cuirassé*. "A tardy try at a Panzer Division," he would later recall with bitterness. "Late as always."[5] Various units had been assembled under General Buisson, formerly commander of the *3eme Division Cuirassée*, the remnants of 3eme, the *7e Division légère méchanique*, a Polish armoured brigade commanded by Brigadier Maczek, three other battalions of tanks and some infantry.[6] Philippe's older brother Guy was serving with *2eme DC*'s reconnaissance unit. Naively, Guy had not realised how seriously France was threatened until Philippe told him.[7] Surpassing their high water mark of the Great War, the Germans were over the rivers Aisne and Marne. Buisson's tank group now had to defend Reims.

On 10th June, Buisson ordered the remnants of 3e DCR under Colonel Le Brigant to counterattack north towards Perthes, south of Rethel. 3e DCR's HQ came under fire from German tanks so Le Brigant himself was unable to lead the operation. Buisson sent Hauteclocque to take over. Without a radio, Hauteclocque walked among the heavy Char B tanks with just a képi on his head, giving directions with his cane. He led the attack from its start line, pushing the Germans back and achieving a limited local success. Briefing Buisson afterwards, both men were impressed by what could be accomplished with a concentrated armoured force. But it was too late. Two days later Buisson's remaining Char B's were lost cutting a beleaguered infantry division out of Mourmelon.

In many ways the Char B could match a Panzer III; it had heavy armour but its 75mm gun was set low in its hull and lacked 360' traverse. The rotating turret, which was standard to other French tanks, only carried a 47mm gun, which was no match for the Panzers and had to be operated by one over-tasked man.

With little armour left, 3e DCR's role for the 13th and 14th was to hold the Marne crossing points between Vitry-le-François and Saint Dizier. The command post was a large *gentilhommière* at Magnant, owned by a lawyer who was packing to leave with his wife just as the French soldiers arrived. The lawyer took an affable, resigned view of events, and chatted amiably with the young officers setting up their division's HQ in his house.

"I'm not going to lock things up. There will only be more damage when they are broken open." With great dignity they took leave of their beautiful home. Getting into his car the lawyer reached into his jacket pocket.

"Here is the key to my wine cellar. Best to drink the champagne before the Germans arrive."

Sitting around a polished dining table laid with silver, the windows open to early summer sunshine just as if they were in a mess in Paris or Saumur, the officers' lunch that day was surreal. Afterwards Hauteclocque took a little Simca staff car to distribute food and wine around the picket positions. Behind machine guns or in their few remaining Somua and Hotchkiss tanks, the men prepared for the last act in their hopeless struggle, drinking champagne from billy cans and eating *foie gras* with camping forks.

They did not have long to wait. The Stuka dive-bombers attacked the next day. Visiting forward positions with Commandant de Bonaventure, their car was strafed with machine-gun fire, causing Philippe a nasty gash across his head. He was rudimentarily patched up at the aid station and returned to Buisson's command post. There, General Buisson realised the struggle was pointless and tried to withdraw as many men as he could to reduce the risk of capture and save the wounded. He took one look at the freshly bandaged Hauteclocque and ordered him to leave at once. The injury sustained at Magnant might have been avoided if Philippe had worn a steel helmet.[8] He reached a hospital in Avallon, run by the Sisters of Charity, where he passed out. Philippe de Hauteclocque's "Battle of France" was over.

The Germans had reached the Loire. Paul Reynaud's government was now attempting to run things from Bordeaux. French industry continued to churn out war material until the Wehrmacht overran their factories. Weygand, appointed too late, rebuked any politician within range for declaring a war the country was incapable of waging. Damage limitation became his aim. The decision to spare Paris by declaring it an "open city" was taken on 10th June, and by the 14th the capital had been surrendered by General Henri Dentz. Overnight, Paris became a place of ghostly emptiness whose silence was punctuated only by the barking of abandoned dogs.

On 10th June, like a scavenger hovering for leftovers, Mussolini's Italy declared war on France. Italian radio thumped out "*Giovinezza*" incessantly. Brigadier General de Gaulle was appointed secretary of state for war, and, however much he wanted to fight on, it was obvious that France was facing a cataclysm she simply could not handle. Twelve million people, over a quarter of France's population, had taken to the roads, causing a massive displacement crisis.

Marshal Pétain, the eighty-four-year-old hero of Verdun, had joined Reynaud's government on 18th May. He viewed the situation grimly. In the previous contest he had won the affection of his men through parsimony with their lives, after three bitter years that cost French manhood many hundreds of thousands of casualties. This time, after merely five weeks, 130,000 more Frenchmen lay dead. On his last visit to the French government, Churchill suggested that France turn itself over to guerrilla warfare. "That would wreck my country," snapped Pétain. As he left, Churchill noticed the young General de Gaulle. "*L'homme du destin,*" he said quietly in his inimitable "Franglais." Churchill returned to England and Pétain sued for peace.

Many Frenchmen claim to this day that Pétain had no alternative, and that his action saved their lives. In less than six weeks the Wehrmacht had put its jackboot firmly over France's windpipe. While the Germans gauged what terms to demand of the new French administration, Churchill's main concern became the future of the French fleet.

When Brigadier General de Gaulle arrived in England on a de Havilland Dragon Rapide aircraft, accompanied only by his ADC, Lieutenant de Courcel, and the veteran British liaison officer General Sir Edward Spears, he entered the world of international politics for the first time. Until that flight, during which he looked down on sinking ships and the smoking

wreckage of his nation's defeat, de Gaulle had only ever been a professional
soldier. Now he was the leader of all Frenchmen who refused to accept a
Nazi-dominated Europe. The British helped him set up a headquarters,
find lodgings and arrange salaries for his supporters, however few or many
they might be. While this went on, de Gaulle drafted the first of his famous
appels (appeals) to the French forces. At 6pm on 18th June he arrived with
Courcel at studio 4B in the original BBC building in London, immacu-
lately dressed but exhausted and reeking of cigarette tobacco like all chain
smokers. He stepped up to the microphone and took upon his shoulders
the soul and dignity of his defeated nation:

> The leaders who have been at the head of French armies for many
> years have formed a government. This government, alleging the
> defeat of our armies, has entered into communication with the
> enemy to stop the fighting. To be sure we have been submerged, we
> are submerged, by the enemy's mechanised forces, on land and in
> the air. It is the Germans' tanks, planes and tactics that have made
> us fall back, infinitely more than their numbers. It is the Germans'
> tanks, planes and tactics that have so taken our leaders by surprise
> as to bring them to the point they have reached today. But has the
> last word been said? Must hope vanish? Is the defeat final? No!
>
> Believe me, for I know what I am talking about and I tell you
> that nothing is lost for France. The same means that beat us may
> one day bring victory. For France is not alone. She is not alone! She
> is not alone! She has an immense Empire behind her. She can unite
> with the British Empire, which commands the sea and which is
> carrying on with the struggle. Like England she can make an
> unlimited use of the vast industries of the United States. This war
> is not confined to the unhappy territory of our country. This war
> has not been decided by the Battle of France. This is a worldwide
> war. All the faults, all the delays, all the sufferings do not do away
> with the fact that in the world there are all the means for one day
> crushing our enemies. Today we are struck down by mechanised
> force; in the future we can conquer by greater mechanised force.
> The fate of the world lies there.
>
> I, General de Gaulle, now in London, call upon the French

officers and soldiers who are on British soil or who may come onto it, with their arms or without them, I call upon the engineers and the specialised workers in the armaments industry who are or who may arrive on British soil to get in contact with me. Whatever happens, the flame of French resistance must not and shall not go out.

Tomorrow, as I have done today, I shall speak again from London.

According to the BBC's official history, this broadcast went out at 10pm on 18th June. It is often said by French historians that few heard it.[9] Amidst the relief that those disastrous five weeks were over, it can only have reached the ears of an exhausted population, and even then it would have had an air of unreality. Here was a seriously winded nation being told by a junior general they had never heard of to carry on the fight, when most of them just wanted to clear up the mess and get back to normal.

De Gaulle's original target audience were French forces on British soil, but the only significant unit that rallied to him was the 13e DBLE (*demibrigade Legion Étrangère*) formerly part of the French expedition to Norway. These were rootless men with nothing to lose, often Spanish republicans. The Norway task force included mountain troops from Metropolitan France, but under French military law soldiers conscripted to defend the homeland can not be compelled to fight elsewhere. Their commander, General Béthouart, had been at Saint-Cyr with de Gaulle, and allowed him to address his men. This yielded a few more recruits, but the vast majority simply wanted to go home and pick up the pieces of their lives. It would be a long time before early *gaullistes* shook off the "men with nothing to lose" image in the eyes of their fellow countrymen.

Of Philippe's future command, only a handful date from this earliest period of "Free" France. Christian Girard, from a sophisticated Parisian Huguenot background, fresh from university with excellent English skills, would have gone straight into the diplomatic service. During the Battle of France he had been French liaison officer to an British cavalry regiment, the Queen's Bays, which had been pushed down as far south as Le Mans. Was he a man with nothing to lose? Far from it. Pétain's Vichy government would need diplomats and administrators. So why did Girard opt for de Gaulle? If there was a deep sense of moral revulsion at Pétain's armistice, he does not declare it in his war journal except to say that he was "*boule-*

versé" by the fall of France and that his choice was based on "*un refus viscéral*"—a gut refusal. He saw images in his head of "a *Schupo* [Schutz-polizei] on duty at the corner of the Rue de Varenne and the Boulevard Raspail. "It seemed impossible for me to pass him when walking out of my house. That is all."[10]

Philippe de Hauteclocque had no idea that de Gaulle had made his first broadcast. He spent the previous day being patched up by the Sisters of Charity at Avallon, and persuaded one of them to swap his officer's tunic for that of an ordinary private. Avallon was now under Wehrmacht control. In his second escape from German custody, Philippe jumped through a hospital window into a nettle patch and set off for his youngest sister-in-law at Étaules, a few kilometres away. On the way he asked a farm worker for civilian clothes, only to be told not to worry about that any more since the ceasefire had been declared. Stopped by a German soldier further on, Philippe said he was going home and was allowed to proceed.

The Baynast de Septfontaines family chateau was sprawling with Germans drunk on the contents of the Count's wine cellar. When Philippe arrived dressed as an ordinary *poilu*, the *landsers* took a happy-go-lucky attitude to him, little knowing the outrage boiling inside him as he watched them swigging the Baynast's rare vintages. For the fit, confident young men of the Wehrmacht, the war was over. "Have a drink," they said. "We'll take back Alsace and Lorraine and then we'll all be friends." When they found he spoke reasonable German they were even warmer towards him. Taking care not to drink too much owing to his throbbing head wound, Philippe mixed in. One German soldier turned out to be a Czech, conscripted into the Wehrmacht *malgré lui*—"in spite of himself." He spoke to Philippe pityingly over what had happened to France. Without letting on that he was related to the chateau owners, Philippe persuaded the Czech to find him some civilian clothes, saying he could not wait to get out of uniform. The Czech promptly stole a country suit and trilby from the Count's wardrobe. Not knowing whether to be angry or amused, Philippe left them and set off down the drive to continue his odyssey, pausing on the way to remonstrate with a German who was larking about on a looted bicycle. "That's mine actually," said Philippe with sufficient authority to command compliance. Now he had to try and find his family.

To reach Thérèse and the children Philippe would have to cross the Loire, but most of the bridges were down after the fighting. So he returned to Paris where he could be sure to find a relation who would put him up. Arriving at 3 Rue Paul Baudry, which belonged to the Wendel family, relations of the Gargans, he found their concierge, Madame Zing, quite unaware of his connection to the owners. Nevertheless she allowed him to escort her to the offices of another acquaintance, Monsieur de Mitry, who could vouch for Hauteclocque. Only then did the concierge allow him a bed and take care of him. Another old friend helped Philippe obtain a new identity card from the Prefecture, describing him not as a soldier but as an employee of Wendels,' giving him a good reason to cross the Loire to work at Wendels' business in Bordeaux.

It was while he was in Paris that Philippe first heard about de Gaulle's appeals. But however angry he was at France's defeat, Philippe had to find out what had happened to his family before committing to anything else. On 26th June, having recuperated and visited a barber, he set off to find his wife in a car lent by the Wendels, with the bicycle "looted" from the Baynasts strapped to the rack. This was a sensible precaution in case it was impossible to refuel. By evening he had reached his sister Yvonne's home, the Chateau de Champiré, near the village of Grugé-l'Hôpital in northern Anjou. He had missed Thérèse by a few days. With the Wehrmacht ranging south of Paris, she had gone on to Les Vergnes in the southwest, along with Guy's wife Madeleine and assorted children carried in a Ford V8 and a Citroen C6. Later that same evening, after supper, Philippe first heard de Gaulle's voice on the radio, strong and firm, convinced that the United States would eventually join in the war and that the Allies would prevail.

Was Philippe de Hauteclocque a man with nothing to lose? Far from it. He was a member of a large and well known family; he had a lovely home, an attractive wife, six healthy children and elderly parents. Other members of his family had found alternative occupations after leaving the army. There were other things in life. So why did he become a *Gaulliste de la première heure*? Was it simply that during his temporary imprisonment he had overheard German officers speaking of France as a decadent country that could not be bothered to defend itself? Even if he could not conceive of a life for himself outside the army, many officers with distinguished careers ahead of them, some of whom would later serve under him in the

2e DB, rubbed along with Vichy until November 1942, when their hand was forced by the Torch landings. Could Hauteclocque have been one of them? And if not, why not?

Unlike another of de Gaulle's early supporters, the uxorious Gaston Palewski, whose conquests included British novelist Nancy Mitford, Philippe de Hauteclocque had no need of personal liberty to pursue the *louche* life of a libertine. Nor was he a "devout liberal," the sort of person who could never imagine Paris without the Moulin Rouge, the Folies Bergères or its de luxe brothels endearingly euphemised as "*maisons serieuses.*" In fact Philippe was the opposite, the sort of Frenchman who might believe in the Vichy slogan *Famille, Patrie, Travail!*—"Family, Homeland and Work!" His past subscription to *Action Française* suggests he had a taste for authoritarian values. So why did he become a *Gaulliste de la première heure*? Part of the answer must lie in his immense moral similarity to Charles de Gaulle himself. Both men came from families that had fought for France over many centuries even as far back as the Crusades. Only political realism stopped either of them from being full-blown monarchists. They were completely unable to conceive of a France that was not in absolute command of her own destiny. As de Gaulle would say on the first page of his war memoirs, "*la France ne peut etre la France sans la grandeur.*" ("France cannot be France without greatness.")[11]

Other officers felt the loss of French prestige just as deeply without joining de Gaulle. Some felt it could only be recovered by collaboration with Nazi Germany. We can not forget the Christian moral dimension, but both Hauteclocque and de Gaulle were furious that their political masters had not made France's armed services modern enough to face the threat. Thus they were not only morally outraged by Nazism but also sickened at not being able to defend their homeland when France is, then and now, a rich nation.

However, in June 1940 France could not have continued fighting without being annihilated. This has to be accepted by moralists and pragmatists alike. In that instance, the seeking of an armistice by Marshal Pétain was entirely reasonable and has to be respected. It was only later, as Nazi pressures grew, that Vichy slid into shamelessness.

The Armistice had been in force since the evening of 22nd June, and the Loire valley represented, roughly speaking, the parallel along which most of France, except the Atlantic seaboard, would be divided between "occupied" and "free" zones. In some areas, Wehrmacht units had advanced so far south they outstripped the area Germany demanded for her occupied zone and had to be withdrawn. Pretty little towns like Loches in Indre-et-Loire received their first "liberation" on July 12th 1940.[12]

The Demarcation Line remained, for all practical purposes, the front line at the time of the ceasefire on the evening of 22nd June until finalised by the Armistice Commission in Wiesbaden. Philippe de Hauteclocque and his wife and children were on opposite sides of it. The line was strictly guarded by the Germans, and administered from rapidly installed local Kommandanturs, one of which had been set up in the *Mairie* of Grugé-l'Hôpital. The identity card that the Wendels had organised for him in Paris might have been good enough to enable him to go to Bordeaux or even on to Bayonne, both of which were on the German side of the line. But for crossing the demarcation line he needed something better.

It may be here that Hauteclocque's *nom de guerre*, "Leclerc," first originates. Local records for the province of Maine et Loire, where Grugé-l'Hôpital is situated, specify that he was issued a pass to the unoccupied zone in the name of "Leclerc—wine merchant," by the Kommandantur in Grugé-l'Hôpital.[13] "Leclerc" is an unremarkable name, equating to the English "Clark" with its nickname "Nobby." That he should have called himself a wine merchant is equally unremarkable. Wine is often traded between French provinces, as well as between France and Spain; the Spanish are not good at brandy and the French make neither sherry nor port. The wine trade certainly did not stop for the war. Explaining that Philippe was no longer fit for military service and wished to rejoin his wife and children, Yvonne de Bodard and the local priest, Abbé Brossier, took the completed forms to the Kommandantur.

"What are you going to do?" asked Yvonne. "Pétain is in power. The Germans are already at Bayonne."

"I've been thinking," said Philippe. "I am going to join General de Gaulle." His sister Yvonne ("Vonnette") was the first person he told.[14]

Armed with the new pass, he set off for Les Vergnes on the bicycle taken at Étaules, but it was a lady's model and too uncomfortable for a long ride. After two days' of walking he arrived exhausted on the 30th of June, weeping with joy to see Thérèse and the children again. Staying there for four

days of borrowed time amid the unfolding cataclysm of war, he told
Thérèse his experiences since 10th May and his decision to join de Gaulle.
In his opinion, everything possible had to be done to defeat the Nazis and
make France free.

Thérèse told him how she had packed and left Tailly once it became
clear the German breakthrough was serious. The journey south from
Champiré was made with two cars full of younger children while the older
ones, including Henri and Hubert, followed on bicycles towed by the cars
to save their legs, everyone singing psalms to keep their courage up on
roads crammed with refugees.[15] It had all been quite an adventure.

Their plan was that she would return to Tailly and see how the political
situation evolved. If necessary she would, with her husband's blessing, sell
Tailly and relocate herself and the children out of harm's way. If she had to
abandon Tailly without selling it, she had the option of contacting her relations in Canada, the Vaniers. She saw that Philippe's decision to join de
Gaulle was firm. She understood his inner turmoil at the fall of France and
Thérèse never tried to stop him in any way. When he worried for her and
the children she told him, "You've decided. You can't go back on it." Showing that particularly feminine brand of enduring courage, she simply said
in formal French, no "*tu*" or '*toi*,"—"*Philippe, allez là ou vous pensez que le
devoir vous appelle, je m'occuperai de nos enfants.*" No lack of affection or
coldness should be imputed from the use of "*vous*" between them; both
their families were "Old France." Nor was it a remarkable burden for
Thérèse to look after their six children. Had she become a nun in the
1920s, instead of taking her confessor's advice to marry, her lot in the summer of 1940 would probably have been similar, looking after displaced
children.

Philippe rose early on the morning of 4th July. While the children slept
Thérèse made him a quick breakfast before seeing him off. "Courage
Thérèse," he said. "Our separation may be long." Then, armed with every
pass, including his original passport, which Thérèse had presciently
brought from Tailly, he set off for Bayonne by bicycle. Bayonne was in the
occupied zone, but he hoped it had better facilities for getting into Spain.
The local representative of Wendels, Monsieur Petit, booked him into the
Hotel du Panier and furnished him with some cash. Finding his passport
a little out of date, he altered some of the stamps with a child's printing

kit.[16] Next he needed a visa to get into Spain and Portugal. The Portuguese consul was happy to issue a visa, as he had provisionally booked a berth on the liner *Exeter*, due to leave Lisbon for New York on 18th July. The Spanish, however, were less helpful; he would have to try elsewhere, back in the "free zone" perhaps.

Before leaving Bayonne, Philippe wrote one last letter for Monsieur Petit to give Thérèse. He began by telling her of his problems leaving France, and that he would have to start again. "Nevertheless, strengthened by your unshakeable confidence I am sure to succeed," he wrote.

During this time he heard how on 3rd July the Royal Navy had issued the French squadron at Mers el Kebir the ultimatum to rejoin the war or be sunk. Receiving no reply by 5.30pm, British Admiral Somerville gave the order to open fire. Churchill calculated that this attack would underwrite Great Britain's determination. Philippe wrote soberly, "I have had the time to consider and reconsider my decision. I have had moments of heavy discouragement due to the sad events of these last few days. But in spite of everything, nothing has changed my initial decision." In fact, later events suggest that he respected the British decision to attack the Mers el Kebir squadron. Nor was Philippe immune to a sense of historic irony. One hundred and thirty years earlier, German soldiers had fled their homeland to take up arms alongside Great Britain against Napoleon in regiments such as the "King's German Legion." "Our situation is like that of old Prussia, on its knees before Napoleon after Jena . . . which wasn't overturned until after Waterloo. So nothing has changed.

> I will not renege on the principles of honour and patriotism that have sustained me for twenty years. If you receive no more news of me, or only rare and indirect news, that will be a good sign that I have succeeded. What a test to be separated like this. I know you will hold firm and realise how fervently I will pray for you . . . I reproach myself for not having said enough the other day that you should not hesitate to sacrifice Tailly if you have to for your own security and the little ones. . . . I very much hope that you won't be bothered [by the Germans], for it seems Adolph has understood with genius that he should avoid completely crushing the French in order to turn them into a proper protectorate. . . . Like I have

already said, turn as much as you have to into cash, horses, cows, poultry, fat, whatever, because the shortages next year are going to be hard. If you can find a little Simca to buy, do so, because petrol will probably be almost non-existent . . . More than ever I shall be supported by your prayers, and I assure you that I will have a truly fighting heart for what lies ahead. . . . Don't worry about me and I will find you again when we are on the path to victory. . . . Continue to develop the characters of our children, for they are everything.[17]

This letter shows that Philippe de Hauteclocque guessed that life under German occupation would not be impossible. Obviously Thérèse and the children would have to retrench both financially and practically, selling things to raise cash, swapping their existing car for a small Simca and, when it came to foodstuffs, shortages during the occupation would be felt most keenly in large towns and cities. Country people would get begging letters from long forgotten relations in Paris and other large cities. Both the German and Vichy authorities found ration quotas almost impossible to enforce in the countryside. Local farmers' organisations were skilled at hiding their produce. Philippe's last letter to Thérèse before becoming "Leclerc" also reinforces the essential point about so many early *Gaullistes*. Though recognising that wives and children could remain in France in relative safety, they knew Hitler was evil and could not countenance compromise.

On 10th July Philippe crossed back into the "Free" Zone and made for Perpignan, hoping to get a visa for Spain there. This time he was successful, but Spanish customs still refused him entry for carrying too much cash. Only 3,000 French Francs were allowed, and he carried 15,000. Accused of transferring assets, he was forced off the train at Figueras and most of his money was confiscated. He was locked up for the night in a police station, sharing a cell with an elderly Jewess fleeing for her life. Freed by a local magistrate in the morning, he was told to wait for permission before continuing to Madrid carrying such a large sum, even if the value of the Franc was plummeting. Philippe, however, decided to get himself to Madrid with what he had left without delay. Once there he resorted to the gold dollars hidden about his person, exchanging ten for enough pesetas to buy himself a train ticket on to Lisbon.

Before leaving Madrid he wrote a last letter to Monsieur Petit, Wendels' representative in Bayonne. Obliquely worded, it was clearly intended to confirm his safe departure from France: "Dear Sir, Just to be sure that you have heard, I can confirm to you the good news concerning Maurice which I sent you in Bayonne. The fight back begins! Tomorrow I lunch with André, we will talk of you." Again he used the name "Leclerc."

On 17th July, Philippe de Hauteclocque arrived in Lisbon and promptly reported to the military attaché at the British Embassy. A passage was found for him on a British merchantman, the SS *Hilary*, which departed on 20th July. On 25th July 1940, he presented himself to the man who would define his future, Charles de Gaulle.

CHAPTER THREE

DE GAULLE'S MAN IN AFRICA

The SS *Hilary* docked in Liverpool on 25th July 1940. The infrastructure of "Free France" was developing fast, and a quayside office run by a French former shipbuilding engineer from Cherbourg already existed. Philippe reported his arrival and that he had run out of money. He was given a £5 note to cover his rail fare to London.[1]

Later that same afternoon, as General de Gaulle was pondering his options in central Africa from within Free France's smart new Carlton Gardens offices, there came a knock on his door. It was his ADC, Lt Geoffroy Chaudron de Courcel, who wanted to introduce an officer freshly arrived from France. De Gaulle met Captain Philippe de Hauteclocque for the first time. Having read de Gaulle's books *Vers l'armée de métier* and *Le fil de l'épée*, Philippe knew he was facing one of France's foremost military intellectuals, though de Gaulle had not yet evolved into the accomplished politician he became. De Gaulle had definitely heard of the Hauteclocque family, which was well known in the French northeast. For a while he listened as Philippe, travel-worn with his head still bandaged, described his escape from the debris of defeat. De Gaulle always valued these stories as they helped him gauge a man's commitment and value. Eventually he re-summoned Courcel.

"Here is Captain de Hauteclocque. I am promoting him *chef d'esca-*

drons.[2] Sort him out with uniform, pay and everything."

Taken to an office on the fourth floor, the first person Philippe was greeted by was a lieutenant with Foreign Legion collar patches.

"Hello, you don't recognise me do you?"[3]

This was his cousin Pierre de Hauteclocque, son of uncle Wallerand and younger brother of the journalist Xavier. Pierre had been on the infantry course at Saint-Cyr in the promotion "Joffre" when Philippe was commanding a cavalry squadron. After Pierre told him how the 13e DBLE, finding itself in Great Britain after the failure of the Narvik operation, had opted for "Free France," Philippe decided to join them as well. Reporting to Trentham Park, he presented himself to the 13e DBLE's commanding officer, a Hungarian named Raoul Magrin-Vernerey, who had been in the Legion all his adult life. The two men did not get on. Either it was a simple personality clash, or perhaps Magrin-Vernerey did not think Philippe was ready for the culture shock of commanding left-wing Spaniards; in any case he rejected Philippe as over-qualified, too grand, and worst of all, a cavalryman! He may not have realised it but, by giving vent to his own cussid and difficult nature, Colonel Magrin-Vernerey had changed the course of Free France.

On 27 July, de Gaulle called upon the French Empire abroad to join him, addressing not only governors and administrators but ordinary people as well.[4] In Brazzaville a group of Frenchmen formed themselves into a "patriotic association for freedom and honour." Informed of such developments by the British, de Gaulle decided to make his first move on the African mainland. Time was pressing. Compared to Vichy, de Gaulle had fewer troops to put into the field. If it came to a fight, those obeying Pétain could call on ships from Toulon or military support from all over French Africa. For French Equatorial Africa to be taken and kept, speed and British support would be essential. Yet, after the attack on the French fleet at Mers el Kebir, French public opinion had polarized, and many were violently anti-British. Servicemen returning to France were seen on newsreels exclaiming that only traitors could countenance being paid in "*livres sterling.*" Any *coups de mains* needed to be low key for the Free French to avoid being called British poodles. De Gaulle needed the best Frenchmen he could find, capable of functioning in delicate situations. Without mentioning Hauteclocque's false errand to the 13e DBLE in his war memoirs, de

Gaulle simply writes "He arrived from France via Spain, his head bandaged from a wound received in Champagne and obviously exhausted. Presenting himself to me, I saw he was someone I could deal with and ruled his place was in the field."[5] So Philippe was bolted onto an expedition de Gaulle was sending to Africa, immediately becoming its leader.

Philippe also had to change his name. Like most Free French, his family was still in France and the mission could end up in the newspapers. If he used his real name he could put Thérèse and the children at risk. So the name first taken to cross the Demarcation Line at Grugé-l'Hôpital was re-used. Captain de Hauteclocque became "Captain F. Leclerc" on Identity Card number 05175 (No 20 Military Mission) "Officer in the forces of General de Gaulle" with the official address of "4 Carlton Gardens London."[6] A few later days the promotion given by de Gaulle came through.

He used his new pseudonym before leaving London. Short of money to buy tropical kit, he telephoned a cousin of Thérèse, Madame Pauline Vanier, wife of the former Canadian ambassador to France. "Tell Madame that François Leclerc would like to speak to her," he told the maid who answered the telephone.

Madame Vanier had no idea who he was until she recognised the deep, teasing voice on the other end.

"Hello, Limpopo," he said.

"Philippe, you are in London?"

"Yes, I need your help to buy a few things."

She gave him a generous subsidy with which Philippe visited various military outfitters around Piccadilly and Savile Row, acquiring, among other things, a pair of Huntsman lightweight breeches. Pauline Vanier next saw him in full British tropical kit superimposed with French insignia, no prizes for guessing where he was going.[7]

Asked to recount his exploits leaving France to the BBC's new French Service before leaving for Africa, Philippe elaborated on two themes. First, he said there was no excuse for capitulation. Given the size of the empire and France's gold reserves, many Free French thought that way. Second, recounting his conversations with German soldiers, he emphasised their intention to enslave France permanently. "We will arrange matters so that France will never again recover her power," Philippe said, quoting Germans he overheard in St Quentin, Bohain and the Baynasts' chateau. As for the old held German view that "France isn't our enemy. It is England that we want to sort out," Philippe said it made little difference to a man who simply wants his homeland free. Finishing, he struck a mediaeval note of which de Gaulle himself would have been proud, regarding France as a distressed damsel, Marianne in chains. "The heart bleeds when thinking of the suffering of imprisoned France which I saw for several days. At least I will have the joy of fighting beside other Frenchmen of stout heart to give her back her independence. Our children will be able to affirm in the future that at every moment of the struggle Germany found French troops facing her. This is the comfort that every Frenchman here holds onto until the final victory in which our faith is complete. This victory, hasten it by every means that are and will be in your power!"[8]

On 28th July the British Government recognised General de Gaulle as chief of the Free French, and was keen to give his African project every assistance. The establishment of a Free French base maintaining a strategic link between Africa's west coast and the Middle East was something on which the British would also depend. Given the highly important diplomatic nature of the task in which Leclerc's team would soon be involved, de Gaulle instructed René Cassin to draw up proper orders. An elderly jurist who had escaped France via Saint Jean de Luz, reaching London a month before Leclerc, Cassin drafted orders for de Gaulle's African mission with a theatrical yet flexible grandiloquence.

Assisted by Lord Lloyd, British secretary of State for the Colonies, the Free French mission made their last preparations before leaving. Thanks to the British Colonial Office, news was reaching Carlton Gardens from the targeted colonies throughout July. In the Congo, many *anciens combatants* favoured joining de Gaulle. Their leader, Governor General Boisson, with a fine Great War record, informed the British consulate of his preference for bringing his colony over to Free France rather than bow to a "dishonourable peace." But Vichy was better placed to offer patronage, and Boisson was given the more prestigious governorship of French West Africa based in Dakar. De Gaulle and the British hoped that Boisson's replacement, Husson, would rally to Free France, but unfortunately Boisson kept him in line. Husson confirmed the Congo's acceptance of the Armistice on 26th July.[9] In Bangui, Governor Saint-Marc was happy to follow de Gaulle, but felt unsure of support from his military subordinates. In Gabon, Governor Masson teetered on the brink of joining the Cross of Lorraine before thinking better of it.

Chad was the most favourable. Governor Félix Eboué and Commandant Marchand were only waiting for the signal to make a concerted effort. Whereas in the Cameroons (the former German colony under French mandate since 1919) High Commissioner Brunot and his military subordinates were hesitant, though leaning towards the English. A small but definite Vichyite following called for public mourning over Mers el Kebir and total loyalty to Pétain. They were led by a pro-German businessman called Mauger and an extreme right-wing Catholic priest named Father Carol who exhorted his fellow Frenchmen to "transfer their allegiance to the virile German race."

However, even by Vichy estimates, eighty percent of the Cameroons' population preferred de Gaulle rather than risk seeing their colony returned to Germany. With the assistance of British consul Miles Clifford in the Cameroons' second town, Douala, the pro-Gaulliste clique led by public works director René Mauclère could call on the Royal Navy for local flag-waving. HMS *Dragon*, commanded by Captain Bowes-Lyon, put into Douala with its band playing the Marseillaise to rapturous acclaim.[10] Cock a snook at Pétain as they might, Vichy's fear that Germany would occupy the "Free Zone" of France was so great that it was only a matter of time before Vichy forces were sent from Dakar, while a German U-Boat was already rumoured to be patrolling off the Spanish island of Fernando Po.

The loyalties of local troops were mixed. The officers commanding *Garde Indigène* Congolese levies at Brazzaville, Commandant Descayrac and Captain Peyrières, were both Pétain men to the core. On the other hand, 750 Sarras, who should have been disbanded following the Armistice, were devoted to their officers, Commandant Delange and his lieutenants, de Boissoudy, Rouge and Coupigny, who were all openly scornful of Vichy but sadly lacking adequate armament. In northern Chad there were enough troops to face down Italian infiltration into the mid-Sahara's Tibesti area, and although the Armistice terms required that these forces should be reduced or even disbanded, Governor Eboué had countermanded this on his own authority.

The Cameroons merely had their local militia, but here the main asset turned out to be their officers, especially Colonel Jean Calonna d'Ornano, a Corsican gentleman, and Captain Louis Dio, thickset, dark and practical. Both were addicted to colonial soldiering and afraid of nothing. After the frustration of spending the "Phoney War" on stand-by to sail to the Métropole (they were still awaiting transport when France fell) these officers and their black rank and file were available to de Gaulle whenever he wanted them.

Hoping to pull the Cameroons into line without conflict, Vichy sent Admiral Platon, a man of Protestant stock who had distinguished himself at Dunkirk. Two months later he had become a staunch *Vichysois*, browbeating Governor Brunot that further dealings with the British would bring armed intervention from Dakar to reaffirm Pétain's authority. Knowing that many French colonials had relations in "occupied" France, Platon blackmailed them with the prospect of German reprisals. Shaken, Brunot ordered HMS *Dragon* to leave Douala, and demanded that German and Italian prisoners sent to British Nigeria should be returned. Following further protests, Platon addressed a deposition of René Mauclère's patriots before leaving Douala airport. "Our Motherland, France, has been utterly defeated by the Germans," he sneered. "You need have no illusions about what will happen to Britain now—she will suffer the same, and worse, fate within the next few weeks. They are without hope. They are foolish to pretend otherwise. The only possible policy for France now is to cooperate with the conquerors fully in the hope that in about eighty years time the opportunity will come for us to get our freedom back. Any recalcitrance by Frenchmen anywhere will surely lead to reprisals by the Germans and will as surely bring retaliatory measures upon them from the Vichy government. It is up to every Frenchman, therefore, to follow the wise and dignified lead of our great Marshal Pétain."[11]

Bristling with anger, the Gaullists recognised that only a local *coup d'état* could prevent Vichy returning the colony to Germany if pressured. But René Mauclère admitted he was no soldier. In despair they approached British intelligence officer Godfrey Allen, asking him to lead them. Flattered, Allen declined graciously, saying "It *must* be a Frenchman who leads you if France is to regain her true glory."[12] In an urgent plea to London, passed to Carlton Gardens, Allen claimed with prescience that a suitable leader need only appear at their head for the Cameroons to be his!

In a last-ditch effort to keep control, Vichy's inspector for the colonies, Monsieur Huet, arrived aboard the submarine *Beveziere*. Led by Mauclère, Gaullists shouted at the submarine, waving *Tricolores* and Union Jacks, making such a din that Huet did not dare step ashore until the crowd dispersed. Taking over the administration, Huet expelled the British attaché and forbade Godfrey Allen from sending any further radio messages. Allen's attempts to subvert the *Beveziere*'s captain were unsuccessful, and when he heard from Mauclère that the Gaullists were preparing to attack the *Beveziere*, he advised against it. Seeing Mauclère's men becoming increasingly depressed, Allen smuggled messages across the border to British telegraph offices in Nigeria, begging the Free French to send a leader.

Though fully occupied with the Battle of Britain, Churchill was keeping in touch with de Gaulle's affairs. Inviting him to Chequers, they watched an aerial dogfight from the garden. "Now you can understand why I couldn't send any more fighters to France," Churchill said.

"But if you had, France might have held the Germans," de Gaulle replied.

De Gaulle watched Churchill shake his fists, shouting "Come on then" at German bombers. Churchill's concern was to get the USA into the war by demonstrating that the British war effort was worth backing. De Gaulle's strategic initiative in Africa was part of that. Accordingly the *Clyde*, an Imperial Airways Sunderland seaplane, originally earmarked to spirit the Royal Family to Canada, was placed at Free French disposal to carry de Gaulle's emissaries to French Equatorial Africa.

Philippe's life was now moving fast. After leaving a cryptic message to his family with the BBC French Service: "Philippe embraces his half-dozen, Tom, Croc etc" (Tom and Croc being Henri's and Hubert's nicknames) he departed for Poole harbour in Dorset. On the evening of 6th August, Commandant Leclerc, René Pleven, a former assistant to economist Jean Monnet, and Captain Claude Hettier de Boislambert—a dashing game hunter who had been a liaison officer during the Battle of France—climbed the *Clyde*'s ladder in Poole Harbour to take their seats in the comfortable passenger cabin, which amounted to executive class for the times. Weighed down with full fuel tanks, the seaplane took off into the setting sun. One of the few aircraft of its day capable of extreme distances, the *Clyde* crossed the Bay of Biscay through the hours of darkness, landing at the mouth of Portugal's River Tagus in the early morning to refuel. As the aircraft took off again, its wing clipped the mast of a fishing boat, luckily without causing serious mishap, and the *Clyde* flew out over the Atlantic to avoid air patrols from French North Africa that might report its presence. The fishing boat episode nevertheless necessitated a stopover at Bathurst in Gambia for repairs.

That repair was only temporary, necessitating a further stop in Sierra Leone, where Leclerc met up with Frenchmen who had answered de Gaulle's *appel*. This was cheering evidence of support for de Gaulle, but they also encountered the widely held French viewpoint that the English were unable to hold out much longer. Mers el Kebir had not helped either. Many French felt their defeat by Germany in Europe simply made their empire vulnerable to British landgrabbing. Initial enthusiasm for their expedition was being replaced with a chill sense of reality.

They arrived in Nigeria on 12th August and were greeted by Miles Clifford before being introduced to Governor General Sir Bernard Bourdillon and General Giffard, the resident British commander. Bourdillon was the soul of affability and helpfulness. Giffard was more circumspect, given the practical military realities to be faced if war developed between Britain and Vichy, frankly preferring that France's African empire "be left to stew in its own juice." This did not fit in with de Gaulle's thinking at all; Leclerc spent the following day being put in the picture by Miles Clifford over escalating hostility between Vichy and Gaullist factions in Douala.

On the positive side, Colonel Edgard de Larminat had joined the Gaullist cause from Vichy-held Syria and had made his way to Brazzaville, there to arouse Gaullist feeling and depose Vichy's Governor General Husson. Coordination, however, was essential. If Felix Eboué ran up the Gaullist flag in Chad too soon he might become a focus for Vichy countermeasures. De Larminat persuaded Eboué to wait until the other equatorial African colonies were ready.[13]

Following his discussions with Miles Clifford, Leclerc decided that he and Boislambert should take up a British offer to move further along the Nigerian coast aboard the HMS *Bridgwater*. They reached Victoria and set off for the little frontier station at Mondane to meet Godfrey Allen and Vice Consul Hooley, who had crossed the Wourie estuary from Douala to

meet them. Again, Godfrey Allen insisted that it must be a French operation for France's sake as well as the British. This suited Leclerc fine.

Treading warily after Mers el Kebir, the only vessel the French Navy
had in the vicinity capable of guarding the Wourie estuary south of Douala
was the escort frigate *Side-Ferruch*. Then Vichy reshuffled their key players:
Cameroons' governor Brunot was replaced on trumped-up grounds of ill
health while the local army commander Colonel Bureau, known to have
Gaullist sympathies, was also replaced. Bureau promptly arrived on British
territory bringing fifty officers and NCOs along with most of Douala's
arsenal at a time when Leclerc hoped such assets would be available to his
own force when it arrived in Douala. Leclerc's next setback was the dis-
covery that the Senegalese troops he hoped would be available had refused
orders, and been sent back to their villages by the British. Everything now
hinged on how far Douala's indigenous troops, reluctant to see the
Cameroons returned to Germany, could be relied upon to follow their
instincts.

In spite of General Giffard telling him that such meagre forces were
insufficient to seize key points in Douala, Leclerc nevertheless decided to
cross the River Wourie with a selection of tough officers and NCOs who
self-deprecatingly called themselves the *gonflés*—"puffed up ones."

Installing himself in a bungalow on a former German-owned plantation, Leclerc set about planning his *coup*. In utmost secrecy they assembled
weapons under the noses of the plantation manager and his workers, greeting any curiosity with "ssshh!" At night Leclerc rowed across the crocodile-
infested Wourie to confer with Godfrey Allen over details—how Vichy
dignitaries spent their evenings, in whose houses, how long they stayed,
what they did, what they drank and how much, and how long they could
be kept distracted by activities such as bridge or the gramophone.[14]

With Leclerc, the *gonflés* included seventeen escapees from the Cameroons, a priest called Père Dehon and five officers, some of whom, like
Quillichini, Son and Tutenges, were *anciens petits-cos* from Saint-Cyr. Quillichini in particular remained with Leclerc throughout the war.

By the 26th of August, they were ready to go, loading everything into
a truck borrowed from the Ekona plantation and saying cryptic goodbyes
to the English manager to conceal their real intentions. Lastly, Leclerc and
Boislambert promoted themselves: Leclerc to Colonel and Boislambert

from Captain to Commandant. Re-sewing their *gallons*, there was just enough tape to give Leclerc five bars on each cuff and only one complete sleeve for Boislambert.[15] "Colonel now!" Leclerc said to Lt. Denise in the early morning of 26th August, "we leave at 8 o'clock. I'll give out orders on board."

Embarking the team on a British riverboat, a pistol and ammunition was given to each man. As they made their way up river that morning, Leclerc held an orders group. The plan had been formulated with Lt. Son and 2lt Penanhoat, both of whom knew Douala well. A group of five, Fougerat, Frizza, Laumonnier, Arnal and Martin, would seize the post office. Penanhoat and a small party would take over the military camp and various government offices, while Lt. Denise arrested two dangerous Vichyites, a customs official and a civil servant. "In short," Denise wrote many years later, "everything was in place to isolate Douala on the one hand and prevent any resistance on the other. It was intended that we should present our compatriots with a *fait accompli*."[16]

At 4pm the British launch left them on a small island and returned to Tiko. Towards dusk, hired river canoes arrived just as a torrential rainstorm began. The canoe men usually ferried smugglers and were used to clandestine activity. Split into crews of eight, the *gonflés* paddled upstream through rain and pitch black. In the dark the canoes could only keep contact through hearing shouted orders somewhere in the shadows close by. Eventually the lights of Douala appeared in the distance. At first the canoe owners refused to land at Douala itself. Being smugglers, they were worried that Leclerc's men might hand them over to the authorities; it was only when a French officer menaced them with a pistol that they steered for the quayside.

Godfrey Allen was giving a bridge party that evening and plying his Vichy guests with plenty of drink. His boredom was broken by a knock on the door and the message that "they" were coming that night. Once his guests had gone, Allen went over to Mauclère's house where they began calling the Gaullist clique together.[17]

At the quayside, the *gonflés* hardly knew where they were. They disembarked at a mole and walked towards the dock gate, which was guarded by a black *tirailleur*.

"*Qui va là?*"

"Returning patrol!" shouted Lt. Denise.

Fortunately, as the *gonflés* reached the dock gate, some Mauclère supporters turned up at the quayside bringing Leclerc an unhelpful message from Dr. Mauze. Not all Gaullists in Douala knew they were coming, and their arrival was premature.

They could hardly go back! Gathering the *gonflés* around him in the light of the half moon, Leclerc gripped the situation.

"We are here on French territory," he said. "We have succeeded in disembarking without incident. Now we have no choice but to stay here to the end, as there is no question of leaving." In the distance cars were drawing up outside French garrison buildings, disgorging Vichyite officers. Giving the *gonflés* their last orders, Leclerc said, "Stick your chests out, hold your pistols firmly and convince them you are utterly determined to continue the struggle. The other colonies will certainly follow the example of this territory. This will lead to the whole of France, reborn through her Empire, continuing the fight alongside England. Do you all agree?"

"*Oui!*" replied the *gonflés*.

Looking round, Leclerc saw Captain Louis Dio of the local garrison.

"And you Dio," said Leclerc. "What do you think?"

"*Mon Colonel*, I am with you," said Louis Dio.

"Good, I congratulate you Captain Dio, and I am happy you're with me because someone told me 'If Dio is with you, you are sure to succeed. If not it will be very hard.'" They were friends from then on. Leclerc finished by saying, "Gentlemen it is 4.30 in the morning. You have only one hour left before daybreak. Let's go!"

Things went smoothly. Dio, formerly one of Colonel Bureau's subordinates, went to find native troops to co-opt. Communications centres were taken. When Vichyite Commandant Pradier was woken in his bed he quickly took in the new situation and shouted "*Vive la France,*" becoming a Gaullist immediately. With Pradier on their side, the garrison fell in without a fight. The only violence occurred when Dr. Le Breton, momentarily forgetting his Hippocratic oath, laid out the pro-German Captain Mauger and broke his jaw.[18]

By daybreak, Douala had a new governor, Colonel Leclerc. The mayor quickly became a Gaullist, and arrangements were made to repatriate the unrepentant Vichyite regional governor. Everything had happened without bloodshed or assistance from the English. Calling Douala's white population together later that morning, Leclerc declared that his mission for General de Gaulle was to rally the Cameroons and all its resources to fight alongside the English for the liberation of France. Douala's expats were delighted, especially since Vichy was now prevented from handing the Cameroons back to Germany. Chad's intrepid black governor, Félix Eboué, declared for de Gaulle on the 27th August.

Although the Cameroon capital Yaounde remained to be taken, Leclerc quickly took stock of the military equipment in Douala now available to Free France. This included an elderly Potez bomber which was used to drop leaflets over Yaounde. Dio's men took the train. As soon as they arrived they took guard positions at all public buildings. By 4pm it was all over.

Governor Brunot handed over formally to Leclerc the following day, asking to become a Gaullist and to be sent to England for health reasons. Leclerc gladly agreed. Of the other "overnight" Gaullists, Leclerc neither forgave nor forgot how Colonel Bureau's vacillations forced him to carry out the operation on a shoestring, and promptly dismissed him to England where he became a valued member of staff at Carlton Gardens.

Thanks to Leclerc's commanding presence, the whole colony was under Gaullist control within a week. He left Captain Dio to organise his men as the first Free French unit on African soil, and ordered the editor of *L'Éveil du Cameroun* to make three hundred wall posters. The editor protested that Douala, being the sticks, did not have the means, but Leclerc insisted. The posters were duly put up, reading as follows:

This morning, 27th August 1940, on the soil of Africa and in a French territory, France continues the struggle with its own arms and returns to the Second World War at the side of Great Britain and her allies.

She will be present at the hour of Victory after the battles with Honour."

Long live fighting France.

Leclerc installed himself in the governor's palace at Yaounde, taking Madame Crognier, the former Renault branch typist, as his secretary. Leclerc gathered many future subordinates at this time. Along with Robert

Quillichini and Louis Dio came artillery officer Captain Jean Crépin, commander of the Wourie estuary's coastal guns, and Lieutenant Raymond Dronne, a highly qualified administrator and former journalist whose humble background prevented him achieving higher office in France, and who had been a reserve officer in the Cameroons.

For these first Gaullists the 26th–28th August 1940 became their "Three Glorious Days." Assisted by René Pleven, Felix Eboué rallied Chad on the 26th, Leclerc the Cameroons on the 27th, and de Larminat brought in the Congo on the 28th after a coup in Brazzaville whose comic moments verged on slapstick. De Larminat, senior to Leclerc at this stage, was promptly appointed governor general of all French Equa-torial Africa, leaving Leclerc free to plan further missions. In de Larminat's words, "the flame of resistance" lit by de Gaulle's first broadcast on 18th June "leapt and danced like a torch."[19] Now de Gaulle had a land base, provided he could hold onto it.

Celebrations in Douala, which included a solemn Mass at the cathedral, emphasised the "Old France" timbre of early Gaullists. Sometimes regarded as extreme "Maurrassians" by their compatriots (after Charles Maurras, founder of *Action Française*), it took them well into 1941 before their politics became more broadly based. Now Leclerc, as governor of the Cameroons, had a threefold task: first to participate in the liberation of France and her Empire; second, to develop Free France's military capability in the region; and third, to develop the Cameroons' economy in liaison with the British.

Formally speaking, the forces now available to Leclerc had never been part of the French Army, and the rules of France's 1919 mandate in the Cameroons did not authorise the raising of indigenous troops. There was a police force of a type and a handful of artillerymen to man the guns covering the Wourie estuary, all recruited locally. Leclerc's solution was simple: true to La Coloniale's tradition of resourcefulness, his experience as *goum* commander, and to the prophecy of one of his seniors at Meknes that he clearly wanted to create units, he turned the police force into a Régiment de Tirailleurs du Cameroun (RTC). To complement this, on 18th September he formed a Légion des Volontaires de Cameroun open to "all Frenchmen and foreigners who, not being incorporated in the units of the RTC, are ready to undertake any mission either interior or exterior to serve Free

France. The colonel-governor appeals to the patriotism of those who place the safety of their country and their liberty above all else and who are not already serving in the RTC to enlist in the Légion des Volontaires du Cameroun."[20] Over the next few days Leclerc recruited eighty men, including foreigners and enough natives to act as lorry drivers.

The stridency of the new Gaullist atmosphere in the Cameroons and other parts of French Equatorial Africa alarmed some French who worried about reprisals against their relations in France. Some preferred to return to Vichy-governed territory. By early August de Gaulle had been condemned to death *in absentia*, and by September some of the repatriated Vichyites had recognised Leclerc as none other than Captain Philippe de Hauteclocque, former cavalry instructor at Saint-Cyr. High Commissioner Boisson contacted Leclerc from Dakar and proposed that he resubmit to Vichy authority. But Boisson was wasting his time. Leclerc was for "Free France," and he declared to whoever would listen, "Vichy is the hook on which men hang their cowardice." More vituperatively, "They [Vichy] only speak to us of pretending to defend the empire against English aggression. Have they defended Syria, Djibouti and Tunis against Italian aggression? Have they defended Indo-China against the Japanese? Their enemies are Hitler's enemies. Their allies are Hitler's allies. That is the brutal fact that dominates this drama. When one speaks of the Berlin-Rome axis, I think we can equally well speak of the Berlin-Vichy axis."[21]

Through the second half of September, Leclerc flew all over the Cameroons impressing upon everyone that his way was the natural way for freedom loving Frenchmen and indigenous alike. However the desire of some to accept Vichy's authority was not always derived from an amoral taste for Nazism. Free France was backed by British sterling, so with problems of trade and exchange rates, de Gaulle represented a huge risk. Many who had plenty to offer Free France simply left. More assertive appeals to their patriotism might have made a difference. Dronne wrote subsequently of his regret at not being able to persuade more to remain.[22] However Leclerc, like de Gaulle, had a talent for recognising who could be useful, and he held in contempt with equal measure the weak and those who vascilated. Only in 1943 did Leclerc take a more accommodating view of former Vichy supporters, when to do otherwise would have been an obstacle to reuniting the army.

In the meantime, for the young Picardian aristocrat, colonial life in such a backwater represented a severe learning curve. Only having soldiered in Morocco, Leclerc found La Coloniale's independence of mind exasperating. Fulminating that two pilots in succession refused to fly him to a conference with General de Larminat in Brazzaville due to stormy weather, he screamed, "What does one do? Is this an army?"[23] When he got there, everyone who met him at Anglo-French cocktail parties found him well mannered, but with little time for anyone not in uniform and absolutely committed to the war. Happily married but facing a long forced absence from Thérèse, Leclerc was punctilious in avoiding any suspicion of impropriety. He never allowed himself to be entertained by a woman alone, and lived like a monk.[24]

"I am a soldier," he told Godfrey Allen. "Nothing else matters to me but waging this war. Nothing else should matter for all soldiers." With Radio Cameroun underway within a week of his seizing power, Leclerc's first broadcast began by defining Gaullist intentions. Chiefly this meant returning to the struggle with as many means as possible to defeat the "barbarians." He also wanted to reassure the indigenous population that, with British support, normal life would continue and they would not be forced to abandon their traditional cultures. He announced that Douala would become the Cameroons' capital since it had better communications, and again told the story of the German officer telling him Germany would make France incapable of waging war ever again. "The soldiers of Mangin[25] once stood guard in Mainz. Those of the Cameroons will succeed him. I don't care how many months and how much effort it takes to claim Victory, but we will have it. If you have heard French men and women, under the German boot, the day after the armistice, declaring 'we are sure of Victory,' despite the treason of Vichy, you wouldn't doubt it. The Cameroons is free. It must fight."[26]

Hearing of the Gaullists' "Three Glorious Days," Governor Masson of Gabon declared for de Gaulle on 29th August. Three days later, due to pressure from the influential Pierre Boisson in Dakar, he changed his mind. Well aware that de Gaulle's seizure of French Equatorial Africa had been accomplished with precariously few forces, Vichy sent 1,300 *Tirailleurs Sénégalais* to Gabon. The Vichy escort ship *Cap des Palmes* and the gunboat

Bougainville were guarding the approaches to Libreville, while the submarine *Poncelet* patroled the coastline from Port-Gentil. Vichy air power consisted of three Glenn Martin bombers commanded by air force General Tetu, whom Vichy intended to appoint as governor of French Equatorial Africa if Free France's General de Larminat could be dislodged.[27]

Could Free France do without Gabon? Leclerc believed not. Isolated from other parts of French Equatorial Africa by a large belt of rainforest and Spanish Guinea, Gabon's economy was small compared to other colonies that rallied to de Gaulle. But if Vichy took Port-Gentil as a naval base, de Gaulle's communications, and even his tenure in French Equatorial Africa, could be threatened. Furthermore, it could even bring German U-boat activity into the South Atlantic.

Aware of the strategic threat following a long conversation with British diplomat Fred Pedler, Leclerc had Louis Dio make inroads into the colony from early September. Dio's deputy, Gardet, began infiltrating the north. He was soon joined by groups led by Dio himself and Raymond Dronne. From Brazzaville, General de Larminat sent a column under Lt. Col. André de Parant, which seized the southern town of Mayumba from land and sea on 15th September. This represented an early success for Parant, but as they neared lower ground behind Libreville and Port-Gentil, both groups found their progress slowed by thick rain forest, some roads being little better than grassy tracks. Parant's unsuccessful attempt to parley with the local Vichy chief, Captain Brunet, at Lambaréné indicated stronger forces would be needed to dig out Governor Masson, and short of stripping troops from Chad's border with Italian occupied Libya, Leclerc had none to spare. For the time being the Gabon operation stalled.

In the meantime, the British believed de Gaulle's best chance of securing his African foothold lay in pursuing the far more ambitious project of deposing Governor Pierre Boisson, then rallying Dakar and with it the whole of French West Africa. Dakar also held 90% of France's pre-war gold reserves that had been spirited from Brest following *la Chute*. While the Battle of Britain raged above southern England, Churchill gave de Gaulle a large task force consisting of two old battleships, four cruisers, the aircraft carrier *Ark Royal* and various destroyers, which they hoped would be enough to rally France's largest African colony by simply appearing off the coast in full view of Dakar's population. Then, it was hoped, landing forces, consisting of British infantry and the Free French 13e DBLE, would go ashore to a heroes' welcome prepared by Claude Hettier de Boislambert, sent from Freetown to subvert Boisson's power base.

Unfortunately the weather was so bad that the people of Dakar could not see the Anglo-Free French task force even if they wanted to. The operation began in the early morning of 23rd September with aircraft leaving *Ark Royal* to drop leaflets signed by de Gaulle exhorting the people of Dakar "to show their patriotism without disorder and to welcome his soldiers heartily." Next de Gaulle sent the very man who had suggested the Cross of Lorraine as Free France's emblem, Captain Thierry d'Argenlieu, who was both priest and naval officer, accompanied by Marshal Foch's grandson, Captain Bécourt-Foch, in a motor launch with a personal message for Governor Boisson.

Stiffened by naval personnel wanting vengeance for Mers el Kebir, Governor Boisson watched the launch arriving through binoculars, and ordered that de Gaulle's emissaries should be arrested immediately as they stepped ashore. Once landed, d'Argenlieu recognised that things were not proceeding as hoped, and ran back to the launch followed by Bécourt-Foch as bullets pinged around them, one injuring d'Argenlieu in the leg.

With heavy heart, de Gaulle asked Admiral Cunningham to fire on the modern and heavily armed battleship *Richelieu*. In spite of being disabled by the British in early July, the *Richelieu* fired back, badly damaging HMS *Cumberland*. Then a second landing ended in failure, this time with fatalities. Mindful of casualties among the British fleet and in Dakar itself, de Gaulle conferred with General Sir Edward Spears and Admiral Cunningham. With Churchill's support, they decided to call off the operation. It has been said that Dakar was the saddest episode of Charles de Gaulle's life, and that he was never really happy again. He never forgave Boisson, and feared the British would cease supporting Free France. Churchill, however, still supported de Gaulle; he had no one else to keep France in the war, however nominally.

For Leclerc, the Dakar operation merely reinforced his contempt for the French Navy. Whereas French Equatorial Africa had largely rallied to Free France without fratricidal bloodshed, at Dakar Frenchman had fired on Frenchman. Free France hardened, and the atmosphere of the next two years was set. As Governor of the Cameroons, Leclerc issued a proclamation on 3rd October saying further requests for repatriation would not be allowed, nor would any obstruction of the war effort, however passive, be tolerated.

Arriving at Douala aboard the *Commandant Dubosc*, de Gaulle was crestfallen. He had not yet set foot on "Free French" soil. Luckily the crowd was ecstatic, their warmth going some way to heal the wretched disappointment of Dakar. With him came the 13e DBLE, a company of Hotchkiss tanks retrieved from the Narvik expedition, and the latest batch of young Frenchmen who had escaped from France, including Lt. Christian Girard.

"Beautiful reception," Girard wrote in his diary entry for 8th October 1940, "simple but perfect. Troops impeccable, crowd enthusiastic, *Marseillaise.* . . . The general [de Gaulle] jumped from the boat onto the quay to be welcomed by Leclerc in dazzling whites and dress sword. Once again we were in France."

Two days later, all Free French troops paraded together, and the newly formed Tirailleurs du Cameroun and Légion du Cameroun were presented colours, newly embroidered with gold thread in London. De Gaulle was particular about such things, and had his aides liaising with those companies that accoutre the British Army from Free France's earliest days in London.

With tanks and the 13e DBLE now available, Leclerc broached his plans for Gabon. After Dakar, de Gaulle was unenthusiastic, but Leclerc insisted that such a threat to their southern flank from fellow Frenchmen was unacceptable. More irksome, some officers and NCOs of the 13e DBLE, including its commander, the same Colonel Magrin-Vernerey who had refused Leclerc's services during July, expressed repugnance at bearing arms against fellow Frenchmen. The more tough-minded Free Frenchmen such as Pierre Messmer, an officer with the 13e DBLE, regarded such scruples as feeble, while the mainly anti-fascist Spaniards of the rank and file did not care. Even so, a British offer of artillery backup from two cruisers had to be refused on the basis that it was more likely to provoke unwelcome Vichy retaliation.[28] Like the Cameroons, the affair had to be as French as possible. D'Argenlieu commanded the Free French naval element, consisting of just three gunboats and three merchantmen. Colonel Lionel de Marmier commanded the embryonic air force; six Blenheim bombers and twelve Lysanders arrived at Douala in crates to be assembled *in situ* and were given Free French paintwork. Commandant Marie-Pierre Koenig would take Magrin-Vernerey's place as head of the 13e DBLE.

September's operations ground to a halt in the green lushness of mid-Gabon (Dio at Mitzic and Parant at Lambaréné), so each side took to dropping leaflets on the other. To break the deadlock, Leclerc devised a plan containing as much surprise as possible. The least approachable piece of coastline near Libreville was Mondah Point, in the shelter of whose bay Free France's cargo ships could be protected while Free French frigates *Commandant Dominé* and *Savorgnan de Brazza* bottled Vichy's *Bougainville* and *Cap des Palmes* in the Gabon estuary. Only the submarine *Poncelet* could threaten the landings.

Leaving Douala on the 7th November, Leclerc's force arrived off Mondah Point the following night and spent all the next day disembarking men and material in an atmosphere of appalling chaos. The worrying appearance overhead of a Vichy airplane indicated surprise was lost, but the landings went ahead unopposed. By evening the force was threading its way through Mondah Bay's fishing villages and jungle to the narrow isthmus separating the bay from Libreville and the airfield at Gué-gué.

Offshore, Vichy ships arrived to attempt a quixotic defence. The colonial sloop *Bougainville* attacked the Free French destroyer *Savorgnan de Brazza*, which sent *Bougainville* to the bottom. North of Mondah Bay, the submarine *Poncelet* attempted to torpedo *HMS Milford*, but depth charges and strafing by a Walrus seaplane forced her to the surface. Her commander, Bertrand de Saussines, who began his war so well by capturing the German merchantman *Chemnitz* off the Azores in September 1939, then ordered his crew to save themselves before closing the conning tower hatch over his head as *Poncelet* sank.

When Leclerc's force emerged from the jungle onto Gué-gué airfield they found an aircraft already prepared to spirit Vichy dignitaries away. A brisk engagement followed, causing thirty casualties between the two sides before Vichy Colonel Claveau presented himself at Leclerc's advance CP saying there was nothing more he could do. Leclerc replied shortly that all he wanted was an end to fratricide among Frenchmen.[29] The following morning his newly formed Tirailleurs du Cameroun captured Libreville.

There now remained Port-Gentil. Boisson had ordered the garrison to resist as long as it had the means to do so. Luckily he was disobeyed. Within an hour of the Free French landing, both sides were drinking to France. Leclerc's men took over various government buildings in Libreville, and were shocked at the propaganda methods of Boisson's men. Bitten by the same fascist fanaticism as the Germans and Italians, documents accused de Gaulle's followers of being traitors in the pay of England. Indeed, the British treasury was paying their salaries, but the arrangement was structured as a loan to be paid back once France was liberated.

Forty-eight hours later, as in the Congo, Cameroons and Chad, the *soi-disant* traitors were in control, and Governor Masson, General Tetu, Colonels Crochu and Claveau, Commandant Raunier, Captain Mordacq and Monsignor Tardit were under arrest. Except for Claveau, Leclerc refused to speak to any of these men. He had nothing to ask them and no comfort to offer. If Frenchmen acted as Germany's slaves he saw them as enemies, simple as that. Instead he concentrated on garnering more Free French recruits from among their subordinates.

Dakar and Gabon put an end to any notions Vichy had of not taking de Gaulle seriously. It was no longer merely an honourable difference of opinion. In the past, Vichy supporters had been courteously repatriated, but new Vichy laws stipulating that captured Free Frenchmen would be executed now meant Vichy prisoners had to be kept as hostages. However, de Gaulle was happy to visit the hospital where both Vichy's and Free France's wounded were treated side by side. The dead were buried in neighbouring graves.

In Libreville the reception given the Free French was sombre. Captain Thierry d'Argenlieu was bitter at Leclerc's apparent lack of appreciation at what Free French naval forces had accomplished, but, in his capacity as a Carmelite priest, he acted as celebrant at the victory Mass held in Libreville's big church. Commandant Koenig played the organ as they sang the *Te Deum*. In the town jail, Governor Masson, who had first declared for de Gaulle and then for Vichy, had run out of credible options. He hanged himself.

In Libreville, as in Douala, Leclerc showed his administrative capabilities. What struck de Gaulle most was not only Leclerc's military skill but how he took the Free French cause and ran with it, giving it all his energy and ideas. It saddened him that they had fought against fellow Frenchmen, but Free France had won. De Gaulle now formed a "Defence Council of the Empire." This was the forerunner of the French Council for National Liberation (CFLN), to which Leclerc, de Larminat, d'Argenlieu, Muselier, Sice, Sautaut and General Georges Catroux were all appointed. Strictly speaking, Catroux was senior to de Gaulle, but recognising the latter's political pre-eminence, Catroux unhesitatingly placed himself under de Gaulle's authority.

De Gaulle was well aware that his forces could be committed to fighting elsewhere. The British were far from strong. Italy had invaded Egypt on 13th September with a hundred thousand men, and de Gaulle shuffled his senior officers so that "administrators could administrate and soldiers could fight."[30] He confirmed de Larminat as High Commissioner of French Equatorial Africa, with Félix Eboué as his deputy and Colonel Marchand as garrison commander. At first, Leclerc thought his efforts were going unrewarded until de Gaulle explained to him that, since the Cameroons were rolling along nicely, he was needed elsewhere. While the Free French "perched on coconut palms in central Africa," flinging "impudent defiance at Hitler and Vichy,"[31] Churchill still had to balance the whole war effort, of which de Gaulle, be he poodle or pest, was merely a part.

Vichy desperately hoped that Great Britain would agree to a colonial status quo. After major attacks by the Royal Navy, the only retaliation Vichy could muster had been a token air raid on Gibraltar. In late October, Vichy envoy Louis Rougier arrived in London hoping to obtain an agreement whereby French merchantmen could cross the Mediterranean unimpeded. Churchill agreed to see Rougier, but by the time the meeting took place Pétain had been infamously photographed at Montoire in full marshal's uniform shaking hands with Hitler. Fear of French concessions to the Nazis filled British newspapers. Churchill was furious and threatened "bombarding Vichy." Nevertheless Rougier, an experienced negotiator, did not panic before Churchill's lambasting. He was frank about Laval's desire to join the war at Germany's side; equally he explained that de Gaulle's antics were more likely to bring Germany to France's colonies and that France would be powerless to resist. Rougier also pointed out a reality supported by President Roosevelt and the US State Department that, distrust them as Churchill did, Pétain and Weygand were the likeliest guarantors of the French fleet staying out of German hands.

Then came Rougier's suggestions: first, that Great Britain and France should accept a status quo over the colonies; second, any attempts to blockade French access to her colonial possessions should cease forthwith; and third, that radio attacks via the BBC French Service on Marshal Pétain should cease as well.

Deciding not to handle the matter directly, Churchill passed Rougier on to the Foreign Office. Sir Alexander Cadogan's deputy, William Strang, drew up a protocol which made clear Britain's unwavering determination to continue the war until the Reich was crushed. It also declared Britain's intention of re-establishing French sovereignty both in the Métropole and empire, but Britain "would be answerable for nothing if Vichy were to hand bases over to the Axis."[32] Next, and here was the breakthrough that gave de Gaulle a free hand for the next year: there was to be no attempt by either Vichy or Free France to take each other's colonies. Thus, under the Rougier-Strang protocol, French Equatorial Africa, furnished to de Gaulle by Leclerc and de Larminat, became a separate "Free" French Empire by agreement between London and Vichy.

Churchill refused to sign the protocol himself, especially given the reports of increasingly wicked treatment of Jews and other shameful concessions by Vichy, but he added a couple of comments written in the margin. The first, regarding French North Africa, was directed at Weygand "If Weygand raises the standard in North Africa he can count on our total support and a share of the United States' aid." Further down, regarding possible Vichy concessions to the Axis in the Mediterranean, Churchill penned, "In that case we should do everything to bring down a government guilty of so base a betrayal."[33]

Armed with this document, Rougier, a true servant of his nation though he never became a Gaullist, made his way to Algiers carrying a personal letter from Churchill to General Weygand, urging him to "raise the standard of revolt."[34] Weygand, however, never possessed the moral clarity of de Gaulle or Leclerc. An adopted Frenchman and a pragmatist, Weygand's remarks when dismissing Rougier's approach sum up *attentisme* as practised by the old *Armée d'Afrique*. "If the British come here with four divisions, I shall fire on them. If they come with twenty, I shall embrace them."[35] In fairness to Weygand, he was also resisting Germany in his own way, getting as many men and as much equipment to Africa as possible. He knew

France could not handle Nazi Germany alone, and until others were strong enough to do so, the Gaullist path seemed impractical. After the whole sickening experience of these negotiations, Rougier went to sit out the war in the United States.[36]

De Gaulle, having set up his Council for the Defence of the Empire at Brazzaville, was growing in stature since taking on the mantle of the *soi-disant* "Constable of France." Hearing about the Rougier-Strang agreement from Churchill, de Gaulle said somewhat disdainfully that he "understood the reasons that may at present induce the British government to adopt the appearance of handling the government of Vichy tactfully, so long as it cannot be proved that the latter has not made any fresh concessions to Germany or Italy." Assisted by Captain Paul Repiton-Préneuf, de Gaulle would reveal Vichy's treacherous concessions in Syria the following year.

Marshal Pétain was unambiguous over having Germany's knife at his throat, but Lord Halifax managed to send the Canadian diplomat Pierre Dupuy to Vichy. Pétain made it clear to Dupuy that any attack on French bases would be defended. When Dupuy asked whether bases would be made available to Germany, Pétain replied, "It all depends. If I am offered a satisfactory compensation I may be obliged to do so."

Dupuy then asked, "But would not that amount to taking Germany's side against Britain?"

"Yes, passively, but not actively," said the Marshal. Pétain then told Dupuy he hoped for British victory and would do nothing to hinder Allied interests.[37] The following week Churchill debriefed Dupuy, who advised the Prime Minister that de Gaulle should leave the Vichy portion of France's empire alone and annoy the Italians instead.[38]

Had Pétain used Dupuy to give "Free" France the green light? Even if de Gaulle had been condemned to death *in absentia,* Pétain still had a father's feeling for the former subaltern fresh from Saint-Cyr whom he had welcomed into the 33rd Infantry Regiment over thirty years before, even ticking off some who called de Gaulle a traitor.[39]

It would henceforth fall to Philippe Leclerc to take "Free" France's war into Italian-occupied Libya.

CHAPTER FOUR

ANNOYING THE ITALIANS

After their invasion of 1911, it had taken the Italians over twenty years to pacify Libya. Further ambitions in east Africa led to the invasion of Abyssinia in 1936. Yet during this period Italy had been a friendly neighbour, an ally even, of both France and Great Britain. The Pact of Steel, which created the Berlin-Rome axis between Hitler and Mussolini, changed all that. Lest the number of Italians living in French Tunisia provide a pretext for aggression from Libya, France built fortifications in the coastal area that were called the Mareth Line. Both Great Britain and France became wary of Italian encroachments in southern Egypt and northern Chad. The Sarra Triangle was reckoned an obvious flash-point.

In June 1940 many Italians had been surprised to find themselves taken into the war as Germany's ally. Their reward, following France's defeat, was to occupy a few bites of the Alpes Maritimes area between Lake Geneva and Nice, much of it former Italian territory until the *Risorgimento* of the 1860s. In September 1940, as the Royal Air Force fought the Luftwaffe over southern England, General Rodolfo Graziani launched his attack on British-occupied Egypt from Cyrenaica in northeast Libya. For the next three years, Italy's African territories became the only theatre where both

British Commonwealth and Free French forces could maintain active hostilities against the Axis.

"*Au revoir, Madame!*" Leclerc said to his secretary, Madame Crognier, before leaving Douala. "On to Paris!"

He flew north to the Chad capital, Fort Lamy, in a Bristol Blenheim of the Groupe Lorraine, piloted by Colonel Lionel de Marmier and navigated by Lt. Jean de Pange. On 2nd December, Leclerc, now wearing the anchor badge of La Coloniale on his pith helmet, participated in a parade to celebrate the 135th anniversary of the Battle of Austerlitz.

Chad is an enormous country, covered by wooded savannah in the south, while sixteen hundred miles north its border with Libya reaches into the southernmost expanses of the Sahara. The capital, now called Ndjamena, was then named after one of France's late nineteenth century explorers, Major Francois Lamy, who was jointly instructed with Fernand Foureau in 1897 to lead an expedition to Lake Chad, which, at that time, had still never been visited by white men.[1] After a tough journey across the desert, dogged by tribesmen led by Rabih Zubair, Lamy reached the lake only to die of his wounds following the final skirmish with Zubair, whose head was brought to him before he expired.[2] Such are the tales with which the French Army's African culture is laced.

In Fort Lamy Leclerc found an officer whose family he already knew from Picardy. Aged 31, tall, fair and taciturn, Captain Jacques de Guillebon had been to the same schools as Leclerc, liked shooting, and shared most of Leclerc's other values. Their friendship was spontaneous and Guillebon became a trusted confidant throughout the war. Otherwise the social gap between the new colonel and Chad's Coloniale officers could not have been wider. The latter were reassured by the arrival from the Cameroons of Louis Dio, Robert Quillichini, Jean Crépin and Raymond Dronne. Leclerc's cousin, Pierre de Hauteclocque, whom Leclerc had encountered at Carlton Gardens, had been transferred from Dewavrin's office out to Chad. Pierre had also taken a *nom de guerre*: "de Rennepont."

Of the potential targets in Italian Libya reachable from Chad, the most obvious were Murzuk in the Fezzan and, several hundred kilometres east, Kufra, an Italian stronghold since 1931. The empty distances involved meant that the British Long Range Desert Group (LRDG), operating from Egypt, was not strong enough to take these bases alone. Any trip from Egypt into southern Libya had to pass south of the Gilf Kebir massif, and their trucks could not carry enough petrol and water to go further without help from Leclerc's Free French to the south.[3]

The Kufra Oasis, with its little town, Italian fort and airfield, stands virtually astride the Tropic of Cancer on what the Italians called the *Pista Palificata*, a historic caravan route running north from Tekro in Chad to Jalo, northwest of the Calanscio Sand Sea, and thence to Agedabia on the Gulf of Sirte. Between Kufra and Jalo the Italians had usefully marked it out with iron posts, *pali*, every kilometre.[4]

After the little town of Faya-Largeau, Chad's northern border was another several hundred kilometres north of dusty, dry and uncomfortable tracks. Towards Niger the border runs through the Tibesti massif, while to the east lies a triangle of Libyan territory bordered by Chad and the Sudan called the Sarra triangle. This area is known for its freshwater wells and was annexed by the Italians during the 1930s. Hence, British intelligence tasked the famous Major Bagnold, who had explored the Gilf Kebir in the 1930s hoping to find the lost oasis of Zerzura, with making cartographic studies for the British government.

Mindful that Italy might become an enemy in the near future, the British explorers were nevertheless friendly towards Colonel Lorenzini's Italian camel corps, *Meharisti*, when they encountered them in the desert.[5] Lorenzini always travelled in style, with mess silver and a liberal supply of wine, often used to entertain the British.[6] The downside was that British explorers inevitably witnessed sickening sights east of Kufra, where Senoussi and Zwaya refugees from Italy's dirty war had fled into the sandy wastes to die of thirst and exhaustion, leaving their sun bleached bones dressed in rags next to those of their dead camels. Compared to the British and French, the Italians were relative newcomers to the colonial game, and slow to learn that rules of acceptability regarding the treatment of native peoples had changed since the nineteenth century. Senoussi tribesmen, led for much of the time by Omar Muhktar, an elderly school teacher, waged a drawn-out guerrilla war until 1931, when Graziani eventually captured Muhktar and hanged him in front of his own people. Many Senoussi fled to Kufra in the vain hope that distance would deter the Italians, allowing these dignified, tribal people to continue their way of life. However, knowing the Senoussi were buying guns from Arab sympathisers in Egypt, the Italians cordoned off the border with barbed wire for many miles inland and then attacked Kufra with artillery and light tanks. This wrecked forever this simple community and forced the survivors to flee into the desert. One of Xavier de Hauteclocque's books had covered the Senoussi War, so Leclerc was well aware of the depth of feeling among the indigenous population.

Thanks to Félix Eboué's refusal to obey directives from the Armistice Commission in Weisbaden insisting that he demobilise his indigenous levies, the highest quality troops available to Leclerc were the Régiment de Tirailleurs Sénégalais du Tchad, of which the word *sénégalais* was "more historic than real."[7] The RTST consisted of 6,100 men, of whom 460 were Europeans. This enormous regiment, whose functions were both military and civil, consisted of thirty companies divided into four groups centred on Beau Geste style forts. Group I was based at Fort Archambault in the south; Group II at Abéché; Group III at Faya-Largeau in the north; and Group IV at Mao facing the border of Niger which was held by Vichy, were all commanded from Fort Lamy.

At first the Chad officers did not take to Leclerc, nor he to them. Apart from Lt. Colonel Jean Colonna d'Ornano, they were largely from lower middle class backgrounds who had chosen La Coloniale for the freedom and independence from Metropolitan France which it offered. They had, of course, missed the Battle of France, but Leclerc quickly formed an overwhelming impression of their toughness. Their men were mainly indigenous Sarras or Hadjerai Moslems. Little motor transport was available, so dromedaries, the single-humped variety of camel, were in common use. What motor transport they had was largely obsolete and ill-suited to sandy trackless conditions—Matford and Laffly trucks whose engines were simply not powerful enough to get them out of trouble if things went wrong in the desert. The only heavy guns were vintage 75mms, the workhorse of French artillery for many decades. Luckily the Chad garrison had the mountain troops' variant which could be dismantled into carriable parts, but in general, weaponry was old-fashioned infantry issue and there were virtually no radios.

The main problem of prosecuting the war against Italy's south Libyan outposts from northern Chad was the nitty-gritty of getting food, water and petrol to isolated and forbidding places.[8] Fort Lamy to Kufra is a thousand miles over rough, barren, rocky desert, and the stifling heat for most of the year meant campaigning could only be undertaken during the cooler months from December to March. By contrast, Kufra and the Fezzan were, from the Italian point of view, at the end of a less tortuous supply line running south from Mediterranean ports such as Benghazi and Agedabia. By 1941 Kufra was no longer the little oasis town populated by devout Senoussi living on dates and goat meat. The Italians had totally transformed the place with a barracks built around a square, a high radio mast and an airfield.

The British were concerned that Italian bases in southern Libya could be used to threaten the increasingly valuable air route between Takoradi and the Middle East. But an operation against Kufra would be at the limit of the LRDG's logistics, and any thoughts of attacking Murzuk were simply unfeasible.[9] So, once Free French power was established in French Equatorial Africa, the Long Range Desert Group's Major Ralph Bagnold visited Félix Eboué in Fort Lamy. On arrival, Bagnold was suffering a malarial attack, which sporadically plagued many white officers, including Leclerc, and was put to bed by Madame Eboué. Nevertheless, Bagnold received guests from his bedroom at Governor Eboué's residence. First was Lt. Colonel d'Ornano, red haired, with a tinted monocle and dressed in the dark baggy trousers worn by camel riding members of La Coloniale.[10] Bagnold explained that he needed French cooperation to take Murzuk and Kufra. D'Ornano had already been impressed by a LRDG patrol that visited his outpost at Tekro,[11] and promised to help Bagnold, provided the LRDG took French soldiers including himself on the operation and they flew the *Tricolore* with Cross of Lorraine alongside the Union Jack. Bagnold readily agreed.

One of the men d'Ornano had in mind for the operation was Captain Jacques Massu, a dark, heavy browed man with a large nose, fierce eyes and small moustache, whose surname roughly translates as "Masher." Massu, who commanded the 6e Compagnie of the RTST based at Zouar, had been horrified by *la Chute* and welcomed Eboué's rallying of Chad to de Gaulle. He had heard of Leclerc long before meeting him on 15th December, and knew his real name was Philippe de Hauteclocque, whose bravery in the Haut-Ziz during the 1930s was common knowledge.

Leclerc touched down at Zouar and found Massu waiting with six camels to take him across the dried bed of the River Enneri to the barracks. Leclerc dismounted to inspect Massu's men, saluting the black, brown and white faces as he marched along their ranks. Next, he insisted on seeing them strip down and reassemble a Hotchkiss machine gun; a little display intended to demonstrate that he was not going to miss a thing. Leclerc was absolutely the stickler from Saint-Cyr that Massu had heard.

Jacques Massu was an aggressive man who had been in Africa since before the war, and he craved action. Yet, he had not seen German troops making themselves at home in his homeland as Leclerc had done, so his views on Vichy were less extreme. Leclerc often said, "It is necessary to treat your former comrades as enemies if the scales are to fall from their eyes." By contrast Massu seems, at this time, to have regarded "*Gaullisme*" as a matter of choice, hugely dependent on an individual's circumstances, rather than as a moral imperative.

Of the few trucks in Chad, most came from Vichy-held parts of French Africa, bringing men, supplies and materials. Massu and other officers had many friends in neighbouring Vichy Niger, who were slipping things to the Gaullists and helping comrades join them in Chad. On one occasion Massu received a message from his friend Commandant Nicloux, a *Vichysois* in Niger, "Are you ready to receive fifty litres of oil?"

"Yes, but I cannot guarantee their return," replied Massu. Soon afterwards General Cornet landed at Zouar airfield offering his services to Free France along with the aircraft and all its crew. "An airplane and a general seemed to me a good prize for the still embryonic Free French Forces," Massu wrote.[12] This affable approach was more likely to win recruits than confrontation.

Massu remembered Free French radio broadcasts aimed at Niger's Vichy garrison more for their extremity and level of moral insult as anything else. "Discipline stops at the limits of dishonour and treason. The senile cowardice of our leaders can do nothing to save the pain. Consider your orders null and act accordingly." Whereas Leclerc's standpoint was uncompromising principle, Massu's tolerant approach had its place and made human aspects of the war easier to deal with. Indeed, Commandant Nicloux delivered Massu's last letter to his dying mother.

Massu had also been warned about Leclerc's strict personal morals.

Leclerc was from a Catholic aristocratic family and was happily married to a social equal with six children. By contrast, Massu was a soldier's soldier from a *petit bourgeois* background and, like so many officers stationed in France's colonial backwaters, he followed the unofficial tradition of taking a temporary native wife. In his case she came from the Toubou tribe and was called Moido. Leclerc soon learned that his personal morality was irrelevant among La Coloniale and that he should only concern himself with his men's fighting abilities. Godfrey Allen remembered Leclerc saying, "All French soldiers need is a bag of dates, a bottle of wine, a woman, some enemy and '*Vive la France.*'"[13]

During early December 1940, d'Ornano managed to convince Leclerc that while Gaullist dignity preferred a wholly French operation against the Italians, the British LRDG was superbly equipped and experienced. Their appearance out of the dunes at Tekro during October was a sight to behold. Using columns of Ford and Chevrolet trucks, stripped down to their essentials, fitted with wider desert tyres, extra water condensers and sun compasses, only the Long Range Desert Group was capable of showing the French what could be done in the desert. Leclerc upped the game. In November, Bagnold had asked for a supply depot in north Chad capable of giving him 3,000 litres of petrol, food and water in order to attack Murzuk, but now Leclerc wanted to do something altogether bigger.

In the desert, camels can go where vehicles cannot. And anxious not to waste La Coloniale's experience in camel mounted operations, Leclerc ordered Captain Maurice Sarazac to prepare a nomad company-sized patrol to journey to the Italian outpost of Tedjéré in southwest Libya, a round trip of over a thousand kilometres. The question of horses and camels versus machines was so fixed in Leclerc's cavalryman's mind that when Lt. Christian Girard arrived at Fort Lamy after a three-week journey from Brazzaville, Leclerc began by asking him whether he thought the horse was finished in modern warfare. Girard gave such an evasive, tactful answer that Leclerc did not know what to make of him.[14] He knew, however, that motorised transport was less demanding of his men's endurance, if the vehicles were up to the task. So at the same time as ordering Sarazac's patrol, Leclerc ordered a discreet motor reconnaissance of Kufra by Commandant Pierre Hous.

Leclerc was in continuous radio contact with Cairo and Brazzaville throughout this period. Apart from planning the LRDG's contribution to the Murzuk and Kufra operations, at the same time Leclerc was also garrison commander. This entailed visiting outlying bases to ensure troops were operational, often by air. In the desert this could be hazardous. On 23rd December, the same day Sarazac set off with his camels for Tedjéré, and Hous departed to reconnoitre Kufra, Leclerc flew to eastern Chad in a Bristol Blenheim of the Groupe Lorraine. Departing at dawn, he was piloted by Captain Lager and his navigator, Lt. Pange. Both were inexperienced on Blenheims and lucky not to crash in the desert, never to be heard of again. Flying instinctively, by the seat of their pants, they got Leclerc to Abéché where he inspected Commandant Garbay's new "bataillon de marche" before its departure to Eritrea.[15] Unfortunately, during the inspection, the Blenheim's wheels sank in the soft sand beside the airstrip. Given the paucity of such aircraft, which were second-hand from the British anyway, Leclerc was incandescent.[16]

He was even more concerned by shortages of men and the necessity to commit experienced soldiers to watch the border with Vichy Niger. The Vichy commander, Colonel Garnier, had previously held Marchand's post in Chad until April 1940, and knew most of Leclerc's officers. Massu's letters got home via Vichy Niger, and in turn Colonel Garnier wrote to "Free French" officers individually, reiterating the Vichy viewpoint. Garnier even buttonholed Louis Dio face to face by Lake Chad. Dismissing what he called the *Vichysois* as "bandits following Hitler's orders," Leclerc banned such contacts.[17] He also insisted that Carlton Gardens give him priority when the *évadés* were allocated their units.

He put Chad's manpower on a war footing with as many Europeans as possible being pressed into uniform and more natives taking over administrative tasks. Operations against southern Libya were gearing up, and Chad's centre of gravity shifted northwards. Three thousand camels, all types of trucks, weapons and petrol were all stocked. Faya-Largeau with its picturesque fort was the first assembly point. Supplies were then moved 250 kilometres further north to Ounianga Kebir, whose crenelated fort beside a lake of shimmering blue water became a massive supply dump.[18] Another twelve Blenheims arrived in Fort Lamy to reinforce the Groupe Lorraine. However, young and inexperienced crews, lack of sand filters, and mechanics seconded from the RAF who were unused to maintaining aircraft in desert conditions took their toll: three aircraft disappeared with their crews before operations even began.[19]

On Christmas Eve, Captain Moitessier returned to Fort Lamy from Cairo bringing the most up-to-date maps the British could offer. Other intelligence on southern Libya came from Fezzan natives, who had fled from the Italians into north Chad. In a meeting with Leclerc their chief, Ahmed Bey Seif en-Nasr, agreed to furnish the French with Fezzanais guides.[20] Whatever religious importance Christmas held for a devout Catholic such as Leclerc, the war was not stopping for anyone.

On Boxing Day morning in Cairo, two patrols of the LRDG, the Guards' "G" and the New Zealanders' "T," seventy-six men altogether, mounted twenty-three stripped-down Chevrolet trucks loaded with everything necessary for a long expedition. Leaving their base in the citadel, they drove southwards through crowded streets towards the open desert. Major Pat Clayton, a forty-five-year-old desert veteran, was in overall command, while Captain Michael Crichton-Stuart, a twenty-three-year-old Scots Guards' officer, commanded "G" patrol.

During the 1930s Clayton had become acquainted with the Hungarian Count Laszlo de Almasy,[21] who gave him photographs of installations the Italians built at Kufra following their defeat of Omar Muhktar in 1931. Since Almasy subsequently became an intelligence officer for Rommel's Afrika Korps, his motives for this gift are harder to quantify in retrospect than at the time. Almasy was undoubtedly pro-Arab, though the Austro-Hungarian Empire, unlike others, was purely European, never having a colonial imprint. Otherwise, in the 1930s, a liberal and bisexual Hungarian aristocrat might have regarded Italy as a longer-standing enemy than Great Britain, and thought Mussolini's brutal, intolerant régime especially obnoxious.

In the interwar years, and earlier, Kufra had been a place of fascination for explorers. During the 1930s Pat Clayton had visited Kufra's Italian garrison to replenish the Zerzura Club's water supplies as they continued their researches in the Gilf Kebir. Two years earlier, Clayton had been in the Gilf Kebir-Uweinat area as refugees fled Kufra after General "Butcher" Graziani's attack. Approaching one exhausted family in his truck, Clayton found them so frightened of his white face that it took several minutes to convince them he was not Italian and that they could safely lower their rifles and accept help.[22] Clayton's knowledge and experience were now at Leclerc's disposal.

Shortly after leaving Cairo, Clayton's patrol stopped on the Mena road to pick up their Arab liaison officer and Sheik Abd el Galil Seif en Nasr, a sixty-year-old veteran of battles against the Italians, whose brother Ahmed had taken refuge with the French in Chad.[23] "G" Patrol navigator Bill Kennedy-Shaw remembered the Sheik as a big man with a "fine, fierce face" like one of Kennington's illustrations in T.E. Lawrence's *Seven Pillars of Wisdom*, along with "one claw-like hand shot to pieces in some distant battle . . . who chewed tobacco and spat incessantly and the doctor's temper for the day varied with the direction of the wind."[24] The British had no intention of using the Sheik to start an uprising by the Fezzanais, whose fighting qualities were slight in any case. Instead they used him as a guide and for propaganda, to rile the Italians once word got round that he was back. "The old man had accepted the invitation of a trip to his old tribal lands on condition that he got a shot at an Italian."[25]

On 23rd December Captain Maurice Sarazac set off for Tedjéré with a raiding force. He had forty-eight men: twenty-five tirailleurs, nineteen so-called "guides"—Fezzanais recruited in the belief that they knew the terrain and wanted to hit back at the Italians—a single "bellah" to look after sixty-three dromedaries, and three Europeans: Sarazac himself, his deputy Lt. de Bazalaire and Sergeant-Major Marson. Their route took them first to Kourizo and then to Lebo in southern Libya. They were beset with difficulties from the beginning. The route was stony and uneven with few grazing places, and they reached Afafi, in Free French territory, to find the well had been drunk dry, which meant a twelve-hour detour to Toummo on the Niger-Libya border to replenish their camels. They only reached Domazé, sixty kilometres from Tedjéré, on the 9th January with their camels beginning to fail.[26]

If that was not enough, on 11th January the chief guide informed Sarazac that their "bellah" had absconded, and it had to be assumed he had gone to warn the Italians. Then the Fezzanais guides turned out to be a disappointment, with false alerts and ignorance over places they had claimed to know when recruited. In spite of this, Sarazac got close enough to Tedjéré on the 12th to evaluate his chances of a successful raid. Finding the Italian fort larger than expected, and in some state of readiness following the simultaneous operation against Murzuk, Sarazac decided on a night attack from three directions: he took the centre, de Bazalaire the north and Sergeant Major Marson the southeast. The attack began at 1.30am on 13th January. Italian return fire was heavy. The air was thick with machine-gun fire, and although Sarazac's men got to within fifty metres of the fort, they were forced to fall back to their regrouping point. They lay up among palmeries the following day, evading detection by Italian aircraft, and when night fell they began their return march. En route they were hit by a sandstorm and took two days to regain the well at Toummo. By then their camels were in a dreadful state and would need to be well rested before any future effort.[27]

Leclerc had given the go-ahead for the Murzuk raid in combination with Clayton's two LRDG patrols on 21st December, and Captain Jacques Massu was tasked with organising resupply for Clayton's men when they reached the Tibesti. After the Groupe Nomade de Tibesti's camels had carried petrol, food and water up into the Tibesti massif, ten Free French awaited their rendez-vous with the British: d'Ornano, Massu, Lt. Albert Eggenspiller, the sergeants Bourrat and Bloquet, along with five indigenous Fezzanais and Toubou specially chosen by Massu.[28]

Clayton's LRDG arrived on 6th January. D'Ornano took his place in Clayton's truck, the Free French pennant flying on the antenna beneath the Union Jack. Massu was struck by the New Zealanders' independence of spirit, and how they mainly came from farming backgrounds. After spending the following day getting organised and checking plans, they considered a preliminary prison-busting raid on Ouau el Kebir in the southeast Fezzan to release its inmates. But, wisely perhaps, recognising that the Italians would soon respond to their presence, they prioritised principal objectives.[29] En route, d'Ornano again found himself impressed by the LRDG style of soldiering, agreeing with Massu that the Free French should consider this way of operating. Their men—*blague volontiers*—would be most suited to it.

Driving on hard sand, they avoided the Italian-occupied Hofra oasis to their east, and by 11th January they could see Murzuk's radio pylon and aircraft hangar shimmering three kilometres away. While they ate—the

French couscous prepared by their natives, the LRDG their usual tea, corned beef and army hardtack—Lt. Kennedy-Shaw drew a diagram of Murzuk in the sand. An Italian bomber landed at the airfield while they squinted through binoculars at their target. Murzuk had been the Italian headquarters in the Fezzan since their final pacification of the Senoussi and Zwaya in 1931. The town contained about two thousand inhabitants, and stands at the junction of ancient caravan routes.[30] However, it was the fort and the airfield outside, manned by two hundred troops, ordnance and fuel stores, that the French and LRDG wanted to wreck.

The New Zealanders began the attack in two groups, one of which was led by the Clayton-d'Ornano truck, while "G" Patrol took up positions behind gardens southeast of the fort. *"Dans cette armée les chefs s'exposent,"* remarked Colonel d'Ornano, taking over the machine gun in Clayton's truck. Massu and two Fezzanais had taken places in the next Chevrolet commanded by New Zealand Sergeant Hewson. The other French, Sergeants Bourrat and Bloquet and three Toubous spread among "T" patrol's other trucks.[31] Crossing the stony ground between the crest and the town without incident, "T" patrol weaved through little streets in the direction of the fort, passing Murzuk's Fezzanais civilians who, assuming they were Italian, called out *"buon giorno."* Passing a well, they spotted an Italian on a bicycle. Clayton and his driver grabbed his shoulders and hauled him into their truck. Their hostage, Italian postmaster, Signor Colicchia, would be their guide. Partly obscured by palm trees, the fort's garrison and dependants sunned themselves while taking siesta. As it approached, Clayton's truck veered left, with d'Ornano firing tracer rounds at the fort.

Hewson's trucks halted and began hosing the fort's walls and gates with fire. From the east, "G" patrol gave support fire with mortars[32] and their Bofors gun, hitting a car later discovered to be carrying the Italian garrison commander, his wife and child—all dead.[33]

The next priority was to shoot up the aerodrome before Italian guards could reach their machine guns. Two trucks under Lt. Bruce arrived first, finding most of the Italians already putting their hands up. One Italian reached for his machine gun and was immediately shot in the head. On the other side of the aerodrome the Italian reaction was quicker. Clayton's truck, speeding across the runway to join Kennedy-Shaw, was liberally hosed with machine gun fire, bullets hitting everything. D'Ornano was hit in the throat, dying instantly. The truck continued amid a withering hail of bullets from a hangar, only suppressed by a timely shell from "G" Patrol's Bofors.

Thoroughly alerted, the Italians were now arming themselves and returning fire. This went on for about fifteen minutes, with the LRDG and Free French shooting up the fort's ramparts and the barrack house used by Italy's Libyan levies. Behind Massu, Sergeant Hewson, firing the truck's Vickers machine-gun, was shot through the heart, falling back dead on the floor. Massu himself suffered a light leg injury. In return, "T" Patrol's suppressing fire destroyed three Ghibli light aircraft, a Savoia-Marchetti bomber and the fuel dump. Seeing that further resistance was futile, the remaining forty Italians surrendered.

With space for only two Italian prisoners on the trucks, the rest, including fifteen aircrew, were left behind to fight for Mussolini another day; something Jacques Massu regarded as impractically merciful. By 5pm all the trucks had regrouped for the return trip. Once underway, when they felt sure that no Italians were pursuing them, they stopped to bury d'Ornano and Hewson as a cold sandstorm began to whip up. In a scene redolent of Charles Wolfe's poem about the burial of General Sir John Moore, they gently lifted d'Ornano off the truck. Massu noticed the serene palour of his face caused by loss of blood. Sentimental as tough men can be, once the Corsican was wrapped in a blanket, Massu pinned the anchor badge of La Coloniale and the Cross of Lorraine to his body. To the New Zealander, Sergeant Hewson, Massu gave his *galons*, later writing, "I had time to appreciate this energetic and gentle farmer-turned-soldier who had welcomed me into his team with such kindness." The cross was made from two pieces of plank and driven into the sand. As Major Clayton read the Church of England's prayer for the dead, the British and French saluted their fallen.

The LRDG reported the raid almost immediately, and British HQ in Cairo maximised Free France's participation. Vichy might feign embarrassment, but the Rougier-Strang protocol, though unsigned by Churchill and Pétain, meant that the French were committed to a dual role as both hostages and unofficial belligerents. If Italy complained to Vichy about Free French activities in southern Libya, Vichy could reply they were a different France. Disingenuously, the Italians put out a communiqué claiming the raiders had been successfully beaten off, but nevertheless admitted damage to the airfield.

Next, the combined British-Free French force made a detour thrust into the desert to raid the small Italian outpost at Traghen. While they laagered under the palms of a mini oasis to hide from aircraft, an Arab camel train appeared from the dunes, tambourines playing, and fluttering green banners emblazoned with symbols of Islam, crescents and pentacles. This was Sheik Abd el Galil Seif en Nasr and the nomadic Ouled Sliman tribe demanding their share of glory. The two groups embraced each other, and the old Sheik introduced each British and French soldier to his fellow warriors, while the Italian prisoners stood motionless.[34] In the meantime Clayton quietly visited Traghen and easily persuaded its two-man Italian garrison to surrender.

Continuing like characters from folklore, they drove on to attack the Italian outpost of Oum el-Araneb (mother of hares). Preparing the trucks for battle in the shade of a palmery they suddenly heard aircraft overhead and bullets ripped through the green palms. The vital element of surprise was gone. In Massu's words, "We weren't in armoured cars and found that we had amused ourselves for long enough." Oum el Araneb would have to be left for another time. On top of which some, including Massu, had injuries needing treatment, though for the time being Massu cauterised the bullet wound in his leg with a cigarette.[35]

They drove on to Toummo where they linked up with Sarazac's Groupe Nomade returning from Tedjéré. After a further 400km around the northeast corner of Vichy Niger, they finally reached Zouar by mid-morning on 19th January, where Massu happily offered the hospitality of his little kingdom. After a parade at which the French, Guards and New Zealanders saluted the Union Jack and Croix de Lorraine flags, the indigenous cooks prepared a *méchoui* of goat meat roasted whole over an open fire, with freshly baked bread. The following day a Bloch aircraft arrived at Zouar. Bagnold had arrived to congratulate them and evacuate the wounded.

Before Clayton's trucks departed, Massu gave them a French 81mm mortar with eighty rounds, since he had been unimpressed by the smaller British mortars used at Murzuk. As they drove away, Massu, a French *méhariste* grateful for being initiated into the new era of desert soldiering, saluted them. He had covered 2,141km in thirteen days. The LRDG covered 4,122km in twenty-four days.

A few days later, Clayton's force was surprised at Jabal Sherif by a motorised Italian Sahariana directed onto them by patrolling Italian recce aircraft. Clayton and two others were wounded and taken prisoner. Several, including two Italian prisoners, were killed. The rest escaped into the desert—some to die in the arid barrenness; others only reaching Sarra wells after the grimmest ordeal. Two Britons and a New Zealander walked for ten days, only to find a well poisoned by the Italians with a dead camel. When finally the French found them, Easton was at death's door, Winchester was maddened by thirst, and only Moore, the New Zealander, was in any sort of reasonable mental condition in spite of a bullet wound in his foot.[36]

This type of tragedy was inevitable. If Kufra was important to the Allies, then it was important to the Italians as well. Their army had developed a Saharan tradition just like the LRDG. Furthermore, the duality of French colonial politics between Vichy and de Gaulle meant that operational security was not what it should have been.

On 26th January Massu arrived in Faya-Largeau to de-brief with Leclerc. *Le Patron*, as Leclerc became known, listened intently as Massu described his experiences. Seeing a Chevrolet truck left with the French by the LRDG, Leclerc was forced to concede its superiority to the Matford and Laffly trucks with which he might have attempted the Kufra operation. At the same time, the senior Free French officer did not see anything that could not be improved. The combination of manoeuvrability and machine guns for shooting up enemy personnel and installations was fine up to a point. However, experience at Murzuk suggested heavier firepower could have been useful. Furthermore, Commandant Hous' reconnaissance to Kufra with merely two vehicles had had to turn back following a warning that Italians were always watching the Sarra area.

The conclusion was obvious. Kufra was the most important target in southern Libya, and if it was going to be taken and held, Leclerc had to mount the largest, best-equipped operation he possibly could. On Boxing Day, while still in Fort Lamy, Leclerc had ordered an aerial reconnaissance over Kufra to supplement the Hous expedition. Groupe Lorraine airmen,

Lager, Stadieu and de Pange carried out two deep-penetration reconnaissance flights over Kufra and Uweinat. The best maps Guillebon could find showed Kufra at the centre of a large yellow coloured area described as "lacking water and vegetation," and were last updated in 1913! From the air, direction-finding could be hazardous owing to sandstorms covering reference points and road markers on the ground.

Undeterred, Leclerc ordered the flights anyway. Jean de Pange, the navigator, later wrote, "Leclerc, who knew nothing about aerial navigation, asked us to go without radio, without direction finding equipment, without radio beacons, with maps that were little better than sketches, to the limits of what was possible. He probably didn't know what he was asking. At Saint-Cyr he would have heard of a compass, but not the other essential elements such as declension, deviation, drift, ground speed, etc."[37] Getting to Ounianga-Kebir was quite a performance. In Fort Lamy, Jean de Pange found a surveyor who knew the territory and persuaded him to fly with them. Their Bristol Blenheims, named after Marlborough's 1705 victory over Louis XIV, were already obsolete in 1939. The 1930s and 40s were a time of huge leaps in aircraft development, speeded by the exigencies of war. In 1940–41, sand filters for aircraft engines had not been perfected. The bravery of these young flyers—for whom a forced landing in the desert would most likely be fatal—should not be underestimated, but Leclerc had to order these missions even if the risks were high. Such is the lonely courage of command.

Leclerc would never ask anyone to take risks he would not entertain himself, but his attitude to aircraft was that they "flew" just as automobiles "roll," and that was all there was to it. On 28th December 1940, Lager and de Pange took off with Leclerc, followed by a second Blenheim crewed by Stadieu, Meurant and Privé with the surveyor. Their flight first took them to Faya-Largeau to refuel. The crews wanted to pause at Faya to allow winds further north to die down and partake of a festive *méchoui*. Leclerc would have none of it. He made them carry on to Ounianga after a single cup of coffee.[38] The journey to rendez-vous with Hous at Ounianga was beset by sandstorms reducing visibility at times to five metres. On arrival, Colonel Leclerc got out of his aircraft, as a flurry of wind and sand struck its wings, and fell heavily on the ground. Le Gall, an infamous colonial doctor who didn't know who Leclerc was, helped him up saying "hello *cuckold*."[39] A character, this medical lieutenant could not say three words without using slang, but Leclerc recognised the eccentricity and did not take offence. Le Gall's experience among La Coloniale was that most white men, given the distances and separation of service life, were cuckolded by their wives.

After debriefing Commandant Hous at Ounianga, with the *méhariste* Captain Barboteu of the Groupe Nomade d'Ennedi in attendance, Leclerc ordered the Blenheims to carry on with the plan to reconnoitre Kufra, taking Barboteu, who had never flown before, with them. However, a heavy sandstorm prevented flying for three days. When it cleared, "Leclerc was present at the take off," wrote Jean de Pange. "We saluted him at six paces and he returned our salute with a gesture of extreme elegance which only a cavalry officer can achieve. I was surprised by his attitude, but I have since learnt to understand it. It wasn't us, poor kids, that he was saluting, but we who were taking the first steps on the road to Strasbourg."

Leclerc, like de Gaulle, had an immense sense of history, and understood the significance of what he took part in. By midday Lager and de Pange's Blenheim was over Kufra, with its fort and the aerodrome of El Giof clearly visible. Lager made two passes so that de Pange could count Italian aircraft and take photographs. On neither occasion did they draw fire from the Italians, and returned uneventfully to Ounianga. The second Blenheim, however, developed a technical problem over Uweinat and was forced to crash land near the Libyan border. The crew wandered in the desert for twelve days before being captured by an Italian patrol and taken to Kufra, from where they were flown via Benghazi to a prison camp in Italy.[40]

Leclerc wanted to know everything; how large was the garrison, how many aircraft, what artillery pieces, as well as the number and type of vehicles. De Pange remembered, "Since Barboteu could not be found, I did my best to answer, feeling the worse for wear after the long hours of flight. I felt the mysterious Kufra had suddenly become real for the *méharistes* and Leclerc. It wasn't me they were looking at, it was 'the man who had seen Kufra.'"[41]

Leclerc spent New Year's Eve 1940 examining aerial photographs. The previous winter he had been in the Forêt de la Warndt spicing up the *drôle de guerre* by leading patrols into no-man's land. Now he was in a backwater of northeast Chad. On New Year's Day he asked de Pange to take him back to Fort Lamy via Faya-Largeau. Since both places were again hit by sandstorms, it was another hair-raising flight. On landing at Faya amid thick flying sand, de Pange protested to Leclerc that he could not navigate if the ground was invisible. Nevertheless, Leclerc insisted they continue to Fort Lamy. The pilot, Captain Lager, had to climb four thousand metres to find usable gaps in the whirling columns of sand. De Pange guessed a bearing which he gave to Lager and, knowing it would vex Leclerc, left all his maps and crawled down into the Blenheim's perspex nose cone. After an hour, Leclerc, visibly agitated, crawled into the nose himself and grabbed de Pange by the arm.

"Why aren't you navigating?" asked Leclerc.

"I can't because I can't see the ground," replied de Pange drily.

Leclerc said nothing and crawled back, leaving de Pange to stare at the featureless sand sliding by below him. A couple of hours from Faya there was a break in the sand flurries, and de Pange recognised the little village of Moussoro. The bearing he had given Lager was accurate. After the tension of the previous hours, Leclerc was thrilled.

Reaching Fort Lamy, exhausted by three hours flying blind, Captain Lager made a dreadful landing. Leclerc left the Blenheim in total silence. Eventually he admitted to Lager his mistake for flying in such appalling conditions. De Pange took the reel of Kufra film to amateur photographers and warned them that if his pictures were not processed properly, he would chuck a grenade at them. Luckily they came out well, and de Pange settled down in the searing daytime heat of the aerodrome office to add details to their map of Kufra. It was hot work. With refrigerators broken, de Pange could not even have a cold beer, but soon the picture of Kufra was all there: areas cordoned off with barbed wire, machine gun nests, the heights of the fort walls, aircraft hangars and gun emplacements. He estimated there were four hundred Italians at Kufra, plus a company of Sahariana, but no artillery. As he worked, de Pange heard hooves outside. Leclerc often found some kind of horse or donkey to ride during his Africa years. Having dismounted and hitched up, he came in to view de Pange's progress. "Carry on, I just want to look at this for a moment."[42]

Leclerc wrote to de Gaulle, "The fort at El Tag appears solid and well built. I am not counting on taking it, but will do the maximum damage to the air base and other facilities outside the fort. Whatever the difficulties we will go and we will succeed."[43]

While Murzuk was happening, Leclerc concentrated his forces for the Kufra operation, placing several companies from the Régiment des Tirailleurs Sénégalais du Tchad at Ounianga, and sending up as many supplies and fuel tankers as would be needed. The attack itself would be carried out by the mobile company of the RTST and the Groupe Nomade de Tibesti. The RTST contingent would be commanded by Leclerc's cousin, Captain "de Rennepont," assisted by Captain Geoffroy and Lt. Arnaud, while Captain Barboteu commanded the Groupe Nomade. By now Leclerc was receiving new Ford and Bedford trucks in sufficient quantity that he could relegate the pre-war garrison's Matford and Laffly trucks to less strenuous tasks. However, it became a hallmark of Free French forces throughout the North African war to make do with whatever could be found, be it old or captured, a mentality which applied to vehicles and weapons alike.

Twenty-five Bedford and thirty Ford trucks, two armoured cars, a recovery section, a medical unit, and an artillery section with two mountain 75mm guns were earmarked for Kufra. For two months, Faya-Largeau's workshops prepared new trucks for the desert, removing cabin roofs, doors, anything reflective and all inessential weight.

A little over four hundred men—one hundred Europeans and the rest indigenous RTST and Groupe Nomade—would take part. Their logistics train required another hundred vehicles and another hundred and fifty men. Everything had to be carried over three hundred and sixty-five miles, especially water. The last usable well was at Tekro. Sarra's wells, being closest to Italian-controlled territory, could not be relied upon.

In a country as dirt poor as Chad, with the British Commonwealth at the limit of what it could offer in terms of manpower and material, Leclerc did well to put such a force together.[44]

De Gaulle was back in French Equatorial Africa following a visit to the Free French contingent supporting the British in Abyssinia, and he was anxious to see Leclerc's progress. He was accompanied by Major-General Sir Edward Spears, the veteran British liaison officer, who had not yet met Leclerc. He was struck by Leclerc's slight limp caused by his horse slipping on Saint-Cyr's parade ground, and "gave him the very fine Malacca stick I had with me." Later, Spears told Henry Maule: "I think sometimes that I have the gift of second sight. I said to him 'as long as you carry that stick with you, you will always be safe.' He seemed really to believe what I had said, for he always did carry it about with him, everywhere, except once."[45] Leclerc called that stick "baraka." In fact, Leclerc went through several walking sticks; they often feature in photographs of him, even pre-war ones—always held in the same way, on the outside of the bend if in his left hand, like a sword if in his right.

Conflicts between British and French interests in the Levant eventually undermined de Gaulle's friendship with General Spears. Leclerc recognised that Free France must cooperate closely with Great Britain, but shared de Gaulle's irritation at being dependant upon France's former greatest rival. When Lt. Kennedy-Shaw, departing for Cairo with Bagnold, complimented Leclerc for being "almost an Englishman," it rankled terribly! However shortly afterwards, Leclerc was sent his own British laison officer, twenty-four-year-old Lt. Mercer Nairne[46] of the Scots Greys, who spoke fluent French. Both aristocrats and cavalry officers, Mercer Nairne and Leclerc got on well. "Under normal circumstances," said the Englishman, "he [Leclerc] would have been shocked at the troops he was now commanding. French colonial soldiers serving in remote stations were apt to be rough and tough and look like a gang of pirates!"[47]

After the Italian ambush and Clayton's capture, remnants of the British contingent retreated to the border. When the LRDG finally left Chad, "G" Patrol's Lt. Chrichton-Stuart remembered Leclerc: "He thanked us for saving his force from ambush and said good-bye. We felt bad leaving him and the scene has always stuck in my mind. The sun was near setting. . . . All around the scruffy little force were cooking their evening meal on small fires. Nearby a coal-black Senegalese was messing about with a repulsive looking piece of dried meat which was to be Leclerc's own supper. He stood there with George Mercer Nairne, smiling and waving as we turned and drove off."[48]

On 2nd February and again on the 5th, Leclerc ordered the Groupe Lorraine's Blenheims to attack Kufra, resulting in the destruction of some aircraft, petrol tanks and supply dumps at the base. But the crews were inexperienced at desert flying, especially with their wholly inadequate maps, and the Blenheims, at their furthest range, could only carry a picayune payload. Two crews failed to return. In a moment of apparent heartlessness, Leclerc refused the airmen time to search for the missing men, muttering, "One does not need incompetents."

"*Mon colonel*, don't you think the skin of an aviator is worth the same as a '*biffin*' [footslogger]?" retorted the Groupe Lorraine's Captain Goujon de Thuisy.

Rendered intensely autocratic by his authoritarian upbringing, Leclerc fumed back, "And you think the air force is the same as the cavalry?" He thwacked the tailplane of a Lysander with his cane. "If so, they need whipping!"

A search was nevertheless carried out, and one crew was recovered. Blenheim T-1867, however, had strayed 360km from its return bearing for Ounianga. When the wreck of T-1867 was discovered 18 years later, notes found on the dessicated bodies of the crew showed they had survived for over a month before finally succumbing to thirst and hunger.[49]

In the meantime the intrepid *méhariste*, Lt. Corlu, who joined the Free French in Chad in August 1940 following a thirteen-day camel trip from the Groupe Nomade de l'Air at Agades, reported back to Leclerc.[50] He had set out with the LRDG's "G" Patrol, and then split off at Sarra Wells to reconnoiter Kufra after the Groupe Lorraine's raids. Corlu reported that the Italians were thoroughly alerted. Leclerc consulted with Guillebon, now his chief of staff, and Lt. Mercer Nairne, who both believed the Italians would reinforce the oasis. But, as at Douala, Leclerc did not flinch. The operation would go ahead, though with the modification of greater firepower. Determined to show the Italians that he would do as he pleased in the desert, and not they, Leclerc decided the following programme: first he would execute a reconnaissance in force to Kufra; second, he would destroy the Italian Sahariana force; third, he would take the oasis itself.

On 5th February they set off without further delay, reaching the oasis of El-Zurgh, only seven kilometres south of Kufra's fort El-Tag within forty-eight hours. On the night of 7th February Leclerc sent out patrols under captains Geoffroy and de Rennepont, while personally leading a patrol into the village of El Giof. Stealing into the house of the village elder, Leclerc woke the old man by shining a torch in his face, and asked him in Arabic for information. Usefully, he learned that at night the Italians returned from their outposts and locked themselves in their fort.[51]

About 2am the other patrols made their rendez-vous with Leclerc. One had taken a prisoner at a lookout post, destroying his radio. Hearing that the road to Kufra's aerodrome appeared clear, and with several hours remaining before sunrise, Leclerc decided to attack the airfield at once with thirty men in six trucks. They found the airfield perimeter badly guarded. Guillebon led a section into a hangar where they destroyed two aircraft and let off a couple of flares to signal their success. In response, the Italians set off a flare of their own: green. Seeing this, the other Frenchmen believed it was the signal to regroup as soon as possible.[52]

On regaining their fallback position, Leclerc ordered them south. At daybreak, Italian Ghibli aircraft were out looking for them. However, the broken terrain offered enough cover to make such efforts ineffectual. Of thirty men who raided El Giof, one was killed and four wounded. Lt. Arnaud was badly hit in the arm, and operated on without anaesthetic by *médecin-lieutenant* Mauric, assisted by the chaplain, Father Bronner.[53] Returning via Jebel Sherif, they discovered the LRDG trucks that had been abandoned when Clayton's group was ambushed, along with two dead. Always punctilious in religious matters, Leclerc ordered these men properly interred. Father Bronner officiated.[54]

On the North African coast the British counterattack by Wavell's "Thirty Thousand" was turning into a roaring success. Leclerc hoped the Italians would be so preoccupied with the British they would be unable to spare reinforcements for Kufra. The French had to keep the initiative.

Leclerc returned to Faya-Largeau on 10th February and telegraphed de Larminat his estimation of Italian forces at Kufra as 250 Europeans and 400 indigenous Saharans living in the fort. Each strongpoint had three 20mm machine guns. He reiterated that, despite repeated raids from land and air, the airfield was fully functional, and Italian air links with Ethiopia were maintained from there. Leclerc recommended a new, stronger raid as soon as the supply situation was favourable. With continued British success in the north, Leclerc hoped they could chase the Italians into Tripolitania so Free France could occupy the Fezzan. But for the time being his main priority remained the elimination of the Italian force at Kufra.

Another air raid by the Groupe Lorraine brought disappointing results, which Commandant Astier de Vilatte covered up from Leclerc. Four days later, de Larminat telegrammed Faya-Largeau: "British advise Italians evacuating Kufra. Act promptly to sieze and occupy!" Spurred that British success meant Free France increasing her African Empire, Leclerc had his attack force ready at Sarra by 16th February. In fact, the Italians had no intention of evacuating Kufra.[55]

On 17th February they set off with Leclerc in the lead and the rear brought up by Commandant Dio. The column made good progress until one of Lt. Ceccaldi's trucks broke down. These carried the column's two valuable 75mm guns and ammunition.

"Ceccaldi, I said 'no stragglers,'" said Leclerc, who had driven back down the line to investigate. "Better to abandon the kit."

True to La Coloniale's spirit of resourcefulness, Ceccaldi and three others began repairing the truck's motor with their bare hands. Job done, they caught up.[56]

They reached the outskirts of Kufra oasis by midday on 18th February. At once, Leclerc and the advance guard, two detachments of twelve Bedford trucks commanded by Captains de Rennepont and Geoffroy, found themselves under heavy machine-gun fire from a Sahariana patrolling out from Kufra fort.

"Take cover!" Leclerc shouted. Men and trucks placed themselves in dead ground behind a dune's undulations and ridges. The dust and sand whipped up during the drive covered everything, and the French found themselves unable to fire back until the grit had been wiped from their weapons' mechanisms.

As Italian machine guns ripped into some of his trucks, Rennepont wryly suggested they go in "*à la baïonette!*"[57] Soon, however, the French were firing back. Leclerc ordered Rennepont's squadron to hold the Sahariana troops down in a firefight, then he and Geoffroy's squadron outflanked them from the northeast.[58] Though not strong enough to dislodge the Sahariana, this attack was sustained for ninety minutes while Rennepont's squadron regrouped and attacked again, forcing the Sahariana to withdraw southwest before turning about and taking the road to Tazerbo, pursued all the way by Rennepont's squadron.[59]

Throughout the afternoon Geoffroy's squadron closed in on the fort from the north. Despite the possibility that the Saharianas being chased off by Rennepont might turn back for a counterattack, the night was calm. The Italians attempted no relief until morning, when seven Savoia-

Marchetti bombers attacked Geoffroy's squadron. He had dispersed his men and vehicles sensibly among the dunes so there were no losses. One of these bombers departed to attack Rennepont's position but was hit by small arms fire and flew off spewing smoke.[60]

At 8am, Leclerc was at Rennepont's position when it was attacked by thirteen Sahariana vehicles. Leclerc ordered half of Rennepont's squadron to face them down while he led the balance in a flanking movement. Leading his Bedfords away towards defendable hillocks, Leclerc lured the Italians in their excellent SPA trucks after him. After losing two trucks, the Italians recognised they were going to come off worse and withdrew along the Tazerbo road a second time. This time Rennepont pursued them for two days and a hundred and fifty miles. French losses were six wounded. Although the Saharianas had been beaten away from Kufra, this was not quite the elimination Leclerc wanted. So far, per his cavalryman's training, he had kept the initiative.

By now Commandant Dio had arrived with the balance of the force to lay siege to Kufra itself. With Rennepont keeping the Saharianas away, Leclerc had a window of time during which to take Kufra. From inside the fort the Italians could easily reckon that the French, subject to the same logistical constraints as themselves, could be worn out. But Leclerc had already thought of this and ordered his men to give the Italians the impression of a long siege, as though they had all the time in the world.

Taking up residence in the deserted *Carabinieri* post at El Giof, lying between the Fort and the airfield, from which he could see all the details of the siege, Leclerc had the benefit of a *pigeonnier* there for fresh poultry and other comforts as well as taking possession of twelve camels.[61] To the northwest he placed an observation post to warn of Italian reinforcements. Although this eventuality was unlikely while the Italian Tenth Army was in full flight from the British in Cyrenaica.

Inside the fort, the Italians possessed mortars and some heavy Breda machine guns, excellent weapons, which they fired on the French— seriously wounding Commadant Dio—as they established control of the surrounding area. Artillery Lieutenant Ceccaldi found that a French 75mm shell could punch a neat circular hole in the fort's earth walls and explode inside. Unluckily, they only had enough ammunition to feed one gun twenty rounds a day—but it was convenient because one of his indigenous gun crews had turned out to be windy when the bullets were flying. The 75mm mountain gun was fired at the fort, moved and fired again, thereby protecting the gun from return mortar fire and giving the impression of greater artillery strength than there was. Some of Ceccaldi's shells hit the fort's mess, others the magazine, all with the aim of diminishing Italian morale.[62] All patrols close to the fort were carried out aggressively on foot, while those of wider radius, checking for Italian reinforcements or relief, were carried out by truck using headlights at night to give the impression of confident superiority.

Leclerc launched a "hearts and minds" campaign among the surrounding villages, saying the French had only come to deal with those who had attacked France and that France wanted peace. The local tribes, caring little for the rival colonial powers, were uninterested by comparative judgments between French and Italians. They simply wanted to carry on their daily business and avoid the incoming and outgoing fire around the fort.

Rumours circulated that conditions inside the fort were deteriorating rapidly. On 26th February, Ceccaldi alerted Leclerc to a white flag raised over the fort. However, when Leclerc approached to parley, the artillery duel erupted again. The Italians were not ready to give up yet. Then, on 28th February, the Italian commander sent a native soldier out to French lines with a letter on "Presidio Militare, Cufra" headed paper, imploring Leclerc to avoid hitting the northwest corner of the fort where the Italian wounded were situated, and asking to evacuate the worst cases to the first aid station he knew Leclerc had established. The letter was dated 27th February, so either the Italian commander had taken his time delivering the note or lost his sense of time altogether. Leclerc replied that such a request should be the subject of a parley between officers.

That afternoon, under a white flag of truce, an Italian officer appeared, making the same request to Guillebon and Sammarcelli. Sensing a weakening, the two French officers debated notions of truce and giving quarter in front of the Italian, nonchalantly declaring that only a formal surrender would mean anything. The downcast Italian returned to the fort. For extra pressure, Leclerc ordered his 81mm mortars and 75mm mountain gun to fire intensely.[63]

At dawn on 1st March 1941, Captain Colonna, commanding Fort El-Tag at Kufra, ordered the white flag raised and sent envoys to the French lines. Once again the Italians attempted parley until Leclerc appeared. Declaring that parleying from a position of obvious weakness was ridiculous, he cut short the discussion and made the Italians get back in their car. Then, jumping onto the running board beside the chauffeur, joined by de Guillebon and 2nd Lt. Ruais, Leclerc directed the Italians' return to the fort. As the gates opened Leclerc found himself facing the ageing Captain Colonna, whose medals included a Croix de Guerre from 1914–18.

"I simply wanted to talk, you have no right to enter," said the peeved Italian.

Leclerc, accompanied only by Guillebon and Ruais, ignored Colonna's complaint and curtly ordered him to gather his men in the courtyard. Further protests were brushed off with, "Do as I tell you." The young Rommel had found that a similar show of self-assurance earned laurels against both Italians and Romanians during the Great War. The Italian garrison, including many who opposed surrender and were reasonably well armed, began to obey Leclerc's orders.[64] Looking around the large open courtyard of the fort's interior, with its absurd *fasces* statue in the middle, Leclerc's mood changed. Standing in his pith helmet, double-breasted *vareuse*, baggy trousers and sandals, and leaning on his stick, he spoke reassuringly to Colonna's junior officers, saying it was not dishonourable to surrender when well beaten, abandoned by their senior command, and with wounded needing treatment.[65]

Leclerc then dictated surrender terms. First, a Franco-Italian hospital would be set up immediately to tend wounded from both sides. Second, the fort's heavy weapons would be left in place, while those outside would be brought in. Third, after the surrender a garrison of European French would take control of Kufra. Fourth, after sending personal messages, the Italian radio would be destroyed. Fifth, all indigenous troops serving the Italians, the Askaris,[66] were to be disbanded forthwith; those from the Kufra area were to be released back among their own people; those from elsewhere were to be released at the oasis. Sixth, the Italian officers, NCOs and other personnel were to be taken to Faya-Largeau, and their captivity decided by the French senior command. Seventh, Italian personnel must see that all terms were carried out properly.

By afternoon everything was in French hands. They were so few that even the chaplain, Père Bronner, had to stand a shift of guard duty with his long beard flapping in the desert breeze. At 2pm the Italian garrison paraded in front of Leclerc: eleven officers, eighteen NCOs and lastly, two hundred and seventy three Libyans soon to be leaving Mussolini's employ. Italian losses were three killed and four wounded.

The North African campaign saw much use by each side of captured equipment. At Kufra, Leclerc's force took charge of four 20mm cannon, three 12.7mm Breda machine guns,[67] eighteen Schwarglose machine guns, thirty-two other machine guns of various types, fourteen vehicles and a stock of supplies. When the thirty Italians, shorn of their Libyan levies, were marched to the lorries bound for captivity, they saw the ramshackle and tiny nature of Leclerc's command and were horrified.

French losses were four killed, including one European Frenchman, twenty-one wounded, including Dio and Corlu, and four trucks destroyed. Equipment losses were well compensated for by the haul of captured kit.

The following morning Leclerc's force held its first parade in the captured desert fort. The *Tricolore* with its Cross of Lorraine was raised on the flagpole which had so recently held the red-white-green tricolour of the House of Savoy. After saluting Free France's first real victory against Axis forces since de Gaulle's *appel* of 18th June, Leclerc had something to say to them: "Swear that you will never lay down your arms until our colours, our beautiful colours, are flying afresh on Strasbourg Cathedral."

"We swear," replied the men gravely.

There are slightly differing versions of the precise wording of Leclerc's *"Serment de Koufra"*—"The Oath at Kufra." Whatever the exact words, this oath became as important in the history of the Free French as Nelson's "England expects that every man shall do his duty" at Trafalgar one hundred and thirty-six years earlier.

The fall of Kufra was quickly broadcast throughout French Equatorial Africa. On 3rd March, the news was dispatched worldwide by Reuters:

> *The General Headquarters of the Free French Forces in London reports:*
> *General de Gaulle has received from General de Larminat, the Free French High Commissioner in Brazzaville, the following telegram:*
> *"I am happy to inform you that Kufra capitulated on the 1st March at 9 o'clock. The taking by French arms of this enemy position is one step towards victory. Vive la France!"*

Also, General de Gaulle has received from General de Larminat a telegram sent to him by Colonel Leclerc, commanding the troops involved in the Kufra operation: "The French troops of Tchad and the Cameroons express their faithful attachment to the allied cause until the final victory."[68]

De Gaulle sent a private telegram to his favourite officer, telling him the hearts of all Frenchmen were with him and his men. Given the political views of Frenchmen loyal to Vichy then, and in years to come, this was not strictly true, but an early indicator of the white lies de Gaulle was prepared to tell in order to rebuild French dignity during and after the war. Not long afterwards, the Free French were successful at Cub-Cub in Eritrea, another source of pride for de Gaulle, except that this operation took place under British operational command, from British Imperial territory. Kufra, on the other hand, was an entirely French operation.

Afterwards Leclerc had tough things to say about his equipment. In mid-March he returned to Fort Lamy and sat down to write a report for his superiors, principally de Gaulle.

The Blenheim aircraft which the British had allocated to the Groupe Lorraine had originally been intended as a versatile basic aircraft which could be used either for night-fighter or bomber roles. However, it was hardly up to desert conditions, any more than French aircraft were.

Infantry weapons also demonstrated serious shortcomings. There were not enough heavy machine guns, and the standard French Hotchkiss was inadequate. On the other hand, the 81 mm mortar gave useful results.

Leclerc felt that British trucks were better than France's pre-war Lafflys and Matfords, but that would hardly be difficult. He was most impressed by the way the Italian motor industry had addressed itself to desert problems. The SPA truck had four-wheel drive and power steering, enabling the vehicle to avoid getting stuck in soft sand, and its engine did not overheat. The Bedfords supplied by Great Britain were the best available on the Allied side, but there were not enough of them.

Overall, Leclerc felt that French infantry had an equipment problem which should be placed "with all possible vigour and urgency before the British High Command."[69]

Tactically, Leclerc believed his experiences of commanding motorised troops in desert conditions confirmed German methods of ten months earlier. The command of mobile forces required energetic leadership at all times. Furthermore, Leclerc felt that indigenous forces levied in French imperial territories, while better than nothing, were ill-suited to mechanised desert warfare. Once again he requested that Carlton Gardens give him as many European French soldiers as possible.

Among the officers of La Coloniale and those from the Métropole who had "done Kufra," a strong bond would grow over the coming years, which would eventually imbue the spirit of the 2e DB. In the very early days of Free France, there might have been a rivalry, not to mention an obvious social gulf, between officers from smart cavalry regiments such as the Cuirassiers, and men from peasant and lower middle class backgrounds who saw La Coloniale as a path to social acceptance; the social fabric of France had not changed so very much since the Revolution. Now there was a new spirit. Any man could be one of nature's aristocrats if he had guts, spirit and an overwhelming desire to see his homeland free. The men of Chad like Massu, Dio, Guillebon, Barboteu, Arnaud, Geoffroy, Dubut, Sammarcelli, Florentin, Eggenspiller and others were to become the core of the 2e DB.

De Gaulle covers Kufra in that part of his memoirs entitled *Londres*. Though excellent history, it is the moments of distrust towards the English which are so telling. Negotiating the minefields of British patronage and condescension was a serious endurance test for such a proud man. "One cannot imagine," he would write, "the lengths the English will go to in order to obtain satisfaction . . . sometimes charming . . . sometimes menacing." For every Antony Eden, who was always "sugar and honey," there would be a scathing general who regarded French troops as useless, not worth wasting resources upon. Nevertheless, de Gaulle admits that his men received equipment fresh from the factories. Even if he did find the British insufferable, they were at the very least Free France's bankers, aside from her closest military collaborators, and the conquest of Kufra could not help but be seen as a good example of Franco-British military co-operation. De Gaulle knew only too well that France in her *faiblesse* could only do what was possible. If the North African war continued westwards, the Free French would have the opportunity to take the Fezzan from Mussolini's African empire. In which case, provided "*L'Angleterre reconnut*

notre droit a y demeurer, nous pourrions évacuer Koufra."[70] Subject to the
Free French flag flying at all times, the first prize won by Leclerc would
be garrisoned by the Long Range Desert Group.

Free France had succeeded in most of what she had undertaken so far.
The balance sheet was mainly in the black. Thanks to Leclerc, de Gaulle
was a different man when he set off for the Middle East in March 1941
than the crestfallen foundling he had been after Dakar.

CHAPTER FIVE

CONSOLIDATING, RAIDING, AND PLANNING

Ever conscious of French prestige, de Gaulle invited the Long Range Desert Group's Colonel Ralph Bagnold to a meeting in Cairo. For de Gaulle, even the French language was an integral part of national identity. Speaking in slow, precise French he informed Bagnold that Kufra belonged to France, his France, until a treaty decided otherwise. On a deeper level however, de Gaulle knew that Free France could not thrive as merely a clique of nationalistic officers over a rank and file of Foreign Legion desperadoes, black African troops fearing Axis racism, and a sub-set of the bloody-minded that exist in any nation. Tentacles of the emerging resistance in the Métropole were making contact with him, men who were not only from the military but also highly respected members of France's civil service and professions. They took a longer view on the kind of France they wanted to see once peace came. De Gaulle recognised that these men required something more reflective than "Old France," the views of *Action Française*, irrational hatreds of Jews and Freemasons, or street fighting with a *Front Populaire* government. In all but name, de Gaulle became a "New Deal" politician. He pondered over the French empire, concluding that it meant nothing unless it improved the lives of its citizens.

In Chad the euphoria of a victory following twenty months of national humiliation made some of La Coloniale's officers insufferable. They lived like pashas in their little colonial fiefdoms with temporary native wives; were waited on by house boys who were often less than benificently treated; and, whatever their fighting qualities, had to be called to order. Some had the nerve to tease Leclerc for his sexual loneliness by slipping girls into his room. But Leclerc never succumbed to such temptations, telling his aide Troadec that abuses must cease. All this, along with the wretchedness of his isolation, made Leclerc hate Vichy the more. He wrote vehemently to René Pleven of "a rage in the heart when I think of our cowardly compatriots. They will pay one day." The sordidness of some aspects of *la vie coloniale* also took its toll on his cousin, Pierre de Hauteclocque (aka "de Rennepont"), who finickily demanded that a punishment section be set up for dealing with "conduct unbecoming." Cousin Pierre found his way back to the 13e DBLE which, despite now being commanded by Marie-Pierre Koenig who was having an affair with his English chauffeuse, was more to his liking.[1]

Leclerc however, unable to apply the "Old France" rules of his caste, had no choice but to see it through. News emerging from France indicated how far *Action Française's* creator, Charles Maurras, had taken the collaborationist path. Finally understanding Pius XI's interdiction, Leclerc wrote to Pauline Vanier in London that "ultimately the Sacred Father was correct a few years ago in condemning the disastrous Maurras. My poor mother-in-law must be in a state." Like de Gaulle, Leclerc came to recognise that a truly "Free" France had to be inclusive, that liberation would not happen without rejuvenation, and rejuvenation had to be broadly based. Recognising that the social anti-Semitism of his class no longer had a place, Leclerc did nothing to prevent a Jew being elected unopposed to run Fort Lamy's mess.[2]

With Kufra taken, it became necessary to secure the route along the old caravan trail, so Sarra was garrisoned as well. Though the LRDG would occupy and have use of Kufra, *méhariste* Captain Barboteu was nominated its first Free French commandant, while Leclerc's role was recognised fulsomely by the British with the award of a DSO (Distinguished Service Order). It fell to Ralph Bagnold, however, to run the place and revitalise its peasant economy.[3]

As the Free French consolidated their gains, things were changing for the British in the north. By 7th February the British capture of Cyrenaica was complete. Place names that would fill two years of British military history—Mersa Matruh, Sidi Barrani, Bardia, Fort Capuzzo, Tobruk, Gazala, Derna, Barce, Benghazi, Beda Fomm, Agedabia and El Agheila—became known for the first time. The British took so many Italian prisoners that one Coldstream Guards officer counted them in acreage.[4]

In the Mediterranean, Britain, having cowed the French fleet into sullen inactivity, now asserted her naval superiority over the Italians by striking the Italian fleet at Taranto.[5] This drew Luftwaffe reinforcements onto North African soil to support Italy's Regia Aeronautica. From 17th January, Stukas operated from a base near Benghazi, but their presence alone could not halt the routing of Graziani's Italian Tenth Army by General Richard O'Connor. Knowing the Italians were coming off worst against British forces at a time when he wanted his southern flank secure before invading the Soviet Union, Hitler did not wait for Major General Werner von Funck's report before ordering advance elements of what would become the Afrika Korps to Libya. Lt-General Erwin Rommel and the 3rd Berlin-Brandenburg Reconnaissance Regiment landed in Tripoli on 11th February 1941. For the next six weeks Rommel's Afrika Korps built up, its most important units being the 90th Light Division and 15th and 21st Panzer Divisions. By 31st March they were ready to move.

The British were sent reeling by the Afrika Korps' first attacks on their Second Armoured Division at Marsa el Brega. They also suffered an immense setback when Generals Sir Philip Neame and Dickie O'Connor took a detour into the desert to avoid a traffic jam and drove smack into a German patrol. Within a fortnight, Rommel had recovered all of Cyrenaica except Tobruk, whose garrison held out stubbornly until the following winter.

The British reverse meant Leclerc's hopes of leading an operation to join up with them in Tripolitania were dashed for the time being. While the British Empire was at full stretch, de Gaulle suffered a bout of hopelessness, and indulged himself with the cranky belief that the British wanted to snatch France's colonies, much to the consternation of his liaison officer, General Spears. The military reversals also meant that, far from initiating further operations from Chad, Leclerc now had to reinforce the British in Egypt. The Blenheims of the Groupe Lorraine departed for the Middle East.[6]

For the next few months Leclerc had to wait and prepare. Swashbuckling souls like Massu found maintaining an active presence in the Tibesti
very boring. More intellectual officers like the recently arrived Christian
Girard wrote of "*Un ennui mortel*." With the Groupe Nomade de Kanem,
Girard got to know each of the 20e Compagnie's horses in detail, but found
it harder to build a rapport with camels! The French Army in Africa always
had a problem with the mind-crunching tedium of desert postings once
the initial fascination had worn off.

All too aware of these frustrations, Leclerc wrote an open letter to his
men on 21st March 1941:

> . . . I feel that I need to respond to various disquieting questions
> which I feel are on all of your lips: 'When are we going? When are
> we going to fight again?'
>
> Our forbears, in October and November 1914, were horrified
> at not yet having been sent into action. . . . Later they were repre-
> sented by the wooden crosses of Verdun or the Somme! At Douala
> a few months ago I threw a young officer out of my office who
> wanted to return to England because there was 'nothing to do.' A
> few days later, that officer was killed at Libreville.
>
> There will be a place in combat for everyone before our colours
> fly again over Strasbourg Cathedral.
>
> How long do we have to hold on? Predictions are impossible but
> all the signs are that it is going to be a long war.
>
> I understand that the noise of combat . . . in Abyssinia makes
> you envious, but . . . hold on as long as you have to.
>
> The final victory is certain and deserves all sacrifices. . . . You
> are taking part in the battle, because, in line with Hitler's wishes,
> this war is total.[7]

As infected by *ennui* and frustration as anyone, the energetic Jacques
Massu spent the time usefully, searching out old camel tracks which
vehicles could use through the Tibesti massif between Wour and Aozou,
essential for an advance into southwestern Libya once the British reversed
the situation.[8] There was a lot to wait for. The United States of America
would not be sending soldiers for another eight months, but Anglo-

American logistics were beginning to hit their stride.

On 16th April Leclerc arrived in Zouar by Lysander. After picking up Massu, the pilot, Captain Noel, flew over the outposts of the Groupe Nomade de Tibesti, dropping messages in weighted bags calling their garrisons to Zouar. By early afternoon, Massu's scattered *méharistes* arrived for Leclerc's inspection and an in-depth discussion of the way ahead. Following a *méchoui*, they gave *le Patron* the anchor badge of La Coloniale. Setting aside his cavalry officer's *hauteur*, with a light smile Leclerc accepted what his cousin Pierre disdained. He recognised the pride of these men in the backwaters of France's empire. Besides, they were all he had.[9]

A few days later Leclerc welcomed de Gaulle to Faya-Largeau. With new Ford and Bedford trucks arriving at Douala, there was a lot for him to see. By 1st May, following their sudden mechanisation, Massu's men were ready for their first important parade. At 9am, de Gaulle's Bloch landed at Zouar and he appeared at the top of the aircraft stairs in tropical khaki, followed by his ADC, Lt. de Courcel. For the first time Massu saw the man who would shape his destiny for thirty years. De Gaulle took a parade of dark-skinned Chadiens in strange uniforms mixing tribal and French styles accompanied by the sound of "tam-tam" drums.[10]

Two hours later, four camels appeared carrying an artillery officer and three junior air force pilots. Commandant Lanusse and Lts. Brisdoux, Louchet and Jourdain had arrived from Vichy-controlled Morocco. Facing disbandment under terms imposed by the Armistice Commission, they had taken two cars across the Sahara to offer their services to Free France. Inevitably the cars broke down. Luckily, by the time their second car gave up the ghost, they were near enough to the Tibesti settlements to obtain camels. Never in their wildest dreams did they imagine the short camel ride to Zouar would bring them face to face with de Gaulle himself.[11] Massu took the opportunity of inviting the new arrivals to join a lunch already too frugal to share. Later de Gaulle toured Massu's defensive positions, smiling as the tough colonial officer explained how to avoid a surprise attack in such forbidding territory.

That night de Gaulle stayed in Massu's plain bungalow, another Métropolitan officer sharing the discomforts of La Coloniale amid beds of animal skin, makeshift showers and camp-style latrines. Giving the general his own bed, Massu lay wrapped in a blanket by the bungalow's door, guarding "the man who was the incarnation of eternal France" as shooting stars burned out in the blue African sky and the excited village of Zouar fell asleep around them.[12]

Bloodletting between Frenchmen was not over. There still remained a sizeable Vichy French garrison in Syria, commanded by the same rabidly anti-British General Henri Dentz who had surrendered Paris to the Wehrmacht on 14th June 1940.[13] The arrival of Rommel's Afrika Korps gave the German intelligence service, the Abwehr, important reasons to support an Arab revolt in Baghdad and pressure Vichy to allow Luftwaffe access to bases in Syria from which to operate against the British.

During the 1930s de Gaulle had been a staff officer in Syria, an appointment he used to educate himself in Middle Eastern history. Several of his senior officers, including Georges Catroux and Edgard de Larminat, also had experience of the colony. Catroux had drawn de Gaulle's attention to the dangers of the Syrian situation the previous autumn following the Italian invasion of Egypt. After further incognito visits through early 1941, Catroux advised de Gaulle that, given Dentz's pro-Axis bias and Germany's need to support Rommel, further conflict with Vichy was inevitable. The British Middle East CinC, General Sir Archibald Wavell, was reluctant to commit forces already disastrously thinned by the need to fight the Greek campaign. But, on 12th May Vichy Admiral Darlan ceded French air bases in Syria to the Luftwaffe. This was too late to save Raschid Ali's abortive pro-German rebellion in Iraq, but a Luftwaffe presence in Syria represented an unacceptable threat to British interests. Wavell and the Free French prepared to act.

A month later, at dawn on 8th June 1941, a combined British and Free French force attacked Syria. Wavell's forces were so meagre that a quarter of the men and a third of the available air power had to be Free French. Dentz's men fought unevenly, yielding before the British, yet the Vichy Foreign Legion fought furiously against their Free French opposite numbers. This is probably because the Vichy Foreign Legion consisted mainly of Germans and White Russians, while the Free French Foreign Legion was composed largely of anti-fascist Spaniards. Within ten days, Dentz, who had kept Gaullists in chains in Syria's prisons, approached the American consulate in Beirut to seek terms from the British. It had lasted three weeks and was all over bar the shouting. Dentz only wanted to surrender to British forces, so de Gaulle was cut out of the surrender negotiations and given little opportunity to persuade the Vichy garrison to come over to him. Thirty-five thousand preferred to be shipped back to France, while most of those who remained in the Levant had business interests there. Syria's airfields yielded up German aircraft, as de Gaulle had warned, and he felt his Britsh allies were ungrateful. Once again General Spears was left to pick up the pieces of de Gaulle's latest tantrum. The next eighteen months, during which the British would take their toughest action against his Vichy compatriots, would be the low point of de Gaulle's relationship with Churchill.

Syria also strained the unofficial cooperation between Vichy and the Free French along the Niger-Chad border. Lt. Girard was in the habit of talking across the barbed wire to a *Vichysois* captain whose slavish devotion to Pétain was, he felt, pathetically chaotic in its reasoning. Information confirming the fallacies of Axis propaganda bounced off him, "Like water off a duck's back." If he became exasperated by what Girard told him he simply yelled, "The BBC lies!" In March 1941, this officer declared, "The English are after our colonies, it's obvious! They haven't changed!" After Syria his attitude became, "The English were right to go into Syria to stop the Germans installing themselves there, but it was inadmissible for the [Free] French to take part in such a campaign on the side of the English! We all hope that England wins. Victorious, she will be just as exhausted as Germany. And then we, who during this time will have been waiting quietly, will be the real victors, much more than de Gaulle's adventurers."[14]

Within a fortnight of General Dentz's surrender in Syria, the strategic balance of the war changed. Germany invaded the Soviet Union. The Free French, and even some Vichy generals like Weygand, finally realised that Germany had gone too far, but many on France's "old" right wing regarded the Franco-German conflict as superceded by a new and greater struggle between Europe and Bolshevism.

In this new strategic climate the British beefed up their presence in Egypt. The ports of the Red Sea received plentiful supplies, and Wavell's original "Thirty Thousand" became a fully mechanised army with a new commander: "sepoy" General Claude Auchinleck of the Indian Army.

Sensing his allies were preparing a large-scale offensive, Leclerc sent Jacques de Guillebon to Cairo as his liaison officer. Guillebon got the distinct impression the British underestimated what the Free French could do from Chad. The British were pleased with Kufra, but doubted Leclerc could deal with the Fezzan on his own. "I thoroughly reassured them," Guillebon reported. "I said we wanted equipment as soon as possible in order to be ready for the future when the British resumed their march to the west." The British protested that their equipment losses in Greece and Cyrenaica still had to be made good, to which Guillebon retorted, "At that rate we're never going to have more than a box of matches!"[15]

Luckily, support came from the British military attaché in Fort Lamy, Colonel Archdale. "[Leclerc] is, I think, the man we need here," he wrote to his superiors. Even so, there were grades of equipment which, given British needs, Leclerc was never going to receive in anything approaching the quantity he would have liked, such as Bofors anti-aircraft and 25-pounder guns. Leclerc demonstrated a fine sense of irony by remarking to Mercer Nairne that while the malacca cane given by General Spears was very kind, "He worried that it was not enough!"[16] The ding-dong over equipment continued through the summer, and the British eventually stumped up four Bofors guns, six US 75mm guns, ten Marmon Herrington armoured cars and over four hundred trucks. The War Office regarded all this equipment as needed for defensive purposes only, and Leclerc as someone who would always complain because it was, "In the nature of the beast." Some even wondered if he was a fifth columnist intent on diverting valuable kit to a tropical dead end like some malign character from an Evelyn Waugh novel, or simply a heat-crazed dreamer.[17]

Meanwhile, in the stifling summer heat of northern Chad, officers and Tirailleurs alike tackled the *ennui* of garrison life as best they could. A sophisticated Parisian, Lt. Christian Girard was surprised to see a black corporal reading a yellow-covered *Revue de Paris* edition of Jean Giraudoux's *Ondine*. Another officer, however, used to reading to kill time in imperial backwaters, did not find it *particulièrement drôle* and began explaining the storyline until Girard stopped him.[18]

Nor did heat, dust and *ennui* help the testing domestic situations which Leclerc's cousin Pierre found so distasteful. One officer who, like Massu, had taken an indigenous temporary wife, returned from a remote outpost to find her sleeping with his African batman who was also her ex-husband. Losing his temper, the officer beat up, trussed and castrated the hapless African, who bled to death. A court martial ensued which reached Leclerc's ears. He saw at once that executing a French officer for such a brutal murder would do immeasureable damage to morale, and ordered the man's discreet removal to a desk job in Douala—"In the general interest."[19]

As always in Africa, distances and terrain meant logistics were Leclerc's major concern. He would never forget the state of French resupply during *la Chute* in 1940 with intact, combat-worthy tanks abandoned for lack of petrol, and was determined never to let his operations come to grief through similar shortcomings if he could avoid it. The distance between Fort Lamy and northern Chad alone meant huge quantities of petrol were expended simply bringing up supplies. The depot at Zouar, where Leclerc lodged himself from mid-April, needed enlarging. Roads which had only ever seen camels were now a stream of British and American-built trucks of which there were never enough, so camels were still used to carry petrol to Kufra.

In the Fezzan, Leclerc had two options. Either he could repeat the Murzuk raid several times over, harassing the Italians and drawing retaliation; or, with properly planned logistics, he could take and hold the Fezzan, if he gave himself a more northerly start line from which to advance into southern Libya and link up with the British once they defeated the Axis in Cyrenaica. Leclerc first needed to establish a staging post in southwest Libya. Uigh el Kebir, a small, ungarrisoned oasis in little known territory, 620km north west of Zouar, was the obvious place, if it could be seized and held.

Using heavy Bedford trucks, European drivers and a few *goumiers*, the "king of noses" Jacques Massu spent July and August establishing the Uigh el Kebir base. He recorded in his affable memoirs that this *balade* was not a "pleasure trip." Heat took its toll of men and machines. As so often happens in the desert, when vehicles are not fitted with condensers, radiators sprang leaks; but with the resourcefulness typical of La Coloniale, these were repaired with gazelle skins![20]

French Equatorial Africa's growing strategic importance made it necessary to divide military logistics into two halves: North and South "Transport Sections" with Fort Lamy on the dividing line. Even civilian trucks, whether by agreement or coercion, had to carry military supplies, leaving the civil economy with the barest minimum. The ensuing economic chaos worsened during the rainy season when petrol supplies had to come over-land from Nigeria instead of from Douala and Pointe-Noire. Even more lorries had to be requisitioned, placing greater pressures on the civil econ-omy. Leclerc's successes made his soldiers believe he was lucky. But they were always the result of careful planning using both intelligence and logistics, ably headed by Captain Lantenois.

Kufra had taught Leclerc the need for motorised troops capable of fight-ing from vehicles, so he created two companies for combat and reconnais-sance whose task would be to seek out enemy patrols and engage them in combat immediately, thereby maintaining surprise. Each of these compa-nies was split into four platoons, which in turn could be divided into two half-platoons. During a desert engagement, one half of a platoon would pin down the enemy in a firefight while the other outflanked. For company commanders, Leclerc chose Geoffroy, who had distinguished himself at Kufra, and Massu whom he recalled from Zouar in October 1941. Massu thus left behind him a phase of his life which had begun in 1938 when he first came to Chad and met his indigenous "wife," Moido.[21]

Leclerc formulated his ideas for "reconnaissance and combat" compa-nies largely from LRDG methods he had seen that summer, but he kept his thought processes to himself. Many of the 77 officers and 189 NCOs from France, who had been in the tropics for over two years, found him impenetrable. Men like Massu would always find something to do in a lonely outpost, whether tinkering with a vehicle, talking to natives or shooting gazelle. But others, like Captain Hausherr, placed in charge of a garrison outpost at Ati, still complained of their lot. Leclerc wrote to him, "Would you rather have a Vichy officer commanding the subdivision at Mongo? . . . If you have not yet understood that this war will be long, requiring enduring effort and patience rather than a frenzied dash like in a Dumas novel, then I am sorry! . . . I made you independent at Ati because you are difficult to command and prefer your liberty. Therefore you should be thanking me."[22]

Following his earlier requests to be given priority with new Free French volunteers, a steady trickle of those young Frenchmen—*evades*—who had got out of France clandestinely, began to arrive at Fort Lamy. Some had reached England by fishing boat directly from the French coast, others had quit France via Spain and Portugal like Leclerc himself. They had heard of Leclerc and were more than happy to serve under the man who had taken Kufra. Some were newly commissioned officers who had undergone a Saint-Cyr-style short course at Old Dean in England—men such as Paul Batiment, Yves du Daruvar, Robert Dubois, Roger Pons, Roger Podeur and Jean Silvy. Like de Gaulle, Leclerc had come to enjoy hearing their adventures reaching Great Britain. Interviewed singly, each was confronted by *le Patron* sitting elegantly cross-legged in a fetid, dusty office under a whirring fan with lizards scrabbling about on the walls. Yves de Daruvar did not know whether to be delighted, charmed or intimidated.

"How did you get out of France?" Leclerc asked.

After a long bicycle ride from Paris to Saint Jean de Luz, Daruvar had found passage to England on a Polish liner.

"Ah," said Leclerc. "You as well. You did a bike ride just as I did."

Then he briefed Daruvar on the garrison role awaiting him. Like many others, this young lieutenant had not realised that the war would involve a lot of waiting.

"*Mon colonel*, I have not come all this way for that. I want to fight!"

Another, Lieutenant Robert Dubois, imagined he was going to become a *méhariste*.

"But you're not, old fellow," said Leclerc, laughing heartily while tapping the ground with his cane. "All that is over! Those units are disappearing. These camels, one can only have too many. It's vehicles we need. And men like you to run them."

Dubois subsequently became a vehicle supply specialist.[23]

Other ranks, young men like Emil Fray and Gaston Eve, were usually thrilled just to be there. They had not served in the French Army before, but Fray and Eve were already in England when de Gaulle paraded the 13e DBLE in front of Marshal Foch's statue on 14th July 1940. The prospect of serving "Free France" had genuine appeal so they turned up at 4 Carlton Gardens to be told by de Gaulle himself, offering a rare smile, to report to Olympia. Fifteen months later, after basic training in England, a tortuous voyage to French Equatorial Africa, a fortnight's trip up from Brazzaville by train and a wood burning paddle steamer, they arrived at Fort Lamy. A few days later Leclerc flew in to inspect them at the airfield. He cast steely eyes over every man before giving them an inspiring lecture about the strategic situation in Africa and the Middle East. He made every one of them feel important.[24]

Like all soldiers at war, these men realised they might never see their homeland again, and they embraced comradeship as a substitute for family. Getting messages home to their loved ones in Occupied France may not have been impossible, as Massu had found, but it was nevertheless extremely problematic. Letters from Free France's portion of the empire were opened and inspected by Vichy or German censors. Often a carefully chosen postcard with a simple greeting in the sender's distinctive handwriting was the best that could be managed without leading to awkwardness or worse for the recipients. Even in the Métropole, communication between the occupied and free zones was severely restricted, let alone between the occupied zone and Vichy's portion of empire.

However much he shared his men's worries about families back home, Leclerc never allowed his personal anxieties for his family to show. From time to time those close to him would notice him quietly reading a prayer book or slipping one discreetly from a desk drawer into his great coat pocket. But the only family contact he had was with Pauline Vanier in London. She became the "ear" with whom he shared thoughts that would otherwise have gone to his nearest and dearest. So it was Pauline who heard of his fears over "poor Thérèse burdened with six children," and the traditional complaint of French soldiery over Africa's climate, hard work and *le cafard*—that peculiar *ennui* particular to the French Army's African subculture. And, when his British liaison officer, George Mercer Nairne, asked Leclerc to be godfather to his newborn son, she found a suitable present from Leclerc for the child in London. Pauline Vanier always did this when officers asked Leclerc to be godfather to their children.

"Perhaps I am going to be able to send some very indirect news to my wife through my British liaison officer," Leclerc wrote to René Pleven. "She does not even know if I am alive . . . What a nightmare!"[25]

News was not coming out of France either. In his traditional role of *seigneur* of Belloy-Saint-Léonard, Count Adrien did his utmost to maintain French dignity under the noses of the occupiers. In March 1941 he held a ceremony of remembrance for Senegalese soldiers killed in the fighting around Amiens the year before, because their sacrifice had saved his chateau from destruction. In February 1941 his wife was the first to hear news of Leclerc from a cousin who told her that her beloved son Philippe had been promoted and given an important command.[26]

Patriotic to the core, the Hauteclocque family were unwilling subjects during the Occupation, and it was their cousin François de Hauteclocque who had the first run-in with the German authorities, during the winter of 1940–41. Francois had been a high-ranking member of Colonel Count Francois de la Rocque's right-wing paramilitary Croix de Feu during the 1930s, and had small arms hidden on his estate. Sadly he was denounced by some of his compatriots and was imprisoned with his wife in Germany for six months.[27]

It was also only a matter of time before the Vichy authorities and German intelligence realised that "Colonel Leclerc" was none other than Captain Philippe de Hauteclocque, former staff officer of the 4e DI and instructor at Saint-Cyr. After collating reports of officers repatriated from the Cameroons, Chad, Congo and Gabon, a Vichy official confronted another cousin, the diplomat Jean de Hauteclocque, with photographs of officers serving with de Gaulle. "That's 'Leclerc,'" they told him, slapping Philippe's photograph down on the interview room table. It would still be some time before Leclerc realised it in his lizard-infested office out in Chad, but the pseudonym game was up. Despite first-rate reports on Philippe by General Buisson, written while he was a prisoner in Germany in June 1941, a court martial sitting at Gannat stripped Captain Philippe de Hauteclocque, *devenu "Leclerc,"* of his nationality. Four months later he was sentenced to death *in absentia* for "crimes and other actions against the unity and safety of *la Patrie*."[28]

Though objectively immensely serious, such condemnations by Vichy, by those "chance gathered governors" as de Gaulle called them in his *Appel* of 18th June 1940, were regarded as the highest decorations imaginable among the "Free French." But, for relations at home, they were no laughing matter. As early as April 1941 Thérèse heard from her brother-in-law, Guy de Hauteclocque, that the "Leclerc" of Kufra was none other than her husband, and she spent the rest of that year living in dread of arrest. The pressure did not stop there. For the sake of her children and the people on the estate at Tailly, she forced herself to maintain an outward appearance of calm. After June 1941, once Philippe was stripped of his nationality, Thérèse was under further pressure. Under Vichy law her husband's property and goods were now forfeit to the state. An old family friend, Paul de Bonnault, "bought in" Tailly for 1.2M FF, intending that Thérèse and the children should retain the benefit of it. The Vichy authorities easily saw through this wheeze. Nor did Thérèse's forthright protests at the Wehrmacht grazing their horses on the estate without permission endear her to the local Kommandantur in Warlus. For that she spent thirty-six hours locked in a sweltering cell during the July heat wave. She was only released after her father-in-law bribed the local Kommandant with bolts of velvet plush provided by another family friend, Paul de la Royère, an Amiens textile magnate.[29]

Finally, in November 1941, Thérèse obtained Pauline Vanier's London address through which she hoped to get a message to Leclerc. The second winter of the Occupation was bitterly cold, and made worse by shortages. Count Adrien was by now 76 and under similar pressure because of his son "Leclerc." However, he worked flat out to ensure enough firewood both for his own home and for Thérèse at Tailly, weakening his heart. Philippe's parting advice to Thérèse was that she should keep as much livestock as possible, but by December 1941, while facing further attempts to evict her, Thérèse only had one cow for milk and one horse for work and transport. When her three youngest children went down with flu she fed them on chicken, eggs and rabbit. Nevertheless she sent a message to Philippe via Pauline Vanier that she did not despair.[30]

French administrative practice is a strange beast to Anglo-Saxons. In the departments of France, prefects are all-powerful, even having the right to suspend, or at least not enforce, the law, if doing so would cause an upsurge of ill-feeling that would threaten "the general interest." Under Vichy law, Thérèse could have been evicted from Tailly at any time; however, despite exceedingly unpleasant pressures, this never happened.

On 9th January 1942, Pauline Vanier sent a postcard to Guy de Hauteclocque, written in the roundabout semi-coded way everyone used when writing to anyone who mattered to them during the Nazi occupation, which succeeded in saying nothing but everything at the same time. "When I received your first letter, I cabled Philippe at once to give him news of you all, because I knew he would not have received anything from anyone for well-nigh eighteen months. Back in September I had a letter from him in which he told me of his anxiety and regret at being without news. He said he was in very good health and I know from others that he is working with unstoppable energy in a place he knows well."[31]

Leclerc spent the autumn of 1941 hassling the British for more trucks, particularly Canadian Chevrolets similar to those used by the LRDG, which he wanted stripped down and made desert-worthy in the same way. When he felt the British did not value him or regarded his Chad-Libya front as unimportant, he vented his frustration on Mercer Nairne. "He would be a bad leader if he only thought his command was important," wrote the Englishman. Eventually Colonel Le Mesurier, head of the British military mission in Brazzaville, put his weight behind Leclerc's unceasing demands for trucks, observing, "When the French are good, they are very very good and when they are bad they're horrid."[32]

The problems Leclerc faced were those faced by de Gaulle and "Free France" generally. They were materially dependant on Great Britain and her empire. In their turn the British were increasingly dependant on their Lend-Lease arrangement with the United States. The Americans agreed to extend this arrangement to de Gaulle's forces from November 1941, but the stance of both President Roosevelt and his State Department was firmly anti-colonial and remained so into the post-war period with hugely destructive effects on both the British and French empires. In this delicate political environment, de Gaulle's *hauteur*, distance, pride and bloody-mindedness could only complicate matters further.

Results, however, spoke for themselves. The senior British generals in the area, Giffard and Hawkins, ensured that Leclerc's forces received all the weapons, ammunition and supplies they could spare. This covered everything from tinned bully beef to British military G1098 rum.[33] Many thought Leclerc was puritanical or barmy for disallowing wine when his force loaded their vehicles for the Fezzan operation, but by late 1941, there was little or no wine available in French Equatorial Africa. Instead his force was allocated three litres of rum per man each month! Other provisions included tinned fish, tinned fruit and the usual tea, coffee and sugar. Leclerc's men made do with their original French uniforms as far as they could, but increasingly British items such as soup-plate tin helmets crept in of necessity. American weapons such as Thompson sub-machineguns were greatly prized by the NCOs issued them.

Erstwhile *méhariste* Lt. Dubois was awestruck when sent by Leclerc to collect eighty brand new lorries from the quayside in Douala. At Faya-Largeau the trucks were made desert-worthy, stripped down, fitted with condensers, and their chassis were reinforced with steel straps sent up from South Africa.[34]

As the new "Reconnaissance and Combat" Companies trained for the Fezzan, news came through of the British "Operation Crusader," which pushed Rommel back through Cyrenaica and relieved Tobruk on 27th November. Leclerc's hopes of taking the Fezzan and then leading his men to join up with the British in Tripolitania looked possible again. Leclerc kept fit, though he suffered the disagreeable experience of having a molar removed by the nearest thing Fort Lamy had to a dentist, a stateless Armenian.

The day after this minor operation, Leclerc went off to inspect Massu's Company in the Tibesti. The old Potez flew through a sandstorm and, without any radio, the pilot got lost. He managed to land intact on an area of flat, hard desert where he and Leclerc spent the night by the aircraft. Airport staff and officers at Faya and Zouar also spent an anxious night with no news. The following morning the wind had dropped and, rather than stay put to die of thirst, they took off again with the little petrol they had left and flew on a bearing certain to bring them to a road, if they could stay airborne long enough. Luckily they saw a tanker lorry and landed. It even carried aviation fuel. Airborne again, they reached Faya-Largeau considerably later than expected, though much to the relief of Massu and his men.[35]

New *évadés* freshly arrived from Great Britain were, as Leclerc intended when he first requested them, put in vehicles. Some, such as Gaston Eve, acquired a little tank training on old Hotchkiss machines left over after Dakar. Eve was sometimes sent into the bush on recruiting drives for African soldiers. This entailed telling a local chief how many men were needed, and then picking the best from a parade of naked black men who were marched away to serve de Gaulle while their womenfolk wept.[36] Small wonder that the highest incidence of vehicle wastage on the supply trails was among African drivers, but after perseverance and training these indigenous troops made useful soldiers for France.

On 4th December 1941, de Gaulle explicitly ordered Leclerc not to launch an attack into the Fezzan or place himself under British command without his express approval. In discussions with High Commissioner Sicé, de Gaulle had aired his belief that it was too early to attack the Fezzan.[37] Fearing the British might face a similar check from Rommel as in March 1941, de Gaulle had no doubt the British would be grateful if Leclerc made a diversion, but he did not want Free France's slender manpower squandered. Leclerc responded to these views via Sicé on 9th December, saying he had never considered placing his men at Auchinleck's disposal but that naturally he was in constant touch with Cairo to keep abreast of British successes and developments.[38]

For the second time in six months, world events rendered such arguments quite academic. While "Operation Crusader" swept through Cyrenaica, on 7th December 1941 the Japanese attacked Pearl Harbor, simultaneously attacking various Pacific Islands, Malaya, Singapore and Hong Kong. At once, Field Marshal Wavell was asked by the Australian government to return two Australian divisions to halt the Japanese onslaught in New Guinea and Bougainville. Reinforcements originally intended for the Eighth Army in North Africa now went to the Far East.

If that was not enough of a blow, Rommel's Afrika Korps received reinforcements and new equipment, including Panzer Mark IV "Specials" toting a long-barreled 75mm Pak gun. In spite of British hopes that Auchinleck's Operation Crusader would finally achieve what Wavell and O'Connor failed to complete a year earlier, they found German morale that Christmas surprisingly robust, with signal flares liberally shot into the air on New Year's Eve. In Chad, the Free French had prepared for a full scale British success. Arriving in Fort Lamy from Foyo on 4th January, Christian Girard found the town empty. "Everyone had gone to the north where they were awaiting an operation."[39]

Expecting his Chadien existence shortly to be at an end, Jacques Massu had taken a solitary hike into the Tibesti to leave sentimental items buried among the arid rocks. His company, platoons commanded by Lts Dubut, Gourgout, Poyet and Tommy-Martin, each equipped with Bedford and Italian Spa trucks captured at Kufra, which were much prized for having four wheel drive, were all impatient for orders to leave their start line.[40]

The two "Reconnaissance and Combat" companies camped around Bardai were under strict orders to stay under cover during daylight to avoid being spotted by Axis reconnaissance planes. Stuck in their hides, condemned to inaction by prudence and discipline, and oblivious, if not uncaring, of the reasons for the wait, the men inevitably lapsed into complaint and speculation. Further, as the wait went on, it became necessary to use supplies intended for the operation itself.[41] When Leclerc visited them to gauge morale and check what logistical adjustments were required while they waited, he was unable to hide his worries.

The problem was that Rommel had turned on the British Eighth Army when it was at its most extended around Agedabia and Mersa el Brega. His reinforced and re-equipped Afrika Korps was now pushing back through Cyrenaica in the directions of Msus-Mechili and Benghazi.

Nor had Free French preparations in Chad escaped German intelligence. On 21st January 1942, Christian Girard and Lt. Robert Quillichini had just finished lunch at Fort Lamy when they heard explosions. Unable to believe such noise could be a training exercise, Girard stepped onto the verandah of his bungalow to see a second stick of bombs fall on the aviation fuel depot north of the town. A column of black smoke signaled the destruction of Leclerc's laboriously assembled fuel store. Donning his tin hat, Girard persuaded a lorry to give him a lift to the depot, where heroic efforts were made to save the fuel in spite of the heat and suffocating fumes.[42] Luckily only a few installations were hit and casualties were light, but vital fuel supplies, essential for Free French operations and the RAF's reinforcement shuttle between Takoradi and Egypt, had been slashed by more than half.

Recognising the importance of Fort Lamy's airport to Allied operations, Captain Theo Blaich, a former German plantation owner in the Cameroons, and Italian desert expert Count Vimercati San Severino had been the brains behind this attack. Using a patch of flat hard sand at Bir Meshru (rechristened "Campo Uno") 135km south of Gatroun as a resupply airfield, stripped-down Heinkel-111 bombers from II/KG4 had made a sixteen hundred-mile round trip across open desert.[43]

Inconvenient it may have been, but it was the kind of operation Leclerc had to admire. Lying between Gatroun and Toummo, Sonderkommando

Blaich's "Campo Uno" was uncomfortably close. Leclerc was justified in asking for more Bofors anti-aircraft guns for Fort Lamy. In the meantime, his men, who had been keyed up for the Fezzan operation, had nothing to do. Were they simply going to go back to their colonial mud forts? Nine months had passed since the Axis last felt Free French teeth at Kufra, and Leclerc felt action was necessary for morale.

So he decided a campaign of "*va et vient*" (hit and run) and "*harcèlement*" (harassment) against Italian garrison posts in the Fezzan would be the next best thing. On 4th February de Gaulle gave his approval for this operation, while warning that it should not go ahead unless the enemy was thoroughly tied up in Cyrenaica. He did not want Leclerc getting stuck in a protracted struggle, since he had so few men and little air support. "*C'est donc une affaire de va-et-vient*," insisted de Gaulle.[44]

This certainly appealed to the former cavalryman in Leclerc, but once the attacks were executed, he knew they would have to get back to Chad as quickly as possible since Axis retaliation would inevitably take the form of air patrols. De Gaulle, whose distrust of the British had escalated to new heights since being cut out of the surrender negotiations following the Syrian campaign, now saw no reason why Leclerc should liaise with the British at all, ordering him to act in total independence.

Leclerc's idea was for his "Reconnaissance and Combat" companies to operate in platoon or squadron-sized groups and attack a dozen Italian posts in southwest Libya. Surprise was essential, so radio silence had to be maintained since Italian radio direction-finding equipment was excellent. They would also have to lie up under camouflage netting during the middle of the day in order to avoid detection by Axis Ghibli and Fieseler Storch recce planes. Once the attacks had been carried out, the companies would have to fall back to Uigh-el-Kebir at once.

The "Reconnaissance and Combat" companies would produce four patrols: A under Geoffroy, B and C jointly under de Guillebon, D under Massu. There would be an attack support group under Commandant Dio with all the available artillery, and a motorised Groupe Nomade under Poletti. This group would also have a supply tail of lorries. Commandant Hous would command a group consisting of two of Massu's original platoons, strengthened by two armoured cars and also supported by supply lorries. The camel-riding *méharistes* of the Groupe Nomade de Tibesti,

under Captain Sarazac and Lts. Florentin and de Bazelaire, would protect
the fall back position at Uigh-el-Kebir, and patrol the area around Tedjéré.
At Uigh-el-Kebir itself would be twenty lorries carrying petrol, aviation
supplies and a section of Tirailleurs under Commandant Hausherr whose
task was to guard the depot with its vital water, food and fuel supplies.
They were told on no account to retreat, however hard pressed, except on
Leclerc's orders. The aircraft available for the operation were four
Lysanders, three Glenn Martin bombers, two Potez transports for the evac-
uation of wounded, and a Potez light bomber.[45]

In total there were 150 vehicles (of which 100 were for combat and 50
for logistics) and 500 men to carry out a motorised-style assault in an area
of empty desert the size of France, using compass and star navigation.[46]
Geoffroy's patrol had to cover the area between the two crossroads at Hon-
Brach and Hon-Sebha and return via Ouaou-el-Kebir—a round trip of
about 3,000 kms. Guillebon's two patrols, commanded by Lts. Eggenspiller
and Maziéras, would venture northeast to Ouaou-el-Kebir before turning
west to raid Italian posts at Tmessa, Zuila and Oum-el-Araneb, and, petrol
permitting, hit Traghen and Goddoa as secondary targets, returning either
via Uigh-el-Kebir or Ouaou-el-Kebir. Massu's role would be to guard the
west flank of the force by crossing the border into Vichy-held Niger ahead
of Dio's group and driving to Toummo, whose well had provided welcome
relief to Sarazac's *méharistes* a year earlier. Dio's group would take out the
Italian post at Tedjéré. Commandant Hous was to attack Gatroun, after
which he would either reinforce Dio against the strongly held Italian post
at Tedjéré, or join up with Massu.[47]

Following the entry into the war of the United States, Leclerc now had
an American liaison officer, Colonel Cunningham. Cunningham thought
the planned LRDG-style raids were suicide, but then he had not been at
Murzuk or Kufra. "*Qui ne risque rien n'a rien!*" ("Nothing ventured, nothing gained!") exclaimed Leclerc.[48]

On 17th February, bristling with machine guns and loaded with everything
necessary for a month in the desert, columns of trucks began leaving Zouar.
Those with furthest to go, such as Geoffroy, departed first, reaching the
Libyan border in three days. Massu's patrol headed out on 21st February,
reaching Uigh-el-Kebir six days later. Dio's and Hous' groups arrived later

that day, having taken two days from Toummo. As soon as he joined them Leclerc prepared to launch the second part of the operation; the attacks would start on 28th February.

Caporal-chef Béné remembered Leclerc carrying the now habitual malacca cane—for which he earned the nickname *Père la canne* ("Father walking stick")—walking among the men as they lay under camouflage preparing a meal of rice and dried meat in the midday sun. He stopped here and there to sample a small mouthful of food with the soldiers, showing genuine concern for their welfare. He looked very "tribal" except for the telltale sign of an army shirt collar visible under his sheepskin jacket, and a forage cap bearing a full colonel's five gold *galons*. In fact, Leclerc had been promoted *général de brigade*[49] five months earlier but was unsure whether de Gaulle or Vichy was properly entitled to award field rank, and remained slow to alter rank insignia right up to the liberation. This led to some confusion and the men did not know whether to say "*oui mon colonel*" or "*non, mon général.*" He had come far in the eighteen months since he had said *adieu* to Thérèse as a senior captain, and he was still only thirty-nine.[50]

Massu's patrol was first to make contact with the enemy in the broken, dusty outcrops of Djebel Domazé. Despite a sandstorm, his Fezzanais interpreter Abdessalam spotted fresh camel tracks leading to a shelter where indigenously recruited *askaris* (as Bené calls them, or *lascars* in Massu's terminology) were playing cards, oblivious to the approaching French. Treated little better than dogs by the Italians, these indigenous soldiers of the Duce had no qualms about immediately telling the French of another lookout post at Uigh-el-Serir. After parley by Abdessalam, this was also taken without gunfire, or any raised alarm, with eight prisoners.[51] This episode ended Massu's first phase as Dio's advance guard. Next, in order to attack Oum-el-Araneb with Guillebon's men on 1st March, he had to drive all day across open desert.

By evening on 28th February 1942, each attack group was in position near its objective. The only group to attack that evening was led by Commandant Hous, who took the fort at Gatroun by surprise. Still there, the fort at Gatroun is a large, rectangular desert fort made of dried mud bricks with circular corner towers, surrounded by dunes. Covered by machine guns, Lt. Dubut and two African soldiers bluffed their way up to the fort disguised as nomads before silencing a sentry at the gate and rushing in. A Sahariana pay parade was in progress with every man assembled in the square. In moments Dubut and his two soldiers had them surrendering. Then Hous drove in with the rest of the patrol to take the Italians, and their pay chest, into French custody.[52] While the garrison was properly disarmed, Dubut rummaged in the radio room, finding Italian codebooks and ground-to-air signal schedules which told the French which colour panels to put on their vehicles to avoid the Regia Aeronautica's recce aircraft. They removed all the loot they could carry, and then Hous' men torched everything combustible before pulling back 25km into the desert. When Italian aircraft came looking for them, the French tried the colour panel ruse but they were quickly rumbled and shot up, losing their *camion dépannage*—breakdown truck.[53]

The following day, near the Hon-Brack-Sebha crossroads, Geoffroy's patrol spotted two lorries approaching in the distance. The French quickly organised an impromptu ambush and destroyed these vehicles with their cargoes of 5,000 litres of aircraft fuel and thirty-two cases of German 50kg bombs, doubtless intended for the next Axis effort against Fort Lamy.[54] The vast column of black smoke and explosions alerted a Sahariana patrol, which called up Italian air support. Geoffroy's men disengaged successfully on the ground and scattered to all points of the compass to avoid the air attack, a trick learnt from the Long Range Desert Group. After dark they reassembled and promptly moved off to attack the Italian airfield at Ouaou-el-Kebir. In the moonlight Geoffroy, accompanied by one native soldier, managed to get under the airfield perimeter wire and then sent the African back to get the rest of the men. Unfortunately, as they sneaked forward in the darkness, one of them accidentally discharged his rifle, alerting the Italians who stood to at once. They had no option but to withdraw.

Hoping for celestial assistance from a lunar eclipse, Guillebon's group reached the fort at Tmessa half an hour before the eclipse began, and started their attack as the sun disappeared. Believing the end of the world was nigh, the indigenous Sahariana troops panicked.[55] Guillebon's men jumped from their trucks close to the fort, and carried on with fire and movement on foot. One machine gun nest was destroyed by Aspirant Roger Podeur, newly arrived from England, and once inside, the French torched the place, destroying documents, the radio mast and any equipment they could not remove.

The following night, under a full moon, Guillebon's men attacked the post at Zuila. This time the Italians were ready, and a furious exchange of gunfire and grenades followed. In the confusion, Lt. Vuillaume suffered three bullet wounds while recovering the body of a popular black sergeant, Tom Mahamat. It was impossible to evacuate Vuillaume by air, so the poor man had to endure several days laid out in the back of a truck in considerable discomfort.

Though carrying wounded in need of treatment, Guillebon patrolled this region for a few more days. Then he returned southwards to attack Ouaou-el-Kebir, which had been hit by Geoffroy two days earlier. This time Guillebon's heavy mortars inflicted considerable casualties, and the Italians capitulated. After rounding up prisoners Guillebon searched the buildings. Opening a drawer, he found a box of white pressed metal star insignia worn by Italian soldiers on their collar points, and took them for Leclerc to use as temporary rank stars on his coat cuffs and makeshift képi until he could obtain proper ones from French sources.[56]

Early on 1st March, after his intial success at Djebel Domazé, Massu crossed the Ramla, a mighty dune of deep, soft sand. At midday his group reached dead ground among palm trees by the track towards Traghen, and observed the fort of Oum-el-Araneb through binoculars. Some of Guillebon's patrol had already mistaken Oum-el-Araneb for Zuila and alerted the Italians, so they needed to see whether the garrison was still alert. Massu considered using Abdessalam to parley the Italians into surrender, but soon dismissed the idea. Italian air force Savoia-Marchetti bombers and Ghibli spotter planes appeared overhead and began firing at random into the palm trees. Undeterred, Tommy-Martin's platoon led the attack on foot across 200 metres of sand, quickly coming under spirited fire which cost two dead Frenchmen and two wounded Tirailleurs. Massu responded at once by bombarding the fort with twenty 81mm mortar shells and heavy machine gun fire, forcing the defenders to duck under the fort's battlements.[57]

During the firefight, an indigenous NCO had reached the fort's walls and began shouting up in Italian, but Massu, sensing that most of the garrison were patrolling somewhere in the surrounding desert, decided not to waste men's lives on the fort itself when their main fight ought to be the destruction of the Sahariana force out among the dunes. He broke off the engagement and withdrew for the night, disguising their tracks as they went. As his men slept in their sheepskins and djellabahs, Massu was woken by his sentry who reported distant engine noises. At first light they packed up and followed double-wheel tracks with large, plain, desert tyres. These led north of Oum-el-Araneb and Zuila. Massu now hoped to engage the Sahariana. However Italian aircraft appeared again and shot them up. Massu's group spent the afternoon playing a deadly game of scattering into the desert, swerving to escape swooping Ghiblis and Savoias. Eventually, and not too soon, they drove into the protection of nightfall.[58]

Massu tried to raise Guillebon's patrol by radio, but the only truck hit by Italian strafing had been the radio truck, wounding the radio operator. His ten lightly armed trucks drove on through the dark until checked by an unmarked wadi, for which their gap-crossing equipment was insufficient. After three unsuccessful attempts to cross, Massu decided his best option was to turn back southwards to Hofra. He still had no news of Guillebon, the Sahariana force was still somewhere out there looking for them, and Italian aircraft would resume their search for them at sunrise. Massu fell back southeast of Oum-el-Araneb, his start point two days earlier.[59]

Any sense of relief on reaching safety was short-lived. Vehicle noise in the distance immediately put everyone on the alert. Was this Guillebon's patrol or the Sahariana? Eyes straining through binoculars in the dark, eventually they recognised the trucks as Italian, heading straight for them, tracer from their Breda machine guns already stabbing the darkness. At once Massu divided his force into two groups and moved off. After a couple of kilometres he realised he had lost a truck. Ordering half his patrol to get away, Massu turned back and found that 2nd Lt. Lévy's truck had run out of fuel and stopped. As the young aspirant refilled his tanks, Massu reprimanded him severely for his negligence and told him to catch up as soon as possible. Rejoining the main group, Massu had hardly gone 500 meters when the Italian vehicles began firing again. When he looked back he saw that the Italians had taken out Lévy's truck with a heavy burst of tracer.[60]

After waiting an hour in case any of Lévy's men managed to escape, Massu decided to drive on and warn Leclerc about the Sahariana following him. En route he met up with one Hous's patrols and they drove to Gatroun together.

Reaching Gatroun from Tedjéré, Leclerc and Dio found the fort still smouldering from Hous's attack, but its walls remained intact. He set up his HQ inside and took Commandant Hous's men under his direct orders. Arriving from Oum-el-Araneb, Massu found Leclerc's welcome worryingly cool, but *le Patron* simply wanted to know how they had coped. Massu explained the problems at Oum-el-Araneb, and how the Sahariana had followed them. Leclerc decided to engage the Sahariana himself. This time a Lysander would hunt down the Italian force and report their position. Happily, the first thing the Lysander spotted was two black soldiers from Lévy's truck. Having escaped the firefight with the Italians, they walked across the desert for three days, surviving through fitness, cool-headedness and fieldcraft.

Leclerc managed to contact Guillebon's patrol, which had been 200km east of Massu. After regrouping on the night of 5th–6th March, Leclerc set off with eight trucks, intending to call in Massu with the balance by radio once he made contact with the Italians. However, after a night at Magedul and Oum-el-Araneb, he returned to Gatroun. The Sahariana had retreated back inside Oum-el-Araneb, where they had heavier weapons. On the way back he found Lévy's burnt out truck. Chatting to Massu afterwards, Leclerc left the younger officer in no doubt that he understood the problems and was pleased with what Massu had done. However, he was disappointed at not hitting Oum-el-Araneb harder, and ordered a bombing raid by the FAFL's Glen Martins.

Overall the operation was never intended to become a fight for ground, but a *va et vient* as agreed with de Gaulle—and to learn lessons for the future. New soldiers had been blooded, but when Leclerc congratulated 2nd Lt. Yves de Daruvar on his baptism of fire, the young officer disabused him, saying the Blitz on London had been a far more formative experience.

The learning curve also demonstrated to *le Patron* that, while the days of camel soldiering might be numbered, Captain Sarazac's Groupe Nomade de Tibesti could give worthwhile service. Separated from the main operation due to their camels' slower pace, the GNT reached the area around

Uigh-el-Kebir on 27th February, and patrolled between Gatroun, Tedjéré and Uigh-el-Kebir throughout the intense fighting of early March. Their mission complemented the motorised patrols perfectly.[61]

The phased withdrawal from Uigh-el-Kebir began early on 8th March. Leclerc ordered Massu's company and some of the armoured cars to provide rearguard in the Uigh-el-Kebir area, keeping up the pressure on the Italians. Captain Savelli's Marmon-Herrington armoured cars patrolled as far north as Domazé, beating off any Saharianas they encountered.

Leclerc himself left Uigh-el-Kebir for Chad on 9th March. Renewed Italian air attacks forced Massu to leave soon after. When a radio truck and one of the Marmon-Herringtons was shot up, killing Sergeant Debeugny, Massu ordered his company away to the south, the second platoon and all supply vehicles to Kourizo, zigzagging between the Toummo track and the route to Kourizo.

At Kourizo, Massu took up new positions, enabling Sarazac's *méharistes* to withdraw. At 9.30am the following day, a single Savoia-Marchetti bomber flew over, releasing a few bombs and machine-gunning erratically. Massu reckoned his men were sufficiently well camouflaged to sit it out for a few hours, but at about 3pm a bomber and two fighters returned and shot up six Bedford trucks, the ambulance, one of the Spa trucks and a supply truck. Casualties were three African soldiers badly burnt trying to save the trucks—bravery that Massu acknowledged fulsomely. At least French return fire was sufficiently accurate to bring down one of the fighters.

Massu now ordered the final pull out. His men transferred all useable equipment onto trucks that were still running—every vehicle had a bullet mark somewhere—and the wounded were tended and made as comfortable as possible for the last leg of the journey. For a man inured to most forms of mental vulnerability, Massu would later write that the last night of "Fezzan 1"—as the Fezzan raids of March 1942 are called by French historians—gave him nightmares for years afterwards.[62]

The journey from Kourizo back to Zouar and the dramatic desert peaks of the Tibesti took two days, during which two of the three burnt Africans died. Massu's group reached Zouar on 14th March. His men were bearded, filthy and heavily suntanned, and Leclerc welcomed them back himself, sensing it had been a tough time for them all and that Massu had been deeply upset by the wretched experience of watching his injured men die.

Guillebon's patrol had brought Lt. Vuillaume back alive, only for him to die of his wounds at Faya-Largeau. Leclerc reminded Massu that such losses were normal, even on the light side for such a mission. Both officers were loved by their men for their obvious concern to keep casualties to a minimum.[63]

Between all units, Free French losses were eight killed and fifteen wounded. For fifteen days they had raided and terrorised Italian forces in southwest Libya, ranging within 300km of south the Mediterranean coast. Four Italian bases, Tedjéré, Gatroun, Tmessa and Ouaou-el-Kebir, had been destroyed. Much information had been gathered which would be used a few months later in the actual conquest of the Fezzan, and, most importantly, Leclerc's men had gained useful experience.

Leclerc's report was simple and to the point:

> A detachment of ground and air forces from Chad operated for several weeks in enemy territory, among important organised defences, several hundred kilometres from its own bases.
>
> Four fortified posts were taken, as well as fifty prisoners, several important depots of fuel and ammunition were destroyed, a number of automatic weapons taken and three aircraft destroyed.
>
> Three colours have been taken, one of which is somewhat shredded by our projectiles, and now take their place in the hall of honour of the regiment, alongside those from Kufra.
>
> These results are due to the daring and bravery of our soldiers and the hard work of all those who helped them.
>
> Vive la France!
> Largeau, 17 March 1942.
> General Leclerc.
> Military Commander,
> Chad.

On the same day, General de Gaulle sent Leclerc the following message:

> The victorious operations executed under your orders in southern Libya are a complete success. General Leclerc, you and your glorious troops are the pride of France.[64]

Shortly afterwards, Leclerc pinned two Italian white metal stars from the box looted by Guillebon on the front of his makeshift khaki képi. So ended Fezzan 1.

The following month de Gaulle appointed Leclerc senior commander of all troops in French Equatorial Africa. Command of Free French troops in Chad fell to Colonel Ingold. Leclerc hated the thought of his new appointment, perceiving it as a desk job in Brazzaville where there was nothing to do.

"Your previous service as governor [in the Cameroons] amply demonstrated that you are better qualified than you say in the politico-military sphere," wrote de Gaulle on 2nd April. "Do not be intimidated by your rapid promotion. It does not follow that you should be pleased despite my friendship for you. There is only the higher necessity which forces me to use each to the utmost according to his abilities. We are in a revolution. It is a unique role to judge functionality, and I am that judge."

Then, taking Leclerc into his confidence, de Gaulle continued: "It now looks exceedingly likely that, in the course of the coming summer, the Allies will undertake something important for France. In the short time available we can only contribute the forces in French Equatorial Africa. This should help you understand the importance of the actual and eventual tasks that I have decided to give you and the confidence I have in you."

Following the USA's entry into the war on 7th December 1941, Churchill and Roosevelt agreed that Germany should be defeated first. It was inconceivable to de Gaulle that their first move would not impact on the French interest. He was right, but he was cut out of those strategic discussions. Instead he became the focus of Free France and resistance activity in the Métropole, and, like all Frenchmen, speculated over what kind of France would exist after liberation. Leclerc's own letters to René Pleven indicate that his attachment to "Old France" with the Catholic Church at the core of daily life was still dear to him. In his opinion, *la Chute* accentuated France's manpower problems, thereby making it necessary for married couples to have large families. Leclerc also believed fervently in strengthening the Catholic Church throughout the empire. He even launched an appeal for the construction of a small church in Fort Lamy, roping in Pauline Vanier in London to help fundraising, to provide a focus for their isolated lives.[65] To British and American liaison officers

George Mercer Nairne and Colonel Cunningham, whose countries faced an impressive array of enemies, such thoughts seemed somewhat self-indulgent.[66]

Leclerc's command was effective, but was only a small part of the overall strategic picture, so he suffered various attempts to subsume it under British command. Naturally de Gaulle resisted, bristling with anger and Gallic obstinacy, even though Koenig's brigade was already serving under Eighth Army's orders. Leclerc's new American liaison officer, Colonel Cunningham, was more than happy to speak up for Leclerc and his needs to the Pentagon, decribing him as "a remarkable soldier, young, energetic and absolutely adored by his officers and men." This view was reiterated by American journalist Hassoldt Davies: "It is [Leclerc] and his men alone who actively defend the great block of central Africa and the Allied lines of communication there with the North and East."[67]

On the North African coast, the British Eighth Army was stuck in Cyrenaica. This meant Leclerc was faced with another summer of "holding on" in French Equatorial Africa's remote desert camps with precious few of even the basic comforts of normal life.

Frustratingly for Leclerc, another Free French general now had his chance at glory. General Sir Claude Auchinleck had managed to stop Rommel at Gazala, and the Eighth Army had dug in along a sixty-mile line stretching directly south into the Libyan desert. Rommel's expected line of attack was to outflank the British at the southern end of the Gazala line at the fort of Bir Hakeim, which had been garrisoned by General Marie-Pierre Koenig's First Free French Brigade. This now included the 13e DBLE and Colonel Garbay's Chadiens.

These men had been given very little chance to do much following the Syrian campaign, and it had taken months of badgering by de Gaulle for them to even be included in the British order of battle in the Western Desert. Perhaps de Gaulle offering Free French pilots to the Russians had helped. He had been trying to get the British to use and equip a large contingent of French fighter pilots, but the British dragged their heels so he offered them to the Russians instead. The Russians were delighted, equipped them with their new Yak aircraft, and they became the famous Normandy-Niemen Fighter Group. After that, Eighth Army HQ in Cairo promptly found Koenig's brigade something to do by garrisoning Bir Hakeim.

But British hesitancy over employing French formations was not without cause. The bitter division between de Gaulle's Free French and Vichy, which still controlled the fourth largest navy in the world and a land empire second only to the British, meant the potential for information leaks could not be underestimated.[68] Churchill admired de Gaulle, but he had to be realistic. Roosevelt, who did not warm to the prickly, unelected leader of "Free France," regarded de Gaulle and his followers as little more than a gesture, while the real goal was landing in France, and if that meant taking a forgiving view of any Vichy followers prepared to change sides, then so be it. Roosevelt even felt that the antagonisms between de Gaulle and Vichy ran so deep that, practically speaking, another French leader ought to be found if the French Empire and her forces were to be reunited. When Leclerc's former commander in Morocco, General Henri Giraud, escaped from captivity in Germany, Roosevelt thought he had found the perfect candidate to replace de Gaulle.

Shortly before General Koenig brought fresh glory to Free France, de Gaulle's relationship with Churchill entered one of its most painful periods. Taking advantage of Vichy weakness, the Japanese navy had infiltrated the numerous bays of Madagascar, enabling their submarines to range freely across the Indian Ocean and even threaten Allied supply routes through the Mozambique Channel. It was intolerable to both the British and Americans that this jewel of the French Empire could be used in such a way. Remembering that Leclerc had taken the Cameroons with a handful of men, Churchill considered allowing de Gaulle to take control of the island. But equally, Churchill could not forget that, during the Syrian campaign, Vichy troops had wanted to surrender to anyone but the Free French. It was also imperative that Madagascar be taken irrespective of de Gaulle's sensibilities. He was therefore cut out of the affair from the outset. The seizure of all Vichy-controlled islands in the Indian Ocean went ahead as an entirely British operation.

As with Mers el Kebir, de Gaulle was outraged when he realised what the British had done. Churchill, whose attitude to de Gaulle alternated between exasperation and affection, retaliated by cutting off de Gaulle's communications. Although Leclerc understood the necessity for action against Vichy forces in Madagascar, he could not allow de Gaulle to be humiliated, and ordered Guillebon to shut down all facilities in Chad that benefitted British forces in Egypt, including overflights from Takoradi and closing the airports at Fort Lamy. Leclerc also ordered Guillebon to make preparatory orders to intern British servicemen stationed in Chad. Once these orders were drafted, Leclerc invited the British Consul-General, Robert Parr, to his residence in Brazzaville. Arriving in morning coat and tails, Parr was shown the draft orders by Leclerc and was warned that unless General de Gaulle's communications were restored, these orders would be carried out. Communications with Carlton Gardens were reconnected.[69] In the meantime, Madagascar's Vichy garrison went behind British barbed wire, where they were given the option of joining de Gaulle. By the end of the year there was little point in doing anything else.

On 26th May Rommel launched his attack on the Gazala line. This began in the north with a feint by mainly Italian divisions against the 1st South African Division dug in to the west and south of Gazala. Rommel's strongest force, consisting of the Italian Ariete Division and 15th and 21st Panzer Divisions, swung around the southern end of the Gazala line in a huge outflanking motion, encircling the Free French fort at Bir Hakeim. Then they moved northeast to engage British forces in a series of "box" battles whereby Rommel's panzers endeavoured to break down the modern equivalent of Napoleonic infantry squares. When the squares could hold no longer, they broke and their men did their best to pull away to the east and retreat into Egypt. Koenig's 1st Free French Brigade held for a fortnight. At the height of the battle, de Gaulle cabled Koenig that his men should take courage in the fact that the eyes of France were upon them and they were "her pride." Koenig replied, "We are surrounded. Our thoughts are always with you. Long live Free France." When they had held long enough for Eighth Army HQ to effect a planned retreat, Koenig's operational superiors, the 7th Armoured Division, ordered the Free French Brigade to break out.[70] Koenig led the breakout himself, sitting on the roof of his staff car with his legs dangling through the sunroof hatch so that his feet could tap the shoulders of his chauffeuse, Susan Travers, to indicate a left or right turn. White Russian Prince Dmitri Amilakvari brought out the 13e DBLE, and Colonel Garbay's Chadien regiment followed behind.[71]

A few days later, the British lost Tobruk. In the ensuing criticism that enveloped Churchill, the steady performance of the Free French at Bir Hakeim was one of the few happy affairs to come out of the whole sorry withdrawal to a line only sixty miles from Cairo. De Gaulle's men were, for once, given maximum publicity. When the German high command announced that their French prisoners (including many wounded left behind at Bir Hakeim) belonged to a country that had signed an armistice, and therefore were not entitled to prisoner of war status and would be executed, de Gaulle announced through the BBC that such an event would leave him no alternative but to order his men to execute their German prisoners.

The British withdrawal to a new line stretching from El Alamein on the coast of Egypt fifty miles southwards to the Qattara Depression, left Leclerc's hopes of an operation to conquer the Fezzan and link up with the British in Tripolitania as far away as ever. The British commander, Sir Claude Auchinleck, won one last vital battle, holding Rommel at Alam Halfa, before he was replaced, but after the mauling the House of Commons had given him over the loss of Tobruk, Churchill had had enough. For two years running, he had stripped forces away from North Africa, first to prop up the Greeks, then to face the Japanese menace in the Far East, and he would not do that again. From now on, the British Eighth Army got priority, and a new leader: General Bernard Montgomery.

In late July 1942, *Time* magazine ran an article on the Free French in central Africa crossing the desert to attack Rommel's rear echelons. Leclerc's role was quite clear. Whatever Leclerc originally hoped for by changing his name, pretty much everyone in France now knew who this general really was. His sister Colette de Baynast was asked by her hairdresser to bring him to the salon after the war, and Thérèse found herself given presents of food: sugar, chickens and turkeys, *"pour le général."* At last, that same July, Leclerc received a letter from her. In the tropical heat of Brazzaville and suffering from recurrent attacks of malaria, news from his beloved wife had a tonic effect on him. Delivered via several pairs of trusted hands to avoid the censors, it told him of his children's progress through school and also warned him that various relations of his and Thérèse's family had opted for Vichy. His older brother Guy had become head of the *Chantiers de Jeunesse* (youth workers) in the southwest, with particular responsibility for supplying horses to French industry, most of which was in full collaboration with the Germans. "It does not surprise me . . ." Leclerc wrote back to Thérèse. "Don't worry. In any case we have chosen the right path." Meantime, Leclerc's mother supported Marshal Pétain as well as her sons, seeing no conflict of interest whatsoever!

Following Fezzan 1 and the anniversary of Kufra, the name "Leclerc" had become synonymous in France with that of de Gaulle and Gaullism; even German radio acknowledged his military competence, to the chagrin of their Italian allies whom he had defeated.[72] By this stage Leclerc's achievements were almost legendary, certainly matching those of T.E. Lawrence during the Great War. If Kufra was Leclerc's Aqaba, then Fezzan 1 was his equivalent of Lawrence's campaign against the Turkish railways. Tripoli might be his Damascus, and yet, for Leclerc, this was only the start.

CHAPTER SIX

A VERY ENGLISH FRENCHMAN

General Auchinleck not only held Rommel at Alma Halfa but, having sensed that a disaster like the Gazala battle might happen, had ordered the line at El Alamein to be fortified many months earlier. He also knew that despite its uncomfortable proximity to Cairo and the Suez Canal, a southerly outflanking move by Rommel was now impracticable on account of the impassable Qattara Depression. The Afrika Korps had also become fully extended from its supply lines emanating at the ports of Tripoli, Tobruk and Benghazi. The Alamein line was absolutely the Axis high watermark in North Africa. Secure behind it, General Montgomery, Eighth Army's new commander, refused to move until he had achieved total superiority in both men and material. A new régime of training was instituted and new equipment arrived from America, the most important item being over three hundred new Sherman tanks taken from the U.S. First Armoured Division. Though far from perfect, for the first time, British Commonwealth forces had a tank that was a match for Panzer Mk IIIs and IVs. Thanks to America's ruthless standardisation of components, the Sherman could also be produced in considerable quantities, a factor that would benefit Leclerc's Free French within a year.

Meanwhile, the Pentagon and the British Imperial General Staff were comparing the merits of a large cross-Channel attack (the difficulties of which were highlighted by the disastrous Dieppe raid of 19th August 1942) and a less ambitious but more feasible Mediterranean venture of strategic benefit. Eventually, at the end of July, the Allies decided that an invasion of Vichy-controlled French North Africa would take place during the late autumn of 1942. The newly appointed American supreme commander, General Dwight D. Eisenhower, was installed in the miserably damp underground command centre hewn inside the Rock of Gibraltar, and large numbers of U.S. soldiers began crossing the Atlantic to Great Britain in readiness for what would become known as "Operation Torch."

The immediate problem facing the Allies was the likely Vichy French reaction. Notoriously, Pétain's Prime Minister Pierre Laval announced on French radio that he hoped for an Axis victory. Yet the Nazis still saw Vichy as former enemies rather than potential allies, while most of Pétain's supporters were horrified at what Laval had said. On the other hand, many Vichy officers saw themselves as defenders of the remains of France's empire against an ever-perfidious British lion. They were also afraid that any attempt at collaboration with the Allies in French North Africa would bring the Germans there, and most definitely into the "free" zone of southern France. Trapped between a rock and a hard place, the Vichy French could make no formal agreement with the Allies nor indulge in any form of secret protocol.

If the British and Americans wanted their invasion to be a success, then strategic surprise was essential as always, but so was good intelligence. In a brief clandestine operation, US General Mark Clark was put ashore by British submarine HMS *Seraph* to meet up with Roosevelt's roving diplomat Robert Murphy, by now an experienced hand in the Vichy-controlled world, to ascertain as far as he could how much resistance the Vichy French would put up. His information from sources in the French Navy and the *Armée d'Afrique* was that resistance would be strong at first and then slacken off sharply. The Allies went ahead with preparations on the basis that their troops would disembark onto a hostile shore, which would cost casualties even if resistance was only intended to satisfy Vichy honour and convince the Axis of France's genuine collaboration.

As before, de Gaulle was kept out of it because British and American planners were worried about operational security being compromised by right-wing French links to the Germans in occupied France. But de Gaulle had his suspicions following a meeting with Anthony Eden on 28th July. When the British Foreign Secretary told him that a second front in France could not be contemplated for the time being, de Gaulle declared that he would visit Syria. Eden replied cryptically, "Come back as soon as possible. It would in fact be a good thing if you were here at the time important decisions are made." In Syria de Gaulle conferred with General Georges Catroux, now French Governor General there, and made inquiries among other French North African sources. He was convinced Pétain would order resistance to an invasion, and cabled Pleven in London, but the Allies continued to cut him out.

The reason became obvious. Since the Vichy *Armée d'Afrique* saw de Gaulle as a maverick adventurer, the Americans were looking to the less heavyweight but more affable General Henri Giraud as a more acceptable alternative for rallying French North Africa to the Allies once the invasion succeeded. Robert Murphy had rashly even gone so far as to write to Giraud on 19th October that if the Axis intervened in any part of French North Africa he would be entrusted with the "coordination of command." This piece of paper caused both Eisenhower and Giraud much embarrassment in the coming months.

In Egypt, Montgomery's preparations for the Battle of El Alamein went ahead. Once again Koenig's 1st Free French Brigade were on the southern end of the line facing élite German reconnaissance troops and paratroopers.[1] Further north, Lt. Colonel Allesandri's 2nd Free French Brigade came under the command of the 50th Northumbrian Division.[2] The main infantry fighting would fall to the Australian and Highland divisions, while newly equipped armoured divisions would engage the 15th and 21st Panzer Divisions in a killing match.

In southern Libya, the Italians had reoccupied their forts and outposts destroyed during "Fezzan 1," but it was a reflection of Italian priorities and methods that replacement garrisons were in fact no stronger than before and even less well equipped. The Italians beefed up a few strongholds, like Fort Elena at Sebha, which were well sited on high ground, protected with gun emplacements, heavy machine guns, barbed wire and minefields. Such strongholds also had new, hastily dug wells to provide for battalion-sized garrisons, comprising around fifteen Italian officers, one hundred Italian troops and five hundred indigenous *askaris*. Leclerc's information network also discovered that the Italian artillery consisted of 77mm and 65mm cannons and lighter pieces. Whatever happened in the north, Leclerc certainly intended to hit the Italians again that winter.

Finding the menace on their southern flank unsettling, particularly since the Italian troops were so much less effective, Rommel's Afrika Korps increasingly ordered its Sonderkommando Dora to patrol south of Hon, and sometimes even as far south as Gatroun and Ouaou-el-Kebir. After '"Fezzan 1," the Italians no longer kept airstrips so far south, which deprived the Luftwaffe of staging posts from which to mount further raids on Fort Lamy. However, the Regia Aeronautica still carried out daytime recce flights which restricted French activities in north Chad and southern Libya during daylight.

French defences in the gorges and passes of the Tibesti mountains had become formidable, with machine gun nests, barbed wire barriers, prepared rock falls and a few minefields. Forward petrol and supply depots were built up again to replace what had been used during "Fezzan 1," ready for the operations ahead. The tracks north from Fort Lamy were improved, and traffic doubled compared to 1941.

In fact, Leclerc's new job, conferred by de Gaulle after "Fezzan 1," proved useful. He delegated more than before, placing preparations for "Fezzan 2" under Colonel Ingold, a fiercely patriotic officer promoted through the ranks during the first war who had become an experienced colonial soldier and *gaulluiste de la première heure*. He also gave a new *bataillon de marche* to Colonel Delange. This gave Leclerc more time for thinking and reading. French journalists who had opted for Free France were now writing books on *la Chute*, risking opinions on how it had come about. Brazzaville, more than Fort Lamy, was where the French community in equatorial Africa mainly gathered, and most had not received any news from their families in the Métropole for two years. Men on Leclerc's military operations badly needed freshening up, so he arranged holiday facilities in South Africa which were well received.

On 13th September de Gaulle, whose anger at being excluded from Allied planning was becoming a crisis in itself, arrived at Fort Lamy in an Air France[3] Lockheed Lodestar for a ten-day visit to French Equatorial Africa.

Immediately after inspecting a guard of honour led by Guillebon, he went into consultation with Leclerc.[4] After outlining the strategic situation unfolding in the north, de Gaulle confirmed that Leclerc's next mission was to conquer the Fezzan and move northwards into Tripolitania. This time he was to take a force of three thousand men as opposed to five hundred. When he reached the British in Tripolitania he was to come under the command of British generals Montgomery and Alexander. But, if the unthinkable happened, if Laval threw Vichy's lot in with the Axis, then Leclerc was to seize any Vichy territory he could, starting with Niger and then taking Dakar from the rear.

First, Commandant Crépin's artillery force was beefed up from its existing complement of old mountain 75mm guns by the addition of captured Italian 47mm guns and a couple of British 25-pounders. These were collected from Wadi Halfa on the Nile, via Sudan, in a six-week expedition led by Captain Dubois.[5] Infantry weapons also needed improvement. Once again Leclerc looked to captured stocks of Italian weapons from the Abyssinian and Eritrean campaigns, and asked the Free French liaison officer in Khartoum to find Breda heavy machine guns with ammunition. At first this officer, a French Armenian named Haig-Torgomian, reported that he could not find any. Fuming that Free France should pay the salary of someone unproductive, Leclerc telegrammed him, "If you're incapable of doing a proper job, give your place to someone more competent!" The Bredas and ammo arrived. Next, Haig-Torgomian exceeded himself by getting four 75mm guns to Fort Lamy on a Dakota: the guns passed through its cargo door with only three centimetres to spare.[6] When Haig-Torgomian eventually met Leclerc at Fort Lamy, *le Patron* graciously said, "Forget that letter. You understood my needs in the end." With a few Bofors guns making up the anti-aircraft capability, Commandant Crépin's artillery was now plentiful, if eclectic.

Following the departure northwards of the Groupe Lorraine the previous year, Leclerc's air capability was reduced to Commandant de Saint-Péreuse's Groupe Bretagne, consisting of the "Rennes" squadron's five Lysander single-engined reconnaissance aircraft, and the "Nantes"[7] squadron with five Blenheims and three Glenn Martin light bombers. There were no fighters, meaning that Saint-Péreuse's aircraft would inevitably be vulnerable to Axis fighters as ground operations took them further north.

Requests for fighter support from Cairo were unsuccessful, and Leclerc felt let down by the British.[8] This did not wholly displease de Gaulle, who wanted the conquest of the Fezzan to be a French operation carried out with French forces, except for the obvious necessity of a British liaison officer in radio contact with Cairo.[9]

More *évadés* arrived from England, and the mobilisation of French Equatorial Africa's civilian population and European reservists, men who had never been in the forces before, all added to Leclerc's manpower.[10] Morale had improved since "Fezzan 1," but some old hands were starting to get on each others' nerves. A petty disgreement between Commandant Hous and Captain Massu over decorations and mentions in dispatches threatened to boil over. Hous believed that no one on Fezzan 1 did anything more than his job, while Massu thought many who took part, both European and indigenous, deserved some kind of gong, even though he found medal hunting anathema himself. He particularly felt that Lt. Dubut deserved an award for his role at Gatroun. In truth, Massu's passion probably got the better of him, and since he was merely a captain with three *galons,* Commandant Hous threatened him with transfer to the Levant if he did not rein himself in. Dubut was already being sent there, and Tommy-Martin and Gourgout were asking to be transferred as well. Contemplating his future bleakly, Massu did not relish being driven by truck down to Fort Lamy and thence to obscurity, like a bad dog dumped in the wild. The order had even been signed by Leclerc and witnessed by Lt. Quillichini. In desperation, Massu complained to adjutant Commandant Blochet. Later that day he was in Leclerc's office. *Le Patron* offered Massu two options: a period of "time out" in Brazzaville, or the reconnaissance job for a new, more direct route for supply traffic between Fort Lamy and Zouar. Leclerc knew not to waste good people.[11] Massu did the recce, had a spell of leave, then set about picking up where he had left off and retrieving his scattered lieutenants.

As the strategic balance increasingly pointed to an ultimate Allied victory, Vichy-held Niger increasingly became an important source of manpower for Free France. In April 1942, Vichy Prime Minister Laval had begun a new era of enhanced collaboration with Germany, both at home and abroad. French labourers became subject to *Service Travail Obligatoire*—

work in German industry—and Vichy also took a more ferocious attitude to France's Jews.

The human leakage to de Gaulle in Africa was politically embarrassing, so Vichy units along the Niger border were given orders to fire on their Free French brethren if the opportunity arose, and even a Vichy attack on Chad seemed likely. Since future operations into the Fezzan would need the use of roads near the Niger border, especially those around Wour and Kourizo, Vichy troops in northeast Niger would have to be watched carefully. This unpleasant but necessary task was assigned to Massu, who took command of the horse-mounted 21e Compagnie Montée. The demands of such terrain made horses or camels essential. Having taken riding lessons both at Prytanée de la Flèche and Saint Cyr, and finding his deputy, Captain Pinhede, congenial company, Massu found this mission less unpleasant than it might have been. What he did not like was being shot at by fellow countrymen, whose fire across the Niger border caused sporadic casualties.

As autumn drew to its cooler end, Massu learnt that Leclerc had promoted him to Commandant, while Jacques de Guillebon became chief of staff at Fort Lamy. On the Niger frontier, however, *le cafard* was biting. The men of the 21e Compagnie Montée and the Groupe Nomade de Kanem—now also under Massu's command—wanted action, any action, preferring to fight Vichy than not fight at all.

On 8th November, the news came that the British and Americans had invaded French North Africa.[12] An Anglo-American task force had landed at Oran and around Algiers, while a "western" task force under Patton had landed at Safi, Medala and Mehdia in Morocco. General Mark Clark's information that resistance would slack off after a token effort turned out to be very wide of the mark. Taking their orders from Vichy's Admiral Darlan[13] and General Nogues, resistance by the French Navy and the *Armée d'Afrique* continued for almost five days until a cease fire was finally agreed. The reason Darlan gave for such fruitless fighting was the realistic belief that the Germans would invade the "Free Zone." If not actually lying, Darlan was being elastic with the truth: the "free zone" in France never was "free." Undoubtedly, the taste of Mers el Kebir in July 1940 was still bitter in French mouths. The underlying bitterness cost 2,225 Anglo-American casualties, of which 1,100 were dead, and the French 3,000 in killed and wounded. Vichy forces lost over half their tanks, armoured cars and aircraft.[14] Though mostly obsolete, this kit had been transferred to Africa under the noses of the Armistice Commission at General Weygand's instigation in the hope that it would be used for France's return to the war on the Allied side. Nevertheless, such losses ensured that America's re-arming of the French would have to be total.

In Egypt, after a fortnight of hammer blows at El Alamein from the newly trained and equipped Eighth Army, which began its offensive on 23rd October, Axis forces finally broke and retreated. There would be no coming back this time. On the south of the line, Koenig's 1st Free French Brigade took their target Himeimat, but were chased off again by an Afrika Korps counterattack using captured Stuart tanks. As so often happened with the Free French, the 13e DBLE was badly shaken by the death of its charismatic leader, Prince Dmitri Amilakvari.[15] Unfairly perhaps, Montgomery felt the 1st Free French Brigade had let him down. In any case, General Koenig's star dimmed compared to Leclerc's.

Bitter at his exclusion from the planning of Torch, de Gaulle's initial reaction on hearing the news was characteristically dog-in-the-manger. "I hope the Vichy people push them back into the sea," he told his aide Captain Pierre Billotte. "You do not get France by burglary."[16] Yet he quickly acknowledged that the development was in his interests, though he hated the subsequent brokering of loyalties among the French Navy and the *Armée d'Afrique*. Staunch as ever, Leclerc telegrammed him, "At the moment the traitors change sides because victory approaches, you remain for us the champion of honour and French liberty. It is behind you that we will return to our country with our heads held high. Only then will the French nation be able to chuck out the shits!"[17]

On 12th November, as soon as it became clear that Vichy was a spent force in Africa, de Gaulle gave Leclerc the order to reinstate the plan for "Fezzan 2." Four days later in Fort Lamy, Leclerc and General Hutchinson (General Alexander's emissary sent from Cairo) agreed that French troops would begin their build-up in the Uigh-el-Kebir assembly area once Eighth Army reached El Agheila. Success would depend on the perfect synchronisation of the two operations, to which end Leclerc would have a British liaison officer provided by the LRDG with a radio link to Eighth Army Headquarters.

However, in line with de Gaulle's strictures on French sovereignty, Leclerc refused British offers to help administer the Fezzan once his men had taken it. Not only had the Fezzan been an area of interest to France during the interwar years, but Italian cruelty meant many indigenous leaders (among them Bey Ahmed Sif en-Nasr, who had been involved in the Murzuk and Kufra operations in 1941) welcomed the prospect of a French protectorate. Thinking of everything, Leclerc had even raised a *goum* of forty Libyans into which new recruits could be drafted. Les "*amis*" *britanniques* would not be given a pretext for intervention.

Logistics had to be planned so that French forces could move quickly from their main bases without spending too much time using up food supplies in the forward concentration area around Uigh-el-Kebir.

On 21st November, General Harold Alexander wrote to Leclerc saying that he would give him eight days' notice of the British Eighth Army's move into Tripolitania. Some of Leclerc's troops, however, needed anything from a fortnight to two months to get ready.[18] By contrast, de Gaulle's orders were that Leclerc should not advance into southern Libya until it was certain that the British offensive into Cyrenaica was successful, and that Tripolitania be as good as conquered as well. As ever, de Gaulle was anxious that his miniscule forces not be wasted on false errands. After the fruitless fighting between the Anglo-Americans and Vichy French in Morocco and Algeria, de Gaulle was also aware that the Allies were now facing tough new resistance in Tunisia.

The Germans had moved quickly to take over Tunisia after Vichy's loss of control in northwest Africa, sending in the 10th Panzer Division, paratroopers and sufficient Luftwaffe reinforcements to give them local air superiority. Tunisia's Vichy commander, an ascetic and religious bachelor named Vice Admiral Jean-Pierre Estéva, vacillated tragically at the news of the Torch landings, allowing the Axis to seize the port of Bizerta along with several large airfields.[19] After his defeat at Alamein, Rommel had refused Hitler's order for a last-ditch defence, and began to retreat across Libya in an orderly fashion, turning when appropriate to fight rearguard actions. These factors would mean that Leclerc would neither be too early nor too late.

Following de Gaulle's orders, Leclerc prepared use his forces as follows: Groupement G under Geoffroy, consisting of two reconnaissance and combat patrols, a 75mm gun and a supply train of fifty trucks, would depart from Bardai in a northeasterly direction on 16th December. They would hold the area east of the Italian fort at Sebha, harass the enemy, attack airfields, and hold themselves in readiness to support Groupement D under Dio when it arrived.

Dio's groupement, consisting of the Groupe Nomade de Borkou (which had now swapped camels for trucks), two reconnaissance and combat patrols, the 12e Compagnie portée, two 75mm cannons and a supply train of one hundred and ten trucks, would leave Zouar for Kourizo on 18th December, heading up into the Uigh el-Kebir area to take the Italian airfield and base at Oum-el-Araneb, followed by the "Forte Regina Elena" at Sebha.

Groupement M under Lt. Col Delange, consisting of the 1st Bataillon de Marche, Massu's four companies, the Compagnie portée de Cameroun, two reconnaissance and combat patrols, two British 25-pounders, two Bofors 20mm anti aircraft guns, and the rest of the logistics trucks would set off from Zouar on 24th December. Resupply from the advanced base at Uigh-el-Kebir would come under Commandant Vézinet. Leclerc's meagre air corps would bombard Murzuk and Sebha when ordered.[20]

Captain Sarazac's *méharistes* would once again patrol the dunes around the build-up area between Uigh-el-Kebir and Gatroun by camel, just as they had done during Fezzan 1. This time, however, they would be supported by Ahmed Sif en-Nasr and the Libyan *goum*. Supply preparations began on 15th November with the establishment at Kourizo of a large fuel dump from which groupes D and M would take their fill before heading into Libya.

Massu was delighted to be under "Père Delange," who was the type of character he admired; a man who volunteered for anything, especially if it involved the desert's vast openness.[21] Massu's company commanders were reservists who had been colonial administrators: Colonna d'Istria, Soulé-Susbielle, Guéna and Diffre, each of whom were good men. For physical and pastoral care, Groupement M had Dr. Coupignies[22] and Père Houchet, who would become the divisional chaplain of the 2e DB. Groupe M also acquired several officers who would become famous once *la Colonne Leclerc* evolved into the *Régiment de Marche du Tchad*, Lts. Sorret, Sammarcelli, Rogier, Vigneux and Captain Jacques Langlois de Bazillac, who was from an Indo-China colonial family, and had quit Niger to become a liaison officer with the British before joining *la Colonne Leclerc*.

The rank and file were three quarters Sarras and a quarter Adjarais, all tough and keen, while vehicle and truck drivers were *Camerounais* tasked with getting their new Ford trucks through difficult terrain with narrow tracks and ramshackle bridges to their operational start points. Massu struggled to teach these Cameroon drivers skills that had taken him many years' experience to acquire, and it took fifteen days' hard driving along the rough track road between Moussoro and Zouar to get his battalion to its start point. When the heavy, twinned rear wheels of these large American trucks got bogged down—they were too wide for the usual sand tracks—the drivers placed lengths of palm trunk under the gap between the twinned tyres. If a lorry was badly stuck they would use sand ladders for the front wheels and logs for the rear combined. Once the lorry got moving, the driver had to keep it going so *tirailleurs* had to pick up the sand ladders and logs and run after the trucks to chuck them all on the back and jump on while the vehicle was on the move.[23]

In spite of American deliveries, the vehicles available to Leclerc for "Fezzan 2" and the march to Tripolitania were still pretty eclectic. Many were not designed for military use, having been requisitioned from haulage contractors throughout French Equatorial Africa, and had no four-wheel drive, which LRDG experts regarded as essential for desert conditions. If the LRDG took a perverse pride in keeping clapped vehicles in working order, *la Colonne Leclerc* took this a few stages further. They would scavenge vehicles the LRDG had dumped as "beyond local recovery," and *le Patron* called them "the pick of his fleet."[24]

For his radio link with Eighth Army during the trek, the Long Range Desert Group gave Leclerc a Rhodesian half-patrol of sixteen men and six trucks commanded by Lt. Jim Henry. They arrived at Faya-Largeau in late November. Still frustrated that his requests for RAF fighter cover were going unheeded, Leclerc hoped Henry's patrol would at least be able to call up a flight of Hurricanes if the need arose. Peers Carter was the only Englishman who went the full distance with Leclerc, and specifically remembered Leclerc's frustration at RAF refusals on grounds of insufficient staging posts. In all fairness to the RAF, airfields in southeast and southern Libya were inadequate, even if they could be taken and prepared in advance.[25]

From 3rd December, the exact nature of the operation—the conquest of the Fezzan and an advance northwards to join up with the British—was known to everyone. Lt. Christian Girard was working for the 2e Bureau[26] in Fort Lamy. Fearing he might get left behind, Girard had a chat with the increasingly influential Jacques de Guillebon in the hope of something better. Guillebon came up with more than the young Parisian expected: he was appointed Leclerc's *aide de camp*. Girard protested, because by its nature the role of ADC tends to keep junior officers out of immediate danger, and his predecessor at the 2e Bureau had been given a field command.[27]

Girard had been a trainee diplomat before the war, and had served through the Battle of France as liaison officer to the Queen's Bays. His well developed social skills and ability to tactfully step outside the confines of rank made him an obvious choice. No one performed the role better. From the moment of his appointment he was virtually inseparable from Leclerc. On 14th December they flew from Fort Lamy to the southern Tibesti to see the superb job Colonel Adolphe Vézinet had made of hiding *la Colonne's* supplies among the oases and rocky outcrops, making them invisible from the air. The following day they flew on to Bardai where Geoffroy's group was making final preparations before leaving the shelter of the dry cliffs around the base. That afternoon they returned to Zouar to see Dio's group depart northwards. Everything was on the move. For the next two days, Leclerc and Girard went everywhere over the vast expanse of sand, often overflying the road from Faya-Largeau to Moussoro. Occasionally, drivers lost their way and wandered off the track. Since the trucks had been stripped of anything reflective, finding them by plane was much harder. Once, the dried bodies of one truck crew were only found after a fortnight's searching. Girard never forgot their last message: "If you don't come within two days, we're dead. *Vive la France!*"[28]

Geoffroy and Dio's trucks arrived at Uigh-el-Kebir to find the descendants of Henri Laperrine's élite, Captain Sarazac's *méharistes* of the Groupe Nomade de Tibesti, already patrolling between the oasis and Gatroun. On 21st December, Leclerc and Girard left Fort Lamy for the operation itself.

Shortly after midday they boarded the old Potez with Colonel Bernard and Lt. Quillichini. Growing into his role, Girard had presciently arranged a picnic of a large poached fish on ice to eat during the flight; not quite up to Air France cabin service, but much appreciated. A couple of hours later they landed at Zouar and found Delange's and Massu's men still there, muffled in great coats against the Saharan winter chill. Colonel Ingold had already set off.

The war could not have dictated a colder time of year for the operation. Raymond Dronne wrote, "The nights are glacial and, during daytime, the sun is barely warm. The men are frozen. At nightime they wrap themselves up, in an old coat, a blanket or a 'faro.' They huddle against each other, their chechias pulled down over their heads and faces. . . . To sleep, each makes a groove in the sand and wraps himself in his 'faro.'" A "faro" was made from four sheepskins or from "kanamaye"—the big saharan goat.[29]

The Axis had not the slightest inkling of the preparations for "Fezzan 2." This would not last. On 23rd December, Dio's group reached Uigh el-Kebir, but this time the Italians were not taken by surprise, and their patrols quickly retreated northwards to raise the alarm. After that, radio silence was lifted since it became more important to be able to coordinate movements. Back at Zouar, Leclerc saw Delange's and Massu's group setting out.

On Christmas Eve, Leclerc and Girard flew back to Uigh el-Kebir. They celebrated Christmas as best they could in a chill wind in the stony bed of a wadi, with Guerin and Laffolay and their pilot, Commandant Bonnafé. Girard, ever resourceful, produced an old box of chestnuts from his baggage, which provided a *soupçon* of festive cheer, while freezing gusts blew Leclerc's maps about as they huddled in greatcoats, scarves, képis and even goggles.[30]

Throughout all this, logistics chief Adolphe Vézinet was ever-smiling and imperturbable. The success of the whole operation depended on reliable supply lines. Fortunately, no enemy aircraft ever spotted them, even though their lines of communication were lengthening.

News that *Vichysois* Admiral Darlan had been assassinated by a monarchist clique within the Algiers resistance gave Leclerc unexpected festive cheer. "They have given us Darlan for Christmas," he exclaimed to the US liaison officer Colonel Cunningham. "Now they only have to give us Boisson [governor of Dakar] and we will be well served."[31]

On Boxing Day morning, Dio reached Gatroun after driving through the night to avoid Axis aircraft. Then, as the Rhodesian LRDG patrol and two French trucks edged closer to the oasis in the pale, early morning light, Italian artillery and Breda machine guns opened up. More French trucks arrived to provide suppressing fire with the group's 75s. Then the French withdrew twenty miles to consider their options.

The original plan was to demoralise Gatroun's garrison with artillery fire and then leave them for Delange to deal with. Instead, Dio decided that the Rhodesians and a French patrol would recce north of the oasis to lure the Saharianas into a trap out among the dunes. However, only six miles from the northern edge of the oasis, the Rhodesians and French found themselves strafed by Italian fighter and bomber aircraft. Happily, the desert was firm so the trucks were able to weave and dodge while returning machine-gun fire. A column of black smoke billowed up a few miles north of them, and turned out to be an Italian fighter, brought down by LRDG machine guns. Colonel Ingold congratulated the LRDG men on their conduct and good example to the French. Hard-pressed, some Saharianas broke out of Gatroun towards the southeast, where they encountered more French; but Italy's indigenous troops could hardly be expected to sacrifice their lives for a colonial power in danger of being ejected in the near future, and consequently gave a poor account of themselves.[32]

German and Italian pilots were a different matter. The following day they came at the French and LRDG advance guard again. First a Heinkel-111 hosed them with its machine guns, and next came Italian Savoia Marchetti bombers and CR42 fighters. The LRDG drill when under air attack was to scatter in all directions while firing back. Leclerc's men now did this too, but some casualties were taken. The Englishman Peers Carter and two Rhodesians were wounded and their truck wrecked. These attacks were ferocious enough but they soon got worse, so Leclerc's troops switched to moving only at night. In daytime, the French, like the LRDG, had become camouflage experts, hiding vehicles laid up for the day, dragging palm branches to brake up vehicle tracks, or setting up false targets to waste Italian bombs and bullets.

On 28th December, Blenheim bombers of the Groupe Bretagne attacked Forte Regina Elena and its adjacent airfield at Sebha, and established local air superiority around Oum el Araneb for a few days. Subduing Oum-el-Araneb would be one of the key actions of the whole operation. For the French coming up from the south there was the Ramla to cross. No sooner had Dio crossed this long, wide and dangerous series of dunes than he immediately collided with a Sahariana patrol sent to watch him. In spite of Dio's attempts to envelope them the Saharianas slipped away, back inside Oum el Araneb's massive stone walls. That night the French launched an attack, but Italian light artillery and emplaced Breda machine guns forced them to go to ground until dawn. Then, daylight merely made the French easier to spot and they remained pinned down.[33]

Leclerc heard about this at Uigh el-Kebir, and immediately decided to fly up to Oum el-Araneb in a Lysander. However, the only practicable landing place was occupied by the enemy, so he and Girard were driven up to the French forward positions, wrapped in their djellabahs to their eyes against the bitter cold. Stripped-down trucks without even a windscreen were no fun at that time of year. To make matters worse, their navigator, Poyet, veered too far east and they had to negotiate a moonscape of abrupt, sharp rocks and soft sand to get back on track towards the main force. By midday they had only reached the little oasis of Um-es-Seghir, where some of *la Colonne* were bivouaced, and stopped to eat. They crossed the Ramla dunes uneventfully, and drove on across empty, cold desert without an Italian aircraft or Sahariana truck in sight. They passed the wreckage of the LRDG truck in which Peers Carter had been wounded, and Gara Magedoul. They found neither Italians nor French. Two hours later Leclerc was worried. Where was everyone? At Hammera, some vehicles could be seen on a ridge to the northeast which could only be French. Leclerc, who was now driving, took off like an arrow, promptly getting stuck in sand. They finally reached *la Colonne's* advance positions outside Oum el Araneb after nightfall.[34]

Throughout the morning of New Year's Day 1943, Leclerc behaved like a true commander, visiting every group to see how they were and giving encouragement. Crépin placed his artillery in position 2.5km from the Italians, quickly provoking an exchange of gunfire. Commandant Troadec noticed some Saharianas leaving the fort, so Captain Farret was sent after them, but the Italians got away. The artillery exchange continued towards midday without causing any French casualties, except Dio, who had his trousers torn to shreds by a shell blast![35]

That night it rained. Those Frenchmen not pinned down in front of the fort attempted to make shelters for themselves. Two days of silence and miserable cold, with no movement on either side, followed, until the weather cleared up on 4th January. Then, southwest of Oum el-Araneb, the Groupe Nomade de Borkou managed to make progress. Artillery support called down by Colonel Ingold succeeded in breaking the *impasse*, and Sergeant Briard of the GNB managed to crawl sufficiently far forward to lob a grenade into an enemy position, which enabled a company of nomads to rush the fort. Like at Kufra, the Italian commander now teetered on the verge of surrender. When Raymond Dronne ordered sections to cover both gates of the fort, he realised he was trapped. White flags appeared on the walls and were spotted from Ingold's CP, where Girard, Guillebon, Guérin and Peers Carter were waiting.

"There's a white flag over the enemy position."

"Ah, good," said Guillebon. "Give me my shoes!"

Suddenly Italian bombers appeared overhead and swooped in to attack. No damage was done. French small arms fire brought one of them down, but their appearance made the Italian commander change his mind. The Italians' white flags vanished and they began firing again. Ingold ordered Crépin's artillery to recommence firing, and another ten minutes was enough for the Italians. About fifty came out of the fort waving white handkerchiefs. But this time Dio was taking no chances, insisting that his artillery maintain sporadic firing until an indisputable white flag flew above the fort. This appeared at 4.25pm. It was all over. Dio and Ingold went into the fort to see what they had captured—ten artillery pieces, twenty machine guns, ten officers and one hundred and ninety askaris, along with several days worth of food. Reaching the Italian commander, who sat on the ground with his head in his hands repeating, "*Resistanza, resistanza,*" all the while claiming he had really been waving a red cross flag, Dio and Ingold were furious with him.[36]

On the 5th February, Leclerc joined his men inside Oum el-Araneb fort, making it his temporary HQ. From then onwards the conquest of the Fezzan accelerated. The desert veteran Sarazac and his *méharistes* of the Groupe Nomade de Tibesti took over from Massu's men facing Gatroun, and harassed the Italian defenders with their portable 75mm guns and called in air strikes. Isolated due to the fall of Oum el-Araneb, the garrison surrendered on 6th January.

The same day, Captain Alaurent, who had split off from the main force on 2nd January, reached the Italian post at Brack, 420km north of Oum el-Araneb. He found the Italians had cut and run the previous evening. Alaurent immediately turned it into a forward base for harassing Italian convoys supplying central Libya. Further north still, Lt. Eggenspiller's patrol had reached Hon.

Leclerc was well satisfied with their progress. Where things seemed to be going too slowly, his stock criticism was, "Army of 1939!" In the meantime, Leclerc could make no contact with General Montgomery's Eighth Army fighting its way along the north coast. The LRDG advised Leclerc that there would be no contact before 13th January, and the French immediately jumped to the suspicious conclusion that *les amis britanniques* did not want them venturing any further north. In fact, nothing could have been further from the truth. The division of powers between generals Montgomery and Alexander was that Montgomery had command of Eighth Army while Alexander was Commander-in-Chief of the Middle East, which included how to use the LRDG, SAS and Leclerc's Free French. This latest bout of paranoid Anglophobia saw Guillebon despatched once again on a journey to Cairo to find out what the British were doing.

Late on 7th January, some Fezzanais elders arrived at Oum-el-Araneb by camel and told the French that the Italians had evacuated the magnificent mock medieaval Forte Regina Elena at Sebha. At once Leclerc ordered Captain Guérin to go there, driving all night if he had to. By 6pm the following day, Sebha was in French hands and Delange's group moved in.

Massu sent a company under Captain Guéna to occupy Murzuk. Entering the fort on 8th January they found it had been hastily vacated by the Italians. Instead, they were met by village notables in white and blue robes bearing a welcome address. The next day the Murzuk Italians were spotted marching north across the desert by a Groupe Bretagne Glenn Martin bomber piloted by Lt. Mahé. Mahé fired his machine gun at them, but his firing control broke. Improvising, he dropped a message to them saying he would fire on them unless they surrendered. Soon the column was blooming with white handkerchiefs, and Mahé used his aircraft to shepherd them back towards Murzuk until a patrol from Guéna's company took them into custody. Once the link-up was achieved, Mahé landed on the track to help count his prisoners: 110 Europeans, of whom ten were officers, plus thirty askaris.[37]

By the 9th Leclerc received an unpleasant reminder that desert warfare is about supply lines. A shortage of petrol immobilised the 1e Bataillon de Marche. However, with Murzuk and Sebha now in French hands, and Brack in use as a forward base, Leclerc decided it was time to send Colonel Ingold to meet up with the Eighth Army.[38]

Leclerc wanted to see Sebha's Forte Regina Elena for himself, and got Lt. Mahé to fly him up in his Glenn Martin. On arrival, he appointed Colonel Delange as the new French military administrator of the Fezzan. Italian rule, which had begun in 1911 and was only consolidated by 1931 with immense cruelty, was over. Bey Ahmed en-Nasr returned joyfully to his people, and the French bathed in the warmth of the Fezzanais welcome. Next, Mahé flew Leclerc on to Brack, a very pleasing little fort compared to Sebha, built beside an oasis in the style of a colonial chateau, and containing reasonable amounts of Italian material. They needed it: desert fighting was taking its toll of vehicles, especially their tyres.

Leclerc allowed himself a few hours at Brack to take a pot at the ducks on the oasis lake, but the pace did not slacken. Captain Alaurent, who had found Brack empty on 6th January, was ordered to continue the advance along the Schiuref-Mizda road. He left with eight trucks at dawn on 8th January, covering 380km in two days. On 10th January he arrived at Schiuref and immediately attacked the fort with his 81mm mortars before seizing it. Then he moved on to a crossroads and ambushed an Italian convoy, taking it completely by surprise.

When the rest of Geoffroy's and Dio's men reached Schiuref, Leclerc ordered the push towards Mizda, with Geoffroy taking the main axis while Dio provided flanking cover from the west and north.[39] In the small hours Girard was woken with the news that a German message had been decoded saying Rommel would sort out the Free French at his pleasure. This did not tally with news from the Hon area.

That same day, Massu returned to Murzuk and visited the grave of Colonel d'Ornano, who had been killed exactly two years before. The Free French had done much since then. At the end of the day Leclerc issued the following communiqué: "The conquest of the Fezzan is complete. The forces under Colonel Ingold have occupied Murzuk, the religious capital, and Sebha, the chief military base. Almost the entire garrisons have been taken prisoner. Our advance elements are progressing towards the north, already engaging in the battle of Tripolotania."[40]

There was still one detail to be settled in southern Libya. The little towns of Ghat and Ghadames on the Algerian border were still in enemy hands, without which the conquest of the Fezzan would not be complete. However, they were too far west to be objectives of the main operation. Relying on British intelligence that the advance into Tripolitania was a success, Leclerc no longer needed Oum el-Araneb as his forward base, but the last mission launched from there would be an air-landed operation to seize Ghat. A section of Massu's 1e Bataillon de Marche embarked on a captured Italian Cant heavy bomber, hastily painted with Free French markings and accompanied by Lt. Mahé's Glenn Martin flying ahead to give the green light if it was safe to land. Instead, Mahé's aircraft was welcomed by fierce machine-gun fire, taking six bullets in an engine cowling, which forced both planes to return to Oum el-Araneb.

Leclerc decided that such an operation could not be carried out at so great a distance, and ought instead to be tasked to French forces in Algeria, now that the *Armée d'Afrique* was back in the war. It was time to attempt a little diplomacy to see if they could sink their differences in a joint operation. He sent Colonel Carretier as emissary to the French in Djanet, east of the Hoggar mountains, the bleak desert outpost contested with the Senussi by Henri Laperrine in 1918.[41] The commander of the *méharistes* company at Djanet, Captain Mougenot, replied, "We are all proud to re-take our arms again. *Vive la France!*" Leclerc offered air support, and the French flag was flying over Ghat by January 25th.[42]

The field of operations was now in the north. Lt. Eggenspiller joined up with elements of the Eighth Army at Hon on 13th January, and British patrols now reached Schiuref and Ghériat from the north. On 22nd January, Dio took Mizda. The Mediterranean coast was only 200 km north of Leclerc's forces. Without stopping, Dio ordered Troadec's patrols on to Tripoli, which they reached by midday on Sunday, 26th January, meeting old friends from the LRDG's Guards patrol on the way.

The Libyan capital had ended its thirty-two years as an Italian colonial city earlier that morning. The first Allied troops to enter were the reconstituted 51st Highland Division's Gordon Highlanders, riding Valentine tanks. The liberation process got under way quickly, and 2,500 Jews were quickly liberated from a small concentration camp.[43] When the Free French drove into Tripoli from the south, the population was stupefied, calling out "*Francesi*" and "*Gaullisti!*" The Frenchmen, wearing sheepskins, bearded, and driving a mixed bag of battered trucks in their eclectic convoy, looked so different from the dusty but uniformly equipped British Army. The French weaved their way through the narrow, grubby streets to the sea front. Many of them had not seen the Mediterranean in years.[44]

Leclerc received a signal from General Montgomery requesting a meeting. Accompanied by Girard, de Guillebon and Bonnafé, he took one of the Lockheed Lodestars that de Gaulle had squeezed out of the Americans to rebuild Air France for the short flight to Castel Benito airfield, which was still littered with wrecked German and Italian aircraft. Leclerc tried to look his best in his battered képi, old single-breasted greatcoat with rank badges roughly sewn on the cuffs, his Huntsman[45] tropical breeches, bought with Pauline Vanier's loan, and old but handmade riding boots. After the brief drive from the airfield in a gun tractor,[46] they arrived outside Montgomery's command caravan, which was parked in a circle of khaki tents. After two hard and remote years in Chad, Leclerc finally had his victory and the long awaited link-up with the British in Libya. Montgomery's ADC, Etonian cavalry officer Lt. Johnny Henderson, greeted him, and Leclerc gave vent to the pleasure of this supreme, long-awaited moment with a bout of enthusiastic French. British public schools give an excellent grounding in languages, but Henderson's ear was not quick enough and, since Leclerc's second language was German, not English, it took Montgomery's chief of staff, the part-French, Ampleforth-educated Freddie de Guingand to ensure both sides understood each other.

Years later de Guingand wrote, "At first I thought one of the characters of Wren's *Beau Geste* had come along to pay a call. His appearance personified the hardened French colonial soldier. He was thin and drawn but intensely alert. His clothes had long since seen their day. Thin drill uniform with threadbare breeches and old but shapely riding boots. A French képi completed the picture. He told me who he was and from whence he came.

He said this just as you might say you had dropped over from the next village to tea."[47]

As planned, Leclerc offered to place his force under British command.

"Well, you can never have too many soldiers," Montgomery replied, to the point as ever. Then they chatted in his caravan for forty minutes, exchanging anecdotes and laughing loudly before emerging smiling and in good humour. Montgomery and Leclerc had considerable character traits in common: austerity, seriousness and personal conviction. Girard remembered Montgomery as being small, with grey hair and a large nose, particularly remarking on an "air of craftiness and sympathy!" After the meeting, Montgomery's GSO1, Colonel Charles Richardson, took Leclerc to one side and asked him if there was any kit he wanted to continue with operations. The Frenchman took out a small piece of paper from his coat pocket. .

"*Deux camions,*" said Leclerc.

"*Oui, mon Général, c'est possible,*" replied Richardson.

"*Cinq [auto]mitrailleuses?*" Leclerc asked, looking at Richardson as if he thought the British colonel might turn down his modest request to augment Savelli's clapped Marmon-Herringtons.[48] In fact, the British agreed to all Leclerc's wishes and more.

Whereas Montgomery was usually scathing about the Free French or any of the various foreign units bolted onto Eighth Army, Leclerc undoubtedly left a good impression, eliciting "he was a very English Frenchman really," from Colonel Richardson, and a nasal "I think we can do something with these men," from Montgomery himself.

British accommodation officers were busy in Tripoli, requisitioning any building they fancied for accommodation. Following a quick lunch, Leclerc's party was advised that an apartment had been found for them. On the way they met up with Dio, Troadec and the bearded Captain Farret, chatting in the shade of some eucalyptus trees about the extraordinary past five weeks. The apartment was a plush three-room affair on the third floor of a modern Italian building on the sea front, furnished in a mock renaissance style with an enormous stiff sofa trimmed with lace and similar chairs. Leclerc, never a self-pampering type despite his squirarchial background, burst into laughter at the sight of all the satin in his bedroom, while Girard rearranged the chairs and sofa, draping their goatskins over the lace to make the ambience less fanciful and more military. They were all shattered, so they grabbed some kip, sleeping well into the hours of darkness when they were disturbed by stores exploding and ack-ack fire. Realising this was nothing special, they returned to their beds, but Girard decided he would be safer sleeping on the parquet floor.[49]

This was only the beginning of Eighth Army's generosity to its new French unit. Montgomery personally ordered his quartermaster's department to send Leclerc a new British Army battledress.[50] Leclerc spent the morning of 28th January in conference with the British High Command, discussing his equipment needs and how his force could join in British operations. In the end, Eighth Army supplied considerably more than the modest list Leclerc first gave to Richardson. Once the desert's attrition of *la Colonne's* vehicles had been assessed more fully, Eighth Army provided thirty Bedford lorries, and agreed to exchange *la Colonne's* captured Italian anti-tank guns for British.[51] Eighth Army also added to Leclerc's numbers by bolting on a squadron of eighty British Royal Engineers and the tiny "free" Greek contingent. Colonel Gigantes' "Sacred Squadron" had served under the Eighth Army since the fall of Greece in 1941, and were now mounted on SAS-style pink Jeeps with Lewis machine guns. Lastly, Leclerc received the 159th anti-aircraft battery, Royal Artillery.

Chad was now behind them. Though he prevailed on Colonel Bernard to garner a few souvenirs (ebony and ivory carvings as presents for his loved ones), Leclerc's main concern was the future role of his men. Girard, Guillebon and Bonnafé enjoyed a few brief days of civilization, living like flat-sharing bachelors in their sea front flat, cooking their own food and seeing the sights while Leclerc held several conferences with Montgomery. As a result, his Free French became "Force L" and would enter Tunisia on Eighth Army's left, inland, flank.[52]

Montgomery was often scathing about the French after Alamein, saying that he only used them to guard airfields,[53] but Leclerc does not seem to have had a problem with him in early 1943. In fact, the Frenchman's memories of Montgomery at this time were sufficiently positive for him to ask to serve under Montgomery again in northwest Europe a few months later. However, whatever similarities British officers like Colonel Richardson saw between Leclerc and themselves, he was still a continental Frenchman with an outlook born of authoritarian Catholicism.

In early February, *la Colonne* regrouped around Mizda, officially becoming the British Eighth Army's "Force L" on the 10th of February. Poor-relation status nevertheless continued. Not for Force L the new six-pounder anti-tank gun whose breach blocks were kissed in gratitude by their crews following the Snipe engagement at Alamein the previous October. Instead, outmoded two-pounders carrying the first bloom of rust were sent from Eighth Army's junk yard at Tripoli, leading to sarcastic quips from Leclerc's men that the British would send them to reinforce the Chinese Nationalists, even then commonly known to receive the least effective weaponry from the Anglo-American arsenal.[54] But Montgomery, however, only envisaged that Force L would face light opposition and, once British instructors taught their new French comrades how to use these two-pounders from the back of a "portee"—an adapted lorry—they could still wreck trucks and armoured cars.

Of the 3,500 Free French who invaded the Fezzan in early December, 1,000 stayed in Libya to garrison France's new protectorate south of the 28th parallel. The rest needed British uniforms—onto which French insignia would be sewn—by the 22nd February.

"We were no longer a horde of ragamuffins," wrote Raymond Dronne. "We were now a unit, a properly uniformed unit. The British gave us beautiful uniforms of warm material: the khaki battledress of the English army, long trousers and a short waist-length tunic, a tin helmet, comfortable boots and webbing gaiters. The boots were an absolute joy to the *tirailleurs*, replacing strange sandals made of rubber tyres. The English had certainly found takers for their extra large boot sizes. The Sarras mostly took sizes larger than 45. The boots didn't always suit their feet but they were well made and warm, and the Sarras sang with good heart. The boots were even more welcome among us Europeans who sported terrible old shoes split with holes; some only had Saharan sandals."[55]

British clothing was only supplementary, and not everyone was lucky. "If you thought they would send us warm clothes you were fooling yourself" was a remark often made to those still left with only shorts for the cold North African winter. Leclerc himself received a new Bedford 750 lorry, but still had to make his HQ under a lean-to awning attached to the side of a breakdown truck, which no British brigadier or major-general would have suffered.[56]

Such problems had their root in de Gaulle wishing to keep "Free France" as autonomous as possible. Had French units come under British operational command (or Russian, as in the case of the Normandie-Niemen fighter squadron), they would have been equipped as far as possible on a parity with their host's forces from the start. This would inevitably lead to the absorption of French forces into those of Great Britain, which de Gaulle wished to avoid. However, once the Americans arrived, de Gaulle found himself fighting a losing battle. The *Armée d'Afrique* fought alongside the U.S. Army in Tunisia, so it was naturally given equipment by the Americans, who rapidly grew into their role as quartermasters and bankers. On 2nd February, Leclerc flew to Ghadames with Colonel Delange to confer with General Delay, senior *Armée d'Afrique* officer commanding the east Saharan front (the first liaison between Free French and formerly Vichy-controlled *Armée d'Afrique* at that level). There he noticed a new form of "can do" positivism, which he put down to three months' exposure to American influence. The old loyalty to Marshal Pétain was, however, still strong among many *Armée d'Afrique* officers. One even confided to Colonel Delange that he "would never forget that it was thanks to the Marshal that he had been able to watch a German military parade in the uniform of a French officer."[57] Small amounts of liaison were one thing, but the military reintegration of two parts of a deeply divided nation were quite another.

The Afrika Korps and other German troops now pouring into Tunisia, many of whom had first-class and bitter experience of the Russian front, were far tougher enemies than the Italian Saharianas. In addition, the fast moving campaign unleashed by Montgomery after Alamein was turning into a defensive slogging match in Tunisia.

Montgomery and Leclerc were great believers in proper training, and so Massu found his battalion being given a crash course in land mines. These had not much bothered *la Colonne* in Chad and Libya so far, but had been a significant and costly aspect of the Alamein battle.[58]

Leclerc's *méharistes*, and the Groupes Nomades de Tibesti, Ennedi and Kanem had to be motorised and surrender their camels. Mercifully, there were plenty of Arabs prepared to take these doughty animals, which avoided gut-wrenching tragedies similar to the British Household Cavalry's bloody disposal of its Irish black horses in Palestine.

On 20th February 1943, Force L's advance guard set off for the south Tunisian front. Their orders were to hold the area of Ksar Rhilane on the southern end of the broken mountain spine that runs north to south through Tunisia. Ksar Rhilane is a corridor between the mountains of Matmata, which themselves stand fifty kilometres inland from the sea, and the great dunes of soft, fine, impassable sand of the eastern Great Erg, or *La Grande Erg Orientale* (known to British Tommies as "the Great Oriental Urge"). It was Leclerc's task to bar this corridor to the Germans, thereby preventing them from outflanking Eighth Army on its western, left flank.

The majority of Eighth Army was on the seaborne side of the Matmatas, facing a former French fortification called the Mareth Line. Dating from the 1930s when France began fearing Italian ambitions, this was a chain of ditches and blockhouses running from the mountains to the sea. Rommel had retreated behind this line after quitting Libya. At his most dangerous when cornered, Rommel had given a bloody lesson to the Americans and the British First Army at the Kasserine Pass during mid-February. The Americans had been horribly green, but the scale of their equipment had impressed Rommel. Next he had to deal with Montgomery to the south.

On 22nd February, Force L's 1st Reconnaissance and Combat Company, supported by the Greek "Sacred Squadron," arrived at Ksar Rhilane and began patrolling at once. German armoured cars and light tanks appeared at the north end of the corridor, showing that the French had not arrived a moment too soon. The German force was engaged and turned back towards Djebel Hallouf, leaving the French and Greeks to hold the pass until more units under Vézinet and Dio arrived and took up defensive positions with their backs to the dunes and facing the Matmatas. The next day Leclerc arrived, thinking the roads were good until the Jeep in front of him was blown up by a mine. The Royal Engineers seconded to Force L got to work with their mine detectors.

Leclerc correctly perceived that the only way for the Germans to turn the Mareth Line would be to make an outflanking manoeuvre through one or other of the Matmata passes, so he positioned his main force in a curve facing the pass between the Djebel Mahalla and the lesser djebels of the Tebaga Gap. His back faced the soft sand dunes of the *Grand Erg Orientale*, from which he would be less likely to be outflanked or taken from the rear.

However, he ordered this area to be patrolled by Algerian *méharistes* after liaison with the *Armée d'Afrique* at the Ksar Rhilane well. Force L dug in and camouflaged their positions, while a recce company operated 30km farther north to watch for enemy movement.

Montgomery felt a pang of conscience at leaving the lightly armed French out on the very limb that offered Rommel his most obvious opportunity for turning Eighth Army's flank. On the evening of 25th February, Leclerc and Girard were invited to Montgomery's HQ for dinner with the British general in his map room caravan, and were afterwards put up for the night.[59]

Leclerc found the tension unbearable, knowing that a strong German attack could annihilate the force he had nurtured for two years. When a French journalist and photographer, Messrs Bénard and Costa, arrived at his CP looking for a story, he told them abruptly to "Push off!" Girard, on the other hand, advised them to follow Force L from a discreet distance. Shortly afterwards, Leclerc caught his ADC reading an article written by the two newsmen on Larminat's and Koenig's units. "Something similar about our troops would be a good thing," remarked Girard. Leclerc agreed, telling Girard to recall the reporters. The newsmen were allowed to interview Leclerc, and their presence in fact turned out to be a welcome distraction. Otherwise, Girard found Leclerc's moodiness before the Mareth battle one of the worst times of the whole war.[60]

It was indeed Rommel's intention to hurl his re-equipped and reinforced Afrika Korps at Montgomery after the successful Kasserine battle. Ultra decrypts gave Montgomery warning of this, and he prepared to meet the attack with 600 anti-tank guns, 400 tanks, and infantry in well prepared positions around Medenine, with the Matmatas on his left and the sea on his right. Giving Eighth Army a headmasterly "no withdrawal" and "no surrender" order of the day, Montgomery waited. The attack came in the early dawn of 6th March. The British held their fire until the German tanks were 400 yards away before inflicting murder. After this, Rommel wanted to retreat 250km to the north but Hitler would not hear of it. Instead he called Rommel home. On 9th March the Desert Fox left North Africa for good,[61] to be replaced by Prussian Junker, General Jurgen von Arnim.

On that day Leclerc received a call from de Guingand. Montgomery wanted to see him. British intelligence indicated a new attack would soon develop in the Ksar Rhilane area to outflank the British position at Medenine. This would be the Axis' last chance to defeat Eighth Army in Africa. Knowing that his new French unit from Chad was not well equipped, and that the two-pounder anti-tank guns he had given them were outmoded leftovers, Montgomery ordered Leclerc to pull back 90 km. Leclerc refused, knowing how vulnerable his force could be if caught in the open. He told Montgomery he would be better off staying in a position which had been well prepared for the previous fortnight if he could have plentiful British air support. Montgomery agreed. A radio air liaison van from "Air Tentacle" was ordered to Ksar Rhilane straight away. Arriving back at the position in a British aircraft, Leclerc warned his staff of the impending attack, but ordered them not to tell the men until the morning so they could have a good night's sleep and be in top form.[62]

As predicted, at dawn a German armoured reconnaissance force consisting of tanks, armoured cars and panzer grenadiers appeared in front of Force L's advance positions at Djebel Outid, making contact at 6.30 am. His advance guard was not strong enough to face this force, so Leclerc ordered them to disengage and retreat south at once past Force L's main position but without revealing it. The German formation under Major Hans von Luck followed, continuing past the north corner of the French position without realising the impending danger. Leclerc was in the middle of his troops, watching everything and making sure no one opened fire until German vehicles and tanks were within range.[63]

Then, on Leclerc's command, Crépin's gunners, the 159th battery's Bofors guns and Vézinet's tirailleurs opened fire on the German tanks, aiming at wheels and tracks, and the panzer grenadiers advancing on foot beside them. The range was short. Unable to see the French positions, the Germans' return fire was erratic. At 8.20 a.m. air support was called in from Leclerc's British liaison van. Hurricane-IID anti-tank aircraft of No. 6 Squadron RAF appeared in the skies overhead and began to shoot up the German force. The Germans retreated, leaving wrecked vehicles everywhere, not to mention many dead and wounded. Instinctively, Leclerc knew this was only a first attempt. The Germans had to open the corridor in order to have a realistic chance of breaking the deadlock after the Mareth battle.

Sure enough, in the late morning, the second attack developed against the south of the French position held by the Groupe Nomade de Tibesti. Leclerc did the same as before, waiting until the attackers came within range without revealing his positions, and then hitting them with murderous fire at short range, supported once again by RAF Hurricanes called in by radio. Again the German attack failed.[64]

Opinion at Eighth Army HQ was that Force L was doomed. "It's going to get hotter around Ksar Rhilane. This brave man Leclerc, he's very nice, but now we won't see him again," Montgomery remarked.

Regrouped by mid-afternoon, the Germans made a third attempt, attacking the centre of Leclerc's position, held by former *méharistes* of the Groupe Nomade de Borkou and 2e Compagnie. This was driven off in the same fashion; fire opening at close range and RAF support. This time the German armour did not return, retreating north pursued by RAF anti-tank Hurricanes.[65] For the first time troops under Leclerc's command had beaten off a major German attack. "The enemy is retreating northwards," he signaled to Montgomery. "He has lost sixty vehicles, ten cannons, and never penetrated our position. We have a dozen casualties."

"Well done," Montgomery signaled back to Leclerc, and recorded in his diary that it was a "fine performance."

In 1983 General Sir Charles Richardson said, "He [Leclerc] was very savagely attacked. I had a wireless set on his command net throughout that battle. There was nothing I could do to help them really. He was a very phlegmatic Frenchman, reporting his casualties, saying he was sure he could maintain his position there."[66]

That night Leclerc toured the position, congratulating his men, gunners, tirailleurs, Greeks and British sappers alike, radiating the exhilaration of victory.

That night in his command post he wrote the following communiqué:

The Germans wanted to take Ksar Rhilane. They attacked with about fifty armoured vehicles. The troops from Chad, helped by their Greek and British comrades, inflicted a definite check on them and made them suffer serious losses. The first contact with the Germans has been a victory. The others will be as well. Vive le Général de Gaulle. Vive la France.[67]

Montgomery now decided to take Eighth Army over to the offensive again by outflanking the Mareth line from the western side of the Matmata hills, using General Sir Bernard Freyberg's New Zealand Division. They were to advance through Wilders Gap south of the Mareth position, link up with the French, and push up the Ksar Rhilane corridor as far as the Tebaga Gap, then swing back to the right through the Matmata range north of the Mareth Line to cut the Germans off.

Freyberg was not only a winner of the Victoria Cross in the First World War, but had two and a half years experience in the Mediterranean theatre with many important actions behind him, including the defence of Crete. He wanted Leclerc's Force L to take Djebel Outid from those Germans who survived the Ksar Rhilane action, which would help the New Zealand Division's progression to the Tebaga Gap. On the afternoon of March 22nd, Freyberg's men made their way to their start line and Leclerc realized the New Zealanders might be held up by German and Italian pickets in the mountains. He saw an opportunity for Force L to get more involved, and drove with Peers Carter to Freyberg's HQ. With Carter acting as interpreter, Freyberg asked Leclerc to clear the Germans off the Djebel El-Matleb. Leclerc's reply was that it would be better to clear them off the whole range.

"But you can't do that with only one brigade group," said Freyberg.

"I can and I will!" Leclerc replied.

Next, Leclerc went off and did the reconnaissance himself, then ordered his men to attack.[68] Leading and directing his men through the slopes of the djebel, in an action reminiscent of his attack on the Ait Hammou in 1931, Leclerc quickly had the hills under French control. Recognising their danger, the Germans tried a counterattack but were faced with a *Tirailleurs* bayonet charge. The New Zealanders were now able to set up observation points with a view for miles around.

But Freyberg had become cautious with old age. On reaching the Tebaga Gap, he failed to exploit the opportunity it offered. After blocking him with the 15th and 21st Panzer Divisions, the Axis quickly consolidated their position so that when Montgomery ordered a general attack for 26th March, the British only penetrated four miles amid fierce resistance. The Axis commander, General Messe—one of very few competent Italian senior generals—recognized that his troops at Mareth would soon be cut off between the hills and the sea, and ordered a measured withdrawal to Wadi Akarit on 27th March to avoid encirclement.[69] Montgomery had won a victory, but not a resounding one.

For Force L, the last weeks of the Tunisian campaign were a mix of minor actions amid the reassessment of French priorities. They remained under New Zealand command, with the British 4th Indian Division on their right. Freyberg's liaison officers, O'Rorke and Nuncarrow, were genial and friendly. The British also gave them a Royal Artillery anti-tank regiment under Colonel Hindley.[70]

Poor relations status remained a nagging problem. Leclerc lacked a proper command car, and vehicles which had lasted since Chad were breaking down with increasing regularity. Girard scoured British depots, finding a Bedford here, a Chevrolet there, while supply officer Bagneux, an expert scavenger, offered his general a captured German Horsch, which Leclerc loved while it lasted.

In the few days' respite between Mareth and the April battles, Leclerc caught up on administrative paperwork and bravery citations. There were also command changes. Force L was transferred from Freyberg to Eighth Army's 10th Corps under Lt. General Brian Horrocks.

Leclerc now acquired Colonel Rémy's 1er Régiment de Marche des Spahis Marocains, who had served at El Alamein in General Koenig's First French Brigade Group. He was impressed that the Spahis' equipment was standard for a British reconnaissance regiment. Colonel Rémy even had a proper command car—which Leclerc appropriated until Eighth Army provided something for him.

If Rémy's Spahis Marocains could integrate with Force L without trouble it was because they felt part of the Free French brotherhood. Sadly, while Churchill's support for de Gaulle was genuine, if exasperating at times, Roosevelt took a different view. He hoped that a different leader could be found who stood a better chance of uniting all Frenchmen against the Axis. His choice was Leclerc's old commanding officer from 1930s Moroccan days, General Henri Giraud.

While Giraud was a good soldier and undoubtedly brave, having escaped from German custody in both world wars, he nevertheless lacked de Gaulle's political sophistication, and seemed not to understand how hard-bitten those Free Frenchmen who fought in the desert or came up from Chad in worn out clothes and clapped vehicles had become. By plumping for Giraud, Roosevelt ended up satisfying nobody.

Nevertheless, from late 1942 until early 1943, Giraud was Roosevelt's chosen Frenchman. On 2nd April, Montgomery invited Leclerc and Giraud to dine at his Gabes HQ. Montgomery sat at the head of a U-shaped table, with Giraud and Leclerc on either side of him. The atmosphere was frosty. In spite of Leclerc's past friendship with Giraud, a lot of water had flowed under the bridge since the 1930s. Since 1940 Leclerc had been a faithful Gaullist, and was irked that Giraud should now think of supplanting his political master. Nor, as he told Girard afterwards, did he appreciate the older man calling him "Hauteclocque," as if he was still an eager subaltern in the High Atlas. Burdened with the role of interpreter, Girard found the occasion highly embarrassing. Montgomery, radiant from his victory at Alamein, and his aides de Guingand, Poston and Henderson, had to listen for a solid half hour while Giraud recounted the story of his escape from Schloss Konigstein. Gaullists were united in their hatred of *la belle France* being occupied, and here was Giraud, in front of a British general who had never been captured and whose country had successfully resisted all hostile invasions since 1066, delighting in the games he had played with the Vichy and Occupation administrations. Worse, he kept stopping like a "circus pony" at intervals so Girard could translate. Visibly appalled, Leclerc interjected, "Meanwhile, we have been fighting here these last three years!"

Girard wrote in his diary, "I was terribly disappointed, and the fox-like smile of Montgomery put the lid on my humiliation."[li] The evening ended frostily. Giraud left, muttering, "I cannot understand him, the little Hauteclocque. Why should he be like this? After all it was I who gave him his *Légion d'Honneur* in Morocco!"[72]

During the Jeep ride back to their quarters, Leclerc could not hide his uncompromising view from his young ADC: "Giraud has become very full of himself!" Leclerc was naturally respectful of superiors but, from that evening on he found himself resenting Giraud.

Force L had remained on standby for several days since the Mareth battle, and badly needed a rest. The attachment of the Spahis Marocains Regiment meant existing staff arrangements run by Guillebon were no longer adequate. Furthermore, 10th Corps had not yet assigned Force L a liaison officer, forcing Leclerc to spend more time at Horrocks' HQ until he got one. In fact Leclerc's purpose was to ensure that his Frenchmen deserved a place in the victory parade.

On 9th April, Leclerc's Spahi armoured cars, commanded by the White Russian Commandant Roumiantsoff, out on 10th Corps' left flank, made contact with General Anderson's British First Army. This brought Force L more attention from journalists who wanted to see the join-up of the army which had fought through Tunisia and the Eighth Army which had fought its way up from the south, all against the backdrop of the welcome they received passing through Kairouan. Leclerc was never a fan of newshounds, but he acknowledged that Free France and the Gaullist cause needed publicity, and endeavored to treat them graciously.

With the Tunisian campaign slacking off, Leclerc was concerned that his men should take part in whatever action was left. Flank-guarding *une division hindoue*—Tuker's 4th Indian Division—at Djebel Fadeloun in mid-April, Leclerc watched enemy positions from Vézinet's observation post and grew visibly impatient for information from the British. Exasperated, he visited 10th Corps HQ and was finally ordered to join Tuker's division for the push from Djebel Garci into the mountains of the northern dorsal. Tuker's men were experts at hill and mountain warfare, and from Force L's standpoint, enviably well equipped. Tuker, for his part, could not help but admire Leclerc. Once, when arriving at Force L's HQ, Tuker found Leclerc was sleeping. Knowing he suffered from periodic bouts of *palu* and had not stopped for months, the British general said not to disturb him. Tuker could not help noticing the French lack of kit, and sent a liaison officer to ask Leclerc how many machine guns he had per battalion.

"What's he meant to do?" Girard asked on behalf of *le Patron*.

"Haven't the regulations for the constitution of a batalion been made clear to you?" Tuker's emissary asked Girard.

Feeling like second-class citizens yet again, Girard replied proudly, "We take the field with what we've got!"[73]

On 19th April, to protect their evacuation from the Tunisian ports, the Germans counterattacked. Their newly arrived *Nebelwerfers* (multi-barreled rocket launchers) rained down hammer blows of incessant shell fire, which luckily fell mostly on open ground, though Dio lost a lorry and eight wounded. A German artillery barrage was nothing like as powerful as the Eighth Army's artillery at that stage in Tunisia, but unpleasant enough. Force L held its position for four days under sporadic shell fire, which was hardest on Dio's group. In the evenings, Leclerc would tell Girard about the early days of Free France; de Gaulle's disappointment at seeing General Béthouart's mountain troops return from England to France; then the rallying of the Cameroons and Gabon; and how Leclerc could not have done it without Louis Dio.

Shells continued to fall, even during Force L's church parade on Sunday, 25th April. But the German counterattack, while sharp and requiring classic North African ridge clearing tactics, eventually failed. Soon Force L received orders to move on to Sousse, where they were welcomed by the Mayor, Maitre Zévaco, and a strong crowd, including uniformed officials, assembled by the war memorial waving *Tricolore* flags.

Maitre Zévaco's speech demonstrated the muddled political priorities of French North Africa. He seemed unsure whether France was suffering under *la botte britannique* or *teutonique!* To Leclerc's annoyance, not once did Maitre Zevaco mention de Gaulle. When Leclerc took his turn to speak, he stood up in his battered képi and battledress and said simply and clearly, "There is only one thing that matters. That is to liberate France, and for that there is only one possible leader, General de Gaulle. Everyone say, '*Vive le Général de Gaulle!*'" Then he walked into the crowd, motioned for silence and shouted again, "'*Vive le Général de Gaulle!*'" until the shouts echoed around the little dusty square.

After this, Leclerc was shown around a hospital. There he saw a nineteen-year-old boy lying in bed who had wanted to be the first man to raise the *Tricolore* over Monastir but had trodden on a landmine, losing a foot. Tapping the lad on the cheek, Leclerc reassured him, "You will still be able to serve your country."

Maitre Zévaco gave a formal luncheon at his house for Leclerc and his staff and local dignitaries. Girard was amazed. Formally laid dining tables with linen and crystal were a *spectacle oublié*. Leclerc was sitting in the drawing room as other guests assembled, when suddenly the well-known actress Francoise Rosay arrived. She had been stranded in French North Africa at the time of the Torch landings and delighted in giving her views on conditions in Occupied France to anyone who would listen, sometimes making reckless utterances and denunciations that mired the reputations of celebrities such as Sacha Guitry when the liberation came. Eleven years older than Leclerc, she was still elegant and attractive, dressed in a Prince of Wales check ensemble, sporting the white blond hair for which she was famous. She gave Leclerc a letter which he opened and read while she looked at him intently.

"Well, Madame, what do you want?" asked Leclerc appearing a little embarrassed.

"Me? Nothing, General. I wanted to see you. I have seen you. That is all," replied the silver haired actress disingenuously.

"Good . . . Well, er. . . . That's fine," said Leclerc, plainly ill at ease.

Girard watched them chatting. It was obvious that Leclerc had become an object of fascination for Rosay, though nothing was likely to come of it. Nonetheless, after luncheon, she took Girard to one side.

"I would like to get to know him a little," she said. "Do you think he would?"

Girard did not record his reply, but she went on, "No, really, you're right. What am I to him? An old silly with bizarre ideas, who wants to distract him when he has other things on his mind. I shall not spoil things, I will talk about what I have seen. His youth, his simplicity, his tunic that sticks out backwards. And that képi! When I think of all those generals who ponce about in Algiers with their gold braid everywhere and who do nothing all day . . . and I shall tell people what he would want, that we should look to de Gaulle!"[74]

On 7th May, when Tunis and Bizerta finally fell to the Allies, over a quarter of a million Axis troops went behind Allied barbed wire, a loss of personnel greater than February's defeat at Stalingrad. Force L saw its share of this human sea of Axis prisoners. On one occasion a German prisoner went berserk, grabbed a rifle from a Senegalese tirailleur, and shot dead a French officer. The Senegalese promptly shot all twenty-five German prisoners they had. "Those African soldiers loved that officer," one of Leclerc's staff told the Royal Artillery's Colonel Hindley.[75] The upshot of this ugly episode was that German prisoners requested not to be handed over to the Free French. By comparison, former Vichy soldiers used Axis prisoners to clear minefields, and were not very good at feeding them either![76]

General Giraud's self-importance caused a row over the Victory parade in Tunis planned for 20th May. Leclerc was incensed at hearing that the only French to be included were the ex-Vichy *Armée d'Afrique*. So he ordered Colonel Ingold and the Spahis Marocains' Commandant Rouminatsoff to infiltrate a dozen vehicles into the parade. Giraud, still smarting at Leclerc's behaviour at Montgomery's dining table, heard about this plan and countermanded his former Moroccan *protegé*.

Furious, Leclerc turned to American reporter Hassoldt Davis, "Why does your country undermine France by encouraging opportunists, coat chasers of the victorious Allies and former Vichy functionaries who have so loyally collaborated with Berlin, right up until they saw that their treason risked their own security?" Eyeballing the American journalist intently, he demanded, "Listen Davis, I want it known above all that we are undefeated. We, the fighting French, have never given in. We have never signed any armistice. *Les Boches* have never beaten us. We have never made any compromise. Our children will not be able to reproach us on our return. France knows only one leader, de Gaulle, and she demands that the Allies recognise the same!"[77]

The groundswell in French North Africa in favour of de Gaulle was gathering momentum. Recognising the slight to the Free French, no one tried to stop Leclerc from bolting his men on to the end of the Eighth Army's march past. Square bashing practice was out of the question. Leclerc's men would join the parade in the most presentable of their vehicles. On the dias stood Generals Eisenhower, Montgomery, Anderson and Giraud. The ex-Vichy *Armée d'Afrique* marched past them in their old pre-war uniforms, long bayonets looking like fishing rods, dressed as what they were, France's past. Then Leclerc's men emerged from side streets in their Bedford trucks, now bearing the word "Tchad" in metal strips on their radiator grilles, in British uniforms, sun blackened faces and limbs, looking the essence of modern, victorious soldiers. They received a rapturous welcome, and the cheers of their Eighth Army comrades.

CHAPTER SEVEN

"A GIGANTIC EFFORT IS
REQUIRED OF US"

After victory in Tunisia, Leclerc expected to lead his men triumphantly into Algiers, the capital of France's most important African colony, where a Frenchman could feel almost as "at home" as in France. Perhaps he also wanted to shame former Vichy officials for the previous three years. However, while such sentiments were understandable, the Allies were not going to let anything so contentious happen. There was even concern that de Gaulle might initiate a *coup* against General Giraud rather than allow time and negotiation to work through the effects of Roosevelt's unfortunate meddling. Fortunately, by mid-1943 however, Roosevelt began to recognise Giraud as a "dud" and "a very thin reed." Even the American supreme commander, General Eisenhower, found it increasingly difficult to understand the American president's aversion to de Gaulle. But there were no immediate U-turns. The Allies were playing for higher stakes.

Leclerc finished the Tunisian campaign as part of General Horrocks' X Corps, and its orders were to return to Tripoli. When Horrocks sought confirmation that this order should include the two French divisions (Force L had become the 2nd Free French Division on 13th May), Allied HQ insisted that the Free French should go to Tripoli with the X Corps. Leclerc refused to go. Horrocks quite understood that a march-past in Algiers would make a fitting end to *La Colonne*'s African war but he advised Leclerc that if he did not return to Tripoli the British would cut off his supplies.[1] Leclerc toughed it out for eight days while shortages became acute, until he reluctantly accepted that he would have to come to heel. He signaled to Horrocks, "Moving to Tripoli. Please start supplies again."[2]

Among the French, Leclerc was becoming a victim of his own success and a focus for resentment among the Giraudists. On the other hand, de Gaulle regarded Leclerc's division almost as his Praetorian Guard. They were also becoming chic, the division which all *évadés* wanted to join when they reached Algeria. French North Africa had received a sizeable number of *évadés* before the Torch landings and after the occupation of France's "Free" Zone by the Germans, but after the victory in Tunisia such young men no longer wanted to join the *Armée d'Afrique*. They wanted to fight under de Gaulle. More embarrassing for the *Armée d'Afrique*'s high command was the increasing problem of desertion, but these so-called deserters were not leaving army life. They were joining the two Free French divisions as well, and were dubbed *spontanément mutés* — "spontaneous transfers." Accused of suborning the ex-Vichy *Armée d'Afrique*'s soldiers, Leclerc had immense pleasure explaining that such men could hardly be called "deserters" for wanting to join the best unit.

In Algiers, de Gaulle was slowly but surely routing Giraud and the remnants of French North Africa's Vichy establishment, getting rid of Peyrouton and, more importantly, General Nogues—the senior army general responsible for the wasteful *baroud d'honneur*. While Giraud was not in any way responsible for this tragedy, he certainly dragged his feet when it came to reversing Vichyite anti-Semitic measures in force throughout French North Africa. De Gaulle put a stop to this. One result of Giraud perpetuating these obnoxious policies was yet more recruits for Leclerc. Another result was that Giraud became increasingly regarded as no different than Pétain and Darlan among both the Free French and even the ex-Vichy *Armée d'Afrique*, where Pétainism was always strongest among senior officers.

However nauseating President Roosevelt's ill-judged attempts to push Giraud and de Gaulle into political marriage,[3] Giraud had done some good for French arms. By pleading the simple cause of re-arming of the French

Army at the Anfa negotiations, Giraud had persuaded Roosevelt to re-equip eleven French divisions. It was true that, once it was realised that transporting so much Class A military equipment would require the cargo space of no less than 325 Liberty ships, which even the arsenal of democracy could not afford in 1943, eleven divisions became eight: five infantry and three armoured.[4] However, French levels of equipping were less generous than American levels, and the *Armée d'Afrique* still possessed stocks of French uniforms and some small arms so the new equipment would go further than expected.

Many of France's most intellectual officers who, like de Gaulle, had seen the importance of developing armoured warfare had remained with Vichy after 1940. Some came to North Africa under Weygand, and now served Giraud. These included the highly intelligent General Leyer who set about re-building France's tank arm with the comforting certainty of a plentiful supply of US Sherman tanks and support vehicles.

Who would command these three new armoured divisions? Leyer's old friend General Jean Touzet du Vigier was an obvious candidate, and General de Saint-Didier another. De Gaulle only had one obvious armoured division commander among his followers with the élan and youth to count, and that man was Leclerc. He was duly promoted *général de division*. Pleased but embarrassed, Leclerc protested to de Gaulle that such a promotion was "too early and too precocious" since men senior in age and service would be his subordinate *générals de brigade*. It also meant he would get his third star before General Koenig, an officer he much respected. However, with the "general interest" of France in mind—his "Free" France—de Gaulle ordered Leclerc to do as he was told. With a modesty that never left him, Leclerc remarked to Girard, "*Le Général de Gaulle* has no-one else!"[5] And he only put up his third star a year later at de Gaulle's insistence.

Whatever contempt Leclerc felt for Vichy, serving de Gaulle had given him a career outside the traditional hierarchy of the army he joined in 1924. Yet he was still a man of tradition and obedience. The rifts between Frenchmen took on a new complexity once the US military machine was ensconced on French imperial soil. No longer could Leclerc call Vichy, "The hook on which men hang their cowardice." That hook no longer existed in North Africa. To paraphrase Napoleon, "After a battle there are only men." However much Leclerc wanted the moral satisfaction of seeing the formerly pro-Vichy *Armée d'Afrique* knuckle under to de Gaulle's Free French establishment, for the time being he had to live in an American-funded real world and accept as comrades French soldiers he had recently branded cowards.

Frustrated that his 2e DFL should kick its heels in Sabratha, the old Roman site near Tripoli, there were times when Leclerc also fell victim to de Gaulle's periodic bouts of paranoid Anglophobia. Girard, a fluent English-speaker with many British friends, managed to talk him away from that mindset's worst excesses, but face to face with the reality of Anglo-Saxon predominance, Leclerc wanted "Free France" talked up as much as possible. *Les Anciens* from Chad such as Guillebon, Massu, Dronne and Girard were his closest comrades, so when Leclerc co-opted any photographers hanging around the 2e DFL's camps wanting to see him, he made them include these comrades in the picture and then photograph the rest of the men.[6]

The friction between General Giraud and de Gaulle continued. De Gaulle thought the situation was entirely caused by American high-handedness but Roosevelt stubbornly refused to recognise de Gaulle's higher view of himself and France. The American president and his State Department did not subscribe to the analogy that Germany's occupation of France was a modern equivalent of the Hundred Years War. "You are not Joan of Arc and you are not France," the Americans repeated to *le grand Charles*. Exasperated, de Gaulle asked Leclerc to visit Eisenhower, but the younger general advised against this, believing such action might smack of desperation. Leclerc was, however, prepared to tell Giraud that, while formally out-ranking de Gaulle, he should graciously accept de Gaulle's political pre-eminence, just as General Catroux had done.

In any case Leclerc, whose parting advice to Thérèse had been, "Listen to the peasants," was not worried about the eventual outcome of the Giraud affair. He detected the murmurings of a groundswell in favour of de Gaulle across the Maghreb. After visiting the offices of the new Free French journal *Combat*, run, in fact, by communists under a rosy-cheeked, white-haired colonel, Leclerc exclaimed to his staff, "What do you want? Someone told me they were communists, fair enough, but one thing I do know, I can talk to them about patriotism and France and they understand."[7] Instinctively Leclerc knew de Gaulle was better placed to carry the day.

De Gaulle had an important supporter Giraud lacked. King George VI arrived in Tripoli to visit Eighth Army, and de Gaulle was invited to a large dinner reception with some of his officers. Leclerc went, along with generals Koenig, Larminat and Girard, still in his battledress tunic but sporting at least a new képi and his medal ribbons. Seated next to the table of honour where the King sat with Churchill, Montgomery, Maitland-Wilson, and Horrocks, the French contingent was delighted when, halfway through the meal, General Horrocks' chair broke underneath him and everyone burst out laughing.

Presenting Leclerc to the King afterwards, Montgomery listed Force L's citations during the Tunisian campaign: Medenine, Ksar Rhilane, El Hamma, and Djebel Mellab. Leclerc was self-effacing as ever but Montgomery kept him in front of the King for a few minutes, finishing off by saying "I couldn't have won the battle of Mareth without him." Monty could be generous when he wanted to be.

"How many men have you?" asked the King.

"About 4,000, Sir," Leclerc replied.

The King nodded his head and turned to the main business of the evening. Montgomery and Maitland-Wilson were knighted. As he watched, Leclerc was impressed by the traditions of serenity and power which this simple ceremony represented. But, as he later admitted to Girard, he felt a pang of bitterness that so much British power had been gained at France's detriment.

"We've had a craze for destroying our proper traditions for ten years or more," the young ADC admitted. "But we must look to ourselves, and not reproach others for our misunderstanding the value of tradition and national cohesion."[8]

But Leclerc had found the display of British splendour harder to take.

"The English, you see, are people I recognise and appreciate in combat . . . but I take no pleasure in seeing them afterwards. I feel a closer affinity to the Germans. But don't tell anyone I said that!"

Leclerc's views, though essentially continental, inevitably reflect a sadness at France's internal divisions. Though France and Germany had been bad neighbours for two centuries, French rivalry with Great Britain was older and, arguably, ran deeper. The ascendancy of English-speaking peoples over the French was decided in the Seven Years War over a hundred and eighty years earlier, and only temporarily retrieved by Napoleon. If Leclerc felt disappointed that there were not more French participating in Germany's defeat it was partly because he knew, once again, that France had let herself down in 1940. He knew France was not Great Britain's equal and must fight simply for the right to fight, and to put an army in the field against the Wehrmacht. The Free French were just a meagre cohort, elbowing each other to get in line, while France itself was, so to speak, "In hospital or a concentration camp or even an old people's home." For a patriot like Leclerc, it was physically painful. "We will get out of it undoubtedly," he told Girard. "But in what state?"[9]

At least the Free French divisions commanded by Leclerc and Koenig knew what they had believed in for the previous three years. By contrast, the *Armée d'Afrique* was in turmoil, not helped by de Gaulle's "open door" policy towards its personnel. Nor had the removal of the Free French to Libya stopped the problem of *spontanément mutés*. Young *évadés* were quite prepared to walk to Libya to join Leclerc, which made a nonsense of planning and materiel provision. Just as generals Giraud and de Gaulle were about to sign an agreement regarding the poaching of recruits, 500 men— including many armed Foreign Legionaires—gathered in Algiers on their way eastwards. Warned by an officer that the loophole was closing, they rested overnight at a farm outside the city before continuing on their way to Tripoli the following day. The following morning they were woken by the *garde mobile* who had been tipped off. Threatened with attack, some of the deserters fired shots in the air, making the *garde* back off.

Admiral Muselier[10] arrived, hoping to break the impasse. Addressing the cornered men, he promised a complete amnesty if they returned with him. Most agreed, except the legionaires who declared their preference for that part of the Foreign Legion attached to de Gaulle. When a young lieutenant presented himself to take command of them, a surly NCO intervened. He addressed the subaltern belittlingly as "*tu,*" saying, "You have never heard a shot in anger. You will not take command. I will take it." Then he turned to the legionaires, "Where shall we go?"

The officer suggested the railway station, but the legionaires left with their sergeant, crossing the line of *garde mobile* and no one raised a finger or a rifle to stop them. They eventually reached the Free French divisions in Libya, and the incident says much about the state of disunity afflicting the French Army during mid-1943.[11]

Whether or not he poached personnel from other units, Leclerc's so-called division was little more than brigade strength. Girard often thought he seemed discouraged, his eyes half-closed, weighed down by his responsibilities and the pain he felt at seeing the army and country he loved in such a mess. As if to reaffirm and justify his actions, Leclerc would often spend the evenings relating to his officers the odyssey which took him from Les Vergnes to London and the colonial *coups* of autumn of 1940.

While French generals quarrelled, the rank and file of Leclerc's Chad veterans had time to kill and were entertained. The glamourous French singer-actress Germaine Sablon sang for both divisions in the ruins of Sabratha's Roman theatre. Enraptured, the men sat through old favourites like *Vous ne savez pas*, *Mon légionaire* and *Mon homme*, but when she sang *"Lili Marlene"* every man joined in, singing their hearts out in the ancient splendour of their surroundings under a full moon.

Released from hospital after his wound at Ksar Rhilane, Raymond Dronne was attached to Leclerc's HQ to convalesce. It fell to him to arrange a few time-filling jaunts for Leclerc, to the Pyramids and other ancient sights. One evening they went into Tripoli to see *Mrs Miniver*, a British film about a middle-class family at the outbreak of war, starring Greer Garson, Walter Pidgeon and Teresa Wright. "A great film; the English are a great people," Leclerc exclaimed afterwards, contradicting his bitter remarks to Girard the evening Monty was knighted.

On 27th June, General de Gaulle arrived at Sabratha accompanied by Gaston Palewski, Charles Roux, de Maupin and Colonel Pierre Bilotte. Though drained by negotiations in Algeria, de Gaulle was jovial and in good form. First, he invested Commandant Roumiantsoff of the Spahis Marocains with the Order of the Liberation before taking Leclerc and the senior officers away to give them his news. The 1st and 2nd Free French Divisions were henceforth dissolved. Leclerc was tasked to transform his unit into the second of three new French armoured divisions equipped "*à l'Américaine*." Everyone who came with Leclerc from Chad would be amalgamated into the *Régiment de Marche du Tchad*—"the Chad Regiment." They would become the new division's motorised infantry, and the Spahis Marocains its reconnaissance regiment. One of the three necessary tank regiments was already to hand: all armoured companies from Free French forces serving with Eighth Army were amalgamated into the new *501e Régiment des Chars de Combat*, the "501e RCC" under the command of Colonel Cantarel, a surprisingly senior *évadé*. However, to make up the division's full armoured stength, two tank regiments, an anti-tank regiment and artillery support regiments were still needed from elsewhere. That had to be the *Armée d'Afrique*.

Then there was another thing. The new division would come under US command for training and operations, but, since the US Army only used black troops in the support arms at this time, the RMT would have to "whiten" itself—*blanchir*. All indigenous African troops who had marched and fought well all the way from Chad to Tunis would have to be transferred to other units.

For Jacques Massu and many other French officers, this news was shattering. A true soldier of La Coloniale, Massu had only really known military life in Africa commanding *méharistes*, or coloured soldiers of one tribe or another, and he had left his indigenous wife, Moido, behind. "How *could* we leave our black *tirailleurs* who had been with us through everything, Kufra, the Fezzan raids, the march to Tripoli and the Tunisian campaign! Men so devoted, faithful and courageous?"[12]

In fact, this grotesquely racist incident ended quite simply. Many of *La Colonne Leclerc's* black soldiers returned home, glad at least to have ended the Italian brand of colonialism. The rest were transferred to Koenig's old 1st Free French Division which went through its own transformation to become the *1ère Division d'Infanterie Motorisée*, or "1ère DIM." Then, so as not to confuse it with a new Moroccan division, it became the *1ère Division de Marche d'Infanterie*, or "1ère DMI," and became part of the new French First Army, though it always bore the Cross of Lorraine on its vehicles.[13]

Shortly after the Bastille Day celebrations, Leclerc visited Algeria and Morocco to find troops to fill his division. The fissure between the Giraudist and Gaullist portions of the army, each with its own command structure, did not make the task any easier. He needed to find ten thousand men and train them in armoured warfare, but it seemed utterly unrealistic simply to open his doors to volunteers. Various officers from the *Armée d'Afrique* shared this view; others did not. Everywhere he found a sense of anxiety rooted in the divergent paths taken by Vichy and de Gaulle.

Among former adherents to Vichy was Leclerc's old friend from Saint-Cyr, Jean Fanneau de la Horie. La Horie was serving under another old friend, Jean Touzet du Vigier, Leclerc's former commander at Saumur. Du Vigier, newly promoted to command the *Première Division Blindée*, was already forming his division at Mascara when Leclerc called on him in late July to claim La Horie.

Du Vigier, who was lucky enough to have his wife in Algeria with him, invited Leclerc to dinner. On hearing that Leclerc wanted La Horie for the 2e DB, du Vigier was understanding, but he had three things to say to his former pupil, Philippe de Hauteclocque:

"Firstly, I think you are the only person capable of re-uniting the French Army, which is an imperial necessity, and I swear, if you undertake this task, I am absolutely prepared to place myself under your orders and to help you in any way I can."

"Secondly, I think you are the only person who can do this because you have not got French blood on your hands."[14]

"Thirdly, if you want to take command of one of these new armoured divisions you must understand that you must take with you a very strong proportion of those you call Vichyists and Pétainists, men you see as traitors."

Leclerc bridled at this and du Vigier remarked that he had not changed!

"If I am to understand your present position correctly," continued du Vigier, "you see the army in two definitively separated factions, which, if not actively hostile, are irredeemably opposed to one another. On the one side, you have those who responded to de Gaulle's appeal of 18th June. For you they are pure, the patriots, the only ones who did what they could to continue the struggle. On the other hand, there are all the others, the conquered, the opportunists, the "*Vichysois*," the Pétainists and now the Giraudists, whom you regard as weaklings and cowards, if not actually as traitors.

"As for me, I would simply ask you the following question," du Vigier went on, seeing Leclerc was listening intently. "My dear Hauteclocque, I know you well enough not to doubt that, on 18th June 1940, if you had been in my place—that is to say at the head of two regiments which had been rescued from Dunkirk and then held on during hard fighting from Tours to Saumur—you would not have abandoned your men to respond to the call from London. It was not possible to take them all, as a unit, so you would have done as I did, and stayed with your men.

"On the other hand, what would I have done in your place if, completely disengaged from responsibilities towards my subordinates, I had been utterly free? Perhaps I would have done the same as you. Anyway, now I do have the chance of doing something effective, which was unimaginable until recently. I can contribute to the rebirth of the French armoured corps. So, who was wrong?

"I thought that it was my duty to work in this way. And today I am absolutely certain that I can do more towards putting in place a modern armoured army capable of giving us victory than if I had taken up who knows what post in London."

After a moment Leclerc replied, "Yes, general, it is clear you did your duty and I salute you for it. I hold you and your advice in the greatest esteem. If I cannot serve under your orders, let us, at the very least, work in close liaison together."

Du Vigier had one more thing to say. "The bravery, devotion, patriotism and valour of your companions has been magnificent! But they are not enough to form an armoured division that will enable you to keep your oath at Kufra. You need two regiments of tanks, three support groups of artillery, engineers and signals. There is no one but us who can give you these. So instead of mounting campaigns to call our men to desert, let's trust each other. You won't regret it."[15]

Leclerc simply replied, "Trust me general."

"Yes, Leclerc, I know I can trust you." It was the first time that evening du Vigier had not called his former pupil "Hauteclocque."[16]

Leclerc recognised in du Vigier another patriotic officer of aristocratic stock. Later that evening du Vigier explained the "legitimist thread" according to which the majority of the French Army followed Pétain, Darlan, and now Giraud. He told Leclerc that he was regarded as the only proper officer among the Gaullists, and that even so Giraud would have nothing to do with him![17] Du Vigier and Leclerc parted as friends, and a month later Leclerc sent Guillebon and Alaurent over to du Vigier's division to learn American ways.

A few days later Leclerc lunched with de Gaulle in Algiers. René Pleven was concerned for the future of the original Free French divisions. De Gaulle lacked Giraud's charm, but that was all he lacked. If Giraud held most of the French Army under his authority, de Gaulle held the moral and practical leadership of the Resistance in France itself. He had evolved into a populist (though not communist) patriot reminiscent of Leon Gambetta.[18] As such, he became a larger figure than Giraud could ever be.[19]

Whatever the proud standpoints of senior generals, junior officers from both the Free French and *Armée d'Afrique* were tired of the infighting. It had gone on long enough. One such was Colonel Paul de Langlade of the *12e Chasseurs d'Afrique*—12e RCA.[20] Nine years older than Leclerc, Langlade joined the *Chasseurs à Cheval* shortly before the first war. Promoted *sous lieutenant* in 1915, he transferred to the *69e Chasseurs à Pied*[21] with whom he was severely wounded attacking La Ferme de Navarrin. Next he became a pilot, finishing the war with the Croix de Guerre and 7 bars, and a Chevalier of the Legion of Honour; but when the French air arm separated from the army, Langlade returned to the cavalry. Colonial service with the 23e Spahis in Morocco beckoned at the same time that the young Lieutenant de Hauteclocque was an instructor at Meknes. In 1939 Langlade was still in Africa; his *Chasseurs d'Afrique* mounted in Somua tanks. When the Italians attacked the Mareth Line during the summer of 1940, Langlade was one of the tank commanders who saw them off. Spared involvement in the *baroud d'honneur*, thanks to his Somuas being hidden among the farms of northeast Algeria, Langlade led them against the Germans during the Tunisian battles. Now his Chasseurs had nothing to do but sit out the political infighting while their morale sank ever lower.

On the evening of 3rd August Langlade took himself out for dinner in Algiers. Since the influx of wealthy American officers had sent restaurant prices through the roof, Langlade drove out to a restaurant in the suburbs known for its reasonable menu and prices. As he ate, he noticed an officer he recognised seat himself a few tables away, placing a new képi with the stars of *général de brigade*[22] on the table. It was Leclerc. Langlade walked over to his table and stood to attention.

"Would you remind me of your name?" asked Leclerc. "I am sure I know you. But I can't place you exactly."

Leclerc invited Langlade to join him for supper and listened while Langlade poured out his heart over the frustrations of the last three years. He told Leclerc that, but for Mers el Kebir, the *Armée d'Afrique* had hoped to continue the war from Africa. Langlade spoke of their former trust in Marshal Pétain until it became clear the old man was incapable of maintaining French dignity, let alone a modicum of moral independence from the Germans. Leclerc heard how the *Armée d'Afrique* had hidden its equipment from the Armistice Commission only to see much of it stupidly wasted resisting the Torch landings, and afterwards how the 12e Chasseurs d'Afrique retook the field against the Afrika Korps in their outmoded Somuas. Langlade congratulated Leclerc on the march to Tripoli and Ksar Rhilane, and expressed sympathy for Force L's unfair banishment back into Libya after the fall of Tunis.

Leclerc saw his opportunity and asked Langlade if his 12e RCA would like to become part of the 2e DB.

"Yes," replied Langlade without a moment's hesitation, and they were friends from that day forward.[23]

This was a *"spontanément mute,"* not just of a few individuals but a whole regiment of two thousand men, without even waiting for orders! How were Giraud and his staff going to take it? Langlade returned to Rio Salado in the Oranais to await developments. Giraud's staff knew they had been hotted, and Langlade was called to Algiers to see General Leyer, who was not at all pleased to be the last to be informed by his subordinate, General Dewinck. Leclerc had told Dewinck that he wanted to see the regiment and Langlade figure in the make up of his division.

Leyer spoke tactfully, but behind the polite language befitting his rank he reminded Langlade that the French Army was and would remain a very hierarchical place.

"Take care my friend," said Leyer evenly. "Dewinck might be taken in by your *grenouillage*, but not me. In any case, this time it suits us. For that reason alone I will go along with it."[24]

Then Leyer read Langlade a pompous and condescending note from Giraud. "Given the particular psychological difficulties presented by the formation of this division, it would be best to choose homogeneous bodies of troops over which their colonel has total authority, and to build up this division from regiments that constitute entire units, rather than to give it a rabble of new recruits and *évadés* from France," quoted Leyer, fixing Langlade a look of unmistakable malice! However, *attentisme* had turned to *pragmatisme*, and Leyer was now determined that the new arrangement should work. "Do you see any moral or personal difficulty arising out of being attached to this division?" he demanded of Langlade. "Tell me frankly, because General Giraud wants you to take up this appointment and I think I do too."

"General, I thank you infinitely for the trust that you and General Giraud have placed in me," Langlade replied smoothly, perfectly aware of the personality clashes. "I accept this appointment without reservation. I already know General Leclerc. I am confident of his good faith and can vouch equally for my own. For what it's worth, my officers and I feel no shame for what our consciences made us do in 1940. We will join the *Deuxième Division Blindée* with our heads high. I also think that our brothers in arms there, who have followed another path, not necessarily harder, but infinitely more glorious, will welcome us without too many reservations."[25]

Leclerc's staff, including Guillebon and Girard, had set up a small divisional office on Algiers' Rue de Constantine before the end of August, where the Cross of Lorraine fluttered for the first time in the Algerian capital. It was to this new Gaullist oasis that Langlade reported. Leclerc told him that training would begin at once using British Crusader tanks until American equipment arrived.

At a stroke the 2e DB's catalogue of exceptional characters grew with the addition of 12e RCA officers such as Commandant de Furst. He spent the previous three years being so scathing about Pétain that it was a wonder he had not trekked across the Sahara to Chad. Loyalty to his regiment prevented him, and his superiors had protected him from being "seized by the collar and thrown into prison."[26]

"So we're Gaullists now, are we?" Furst quipped sarcastically.[27]

Then there was Captain André Gribius. As tall as de Gaulle, Gribius had been evacuated from Dunkirk, returned to France to fight on the Loire, and spent 1941 as an instructor at the Armistice Army's cavalry school at Tarbes. Later, under Langlade, he distinguished himself as a squadron commander in Tunisia.

If the Americans had not forced French officers out of their usual haunts in Algiers, the fortuitous meeting between Leclerc and Langlade might never have happened. At the Hotel Aletti, Leclerc was given two hours to decamp to another room because the Americans had requisitioned all the rooms on his floor. "Free" France had swapped one "rich relation" for another, whom they found equally insufferable. Compared to the British, the Americans had different failings, such as naivete and greenness, and different qualities, like openness and generosity; and they were the new quartermasters. A meeting with Giraud brought this home to Leclerc. When he gave his former CO a sincere explanation of Free France's uncompromisingly patriotic motives following de Gaulle's *Appel* of 18th June 1940 he found Giraud unmoved.

"The turning point of [French] history was not the *Appel* of 18th June 1940," Giraud stated dogmatically. "The turning point was 10th November 1942 when I appealed to our troops in French North Africa to place themselves alongside the Americans."[28]

That finished it for Leclerc. Never a wind-cock patriot, he remained loyal to those who served with him from the beginning, and refused quarters for his new division in eastern Algeria. He plumped instead for the country where he made his name as a young officer, Morocco.

After the black soldiers had been removed from the RMT there were not enough men to make the three infantry battalions needed for an American-style armoured division. The necessary men would have to come from the *Corps Franc d'Afrique*, an *ad hoc* formation of political odd balls and refugees created by Giraud during late November 1942. They were commanded by Colonel Magnan, who had disobeyed General Nogues' anti-semitic orders during the *baroud d'honneur*, but he was not too fussy over whom he recruited. They had acquitted themselves acceptably in the battle for Bizerta, and Magnan was made a *général de brigade*. [29]

Louis Dio, now colonel of the RMT, reported that they were largely left-wingers with a significant proportion of anti-fascist Spaniards who had fled to French North Africa after the Spanish Civil War. Leclerc sighed, "A toff like me commanding a bunch of reds!"[30]

Designated the RMT's 2nd Battalion commander, Massu set off in an old Renault for Djidjelli, a small seaside town north west of Constantine, to look over the new men. Their officers were Saint-Cyriens from the *Armée d'Afrique*, and the rank and file were indeed a cosmopolitan bunch: Pieds Noirs, Christians and Jews, Armenians, Moroccan muslims, *spontanément mutés* from the Legion and La Coloniale, a considerable number of left wing Spaniards, Tunisian Italians opposed to Mussolini's fascist régime, Corsicans anxious to end Italian Fascist occupation of their island, *évadés* from France who had spent time in Spanish jails, and Algerians who naively believed that, by fighting for French freedom, they would free themselves. In the main they seemed to share a desire to wear de Gaulle's Cross of Lorraine.

The 3rd Battalion's colonel was Spanish Civil War veteran Joseph Putz, a former colonel in the International Brigades and unashamedly left wing; one of his companies, the 9e, consisted almost entirely of Spanish republicans. Raymond Dronne found himself appointed the 9e's commander.

According to French Army regulations, Massu had to surrender command of the 2nd Battalion to Commandant Signard from the *Corps Franc d'Afrique* because Signard was senior, even though markedly less fit. The amalgamated regiment slept under canvas at M'Zair, near Djidjelli, sharing messing facilities. They sang the same songs. A new training programme taught commanders who worked best with whom. The first American vehicles to arrive were Jeeps which the RMT test-drove on desert roads and hilly goat tracks. Then, on 2nd October, Commandant Signard announced to Massu that he was resigning. His sight had worsened since the Tunisian campaign. Regaining command of 2/RMT, Massu led its training through the autumn while the men's imaginations ran riot over what their next mission would be.

An unfortunate spate of training accidents occurred. First, a mishap during grenade training put Captain Fonde and Lts Don José and Salbaing in hospital. Next, one of 2/RMT's company commanders, Captain de Bazelaire, and Lts Postaire and Borruat, were injured by a Hawkins mine while training in the desert. Bazelaire, a veteran *méhariste* from the Groupe Nomade de Tibesti, died in Constantine's Hopital Lavran later that day. Then another grenade accident killed Sergeant Yves Gallioux and consigned Lt Guigon and two enlisted men to the battalion infirmary.[31] Massu, emotional as only truly tough men can be, was shattered by such losses, especially Bazelaire, whom he regarded almost as a younger brother. Such tragic and pointless losses among *anciens* from Chad, the best and bravest, would continue until the end of the war. During late October the RMT was ordered to leave M'Zair for Skhriratplage in Morocco, a few miles south of Rabat.

Leclerc's staff arrived in Morocco on 12th September amid some hilarity. A story was going around that Paul de Langlade had told General Leyer he was happy to serve under Leclerc even though he was a much younger man. The comparison between Leclerc and General Giraud, for whom Leclerc always remained *Capitaine de Hauteclocque*, was obvious.

On the way west they stopped at Rio Salado, where Leclerc addressed the 12e RCA, "You are, from now on, part of the Deuxieme Division Blindée, under my command. This is the first unit in which Frenchmen, separated by circumstances for three years, find themselves reunited. I want you to reflect upon the importance of that reunion. Our country is in a situation that it has rarely known. It has become a second rank nation. We can no longer afford the luxury of internal divisions. Unity is now more important than ever to give France back her national *grandeur*!"[32]

Five days later, after stopping off at Fez and Casablanca, Leclerc and his staff reached Temara, the smithy where the 2e DB would be forged and have its home for seven months. They arrived in convoy, Leclerc driving his new command HQ, a caravan built around a British utility truck donated by General Koenig, followed by Girard and Quillichini in a Chevrolet staff car.[33] Girard found a villa on the sea front and a wooden bungalow on the opposite side of the road for an office. "You want to make me into a *bourgeois*!" joked Leclerc. "I can't work in there. Put my caravan in the garden." Commensurate with his rank he received a full complement of servants from the *Armée d'Afrique*: a chauffeur, Labarthe; a cook, Bergé; soldier servants Kempf and Mollot; two Moroccan orderlies; and Mess Sergeant Loustalot who became as faithful a friend in his way as some of the officers. Loustalot came from Biarritz and, prior to hostilities, had worked himself up to *maitre d'hotel* by the age of eighteen. This team ensured that their general's household ran smoothly.[34]

Soon after their arrival Leclerc was visited by his older brother, Guy de Hauteclocque, who had been posted to Rabat by the Vichy government before the Torch landings. Preferring not to be in his younger brother's shadow, Guy had declined the invitation to join the 2e DB even when

Leclerc told him eagerly, "You know, I've got lots of Picardians with me." Like many veterans of the first war, Guy felt an almost mystical loyalty to Pétain. Nevertheless, when Leclerc sought him out in his lodgings, Guy wisely removed the Marshal's portrait photograph.[35] Girard describes Guy as "very kind, but very different." Once again, when it came to those close to him, *ses proches*, Leclerc could forgive their Vichy past—once he had told them precisely what he thought of it.

Other visits followed from various *Armée d'Afrique* generals like Jacques de Vernejoul, CO of the new 5e DB. Intent on rebuilding bridges, Leclerc was accommodating but, at the same time, uncompromising.

Franco's Spain could see which way the wind was now blowing and, after negotiations with de Gaulle's *France Combattante* (as Free France had now become), and backed by US muscle, the Spanish authorities agreed to release 2,500 French *évadés* from their jails. On 25th September, accompanied by Spahi Nicolas Roumiantzoff and the 501e RCC's Alain de Boissieu, Leclerc went to Rabat for their welcoming ceremony.

"France has recovered her children!" declared the effulgent mayor on the be-ribbonned quayside. The band played the *Marseillaise* and an honour guard presented arms. The mayor went on to describe how the French Army had "re-begun the war in Tunisia and Algeria."

"Don't forget Bir Hakeim!" Leclerc shouted loud enough for all to hear, furious once again that a *Vichysois* functionary should air-brush over Free French achievements. He was "pushing it." But when would he push it too far?

"Well, this morning I definitely muffed my promotion prospects," he commented dourly to Girard.[36]

Many of these new *évadés* wanted only to join Leclerc. By then he had become virtually the second most popular man in France after de Gaulle himself. For getting first pick of these young men, Leclerc's cantonments outside Rabat were well placed. So long as these young men did not sign up with another unit first there was no problem; they were free to vote with their feet. The fledgling 2e DB was the most *chic* unit and its regiments had the best recruiting drives. Things grew tricky when recruits found themselves inveigled towards Giraudist units and changed their minds after induction. On the afternoon of 25th September, Girard found seven teenagers, claiming to be on leave from a unit based at Oujda, walking onto the Temara base begging to join the 2e DB. Their leave permits were due to expire that evening. They said the atmosphere in their unit was appalling: there were no weapons, therefore nothing to do but fatigues, and anyway they were Gaullists. Close to tears, the three youngest said they had always wanted to join Leclerc but had been prevented from doing so. Girard sympathised but he had to insist that the 2e DB was part of a unified and disciplined French Army and there was nothing he could do but send them back.

Treading a narrow path between keeping the Cross of Lorraine flying and open insolence to the *Armée d'Afrique*'s heirarchy, Leclerc could not resist another opportunity three days later. As divisional commander to Colonel Rémy's Spahis Marocains he attended a reception in Casablanca organised by the so-called *Comité de Bir Hakeim*, since the Spahis had been part of Koenig's brigade. Stepping up to the microphone, once again he put his Gaullist boot into the *Vichysois*.

"*Mesdames et Messieurs*, I have agreed to say a few words, given the welcome that you have shown me. This welcome reminds me of the one I received three years ago in French Equatorial Africa, in the Cameroons when they rallied to de Gaulle." He waited for the applause to die down. "Those countries decided to continue the fight. It is thanks to those efforts and the cooperation of all, civil and military, that we were able to take part in the Liberation of North Africa. So, what I want from the civilians of North Africa is that they help the French Army in the same way! This time we are going to liberate the mother country!"

"The army of Giraud, is the army of Vichy, *exactement,*" he told Girard later.[37]

Given that many soldiers under Giraud's command were now wearing gallantry medals for resisting the Torch landings, Leclerc had a point.

Of the original Free French units making up the 2e DB, Colonel Rémy's Spahis Marocains provided the cavalry with an aggressive Gaullist esprit.[38] Langlade's 12e RCA would be the acid test of whether Leclerc could give the 2e DB a viable *esprit de corps*. As usual, badges and flags were important. Leclerc and Langlade agreed in the beginning that the Chasseurs should carry the divisional symbol of a white "map of France" on a blue background without the Cross of Lorraine superimposed in blue upon it.[39]

Nevertheless some crews were painting the Cross of Lorraine on their Crusader tanks on their own volition. On uniforms, the Chasseurs d'Afrique regimental badge of a prancing horse over a map of Africa with the motto *"Audace n'est pas déraison"*[40] remained as before.

Langlade was also involved in forming the third tank regiment in the 2e DB. His 12e RCA numbered 2,000 men, enough personnel for two American tank regiments, so he divided the regiment in two. The second half became the 12e Cuirassiers, a regiment which had been in suspended animation since 1940, and took the old 12e Cuirassiers' badge of a dolphin with the device *Pericula Ludus*[41]—"danger is my pleasure." Under officers like Colonel Noiret and commandants Warabiot and Rouvillois, the 12e Cuirassiers would rekindle the traditions of Metropolitan cavalry regiments and started the process in Morocco where they received the equipment, so lacking in 1940, with which to liberate their homeland.

The 501e RCC was the most Gaullist and socially diverse. Formed around the *Première Compagnie des chars de combat* which had served with the Eighth Army, it contained three companies: the first came from the Levant; the second came from British Nigeria (a collecting point for Frenchmen in Vichy-controlled Africa who opted for de Gaulle); and the third was made up of *évadés* from Great Britain. Officers like captains Jacques de Witasse, Georges Buis and Jacques Branet constitued a *soviet* as recognisable as the strength of their Gaullist views. Leclerc nicknamed Branet a "Russian" since he had reached de Gaulle after escaping from a German prison camp, crossing occupied Poland to the Soviet Union where he was interned until the German invasion Afterward, the release of French internees was negotiated by the British Ambassador, Sir Stafford Cripps. The group which subsequently sailed up the Clyde aboard the *Empress of Canada* on 8th September 1941 included not only future 2e DB officers Jacques Branet, Pierre Billotte, Alain de Boissieu and Jean de Person but also Jean-Louis Crémieux-Brilhac, who joined the BBC's French Service.[42]

The 2e DB's three tactical groups (or *groupements tactique,* GT, as the French called them) each had its own tank regiment. Colonel Rémy's Spahis Marocains would provide a reconnaissance company in each group along with one of the RMT's three battalions. Jean Crépin, who had followed Leclerc since the Cameroons, was promoted to running the division's artillery. Each GT needed an artillery regiment. These were Colonel

Fieschi's *1/3Régiment d'Artillerie Coloniale* —of Gaullist origin; Lt. Col Tranie's *64e Régiment d'Artillerie*—previously stationed in Morocco and reinforced by recruits from depots in Fez and Meknes; and the *40e Régiment d'Artillerie Nord Africain*, commanded by polytechnicien Commandant Mirambeau, which came from Constantine and was the first regiment to receive American equipment from Casablanca. Colonel Delage's *13e Génie* were the division's engineers. There were also signals and logistics cadres.

The division's medical personnel provided a feminine touch previously nonexistent in Leclerc's command. A forthright American lady, Florence Conrad, tall, elegant and white-haired, had been a nurse during the First World War and now led a group of women called *Le Groupe Rochambeau*, named after a French count who fought the British during the American War of Independence. She and Mlle Suzanne Torres, who later married Jacques Massu, commanded the division's female ambulance drivers—*les Rochambelles*. British Quakers were also allocated to the 2e DB. These were conscientious objectors willing to serve as first aid medics and stretcher-bearers in battle, in British battle dress uniform and soup-plate helmets.

Pastoral care was the province of a dozen Catholic chaplains, all bearded, under Pere Houchet from the White Fathers, an order founded in 1873 by Algiers' Archbishop Lavigerie to spread Christianity among the Tuaregs; their white habits and flowing beards were obligatory.[43] Since boyhood Leclerc's fierce Catholicism was topped up with tales of these latter-day monastic knights who administered the last rites to France's dying soldiers of empire. The White Fathers would tend the 2e DB's wounded and dying; three of them being killed in the course of their duties.

Colonel Paul Bernard, who had been Chief of Staff for all French Equatorial Africa, returned to Leclerc to head the division's staff. Leclerc's sometime shooting partner, the caustic Picardian Jacques de Guillebon, would be Bernard's assistant. Chad *ancien* and original *gonflé* Robert Quillichini would head the *1ere bureau* with Boissoudy, who had been badly injured in Syria, as his deputy. Paul Repiton-Préneuf, the *polytechnicien* and former petrol businessman who forewarned de Gaulle of the tragic fratricide in Syria in 1941, became head of the 2e DB's intelligence gathering—the *2eme bureau*. The *4eme bureau*, logistics, was run by Roger Lantenois, whose skills were already well known to Leclerc, assisted by Captain Jean

Compagnon who had been wounded outside the walls of Leclerc's own home, Tailly, during *la Chute*.[44] The *3eme bureau*, the vital operations department, had to be run by an officer with armoured experience. The only man Leclerc could find for such a role was the 12e RCA's Captain André Gribius. Willingly or otherwise, Leclerc was obliged to follow du Vigier's suggestion and give worthwhile appointments to officers from the *Armée d'Afrique*.

Command of these three American-style battlegroups—*groupements tactiques*—was given to Louis Dio (GT Dio), Paul de Langlade (GT Langlade) and Michel Malaguti (GT Malaguti), who had commanded tanks during the Battle of France. The divisional HQ was protected by a squadron of Stuart light tanks commanded by Captain Alain de Boissieu, a former pupil of Leclerc's at Saint Cyr and one of the so-called "Russians." After reaching de Gaulle, Boissieu became a roving attaché around Free France's Indian Ocean possessions, while also romancing de Gaulle's pretty daughter Elizabeth when in London. He had, however, been nagging to join Leclerc for some time, and eventually de Gaulle let him go, recognising Boissieu's disappointment at not having been part of *la Colonne* in Chad and Libya.[45]

With Paul de Langlade, known to his men as *le duc*, now a GT commander,[46] Commandant Jules Minjonnet was promoted to command the 12e RCA element of GTL, becoming a Lt. Colonel. Small, lively and always chain-smoking, Minjonnet was so concerned for his troops' welfare that he was known as *Père Mégot*.

Langlade met his fellow GT commander Louis Dio for the first time in Temara. Both were highly experienced, but there was an age difference of fifteen years between them and any number of pretexts for a major personality clash. Not least of these were Langlade's aristocratic Loire background and two years under Vichy. Their mutual good sense ensured this did not happen. For their part, Giraud's staff also had the good sense to confirm promotions made by Leclerc during the Chad years, and agreed to appoint Dio full colonel rather than lieutenant colonel.[47]

In the late summer of 1943 Henri Giraud stood on the Moroccan shore in full general's tunic, braided képi and breeches, watching Liberty ships steaming towards Casablanca's quayside laden with new equipment for the

French Army. The photographer who caught that moment rightly recognised its emotion. "Old France" was looking at the future. Marked as they left the factories of Detroit and Pittsburgh with long thin *Tricolores* for their end-users, Sherman tanks, White halftracks, Stuart light tanks, trucks and Jeeps by the thousand all smelling of factory grease and fresh paint were disgorged from each ship onto Casablanca's dockside. The old French Army "of rules, hierarchy and black sheep led by half ga-ga patriarchs"[48] that had been trashed in 1940 by the Germans was coming face to face with the arsenal of democracy. Nothing mattered now but the most effective and rapidly obtained result.

The 12e RCA's rank and file had never seen anything like the new Shermans and, some new recruits had never seen the inside of a tank before. Arthur Kaiser from Mulhouse was typical; a lively, freedom-loving young man, keen on cycle racing. Born in Alsace, he was determined to avoid conscription in the Wehrmacht, and managed to reach French North Africa before the Torch landings. His enlistment was followed by two *spontanément muté* style desertions before he finally found himself a Chasseur d'Afrique with the 2e DB in Morocco, being warned gravely by a young captain that he would be armoured crew. He was standing with four others in front of a brand new Sherman and, when the captain asked who would drive the tank, Kaiser stepped forward. All of them simply got stuck in. The following morning their troop sergeant, pleasantly surprised by their enthusiasm, left them to it. An American instructor gave him advice on changing gear, and Kaiser found he could master the 30-ton beast. His first tank was called *Vendée*, his second the *Bordelais II*.[49] Though well aware that a Sherman's armour was less thick than recent Panzer models and that its 75mm gun was half as powerful as the German 88, so the crews of the 12e RCA, 12e Cuirassiers and 501e RCC were advised to play to their tanks' advantages: speed and the Sherman's electronically powered turret.

Colonel Michel Malaguti was put in charge of the division's tank regiments, an appointment that ought to have been inspired. An experienced tank commander, Malaguti had fought during *la Chute*, but seeing his fine regiment annihilated piecemeal had scarred him deeply. He was not from the cavalry like the 12e RCA and 12e Cuir, but he was a fierce traditionalist who expected cavalry regiments to adopt the insignia of the pre-war French

Army's tank arm—the crossed cannons. To initiate a *guerre des boutons*—an argument about insignia when all personnel were trying to get on with each other was less than helpful.[50] Leclerc regarded Malaguti's stance as an unwelcome attempt to return the army to its condition in 1940.

In any case, new American uniforms hardly lent themselves to the pre-war French Army's distinctions between officers and men. The 2e DB's tank officers were not going to war in the shining leather coats and smart jodhpurs of three years before. The whole division was receiving the comfortable and classless uniform of a citizen army. This came as less of a shock to Leclerc's Chad veterans, who had received British battle dress a few months earlier. Even so, they found the US khaki shirts, herringbone twill trousers, boots, canvas spat-style gaiters and Mk 1941 combat jackets and helmets far more comfortable than the clothes supplied by the British. Chad veterans were invariably the most adaptable. Whether riding camels or stripped-down trucks, their apparel was usually devised to address needs rather than sartorial status or obscure military tradition. From Colonel Dio down to the lowliest *tirailleur,* the Chad regiment dressed the same, albeit with La Coloniale's anchor on képis and forage caps.

Massu's former *méhariste*, Lt. Gueritte, had the enormous task of introducing the new range of US equipment. He started receiving Jeeps at Djidjelli, and then White halftracks arrived. This half-track was a maid of all work, whether as personnel carrier, supply wagon, self-propelled artillery base or ambulance, the White halftrack was more than a match for the German Hanomag. The Gaullist nucleus in the division RMT resented being what the Americans called "support infantry," but that is exactly what they became. However, having handed in their eclectic mix of pre-war French, captured Italian and British small arms, they received instead Browning Automatic Rifles, Springfield rifles, M1 carbines, Thompson sub-machine guns and Colt .45 automatic pistols—all as good or better than anything they had before, and most of it was brand new. It must also be said, however, that the Americans held some things back—for example, their excellent gas-powered M1 rifle was not included in the Anfa programme, nor were later models of Shermans and Tank Destroyers.

Military cohesion is acquired through practicalities such as uniform. Once everyone was subsumed by the new American kit, living in rows of tented encampments around Temara, the differences between former Free

French and *Armée d'Afrique* troops were largely subsumed. For some the old rift between Giraudists and Gaullists still rumbled on, but former *Armée d'Afrique* officers like Langlade had the prescience to recognise what the French Army, of necessity, must become. On the other side, Massu and other original Free Frenchmen were generous enough to recognise that not everyone could simply up sticks and make their way to de Gaulle between 1940 and 1943.

Of course, many of the young soldiers now filling the 2e DB's ranks were civilians at heart, an anti-authoritarian bunch, who were obliged to join an authoritarian organisation as the only path to liberating their homeland. This meant flare-ups over discipline and respect were inevitable. On one occasion a couple of Free French originals from the 501e RCC off duty in Rabat were walking along singing a disrespectful ditty about General Giraud. Ticked off by a passing *Armée d'Afrique* officer, they simply ignored him. Frustrated, the officer belted one of them, promptly getting himself beaten up. Strictly speaking, the officer was right to protect the Commander of the French Army's good name, but he had started the fisticuffs. He was also a pompous ass, with no clue how hard-nosed Leclerc's men were by 1943.

"You are responsible for the dissatisfaction and disobedience towards you," Leclerc told the young officer. "The incident that has happened is very regrettable but I am forced to excuse it. Don't think any more that you are going to be respected just because you have *galons* on your sleeves. Earn the respect of my men, because these are soldiers who respect deeds, not mere *galons*."[51]

In the circumstances of an increasingly citizen army whose primary motivation was to liberate their homeland, Leclerc was right. Nor was it the first or last time he took this view. However, many former *Armée d'Afrique* officers were deeply disquieted.

Christian Girard spent early October 1943 arranging a reception for 2e DB officers in Temara's casino. Though tricky to organise while so much remained in a state of flux, about five hundred officers and senior NCOs were present.

"I have brought you together to tell you why you are here," said Leclerc, beginning an address which lasted twenty-five minutes.

Last summer, when General de Gaulle told me to form an armoured division, he asked me if I thought it was possible to form a solid unit with elements from diverse origins. I told him, 'Yes!' because our aim these last four years has always been to see as many French as possible return to the struggle for France.

Now, the decision to open a second front has been taken and General de Gaulle has specifically asked that the French Army should be represented, particularly by our unit. True, we still have less equipment than others and are not yet as fully trained, but, in his eyes, that is no disadvantage. He has succeeded. We have been the first to be designated to take part in the campaign of liberation. For each of us this will be a great honour. We must now rise to the occasion, to combat. The moment Frenchmen are well led and well armed they fight well. You have already shown this.

Remember that success will depend on the actions of junior officers, whether troop leaders or tank commanders.

During the liberation campaign and afterwards, we will find out if France is capable of becoming a great nation again.

Recently I met some of the people who have been involved in the Maquis. One told me about his anxiety over the lack of leaders. Another, from a resistance group of old soldiers, told me about the shortage of ordinary foot soldiers. He summed up the situation by saying 'the maquis has numbers but no leaders while the Resistance has leaders but no people.' In short, Frenchmen under the German boot still have not reached a point of refinding their unity.

Strong leadership is essential. We are lucky to have General de Gaulle. For those of you who do not know him very well, he is a patriot. Without General de Gaulle the unity of the French Empire would be no more than a memory today.

A gigantic effort is required of us and it is your duty to make this clear to your subordinates.[52]

Leclerc underlined the fundamentally Gaullist purpose of the 2e DB just as Gaullism had already stamped its mark, the Cross of Lorraine, across the towns and cities of north Africa.

Leclerc kept abreast of progress in the 2e DB's regiments by dining with their officers, and took the opportunity to iron out issues of divisional and regimental training. On one such occasion, dining with the 501e RCC, Leclerc learnt that Chad veterans Barboteu and Anselmi had been in a car crash and Anselmi was killed. Leclerc was devastated. Dying for one's country was one thing, but car accidents another. The highest priority, however, was the 2e DB showing itself "combat ready" for US military inspector General Kingman, upon which delivery of the rest of their equipment depended.

The tank regiments had their Shermans, but the 2e DB's consignment of artillery pieces had been transferred to the Italian front. Nevertheless all three GTs trained as individual battlegroups, developing tight collaboration between the tanks and motorised infantry. GT Langlade's infantry battalion was Massu's 2/RMT. Compared to the 12e RCA, Massu's officers were more experienced and rambunctious personalities, but 2/RMT got on well with Minjonnet's men as they trained in the forests around Temara. Langlade's robust sense of humour provided a wealth of anecdotes. When young Arthur Kaiser was dressed for guard duty in *Chasseur d'Afrique's* formal red sash and chéchia, Langlade inspected the guard. "Prize cream idiot of a postal chief!" he called Kaiser. "Are you trying to fool me they're protecting a camp?" On another occasion Langlade gave a junior officer two days punishment for being caught in a girl's bed with the dry comment, "This officer has picked a flower that is not destined for him."[53]

Amid the hectic training schedule, Leclerc himself worried about how the 2e DB would be used. There was talk that most of the *Armée d'Afrique*, now reforming as the French First Army under General Jean de Lattre de Tassigny, would take part in either the Italian campaign or in an amphibious landing in southern France. There was also mention that a French division would join in the cross-Channel invasion mooted for the summer of 1944. No one was sure which division would have this honour. Knowing de Gaulle had used Alain de Boissieu as a liaison officer extraordinary, and that he was courting Elizabeth de Gaulle, Leclerc invited him to join a partridge shoot in early December. In the course of the morning Leclerc briefed Boissieu to take a letter to de Gaulle explaining that the 2e DB still lacked essential artillery and he needed to know what they were preparing for.[54]

Arriving at de Gaulle's villa in Algiers' rue des Glycines, Boissieu was welcomed by his future father-in-law. De Gaulle read Leclerc's letter and told Boissieu, "You tell General Leclerc that I attach great importance to the future of his division and that, if necessary, the artillery equipment he needs will have to be taken from another unit. Regarding the regiment of Tank Destroyers, General Leclerc may have to choose from those already formed. Your division will, I firmly hope, be placed at the disposition of the Allied Command in Europe. But make clear to General Leclerc that if it so happens that I need him for another mission of national importance, he must be ready to obey my orders for that too."

For a few minutes de Gaulle ranted about the problems facing Fighting France, not least the high-handed imposition of AMGOT (Allied Military Government of Occupied Territories) which, if it got the chance, would make a nonsense of the CFLN's efforts to create a new French administration ready to slip into place the moment liberation came. Waving his massive arms, the Constable explained intently that more discussions with Eisenhower were necessary before finally he could confirm to Boissieu that "If I can obtain transport for only one division it will be Leclerc's that goes to Great Britain."[55]

Back in Temara, Leclerc was ecstatic at what Boissieu had to tell him, smiling like a schoolboy. The implication was clear: the 2e DB was earmarked for Paris. Thrilled, Leclerc ordered Boissieu back to Algiers with another letter for de Gaulle confirming that he understood what was expected of him. Not in the best of health, Boissieu took off for Algiers again. This time de Gaulle did a remarkable thing, especially since it was so far in advance of the event. Taking a sheet of paper from his bureau, he drafted by hand Leclerc's appointment as "Interim Military Governor of Paris," then he passed it to Boissieu. Momentarily back on autopilot from his days on de Gaulle's staff, Boissieu made to leave the room.

"Where do you think you're going?" barked de Gaulle.

"To get it typed up by Madame Aubert," replied Boissieu.

"I don't want any archive of this," snapped de Gaulle. "If the Americans know that I intend to use the 2e DB to re-establish the French state in Paris they will not let us go. And tell Leclerc *always* to keep that letter with him."

After yet another flight, Boissieu handed the treasured document to Leclerc and then took to his bed with a serious bout of malaria.[56]

Addressing his men at New Year's, Leclerc made no mention of Paris.

> The year 1944 will be the year of Liberation. General de Gaulle told me a few days ago that he has immense confidence in the 2e DB and I replied that the division would show itself worthy of that confidence. The objective I fixed on for those who had come up from the Congo with me three years ago was Strasbourg. My vow for 1944 is to obtain that objective.[57]

Separated from events in France by several hundred miles of ocean, the 2e DB listened to German-controlled French radio in their makeshift messing halls where the diatribes of ultra-collaborationist Philippe Henriot provided just as much amusement as Lord Haw-Haw had for the British. The majority of units got on well but there were, at the same time, individuals who became increasingly isolated. There could be several reasons for this. A pro Vichy soldier would have difficulty fitting into a regiment where the Gaullist imprint was strong. Some were patriotically French but so left-wing that, while appreciating the usefulness of American equipment, they resented having to accept it. This outlook could lead to disputes with comrades who were more realistic about Uncle Sam's largesse. Inevitably the prospect of liberating their homeland led to speculation over what postwar France would be like. Stock characters of pre-war domestic politics like Vincent Auriol and Maurice Thorez might have been dormant during the occupation but were far from forgotten.

Dennis Woodcock, an English Quaker attached to the 2e DB as a stretcher bearer, found that the overriding emotion among the 2e DB was an immense pride that they were "General Leclerc's Division." As exercises in the Moroccan hills intensified, these pacifist medical personnel became increasingly involved in the life of the division. Stopping to talk to them, Leclerc was friendly, chatting about London, of which he had grown fond during the summer of 1940.[58]

The Dodge ambulances, which Woodcock and his fellow Quakers would fill with the 2e DB's wounded, arrived shiny and new in January 1944. Neatly lined up in the car park of Rabat's Club Nautique, their female crews, the Rochambelles, began kitting them out and familiarising themselves. As they did so they were approached by Edith Vézy, a young woman in her mid-twenties, who was surprised to find that these women in new US khaki uniforms were not American but French, and attached to the new 2e DB. A trained nurse, Vézy was widowed young when her husband, a pilot in the French Air Force, was killed in a training accident. After loose-end jobs in nursing and nannying, here was something exciting and, being from Alsace like Arthur Kaiser, she felt the loss of freedom implicit in Nazi rule especially keenly. Wanting above all to contribute something to winning the war, she packed her bags with the little she had and set off for a villa called La Péniche in Bou R'Greg on the seafront, brandishing her state diploma in nursing and a driving license issued in Rabat during 1939. Warned that driving a large Dodge was not quite the same as her brother's old Ford, she was promptly put behind the wheel of one of the ambulances to see if she could drive. A quick foray around the streets of Rabat showed she could drive adequately for the Groupe Rochambeau, though she found parking something so large a little tight. Nevertheless, she was signed in straightaway and soon found herself under the command of Lt. Suzanne Torres, whose standards were high. Any of her girls who slipped up was paraded in front of everyone while Torres lectured and wagged her finger. Now dressed in American khaki, Edith Vézy spent the next three months in fitness instruction, and on courses in vehicle maintenance and first aid.[59]

The balance of the division's artillery equipment finally arrived in January. These weapons should have arrived earlier but a logistics error caused the 105mm self-propelled guns to end up in Sicily. Belatedly, divisional artillery chief Jean Crépin set up a battle school for all three artillery regiments at Camp El-Hajeb south of Meknes, with much to achieve before the whole division was expected to pass its combat readiness inspection by the Rearmament Commission's General Allen Kingman.

Where operational planning was concerned, Leclerc and Guillebon, who both had searing memories of German tactical competence in 1940, found their new operations officer, André Gribius, a kindred spirit. Orders handed out in mid-January emphasised afresh the importance of speed from the tanks and the necessity for the motorised infantry to keep up with the pace to hold the ground gained. Strenuous efforts were made to distribute these orders around the thousands of men and vehicles. Although pieces of paper passed among large groups of young men are often ignored, these were not. So when General Kingman's inspection came, over three days in mid-February 1944, the 2e DB passed. The gap in tactical thinking between France and Germany in 1940 had been closed. Leclerc was so pleased with one of his artillery battalions that he handed out his own stock of cigars to its officers.

He still lacked his anti-tank regiment which, when it arrived, would be equipped with Tank Destroyers, which mounted a more powerful 75mm gun in a fully traversing open turret on a Sherman-type chassis. This regiment's amalgamation would be the most controversial possible between a Gaullist and Vichy unit, and only de Gaulle's insistence made it palatable for Leclerc. The fact is that de Gaulle particularly chose the 2e DB to go to England to join in the main invasion because they were his favourite division and Leclerc was his favourite general. For the British and Americans, their agreement that French troops should liberate Paris was never more than notional. As far as the Americans were concerned, the 2e DB would always be under their operational command and meet battlefield exigencies decided by them. Eisenhower's staff regarded a French liberation of Paris as a "nice idea" if it could be managed, but not something that would unduly concern them. For de Gaulle, on the other hand, it was everything.

Whatever Leclerc thought about the final balance of his division's personnel, de Gaulle decided the 2e DB should represent a new unity between previously hostile factions of the French military. The service that had been the most *Vichysois* and anti-British, when Churchill was de Gaulle's only backer, was now the one he proposed Leclerc should embrace—the French Navy. After coming off worst when Churchill demonstrated British determination in the dark days of July 1940 by ordering the attack on the Mers el Kebir squadron, the French Navy gave de Gaulle his worst humiliation at Dakar when the battleship *Richelieu*'s guns pounded the British and Free French task force into retreating. In admirals Darlan and Muselier the French Navy provided the most dubious and controversial characters in both Vichy and Carlton Gardens. The French Navy had followed Admiral Darlan's orders and offered the most spirited resistance to the Torch landings while losing both men and equipment, both of which were difficult and expensive to replace.

Yet, of his original inner circle at Carlton Gardens, one of de Gaulle's most trusted officers was Admiral Thierry d'Argenlieu. He had first suggested using the Cross of Lorraine as the symbol of Free France. Those sailors who rallied to it in 1940 remained utterly loyal to de Gaulle, carrying out his orders to the letter, however controversial. The seizing of North Atlantic islands Saint Pierre and Miquelon was a Free French Navy operation which hugely annoyed the US State Department, contributing to US reluctance to accept de Gaulle as the true leader of the "Fighting French" in 1943. De Gaulle's own son, Philippe, had taken the naval officers' course devised with British cooperation. By 1944, the Free French Navy was seamlessly integrated in the Atlantic war effort.

However, for naval personnel who had been loyal to Vichy, there were not enough ships to go around, and it was these men that de Gaulle now wanted Leclerc to accept as personnel for his anti-tank artillery regiment. From the Armistice of June 1940 until the Torch landings of November 1942, the Vichy-controlled portion of the navy did very little. Sailors from Admiral Geoffroy's Alexandria squadron had gone over to the Free French in small groups, and been used as anti-aircraft gunners by British Eighth Army. But the majority, that part of the navy based in the French North African ports, which had been attacked by the British in July 1940, had remained absolutely obedient to Vichy, obeying Darlan's orders to resist the Torch landings, although invariably coming off worst.

The crew of the *Tramontane*, a torpedo destroyer of the 7th Squadron, which had been badly damaged and beached, had killed time in Oran's bars while their future was decided, discovering that between British and Americans the latter were more forgiving and happy to buy them drinks. The next thing they knew they were being formed into a battalion of *fusiliers marins*, "marine riflemen." For a young Breton *matelot* like Jean-Marie Thomas, this represented quite a turnaround. He was trained for torpedo destroyers, not as an infantryman. Nevertheless he and his friends re-mustered at Cap Matifou where his sailor's garb, except for the traditional French sailors' *bachi* hat with its red pompom, was swapped for khaki *poilu* garb. His company commander was 1st Lieutenant Guillon, former gunnery officer of *Tramontane*'s sister ship, *Tornade*, and a future admiral.[60]

Other members of the battalion had similar histories to Thomas, though they had fought the British not in North Africa but in Madagascar, and then spent six months in British prison camps alongside captured German U-boat crews. These included the battalion's commander, Captain Raymond Maggiar. His war began with fighting the Germans in the Norwegian campaign. Then, a few months after the Armistice, he found himself appointed to a former banana boat-turned auxiliary cruiser *Bougainville*, which was torpedoed by the British off Madagascar on 5th May 1942. By the time French North Africa joined the Allies, Maggiar had been incarcerated for six months alongside captured German sub-mariners. Finally realising that the only viable path to French freedom lay in following de Gaulle, Maggiar asked to be transferred to Algiers. There he knocked incessantly on French admirals' doors, particularly Admiral Lemonnier, until he was ordered to form a battalion of *fusiliers marins*.

In spite of the bitterness between Frenchmen, and between French and British, the newly formed *fusiliers marins* marched off to fight the Germans in the Tunisian campaign without rancour, having finally recognised that the only thing that counted was an Allied victory. They fought alongside the *Corps Franc d'Afrique*, and a comradely atmosphere developed between the two units. After the Allied victory in Tunisia, the *fusiliers marins* entered Bizerta acquiring the honoured title *Bataillon Bizerte*. Afterward, once again, they had nothing to do. Maggiar tried pestering the US Navy for ships, with no success. In despair he turned to the army. Predictably they said his men were a navy problem, refusing to take him seriously until he went to see General Alphonse Juin.

"Here is something that might suit you," said Juin. "How about Tank Destroyers? After all you have well-trained men, specialists. Tank Destroyers are similar to ships, ships on land."

"Yes," said Maggiar. "That will suit us very well."

The sailors of the *Bataillon Bizerte* could not believe it: from sailors to infantrymen, and now tanks! As with other French forces being re-armed by the Americans, the first vehicle most of Maggiar's men got to touch was the ubiquitous Jeep. But in September 1943 the *Bataillon Bizerte* was ordered to Hangar 14 of the vast US logistics complex developed over the previous ten months in Casablanca. Already wearing GI uniforms except, of course, for their French Navy *bachis* with red pom-poms, the *fusiliers marins,* now numbering 1,000, were introduced to their new "ships!" They formed three companies of tank destroyers, one company of reconnaissance, and a support company in what would become known as the *Régiment Blindé des Fusiliers Marins* (RBFM).

In January 1944, they drove up into the hills around Berkane in northern Morocco to familiarise themselves with their new TDs. On the firing ranges, the RBFM showed they were better gunners than the newly equipped French cavalry regiments in their Shermans. Compared to naval gunsights they found the TD gunsight somewhat basic, so Jean-Marie Thomas was sent to the naval gunnery department for forty sets of naval range-finders, which gave the RBFM a useful edge in the coming months.[61]

Leclerc, however, gave them a very different and brutally frank welcome compared to that which he had offered Paul de Langlade, and the fact that Raymond Maggiar had been his contemporary at École Saint Geneviève counted for nothing.

"Gentlemen," he said, tapping his cane upon the ground. "I have not asked for you. General de Gaulle has foisted you upon me. I have been obliged to take you, but I know what you are and what you have done. You have always defended the interests of the navy but not those of France. Now you have to change. If you can't get on with the other units in the 2e DB, I will leave you on the quayside in England and you will not land in France."[62]

Leclerc left no one in any doubt over his feelings toward the former Vichy-controlled Navy, which he thought had prolonged the war by not rallying to de Gaulle in 1940.

> You are proud to be sailors and are probably congratulating yourselves on being sent to the 2e DB. You may think your technical skill, radio and gunnery training are impressive. Disabuse yourselves. For me you have never made war. I've already got technicians, radiomen and gunnery experts in my division who have fought for three years and more. They are the ones I trust.
>
> Soon you will realise where you fit in from battle-hardened instructors. You are going to be put to work without any let up, and you will not have any rest until your training satisfies me.
>
> The minister for the Navy gave you a regimental colour in Casablanca and told you that you were the heirs of the *fusiliers*

marins of 1914–1918. I will salute your flag when you are installed in England, but I forbid you to wear the red lanyards of your ancestors until you have shown yourselves worthy of them.

"To work," he concluded, uncompromisingly.[63]

CHAPTER EIGHT

THE 2E DB IN ENGLAND

By Easter 1944, the Wehrmacht was retreating in Russia and being pushed north through Italy. However, they had halted the Allies at Monte Casino. The French Expeditionary Corps in Italy was drawn from *Armée d'Afrique* units under General Alphonse Juin, himself of *pied noir* stock, and it fought with competence and courage, especially the *goumiers* from Morocco who proved themselves ruthless and effective mountain fighters. In rear areas, however, US troops running POW stockades found the *goumiers'* practice of demanding payment for their prisoners (with an escalating tariff according to rank!) quaint to say the least.[1] Furthermore, being aware of Italian cruelty in Libya, the *goumiers* lost few opportunities to rough up any Italian they saw in uniform, even the new Italian co-belligerent forces now fighting on the Allied side. Multiple rapes followed, and eventually the Pope intervened.

Fiercely Catholic, Leclerc hated to think of the French Army being reprimanded by the Papacy, even though he retained fond memories of his time as a *goum* commander. In Leclerc's view such men needed firm discipline, so he had little respect for the *Armée d'Afrique* in Italy, nor for General de Lattre de Tassigny's First Army earmarked for "Operation Dragoon," the invasion of southern France.

Though several years senior to Leclerc and similarly educated at

"Ginette," Jean de Lattre de Tassigny had been a brave cavalry officer in the First World War, and one of the few French divisional commanders to cause the Wehrmacht serious problems in 1940. Loyal to Vichy from 1940 to 1942, de Lattre attempted to resist the German occupation of the "Free Zone," only to be arrested for his pains. Subsequently assisted in escaping by his beautiful, much younger and fiercely proud wife, de Lattre reached French North Africa. Nevertheless, much to Madame de Lattre's chagrin, it was the 2e DB, with its core of *Gaullistes de première heure,* who got the most publicity.[2]

In Morocco, Good Friday was a day of brilliant sunshine. Colonel Louis Dio paraded the whole RMT before General de Gaulle. Among them were the *fidèles,* those who had followed de Gaulle since the darkest early days of Free France. There was some emotion as he walked among their ranks. If they were envious of Juin's men in Italy, or perplexed by ten months of inactivity, their purpose soon became clear. That evening, 2e DB officers assembled in Temara's casino where, looking tired and drawn, de Gaulle announced their imminent departure for England. Both they and their general were ecstatic.[3]

Under their movement orders, the division would be split into two echelons. The first, under Langlade, consisting of most heavy equipment— tanks, TDs, self-propelled artillery and halftracks, totalling over a thousand tracked vehicles and 3,000 men. These would embark at Casablanca on 16 LSTs (Landing Ship Tank), which were returning to Great Britain from Anzio. The second echelon, consisting of the balance of the division's vehicles and men, would drive to the dispersal park at Oran and depart a few days later under Dio. A small rear party under Colonel Malaguti would remain at Temara a few days longer to effect the division's final pull-out.

Amid Girard's dismantling of divisional HQ, Leclerc held a small Easter lunch party with René Pleven as guest. After a sumptuous meal of fish followed by pigeon, the packing of boxes and cases continued.[4]

Soldiers on leave were recalled from all over French North Africa. These were mainly Crépin's artillerymen, whose training had dragged on owing to late delivery of their equipment. The newly created RBFM had still not received all their Tank Destroyers; the balance would be taken from de Lattre's army.[5]

On the drive to Casablanca, the 2e DB's Shermans inevitably drew attention. Two days later, Radio Stuttgart announced the departure for England of a French armoured division, though the Germans believed it was du Vigier's 1ère DB.[6]

Nearing the quayside, their arrival had to be staged over the last two kilometres before embarking on the LSTs, "these modern Trojan horses." Langlade controlled embarkation from a cabin on the damaged battleship *Jean Bart*, which was moored further along the dock. Since they were embarking at a friendly port the LSTs were cram-packed. Vehicles and personnel of different units were mixed, so that if any ship was sunk losses would be spread across all units rather than crippling one. An additional advantage was that different regiments got to know each other during the journey.[7]

Leclerc arrived in Casablanca on 10th April, not least to ensure that his command caravan was loaded properly. The following day Girard finally closed down the villa, locked it up and handed over the key. As he got into the car, Leclerc gave him a hearty slap on the thigh. Another stage in the recovery of French arms was over.

Since the ships were returning from Anzio, the only food on board was baked beans and vitamin-fortified chocolate. The first echelon's journey took place during an Atlantic gale, euphemistically called a "fresh breeze" or "touch of wind" by British sailors. The convoy cruised at the pace of the slowest vessel, protected by escort destroyers, and the LSTs rolled abominably in the swell, sometimes creaking so loudly they seemed about to break up. The weather made everyone feel miserable, but by the sixth day the sea calmed. Langlade went on deck to take the view. To all points of the compass were ships, probably about three hundred in all, including aircraft carriers from which Grumman Hellcats took off to patrol the skies.

On the liner-turned troopship *Capetown Castle*, the division's artillery chief, Colonel Crépin, gave gunnery instruction to officers of the RBFM, while the 12e Cuir's Colonel Noiret taught them the finer points of tank manouevre.[8]

The Royal Navy gave the strictest instructions that nothing was to be thrown overboard in case it was picked up by a U-boat or Spanish trawler. Smoking on deck after dark was forbidden; any soldier caught having a quick fag on the rail before turning in at night was slammed in the brig. Once past Cape Trafalgar the convoy turned north on course for Swansea and Liverpool.

At 3pm on Monday, 17th April, Guillebon telephoned Girard at Rabat's Hotel Majestic, confirming that Leclerc's staff had seats on a converted Liberator bomber later that evening. After spending their last hours in Morocco visiting Madame de Boissoudy, Leclerc and Girard joined Guillebon, Weil, Gamet, Renaud and Lavergne for a last dinner in the Air France mess. At 9pm, with everyone in excellent spirits, they boarded the Liberator and took off into the warm night. After a brief halt for breakfast at Prestwick in Scotland, they arrived in London the following morning and went straight to 4 Carlton Gardens, where Leclerc had first presented himself as a captain to de Gaulle nearly four years earlier. Rooms had been booked for them at the Berkeley, and that evening Leclerc dined with General Koenig while Girard looked up an old girlfriend to take to the Savoy grill.

The 2e DB staff were given an office next to General Koenig's with three telephones and a dictaphone. "This is serious," said Weil, impressed. Leclerc was highly amused, walking round the room like a child with new toys, opening empty draws and folders.

"What do these people do all day?" Leclerc exclaimed.

Since the Free French establishment had evolved into the CFLN based in Algiers, 4 Carlton Gardens was not the bustling hive it had been in July 1940.

Leclerc now had to join the 2e DB into the Allied Expeditionary Force without losing French identity. Girard was tasked to arrange divisional badges, a process impeded by officialdom's belief that the division was still in Morocco. Luckily Girard found a *helpful*[9] Englishman and "helpful" entered the divison's argot.

For five days Leclerc's staff gathered details of the 2e DB's cantonments in Yorkshire; places such as Dalton Hall, home of the Hotham family, Sledmere, Wetwang and Fimber Station. To reach these places the 2e DB had to drive three hundred miles from Liverpool and Swansea through the narrow lanes of rural England.

On the afternoon of 23rd April, Langlade's convoy docked at Swansea to find Leclerc and Girard waiting on the quayside. Spotting Langlade and Verdier at the top of a gangway amid the smoke and Welsh drizzle, Girard went up the gangplank and handed them a package containing £500 cash for expenses. The head of "movement control" in Swansea, Colonel Bevan, was sympathetic and *helpful.*

"It's always the same thing," Leclerc observed to Girard. "Once you get down to the minor staff officials, among those who have to do the work, everything becomes easier, because they speak the same language. They are busy, the telephone rings non-stop. They understand and are friendly and put themselves out for you. But as soon as you have to deal with big heads, one finds them sententious, they understand nothing and hand out inexecutable orders."[10]

British "movement control" was an *ad hoc* organisation that transcended regional military divisions such as North, South, Eastern and Western Commands, and designated which routes, whether roads or rail, military traffic should take to their camps. Most tracked vehicles would go to Yorkshire by rail, but there were still 240 tanks that would have to be driven along winding country roads by their crews, some of whom were still inexperienced. Another problem, which they had had since Casablanca, was the lack of tank breakdown support. Langlade discussed this with Leclerc and they both got on the phone to the British and Americans, and were passed back and forth until finally Captain Renaud, by sheer force of personality, managed to get assistance from a British service corps unit.[11]

Most of the 2e DB could not speak English so the British Quaker medics were very useful. They were dropped off at difficult junctions to act as traffic police, but there were not enough of them, and some tanks still got lost. One troop ended up in a Welsh village where no one understood them, but they all got on famously.[12] By 6th May, 237 out of 240 tanks had reached the divisional cantonments in Yorkshire. Fatalities, however, are sadly inevitable when moving large numbers of soldiers and equipment. A TD of the RBFM drove into a house on a tight bend in a village, killing both commander and driver, and a tank commander of the 12e Cuir' was thrown from the turret of his Sherman.

Arthur Kaiser of the 12e RCA travelled to Yorkshire in a first-class rail carriage, a far cry from the travelling conditions he had experienced in

French North Africa. Arriving at Wetwang, the tankers found themselves given large tents with duckboard floors and a warm Yorkshire welcome.[13] For men such as Émil Fray of the 501e RCC and other original Gaullists, without news of their families for four years, being welcomed into British homes meant the world.[14]

The advance element of the RMT found itself at Fimber Station, a large area north of Hull also being used by General Maczek's 1st Polish Armoured Division and the British Guards Armoured Division. The RMT was generously befriended by the Irish Guards' tank group, which five months later would earn fame in Operation Market Garden. Most of the Irish Guards were volunteers from Eire, a neutral country, and they found a great rapport with the Chad veterans and oddballs of the Corps Franc d'Afrique, and the whisky flowed.[15]

While his men settled into their Yorkshire training ground, Leclerc introduced himself to the Allied commanders with whom he would work. On Friday, 28th April, accompanied by Girard, Leclerc set off to meet US General George Patton at a country house near Hull. Patton, ever the prima-donna, greeted them on the steps wearing riding breeches, shining knee boots, ivory handled revolvers and a polished helmet with three stars—the rig for which he was famous. Leclerc inspected a guard of honour while the band thumped out tunes by Souza. Girard, finding the display somewhat excessive, had to suppress the desire to laugh.

The lunch which followed began with soup, after which Patton plunged straight into bread and jam. No sooner had Leclerc and Girard followed their host's example than roast chicken and a gammon joint arrived. In spite of Patton's eccentricities and language difficulties, the atmosphere was relaxed and friendly. Patton regaled Leclerc in French about his time at Saumur before the First World War, and the two men shared anecdotes about North Africa. At this time Patton was playing a role designated by Allied intelligence, pretending to be head of the fictitious First United States Army Group (FUSAG), a *ruse de guerre* aimed at fooling the Germans that the main allied landing would be in the Pas de Calais. Despite his immense tactical skill, Patton's outspoken nature had caused a series of political gaffes ranging from slapping a shell-shocked soldier in a field hospital to his most recent declaration to the women of Knutsford that

Britain and America were destined to rule the world (taken at the time as an insult to Russia). Whatever diplomatic skills Eisenhower demanded of senior commanders, Leclerc's own record of pithy directness made him sympathetic to Patton. According to Girard the two men got on well.

Settling into their cantonment near Wetwang, the men of the 12e RCA were becoming strong Anglophiles. They were given so much food they hardly touched their rations, and there was plenty of butter and sugar on mess tables. The 12e RCA and 12e Cuir's move went best.[16] On the other hand, Massu and his men were still camped out among the rough slopes of Assi ben Okba in Morocco with sand blowing into everything they owned, awaiting their turn at the quayside. They had few amusements save swimming, but the sight of *Les Rochambelles* doing their morning exercises was not to be underrated. It was the 20th May before the *Capetown Castle* and *Franconia* re-docked at Mers el Kebir to take the last of the division to England. Life aboard these former liners was a pleasant dream compared to Saharan wind and dust, and food was plentiful. The Frenchmen found coloured blancmanges quite appalling, but the fare was undoubtedly better than the baked beans offered the first echelon.

Many *Rochambelles* took the cruise as a last chance to snatch civilian comforts. Edith Vézy snuck into her bunk wearing cozy pyjamas rather than US issue. As she nodded off she felt a hand under her blankets confirming her unofficial attire. "Edith, you have eight days until we arrive," said Florence Conrad. "If you cannot accept military discipline you will have to join the Russian ballet!"[17] Amidst the splendour of *Capetown Castle*'s reception rooms, with its staff in white jackets and gloves, there were few quiet corners, and Florence Conrad's nurses were young women in a sea of young Frenchmen at war and far from home. Inevitably, romances blossomed.

Franconia was first to enter the Clyde estuary, sailing past the grey silhouettes of Royal Navy battleships such as *Rodney* and *Nelson*. Everyone knew that the invasion of Normandy was imminent, though they could not have known that it was only a week away.

After disembarkation, they took ten hours to reach Yorkshire by road, where they found they could eat more plentiful US Army rations. The

RMT were not parade ground soldiers but men joined together by their determination to carry out a specific task: the liberation of their homeland. All of them—French, *pieds noirs*, Algerian, Moroccan—found themselves warmly welcomed by the English; all that is except their regimental mascot, a young wild boar called "Jules" who had developed a taste for US Army chocolate mousse.[18] Agricultural inspectors said he had to go.

Throughout May, Leclerc, usually accompanied by Girard or Guillebon, attended a series of meetings with senior figures, lunching with George Mercer Nairne, his former British liaison officer, the future French Prime Minister Maurice Schumann, the longstanding anti-Nazi Sir Robert Van-sittart, and the Allied generalissimo, Eisenhower himself. Much was discussed at these gatherings about life in occupied France; resistance activity, executions and the deportation of Jews. Leclerc was horrified by the reign of terror inflicted on their countrymen by both Germans and the *Milice*, a French fascist para-military organisation formed in January 1943 by the extreme right-winger Joseph Darnand.

Finishing off a day spent visiting southern assembly areas, Leclerc and Guillebon stopped off at a country pub frequented by RAF pilots. Entering the saloon bar they saw two young men wearing raffish mutations of an *Armée de l'Air* uniforms, washing down fried eggs and bacon with pints of Guinness. Guillebon surveyed the two men. "Are you French?" he asked. "Has no one taught you to greet a superior officer and salute? Haven't you noticed there's a French general behind you? Go and pay your respects to him?"

"Right now, *mon ami*, stand up straight!" said Leclerc.

The pilots stood up. Though barely in their twenties they wore several medal ribbons, and one of them sported a luridly decorated silk scarf.

"And what's this around your neck?" asked Leclerc. "You want to look like a dancing girl instead of a French officer? Then why not stick a feather in your arse?"

The pilot was Jacques Remlinger, who would later be involved in shooting up Rommel's motorcade with 602 Spitfire Squadron. His friend was fighter ace Pierre Clostermann.[19]

For the two months he stayed in Yorkshire, Leclerc's HQ was at Dalton

Hall near Beverley, on the estate of the 7th Baron Hotham. Lord Hotham was then a Lt. Colonel of a reserve artillery regiment, as well as being the area's quartering officer. Having moved into the south wing of his home in 1942, he was becoming used to upheavals; nevertheless the 2e DB are fondly remembered by his son, the present Lord Hotham, for being "user friendly."

Leclerc and Girard were met on the doorstep by André Gribius and ushered down a long corridor to take tea with their host. On such occasions Girard could not help noticing how Leclerc played the simple soldier when it suited him, though he was far from unsophisticated.[20] It was obviously an awkward situation for a young general and second son of a papal count, whose own estate was under German occupation, to meet a British peer who was a considerably greater landowner, three years older than himself, and whose home he was taking over.[21]

Lord Hotham's dining table was capable of seating over twenty. Leclerc often had at least fifteen officers dining who had to listen to him pontificating endlessly about the war and drinking nothing but water. Dio, when he first saw the Georgian *grand luxe* into which Leclerc had moved, returned immediately to his own quarters and telephoned back to tell Leclerc it was unacceptable while his men were under canvas. Leclerc's response is not recorded. In fact, many buildings in the area, domestic and agricultural, were made available to the 2e DB, including Dalton Hall's stable block.

Leclerc made the most of Lord Hotham's home, retiring to the library to read the few French classics available, such as Rousseau and Voltaire,[22] while Bagneux and Gribius took to the Grotrian Steinweg piano in the red drawing room to play four-handed duets such as *J'attendrai* and *Clair de Lune*. From time to time Leclerc would appear frostily and demand to speak to one of them, leaving the others looking worried and apprehensive.

Alain de Boissieu's HQ protection squadron was billeted in the nearby village of Etton, while Paul de Langlade was allocated rooms in another stately pile nearby, where the titled owner was grumpy and unwelcoming.[23] Nevertheless, Langlade made sure his men accepted any hospitality offered by "Friends of the French Volunteers" and other well meaning British organisations. His own evenings, those not shared with Leclerc at Dalton Hall, were spent playing country house games like "sardines" with his officers.

Entertainment was another instance where American largesse proved unending. The division received a telegram from the US High Command asking if they needed musical instruments for a band, which provided an unexpected discussion point over the dinner table. For most of the 2e DB, the biggest boost to morale was finding themselves sufficiently well paid to enjoy evenings out and go on jaunts. Restaurants functioned, though subject to rationing, and better fare could be found on American bases. There were cinemas, theatres, music halls, barn dances and village hops. Getting rides on Yorkshire's buses and taxis was the problem. When Arthur Kaiser and his tank crew asked a local taxi owner to drive them around, he declined due to lack of petrol. Kaiser and Co. offered him twenty litres from their Sherman's reserve tank and another twenty litres as a "thank you." The Yorkshireman still refused and gave them a lecture on duty, patriotism and the improper use of war supplies.[24]

Trips into Yorkshire's towns were mostly happy, carefree affairs. On a few occasions there was indiscipline and misunderstandings with the locals. Captain Gui de Schompré, from Repiton-Préneuf's intelligence staff, knew something of English law and was once sent into Hull to represent a couple of *fusiliers marins* who had been hauled before the local magistrate for disorderliness. Schompré got them off their charges.[25]

Then there was the natural desire of fit young men for the opposite sex. The British took a practical, unmoralising view of this, placing "prophylactic stations" near divisional cantonments where "French Letters," known as *capotes anglaises*, and treatment for STDs could be acquired. By contrast Leclerc, faithfully married and devout, was concerned that the local women were seducing his men.

"Bernard, I have already told you that I do not wish to see any more women around the division's encampments," Leclerc told his chief of staff over dinner at Dalton Hall.

Père Fouquet of the White Fathers intervened.

"*Mon général*, leave Bernard to get on with his work, no one's going to change anything."[26]

While it could never be said that Leclerc was rugged in the same way as Coloniale career officers like Dio or Massu, the Hotham family's abiding memory of him was that he was "very austere." Perhaps they detected the traditional difference between a French courtier and a *gentilhomme fesses-*

lièvre, a "gentleman-harebuttocks!" Leclerc did allow himself seasonal country pursuits, which at that time of year only meant some riding. Several local stables hired out horses to 2e DB officers, but the only officer with access to any kind of normal home life was Gui de Schompré, who brought his wife, Eveline, and their children from Morocco and was allocated a garden cottage by Lord Hotham.[27]

In the south of England, D-Day preparations continued apace. Churchill—though aware that Leclerc's division would not land until the bridgehead was well established— asked Eisenhower specifically to ensure any deficiencies in the 2e DB's equipment were made good from US resources. In his war memoirs Churchill covers the 2e DB at some length compared to other formations, thereby demonstrating the kindly interest he still took in Free French affairs. But, owing to a disagreement over diplomatic codes with the British and Americans, de Gaulle remained in French North Africa until June.

Arriving back in Britain on 4th June, de Gaulle met Churchill on his personal train at Portsmouth. The Frenchman was angry that Allied troops had been issued currency for use in liberated France that had not been recognised by his CFLN, the French Council for National Liberation. Such Anglo-American high-handedness, with the spectre of how AMGOT (Allied Military Government of Occupied Territories) would act, once again undermined efforts by the French civil resistance to prepare a new administration. Sharing a bottle of champagne with de Gaulle, Churchill gave him the facts of life about the Atlantic partnership: ". . . every time I have to choose between you and Roosevelt, I shall always choose Roosevelt."[28]

For two days, de Gaulle struggled to keep his temper. As far as Eisenhower was concerned he was commanding a force drawn from many nations, and the French Army was under his orders. He had drafted his own address to the French people and was tactful enough to show it to de Gaulle and ask him if the invasion should be postponed due to poor weather conditions. De Gaulle advised that further delays would be demoralising and endanger security. The 5th and 6th of June provided the best opportunities. Cloud cover was too dense for the airborne aspect of the operation on the night of the 4th and 5th, so it had to be the 6th, even though the weather was not ideal.

Eisenhower made the decision. Two hundred thousand men and all the modern equipment that the Anglo-Saxon world could produce were hurled at the Normandy coast.

De Gaulle spent that night talking to his son, Philippe, who would shortly be joining the RBFM in Yorkshire. The following afternoon he went on the radio.

> The supreme battle has begun! It is the battle in France, it is the battle of France, and France is going to fight this battle furiously. She is going to conduct it in due order. The clear, the sacred duty of the sons of France, wherever they are and whoever they are, is to fight the enemy with all the means at their disposal.
>
> The orders given by the French government and by the French leaders it has named for that purpose must be obeyed exactly. The actions we carry out in the enemy's rear must be coordinated as closely as possible with those carried out at the same time by the Allied and French armies. Let no one capable of action, either by arms, or by destruction, or by giving intelligence, or by refusing to do work useful to the enemy, allow themselves to be made prisoner. They must remove themselves beforehand from danger of being seized or being deported.
>
> The battle of France has begun! In the nation, the Empire and the armies there is no longer anything but one single hope, the same for all. Behind the awful cloud of our blood and our tears, the sun of our grandeur is shining once again![29]

Churchill listened from the Cabinet Room with tears running down his cheeks. General Ismay, who had also been privy to the fortunes of "Free France" from the very beginning, sat motionless.

"You great tub of lard," said Churchill. "Have you no emotion?"

Leclerc's staff heard about the landings at 9am and gathered round their radio. They were interested that operations centred around the Seine estuary, though the broadcast also referred to Calais and Dunkirk. These announcements were no prank of the type played on the 12e RCA a few days earlier.[30] This was the real thing. To a man the 2e DB exploded with joy. Some were invited into private homes to hear the news unfold while their Yorkshire hosts passed cups of tea.

"The battle of France has started," Leclerc wrote Pauline Vanier. "I have no illusions that we will rediscover France somewhat damaged, but anything is preferable to Nazi slavery. Regarding my family I have complete trust in Providence. I would be so proud to see my eldest son take part in the fight. Perhaps he is in the *maquis*."[31]

Aware of the longstanding rift between de Gaulle and Roosevelt, and worried that de Gaulle was now more interested in the interior resistance, Leclerc approached Montgomery's Chief of Staff, General de Guingand, requesting to be placed under British command again. In fact, plans were now too far advanced for this. In any case, dining with de Gaulle on 11th June, Leclerc found him more optimistic than expected. The smooth takeover by new Gaullist prefects in newly liberated *départments* arranged by Michel Debré, which rendered AMGOT superfluous, was the cause. Even so, de Gaulle failed to mention the division's future role, and Leclerc was left wondering whether perhaps the document drafted in front of Boissieu might have been a whim.

"Aren't we going to be used in the end?" Leclerc moaned to Girard.

The men continued to train hard as the days passed. As part of Patton's command the 2e DB had to meet US standards. No allowances would be made for their being the Allied Expeditionary Force's only French armoured division and therefore carrying a unique political significance. Patton knew the 2e DB expected to make its way to Paris, but if they were not up to standard he was more than prepared to take a "to Hell with that!" attitude.[32]

Exercises in late May had shown that the 2e DB needed improvement in tank gunnery. Whereas in Morocco they had trained with machine gun tracer, Anglo-American battle schools set up for D-Day were more realistic, and the 2e DB's gunnery was at the bottom of the league.[33] Furthermore when Patton inspected the 2e DB, their guard of honour consisted of young, fresh-faced Corsicans who had lied about their age.

"Are you planning on going to war with these choirboys?" Patton asked Leclerc in astonishment.

Leclerc was furious that his division might be back-termed for further training and miss the chance at Paris. Although closest to Girard and Guillebon, Leclerc ventilated his frustration once more in front of de Gaulle's *émissaire extraordinaire*, Alain de Boissieu. After consultations with other officers it became clear to Leclerc that the underlying difficulty was training to become part of another army and understanding the operational psyche of that army. The Americans emphasised speed—a fact reflected in their tank design. When a French liaison mission returned from US 5th Armoured Division, the tank crews were reorganised so that commanders and gunners were men most suited to the new objectives, and, helped by an unlimited allocation of shells from Patton, the 2e DB's tank gunnery was turned around.[34] By 12th June the Americans were satisfied, but another ten days of hard training followed.

Political unity in the division still left something to be desired. Leclerc inclined to frostiness towards the RBFM's Captain Maggiar, but since Maggiar mourned Admiral Darlan, whom many regarded as the rebuilder of the French Navy during the interwar years, this was hardly surprising. Nevertheless the Tunisian campaign had created a strong bond between the RBFM and the *Corps Franc d'Afrique*, now integrated with the RMT. Whatever Leclerc thought of the French Navy, de Gaulle did not look back, and the RBFM's highest profile recruit during the 2e DB's Yorkshire sojourn was Ensign Philippe de Gaulle. Many RBFM personnel did not welcome this, so painful were memories of lost comrades and much-loved ships sunk by the British,[35] but gradually these sailors came to realise that the Allies had had no other choice and Vichy's leaders were to blame.

Nothing united Leclerc's men more than anger felt at the single most brutal incident of the whole Nazi occupation of France: the massacre by the SS Das Reich Division at Oradour-sur-Glane, a village near Limoges. The 2e DB trained with heightened determination and, as if to mark their efforts, their divisional badges were ready: a blue and white enameled tag to be hung from the right breast pocket of every man. The outline of France with the Cross of Lorraine, wavy lines signifying the Atlantic and the Mediterranean, while blank space represented Spain and eastern neighbours. Bretons complained that the "nose" of Brittany was not prominent enough, while others regretted it had not been made in France. Even so, this badge, made by British craftsmen, gave every man a sense of belonging to the best, most modern unit in the French Army. Each badge was numbered, the lower numerals going to senior officers and the Chad veterans. No 1 went to Divry, who had joined de Gaulle as soon as he reached Britain from Norway in 1940. No 2 was reserved for de Gaulle. Leclerc gave himself No 3 while giving No 4 to Girard, because, "He has stopped me dying from hunger."

The 2e DB's last big exercise, codenamed "Kestrel," was essentially a battle school manoeuvre against General Maczek's Polish 1st Armoured Division, for whom they felt immense sympathy. Planned for three days, Kestrel began early on 26th June with Polish infantry attacking French positions, followed by a counterattack from GT Dio amid pyrotechnics let off by a phlegmatic British sapper. Both divisions were now ready for a real enemy and their hearts were not really in the simulation. Forces got muddled up and battalions mistaken for one another, so that the exercise had to be stopped, red flares bringing the Shermans to a halt. Half an hour later, a green flare set things roaring again, but it was just as muddled as before, with French Shermans and Polish Cromwells[36] driving nonchalantly through each other's positions. Leclerc did not know whether to laugh or cry. Luckily, rain stopped play. That was not all it stopped: an open-air theatrical soirée had been arranged with actors coming from Hull to perform scenes from Shakespeare in period costume. In the downpour everyone went for refreshments at Dalton Hall, and the day ended with bemused Shakespearean actors wandering among astonished French soldiers.[37]

The last day of Kestrel called for gunnery exercises and the 2e DB passed well. Patton inspected the division again, complimenting Leclerc on the improvements achieved in so short a time. Tank gunnery remained an obsession, especially since news was arriving from Normandy that Allied tanks were still no match for later marks of German Panzers or the dreaded 88mm gun. After hearing Leclerc's explanation why his division's anti-tank regiment was composed of sailors, Patton insisted on watching the RBFM shoot. They were among the best he had seen. This time the guard of honour was formed by the *Spahis Marocains*, and their flamboyant turban-like headdress and red cloaks led to so many American compliments that Colonel Rémy was smiling from ear to ear. Before lunch Leclerc presented his officers to Patton in the garden behind Dalton Hall, and Colonel

Canterel, the commander of the 501e RCC, gave Patton their regimental badge with the motto "*En tuer*"—"In killing."

The biggest occasion for the 2e DB at Dalton Hall was the divisional parade on 3rd July when most regiments received their colours. These had been embroidered with gold thread in London, and paid for by English friends of the Free French who had heard that the 2e DB lacked accoutrements that their own army took for granted. The *3e bureau* chief, André Gribius, organised the event. Many dignitaries from governments in exile, from Prince Félix of Luxembourg to the Czechoslovak minister of war, attended.

Early morning rain had given way to brilliant sunshine. De Gaulle was back in Algiers preparing for his trip to Washington, so it fell to General Koenig, the hero of Bir Hakeim, to present the standards. In cleaned and pressed US uniforms, with only their insignia and head dress to mark them out as French, the regiments formed up. Black berets with crossed cannon badges were the 501e RCC; red forage caps were Rémy's Spahis; sky blue forage caps for the 12e RCA; dark blue forage caps with white piping for the 12e Cuirassiers; dark blue with red piping and the anchor badge of La Coloniale for the RMT. The RBFM wore the same US uniforms but with their sailor hats topped by red pompoms of the French Navy, and *Marine Nationale* on their hat ribbons. The *Rochambelles*, now numbering thirty-five, were there too, parading in the below-the-knee khaki skirts of US female auxiliaries.

Koenig's aircraft landed on Dalton Hall's main drive and taxied to a halt, watched by Henry Hotham and his younger brother who had been scrumping fruit with their old chauffeur's grandchildren. Realising something important was unfolding they ran to the gravelled forecourt from where they watched the parade.[38] Koenig, looking impeccably smart, presented the standards to the Régiment de Marche des Spahis Marocains, formerly with his 1st French Division in the desert, and the Régiment de Marche du Tchad, representing the original Gaullist parts of the 2e DB. The 12e Régiment des Chasseurs d'Afrique, 501e Régiment des Chars de Combat, 12e Cuirassiers and the 13e Bataillon du Génie (engineers) also received their standards. Each one was blessed by the divisional chaplain, Pere Houchet of the White Fathers. A march past followed, which was not as impeccable as it might have been in peacetime, but those who witnessed it, from Leclerc's staff to senior Free French from London such as Admiral d'Argenlieu, Colonel Noiret, Vallin, General Sicé and the owner of Dalton Hall, Lord Hotham, found the occasion very moving.[39]

An American officer called Garretson, ADC to General Cook, took Girard to one side afterwards and remarked how much the French officers had to say about their experiences in 1940 and North Africa, "They think they will not be used, but they are wrong. They will be used and perhaps a great deal more than they think. We only want one thing, to be behind you when you enter Paris. You will be the first to return. We promise."

Once Koenig had left, Leclerc managed to grab a bite to eat before thanking Gribius for organising such an excellent parade. Girard wandered quietly through the ground floor of the Georgian mansion, eventually finding Guillebon sitting silently in the drawing room, staring out over the sunken rose garden towards the big lawn. Usually taciturn and unemotional, often dry and sarcastic in his humour, Guillebon quietly told the young ADC, "I have complete faith in this division."[40]

However, a clash was brewing among the 2e DB's senior officers which Leclerc could not allow to fester. The 2e DB was formed on the American model of three battlegroups consisting of a tank regiment and support elements of infantry, artillery and anti-tank: the results of American evaluation of tank methods by officers such as General Chaffee. Colonel Michel Malaguti, who had bad memories of his tanks being destroyed in 1940, believed the 2e DB's tanks should operate together, even telling Leclerc he was too inexperienced to contradict him. However, the idea of returning tanks to infantry support was never considered by late-war Allied commanders, as equally the existence of powerful anti-tank weapons like the German 88mm gun meant that there was no question of tanks being sent into action *en masse* with no support like Marshal Ney's cavalry at Waterloo. Leclerc had no intention of taking a different view. Malaguti also failed to understand how the French Army needed to change, as earlier disagreements at Temara had demonstrated. Nor did he realise that the 2e DB could hardly sing from a different tactical hymn sheet than the US Army into which it was integrated, and who were, incidentally, also their pay and quartermasters.

Worst of all, Malaguti had been so discourteous to Leclerc that it became clear the 2e DB was not big enough for both of them. Leclerc hated this sort of discord. He felt that the days when he had to chew-out soldiers on an individual basis should be in the past. He would often ask Girard to sort out discipline, forgetting that his ADC was only a lieutenant enlisted for the duration of hostilities, whose real career plans were with the French diplomatic service.

Pre-embarkation tension affected everyone. On Sunday 9th July, Leclerc went up to London for a few days, accompanied by Girard, to get away from the heavy atmosphere at Dalton Hall. They stayed at the Berkeley Hotel and spent the following morning in shops around Piccadilly and Savile Row. De Gaulle was particular about turn-out, and the days when Leclerc and his men could drive out of the desert dressed like raggamuffins were over. When he returned to France, Leclerc wanted to look like what he was, a French general commanding his army's most modern division. Being a good shot, Leclerc could not resist visiting gun-makers Holland and Holland, then at 98 New Bond Street, spending a long time looking over their exquisitely engraved shotguns.[41] Settling on a gun, he tried it against his shoulder while guessing with Girard the height and arm length of his eldest son Henri. Leclerc wanted the safety catch adjusted a little, but otherwise it was fine.

"And what about engraved initials, *Monsieur le général?*" Asked the gun-maker's assistant.

Engraved initials? But which? How could Leclerc explain the French tradition of renaming oneself for the priesthood, the stage, the Foreign Legion, or simply to protect one's family, to a London gunsmith?

"Leave the initials till later," he replied.[42]

Back at Dalton Hall that evening, Leclerc steeled himself to act. He informed Girard that he wished to see Malaguti at 9pm, followed by Cantarel, CO of the 501e RCC, at 10pm. In the meantime, there were celebrations, since Bernard had been promoted full colonel. Arriving as ordered at the big house Malaguti spent an inconclusive and confusing half-hour with Leclerc, after which he joined Bernard's celebrations. Leclerc felt it just was not the moment to metaphorically "behead" a man because his personality was too big for the role he played. He decided to place the matter in de Gaulle's hands.[43] Three days later, Leclerc received a letter from Koenig appealing to his military sentiments: Malaguti was undeniably a brave, patriotic and experienced officer. Discussing the matter closely with Girard, Leclerc felt he was being cruel, but by morning his thoughts had crystalised and the inner turmoil was over. Malaguti had to go. Leclerc dictated the final letter to Girard.

"Is that it?" asked the young ADC.

"*Voilà*," said Leclerc.[44]

Even de Gaulle had received an insubordinate letter from Malaguti, who was clearly unaware of the unbreakable bond between de Gaulle and his earliest followers. "I allow myself in passing to respectfully draw your attention to the inexperience of the commander of this division and of his staff in respect to armoured warfare, inexperience which could be costly and is due to their past service," the jealous colonel had written, doing himself no good whatsoever.[45]

If Leclerc was inexperienced in armoured warfare, so too were many other divisional commanders arriving in Normandy that summer, men who often lacked even Leclerc's three years' continuous service in Africa.

A final letter from Leclerc to de Gaulle saying he would not have Malaguti under his orders "at any price" was the final *coup de grâce*.[46] Leclerc told de Gaulle that Malaguti was to be replaced by Colonel Warabiot of the 12e Cuirassiers. But de Gaulle had his own contribution to make. He had come to greatly value the services of Colonel Pierre Billotte,* the son of General Billotte who was killed in the Battle of France. Pierre Billotte had been captured during *la chute* and escaped to the Soviet Union, finally being allowed to join de Gaulle in the same batch as Alain de Boissieu and Jacques Branet. "I wish to see Billotte serve under Leclerc's orders," de Gaulle wrote. "My reason for this is the 'general interest' above anything else." The matter was closed.[47]

The division was as battle-ready as it was ever going to be, and on Sunday, 16th July, the news finally came through: they would be going to France in not more than twenty days time. In fact it would only be fifteen days. The men were overcome.

"You're moved," remarked Leclerc, noticing tears in the tall Gribius' eyes.[48]

---

*Billotte and Cantarel had served under Malaguti in 1940.

The last regimental colour to be presented before departure was to the shipless sailors of the RBFM. Leclerc had been especially hard on these men, telling them to remove the red lanyards earned at Dixmude in 1914. He was therefore furious to find that the senior petty officer carrying the colour was not only pushing fifty but wearing the forbidden item.

"Why is he wearing the red lanyard?" Leclerc angrily asked Captain Maggiar.

"He won it at Dixmude," replied Maggiar, citing the 1914 battle for which the red lanyard was originally awarded.

Leclerc stepped back without saying a word. Interviewing Petty Officer Renou afterwards, Leclerc apologised for being angry with him. Later Commandant la Horie, Leclerc's *petit-co* from Saint Cyr, who with his brothers had taken the Vichy line until November 1942, reminded Leclerc that since the sailors had performed with excellence during training he should ease up. The Petty Officer Renou incident was the last time *le Patron* humiliated the RBFM for the sins of Pétain and Darlan. Shortly after their arrival in France, Leclerc would open his heart to them.[49]

Some RBFM's Tank Destroyers were named after French battleships and cruisers, but true to French naval tradition when naming squadrons of ships, most of the TDs were named after the winds and by a letter. Jean-Marie Thomas' TD was named after his old ship, *Tramontane*, while others in the same squadron had names like *Tempête* and *Typhoun*. Another squadron had names beginning with 'S;' *Sirocco*, *Simoun* and *Souffleur*. Other TDs were called *Orage*, *Ouragon* and *Astral*. The *Bourrasque* was named after a French destroyer sunk at Dunkirk with many French and British soldiers aboard.

The French Army already had a tradition of naming tanks. The Shermans of the 12e Cuir' were named after Norman towns and villages such as *Caen*, *Evreux* and *Lisieux*. The men of Minjonnet's 12e RCA named their tanks after old royal provinces such as *Vendée*, *Tarentaise* and *Bordelais II*, or else marshals of the Napoleonic era. The tanks of Cantarel's 501e Régiment des Chars de Combat, whose personnel were largely original Gaullists, called their Shermans after famous French victories, with names from the Verdun battlefield figuring strongly—*Douaumont* and *Mort-Homme*.[50] The RMT named its halftracks after heroes from French history like *Bertrand du Guesclin*, who resisted the English during the first half of the Hundred Years War, reversing gains made by the Black Prince. Inevitably some of the vehicles were given names of personal importance to their commanders—Massu's jeep was named *Moido* after his Toubou mistress left in Chad, while his HQ halftrack was called *Mourzouck*.

In the summer of 1944 these names were emblazoned somewhat gaudily on the flanks of 2e DB vehicles. Once they were due for a repaint, following the battles of August and September, divisional insignia became more subdued. Leclerc insisted on one last change to vehicle insignia before the embarkation process began: the blue Cross of Lorraine superimposed over the outline of France in those regiments of Gaullist origin would now become compulsory across the whole division. This was not negotiable.

On the 18th July the Order of the Bath and DSO awarded to Leclerc earlier by the British were delivered to Dalton Hall. *Le Patron* burst out laughing when Girard brought him the sumptuously lined cases. Giggling away, Leclerc hung the Order of the Bath around d'Allonnes's neck and pinned the DSO on Girard's chest, and photographed the two of them in front of the window.

With departure imminent, the 2e DB HQ was dismantled for the second time in three months. Cases and boxes were packed. Surplus papers were burnt in Dalton Hall's marble fireplaces, and the picture-lined corridors reverberated to the sound of hobnailed boots as men staggered along them taking out trunks full of kit.[51]

The impedimenta of their tented life dismantled, the RMT traveled southwards in Jeeps and half tracks, passing through village after village amid clapping and waving from pretty but dowdily dressed English women and old men shouting "Give 'em Hell!" Few of the RMT spoke English, but the gestures and intonations were transparent enough.[52] The Shermans, Stuarts and Tank Destroyers were driven to Hull and went south by rail. Next stop, the holding camps along the southern coast.

On 20th July Leclerc heard from Colonel Divry, who was already in Normandy on a recruiting drive, that the Normans were looking forward to the arrival of French troops. Recruits were coming in, enthusiastic and motivated, but immensely bitter about the occupation and the antics of Vichy.

Leclerc finally left Dalton Hall the following morning. Except for Eveline de Schompré and her children, all the French had gone. There were no guards left, only the cows in the home park to see their departure.[53] Leclerc said his goodbyes to the Hothams, and walked through the large hall to the front porch, his cane tapping rythmically on the wooden floor.

He arrived in London at lunchtime and went to Upper Grosevenor Street, where he heard from d'Allonnes that moves were afoot in the French High Command to deprive him of one of his tank regiments.

"They must be mad!" he exclaimed. "I will simply not allow the staff to interfere with my division!"

Then at lunch he admitted, "Anyway, you know, it can't be nice to know that de Gaulle prefers Koenig, Larminat and myself. We must seem like spoilt brats."

The next day, as the French began to arrive in Bournemouth, Leclerc visited General Wade Haislip at US XV Corps HQ, under whose command the 2e DB would be operating. Leclerc had received conflicting orders on the way down from Yorkshire and hoped this would not continue once the division was in combat. Otherwise the sight of the Channel, and knowing their homeland lay beyond it, was a huge boost for his men.

As Langlade and his chief of staff, Commandant Verdier, reached Lutterwoth[54] they learnt of the failed assassination attempt against Hitler by Colonel Count von Stauffenberg of the Wehrmacht's Home Army HQ in Berlin's Bendlerstrasse. Stauffenberg was also a cavalry officer, devoutly Catholic and a young father to a large family. In different times he would probably have been friends with men such as Leclerc or Langlade. In the early morning of July 21st, lit by lorry headlamps, Stauffenberg and his co-conspirators were shot in the Bendlerstrasse courtyard.

"Long live holy Germany!" shouted Stauffenberg as the shots rang out.[55]

Yet the janissaries of "eternal France" greeted the coup's failure as something to celebrate. Whatever the 2e DB's predominantly Catholic and conservative officers might have in common with the German resistance, the 2e DB wanted to fight to free their homeland, and they wanted all France to see them do it. To have their country's freedom ceded back to them by a new German government headed by a Field Marshal like Rommel or Witzleben was not in their thinking at all.

"The defeat of Germany on it's own soil is necessary for the peace of

Europe," wrote Girard in his diary on 24th July. "It is terrible to write this, but this essential result is worth the human lives that it will cost. Through sparing them in 1918, Foch cost us many more lives than he saved."[56]

In any case, it was fate's decision that Hitler's saga would play through to *Gotterdammerung*.

Reaching Dorchester, Langlade gathered up his GT. They were installed in a large tented barracks which, like most things American, was very comfortable with proper messing and washing facilities. For a few days this would be his home. On the 27th Gribius told them embarkation was now planned for the 29th. Tracked vehicles would be embarked at Southampton; wheeled vehicles at Weymouth. The first members of the division to land in France on an operational basis would be Paul Repiton-Préneuf's *2e Bureau*.

As the Battle for Normandy raged around Caen, and the American right hook built up, the 2e DB set off from the holding areas around Bournemouth and Dorchester for the marshalling area outside Southampton. After a long drive through the rain, passing all kinds of traffic coming the other way, including a circus complete with elephants, the 2e DB arrived in the great port's streets by late afternoon. They found themselves fitted at once into the massive American logistics operation. They parked up their vehicles as directed and settled into the transit camp. Then, by regiment, they filed through canteens for a dinner of roast chicken, vegetables and cheese, officers served last.[57] Freshly laundered, warm bedding awaited the new arrivals in every tent, which was much appreciated on a chilly day of torrential rain. After dinner, Colonel Bernard made his rounds telling everyone that they would not be embarking for at least another twenty-four hours, and the 2e DB thought they had a good night's sleep ahead.

Leclerc had gone to lie down with a mild attack of malaria brought on by the rain. Girard left him flat on his back with a handkerchief over his eyes, *comme d'habitude*, and went off to get some sleep. A few hours later Leclerc woke him, feverish, saying he had been having nightmares. Girard found Dr. Richet. The doctor examined Leclerc and told Girard not to worry. "This kind of malarial attack is normal in a man who lives so much on his nerves."[58]

They got no sleep in any case. Embarkation was brought forward twenty-four hours. They were woken with fresh orders to assemble at once on the quayside. Driving through pelting rain and glistening Southampton streets in full black-out, they reached the docks by 4.30am. All day long the loading and shouting went on as vast cranes and winches swung vehicles of every description into LSTs and landing craft, and the French filed up wet gangplanks in the drizzle.

Rochambelle Edith Vézy was impressed by the sheer magnitude of the operation, with the countless grey ships moored in Southampton harbour and the Solent beyond. For a moment this enormous hive of activity stopped as an air-raid siren sounded. This was the time of V-1 doodlebugs, but the "all clear" soon came.[59]

The 2e DB was not the only armoured division loading that day. General Maczek's First Polish Armoured Division was also being loaded onto ships. The 2e DB would meet these Poles again during the weeks ahead.

At 5.30 pm, Langlade and his entourage were invited to board the *Horace Grey*. Either *le duc* was fussy or else unlucky with captains of the Allied logistical fleet. He later wrote that the *Horace Grey* was the filthiest ship he had ever seen and that captain and crew seemed to be drunk!

For some members of the 2e DB, Southampton would provide their first contact with the enemy. Landing craft were docking and disgorging long files of prisoners in *feldgrau,* guarded by grim-faced military policemen. For the most part 12e RCA's Arthur Kaiser thought they seemed glad to be out of the inferno, that their war was over. Seeing these Frenchmen, fresh, well-fed and rested, some Germans seemed to look on them with pity, while others visibly blanched at the sight of their new and plentiful equipment.[60]

Waiting to embark, Girard walked along the quayside taking in sights and sounds; the ships rocking at their moorings, the giant cranes constantly moving aloft, the tanks driving up the ramps of LSTs in the order they were due to disembark on the Norman coast. He breathed the smell of hot engine oil and diesel fumes, and listened to some of 3/RMT who had formed an impromptu choir on the quayside, singing *"au près de ma blonde . . ."* and other French marching classics. Others found a great hangar nearby with three hundred bunks in it. The Americans really did think of everything. Using packs and webbing for pillows, many Frenchmen crashed out while waiting their turn to board.

In the small hours of the following morning Leclerc boarded his LST, accompanied by Girard. His caravan had been placed on the deck, and the Cross of Lorraine flew from the mast. The captain was honoured to have the famous General Leclerc aboard, and offered the use of his own cabin and bathroom. The captain also offered to hoist Leclerc's ensign if he had one, or if not, the ship's flagmaker would make one during the night. By morning it was flying: blue and white diagonals under the Cross of Lorraine and carrying two stars. Girard watched it fluttering in the dawn sunlight, and for a moment he was overcome with emotion, remembering all they had done during the previous four years. He thought of the *Tricolore* flying in London's Carlton Gardens, and how French military identity had been nearly submerged in the Anglo-American war effort. But they were the *Free French*—those difficult people who had exasperated both the British and Americans, and now they were going home.[61]

Lifting anchor at 10am, their ships moved slowly into the grey Solent and crossed the Channel. It was sunny and the sea was calm. By 8pm, they hove to off the Normandy coast. The land was difficult to see through the haze and twilight, but it was the French shoreline. The ships dropped anchor. The following morning the 2e DB would land on French soil.

Leclerc drafted the order of the day.

"How do we describe our feelings when we put our feet back onto the soil of *la patrie*? This soil we left four years ago, leaving France under the boot of the enemy, with all that this has meant for each and every one of us. We return today as combatants, having continued the struggle for four years under General de Gaulle. We will see afresh the faces of our countrymen who will salute us enthusiastically from the midst of their ruins. We can only guess what they have suffered. My first duty is to salute those Frenchmen who have never despaired, who have assisted our allies, who have contributed to victory. I admire them and I honour them. For ourselves, we have reached our goal, we have come at last to help them, to relieve them and to continue at their sides in the great battle for liberation."[62]

CHAPTER NINE

FIRST BLOOD—ALENÇON

Through the hours of darkness the convoy of ships swayed at anchor as barrage balloons floated above. With three fresh armoured divisions about to come ashore the depleted Luftwaffe threw in repeated attacks, but Goering's weary, petrol-starved veterans were easily chased off by Allied fighters. At dawn, lighters went into the shore first, directed by beachmasters, while larger vessels awaited low tide. Below decks there was an impatient atmosphere as the Frenchmen of the 2e DB made ready to step onto the soil of their homeland.[1]

It was a chilly, windy day. At 9.30am Repiton-Préneuf and Schompré arrived on a DUKW to tell Leclerc a landing craft would take his staff ashore at 11am. At the appointed hour, wearing a US raincoat and forage cap with the two stars of a brigadier general, even though he had long been officially a major general, Leclerc led the way. Clutching a malacca cane, he jumped off the ladder hanging down the ship's side into the landing craft. Girard followed him wearing his 1935 French tanker's helmet and carrying a haversack containing divisional papers.[2] One by one, Repiton-Préneuf, Schompré, Girard, Gribius and Bernard leapt onto the landing craft, soon followed by Guillebon and Quillichini. The landing craft chugged past the fleet of anchored ships and the concrete breakwaters that had been towed across the Channel in June to protect the Mulberry harbour. The gateway to France loomed up in front of them: a long pre-fab jetty of wood and steel along which thousands of soldiers had already marched into the Battle of Normandy.

"A strange impression," Leclerc murmured.

"Awfully pleasing," replied Girard sarcastically, taking in the scene.

Stepping from the jetty onto the sand to be greeted by US General Walker, they found an atmosphere of fierce activity amid the desolation left over from the beach fighting on 6th June. French and US soldiers gathered amid the chaos of vehicles, and photographers moved forward to record Free France's first operational general coming home.

"Can you wave your hand again please, General?" they called out, and asked him to repeat his walk from the jetty.

Leclerc pursed his lips and looked dour. "No, we're here to get on with the war," he replied. "Let me get on with my job."

The photographers still pestered him as they boarded a Dodge command car, and the atmosphere of this unique moment began to touch him. The day Leclerc had waited for so long had arrived and he found himself smiling with real pleasure.[3] He was leading Free French troops back onto French soil to free their homeland and liberate Paris.

Along the shoreline, LSTs beached themselves, opened bow doors and lowered ramps. On their decks tank and vehicle crews were gunning engines and making the air thick with exhaust smoke. One after another the tanks and halftracks came rolling ashore to line up in parallel columns. Amid the roar of engines the Frenchmen's emotions were churning. Most of the 2e DB had not seen France for three or four years. But in the case of Massu and other Coloniale old-timers, it was more like six years. Once ashore, handfuls of sand were put in pockets or small tins and jars. Others laughed with boyish delight, knowing they were making history.[4] From that moment, Massu would write, an immense feeling of elation came over him which lasted throughout the European campaign, sustaining him through fatigue and combat, only ever dimmed by their losses. Here was their chance to pay back some of what the Germans had meted out in 1940.[5]

The 501e RCC's Shermans drove inland from the beach amid the sound of shellfire from the south. When his troop paused near a farm, the 501e RCC's Emil Fray found its owner incredulous to discover they were French.

"A whole division of us are coming ashore in the next few days," insisted Corporal Fray, grinning.

"You must be joking," replied the ecstatic farmer.[6]

Leclerc checked in at the CP set up by Repiton-Préneuf, where he also found Janney, Putz, Compagnon and Colonel Rémy, with an advance guard of Spahis Marocains Greyhound armoured cars, and then set off to lunch with Patton. The route to US Third Army headquarters took him along country lanes clogged with men and equipment. It was fourteen months since any of the 2e DB had seen a battlefield. For the first time since 1940, they saw shattered French villages and homeless peasants loading frightened children and a few sad belongings onto handcarts and wagons.[7]

In a Norman apple orchard, Patton explained the situation in a loud stentorian voice. General Montgomery, commanding Allied land forces, was drawing German Seventh Army onto the British Twenty-First Army Group at Caen on the east of the bridgehead, while US forces on the western flank built up for a large breakout into open French countryside to envelope the Germans from the south. The British and American armies would meet up around Falaise and Argentan. Patton's Third Army, of which the 2e DB was a part, would perform that envelopment, and Leclerc was struck by the simplicity of the plan and the material resources available to carry it out.

After bringing the 12e RCA ashore, Colonel de Langlade found himself drinking a toast that evening with the mayor of Saint-Germain-de-Varreville, and then meeting the local population. Their welcome was warm and moving, though some believed German propaganda that de Gaulle's men were communists bent on revenge against Pétain's former servants. Langlade's reassurances and the discipline of his men did much to mollify such fears. By nightfall, Langlade was settled in GTL HQ with his radio working perfectly. There would, however, be no orders until the division was fully assembled.[8]

Disembarking was a slow business. Even after two days, Leclerc's staff were finding divisional HQ vehicles still waiting to be unloaded, including Leclerc's caravan. Captain Maggiar's RBFM and its Tank Destroyers only embarked in Southampton on 2nd August, the troops' frustration allevi-ated by Hershey bars, chewing gum and drink generously supplied by the Americans. The US Navy captain of Maggiar's LST was an ex-dentist who was incredulous at the trail of misfortune that put French sailors into tanks fighting on the European mainland.

They arrived off the Norman coast at midnight, and within two hours the Tank Destroyers were filing inland, each driver following the rear lights of the one ahead. As the morning sun rose over the shattered villages, Mag-giar was reminded of ancient ruins in North Africa. Few French villagers could sleep amid the racket of passing armour, and stood by the roadside instead to shout words of welcome in broken English. The sailors replied in fluent French, often with Breton accents, *"Nous sommes les marins! Nous sommes avec la division Leclerc!"* The Normans were delighted, unbelieving, a scene which repeated itself in every village all the way to the assembly area at La Haye-du-Puits.[9]

That evening Leclerc dined with his cousin, François de Hauteclocque. Fifty-one years old at the outbreak of war, with a good record from the Great War, François had acquitted himself well in 1940. Afterwards, as mayor of his village, he did his utmost to mitigate the laws of Vichy and the occupiers, even refusing to allow the Germans use of his chateau until they seized it anyway on the false pretext of finding a planted pistol there, and imprisoned François and his wife in Germany. Luckily, they had been released within a year and allowed to return home. When Leclerc arrived he was recognised by an elderly maid. In spite of the *nom de guerre* they all knew who he was. François was too old to join the 2e DB in any useful capacity. Not so his son Wallerand, who had been prevented from reaching Spain by the intense security in the southwest and had lived in hiding to avoid being sent to work in Germany under the *Service Travail Obligatoire* rules brokered by Vichy prime minister Pierre Laval. Wallerand and his friend Herout were the 2e DB's first direct recruits on French soil, much to Leclerc's pleasure.

Less agreeable was a visit to his CP by his brother-in-law René de Toc-queville and his wife Marie, one of Thérèse's sisters. At first, this reunion also went well, but when de Tocqueville started making excuses for Vichy, supported by his wife, Leclerc saw red and had them shown out of his HQ tent as quickly as they had arrived.[10]

None of the 2e DB expected free hospitality from freshly liberated relations, but their pay had been held up. The Allied planners' "invasion francs" currency so loathed by de Gaulle had not reached them yet. As Girard was organising Leclerc's newly arrived caravan at HQ, Langlade appeared, beside himself over the men's pay. "They can hardly march through their homeland with no money in their pockets!" he exploded.

"The French soldier is a chap who likes to touch his money. He doesn't like other people looking after it for him. He hates that. It may seem stupid if you want to see it that way. But that's how it is!" After Langlade's outburst everyone at HQ was silent.[11]

Langlade had positioned GTL's HQ close to a German minefield into which large black and white cows, the pride of Norman husbandry, had wandered, blowing themselves up. Now their corpses were expanding like balloons as grass fermented inside their stomachs. Not far away were German Panther tanks, intact but abandoned by their crews for lack of petrol. The French experience of 1940 was being reversed. Immensely civilised, Paul de Langlade was deeply disturbed by the ravages inflicted on Normandy. Two months after D-Day it was still very much a war zone.[12]

Edith Vézy was also struck by the devastation, but still without a co-driver for "Gargamelle," her ambulance, she was more concerned about managing effectively on her own. When the "buddy" promised by Suzanne Torres arrived, she turned out to be a tall, slim *résistante* with auburn hair and a refined, jolly face who had been evacuated to England for security reasons. Their first casualty evacuation came within two days of landing. A neighbouring American unit had suffered a rare German air attack and the *Rochambelles* were called in to help. Their laughter and pleasure at being back in France again, the hope of which had buoyed them through their training, died away in the face of war's reality. When more German ground attack aircraft inflicted the 2e DB's first casualties, killing twenty and wounding nearly two hundred, including a *Rochambelle* driver whose legs were so badly broken that she became a lifelong invalid, the grim nature of their job came home to them.[13]

Seeing the shattered landscape of Normandy during those first overcast days ashore lowered the 2e DB's morale. Nevertheless recruiting flourished as young Normans heard about the US-equipped French division. At least a hundred joined on top of those recruited earlier by Divry. Since the 2e DB was the only French unit on home soil at this time, there could be no accusations of inciting *spontanément mutés*.

From the 4th to the 6th of August conflicting orders arrived one day after the other, either to move or stand by for forty-eight hours. Feeling the Americans were treating the French cavalierly, Leclerc told Girard, "Go to Corps. Unless I have orders to the contrary, I am moving at 8 o'clock this evening."

The US XV Corps commander Wade Haislip, a scion of Virginia's first families and a fluent French speaker, had been briefed all about Leclerc and his men, and he rightly believed that, properly treated, they would give good service. He ordered Leclerc south, to follow behind Patton's breakout which had already sent German Seventh Army reeling. Their first orders to move brought smiles to every face. Their pessimism began to evaporate.[14]

Leclerc had not yet had time to visit his beloved sister Yvonne at the nearby chateau of Champiré, so he sent Gui de Schompré with a brief letter.

"My dear Vonnette, it is me Philippe," he wrote. "I embrace you very, very strongly. I am trying to pursue the Germans so fast that I will not have time to call at Champiré. I have not changed in myself though I am older physically. No news of Thérèse. Is our father still alive? Kisses to all."[15]

They left Vesly in a convoy with Girard driving Leclerc's Jeep, and the devastation around the beachhead area gave way to unspoiled countryside. Passing through villages untouched by war south of Avranches, Leclerc was cheered and applauded. Some people ran alongside the Jeep to shake his hand while others shouted, *"Bravo pour Tchad!"* and *"Vive de Gaulle!"*[16]

In the lead of Patton's huge right hook, General John Wood's US 4th Armoured Division had made a brilliant advance southwards, facing scant opposition. "You see," he told Repiton-Préneuf and Guillebon, "I do not want the army to push me. I want to pull the army along behind me."

Leclerc later told Girard that Wood and Patton were, "A little bit mad, and that is what it takes to make a good soldier."[17] Patton's Third Army was pushing into the unknown, as Kleist and Rommel had done in 1940. With the German frontline now well behind them and new operational maps slow in the pipeline, the Americans were finding the FFI—*Forces Françaises de l'Intérieur*, the resistance, especially helpful.

Recognising the danger of Patton's corridor to the south, the Luftwaffe attacked Third Army during the night but achieved little more than disturbing their sleep. There were no 2e DB casualties this time, but as day broke, Leclerc heard that German armoured divisions were launching a counterattack against the corridor's eastern flank around Mortain and Vire. Their intention was to push through to Avranches, cut off Third Army at the base of the Cotentin peninsula, and thereby forestall the American right hook.

On 8th August at 3pm, Leclerc confirmed to his senior officers that they were facing a German counterattack by the 1st and 2nd SS and the 2nd and 116th Panzer Divisions, though these units were far from full strength. Earlier in the battle for Normandy, Montgomery wanted German armour to face the British and Canadian 21st Army Group; now he wanted more German troops moving west towards Patton so that, once the envelopment was complete, as many Germans as possible would be roped into "the bag" along with their equipment.[18]

Ordered to face eastwards to meet this threat, Leclerc sent out a mixed tank and reconnaissance detachment under Captain Bort, composed of Spahis Marocains and 12e RCA, to find the enemy towards Mortain. Langlade was ready with the balance of his GT to follow up along the National 177. Langlade recognised Leclerc's anxiety, ordering an advance to contact for his first time as a divisional commander, and knew how scanty was the information he had received before making his decision. In this first engagement the coordination of tank forces by radio worked perfectly, but their opponents were the 2nd SS Panzer Division, *Das Reich*, whose men were responsible for the infamous massacre at Oradour sur Glane.[19]

Rivetted to the command radio, these first few hours of combat seemed to Langlade like an eternity. At about 7pm, feeling he had insufficient information, he jumped into a Jeep and went to Mortain himself. In a war of constant movement, leaders have to be at the front, but they cannot be everywhere. They have to choose where their decision-making powers will be most effective. Langlade found the tail of Captain Bort's detachment among American infantry, and he pushed on along crowded roads until he came across Bort himself. The fighting had been sporadic, but the Spahis and Chasseurs had taken several prisoners, ending the day west of Mortain.[20]

At Leclerc's CP it seemed to Girard that the division's first action had passed in a state of constant semi-alert or waiting for orders. Leclerc gathered his GT commanders in front of his caravan at the end of the day and ordered them to make sure their men got enough sleep and not to give out unnecessary fatigue duties.

Also on 8th August, Colonel Pierre Billotte, de Gaulle's nominee to take over from Malaguti, finally joined the division. Billotte was deeply committed to Free France, but he was a far more political animal than either Paul de Langlade and Louis Dio, with whom Leclerc had a better rapport.

Next day, things began to move fast. Haislip's US XV Corps was ordered south to Le Mans, the home of the twenty-four hour motor race, which was still occupied by the Germans. By dusk, the 2e DB's four thousand vehicles were heading there too, in two columns, while reconnaissance units moved eastwards to the River Sarthe. The US 79th Infantry and 5th Armored Divisions making up Haislip's XV Corps had gone ahead to form a bridgehead on the Sarthe.[21]

Since they were following in US 5th Armored's wake, and poor weather excluded the risk of air attack, Leclerc sent his petrol tankers ahead to provide refuelling depots *en route*. These truck drivers became the first members of the 2e DB to receive the flowers and kisses of the liberated Loire. The division kept going all night. Leclerc caught a few hours sleep in a small deserted house while Girard and Guillebon kept watch downstairs.[22] Driving for ten hours through the darkness and driving rain, the 2e DB's tail stretched thirty kilometres through the French countryside. From time to time there were breakdowns, but these were dealt with quickly and the division kept rolling while villagers lined the roadsides, barely visible in the dark but shouting with joy as "*les Leclercs*" pushed towards the Loire, the garden of France.

The journey southwards did not go smoothly for everybody. Some lesser roads were very quiet and the men felt as though they were plunging into dark, silent enemy territory, constantly straining to see into the night, looking for the guide lights of a convoy in front, or US military traffic control. The RMT's Captain Fonde got fabulously lost, only finding his way again at dawn.

When her new co-driver hitched a ride with the Spahis, *Rochambelle* Edith Vézy was left alone in her "Gargamelle," unable to see any 2e DB ahead of her. Every so often she stopped to ask a civilian if the French had been through, hearing each time, "*Oui, oui, les Français viennent de passer.*" Then, at daybreak, she found herself driving into a village full of Germans. She saw that an officer had recognised her US ambulance and was pulling his pistol. She ducked. Luckily the bullet only went through the draught of her helmet liner.

"*Ach, es ist eine Frau,*" said the German officer. As an *alsacienne*, Edith was bilingual and broke into German, demanding to see someone senior. After a major heard her excuses and accepted that she was of no military value, she was allowed to return to Allied lines under escort, provided she promised not to mention anything she had seen. Taking the view that, "A French promise was not the same as a German promise," she agreed. In the meantime the Germans had searched the back of her ambulance, chucking sheets, blankets and medical supplies on the ground. The glass jars of preserved fruits in calvados given her in Normandy as *bonnes bouches* were thrown against a tree. Two soldiers jumped onto the footboards, one on each side of the cab, and she drove back along deserted lanes. No one spoke. After ten kilometres one of her escorts said, "*Voilà, les Américains.*" The two Germans got down and she drove on until, seeing three Americans, she asked, "Where are the French?"

"The other side of that wood," came the reply. Relieved, she turned a corner only to see her two escorts being marched along with their hands up. Inadvertently, she had brought in two prisoners, and probably saved their lives.[23]

Haislip's XV Corps was concentrated around La Chapelle-St.-Aubin, north of Le Mans, while US Third Army's engineers completed two Bailey-type pontoon bridges, the biggest yet seen since D-Day, which were christened "Miss America." Haislip had been tasked to attack westwards along the German Seventh Army's southern flank and then turn north along the axis Le Mans-Alençon-Argentan to meet up with the British and Canadian armies. Aware of the mounting danger, the Luftwaffe attacked the 2e DB during the night of 8–9th August, hitting several petrol tankers. Some of Leclerc's Shermans were unable to move until replacement tankers arrived.[24]

The attack began on the morning of 10th August, the day many French historians regard as the beginning of the 2e DB's war. Parallel assaults by the US 5th Armored Division and the 2e DB pressed northwards on the east and west of XV Corps' axis, supported by the US 79th and 90th Infantry Divisions. GT Dio would advance on the Ballon-Doucelles-Coulombiers axis, while further east GT Langlade would go through Sablon-Dangeul-Louvigny. Their objective was to envelop Alençon, where most of German Seventh Army's supplies were kept, from both the east and the west.[25] While petrol remained short, GT Billotte would stay in reserve. The final objective of Argentan was on Fifth Armored's axis. Opposite them was the 9th Panzer Division, which had travelled north from Nîmes after D-Day, though with less incident than 2nd SS *Das Reich*. The 9th Panzer Division was fresh and well equipped with Panthers and Panzer Mk IV specials, both carrying high-velocity 75mm Pak guns. Luckily, however, 9th Panzer had no Tiger tanks with their feared 88mm guns.[26]

The countryside between Le Mans and Alençon is *bocage*; small, undulating fields, characterised by sunken lanes running between high hedges, a combination that favoured defenders and not tanks. The Germans had already used such terrain to their advantage further north, causing heavy losses among Allied tank crews. In Alençon there are important bridges over the Sarthe which had to be denied the enemy, while north of the town there is a line of three large woods, where overcoming well-prepared defences would be difficult. To reach Argentan with minimum delay and thus close the Falaise gap, it was necessary to take the Alençon bridges intact and by-pass these woods with armoured thrusts. This was the hard re-baptism of French arms that Leclerc had warned of in Temara's casino.

"Don't let yourselves be stopped by resistance," Leclerc told his GT commanders. "Go around them if you can't break them. Get to the northern edge of Alençon as quickly as you can."[27]

Then Leclerc went to the church of La Chapelle-Saint-Aubin to hear the *Te Deum*. A dark, moonless night, lit only by farms burning in the distance, lay ahead as they waited for their first day of real armoured operations. As usual, Sergeant Loustalot found Leclerc a bed in a pretty village house, while Girard made do with a bedroll on the ground beside *Tailly*, the Sherman command tank which Leclerc named after his home.[28] Exhausted after their two hundred-kilometre march to take part in this enveloping thrust, the men slept as best they could.

GTs Dio and Langlade crossed the Sarthe on US Army pontoon bridges early on 10th August. Starting at 6.40am, Leclerc positioned himself at the crossroads of four routes which straddled the axes of both tank groups. There he found vehicles of Massu's group getting muddled up with Dio's. Massu's subordinates from the 2e RMT, Commandant Marcilly and Captain Philippe, tried to explain to Leclerc why they were on Dio's routes. When Massu himself arrived Leclerc told him, "Don't mess this up!" If Massu is correct, this was the last time Leclerc ever chewed him out.[29]

The GTs headed northwards with Stuart light tanks in the lead. The weather became hot and close. Leclerc installed his CP at La Trugal, north of Le Mans, though he often took off alone in a Jeep, much to the consternation of Girard and the head of the HQ protection squadron, de Boissieu.

The first contact with the enemy was made at the Sablon crossroads. A Stuart from Massu's subgroup was destroyed by a German flame-thrower. The rest of the group stopped a kilometre to the south. Although managing to link up with the Minjonnet sub-group, Massu lost four Shermans along with fourteen crewmen, including two popular lieutenants, Zagrodski and d'Arcangue.[30] To add to 12e RCA's misfortunes, they were attacked by an American fighter-bomber, luckily without fatalities, because the crews had not changed the coloured identification panel on the back of a Sherman, which was destroyed.

The 2/RMT were blooded when they encountered German resistance holding the bridge at La Saunerie over a tributary of the Sarthe. A short and brutal exchange followed, with a German counterattack nearly reaching 2/RMT's half-tracks. It was only when Captain Langlois de Bazillac[31] demanded reinforcements and Massu sent him a section of infantry and artillery support that the Germans retreated, losing fifteen casualties and ten prisoners. 2/RMT lost seven killed and another seven wounded, but their morale remained high.[32]

Leclerc followed everything by keeping close to the fighting, visiting one sub-group after another, each time finding the same faults. There was too much sticking to obvious routes and coming up against foreseeable roadblocks held by infantry armed with *Panzerfaust* anti-tank weapons. Above all, everyone was moving too slowly.[33]

From GT Dio a mixed detachment of 12e Cuirassiers, commanded by Captain de Laitre, manouevred towards Ballon. Sending his light tanks forward to reconnoitre, Laitre outflanked the enemy positions, calling in artillery to deal with them as he pushed on to take Chérancé. Leclerc was pleased: this was what he expected from his commanders. Shortly afterwards Laitre was killed. French soldiers are often inconsolable at losing popular officers, and *témoinages* by 2e DB veterans are littered with the phrase "*le pauvre petit*" for those who died before their time. Leclerc gave his condolences to 12e Cuir' but there would be more losses.

"Don't just think about burying your dead," was Leclerc's severe comment to the 12e Cuir', though he was as affected as anyone. But speed in execution reduces casualties and Leclerc had the whole division to think about.

"This division is the biggest disillusion of my life," Leclerc commented sourly to Boissieu during a black moment. "Tomorrow I will send Commandant de Guillebon and Commandant Repiton-Préneuf (who were in fact lieutenant colonels) to tell all group commanders that if they don't reach their objectives tomorrow I will sack them. And the same for captains commanding smaller units!"[34]

On hearing this, Guillebon interceded with Leclerc that the march from Vesly had been exhausting. Leclerc was unmoved. Guillebon and Repiton visited Langlade and Dio that night to warn them of *le Patron*'s displeasure. Remembering that Boissieu was a "Russian," Leclerc sent him to inform Billotte of the improvements he demanded.[35]

Leclerc decided to visit Dio himself, despite Girard's warnings about snipers. Shouting at Girard not to fuss, they sped off in the Jeep with Girard driving and Sergeant Maurois riding shotgun. Suddenly a German ran across the road 500 metres ahead of them, disappearing into the undergrowth. Passing the spot, Maurois emptied a magazine from his

Thompson into the bushes. Scattered pockets of resistance made it impossible to reach GT Dio, and held up sub-group Farret's progress at La Hutte as well as sub-group Noiret.[36] Leclerc gave out fresh orders at a crossroads as an incoming shell whistled towards them. The men dived into the roadside ditches while

Leclerc stood in the road, insouciantly tapping his cane on the ground as the shell exploded harmlessly in a field.[37]

Leclerc's command style was now to ride around by Jeep wherever possible, although he had use of a White scout car and his command tank, *Tailly*. On the face of it, his attitude to his own safety made a nonsense of Boissieu's role commanding the HQ protection squadron, but it was impracticable for Stuart tanks to follow Leclerc along narrow, winding lanes where small vehicles could barely pass each other. Boissieu was hard pressed to stop Leclerc speeding off in a Jeep with only Girard. On the other hand, Leclerc liked seeing his HQ squadron up with lead units if it made his men think their general was everywhere.[38]

By late afternoon the 2e DB, in concert with the US 5th Armored Division, had fought its way to the line Beaumont-sur-Sarthe and Vivoin-Doucelles-Dangeul. The 5th Armored had met the same difficulties: sunken roads, high hedges and an enemy who inflicted casualties, then fell back to another prepared position and started all over again. All the same, the 2e DB made reasonable progress that day with many German vehicles destroyed and prisoners taken. Leclerc was always impatient, but he said with a smile to Boissieu, "We're going well." By evening, his 2e DB CP was installed at Ballon.

In the dwindling light west of the forest of Perseigne, two Tank Destroyers, ironically named after battleships notorious in the Vichy era, *Strasbourg* and *Jean Bart*,[39] brought the RBFM's first kills. Tasked with cutting off the enemy retreating through the forest, they encountered three trucks carrying German infantry. The commander of the *Strasbourg*, a solid Breton called Le Roux, shouted to the *Jean Bart*, "This one's mine!" When the lorries came within range, Le Roux set them alight with cannon and machine gun fire. With Panzergrenadiers running for cover or looking for the French, the commander of the *Jean Bart*, master range-finder Passaquet, spotted a Panther and ordered an armour piercing round for his TD's cannon. Sparks flew when it hit the Panther's hull, but no kill. The second round struck the German tank amidship, sending a sheet of white flames into the air. A third round had the crew bailing out. This episode lasted less than a minute.[40]

Making use of *Tailly*, Leclerc finally managed to reach GT Dio at dusk. He climbed out of his tank to greet his *comrade de promotion,* the 12e Cuir's Lt. Colonel Marc Rouvillois, who was coolly directing his sub-group from a café at Champfleur. Rouvillois was horrified to see Leclerc so near the front line. "*Mon général,* you are walking in full view of German tanks. You have no right to take such risks. If you are killed who will command the division?"

"Rouvillois," replied Leclerc, "you do your job and I will do mine."

The Champfleur café owner, taking equal risk, wrily passed Leclerc a chair.

"Sit there at least and let me clear the forces still holding out in the village," said the despairing Rouvillois. Gaudet took a troop of Shermans along a railway line, out-flanking the remaining Germans, and the village was soon back in French hands.[41]

Alençon and its bridges ten kilometres to the north were important, so although the men were tired, Leclerc ordered the 12e Cuir's Colonel Noiret to keep pushing into the night. The situation was so fluid they had no idea where the German lines were—if they existed. In the small hours of 12th August, while Leclerc and his staff snatched much-needed sleep, mortar shells landed around the 2e DB HQ. Lying awake on the ground, Girard heard the first shell whistle in but it failed to explode. Jumping to his feet he asked a sentry where it came from but no one knew. The second did explode, setting a halftrack ablaze and lighting up the field. More shells arrived and the explosions sent everyone running to their vehicles. Furious that the Germans had got so close, Leclerc nevertheless recognised the fluidity of the situation. At dusk Noiret's sub-group had been on the 2e DB's point and reached Saint-Gilles three kilometres south of Alençon, where he paused so his tank crews could rest and replenish with fuel and ammo. Leclerc jumped into a Jeep and went to Saint-Gilles, where the 12e Cuir's Captain Gaudet, at the front of the division, had halted for the night after destroying a 88mm gun. Fast asleep on his bedroll like the rest of his exhausted squadron Gaudet was woken by his orderly to find General Leclerc standing in front of him. Impervious to Noiret's entreaties that the

12e Cuir' needed rest, Leclerc shouted, "Get on the road, we're going to Alençon."

Pulling his boots back on, Gaudet ordered his men back into their tanks.[42] Then, as would often happen during the 2e DB's march through France, Leclerc found that a young *résistant* (called Raymond Ciroux) had arrived at Gaudet's position offering to guide the French into Alençon as far as the Pont Neuf.

Driving along the road between Alençon and Mamers, Leclerc and Guillebon sensed something was not right. Gachet slowed the Jeep while they listened intently. A car was coming from Mamers.

"Careful," warned Guillebon, unholstering his 45 automatic. "They might be Germans." Gachet stopped the Jeep.

"They are Germans!" said Leclerc, recognising the language. "Fire!"

Two of them died in the fusillade and the third put his hands in the air. Leclerc's risk-taking, which often worried his subordinates, seemed to have paid dividends.[43] Various documents found in the German *kubelwagen* and words from the prisoner indicated that a Panzer division was coming to secure Alençon and the routes into the town. Back at his CP Leclerc ordered the RBFM's TDs to cover these roads, though in fact, the 9th Panzer Division was more interested in retreating.

Leclerc correctly guessed that the Germans' defensive screen had been ruptured and they had not prepared Alençon for defence in depth. German reinforcements ran into GT Langlade's Shermans while GT Billotte rolled into the town, brushing aside light resistance and taking the bridges intact.

Leclerc set up his CP in a corner house by the river. On the wall was a superb photograph of Marshal Pétain, under which Leclerc gave full rein to his temper over a succession of cock-ups. André Gribius told him that because the Americans had planned a massive bombardment of the forest of Perseigne, which GT Langlade had been due to pass through later that morning, Gribius had, in Leclerc's absence, advised de Langlade to avoid the forest and head directly east and northeast of Alençon. As he spoke, Langlade himself arrived.

"Here at last," said Leclerc crisply.

"We are already in those woods," said Landglade, beginning an explanation.

"Yes, I know. Gribius has explained."

Leclerc told his officers that just because the Americans kept changing their plans was no reason for his subordinates to do as they liked instead of seeking orders from him. Nevertheless, the Americans were quickly asked to call off their airstrike.

The Americans were often planning and calling off airstrikes and para-chute drops that summer, as the ground war was moving so fast.[44] In any event, a bloody friendly-fire disaster had been avoided. The Americans would have obliterated the woods and caused huge casualties with their Flying Fortresses.[45]

Leclerc planned the next phase of the advance, and GT L's sub-groups Massu and Minjonnet spent the morning covering routes northeast of Alençon. Meanwhile, 9th Panzer Division decided against attempting to retake the town and instead took up position in the virtually impenetrable forest of Écouves which separates Alençon from the Argentan-Écouché region. Getting past this forest to Argentan was the 2e DB's next objective. Warned by a *résistant* and former artillery officer of German dispositions, Leclerc decided that crossing the forest would cost too much time and too many casualties. His best course was to bypass it. Dio was already posi-tioned to pass southwest of the forest with Ciral as his intermediate objec-tive. From there he could move onto Carrouges to meet up with GT Billotte coming north from Alençon past the forest on its east side via the town of Sees on National 138. This led to a problem with the Americans, because Sees was not in Leclerc's zone of operations. The town was in the operation zone of the neighbouring 5th Armored Division which was moving north from Mamers. Leclerc was unfazed. In fact, he rather relished the opportunity to show his allies that the 2e DB was a match for their unit by getting to Sees ahead of them. Aware of this, Billotte pushed hard along two routes towards Sees, dealing easily with any Germans emerging from the east of the forest who were mainly supply troops lagging behind the German retreat. With little to impede it, GT Billotte in fact arrived in Sees at the same time as the 5th Armored, which lead to confus-ing traffic jams and a good deal of name-calling between the Americans and French.[46]

Wade Haislip was furious at Leclerc for having the 2e DB running on routes outside his ops area, and at Patton's HQ, Leclerc's attitude was put down to "his inexperience and inability to control his units because he had not commanded an armoured division in combat before."[47] Strictly speaking however, Haislip was right. The incident could have caused serious "blue on blue" casualties.

Langlade was ordered to push north towards the forest of Écouves via the corridor between the forest of Perseigne and Alençon. He sent a group of Spahis Marocains under Lt. Colonel Roumiantsoff into the forest, where Captain Gerberon had reported that the majority of German forces seemed to be on the east side. Bypassing west of the woods, Dio reached Carrouges, running into a jam of Wehrmacht vehicles seeking shelter in the forest from air attack.

The weather turned stiflingly hot which, combined with petrol vapour, oil and dust, conspired to make men on both sides exceedingly uncomfortable. Lt. Bonnet's squadron of RBFM TDs was pushing up the Carrouges corridor running between the forests of La Motte, Monaye and Écouves, when they saw elements of the 2nd Panzer Division laid out in mixed columns of armoured vehicles and trucks, their crews resting on the grass. The shipless sailors could not believe their luck. The Tank Destroyers opened fire with cannon and machine guns, and the Germans ran away northwards or were killed on the spot if they resisted. Their trucks, armoured cars and tanks burned by the dozen along the roadside, and charred bodies lay all around. For a few moments the sailors of TDs *Fantasque*, *Audacieux*, *Terrible* and *Malin* picked up souvenirs, such as pistols, daggers and helmets of some Waffen SS who had been bolted onto 2nd Panzer.

RBFM recce troops led by Lieutenants Molle and Vilarem advanced north to the little hamlet of Mesnil-Scelleur, northeast of Carrouges, in their Greyhound scout cars. Sensing tanks in the vicinity, they dismounted and crept forward silently on foot to find seven Panzers with their crews sitting about on the ground, eating from billy cans. Then Molle and Vilarem were spotted, machine gun fire cracking over their heads. The RBFM scout cars bounded forward, firing back, and they quickly encircled the Germans, killing a good many and taking around a hundred prisoners. Their vehicles were eight-wheeled armoured cars. Suddenly a Panzer Mk IV appeared almost head to head with the TD *Dunkerque* twenty-five

Fort Lamy 1941. Leclerc reviewing his troops. The French Empire's indigenous black troops infinitely preferred to serve Free France than Vichy whose racial policies could not be trusted. *Musée de l'Ordre de la Libération*

Colonel Jean Colonna d'Ornano. A true swashbuckling camel soldier of "La Coloniale." D'Ornano was killed during the combined raid by the LRDG and Free French on Murzuk. *Musée de l'Ordre de la Libération*

Lieutenant Jean-Marie Corlu. During 1940 Corlu was stationed with Groupe Nomade at Agades. With just a camel and a compass he crossed 1,100 km to reach the Free French in Chad. Several other French officers rallied to de Gaulle in this way. Corlu was killed in the fighting for Le Bourget Airport the day after the Liberation of Paris. *Musée de l'Ordre de la Libération*

Leclerc in 1942 attending a parade as a two star general with the anchor badge of La Coloniale on his pith helmet. *Musée de l'Ordre de la Libération*

Free France's Air Force was equipped with British hand-me-downs. Shown here is a Bristol Blenheim bomber of the Groupe Lorraine. The Blenheim was ill-suited for desert conditions and crews suffered accordingly. *Imperial War Museum*

A man with a lot on his mind. *Imperial War Museum*

Leclerc is greeted by Brigadier-General Freddie de Guingand while Captain Johnny Henderson looks on. *Imperial War Museum*

From left to right: Brigadier Freddie de Guingand, General Bernard Montgomery, Brigadier General Philippe Leclerc de Hauteclocque and Commandant Jacques de Guillebon. *Imperial War Museum*

The famous photograph of Montgomery and Leclerc outside Montgomery's caravan (the only photograph from this sequence to pass the censors in 1943). *Imperial War Museum*

Leclerc and Louis Dio make their farewell, confident that their material needs will now be met by the British. *Imperial War Museum*

Now wearing British battledress, Leclerc confers with Colonel Ingold at Kairouan. *Imperial War Museum*

Holding an orders group about the time of Ksar Rhilane. *Imperial War Museum*

Above: Leclerc inspects artillery positions at Djebel Garci during the closing phase of the Tunisian campaign. *Imperial War Museum*

Below: Not Americans but his least welcome recruits. Accompanied by Capitaine de Vaisseau Raymond Maggiar (left) Leclerc inspects the sailors of the RBFM who became the 2e DB's anti-tank regiment. *Imperial War Museum*

Above: Accompanied by Maggiar, Leclerc advises the most Gaullist member of his least Gaullist regiment. The junior officer at second left is Ensign Philippe de Gaulle. *Imperial War Museum*

Below: Forging the 2e DB. The division goes through its final training in Yorkshire, and Leclerc confers with Patton and other officers, including his ADC, Christian Girard on the extreme right. *Musée de l'Ordre de la Libération*

1st August 1944. Accompanied by Christian Girard, Leclerc reaches the end of Utah beach's Mulberry jetty. Four years and a month after leaving France as an unknown captain, Leclerc returns to his homeland at the head of an armoured division. *Imperial War Museum*

23rd August 1944. Leclerc and Girard watch the 2e DB's Shermans roll toward Paris. *Imperial War Museum*

24th August 1944. On the main street of the Parisian suburb of Antony, Leclerc orders Captain Raymond Dronne (on the left), "Dronne, get into Paris. Get right into Paris." The diminutive officer on Leclerc's right is Jean Fanneau de la Horie, Leclerc's *petit-co* from Saint-Cyr, who captured General von Choltitz and was killed at Badonvilliers later that autumn. *Memorial du Maréchal Leclerc et de la Libération de Paris, Musée Jean Moulin, Ville de Paris*

24th August 1944. Later that evening outside the Hotel de Ville, the Sherman *Romilly,* from Lieutenant Michard's troop, is festooned with ecstatic Parisians, many of whom are wearing FFI arm bands. *Musée de l'Ordre de la Libération*

One of the most
iconic images of
Liberation day.
With Girard
behind him,
Leclerc gives
directions from
the back of a
White Scout car
near the Gare
Montparnasse.
*Imperial War
Museum*

25th August 1944. One of many
photographs taken of Jacques Massu
during the liberation of Paris. Always
a Gaullist, Massu was a tough and
honest soldier who later commanded
the 10th Parachute Division in
Algeria and the French Army in
Germany. *Musée de l'Ordre de la
Libération*

Above: 25th August 1944. De Gaulle and Leclerc peruse the surrender document at the Gare Montparnasse. De Gaulle was not pleased that Leclerc should have allowed the FTP leader Colonel Henri Rol-Tanguy to sign above himself. On the right, General Alphonse Juin.
Memorial du Maréchal Leclerc et de la Libération de Paris, Musée Jean Moulin, Ville de Paris

Below: 26th August 1944. *"Quelle foule!"*—"What a crowd!" said de Gaulle, at center, as he made the great march down the Champs Élysées. On his right, wearing British army trousers and gaiters, marches Leclerc. At far right, with bamboo baton, marches General Marie-Pierre Koenig, the commander of the FFI, while on de Gaulle's left marches the ever present Christian Girard.
Memorial du Maréchal Leclerc et de la Libération de Paris, Musée Jean Moulin, Ville de Paris

Pierre Billotte as a two star general. Captured during the Battle of France in 1940, Billotte escaped via Russia to join de Gaulle, becoming his ADC for a while. Following Leclerc's disagreements with Colonel Malagutti, de Gaulle foisted Billotte upon Leclerc as a battle-group commander, in which capacity he commanded the southern advance into Paris during August 1944. *Musée de l'Ordre de la Libération*

Alain de Boissieu of the 501e RCC was one of the officers who reached de Gaulle from Russia with Billotte. He commanded the 2e DB's HQ protection squad during 1944–1945. After the war he married de Gaulle's daughter Elizabeth. *Memorial du Maréchal Leclerc et de la Libération de Paris, Musée Jean Moulin, Ville de Paris*

Above: The Oath at Kufra has been kept and the *Tricolore* flies over Strasbourg. Holding his stick like a sheathed sword, Leclerc salutes a parade of the 12e Cuirassiers on Strasboug's Place Kléber with Girard and Colonel Rouvillois standing behind. *Imperial War Museum*

Below: Decorating his favourite Americans. Leclerc pins French medals to the chests of General Wade Haislip (left) and his staff. *Imperial War Museum*

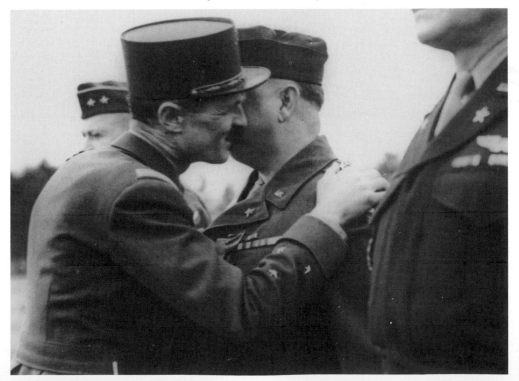

Captain de Vaisseau Raymond Maggiar stands beside a knocked out Tank Destroyer during the winter battles. By now Leclerc had forgiven the shipless sailors of Maggiar's RBFM for their Vichy past. *Memorial du Maréchal Leclerc et de la Libération de Paris, Musée Jean Moulin, Ville de Paris*

General Jean de Lattre de Tassigny. De Lattre was undoubtedly one of France's best soldiers whom de Gaulle had even recommended to defend Paris in 1940, but his failure to modernise the French First Army's thinking and keep proper control of his colonial troops during 1944–45 caused many disagreements with Leclerc that were the talk of Parisian society. *Musée de l'Ordre de la Libération*

Colonel Paul Repiton-Préneuf was a highly skilled intelligence soldier. He warned de Gaulle of the danger Vichy represented in Syria during 1941. He served as the 2e DB's intelligence chief and followed Leclerc to Indo-China where his advice was invaluable. *Memorial du Maréchal Leclerc et de la Libération de Paris, Musée Jean Moulin, Ville de Paris*

Louis Dio as a Lieutenant-General after the war. Another tough soldier of "La Coloniale," Dio's support tipped the balance in Leclerc's favour during the coup at Douala. He continued to serve Leclerc faithfully as a combat group commander both in Africa and Europe, before taking over as commander of the 2e DB. *Musée de l'Ordre de la Libération*

General Gracey (center) welcomes Leclerc to Indo-China. *Imperial War Museum*

Colonel Jean Crépin stands to attention to mourn his chief. Crépin had followed Leclerc all the way from Douala and hand-wrote the famous note *"Tenez bon, nous arrivons,"*—"Hold on, we're coming!"—to the beleagured defenders of the Paris Préfecture on 25th August 1944. *Memorial du Maréchal Leclerc et de la Libération de Paris, Musée Jean Moulin, Ville de Paris*

metres away. The French reacted faster, a testimony to good training, and left the Panzer in flames, hit by seven armour piercing rounds. Next, a Panther tank appeared, disabling *Richelieu,* destroying two Jeeps—grandiloquently called *Impétueuse* and *Dédaigneuse*—and wounding six men. Luckily *Richelieu's* damage did not prevent her crew from firing back at the Panther, putting it out of action. The RBFM had done well and the captured German armoured cars were driven into Carrouges by their own drivers, following behind Lt. Debout's Greyhound.[48]

Leclerc entered Sees with GT Billotte. There Billotte divided his GT into two sub-groups; the first under Colonel Warabiot moved on to Écouché, west of Argentan, reaching the outskirts during the night. This was a significant action, meaning that the route from Vire to Paris—along which much Wehrmacht traffic had to move to escape the looming encirclement—was effectively cut. Billotte's other sub-group, led by Commandant Putz, the Spanish Civil War veteran from the Corps Franc d'Afrique, headed along the northeastern side of the forest to harrass any of 9th Panzer trying to escape northwards.[49] By dusk Putz had reached the crossroads in the forest centre, meeting up with GT Dio coming in from the south.

It was there that Leclerc joined them. After conferring with Putz, a light detach-ment under the "Russian" Captain Jacques Branet was sent to make contact with Warabiot's men at Écouché. En route they surprised elements of the 116th Panzer Division, which was reduced to fifteen serviceable tanks and heading towards Sees to rescue the remnants of 9thg Panzer. The rest of Putz's group joined with sub-group Massu to destroy the remaining 9th Panzer Division artillery batteries in the forest of Écouves.

With the whole division engaged in combat that day, Leclerc was everywhere, usually in his Jeep with Girard, and often on the radio directing artillery support. Moving about so much made Boissieu's job as head of the HQ protection squadron very difficult. The *Rochambelles* worked tirelessly in their first real battle to maintain quick casualty evacuations. Several times Suzanne Torres found herself on the wrong side of the lines, but on each occasion the Germans allowed her to pass. Quaker stretcher-bearer Dennis Woodcock noticed how the success at Alençon and kicking 9th Panzer Division out of the forest of Écouves had given the 2e DB immense confidence.

With the forest of Écouves in French hands, Boissieu ringed the new CP with his Stuarts. Like everyone else, Leclerc slept on the ground that night. Girard slept sitting up nearby, his French 1935 helmet on his head and a Colt.45 automatic in his hand. In the distance, remnants of the 116th and 9th Panzer Divisions could be heard rumbling away to the northeast to join other retreating Wehrmacht units who were being hemmed in at Falaise.[50]

The following day the division reassembled amid sporadic confrontations with exhausted Germans. These were also being mopped up by the US 90th Infantry Division which followed behind the 2e DB. North of the forest, GT Dio linked up with GT Billotte at Écouché, and Roumiantsoff's Spahis entered the southern outskirts of Argentan. From Roumiantsoff's position on the Baise, Leclerc peered at the town through binoculars, taking *Tailly* as close as he dared to the southern outskirts. There were no signs from civilians in doorways or windows to alert the French to enemy movement. The only thing that seemed to be happening was Girard ripping his trousers on the radioman's seat.[51] Then a window rattled and a civilian signaled a German tank nearby, a Panther in enfilade that could have destroyed the unarmed Sherman. Aware of the danger, Boissieu passed an anxious few minutes watching *Tailly* thread its way back through Argentan's streets to comparative safety, Leclerc standing in *Tailly*'s turret smiling radiantly as he watched Roumiantsoff's Spahis probe for German positions. Back at the divisional CP Guillebon chewed out Boissieu.

"When one has the honour to command the unit charged with protecting General Leclerc one does not leave him wandering off alone in his tank," said Guillebon dourly.

There had also been a problem with *Tailly*'s radio, but even so there was nothing Boissieu could do to stop Leclerc from swanning off when he wanted.[52]

Deaf to his subordinates, Leclerc was determined to set up a new CP in full view of the town until a German shell smashed his precious caravan and injured several officers. German patrols were frantically testing the boundaries of the pocket into which they were being relentlessly pushed, but the Spahis' patrolling was also aggressive, and Lt. Duplay's squadron reasserted French control south of Argentan.

North of the town, the eastern end of the Falaise pocket remained open while Field Marshal von Kluge's German Seventh Army was subjected to continuous bombardment from artillery and ground attack aircraft called in cab-rank style. Taking any road they could, German troops approaching Écouché found themselves facing GT Billotte pushing the other way, preventing them from linking up with other German forces still west of the Seine. French patrols pushing into the German pocket west of Écouché, around Serans and Montgaroult, found themselves bringing back an increasingly diverse range of prisoners from Wehrmacht, Luftwaffe and Waffen SS divisions, bearing testimony to the increasing disorder of Hitler's legions. The fighting continued, though, as the Wehrmacht had a skill for creating *ad hoc* units from whoever could be found when the need arose.

Every day that the pocket remained open, the Germans could continue to withdraw men and equipment. The Allies faced a difficult choice: whether to go for a small envelopment which the Germans would be more than capable of fighting their way out of—or else try for a longer envelopment. The first choice put Patton's Third Army into a furious attack northwards to meet up with the British and Canadians around Falaise, a plan upon which Montgomery had agreed during early August. However General Crerar's Canadians got bogged down against stiff resistance on 11th August, which was attributed to leadership problems at the most basic level. Montgomery could have tasked experienced British formations to close the Falaise pocket, but he did not want to withdraw units from one place and move them across the support lines of other formations; what he called "untidyness."[53] Furthermore, seasoned British divisions like the 7th Armoured Division, the "Desert Rats" who had been brought from Italy to take part in the D-Day operation, were by this fifth year of the war not the formations they had once been.

Could the US Third Army have gone further to close the pocket? German strength had built up in Argentan, with elements of the 1st and 2nd SS Panzer redeploying to support the exhausted 116th Panzer Division. German artillery had relocated north of Argentan and it was these guns that were targeting lead elements of the 2e DB.[54] Amid the conjecture whether Haislip's XV Corps could have made faster progress to close the Falaise pocket, it has sometimes been said that Leclerc's infringement on the US 5th Armored Division's operational area in Sees slowed that division by six hours, thereby denying it the opportunity of reaching Argentan earlier.[55] It also seems likely that the Allied high command had not fully appreciated what the French had achieved in reaching Argentan. Patton certainly saw the significance, joking that he could not only reach Falaise but push the British back to Dunkirk again. Allied intelligence believed that a German counterattack was building on the 2e DB's left flank to keep the pocket open.[56]

In fact, it was US General Omar Bradley's decision to halt Patton's army, thereby allowing more encircled Germans to get away. Some say this was due to concern that the British and American pincers might find themselves firing upon one another when they met up. The Allies were always over-cautious of German counterattacks on their flanks. In any case, just as with the Russian encirclement of Stalingrad, where two Russian armies met up at Kalach, the truth was that a wider envelopment was needed with its pincers meeting across less local resistance.

Leclerc was angry at seeing the 2e DB halted at Argentan. He was a cavalryman and did not believe the role of armoured divisions was to remain static. All he wanted to see was an Allied victory as soon as possible, and for this reason he sometimes viewed de Gaulle's political antics among the Allied chiefs with misgiving. "Who does that fellow think he is?" Leclerc once said to Wade Haislip when the American general brought him a telegram from de Gaulle insisting that he put the third star on his képi. However, Leclerc was aware of his Gaullist agenda as well, and was beginning to think the time was ripe for the 2e DB to play the role it was born for— marching on Paris, there to "crown" the leader of Free France.

On 15th August, Haislip told Leclerc that two divisions, including the 2e DB, were to be pushed towards Dreux. Leclerc was unhappy about this and wrote a letter to Patton threatening to pull his division out of the line if it wasn't given the honour of marching on Paris. Next he flew to US Third Army HQ, where Patton first began by promising that he would have his way. However General Wood, commander of the US 4th Armored Division, which had taken Rennes and cut off the Germans in Brittany, was also there. Wood was a similar character to Leclerc in many ways, and Patton said, "You see Wood, well he is even more fed up than you are." Leclerc thought he had Patton's agreement, however, and returned to his division in higher spirits, saying to his cousin Wallerand de Hauteclocque over dinner that he soon hoped to march on Paris. Nevertheless, the day finished without further instructions, though news came through that de Lattre's French First Army had landed at Fréjus.

At dusk on 16th August, Leclerc was called to Third Army HQ again where General Gaffey gave him orders not to march on Paris but to allocate one of his GTs to join an attack the following day by US 90th Infantry Division aimed at finally closing the pocket. The idea of seeing his division split up and passed around did not appeal. The first "2e DB" had suffered such a fate in 1940. Also, looking at the map it became clear to Leclerc that this attack was not a matter for tanks, and that its conception was as an infantry attack. In any case, he felt it was a mediocre plan, which, in his opinion would lead to the massacre of two divisions. "Nothing is ready. There is no resupply, no intelligence, no reconnaissance, no reserves, no back-up, and no possibility of exploitation."

"I am in command and I am giving you an order," said Gaffey, exasperated.

"It is inexecutable," replied Leclerc bluntly. "There isn't a third of what's needed."

"Are you refusing to obey orders?" asked Gaffey as he turned to a clerk. "Make a note of this."

Gaffey said he would put the matter to Patton, but was not going to call him in the middle of the night. In the meantime he expected the attack force to get to its start lines. Girard wrote in his journal that he suspected Gaffey was a bank manager in civilian life, and thought they would be taken to an execution pit. The discussion ended inconclusively at 1am and they returned to Fleuré.[57]

The following morning the attack was suspended, only to be revived again in an altered form by General Gerow, the commander of US Vth Corps, which had been transfered from US First Army. Active, competent and authoritarian, Gerow had come up with a new version of Gaffey's plan to link up with British 21st Army Group, which entailed weaving through known German positions, first west, then northeast. Reluctantly, Leclerc allocated GT Langlade to support the US 90th Infantry. Leclerc was, nevertheless, most unhappy. He wanted to keep the 2e DB as intact as possible for marching on Paris, and, since talk in Patton's HQ was that Paris should be bypassed, he was increasingly coming to the conclusion that he might have to take unilateral action. In the meantime, the 2e DB was under American command and had to be seen to obey.

"We are visiting the headquarters of the US 90th Infantry Division," Leclerc informed Langlade. "You salute. You listen to their orders. You simply say 'understood.' You don't ask for any explanations and you leave. Then you wait for me at your Jeep."[58]

Langlade's orders were to act as flank guard and cut his way towards Trun. Just as Leclerc told him, he replied "understood" and then returned to his Jeep where he found Leclerc.

"It is necessary for us to be in Paris in forty-eight hours," Leclerc told him. "I will go to General Bradley to have this decision overturned. It is essential that you are not involved in a scrap that you will be unable to disengage from, or in which you might come off badly."[59]

Now trying to obey two masters, Langlade took Massu and Minjonnet into his confidence. Together they manoeuvred GT Langlade so astutely between them that they managed to close the gap and meet up with their old friends of 1st Polish Armoured Division, without getting involved in any costly engagements.[60] The 12e RCA called out loud laconic greetings of "Hello!" in mock English upper-class voices to the Poles, doubtless learnt from the Guards Armoured Division while all three divisions were in Yorkshire.[61]

Under a smoke screen, sub-group Minjonnet managed to reach the top of hill 262. From there they had an excellent view of the Chambois basin. Below them, miserable crowds of German soldiers, driving clapped vehicles and horsedrawn carts, were attempting to retreat in a cloud of dust. Having closed the pocket as cost-effectively as possible, GT Langlade was now available to rejoin the rest of the 2e DB to take General de Gaulle, "Charles XI" as they sometimes called him, to his "coronation" in Paris.

Langlade regrouped his men alongside GT Billotte. The latter were still in the Écouche area and had met up with General 'Pip' Roberts' British 11th Armoured Division, as German resistance in the Falaise pocket collapsed. From the 22nd August the 2e DB was laagered up north of the forest of Écouves awaiting its next mission.

The Battle of Normandy was over. Leclerc told Girard, a captain since 14th

August, that, given the huge material advantage possessed by the Western Allies, greater coordination between the Allied armies could have led to a quicker victory and a larger encirclement, trapping another 250,000 *Boches*, which would have seen the Allies in the Champagne region by mid-August. Leclerc dreaded what might happen once the war reached the industrial areas of northeast France.[62]

As for the 2e DB, in less than three weeks it had gone from being a new formation whose troops were a mix of both highly experienced and green as the grass, to being one of the most effective armoured divisions in the Allied Expeditionary Force. This may well have been due to Leclerc's personal style of leadership, often at or near the front line, in full view, wearing a képi and carrying his malacca walking stick. His troops called him, "*le Patron*" or "*Père la canne.*" Asked by General Haislip why he took such risks, Leclerc replied, "Sir, I have a lot of people who do not know how to fight, and I have to show them."[63]

The first phase of their attack from Le Mans to Alençon felt easy to young tankers like Gaston Eve of the 501e RCC, but in and around the forest of Écouves the 2e DB fought an experienced enemy which was facing its own desperate struggle for survival, yet the Frenchmen had won. Colonel Malaguti's insubordinate criticisms a couple of months earlier had proven unfounded. In their first battle the division had cost the Germans over 7,000 in killed, wounded and prisoners at a cost to itself of 550 casualties (circa 3.5% of their effectives). They had destroyed over 600 German combat vehicles for acceptable losses to their own equipment, and had engaged Germans from at least five Panzer divisions.

Numerically, the 2e DB's losses could be replaced by new recruits from the liberated areas. Their training cadre was running full time in Great Britain with young Frenchmen being whisked across the Channel, put into uniform, trained and sent back to the division in France. Losses among experienced junior officers were harder to replace; the 12e RCA's Lt Guy de Valence returned to the 2e DB a few months later minus an arm. In most other armies Valence would have been invalided out.

For most of the men it had been a steep though highly exciting learning curve. At the lowest level they had been pleased with the way their American equipment functioned, and the logistical back-up that kept ammunition, replacement vehicles and supplies flowing to the front. US Army K rations, delivered in boxes, became mind-crunchingly predictable, however high their quality and nutritional content. The 2e DB took full advantage of its status as the only *chez nous* combat formation in northern France to beg and borrow local produce, if it wasn't given to them freely, which it often was. It became commonplace to see 2e DB vehicles festooned with unplucked chickens, rabbits, and strings of onions awaiting the evening *popote*.

On 17th August, the 2e DB was swapped from Haislip's XV Corps to Gerow's Vth Corps, with whom they remained for the rest of August. Gerow understood Leclerc's unique position as the senior French combat officer in northern France at this time. Then there was Leclerc's obvious obsession with Paris and his unspoken threat to disengage the 2e DB and strike out on his own. This was something American generals simply did not understand. Eisenhower and Churchill knew implicitly that this was virtually the 2e DB's only *raison d'être*, though none of them were aware that Leclerc had been appointed interim Governor of Paris by de Gaulle while his division was still in Morocco.

Sensing Leclerc's frustration and the lack of understanding from the Americans, 2e DB supply officers began claiming extra petrol. Fuel was claimed for vehicles that had been destroyed, and if American supply supervisers were unwilling to part with what they wanted, the 2e DB resorted to stealing.

As victor of Alençon, Leclerc had been on the radio announcing to the French people that he had arrived at the head of an armoured division to take part in France's liberation and that soon Paris would be free. At the village of Warlus near Tailly, his home in Picardy, the broadcast was heard by Madame Dumont, the owner of the village café, just as she saw Thérèse de Hauteclocque and the children entering the local church to decorate it for the Feast of the Assumption. Madame Dumont ran out and called Thérèse inside to listen to the radio. In the drab café, Thérèse heard the same voice that said "*Adieu*" to her over four years before at Les Vergnes.[64] The open secret that her husband was "Leclerc" of Kufra was a secret no more.[65] The Vichy authorities had made an inventory of Leclerc's property and possessions during 1943, but the threat to evict Thérèse and the children from their home was never carried out.

De Gaulle was following events closely. His first visit to liberated areas shortly after D-Day had been thoroughly orchestrated by his staff so that when he arrived in the old town of Bayeux[66] there were enough people on the streets for him to make a credible walk-about. Such antics hugely annoyed Montgomery, who threatened to return him to England by force, something for which de Gaulle never forgave him. After visiting Roosevelt in Washington during July, de Gaulle returned to France on 20th August. Roosevelt had exhausted all other French leadership alternatives, such as General Giraud, so by August 1944 he grudgingly accepted the reality of "Free France" and, in his turn, de Gaulle graciously thanked the United States for its prodigious war effort.

With victory in Normandy and German forces withdrawing behind the Seine, a thrust to liberate Paris no longer seemed so distant a prospect for de Gaulle's favourite general. Any reluctance by Allied commanders to take Paris was motivated by logistics. As soon as the city was liberated its population would have to be fed, immediately adding some two million mouths to General Eisenhower's food bill. It would take months before normal French food distribution got back into its stride.

The population of Paris was meantime getting impatient. On D-Day their spirits had leapt and their eyes were naturally riveted upon the drama unfolding in Normandy, bringing with it hopes of liberation. But Parisians, especially the city council, now feared their city might become another Stalingrad or worse. That summer, as Stalin's Red Army neared the outskirts of Warsaw General Bor-Komorowski's highly organised Polish Home Army had risen up against the German occupiers. Polish resistance was non-Communist and Stalin had no wish to see them prevail over the Nazis, so the Red Army was halted on the Vistula while two of Hitler's most notorious SS units, the Dirlewanger and Kaminski Brigades, destroyed Bor-Komorowski's army. Hitler then ordered Warsaw reduced to rubble, SS engineers blowing it up block by block. German news film of this was shown all over occupied Europe, ending rather typically with the threat, "So perish all enemies of the Reich!" Parisians naturally wished to avoid this fate.

It had already been an interesting summer in the French capital. A large part of the drama of July 20th, the unsuccessful German Army officers' plot to kill Hitler and remove the Nazis from power, was played out in

Paris. France's military governor, General Carl-Heinrich von Stulpnagel, had been implicated and subsequently tried to commit suicide with a pistol at Verdun, where he had served during the first war. Having only succeeded in blinding himself, von Stulpnagel was arrested and tortured. Breaking down in his cell he called out, "Rommel, Rommel," thereby beginning a chain of events which led to Rommel's forced suicide that autumn. Other Wehrmacht conspirators were faced down by Admiral Theodor Krancke, the head of the Kriegsmarine in France, though General Gunther Blumentritt managed to negotiate a deal with local SS chiefs which saved many decent Germans from the gallows. Even Field-Marshal von Kluge was implicated, having been well acquainted with Stauffenberg's representative in Paris, the Luftwaffe officer Casar von Hofacker.

By mid August, the Gestapo trail had reached Kluge's door. When Falaise fell on 17th August, putting the seal on Kluge's military humiliation, Field-Marshal Model arrived at Kluge's headquarters carrying a letter from Hitler sacking Kluge and ordering him to keep OKW informed of his movements. The message was clear. Leaving France, von Kluge also told his driver to stop at Verdun, where he successfully ended his life with cyanide.[67]

A few days earlier, during the three-day holiday Parisians give themselves to celebrate the Feast of the Assumption, Lt. General Dietrich von Choltitz arrived in the city to take over the military governorship from the hideously wounded though decent Lt. General Hans von Boineburg-Lensfeld. Unlike Boineburg-Lensfeld, von Choltitz was reckoned a *ganz Harter*, a die-hard, an utterly strict Prussian who did not know how to disobey an order. His record spoke for itself. It was von Choltitz who gave the ultimatum to the garrison of Rotterdam in May 1940 that they should surrender or their city would be bombed. The surrender did not come through in time and Rotterdam was wrecked. Von Choltitz was also responsible for bombarding the Crimean capital of Sebastopol to smithereens with a giant mortar during the invasion of Russia. In early August 1944 Hitler, enraged to new levels of madness by the attempt on his life, was determined that if Paris fell back into Allied hands it would be as a smouldering moonscape. Hence von Choltitz's appointment.[68]

Shortly before his removal, Field Marshal von Kluge had ordered the French Police to be disarmed, including the 20,000-strong Paris Police. As the occupation progressed, many policemen became uneasy at the role Vichy expected them to play, whether it was stamping out the resistance or rounding up Jews.[69] Once it became clear the Allies would win in the end, they began forming their own links with the resistance.

The resistance in Paris knew their hour was approaching, but it was divided between Communists and Gaullists. The Communists wanted to seize power as soon as the Germans looked weak enough for an uprising to have a chance of success, and then present Métropolitan France with a *fait accompli*. The Gaullists, however, wanted to forestall this eventuality by handing the political leadership of Paris, and France, to General de Gaulle. Rivalry between the two factions intensified, with killings and betrayals to the Gestapo becoming a daily occurrence. Paris's prisons were bursting with *résistants* of every hue. Every day another trainload was sent to concentration camps in Germany. The unlucky ones were shot at Mont Valérien.

The Western Allies had been alerted to the political problems in Paris by Jacques Chaban-Delmas, de Gaulle's senior resistance general in the city. Chaban-Delmas (*Chaban* was the last in a long succession of *noms de guerre*) was flown out of France by Lysander in early August. After a visit to London, which included interviews with General Ismay and Winston Churchill, Chaban-Delmas returned to Paris via a quiet sector of the American lines, cycling back into the city dressed in tennis whites, carrying a racket and a freshly killed chicken in his saddle basket. The orders he brought from de Gaulle were that there should be no insurrection in Paris until the Allies were close, whereupon the resistance might be allowed a day's worth of activity to satisfy honour. If the Communists (from whom the rank and file of the Parisian resistance were largely drawn) seized the initiative by rising prematurely, then the Gaullist resistance would have to balance the situation by wresting control from them and the Germans combined. For that there would be a coded message given by the BBC's French Service, "*As-tu bien déjeuné, Jacquot,*" which Chaban-Delmas hoped never to hear.[70]

The Communist resistance had been active as well. Their leader was Colonel Henri Tanguy, codenamed "Rol" after Theo Rol, a lad killed in the Spanish Civil War. His plans were so advanced that only one imponderable remained to be addressed. Would the Paris Police obey him? Von Choltitz's orders were to make the Allies pay dearly for Paris. Key points and buildings were made ready for demolition, including many architectural treasures. A Wehrmacht demolition expert was brought in to mine the bridges, many of which had been fitted with mining pans under a French law dating from the 1870s. The occupants of blocks near these bridges were ordered to leave.

As leader of the Municipal Council, Pierre Taittinger of the champagne family and councillor for the Vendôme district, was effectively Mayor of Paris. He was tipped off about these developments by an anonymous telephone call. Horrified, he immediately sought an appointment with von Choltitz. Taittinger was a right-winger who had founded his own party, the *Jeunesses Patriotes*, during the interwar years. Though losing a son in 1940, he spent the occupation lining his pockets at the expense of the city's dispossessed Jews, and interceding with the German authorities to lessen the unpleasantness of war for his fellow Parisians, usually the rich. Overall, his conduct during the Occupation was not especially commendable, and his Pooterish though fascinating postwar memoir, *Et Paris ne fut pas détruit*, fooled few. Yet, if his life had a moment of true heroism it was when he donned the robe of a burgher of Calais to plead with von Choltitz for the city he undoubtedly loved.[71]

Greeted with a harangue, Taittinger listened with growing distress while von Choltitz emphasised that he possessed the men and the means to turn Paris into another Warsaw. If one bullet was fired at a German soldier, the stocky little Prussian warned Taittinger, he would, "burn down every building in the block and shoot all their inhabitants." Shaken to his core, Taittinger glanced out the window while he composed himself. It was a beautiful afternoon and the gardens of the Tuilleries could be seen in the distance with pretty young women on bicycles and small boys playing with boats by the lakes. In desperation, the mandarin Frenchman exclaimed the beauty of Paris to the immoveable Prussian.

> Often it is given to a general to destroy, rarely to preserve. Imagine that one day it may be given to you to stand on this balcony again as a tourist, to look once more on these monuments to our joys, our sufferings, and to be able to say, 'Once, I could have destroyed all this, but I preserved it as a gift for humanity.' General, is not that worth all a conqueror's glory?

Though Taittinger's standpoint was blatantly self-interested at a time when Berlin was being bombed to rubble, his emotional plea visibly mellowed the German.

"You are a good advocate for Paris Monsieur Taittinger," replied von Choltitz, now calmer. "You have done your duty well. And likewise I, as a German general, must do mine."[72]

The Germans had now suffered two huge reverses that summer: the destruction of their Seventh Army at Falaise, and in the east, against the Russians, the loss of Army Group Centre, a far bigger disaster. In addition, RAF Bomber Command and the US 8th Air Force were bombing the heart out of Germany on a daily basis. So the Germans were hardly open to pleas for quarter.

Whatever document he might have folded into his wallet, Leclerc was not only concerned to reach Paris so de Gaulle could re-establish the French state, he also genuinely loved the city. Like many of his men he had relations there. He also had few illusions about the sort of orders Hitler and the Wehrmacht's OKW were capable of issuing. So on 19th August he sent Weil to SHAEF HQ in another attempt to elicit the Allied High Command's intentions for Paris. SHAEF's latest thinking was to avoid fighting in built-up areas, so costly in soldiers' lives, and to envelop the capital from north and south, meeting somewhere along the Marne.

By now Leclerc was also aware that the Americans preferred not to have the food needs of Paris added to their supply burden. His staff felt understandably bitter at this outlook, already feeling that the Americans cared little about the level of destruction in France. Argentan was a case in point often discussed among the 2e DB. Colonel Crépin, the division's artillery chief, had taken great pains to aim his artillery at known German positions, avoiding unnecessary destruction in Argentan. When the Americans took over that sector, after meeting a little resistance, their heavy guns fired all night and wrecked the town. "Always the same view," wrote Girard in his journal. "It's the big omelette that counts."[73]

In the "*vaste salade*" of corps and divisions, the 2e DB thought no one was interested in their natural desire to march on Paris. They received understanding, yes; but positive orders, no. Leclerc told Girard, who was unaware of the document Boissieu had delivered to Leclerc on 15th

December 1943, that he was considering a rerun of his *marche sur Tripoli* on a grander scale. A *général de division* might say this to his ADC with wry joviality, but both recognised the gravity of any such decision.[74]

On 20th August Leclerc came out of conference with Gerow feeling slightly more satisfied that an American understood his viewpoint.

"You're not just a divisional commander," said Gerow. "You represent the French Army."

But little seemed to change.

"That is not up to me," said Gerow. "You'll have to go higher."

Annoyed that he would have to repeat himself, Leclerc resignedly got into a Piper Cub to visit US First Army headquarters.

"The trouble with the Americans is their puritan sense of discipline," Leclerc moaned to Girard. Leclerc would have to lay it out for them again, going as high as it took. Girard's observation of the American military mind was that, "They would take for indiscipline the crisis of conscience that would make a soldier undertake a course of action for non-military reasons."[75]

General Courtney Hodges, commander of US First Army, was a typical product of the Pentagon hierarchy: applied, meticulous and conscientious. The Allies were going to "regroup," Leclerc was told, a phrase that often puzzled him. And then what? Hodges would not say. Exasperated, Leclerc decided not to hesitate any longer. He would go it alone. He decided to send an advance guard towards Paris under Jacques de Guillebon.

Through the night, Guillebon gathered a mini *groupe de marche* from the various regiments of the division, an eclectic force of halftracks, armoured cars and light tanks that the 2e DB's US liaison officers would not miss. Making sure they had enough rations, ammo and petrol, they slid into their vehicles as daylight was fading. Guillebon gave every officer one simple order, "Avoid the Americans at all costs." Then Leclerc waved them off into the damp, dark night.

Before turning in, Leclerc called for Alain de Boissieu. The following day Boissieu was to take their US liaison officers, Major Loumiansky and Captain Plutschak, for a little sightseeing trip—castles, churches, anything to keep them out of the way.[76]

Leclerc was right to worry about American interference. While Boissieu kept Loumiansky and Plutschak occupied by revisiting the 501e RCC's campaign trail between Alençon and Argentan, Leclerc ordered GT Langlade to regroup with the rest of the 2e DB around Médavy. But no sooner had he informed Gerow's HQ of this than orders came back telling him to leave GT Langlade exactly where it was.

Leclerc's relationship with the Americans was wearing thin. The disagreements with General Gaffey had been noted, and they clearly expected Leclerc to be grateful for their not taking the matter further. Even some of Leclerc's staff, unaware of the secret document in his wallet, felt enough liberties had already been taken towards the Americans.[77]

For four days following the Argentan battle, the 2e DB's HQ did virtually nothing. With orders not to disclose Guillebon's advance guard, Leclerc sent Repiton-Préneuf to US First Army HQ with the complaint that everything was going too slowly and that the 2e DB should be allowed to proceed to Paris forthwith. General Hodges replied that the Germans were reorganising around Paris, and such a manoeuvre would take time.[78] It seemed unbelievable to Leclerc that, at the pinnacle of his career, the misfortune of being transferred from Patton's command to the vacillating Hodges could have the direst consequences for post-war French politics.

Weil's news brought him further frustration. Over a glass of whisky General Bradley had told Weil that things were going well and that the French should be patient. Leclerc felt he was being fobbed off all around, but he admitted to Girard that it was difficult for a *chef d'escadron* such as Weil to take such a message to a four-star general commanding an entire army group.[79]

That evening Vth Corps HQ telephoned André Gribius to ask if the 2e DB had troops in the Senonches area, on the road to Paris.

"No," replied Gribius, unaware of Guillebon's probing advance guard.

"You're sure?" asked the American staff officer.

"I am sure," said Gribius.

"Really sure?" probed the suspicious American.

"Quite sure," said Gribius.

"Ah . . . "

Knowing Gribius was not entirely in the picture, Leclerc thought it best that he explain the 2e DB's position to Vth Corps. Leclerc felt that the sending of Guillebon's sub-group was self-explanatory and they should keep going, though difficulties were inevitable.

It is in the nature of human memory that conversations are not always remembered in detail. When Weil came back from Bradley's HQ the following morning and told Leclerc that the Americans expected to envelop Paris instead of going in, Leclerc was beside himself.

"How?" demanded Leclerc incredulously. "He wants a battle north of Paris and we aren't going to take part!"

The deadlock had to be broken. Leclerc ordered one of the 2e DB's six Piper Cubs to fly him to Omar Bradley's HQ.[80]

CHAPTER TEN

"MOUVEMENT IMMÉDIAT SUR PARIS"

The disarmament of French Police ordered by Field Marshal von Kluge had gone off peacefully in most places, but the Paris Police regarded it as the final indignity after four years of subservience. They went on strike, leaving their *Vichysois* prefect, Amedée Bussière, alone in the Préfecture opposite Notre Dame. Then, on the morning of 19th August, the strikers returned to the Préfecture armed to the teeth. Bussière opened his bedroom shutters to the enormous courtyard below to be greeted by the sight of his policemen in *mufti* waving *Tricolore* flags. A Gaullist agent, Yves Bayet, announced through a loudspeaker that he had taken over the Préfecture in the name of General de Gaulle. There followed a rowdy rendition of the *Marseillaise*.[1]

As it happened, Communist leader Colonel Henri "Rol" Tanguy was cycling to an FTP staff meeting on the Rue de Meaux when he passed the approach to Notre Dame and heard the policemen defiantly singing.[2] Seeing the *Tricolore* flying above the Préfecture, Rol-Tanguy recognised that his long-planned Paris insurrection was running out of his control. Quickly he donned the uniform he wore during the Spanish Civil War, which he had secreted in his bicycle's panier, and presented himself at the Préfecture's great gate intending to take control. He found himself both ignored and pre-empted. While most of the FTP had only resisted the Germans since the invasion of Russia in 1941, Rol-Tanguy and an inner core had been involved in industrial sabotage throughout the occupation, tapping into the militant traditions of the Parisian working class, going back through the *communards* to the Revolution. They wanted post-war France to be Communist, and seizing control of Paris following the German collapse was a necessary pre-condition. For this Rol-Tanguy believed casualties in the region of 200,000 were acceptable.

By contrast, the Gaullists wanted to seize control with as little damage to the fabric of Paris as possible. Arriving back in the city from London, Jacques Chaban-Delmas advised the resistance to delay any rising until Allied armies were close enough to relieve them. However, once it became clear how advanced Rol-Tanguy's insurrection plans were (the FTP had trained for street fighting using old German *Freikorps* manuals from the 1920s) the Gaullist hierarchy gave Luizet and the Gaullist resistance within the Police orders to act without further delay.

Not to be outdone, Rol-Tanguy's FTP furiously printed posters calling for *mobilisation générale* and posted them across the city. With the cry, *"A chacun son boche!"* the FTP went into action alongside their Police compatriots who had previously hunted them, attacking individual German soldiers and mounting assaults on isolated German garrisons around the city.

General von Choltitz had no option but to regain control. The retreating Wehrmacht needed the Seine bridges to get away from the Allies. So Panther tanks were sent to subdue resistance strongpoints and seize back the Préfecture. The first shell fired at the Préfecture tore the large iron door off, scaring the wits out of the flimsily armed policemen. Many bolted towards the comparative safety of the Métro station beneath, but were halted at pistol-point by police sergeant Armand Fournet, who told them soberly that their best chance of survival was to win. Their resolve stiffened. Molotov cocktails were prepared in the Préfecture's cellar by a nephew of the Curies, who ordered the Prefect's wine reserve poured down the drain to provide the necessary empty bottles. Outside, the Germans prepared their assault.

Within a couple of hours of the German attack it became clear that the Préfecture insurrectionists were having a hard time and would soon run low on ammunition. Neuilly's *mairie* had already been subdued and its defenders taken to Mont Valerien.

Many now believed the city would be ruined if fighting continued. Of the neutral foreign diplomats available in Paris, Swedish Consul General Raoul Nordling was prepared to act as an intermediary. Nordling's father had been consul before him and he had spent most of his life in the French capital. In truth, he was as much of a Parisian mandarin as Pierre Taittinger, but the cloak of neutrality enabled him to fix an audience with von Choltitz at the Hôtel Meurice by late afternoon. Virtually reiterating Taittinger's words, Nordling told von Choltitz that destroying Paris would be an unforgiveable act of vandalism. For Choltitz, however, his soldierly duty gave him little choice but to "bomb them out of it [the Préfecture]."

"Near misses will fall on Notre Dame and the Sainte-Chapelle," the Swedish Parisian insisted, conscious of the Préfecture's proximity to the cathedral which, with its flying buttresses—*grand contreforts*—is a treasure of medieval architecture.

"Put yourself in my place," shrugged von Choltitz. "What alternative do I have?"

Nordling suggested a "truce" to attend the wounded and dying. In thirty-five years of soldiering von Choltitz had never heard of such a thing. Yet, if he could be sure of the Wehrmacht's uninterrupted movement through the city for a few hours it might be worth it. But while von Choltitz was confident that he could control his own men, he doubted the resistance could do the same. Therefore, he told Nordling, he would only discuss a truce if the resisters could keep a ceasefire for an hour's trial. In the meantime he called off the attack on the Préfecture.

The *résistants*' morale was sinking low. Hearing from Gaullist sources that the Allies would bypass Paris, a repeat of Warsaw was looking like a distinct possibility. When news arrived of Nordling's "truce" there was immense relief.

"Thank God," said Edgar Pisani, a young law student fighting in the Préfecture. "We've saved Paris!"[3]

In fact, at the end of the Paris insurrection's first round, it was Nordling and von Choltitz who had saved Paris.

That night de Gaulle returned to France for the second time since D-Day, in a Lockheed Lodestar piloted by the same Colonel Lionel de Marmier who, four years earlier, had built the Free French Air Force from obsolete Bristol Blenheims delivered to Douala in crates.

Updated on the Paris uprising by Koenig,[4] de Gaulle immediately arranged an interview with General Eisenhower. Ike knew exactly why he had come before the Frenchman even opened his mouth and, knowing it could slow him down, he had been "damned mad" at hearing the news. From the Lodestar's cockpit, de Marmier watched them tramping in the wet grass, the leader of Free France looking dejected as only he could. Reneging on his conversation with de Gaulle eight months before, Eisenhower's answer was "No." The Allies were there to destroy German armies and get the war over with, not pander to de Gaulle's political ambitions.[5] On hearing that Paris was so important to the Free French interest that de Gaulle was prepared to send the 2e DB into the city on his own authority, Eisenhower smiled. After all, he controlled the gasoline supply. However, Eisenhower had no idea how much fuel the 2e DB had been secreting away. Even so, de Gaulle would rather have gone to Paris with Eisenhower's blessing than against his wishes.

Events in Paris were spiralling out of control. Although the Nordling "truce" held through the night of 19th–20th August, the FTP were determined to have their battle, and after lunch on the 20th they denounced the truce as an act of treason. Violence returned to the streets, the FTP taking potshots at Germans, or the Germans would initiate a firefight themselves. Sadly, as is often the way when guerrilla fighters take on trained soldiers, résistants' casualties were higher than those they inflicted, and ammunition was running desperately low.

Rol-Tanguy did not want Americans in Paris any more than the Germans, but he did want American weapons and supplies. So he authorised Commandant Roger Gallois to reach Allied lines with a request for supply drops. Leaving the city, Gallois called on Dr. Robert Monod, a friend he trusted but also a Gaullist. As a senior physician, Monod was entitled to a car and plenty of German-authorised passes, and, Gallois hoped, like all physicians, Monod had a sense of confidentiality equal to any priest. However, when Gallois told Dr Monod his mission, the doctor was horrified. If weapons were dropped by parachute, he said, there would be heavy street fighting and Paris would certainly be turned into another Warsaw. Monod persuaded the younger Gallois that, whatever his politics, his mission instead ought to be getting the Americans, and especially de Gaulle, into Paris as quickly as possible.

"Robert, I think you are right," said Gallois.[6]

After several hours preparing arguments they decided they were ready. Since Dr. Monod was head surgeon at the Laennec Hospital, passage through the curfew was not a problem. He drove through the night to Perray-Vaucluse where he handed Gallois over to Gaullist supporters. Continuing through the night by lorry, Gallois reached German lines at Courville-sur-Eure by dawn. They saw a German machine-gun nest as they slipped through no-man's-land, but hoped the Germans would not want to expose their position by opening fire, and continued until finally they reached the Americans in the Chalmette valley.[7]

The Americans were not taking chances with Frenchmen demanding to speak to their senior generals. So, it was only after several interrogations that Gallois was finally taken to Patton's HQ at 1.30am on 22nd August.

"The Germans are demoralised," Gallois reported. "Some of their defenses are very feeble. The Parisians are hungry but are nevertheless fighting to cut off the enemy's retreat. They don't understand the idea of a vast encircling movement by the Americans. They are already in a 'cauldron.'"

"You should consider," replied Patton, "that the operations we are undertaking at the moment are not conceived lightly or without considerable planning and reflection. Our objective is Berlin, and we need to end the war as quickly as possible. The taking of Paris is not prescribed and we're not going there. We would have to be sure of feeding a large population and repairing various things destroyed by the Germans. We want to destroy enemy armies, not take towns!" He finished by summing up. "You should have waited for orders from the Allied high command before beginning your insurrection on your own initiative."[8]

But, like any Frenchman who listened to the BBC's French Service throughout the Occupation, Gallois had heard of Leclerc and the 2e DB, and he asked Patton if he could speak to Leclerc. Since the 2e DB now came under Hodges' First Army, Patton had to make a telephone call.

"Are you ready to make a long journey?" Patton asked, having discovered Leclerc's whereabouts and fixed the trip. Before Gallois' departure, Patton's staff found a bottle of champagne and Patton and Gallois drank to "France and Victory."

At Twelfth US Army Group HQ outside Laval, Gallois was received by General Bradley's chief of staff, General Sibert. Again the exhausted Gallois told his story. This time it was also heard by Bradley's French liaison officer, Colonel Lebel. Lebel knew Bradley would shortly visit Eisenhower, and he drafted his own plea for his country's capital. "If the American Army, seeing Paris in a state of insurrection, does not come to its aid, it will be an omission the people of France will be unable to forget."[9] As General Sibert left, taking the memory of what Gallois had said to him, he told Lebel, "Your impatient lion, Leclerc, is coming today. Take care of him, we may have important news for him tonight." With that Sibert climbed into a Piper Cub and left for Eisenhower's HQ.

After hearing de Gaulle's pleas, Eisenhower brooded for a couple of days before writing a note to General Walter Bedell-Smith, Roosevelt's chief of staff, admitting that the Allies might "be compelled to go into Paris." He also cabled General Marshall, in Washington, expressing his concern that liberating Paris would mean delaying the encirclement of German forces in the Pas-de-Calais.[10] On the other hand, as Eisenhower saw it, if the Allies had to go into Paris, there would be a triumphal entry in which de Gaulle would have a place of honour. However, hearing the news from the French capital, and with the spectre of another Warsaw in mind, Eisenhower said, "Well, what the hell, Brad. I guess we'll have to go in." With that, Bradley and Sibert returned to Laval.

By then Leclerc and Repiton-Préneuf had already been waiting at Bradley's HQ for several hours during which they spoke with Gallois at length. Leclerc paced up and down, switching at the damp grass with his cane and saying repeatedly, "I must have orders tonight." His own staff knew, however, that even if permission was unforthcoming, Leclerc would have gone anyway. Whenever there was the sound of an aircraft they stood utterly still, listening and looking into the sky, hoping it was the returning US generals. Eventually a Piper Cub came gliding towards the airstrip, touched down and taxied to a halt. General Bradley opened the fuselage door and climbed down.

"Well, you win," Bradley told Leclerc. "They've decided to send you straight to Paris."

Leclerc was visibly delighted.

Like many Americans, Bradley never really understood the quasi-medieval fervour of de Gaulle's followers, refighting their own private Hundred Years War. Bradley had never visited Paris himself, but he knew it was beautiful and he had one, almost unnecessary, condition.

"I want you to remember one thing above all: I don't want any fighting in Paris itself. It's the only order I have for you. There is to be no heavy fighting in Paris."[11]

Exhilarated, Leclerc and Repiton-Préneuf ran back to their own Piper Cub for the flight back to Fleuré. Striding back into the 2e DB HQ at dusk, Leclerc called for his operations officer and gave the famous order.

"Gribius! *Mouvement immédiat sur Paris!*"

Gribius passed the order to all commanders, and the whole division went into top gear at once. Leclerc found a letter from de Gaulle waiting for him, commending the dispatch of Guillebon's advance party. Next an order came in from Vth Corps commander, General Gerow. Having previously done all he could to hold them back, now the Corps commander demanded that the 2e DB get going within the hour. Gerow wanted the 2e DB in Paris by the 24th if possible or, in the case of serious resistance, to seize the bridges at Gennevilliers northwest of the capital, as they controlled a large loop of the Seine between Billancourt and Nanterre. The US 4th Infantry Division, the "Ivy Division," would advance on Leclerc's right and enter the city from Joinville and Vincennes.[12]

"This time it's 'Paname!'" as the era's *chanteuses* called "the City of Light."

The RBFM heard as they prepared their *popote*. For some the news was more emotional than for others. Captain Charles d'Orgeix of the 12e Cuir', from an old Parisian family, had attempted to defend the city's northern approaches in 1940 with little more than machine-guns and motorcycle combinations.[13] It had been horribly unequal. When the order came, d'Orgeix was close to tears. Commanding a squadron of Shermans built in Detroit, his own was called *Paris*.[14] The news also burnished a desire for smartness. Three weeks of grime, exhaust smoke, dust and cordite were wiped away wherever possible and razors appeared. Those who had never

seen Paris were teased by those who had; many had family there but most
had been colonials all their lives, only returning to the Métropole to fight
wars or be educated.[15]

All night Gribius prepared marching orders. The 2e DB would advance
on Paris along two main routes. The GTs Dio and Langlade would advance
along the route Sées, Mortagne, Chateauneuf-en-Thymerais, Maintenon
and Rambouillet. GT Billotte would make the main push from Mamers,
Nogent-le-Rotrou, Chartres, Ablis and Limours. Some present day French
historians believe de Gaulle wanted Leclerc to favour Billotte, but it seems
equally likely that Leclerc would have wanted to honour his most *Gaulliste*
tank regiment, the 501e RCC, by being first into central Paris.

By 6.30am on 23rd August the 2e DB was ready to move in two giant
columns while Colonel Peschaud's route teams pointed the way.[16]

By now Guillebon had reached Rambouillet, where the French President
had his country retreat. Along with a posse of American journalists, which
included Ermest Hemingway, they found the route clear of Germans. Leaving behind a troop of Spahis under Lt. Bergamain to hook up with the
main force when it arrived, Guillebon now pushed new reconnaissance
patrols towards the capital's southern approaches. German tanks were
encountered near Trappes, but Wehrmacht positions were less strong
around Arpajon and Sceaux, information that would be of signal importance to Leclerc a few hours later.[17]

The 2e DB rumbled along in a haze of dust and exhaust fumes. The
Shermans of the 501e RCC, the 12e RCA and 12e Cuir' were kings of the
road. The division's infantry, the RMT, were split between both routes and
everywhere there were lorries, armoured cars and Jeeps.[18] Leclerc and his
staff were in the lead. Stopping every so often, Leclerc and Girard would
stand at the roadside like traffic policemen, Leclerc leaning on his stick
with his young ADC beside him.

Leclerc reached Rambouillet by early afternoon and found Lt. Bergamain covered in blood after pulling injured crewmen from a knocked out
Stuart near Trappes. A gang of journalists appeared, including Hemingway,
seeming to think Paris was already liberated. Leclerc muttered audibly,
"Buzz off you unspeakables!" From then until Leclerc's death the great but
unfair Ernest would call de Gaulle's best general "That jerk Leclerc!" and

he wrote that Leclerc seemed nervous at Rambouillet.[19] Most journalists were firmly told that their moment would come, and to stay out of the way until then.[20]

It is often the lot of an advance guard to be too small to do anything. So it was for Guillebon. Having ascertained which routes were free of Germans, and having forged useful links with the local resistance, they had to turn back amid exclamations of "What? Are you going again? You're abandoning us? What about Paris?"[21]

At Rambouillet the 2e DB's columns halted. Gribius set up the divisional CP in the chateau park while Leclerc received local resistance leaders brandishing their latest information on German troop displacements. The most useful were the *gendarmes* who had been able to move around fairly freely with a trained eye for military detail. They told Repiton's *2eme bureau* the precise nature of German forces, tank numbers and defensive layout.

At once Leclerc sent Captain Janney to inform de Gaulle of conditions in Paris, and that operations to take the city would begin the following morning. De Gaulle telegrammed back, "in the manner of Bonaparte writing to Lannes,"[22]

> I have received Captain Janney and your note.
> I should like to see you today.
> I expect to be at Rambouillet this evening and to see you there.
> I embrace you.

Through the afternoon of 23rd August it became clear that fighting a defensive street-by-street battle in Paris itself was not a German priority compared to saving their troops from another envelopment. But a Warsaw style destruction of the city was still possible. Paris is at the confluence of several road systems with important bridges. Hitler had ordered the destruction of the city, and the Wehrmacht was compelled to hold onto the southwest banks of the Seine and Marne for as long as possible to delay the Allies' pursuit.

While Leclerc's priority was to prise the Germans out of the city with as little collateral damage as possible, de Gaulle was also concerned that the communist FTP, which dominated the resistance, could create a worse crisis than the Paris Commune of 1870–71. On the afternoon of 23rd

August, de Gaulle visited Chartres Cathedral and then flew on to Rambouillet. He could see Leclerc's advancing columns on the roads beneath him. Landing on the chateau's front drive, de Gaulle found his commissariat officer, Commandant de Lignières, had arrived ahead of him.[23] De Lignières had been busy getting the generator working, and had even found a Paris bus with a *gazogène* converted engine in nearby Dreux.

Inside the chateau, de Gaulle went to the library and picked out a volume of Molière's *Le Bourgeois Gentilhomme* to distract himself before a late lunch of cold C rations in the grand dining room.[24] A conference at 5pm gave him a clear idea of what Leclerc intended to do. Dismissing US Vth Corps' orders to head for Versailles and the Nanterre-St Germain bend, the 2e DB would wheel south of the city, avoiding German defences which now included another sixty tanks.

Gribius drew up Order No. 1. *S'emparer de Paris*—"To seize Paris," followed by Order No. 2 *Tenir Paris*—"To hold Paris."

The 2e DB would attack along two main axes. GT Billotte would move south of the city and make the principal effort along the axis Arpajon-Sceaux-Paris, using small roads where possible, avoiding heavily defended crossroads, and penetrate the city in the direction of the Panthéon, cross the Seine bridges and move on towards Vincennes and Charenton, taking in the bridge crossing of the Marne at Neuilly.

GT Langlade would push through from Dampierre, via Chevreuse, Jouy-en-Josas and Villacoublay to the Pont de Sèvres. From Pont de Sèvres a sub-group was to push towards Versailles and from there towards the centre, along the Champs Elysées to the Place de la Concorde. GT Dio would support GT Billotte's main thrust. The US 4th Infantry Division would be out on Billotte's right flank.[25]

After Leclerc finished his briefing, de Gaulle reflected how other French generals such as de Lattre and du Vigier would have died for such an opportunity.

"How lucky you are," he told Leclerc.[26] "Go quickly. We cannot have another commune!"

During the evening de Gaulle received news of conditions in Paris from Dr. Favreau, an emissary from Charles Luizet. The resistance had achieved a degree of control in some areas, forcing the Germans to retreat into strongpoints such as the École Militaire and Palais de Luxembourg, just the type of buildings the French did not want damaged, from which they launched attacks aimed at retaking control. De Gaulle welcomed a measure of resistance activity since it showed Frenchmen were taking part in their own liberation, which is why he had been irritated at the "truce" brokered by Nordling, whatever its benefits might have been.[27]

That night it rained. Around Rambouillet the evening was spent in constant activity, preparing meals, receiving supplies, and cleaning weapons. The 2e DB slept wherever dryness could be found, in vehicles or makeshift bivouacs. Leclerc was given a bed in the chateau beside which Sergeant Loustalot had placed a bar of dark chocolate.[28] Unaware of the proximity of Leclerc's division, the Germans still believed the activity at Rambouillet and Trappes was caused by a reconnaissance group. Von Kluge's successor, Field Marshal Walther Model, had reappraised the strategic importance of defending the western approaches to Paris, and sent for two panzer divisions which were expected to arrive by the 26th August.

After a brief night's sleep Leclerc, Girard and everyone in the advanced CP were up in the small hours while the men made ready in the green, sopping wetness of the surrounding forest. Leclerc planned to follow behind GT Billotte's main thrust towards Arpajon, while to the northwest a detachment of Spahis under Morel-Deville would attack the Trappes-Saint Cyr-Versailles area, making as much noise as possible to fool the Germans that this would be the 2e DB's main thrust into the city.

GT Langlade's first task was to cross the Chevreuse valley. At dawn Massu's sub-group set off from Saclay in the same joy-ride fashion as the day before, until they encountered a minefield at Châteaufort and artillery at the wooded crossing of the Bievre, losing three tanks from the 12e RCA, and turning to 2/RMT infantry to clear the opposition.[29] By the time they destroyed a dozen anti-tank guns barring their way it was already 11am.

Sub-group Minjonnet did better, reaching Jouy-en-Josas to the sound of church bells by 2pm. But their advance was not without tragedy. Of the two Zagrodski brothers serving in the 12e RCA, the elder had been killed at Alençon. Now the remaining brother was leading his troop up the flower blossomed slopes north of the Bievre. Seeing a 75mm Pak gun, Zagrodski's Sherman destroyed it, but there were more. Opening his turret hatch to get a better view, the younger Zagrodski was quickly shot in the head, collapsing back inside his tank.[30]

The march continued at a slower pace. Next, GT Langlade was held up by German panzers in the bois de Meudon and at the Chatillon crossroads. This did not stop the crowd from taking to the streets to welcome them, but all that would have to wait. The men kept their eyes on their gunsights as officers and NCOs turned away joyous civilians with "Not now! We love you too, but let us pass."[31]

By 9.30pm GT Langlade had reached its objective, the Pont de Sèvres, meeting up with *résistants*. There was a risk that the bridge might be mined, but Massu ordered a 12e RCA Sherman across supported by four *résistants* on foot. Nothing happened. By nightfall GT Langlade was installed at both ends of the bridge. In the western outskirts the news spread *"La division Leclerc est arrivée!"*[32] In truth, GT Langlade, though allocated a diversionary role, could have gone further. Massu knew he had enough fuel to push on towards the Étoile and the Champs Elysées, but Langlade stuck to his instructions, telling the veteran *méhariste*, "That is not your mission."[33]

GT Billotte set off from Rambouillet at the same time as GT Langlade, using the National 20 Orléans-Paris road as its axis. In the lead were Commandant Putz's 3/RMT, consisting largely of anti-fascist Spaniards. They passed through Arpajon and Monthéry without incident, with Leclerc following behind.[34] But from Ballainvilliers, they ran from one snarl into another, with both strong roadblocks and ecstatic crowds contributing to the delay. Annoyingly for Leclerc and his staff, Gerow and other Americans regarded the effusive welcome accorded the 2e DB and the time taken up as yet more evidence of the incorrigible triviality of the French. When GT Billotte stalled at Longjumeau, a policeman walked out from his *gendarmerie* to Leclerc's Jeep and extraordinarily asked Leclerc to come to the telephone. Charles Luizet, who had been a *comrade de promotion* at Saint-Cyr, was calling from the Préfecture. Crépin went with the Gendarme to take the call; Luizet wanted the 2e DB to hurry up as the *résistants* in Paris were running low on ammunition.

By midday, sub-group Putz had reached the southern outskirts of the industrial town of Antony, while on his right, sub-group Warabiot was held up in Morangis, south of Orly airport, and lost two tanks. With GT Billotte fully engaged, Leclerc ordered up GT Dio, which had been held in reserve. After resistance at every crossroads, Antony was taken by 4pm. Further progress was barred by German anti-tank guns at the crossroads of Croix le Berny, and Lt Montoya's platoon of Spaniards was nailed to the ground by machine-gun fire. Sub-group Warabiot managed to reach Fresnes prison, losing the Chad veteran Captain Dupont to a sniper's head shot, but got no further. To Leclerc's annoyance, GTs Billotte and Dio were bogged down in street fighting. Only Raymond Dronne managed to get his 9e Company north of Fresnes, despite being held up by German 20mm guns. The Eiffel Tower was visible, but the day was gone and GT Billotte was five times further from Paris than GT Langlade.[35]

The crowd was everywhere, glad to be liberated, but added to the day's collection of tragic incidents. On one occasion a beautiful girl approached a 501e RCC Sherman, raising her arms to be pulled aboard by the enthusiastic tank commander, when a German machine gun opened up on them. The girl fell to the ground, snagging on the tank's tracks, her summer dress peppered with bloody bullet holes.[36]

This was not how Leclerc wanted it at all. Angry and impatient, he walked down Antony's main street, cane in hand. Things were not going fast enough, and his anxiety over Paris increased after a new message from Jacques Chaban-Delmas once again raised the spectre of a French Warsaw. While Taittinger and Nordling may have persuaded von Choltitz to act with restraint, the Prussian general was nevertheless not going to surrender Paris without a fight, and he had prepared to blow up the Seine bridges. Leclerc decided it was time to get personal. He called for the *résistants'* emissary, Lt. Petit-Leroy, and dictated a note saying he would hold von Choltitz personally responsible for any damage to the fabric of Paris and its monuments. Petit-Leroy was killed later that evening when his Jeep was shot up by a German patrol, but they searched his corpse and Leclerc's message was on von Choltitz's desk by nightfall.[37] (After the war, von Choltitz admitted to Alain de Boissieu that this was the first time he feared being treated as a war criminal.)[38]

After a day of setbacks, the resistance had to be encouraged to hold out a little longer. The division's six Piper Cubs were slow machines, only flying at 110km per hour, making them vulnerable to German weapons such as rapid-fire 20mm guns. However, Colonel Crépin wrote *"Tenez bon, nous arrivons!"* He put the message in a weighted musette bag and Captain Callet flew over the rooftops of Paris, zigzagging all the way, to drop it into the Préfecture's courtyard.[39]

Nor could it be long before German reinforcements arrived.

At the Croix de Berny junction, Leclerc saw Raymond Dronne returning from his successful manoeuvre to envelope Fresnes. Tapping his cane on the ground with every stride, visibly dissatisfied by the events of the day, Leclerc called to the red-haired Chad veteran, "Dronne, what are you doing here?"

"Mon général, I am returning to the axis of advance."

"You know better than to do something dumb like that!" Leclerc snapped, and then explained to Dronne that there was less serious resistance east of Fresnes where the roads into Paris were open. Gesticulating with his cane while the captain stood to attention in US uniform topped by a *Coloniale* képi, Leclerc ordered him, "Dronne, march on Paris! Get into Paris!"

"At once, *mon général,*" replied Dronne, adding practically, "But I have only two platoons and I am going to need more than that."

"Take what you can find and quickly," said Leclerc.

"If I understand correctly," Dronne insisted, "I am to go around the points of German resistance, without letting them hold me up, and my objective is the centre of Paris."

"Correct!" said Leclerc. "Right on into Paris. Any way you like! Tell the Parisians and the resistance not to lose courage and that tomorrow the whole division will be in Paris." For a moment the tension left Leclerc's face and he relaxed, smiling at his old comrade.[40]

With Montoya's platoon ineffective, Dronne's company, the 9e of 3/RMT, was down to Elias and Campos' platoons and its HQ section. The men were mainly Spanish Civil War veterans whose halftracks carried names like *Madrid, Guadalajara, Brunete* and *Guernica.* To these men, who had more in common with Colonel "Rol" than de Gaulle, Dronne was nevertheless *"El Capitan."* Next Dronne needed tanks and combat engineers. A troop of three Shermans commanded by Lt. Michard, a priest with the White Fathers in peacetime, joined him from Witasse's company of the 501e RCC, with the *Montmirail, Champaubert* and *Romilly.* Lt.

Cancel's platoon of engineers brought Dronne's force to a hundred and fifty men in three Shermans, fifteen halftracks and assorted Jeeps.[41]

They set off at 8pm. A young man from Antony called Georges Chevallier stepped out of the crowd watching them and offered his services as guide. He had remarkable knowledge of the tangled network of roads in southern Paris, and helped Dronne's force thread its way through L'Haÿ-les-Rosas, Cachan and Arceuil past the fort of Bicêtre, where they feared they might be held up again by more fighting. Instead there was the rapturous welcome of Parisians unable to believe their eyes, seeing Spanish soldiers in the French Army, driving American vehicles. After Bicêtre they took another three quarters of an hour to reach the Porte d'Italie, which marked the boundary of old Paris where the *ancien régime* had ringed the city with customs houses.[42]

They were now in Paris. "Paname!" *la colonne Dronne* cheered to a man. Dronne himself had not slept for forty-eight hours, he had not shaved, he was filthy, and his US olive-drab uniform was stuck to his body with his own sweat, yet he was utterly thrilled. The only French part of his uniform, his *Coloniale* képi, had developed a jaunty bend on the right of its peak and, all in all, he presented a total contrast to the white-gloved French officers who had sat through the *drôle de guerre* of 1940.

Again and again they were held up by ecstatic Parisians. At first they were taken for Americans, and each time the crowd's joy multiplied on discovering they were *"Les Leclercs! Les Français!"* Dronne needed more information about German positions, but he was finding it impossible to make sense of the contradictory shouted directions coming from the crowd. Again a guide offered himself, a young man in patched clothes, sitting astride a moped for which he had somehow obtained petrol in that capital of food shortages, power cuts and wooden-soled shoes. Even more strange, he was Armenian (ironically, the 9e Compagnie had lost an Armenian earlier in the day). Lorenian Dikran, like Georges Chevallier a couple of hours earlier, was both calm and knowledgeable as he gave Dronne directions into central Paris, avoiding both *résistants'* barricades and German strongpoints. Deciding to trust Dikran, Dronne made the Hôtel de Ville his objective, because it symbolised the rights and liberties of all Parisians and Frenchmen.[43]

Dikran led the way on his moped, followed by Dronne in his Jeep, which now sported a live figurehead on the bonnet. A well-built *alsacienne* called Jeanne Borchert had plonked herself there, cracking the folded-down windscreen. This Jeep had somehow obtained the name *Mort aux Cons*— "Death to Idiots!"[44]

Dronne's force drove quickly along the Avenue d'Italie before threading its way down narrower prestigious streets such as rue Baudricourt, rue Nationale, and rue Esquirol. Next, *la colonne Dronne* turned along the boulevard de l'Hôpital, crossed the Seine at the Pont d'Austerlitz and made their way along the quais alongside the river to the Quai Hôtel de Ville. The streets were empty and the racket of tanks and halftracks on the cobblestones drowned out the gunfire from other parts of the city.

They arrived outside the Hôtel de Ville at 9.22pm before it was fully dark, in the warmth of late summer. At once Dronne put his force into all-round defence. Then he entered the Hôtel de Ville and climbed the main staircase to the *grand salon* which blazed with electric light. All the dignitaries of the Parisian resistance were there: Georges Bidault, Laniel, Marrane, and others. Standing unshaven in his sweat-soaked uniform and battered képi, Dronne felt deeply moved. For the burghers of Paris his appearance signified the end of a nightmare. For the Spaniards of the 9e Compagnie, liberating Paris was not the same as Madrid, but it was something. It was a high point in their struggle against fascism and, that evening, they were winning.[45]

Georges Bidault tried to make a speech but his voice broke with emotion. A radio reporter picked on one of Dronne's men, another Armenian called Pirlian Krikor. "I have in front of me a French soldier," he said, speaking into his microphone live to the people of France, "a brave guy who has just got here. Tell us, where are you from? Where were you born?"

"Constantinople," replied Krikor.[46]

Crowds gathered around Dronne's men in the Place d'Hôtel de Ville, church bells were rung and everyone sang the *Marseillaise*. Then a rattle of machine-gun fire brought them back to reality. By the time Dronne got back downstairs the crowd had vanished into cover. 2nd Lieutenant Bacave radioed back to 2e DB HQ, "We are at the Hôtel de Ville!"

Soon after, two policemen arrived at the Hôtel de Ville to take Dronne to the Préfecture. Leaving his men under the Spanish Lt. Granell, Dronne took Pirlian Krikor and went with the police to the Préfecture where senior

Gaullist *résistants*, Luizet, Chaban-Delmas, the newly released Alexandre Parodi, and others awaited them. Dronne confirmed that the 2e DB would arrive in the city at dawn. Charles Luizet asked if he wanted anything. "A bath," replied Dronne. They showed him to the bathroom in the Prefect's private suite, but there was no time to wallow in that unaccustomed luxury. Soon he was back with his men, and he spent the night slumped against the front of his Jeep outside the Hôtel de Ville.[47]

On the threshold of legend, Leclerc refused the bedroom Girard had requisitioned for him, preferring instead to lie down Sahara-style under a tree at La Croix-de-Berny, where the loyal Sergeant Loustalot had laid out a sleeping bag and djellabah. But Leclerc did not sleep. First his nephew Bernard turned up. The son of his older brother Guy, Bernard had only been with the division a few days, and they talked *en famille* for a few moments. After Bernard left, Leclerc found attempting to sleep useless. He kept thinking of Dronne at the Hôtel de Ville, GT Langlade at the Pont de Sèvres, and Massu's sub-group fighting through the Bois de Boulogne in the small hours. When Loustalot looked in on him at sunrise, Leclerc had disappeared. Worried, Loustalot packed up Leclerc's kit and jumped in a White scout car to look for him. He found his general being professionally shaved in Anthony, sitting in his Jeep with a small crowd gathered round, murmuring "It's him, General Leclerc!"[48]

Spruced up, he issued the day's orders at 4.30am on 25th August. Sub-groups Warabiot and Putz, from GT Billotte, would head into the middle of Paris. Warabiot's three sub-units, led by Branet, Bricard and Sammarcelli, would head respectively for: the rue de Rivoli, Hôtel Meurice and the Place de la Concorde; the Quai du Louvre, Quai des Tuilleries, also converging on the Place de la Concorde; and the rue Saint-Honoré, Hotel Meurice and Champs Élysée. Sub-group Putz, entering through the Porte d'Italie, would get to the Seine along the Avenue des Gobelins, the rue Monge, the Boulevard Saint Germain and the Boulevard Saint Michel. From there it would converge on its objective, the Palais de Luxembourg in two sub-units. The first would go along the Boulevard Saint Michel and the rue de Vaugirard, while the second followed the bank of the Seine on the Quai des Grands Augustins and the rue de Seine.[49]

GT Langlade, then fighting its way through western Paris, was to converge on the Place de la Concorde from the Étoile and the Champs Élysées, with sub-group Massu in front, followed by Minjonnet.[50]

GT Dio, which had been in reserve behind GT Billotte the day before, would be split into sub-groups led by Lt. Colonels Rouvillois and Noiret. Rouvillois would take the Avenue de Maine, la Gare Montparnasse, the Boulevard des Invalides, the Palais Bourbon and the Quai d'Orsay. Noiret was to turn left towards the Porte de Versailles, the Boulevard Victor and the rue Balard. From there he was to take control of the Seine bridges between the Porte de Versailles and the École Militaire, and move on to take the Champs de Mars and the Eiffel Tower.[51]

GT Rémy, with the Spahis Marocains, who had been covering the 2e DB's left flank around Trappes and Versailles, was to take the Pont de Sèvres route into Paris and then get to the north bank of the Seine ready to harrass Germans retreating through the city.[52]

Not only was 25th August the feast of Saint Louis, patron saint of France, but the low air pressure of previous days had blown away, bringing blue skies and sunshine. Parisians had spent a tense night, often sleepless, knowing from chiming bells that their deliverance was nigh. Many had risen earlier than usual to await the day's events.

Hearing that the Porte d'Orléans was clear, Leclerc ordered Alain de Boissieu's squadron of Stuarts to head straight there, followed by Rouvillois' Shermans and he followed behind in a White Scout car with Girard manning the car's Browning 0.5mm machine gun, providing one of the enduring images of the day.

Leclerc met up with Chaban-Delmas, now back in uniform after four years as a *clandestin*, at the Lion of Denfert-Rochereau, and then headed for the Gare Montparnasse where he set up his CP. He chose that great railway station because it had a telephone exchange and could be reached quickly from the south. Since the resistance and allied air forces had smashed the French railway system, this terminus provided an oasis of calm. A long table was set up on the concourse between the ticket offices and railheads. Within minutes of Leclerc's arrival the telephones began ringing without cease, continuing throughout the day.[53]

Information provided by the resistance meant Leclerc's plan could proceed like clockwork. The Germans fell back to their strongholds at the

Palais de Luxembourg, the Chamber of Deputies and the École Militaire. In fact the German withdrawal from the streets was so comprehensive that sub-group Warabiot was able to reach Notre-Dame by 8am, and Billotte was able to set up a CP at the Préfecture by 9am. Jean Fanneau de la Horie was Billotte's chief of staff. He was sent to the Swedish Consulate where he managed to relay a request via Raoul Nordling to the German commander, Dietrich von Choltitz, that he should surrender to the French Army. Cleaving to his notions of Prussian honour, and mindful that if the *Führer* thought he had underperformed his family might suffer under the *Sippenhaft* laws, von Choltitz made it clear the Wehrmacht would make a day of it. There would be no surrender without some show of combat. This was relayed to La Horie, who incorrectly took it to mean that von Choltitz would only put up a token resistance to satisfy honour.

Massu's men had already spent the first few hours of the day in action near the Renault factory where 2/RMT's 6e Compagnie took 200 prisoners and captured a large selection of German vehicles. That operation ended as the morning warmed up and the urge to strip off sweat-soaked uniforms and plunge into the Seine became irresistible. At 10am Massu entered central Paris looking every inch the returning *gaillard*, with forage cap perched on the back of his head and a cigarette wedged between his lips. His driver, Georges Hipp, speeded him through the streets in a Jeep called Moido, and a *Tricolore* with the Cross of Lorraine fluttering from his radio mast. As they pushed forward from the Pont de Sèvres through the Porte Saint-Cloud into the *16e arrondissement,* ecstatic Parisians crowded round them and their progress slowed. Pushing on towards the Étoile, they found the enormous roundabout deserted, though the fire brigade had raised a *Tricolore* on the Arc de Triomphe. The Champs Élysées was also empty, but gunfire was audible from German strongpoints and blockhouses in the roads leading off it. Through the second half of the morning the infantry of the 2/RMT gathered behind 12e RCA Shermans and RBFM Tank Destroyers as GT Langlade took control of the area.[54]

Amid the joy of liberating their capital and of being liberated, there were still moments of terror. When Langlade's men were held up at a crossroads by a German machine gun in a window or a balcony, they fell back and called up a Sherman. The tank edged round the corner, its 76mm gun barrel raised and seeking its target. The crash of breaking glass and masonry signalled another German machine gun destroyed. Where possible the 2e DB kept to small arms fire to keep building damage to a minimum.

By 2.30pm Langlade had established control over all of western Paris. Massu met up with him and Mirambeau at the Arc de Triomphe. Allowing themselves a quiet moment to salute the Unknown Soldier, the three men were interrupted by a tank shell whistling past their heads. It was not over yet.[55]

The Avenue Kléber, where the Wehrmacht had taken over the Hôtels Raphael and Majestic, still bristled with barbed wire. German tanks charged out of side streets to be met with cannon fire from 12e RCA and the RBFM. The tank responsible for disturbing Massu, Langlade and Mirambeau at the Arc de Triomphe was a Panther down on the Place de la Concorde firing at the troop of RBFM Tank Destroyers at the Etoile. Four Tank Destroyers—*Siroco, Cyclone, Simoun* and *Mistral*—split off in twos, advancing down each side of the Champs Élysées. Whatever gaiety may have enveloped other parts of the city, the greatest boulevard in Paris was void of anything but bare pavements and tanks firing at each other from each end. The Panther in the Place de la Concorde was beside the Obélisque, an Egyptian sculpture similar to "Cleopatra's Needle" in London, erected precisely where the guillotine stood during the Revolution. The commander of the *Simoun*, Second Mate Paul Quinon, told gunner Robert Mady to set their 76mm cannon for 1,500 metres. But Mady was a Parisian and he knew the Champs Élysées was 1,800 metres long. He set the gunsight to the correct distance.[56]

The Panther was hit in the track and disabled. But it could still fire its deadly 75mm Pak gun. By now 501e RCC Shermans from Warabiot's subgroup were emerging onto the Place de la Concorde from the Rue de Rivoli. Sergeant Bizien's Sherman *Douaumont* spotted the same Panther and fired at its frontal armour with little effect. Seeing the Panther's turret cranking round towards them, Bizien ordered his driver, Georges Campillo, to ram the German tank. They charged and, after the cacophany, Bizien climbed out of *Douaumont*, pistol in hand, to capture the Panther's crew. Perhaps wisely, they had already fled.[57]

Further west, one of Massu's officers, Holz of 5e Compagnie, managed to work his way around the back of the Hotel Majestic, a German strongpoint whose rear entrance on the Rue la Pérouse was protected by a concrete blockhouse. This could only be subdued with a bazooka, but the Germans inside the hotel indicated a willingness to surrender to regular soldiers rather than the resistance. A German spokesman was brought to Massu under a white flag and, with Langlade's approval, Massu went to the Majestic accompanied by Senior Sergeant Dannic. As they approached, Dannic was shot dead by a German sniper on a rooftop. In spite of this, Massu, showing considerable courage, walked up the steps of the hotel into the foyer where he found himself in the midst of about fifty German officers and three hundred other ranks. Luckily for Massu, they recognised that the game was up and he took their surrender. Langlade consigned them to Mirambeau's artillerymen for transfer to allied POW stockades.[58]

Lt. Sorret, who Massu inherited from the Corps Franc d'Afrique the previous autumn, now reported that the "Abeille," a well known insurance building at 24 Avenue Kléber, was full of Germans. Gathering the rest of 2/RMT, Massu sealed off the area. Then, accompanied by a bi-lingual bell-boy from the Majestic, a Dutch lawyer who offered himself as an interpreter and five men, Lt. Berne presented himself at the "Abeille." Going inside, Berne found they were SS, and he had a Schmeisser poked into his chest. However, through his Dutch interpreter, Berne managed to parley with their colonel. After a few anxious telephone calls confirmed the hopelessness of their position, the SS colonel gave Berne his pistol, and his men surrendered. While these Germans were gathered by the Étoile, an unknown hand among them threw a phospherous grenade among the 2e DB guards, wounding Commandant Mirambeau and burning one soldier so badly he had an arm amputated.[59]

Shermans of 12e RCA advanced down the Champs Elysées supported by 2/RMT's 5e Compagnie. The crowds were not yet confident enough to venture onto this great avenue, but the press was already there. As the 2/RMT patrolled down the Champs Élysées, cradling rifles and submachine-guns in their arms, a microphone was thrust towards Lt. Holz. "I am a Parisian," he said. "I did Kufra and Tunisia. I'm just happy to be back in Paris where my family live. They haven't had any news of me for several years."

After the tensions of taking the surrender at 24 Avenue Kléber, Lt. Berne found a more amusing task—collecting up German supplies of champagne, cognac, and quality foodstuffs he found in the basement of the Hôtel Majestic. Everything, including ten thousand packets of cigarettes, was loaded onto five RMT halftracks. All this would be redistributed to liberated Parisians the following day.

As fighting ended in the western half of the city, Parisians began leaving their homes to meet their liberators from the 2e DB. This was a joyful experience after the previous four years, but there were heart-rending moments. As Arthur Kaiser dismounted from *Bordelais II* he was approached by a lady of middle years asking after her sons, the Zagrodski brothers. Embarrassed and appalled, knowing the elder had died at Alençon and the other at Jouy-en-Josas, Kaiser referred Madame Zagrodski to an officer to receive the tragic news.[60]

Earlier in the afternoon, Leclerc left the Gare Montparnasse to join Billotte at the Préfecture, where an impromptu lunch party was given by Charles Luizet. They were joined by General Barton of the US 4th Infantry Division, which was now pushing into the southeast of the city. Leclerc allowed himself a brief moment to eat some lunch.

Commandant La Horie had remained at the Swedish consulate since mid-morning with his Spahi armoured cars standing watch outside. The consul, Raoul Nordling, was still working hard to end the occupation, helped by an anti-Nazi Abwehr officer, Bobby Bender, who was in telephone contact with von Choltitz at the Hôtel Meurice. Bender knew Hitler had given orders to destroy the city, and most vehemently advised the little Prussian against carrying them out. "You make plenty of noise," Bender told von Choltitz mockingly. "It's just a token defence isn't it?"

Billotte was less patient. While von Choltitz's "nonsense" continued, he ordered La Horie to take the Hôtel Meurice while the rest seized the Jardins des Tuilleries and the Opera House area.[61] The Meurice was the centre of a defensive network around the rue de Rivoli and Tuilleries which included six Panther tanks. Sensing a battle brewing, the Parisians who had thronged around La Horie's sub-group on the Place du Châtelet began to fade away and take cover.

Captain Branet led his detachment along the rue de Rivoli with RMT infantrymen marching ahead on foot and the 501e RCC's Shermans rumbling along behind. Lt. Henri Karcher's platoon advanced between the deserted rue de Rivoli's archways when some Parisians emerged into the street behind them. Then a machine gun opened up, killing a few men from Lt Franjoux's platoon beside Karcher's. The French neutralised it with hand grenades. Moments later, a pre-war Hotchkiss tank, now under German ownership, appeared from the Jardins des Tuilleries and was knocked out by one of Branet's Shermans.[62] Seeing that his platoon was too exposed on the south side of the road, Franjoux brought them over to join Karcher's as they neared the Meurice. Grenades were being chucked out of the windows above them. Karcher's platoon rushed the main entrance up into the hall, hosing the area with submachine-gun fire and phosphorous grenades. The Germans on the ground floor surrendered.

"Where is the General?" asked Karcher.

"Upstairs," replied a German officer on the staircase as he raised his hands.

Karcher bounded up to the first floor. There, surrounded by half a dozen staff officers, in a tight fitting *feldgrau* uniform, wearing a monocle, was the *ganzharter* appointed to destroy the loveliest capital in the world. Von Choltitz knew it was over.

Karcher was quickly joined by Commandant La Horie. "You refused the ultimatum that was sent to you this morning," La Horie told von Choltitz. "You fought and now you are beaten. But some of your soldiers are still fighting. I demand that you give orders to all officers commanding these centres of resistance to cease fire!"

"Yes," said von Choltitz. "But I would like to think that we will be treated as soldiers."

"Follow me," said La Horie bluntly.

Von Choltitz said his farewells, *"Hals und Beinbruch,"* and left the Meurice with the French.

The tension over, Karcher slumped in von Choltitz's chair and telephoned his family that he had captured a general.

Von Choltitz was led through the Meurice's back lobby to a Jeep waiting on the rue du Mont-Thabor. La Horie reproached him for making his resistance more than necessary to satisfy honour. "I have lost a lot of people," said La Horie, his voice hard with bitterness. "I don't know what we're going to do with you."

"After my surrender," von Choltitz insisted, "I have a right to be treated properly!"

The streets began to fill with abusive Parisians. Fearing his prisoner might be lynched before he reached the Préfecture, La Horie transferred von Choltitz to Billotte's White scout car. The crowd closed in, pulling the Prussian's valise from his batman and scattering his personal effects on the pavement where they were seized for souvenirs.[63]

In the area of the Préfecture, agitation and argument reigned between the Police, the Gaulliste and Communist resistance, the 2e DB and the US 4th Infantry Division. Journalists absorbed it all. The billiard room, which Billotte had earlier taken over as his CP, provided enough civic grandeur for von Choltitz's surrender. The commander of the 4th Infantry Division, General Barton, recognised the overriding importance of this event to French dignity and declared graciously to Leclerc, "You ought to be alone in Paris."

In the meantime Barton's soldiers, who had followed up from Arpajon and taken over the Gare Austerlitz, were ranging over the Seine bridges onto the right bank, sharing in the welcome offered the 2e DB.[64]

All across central Paris the crowds were now so great that Billotte's progress with the defeated general was reduced to a crawl. Leclerc waited impatiently. "Right, that's enough," he said to Repiton-Préneuf. "Go and find him [von Choltitz] and bring him to me."

Repiton went to the broken window, looked out and saw the shrieking, whistling, shouting mob swirling around Billotte and von Choltitz in the square below. There was nothing to be done but wait until they arrived. The billiard room door opened. Billotte finally stood there with the stocky Prussian general beside him, relieved to be alive.

"*Le voilà*," said Billotte tersely.

The German general was formally dressed with monocle, breeches with red stripes, tunic with red collar patches and gold-wired insignia. Opposite him, Leclerc wore a waist-length US combat jacket with minimal insignia, a tie and collar pin being the Frenchman's only concessions to sartorial elegance. Von Choltitz offered his hand, which Leclerc refused.

"At last we have it," mumbled Leclerc to himself. Fixing von Choltitz with a cold eye, Leclerc said loudly in German, "I am General Leclerc. Are you General von Choltitz?"

Von Choltitz nodded that he was.

"Sit down," Leclerc ordered.[65]

At this point, in the anteroom, Charles Luizet was confronted by Colonel Rol-Tanguy and the COMAC official, Kriegel-Valrimont, indignant that the FTP and FFI of Paris were being excluded from the surrender ceremony. Luizet slipped into the billiard room for a brief word with Chaban-Delmas. Leclerc had never met Colonel Rol-Tanguy but must have heard of him from Roger Gallois three days earlier. At first Leclerc said, "No civilians." But, after Chaban-Delmas vouched for them, Leclerc allowed Rol-Tanguy and Kriegel-Valrimont to join in.

Under the surrender terms, von Choltitz agreed to the cessation of all German resistance in Paris, and that German personnel who continued to fight put themselves outside the rules of war. Though visibly agitated and breathing deeply, von Choltitz signed. The Communist Kriegel-Valrimont insisted Rol's name be included on the surrender document. At first Leclerc said that, in his role as commander of all French forces in Paris, the FFI were automatically included. But Rol and Kriegel-Valrimont insisted. Exasperated, Leclerc allowed "Rol" to sign, and famously Rol-Tanguy took the opportunity to put his signature above that of Leclerc on the French copy. At the time, Leclerc decided that it was not worth fussing over.[66]

"All the means of command are with my CP at Montparnasse," Leclerc announced. "We'd better go back there at once to bring the fighting to an end as quickly as possible."[67]

The increasingly ill von Choltitz had to make another journey past the Paris mob. Sitting in a White scout car behind Leclerc, Chaban-Delmas, Rol and Kriegel-Valrimont, the stocky Prussian was the target of relentless abuse, which Leclerc did his best to minimise by waving his cane. On reaching the 2e DB's CP on the Montparnasse concourse, Leclerc set about putting the ceasefire into effect across the city. He insisted that Jeeps carrying French, American and German officers visit every remaining German strongpoint, bringing written orders signed by all parties calling on them to cease fire. Again Kriegel-Valrimont prevailed upon Chaban to have the FFI represented on these documents. In the meantime, von Choltitz appeared increasingly uncomfortable. Turning to adjutant Weil, Leclerc said, "You speak German. Take him for a walk."[68]

They ambled down the station platform while the afternoon sun shone stiflingly hot through the massive skylights. Von Choltitz admitted to Weil that he knew Germany would lose the war. Searching in his pockets, he asked for a glass of water. Though worried that the German might have a suicide pill, Weil complied.

"If I might give you some advice," said von Choltitz, composing himself, "when you meet up with the Russians in Germany, don't stop, march on to Moscow!"[69]

Back at the CP's long table, Leclerc was taking stock. He was surprised by Chaban-Delmas, a trained civil servant in his late twenties, wearing the uniform of the French Army and stars of a brigadier general, who spoke with the authority of the provisional government. It was obvious that Chaban was de Gaulle's man in Paris, but Leclerc could not help wondering if he was experienced enough to recognise what men like Rol and Kriegel-Valrimont were about: exploiting the natural drive for French liberation for the good of the Communist Party. Reflecting that it was four years to the day since he began his fight for Free France, Leclerc once again allowed Rol and the Paris FFI to be represented on the documents.[70]

Waking at Rambouillet that morning, Charles de Gaulle knew he was on the threshold of power. Few Frenchmen had seen his face. This was about to change. Getting into an open-top black Hotchkiss to ride into the capital he had not seen for fifty months, he felt "gripped by emotion and filled with serenity."[71]

For most of the journey the roads were reasonably clear, but when the cavalcade reached Longjumeau the crowds thickened in the atmosphere of carnival. At the Porte d'Italie, movement became virtually impossible, and de Gaulle's party had to hoot and barge its way slowly through. Most Parisians awaiting their first glimpse of the man who had encapsulated French dignity for four years expected him to drive to the Hôtel de Ville, and positioned themselves along the Boulevard Saint-Michel. But de Gaulle was scheduled to join Leclerc at Gare Montparnasse.[72] There, at 4.15pm, he was met by the man he had first encountered four years and one month earlier at 4 Carlton Gardens as Captain Philippe François Marie de Hauteclocque, now the famous "General Leclerc." If the hours they actually spent in each other's company were ever counted they would amount to very few, yet no one could doubt their identical sense of purpose. De

Gaulle cast his eyes over Leclerc's staff—Repiton, Girard and Gribius—and also the leaders of the Paris resistance who had witnessed von Choltitz's surrender: Chaban-Delmas and Colonel Rol-Tanguy. De Gaulle was not surprised to see Rol; both the resistance and 2e DB had plenty of his type.* But, eyeing his Parisian representative, Jacques Chaban-Delmas, wearing the same two stars of a *général de brigade* on his forage cap as he wore on his own képi, de Gaulle muttered, "Well I'm damned, well I'm damned!"[73]

Leclerc had ensured Ensign Philippe de Gaulle was also there. De Gaulle embraced his son, asking him to join his entourage for the rest of the day. But Leclerc austerely reminded his leader that even his own son had duties to attend to. Philippe de Gaulle was needed to take the surrender of Germans still holed up in the Chamber of Deputies.[74]

After the formalities, de Gaulle inspected the surrender documents. The sight of Rol's name above Leclerc's on the French copy elicited some irritation. "You allowed Rol-Tanguy to sign!" de Gaulle exclaimed. "Leclerc, why do you think I made you temporary governor of Paris?"

"But Chaban agreed."

"Even so, it is not correct," ruled de Gaulle. "In any case, in this matter you are the ranking officer, and consequently solely responsible. Anyway, the plea that led you to accept this wording comes from those with unacceptable views." Nevertheless, it was clear to de Gaulle that Leclerc had acted on his instincts out of goodwill. "You have done well," he continued. "I will recommend Rol-Tanguy be made a Companion of the Liberation." Then, turning to Jean Marin, the senior French newsman at the BBC, de Gaulle said clearly, "The enemy has surrendered to General Leclerc and French Forces of the Interior."[75]

At 5pm de Gaulle, accompanied by his long term ADC Geoffroy Chaudron de Courcel, left the Gare Montparnasse for the Hôtel de Brienne, the pre-war Ministry of War. On the way there the Hotchkiss, escorted only by a single Greyhound armoured car from the Spahis Marocains, came under fire from the church tower of Saint-François-Xavier. De Gaulle got out of the car and stood erect, staring at his former place of worship, as if

---

*However much de Gaulle may be accused of re-writing WWII history to suit his ideas of French dignity or the centre-right Gaullist cause, his memoir is utterly fair about the role played by the resistance who took to the streets of Paris in August 1944. Though he leaves out the fact that many of them were Spanish!

challenging the gunman, who was either a Wehrmacht sniper or *milicien*. A further two bullets cracked into the Hotchkiss' trunk while de Gaulle puffed a cigarette. "*Eh bien,*" he said to Courcel. "At least we're coming back to better conditions than those in which we left!"[76]

The Occupation had pickled the Ministry of War in a time warp. "Not a piece of furniture, not a tapestry, not a curtain had been altered. Telephones were still in the same places on desks with exactly the same names to be seen under the buttons," de Gaulle wrote in his memoirs[77]

Oddly, in spite of the vicissitudes of the day, the Paris telephone service still worked marvellously. Many members of the 2e DB took full advantage to contact their families. Stuck in the Gare Montparnasse from mid-morning, Captain Girard managed to get the switchboard operator to call his home while he waited in a phone booth on the station concourse. Three times he heard his mother's voice answer and each time he was too emotional to speak. In disbelief and sheer frustration that he could be so tongue-tied, he realised there was only one remedy. He asked Leclerc for twenty minutes time off, grabbed the Jeep and drove to his parents' house at 19 rue du Bac. He rang the bell, but when his mother opened the door, in a lace collared black dress, he was still unable to talk.

"*Te voilà, mon fils,*" Madame Girard said simply, folding her arms around the young man whose Free French odyssey had begun as a liaison officer to the Queen's Bays four years earlier.[78]

The Champs Élysées was now full of people. GT Langlade was gathered around the Étoile when a young resistance fighter with a heavy brow and big nose pushed his way through to talk to men of the RMT.

"Do you know an officer called Massu?" he asked.

"Are you kidding? He's our battalion commander, the King of Noses!"

"Terrific, help me find him," said the young *résistant*.

A few moments later, Jean Massu was led to his brother Jacques, who was sitting by the radio in his Jeep with his driver, Georges Hipp. Jean was younger by a year. For the rest of the day the two men never left each other's side, but there were still two brothers absent: André, a prisoner of war in Germany since 1940, and the youngest, Henri, taken for the infamous *Service Travail Obligatoire.*[79]

The fighting continued in other areas. Leclerc's chief artillery offier, Colonel Crépin, found that the Chamber of Deputies was in the hands of Waffen SS men who arrogantly refused to surrender. Frustrated at the pointless bloodshed and the prospect of further damage to the fabric of Paris, Crépin told the monocled SS commander that if they did not surrender, any survivors of further action would forfeit their right to be treated as prisoners of war. The SS spent the next half-hour shooting the last of their ammunition into the air before throwing their decorations on the ground, shouting *Heil Hitler* and stamping off into captivity. The last German stronghold in central Paris had surrendered.

In spite of a few tragic incidents, the mood of Parisians that evening of 25th August was overwhelmingly euphoric. A tremendous crowd waited outside the Hôtel de Ville as de Gaulle made his way up the steps. On the way he asked Flouret, "How is the purge coming along? This matter must be settled in a few weeks." Drawn out, vengeful bloodletting was not what he wanted. On the balcony he gave one of his best-ever speeches to the waiting crowd with no preparation and no notes.

"Why should we hide our feelings, we men and women who are here in our own city, in Paris that has risen to free itself, and that has succeeded in doing so with its own hands? No! Do not hide this deep and sacred emotion! There are moments that go beyond each of our poor lives. Paris! Paris outraged! Paris martyred! But now Paris liberated! Liberated by itself, liberated by its people with the help of the armies of France, with the support and the help of the whole of France, of France that is fighting, of France alone!"[80]

The last sentence might give rise to resentment in Anglo-American minds. Had de Gaulle forgotten the practical and financial assistance offered by both the British and Americans during the previous four years? Had not the British financed and equipped the Free French in the dark days of 1940–43? Were not the uniforms, boots, small-arms, Jeeps and tanks issued to the 2e DB manufactured in the USA? De Gaulle was perfectly well aware of all this. He was concentrating on the human element of those few, short seven days, which, the assistance of the US 4th Infantry Division apart, had been mainly French. De Gaulle had felt deeply the deficiencies that weakened the French Army's ability to respond to the Wehrmacht's onslaught in May 1940. Now the French Army had three of the four armoured divisions he had recommended in the 1930s, thanks in fact to the rearmament programme brokered by the man whom the Americans had wanted to replace him, Henri Giraud. Now the French needed something to be proud of after their humiliations. Leclerc's 2e DB and the resistance had given it to them.

Among senior American officers, opinion was mixed. Bradley was hardly surprised that the French should celebrate, while First Army commander Hodges and Gerow of the Vth Corps were scathing.

"Who the devil is in charge in Paris?" Gerow asked. "Is it Koenig? Is it de Gaulle? Some one is going to get a kick up the arse."[81]

General Wade Haislip took a more Francophile, realistic and generous view. "If we had been pushed out of our country, then returned, and I had sent the First Infantry Division into Boston it would also be chaos."[82]

As the day ended and Paris came to terms with its newly won freedom, André Gribius, assisted by Gachet and Compagnon, transfered the 2e DB's CP from the Gare Montparnasse to the barracks of La Tour Maubourg, northwest of Les Invalides. With the gathering of prisoners, about 12,000 in all, the liberation of Paris was virtually complete. Koenig invited Leclerc and his officers to dine that evening in the grand mess room at Les Invalides, along with Jacques Chaban-Delmas and senior members of the resistance. Leclerc had not walked the streets of Paris since 1940, so he strolled the short distance from La Tour Maubourg to Les Invalides. Since Girard was spending the evening with his parents, Boissieu went with him. Passing the main gate Leclerc turned to him, "You know, Boissieu, it is extraordinary to have liberated Paris without destroying any of its riches! All the bridges, all the buildings, all the artistic treasures of the capital are intact. Look at Les Invalides! What luck we've had! Do you remember the day when you brought me that letter from General de Gaulle with my mission to liberate Paris? It contained my nomination as interim military governor of Paris. Well, that document, I still have it on me, in this pocket," he said, patting his tunic. "It is there with another letter from General de Gaulle. Whenever I felt unhappy or doubtful, I reread them."[83]

The dinner was disturbed by a rumpus in the rooms above where French soldiers had found some fugitive Germans trying to burn archive documents in the fireplaces, but they carried on dining. Massu arrived late, without having had a chance to clean himself up, bringing news of continued fighting involving Minjonnet's men. He was invited to sit beside General Koenig. Balking at sitting his filthy combat trousers on embroidered chairs, Massu deftly draped a napkin over the seat. Meanwhile Chaban-Delmas began relating the story of the truce and how Raoul Nordling negotiated the exchange of prisoners that led to Alexander Parodi's release. Hearing how the FTP had earlier seized the Hôtel de Ville, General Koenig remarked soberly, "We have narrowly avoided another bloody commune!"[84]

Whatever the US Vth Corps commander, General Gerow's, concerns about increasing German resistance northeast of Paris, Leclerc's next role was purely political. The newly liberated capital needed a day of pure ceremony in which to reaffirm its nationhood and recognise its new political leaders. De Gaulle wanted the 2e DB there to reinforce his power base and make clear to political rivals that the future of France would be decided democratically and not by the Communists of the FTP.

After sending a few patrols north of the city and visiting the wounded, Leclerc swapped his US combat blouse for a formal khaki tunic, though his British battledress trousers and canvas gaiters remained. The Spaniards of Dronne's 9e Compagnie 3/RMT assembled at the Étoile, and the tanks of GT Langlade lined up down the Champs Élysées.

At 10am an American liaison officer, sent by General Gerow, who had installed himself in Marshal Pétain's old office at Les Invalides, arrived at La Tour Maubourg barracks with fresh orders for Leclerc to retake his place in Vth Corps and move the 2e DB northeast of Paris. In reply, Leclerc sent Weil to inform Gerow that the 2e DB had orders from General de Gaulle to parade on the Champs Élysées that afternoon. Hearing the French response, Gerow repeated his order, this time pointing out that refusal to obey would constitute a court martial offence under the laws of the US Army to which Leclerc's division was attached.

Leclerc and his staff were having lunch with de Gaulle at the Restaurant Chauland, a favourite of French officers, on the corner of Les Invalides and the Rue de l'Université, when Gerow's liaison officer found him again. The idea that Leclerc should disassemble his men and call off the first parade by French soldiers in their capital after four years of German occupation was utterly preposterous. One version of this story has it that Leclerc said to Gerow's emissary, "Precisely because these orders were given by idiots, means I don't have to carry them out!"[85] In any case Leclerc referred the American to de Gaulle who said, "I lent you General Leclerc. Surely I can take him back for a little while."[86] The only part of the 2e DB in action that afternoon was a light detachment commanded by Commandant Roumianzoff, operating in the Aubervilliers-Saint Denis area.

Considering the dangers, Gerow might have had a point. De Gaulle planned a parade and fete involving over a million people, with only one regiment of the US 4th Infantry Division and Roumianzoff's Spahis between Paris and the German front line. There were still German snipers and small bands of Wehrmacht soldiers at large in the city. But it was too late to cancel the parade. Printing presses had worked through the night to produce posters emblazoned with *"Vive de Gaulle!"* and hundreds of thousands of Parisians were already assembling along the route between the Étoile and Notre Dame.

Photographs of Leclerc taken at the Arc de Triomphe before the parade show a man exhausted but serene among his comrades of the previous four years. At 3.10pm de Gaulle arrived, getting out of his car to be greeted by Leclerc and Koenig. The leader of Free France saluted the men of the Régiment de Marche du Tchad who, along with the 13e DBLE, were his longest serving followers. Then he rekindled the eternal flame under the Arc de Triomphe and laid a Cross of Lorraine made from gladioli on the tomb of the Unknown Soldier while Leclerc, Koenig, Juin and officers of the 2e DB saluted.

De Gaulle had not wanted this parade to be a purely military affair but to prove his popularity and bathe in the crowd's acclamation. After sending a loudspeaker van down the Champs Élysées declaring that he placed his safety in the hands of the people of Paris, de Gaulle began his long walk from the Arc de Triomphe to the Cathedral of Notre Dame. Four of Boissieu's tanks led the way, then came de Gaulle, followed by senior Free French personalities—Le Troquer, Parodi, Bidault, Laniel, Flouret, Luizet and Chaban-Delmas, and senior military figures—Leclerc, Koenig, Juin, Bloch-Dassault, and Admiral Thierry d'Argenlieu. Four halftracks carrying Dronne's Spaniards brought up the rear and provided for de Gaulle's immediate security.[87]

The crowd fell back in front of de Gaulle like the Red Sea before Moses. All the way from the Étoile to the Place de la Concorde, young men and women climbed trees and lamp posts to get a better view of the immensely tall man who, with only the small, trusted coterie now marching beside him, had represented the dignity of France. From every window and balcony Parisians cheered and waved *tricoleurs* and other Allied flags. Passing the statue of Clemenceau, France's leader during the First World War, de Gaulle paused and saluted.

"What a triumph," said Bidault.

"Yes, but what a crowd," replied de Gaulle.

Taking a car from the Place de la Concorde to Notre Dame, de Gaulle arrived at 4.15pm. Cardinal Suhard, who had managed to get himself stygmatised as a Vichy supporter by the Free French, not least for presiding at the funeral of arch-collaborator Paul Henriot, had been forbidden from taking the Mass and placed under temporary house arrest. Indignant at the treatment of Suhard, the senior chaplain of the 2e DB, Père Houchet of the White Fathers, refused to act as his replacement. Instead, one of the senior priests of the cathedral, Monsignor Brot, took the service assisted by two other 2e DB chaplains.[88]

As de Gaulle entered the magnificent mediaeval church, shots rang out followed by bursts of machine-gun fire. The crowd was seized by panic, throwing themselves flat on pavements and cobblestones or huddling in doorways. Everyone with a firearm began shooting, often into mid air or else at illusory targets in windows or on rooftops, all of which provided Parisian masons with repair work for years to come. Officers tried in vain to stop the shooting. Leclerc was seen hitting one soldier on the back with his cane. The Spaniards, all hardened soldiers, quickly regained their cool.[89]

The shooting was even audible inside the cathedral. The congregation took cover, causing one of de Gaulle's entourage, Le Troquer, to say that he saw "more backsides than faces!" When de Gaulle entered he was greeted by Monsignor Brot, who briefly protested the treatment of Suhard. De Gaulle replied that it was his intention to meet Suhard in due course, but in the meantime the service must go ahead.[90]

As clergy and congregation began to sing the *Magnificat*, more shots rang out inside the cathedral and ricochets pinged off the walls high up, hitting some of the congregation. American journalist Helen Kirkpatrick wrote to her family, "I am not one for believing in miracles, but only a miracle prevented those French generals, and myself as well I suppose, from being killed. A miracle and also the fact that the Germans and the *Milice* were bad shots." De Gaulle decided to cut short the service and go back outside where he was acclaimed with more shouts of "*Vive de Gaulle!*" and "*Dieu sauve de Gaulle!*" He returned to the Ministry of War.

At the same time more gunfire, the causes of which have never been clear, had thrown the crowd into panic around the Étoile and the Hôtel de Ville. De Gaulle took the view that one or other of the resistance factions was behind it, motivated by a desire to provoke anxiety. Other shooters bringing chaos that afternoon were undoubtedly *Miliciens* and *collabos* who prefered to go out with a bang rather than a whimper, and two such *salopards* were shot at dawn the following day. Paris was awash with abandoned weapons. Most probably fell into untrained hands who hoped to fire off a few rounds in celebration rather than anger. It is also certain that many Parisians and soldiers of both the 2e DB and US 4th Infantry Division were drunk.

In spite of shortages, many Parisians had salted a few bottles away for the long awaited liberation. After four years of exploitation, with railways wrecked by the Allies, and not enough petrol to distribute food, many Parisians were painfully thin. Such was the sight that greeted André Gribius when he was reunited with his parents. Hearing that the Versailles area was free of Germans, Gribius sought Leclerc's permission to miss the 26th August parade to visit them. Well aware of the shortages, he loaded a Jeep with basic US foodstuffs: biscuits, jam, cheese, bread and plenty of tins of baked beans. Reaching their apartment, Gribius found both his parents were at least two stone below their proper body weight. Madame Gribius, like Christian Girard, was so overcome with emotion she was unable to speak. She just sat in a chair and marvelled at her immensely tall son dressed in part-US uniform topped by a képi who had come back to her. News of André had been sporadic to say the least during the previous four years. Being an officer in the Chasseurs d'Afrique made him a member of the Armistice Army from June 1940, but private communications between the "occupied" zone and the "free" zone or French North Africa were difficult. Gribius' father had no news of him from December 1940 until

November 1942 when an unnamed emissary brought them a bundle of his letters speaking of new hope and reconciliations with old friends. In 1943 Monsieur and Madame Gribius discovered their son was in the 2e DB. All Gribius knew was that his beloved parents were still alive. For a few hours they told him how they had lived, and the various tricks to which they had resorted simply to eat. His father had always trusted Pétain, whereas at least since late 1942, Madame Gribius had listened to the BBC's French Service hoping for news of her son.

Driving his Jeep through the celebrating crowds back to La Tour Mauborg later that evening, Gribius was stopped by a seventeen-year-old youth who wanted to join the 2e DB. There would be many such recruits over the next few days. This one was called Bernard Frachon: he would die in Indo-China in 1950.[91]

Just as the liberation brought moments of joy, tragedy and triumph, it also brought moments of downright ugliness, as when former French mistresses of German soldiers, especially those who had indulged in *collaboration horizontale* with SS and Gestapo officers, were paraded—sometimes completely nude—for public degradation. Often their heads were shaved, swastikas were painted on their bare breasts, they were tarred and feathered, deluged with abuse and buckets of swill, and sometimes murdered with no process of law and without public outcry. Given the sense of privation which had eaten into French society, such scenes were sadly inevitable.

Fighting continued northeast of the capital. After the ceremonies along the Champs Élysées and at Notre Dame, Leclerc had given orders for the following day. GT Billotte, which had ended 25th August around the Bois de Boulogne, would push towards Saint-Denis and relieve Roumianzoff's detachment, which was facing the possibility of a Wehrmacht counterattack into the capital. Both GT Billotte and GT Langlade were facing severe resistance in the areas of Gonesse and Blanc-Mesnil. GT Dio pushed its way onto the airfield of Le Bourget, sustaining tragic casualties among veteran officers from the beginnings of Free France. These included Commandant Jean-Marie Corlu who, as a *méhariste* lieutenant in August 1940, had left the Groupe Nomade de l'Air based at Agades on a camel to make the solo trip across 1,100 kilometres of desert in thirteen days to reach the

Free French in Chad.[92] Leclerc's cousin, Lt. Humbert de Waziers, and Lts. Pity and de Gaudet were killed in front of Leclerc's eyes. They had gone to take the surrender of Germans holding out in the hangars, only to be shot at from behind by more Germans hiding in a drainage ditch.[93]

In the same letter in which he told de Gaulle of these tragic losses, Leclerc also said his men were exhausted. They had been in continuous action for three weeks since they had taken part in Patton's breakout towards Le Mans. In spite of the disagreements with General Gerow, the 2e DB had done virtually everything that had been asked of them. Leclerc went to see Gerow on the 30th and explained his actions concerning the French capital in a courteous manner that did much to mollify the American.

On the last day of that extraordinary August, the 2e DB buried its dead at Pantin.

The liberation of Paris had cost the Germans 14,800 prisoners and 3,200 dead. The 2e DB had certainly inflicted more casualties and damage than it had suffered, though some, including de Gaulle, believe that the resistance in Paris accounted for about 1,000 of the German casualties. Afterwards de Gaulle would regret that the French people, Parisians particularly, seemed to forget the human cost of liberating the French capital, remembering only the hugging and kissing and handing around of drinks. Philippe de Gaulle would later write, "The 2e DB lost more people than during the whole of the liberation of France. Effectively speaking we lost ninety-seven killed and two hundred and eighty-three wounded out of a complement of twelve thousand men actually inside the old boundaries of Paris alone, and twice as many in the surrounding area, making at least 14% of our strength out of action over eight days."[94]

These would be replaced by the throng of enthusiastic young Frenchmen presenting themselves at the recruitment office, which was quickly up and running near the Bois de Boulogne.[95] Leclerc thought French youth were generally pretty good despite the privations of the Occupation, but his view of the resistance was more qualified: ten percent were "very good, brave and real fighters," the next twenty to twenty-five percent were "acceptable and prepared to follow;" while the rest were "riff-raff and con-artists." The last view he shared with Koenig who, in his turn, advised the Americans that the FFI represented "the worst danger to Paris," requesting the means to bring them under military discipline as soon as possible.[96i]

Other recruits had done nothing at all during the Occupation. After the Armistice, Commandant Jean Lecomte, Leclerc's *comrade de promotion* at both "Ginette" and Saint-Cyr, and co-*goum* commander in the High Atlas, had spent the previous four years as a Cognac salesman in the Charente, and enquiries elicited that he had been a Vichy supporter. Leclerc's first instinct was to send Lecomte packing. Admitting that he was wrong to have supported Vichy, Lecomte persisted. "Couldn't you use an officer with good organisational skills?" And what about forgiveness? "Isn't there more joy in one soul who repents than ninety-nine others?" Lecomte was put back in uniform and onto the 2e DB's staff.[97]

The 2e DB spent the first days of September recuperating, readying for its next task. He never allowed private concerns to distract him from the duties of command, but Leclerc had kept up with the progress of British 21st Army Group, which had been operating with similar speed in northern France since the Battle of Normandy. Tailly, the elegant triple-fronted chateau given to him as a wedding present, was now behind British lines. On 6th September he took one of the division's Piper Cubs and flew to his home, landing in a field nearby. His wife Thérèse and their six children were all there. Since hearing that he had liberated Paris eleven days earlier, Thérèse had lamented to her children that she did not have any presentable shoes in which to go and meet him, but when Léopold Doile, one of Tailly's young tenants, came on his bicycle to tell her of Leclerc's arrival she said, "Give me your bike," and pedalled off into the fields. Their second son, Hubert, had got there first on his own *vélo* and lent it to his father. Each astride the standard transport of the Occupation, Leclerc and his wife bicycled towards each other after four hard years of separation.[98]

Of their six children, the eldest sons Henri and Hubert were now eighteen and seventeen years old, and begging to join the 2e DB.

"Only if you have done something," replied Leclerc. Since Henri had been in the local resistance his father allowed him. Hubert, the second son, had helped bring in the dead when Amiens was taken. Was that good enough? Leclerc was concerned that he had left instructions that no one under eighteen should be recruited. Thérèse suggested that each should say he was a year older. The two presented themselves at the Bois de Boulogne recruitment office in the late afternoon of 7th September 1944, just as it was closing, and the Spahi Marocains' Lieutenant Duplay said, "Too late."

"But our father told us to come and join here."

"And who might your father be?"

"The General."

After an incredibly short basic training, both went on to serve in GT Langlade. Henri joined Massu's 2/RMT and served in Arthur Eggenspiller's company. Hubert served first in Alain de Boissieu's HQ protection squadron before transferring to the 12e Chasseurs d'Afrique to become a gunner in the Sherman driven by Arthur Kaiser, *Bordelais II*. Other relations also joined the division, including the younger sons of Leclerc's older brother.[99]

The Chateau of Belloy, where Count Adrien de Hauteclocque still lived, had suffered collateral damage when nearby V-1 launch sites were bombed, and its chapel was destroyed. When Leclerc visited his parents, "all the locals were there to fete him, from morning until dusk," wrote Countess de Hauteclocque. "He has not changed. He is as kind as ever." Leclerc hugged his father, rare in such an austere family, but the count blew his top the following day when he learned from Thérèse that his son was going to keep the name "Leclerc."[100]

CHAPTER ELEVEN

DOMPAIRE AND BACCARAT

It was understandable that the 2e DB's time in Paris would be an opportunity for celebration and some drunkenness. Though some American generals lacked appreciation of this, few begrudged Leclerc's Frenchmen their celebrations. General Montgomery, however, having been kind to Leclerc's men when they emerged from the desert in rags and clapped-out trucks, took the opportunity to be scathing about such festivities. His 21st Army Group's War Diaries record Monty giving the following order to General Crerar's Canadian First Army, which contained units from other occupied countries: "The Belgian detachment will be the first troops to enter BRUSSELS. They will all get tight in BRUSSELS, and I hope that is the last we shall see of them. The Dutch contingent I am leaving with the Canadian Army as there is a bit of HOLLAND just beyond BRUGES and they can frig about in that!"[1]

Quaker stretcher-bearer Dennis Woodcock said, "Paris was absolutely fantastic. The men of the 2e DB could have anything they wanted: whatever shops they went into, wherever they went, the people would insist they had anything it was humanly possible to provide!" Gaston Eve, from the Sherman *Montmirail*, who entered the city with Dronne on 24th August, found himself shielding a young *parisienne* during the wildcat gunfire of the 26th, and gave her his helmet to wear home. The next day,

323

she traced him to the Bois de Boulogne where the 501e RCC had regrouped, and romance inevitably followed.[2]

However, these days had their darker side, and de Gaulle wanted Leclerc's division to stay a few days to keep order as much as anything. The division's British Quakers found themselves rescuing Wehrmacht personnel from the vengeance of the mob and taking German wounded to hospital. Nor did the party go on forever. Ten days after liberation, things began to return to their pre-war state. The old divisions of French politics quickly resurfaced and, by 7th September, in some quarters, the attitude to Leclerc's men on the street was, "You lot still here?"[3]

With none of Montgomery's selfish puritanism, Leclerc was nonetheless concerned lest the 2e DB forget what they were there for. There was more of France to liberate, and his Oath at Kufra included Strasbourg on the Franco-German border, still in German hands. However, Gerow's Vth Corps was not directed towards the Vosges but Belgium. To be on the correct axis for Strasbourg, Leclerc needed to be back under Patton. He wrote to Wade Haislip, begging for reassignment to US XV Corps. Leclerc was successful.

De Gaulle would have preferred the 2e DB to join de Lattre's First Army which, as part of General Devers' US 6th Army Group, was now pushing up the Rhône-Saône corridor. Leclerc did not share de Gaulle's overview, and only buried his anti-Vichy sentiments when he absolutely had to. "We are the original Free French," he declared. Then, kicking over any conciliatory balm he may have previously offered, the Liberator of Paris continued bluntly, "I will not serve with any commanders who previously obeyed Vichy and whom I consider to be turncoats!" Maybe Leclerc feared for his very command if he allowed himself to be transferred to de Lattre. The only Free French divisional commander in First Army was Larminat, *gaulliste de première heure* and senior to Leclerc. Shortly after arriving in southern France, de Larminat made a punchy *gaulliste* speech for which de Lattre, an egotist of MacArthur-like proportions, replaced him with Monsabert, an old hand from the *Armée d'Afrique*. All de Gaulle could find for the faithful Larminat was command of the *Armée de l'Ouest*, whose men faced German garrisons holed up in the Atlantic ports with captured equipment and patched uniforms.[4]

The 2e DB left Paris on 8th September with Leclerc standing in his White scout car, waving at the crowds. GT Langlade led the way with sub-group Massu providing the screen. In spite of Leclerc's concern that a few days high living might have blunted the men's enthusiasm, even his seriously wounded were discharging themselves from hospital, anxious not to be left behind. Haislip could not believe his eyes: some still had legs and arms in plaster. The division's experience of make do and mend meant that recently captured vehicles had already been given a quick repaint and chugged along beside the rest. Renewed access to French industry meant the 2e DB took over a consignment of *Gnome et Rhône* motorcycles previously intended for the Wehrmacht. However, France's left-wing factory workers had already sabotaged them, which led to frantic calls for spares as they conked out.[5]

With his supplies still coming from the invasion beaches and the ports of the Cotentin peninsula, Eisenhower was anxious to open the port of Antwerp and move German Fifteenth Army out of the Scheldt estuary. In addition, contrary to German expectations, Eisenhower decided to support a British attack into Holland to capture the lower Rhine bridges rather than place full resources behind Patton. The British stood on the banks of the Albert Canal with Brussels liberated not by Belgian troops, as Monty had mockingly suggested, but by the Guards Armoured Division. Now Montgomery planned to grab the Rhine delta by laying an airborne carpet of two US and one British airborne divisions along the main road from Eindhoven through Nijmegen to Arnhem, seizing the road bridges until the paras could be relieved by British Second Army. On paper it was a plan of breathtaking daring. In practice the relief force, with specific orders to stick to one narrow main road as the only axis of advance, was hard pressed to keep to the prescribed schedule as the Germans blocked them time and again. Often with no more than a couple of Jagdpanthers, the Germans took a dreadful toll of British tanks silhouetted against the skyline on the raised dyke road. Although the two US airborne divisions were relieved by advancing armoured forces, General Horrocks' XXX Corps ground to a halt at Elst, leaving the battered remnants of British First Airborne Division at Arnhem to surrender or slip back across the Rhine from Oosterbeek.

The Germans were more concerned with Patton's next move. It was Patton's breakout and mad dash to encircle German Seventh Army at

Falaise that had most won their respect. To face the Allies, Field Marshal Model could only count 239 tanks and assault guns along a front held by three armies. Rather than refitting experienced crews with new tanks, Hitler fortunately chose instead to issue 400 new Panzer Mk IVs and Panthers to new regiments of fresh recruits, four of which went to the Fifth Panzer Army facing Patton in the Lorraine, which was commanded by ex-amateur jockey Hasso von Manteuffel,[6] former commander of the *Grossdeutschland* Division in Russia. Although his Panzer colonels, von Bronsart-Schellendorf, von Usedom and von Seckendorf, were experienced, the greenness of their tank crews, whose training had been dogged by shortages of fuel and ammunition, would prove decisive.

By contrast, the 2e DB had trained with limitless supplies, and the battles of August had turned Leclerc's men into veterans. They also knew to play to the advantages of their equipment. It was well known that Shermans were vulnerable to the firepower of German tanks, so wise commanders in Patton's Third Army, like Leclerc and General Wood of US 4th Armored Division, trained their men to use the Sherman's speed and manoeuvrability to outwit adversaries rather than slug it out face to face.

With the Germans in full retreat, the 2e DB advanced on a narrow axis from Troyes to regroup north of Chaumont. There, Leclerc received fresh orders to attack towards Épinal and seize the west bank of the Moselle. The weather was good but the first chill of autumn was in the air as Roumianzoff's Spahis made the first contact with von Knobelsdorff's fleeing First Army.

Gribius' *3ème bureau* intelligence cell had known that von Bronsart-Schellendorff and von Usedom's Panzer brigades were in the area since 7th September. Their mission was to push towards Dompaire and Darney to halt Patton's advance so the German front could be stabilised, and to delay the impending link up between Patton's Third Army and Devers' US 6th Army Group coming from the south. GT Langlade was moving towards the Panzers, but on 11th–12th September the French were held up for lack of petrol. A tanker convoy drove through the night enabling Langlade's men to move again, and they soon came upon elements of either German First Army in retreat or von Manteuffel's advance units.

Before the armoured clash, Leclerc had a different experience as liberator. This time it was not Parisians ecstatic to meet the new French Army but his first sight of a German internment camp. On the afternoon of 12th September, Massu took the little spa town of Vittel, including an internment camp of 3,000 British and American civilians, largely women, and a few French that Vichy had found politically undesirable, all crammed into a cluster of rundown hotels and villas. Repiton warned him that it was a most degrading sight, but Leclerc went himself to open the gates.

"We've been waiting for you for four years," said an elderly British captain in the remnants of a uniform who came forward to meet him. "I expect you would like to see the French prisoners?"

"No," said Leclerc. "I want to see everyone. In 1940 we were admirably received by the English. The Americans have given us equipment. We are especially pleased that it has been given to us to free you."

They found that former Prime Minister Reynaud's wife was among the inmates, so Leclerc sent Girard to telegram Gaston Palewski in Paris. Soon Madame Reynaud was reunited with her husband and daughter.[7]

Sub-group Massu did not have time to celebrate the liberation of Vittel. The division's right flank was completely exposed both south and east of the town. That evening, Leclerc's CP moved to Valleroy le Sec, 5kms east of Vittel. As GT Langlade pushed eastwards, Massu, Minjonnet and Langlade himself became aware of the strong German Panzer forces ahead of them. In fading light, the Spahis detected Panther tanks on the crests overlooking the river, so Durville's troop of RBFM Tank Destroyers were called forward: *Sirocco, Simoun* and *Mistral*. At first they could not see a thing. German tank crews were accomplished at camouflage and it was almost dark. Then a Panther broke cover. The gunners of *Sirocco*, Le Callonec, and Robert Mady of *Simoun*, the hero of the Champs Élysées, saw it at the same time and both fired, one shot ricocheting off the Panther's frontal armour and the other missing altogether. Mady fired again. This time the Panther burst into flames, its crew taking flight in a hail of machine gun bullets.[8]

The burning Panther lit up the hillcrest in the darkness. In *Sirocco*, Le Callonec kept his eye glued to the range-finder. Suddenly more Panthers broke cover and stormed towards the French. First a Jeep was hit, then a halftrack, then another Jeep, each bursting into flames. Recognising the danger, Durville ordered his squadron to seek cover as *Mistral* hit another

Panther. The TDs fell back and regrouped for the night as the Panthers converged on a little village in the Guitte basin. The battle of Dompaire had begun.[9]

"I heard the noise of numerous tanks in the Guitte valley," Massu informed Gribius by radio. "In my opinion they won't attack tonight because they are too busy pushing tanks towards the crest." Gribius reported to Leclerc. It was imperative that 2e DB did not allow itself to be encircled or have its southern flank turned. GTs Dio and Billotte had to maintain contact with the US 79th Infantry Division to their north while Roumianzoff maintained the division's screen to the south. The US Army Air Force liaison officer, Colonel Tower, was allocated to GT Langlade. As at Ksar Rhilane, ground-attack aircraft could be called in if necessary.

That night Langlade set up his CP at Ville-sur-Illon. Sub group Massu took position northwest of Dompaire, while Minjonnet dominated the heights to the south. Through the small hours the rumble of Panzers went on without cease. Frightened villagers were leaving Dompaire, heading for the French positions where they readily reported what they had seen of the Germans to Repiton's men. Langlade's supply officers made sure that every tank and TD that could be reached was refueled and fully stocked with shells.[10]

Dawn broke in a damp drizzle, but Langlade found that his position on high ground at Ville-sur-Illon gave his staff a ringside seat. Even the Quaker stretcher bearer, Dennis Woodcock, could see the drama unfold through the doors of the old stone barn where they had their dressing station, with a long view down the valley to Dompaire and its satellite hamlet, Lamerey, 4kms away.[11]

The action began with a squadron of Panthers leaving Dompaire and heading up the southern slopes of the Guitte valley past Minjonnet's position. Ensign Allongue watched from his TD hidden in a copse; his crews had hardly slept in expectation of this moment. Though they had missed the glory of the Champs Élysées, Allongue's troop had destroyed a Jagdpanther and two Panzer Mk IVs at Enghien in the *banlieuex* of Paris. Now TDs *Orage* and *Tempête* turned their guns to begin their next battle. "Range 900. Two shots, armour piercing." With a dry clatter, the first Panther was stopped. A second was hit amidships. Then the *Tempête* hit a third. The Germans began to fire back at the French sailors with everything they had, as tanks and infantry broke cover and surged forward only to be halted by further French gunfire.[12]

Colonel von Usedom saw his Panthers burning in the morning rain and halted the advance. He had 59 Panthers and 45 Mk IV Specials against only 40 Shermans and 7 TDs, which were technically inferior, but he had lost the initiative.[13]

A USAAF communications tank was "embedded" with sub-group Massu, and Massu and Minjonnet were in close radio contact. Instead of tasking an American formation of fighter-bombers the TALO radio linked up to a squadron of RAF Typhoons that were already booked and airborne for a mission. They only needed clearance and, once approved, they appeared overhead, smashing rockets into German positions at Lamerey. They accounted for eight Panthers and numerous German personnel. As this was happening, sub-group Massu moved into the little hamlet of Laviéville, cutting off the Panzers' escape to the west. On the south side of the village, sub-group Minjonnet, led by Allongue's TDs, moved down the slopes, destroying two more Panthers and cutting the main road to Épinal.

At 11am, with the weather clearing, another air attack came in, this time by USAAF Thunderbolts. Close liaison between US Colonel Tower and the US airmen prevented them from hitting the French tanks infiltrating the villages. The German crews who escaped their burning vehicles knew their opponents were French, not American and, fearing mistreatment if captured, they burrowed into middens or stole civilian clothes from village houses to get away. In desperation, the Germans trapped in Dompaire called for help from another Panzer regiment to the south.

At Valleroy le Sec, Leclerc heard that a push towards Mirecourt by US 79th Infantry Division had been halted. He was concerned that GT Langlade might be too far south, so he ordered GT Billotte to push its sub-units southwards. Taking Girard, he went over to GT Langlade to see for himself and found that Langlade had made his CP in a convent which was run as both a hospice and girl's school. Von Usedom's second Panzer regiment, 1/Pz Rgt 2112, was now south of Langlade's position, supported by a battalion of Panzergrenadiers. The local population was honoured and delighted to know that Leclerc's Free French division was operating in the area and, in the early afternoon, shortly after a third US fighter-bomber strike departed, Langlade was telephoned by the postmistress of Pierrefitte, the neighbouring village. She warned of a German force heading his way.[14]

In response to a call for help from Langlade, Minjonnet sent some RBFM TDs, half Allongue's squadron, to Ville-sur-Illon. They took up position alongside some anti-tank guns on the southern approaches to the village. After Commandant Weil made a reconnaissance from a Piper Cub, some of GT Billotte moved further south to cover Langlade's left flank.[15]

When the Pz Mk IV Specials approached, the first was brewed up by the TD *Tempête*, but there were still over forty Panzers and only two TDs plus a few 12e RCA Shermans to see them off. Only the two TDs with their 76mm guns and a Sherman Special with a 76mm gun, such as Arthur Kaiser's *Bordelais II,* stood a chance of destroying a Panzer Mk IV head on. Leclerc's men, true to their tradition of improvisation, aimed for tracks rather than frontal armour. "First one German tank, then another, started going round in circles," said Dennis Woodcock. "My impression was half a dozen Shermans were engaged; one could hear their engines roaring all around and the three from the village kept dodging out from behind buildings to shoot."[16]

Then, amid casualties on both sides, there was another air attack on the Panzers from US Thunderbolts. The Mk IVs dashed for cover in surrounding woodlands, falling trees marking their path, easily spotted from the sky, while their supporting infantry still fired on the French at Ville-sur-Illon. This was largely ineffective since the Panzergrenadiers' approach had been interrupted by a looting spree, yielding a considerable amount of home-produced kirsch. When the Panzergrenadiers were within range, the French raked them with machine-gun fire.

Langlade could see his men were giving a good account of themselves, but he was also aware that he faced a grave attempt by the Germans to turn the southern flank of Patton's US Third Army, and he was in the thick of it. He decided to pull his CP further north to Begnécourt, closer to the bulk of the 2e DB and the US 79th Infantry Division. Leclerc sent Gribius to evaluate the situation, but after meeting Massu and Langlade north of Dompaire they agreed there must be no falling back. Manteuffel's Panthers and Mark IVs were an important German asset that had to be taken down, and with the rest of the division still too far north, air support remained the only practical way of reinforcing GT Langlade.

The fourth air strike was called in between 3.30pm and 4pm. Six Thunderbolts attacked German positions in and around the village of Lamerey again. In a desperate effort to retreat eastwards, von Usedom's remaining Panthers pushed across open stubble field and came under fire from Minjonnet's Tank Destroyers and Shermans which had taken cover near Dompaire's cemetery. Six Panthers were rendered inactive while the rest fell back into Lamerey.[17]

Towards the end of the day, Panzer Regiment 29 made a further attempt to break out of Dompaire, losing more Panthers, much of the damage being done by RBFM TDs *Mistral* and *Siroco*. *Siroco* accounted for three Panthers in less than five minutes.[18] Langlade ordered sub-group Minjonnet to disengage for the night and pulled remaining French troops out of Ville-sur-Illon. Only later would GT Langlade's phenomenal kill rate be recognised.

Ordered by Leclerc to go to GT Langlade's assistance, Putz kept his men going through the night, in driving rain with all headlamps blazing. Arriving at Ville-sur-Illon at daybreak on the 14th September, they found the Germans had gone. Sub-group Minjonnet could simply walk into Damas, and Massu could march his men into Lamerey. Massu had spent the night hiding in Dompaire's cemetery, listening to the rumble of the German pullout. Entering the village at dawn, he bumped into one of the inhabitants who was inconsolable at the devastation. The French found 33 brewed up Panthers and another four abandoned intact by their crews. Panzer Brigade 112 had ceased to exist as an effective force.

The German tank had been brand new, their specification plates giving their batch date as 15th August 1944, less than a month before.[19] Langlade sent two of the intact Panthers to General Koenig in Paris, who displayed them outside Les Invalides, trophies to the recovery of French arms, where they remained until tactfully removed at the time of de Gaulle's Élysée Treaty with Konrad Adenauer. Koenig contacted Langlade to thank him for the "slightly banal" gift.[20]

The Germans reinforcements sent to Dompaire were commanded by the veteran Colonel Hans von Luck who had fought Leclerc at Ksar Rhilane, but by the time von Luck arrived, US artillery was ready to join in and, to save further losses, the German counterattack was cancelled. Humbly, Paul de Langlade attributed the victory at Dompaire to air support and lack of training among German tank crews and infantry. On the other hand, von Luck believed that the Wehrmacht had underestimated the French, probably on account of pre-conceptions dating from 1940.[21] The 2e DB had shown that French soldiers with excellent officers like Langlade, Massu and Minjonnet, all under their legendary commander, were second to none.

For a few hours calm reigned at the 2e DB's HQ. During the previous day Cathleen, Lady Queensberry, a member of the Royal Society of Portrait Painters, arrived at Leclerc's HQ as the battle of Dompaire was in full swing. For Leclerc to break off from his duties and sit for a portrait on such a day would have been a monstrous dereliction of duty. However, as arranged, her chauffeur called the following day to enquire if Leclerc was available. Girard asked him to wait while he found the general. Gribius said all was calm in GT Langlade's sector so Girard, knowing de Gaulle liked to see the French képi in Allied newspapers, penned a note to Lady Queensberry apologising for her frosty reception the previous evening.

"What? Are you reproaching me?" asked Leclerc, feeling that his young ADC was being disapproving.

"I just thought it was a pity, *mon Général*," said Girard.

"All right," said Leclerc. "Go and get her."

"But if you have work. . . ."

"No. Go and get her," said Leclerc.

By 9am Leclerc was sitting for Lady Queensberry.[22] But he would not be able to give her long. On his north flank Leclerc had to maintain contact with the US 79th Infantry Division pushing towards Mirecourt. His old friend from Saint-Cyr, La Horie, recently promoted to command a sub-group of GT Billotte, was pushing northeast and liberated the little town of Remoncourt in the face of stiff resistance. This gain had been followed up the next day by the taking of two crossroads at Hymont and Mattain-court. With the Germans reeling from their disaster at Dompaire, on 15th September, La Horie took his sub-group to Nomexy to seize its bridge over the Moselle.[23]

The following morning, La Horie, seizing the opportunities of his new rank, crossed the Moselle to create a bridgehead at Châtel. Manteuffel still wanted to rescue his 16th Infantry Division from encirclement by the advancing French and American forces and, that evening, he sent a force of infantry supported by his few remaining Panthers to kick La Horie back across the river. Once again, the French were warned in advance by the local population. Supported by artillery, La Horie's subordinates, captains Lucien and Branet, inflicted heavy losses on von Manteuffel. The Germans lost 200 men, 5 Panthers destroyed and 10 more damaged against French losses of five killed and twenty wounded.

Leclerc, however, thought La Horie's force was too much out on a limb, and ordered them back to Nomexy after dark.[24] He even went so far as to criticise La Horie for sustaining casualties uselessly, a sanction really aimed at GT commander Pierre Billotte, whom Leclerc regarded as vainglorious with eyes only for what happened in Paris. Billotte sprang to La Horie's defence, calling Leclerc's criticism a grave injustice with which he did not wish to be associated, and asked to be transferred out of the 2e DB. Billotte had waved the red cape and Leclerc, annoyed at having him imposed by de Gaulle in the first place, had no intention of asking him to reconsider.[25] Once the rest of the 2e DB caught up, Leclerc ordered a fresh crossing of the Moselle, this time in strength with Bailey bridges built by engineers.

Unlike his view of Billotte, Leclerc was warming to the shipless, tank-killing sailors of the RBFM after their conduct during August and September. The most tank kills at Dompaire were scored by the RBFM's *Siroco*. Two days later it was reported to Leclerc that two RBFM TDs had been patrolling towards the Moselle when one broke down. The crew dismounted and continued on foot. After a while they came across some German infantry on bicycles accompanying an artillery piece towed by horses. With nothing but small arms and effrontery, the sailors took the Germans prisoner. "Think how events might have turned out if men like that hadn't been stopped in 1940," Leclerc complained to Girard. "The responsibility of their leaders is blatant." The sailors even got on well with original *Gaulliste* units. Leclerc would especially comment to his staff on the rapport between them and the Spahis Marocains. When de Gaulle had foisted the RBFM upon him in Morocco Leclerc had degraded them by making them remove the red lanyards won by their forbears at Dixmude. Now he gave those lanyards back.[26]

Patton was greatly impressed by the battle at Dompaire, and on 18th September Leclerc was invited to lunch at Haislip's HQ. The weather was unsettled and Girard drove the Jeep along country lanes flowing with mud.

As they reached a clearing in a saturated wood, a US Military Police Jeep appeared, followed by a staff car bearing a red plaque with three gold stars—Patton. The American *prima donna* shook Leclerc's hand warmly. A table had been beautifully laid in an olive green messing tent, and chilled champagne awaited them. Having quaffed a few glasses, the three generals soon relaxed, a little *pompette*, but throughout lunch the austere Frenchman was wondering why he was there. As lunch ended Patton, puffing a fat cigar, led Leclerc outside and, after resting his cigar on the Jeep's mudguard, gestured to his ADC to pass him a small rectangular jeweller's box. Patton whipped out an American medal, the Silver Star, and pinned it to Leclerc's tunic.

"What's this for?" Leclerc asked, amazed.

"It is a decoration for courage on the battlefield," said General Haislip. "You have done a lot for the honour of the US Army."

As the generals spoke, Patton's ADC took Girard aside to clarify names, dates and places for official citations. There were another six Silver Stars and 25 Bronze Stars to distribute among the 2e DB. [27] Then the conversation took a more serious turn. Patton wanted the advance to continue the following day. Laying out a mica-covered map on a Jeep bonnet, Patton showed Leclerc his next objectives: Rambervillers and then Baccarat with its bridge over the Meurthe. Leclerc and his division would again be covering the US Third Army's southern flank.

"Yes I can do that but . . ." Leclerc hesitated for a moment.

"You need something?" Patton asked abruptly.

Leclerc enumerated a few things his division did not have, as well as his wish for extra artillery support.

"You shall have them," said Patton.[28]

Later that day Leclerc visited the 2e DB's forward positions in retaken Nomexy. While GTs Langlade and Dio were commanded by officers who accepted his authority, Leclerc was still stuck with Billotte, whose new appointment and with it promotion to *général de division* had not yet come through. His impatience with Billotte began en route to Paris, when he had ordered Raymond Dronne to form his impromptu *colonne* to break the deadlock. Billotte was undoubtedly a courageous officer, but in Leclerc's eyes, he did not have the dash or that little touch of madness to make a good tank commander. Unlike the Malaguti affair, there would be no drawn-out feud. After barely seven weeks with the 2e DB, Billotte was going anyway. The French Army was turning the rabble of former *résistants* into regular soldiers needing generals. Billotte would command the new 10th Infantry Division recruited from Parisians, in which "Colonel" Rol-Tanguy became an officer. Billotte, however, still managed to annoy Leclerc by wearing his new stars before the official date of his promotion, and demonstrating an over-fondness for the fripperies with which some senior officers surround themselves. In Nomexy, Leclerc found him being driven in the swanky Mercedes Benz that had belonged to General von Choltitz.

"Billotte, in combat it is necessary to get around in a Jeep," Leclerc remarked.

"But I am a general now," Billotte replied.

"Me too," said Leclerc. "But to understand situations it is necessary to see. You can't see anything shut in a limousine."[29]

Billotte's use of von Choltitz's Mercedes deserved slapping down. Leclerc gave explicit orders that enemy vehicles taken as booty must be found petrol elsewhere than from divisional supplies (ie, the petrol had to be booty as well). With Antwerp's port facilities still unavailable, Allied logistics were at full stretch. Conscious of their poor relation status, the 2e DB were more frugal and resourceful than other divisions; not handing in damaged vehicles unless they got a replacement, even if it meant towing it, or using a captured vehicle instead. When Leclerc told Patton he preferred equipment to medals he meant it.[30]

GT Billotte became GT Guillebon. Having been at the heart of everything for four years, Jacques de Guillebon undoubtedly deserved to command a *groupement tactique*. But for de Gaulle's intervention after the Malaguti affair he might have had it earlier. GT Guillebon crossed the Moselle on the night of 18th–19th September, expanding its bridgehead towards the villages of Vaxoncourt, Pallegney and Moriville in the face of heavy resistance. Again GT Langlade found itself covering Patton's southern flank, and Roumianzoff's recce detachment had to call upon Third Army's bridging equipment to assist its drive towards Rambervillers. One by one the rivers of central-eastern France had to be crossed. The Meurthe was only 8km away, and next came the Vezouze, which flows parallel.[31]

The US 45th Infantry Division arrived to plug the gap between Patton's army and Devers' 6th Army Group coming from the south, so Leclerc no longer had to worry about guarding Third Army's southern flank. The Americans liberated Épinal, and the front between Switzerland and the Belgian coast stabilised, but there would be none of the trench warfare of twenty-five years earlier.

The *anciens* from African days knew Strasbourg was still in German hands and remembered the oath they had taken at Kufra. Winter was approaching. The liberation phase of late summer was over and the Germans were certain to fight harder as they were forced back to their own soil. Only a small number of the 2e DB had seen their homes again after Paris, and for those whose homes were in or near the path of battle, the sense of nostalgia could be overwhelming. Leclerc himself acknowledged, "It has perhaps been hard for many, after four long years, to have only a few days in which to renew the past, and just as often for others to pass within a few kilometres of a forgotten door without stopping."[32] Yet the morale of the division was good. Newcomers joining since Paris soon acquired the division's attacking spirit, enthusiastic to eject the Germans from *la patrie*, but every so often Leclerc would see the faces of veterans darken, or notice a heaviness in the voice which he knew would have been due to news from home or nostalgia for what they had left behind.[33]

On 23rd September, sub-groups commanded by Rouvillois and Quillichini crossed the Meurthe and pushed reconnaissance patrols towards the Vézouze. Sub-group Putz was the first to link up with du Vigier's 1ere DB near Épinal, still sweeping up Wehrmacht stragglers fleeing the Massif Central trying to reach their own lines in the Vosges. Arriving in Mesnil Flin behind GT Dio, Leclerc and Girard passed many houses still burning, their inhabitants rescuing furniture and stacking it onto carts. In spite of the destruction, villagers came up to Leclerc with tears in their eyes to thank him for their liberation. "*Merci, mon général, c'est bien.*"

Girard noticed that the young general was on the verge of tears himself. Later, Leclerc would tell his staff how this desperately damaged village gave the 2e DB one of its most moving welcomes, his voice breaking as he strove to hide his emotions.[34]

French civilians did their best to minimise fighting on their home patch. North of the 2e DB, the US 79th Infantry Division took Lunéville, only to be turfed out again by a strong German counterattack. Massing to retake the town, the Americans were told by French civilians to save their effort because the Germans had pulled out, this time for good.

On the afternoon of 25th September, de Gaulle made an impromptu visit. With the majority of French forces now in de Lattre's First Army, de Gaulle spent more time with them, and visits to Leclerc's division became a rarity by comparison. Accompanied by former Vichy generals Juin and Giraud, the diplomat Jouve, and the original *Gaulliste* general Charbonneau, the purpose of de Gaulle's visit was to award medals, but many recipients were stuck out on the line and could not be called in before de Gaulle departed. Instead, a proper parade was organised in Nancy for the following day where Massu, Langlade, Dronne, Putz and others received medals for Alençon and Falaise, liberating Paris and the action at Dompaire.

Shortly afterwards, Haislip's XV Corps was transferred from Patton to General Patch's Seventh Army, which had landed at Fréjus alongside French First Army. Leclerc wanted to stay with Patton, and sent Weil to Third Army to ask if the 2e DB could remain. He was refused.

US Seventh Army was less well off for resupply than the armies coming from Normandy. Its commander, General Alexander Patch, had been in the Pacific before being switched to the European theatre, and he had been heavily involved in the French rearmament programme brokered by Giraud. Like Patton, he also had a taste for wearing riding breeches, high boots and helmet but he never cut the same Caesar-like figure. Of those who landed in the south, the most colourful general was Jean de Lattre de Tassigny. De Lattre liked to surround himself with smartly turned out aides, both male and female, from good families: *bon chic bon genre*, as the saying goes. Leclerc also had his share of upper-class officers, but it was never a policy in the 2e DB, where men were judged by their deeds. The transfer to US Seventh Army worried Leclerc that the 2e DB might be *kidnappé* by de Lattre's army with all its Vichy connotations. In his heart Leclerc never put his feelings anti-Vichy feelings aside, whatever du Vigier had said to him at Mascara.[35] However, if the Oath at Kufra was to be kept, he was now better placed to liberate Strasbourg from Patch's sector than Patton's.

Through October the division stood still, holding ground and sending out patrols while decisions were made between Eisenhower and de Gaulle over the best use of French forces. De Gaulle wanted du Vigier's 1ere DB sent to liberate some of the Atlantic pockets such as Bordeaux and La Rochelle, whereas Eisenhower was happy for these German garrisons to whither on the vine while the new French Army's least combat worthy units contained them. Meanwhile, discussions between Juin and the US High Command earmarked the 2e DB for the liberation of Strasbourg. But as with Paris, the Americans only ever saw this as a "nice idea," dependant wholly on the course of the war.

About this same time, the 2e DB had to shoot a spy. An agent infiltrated the division's positions disguised as a priest. In the tradition of the Catholic Church, guest priests are asked to celebrate Mass, and here was his undoing. Attended by the divisional Chaplain, Père Houchet of the White Fathers, the spy stumbled over his breviary; he did not know it. Houchet, a patriotic Frenchman as well as a man of the cloth, questioned the man, who eventually had to admit he was a spy sent by the German SD. His sentence: Springfields at dawn.[36]

Even though the front line was static, patrols and ambushes cost the 2e DB good men. Putz's 3/RMT was fighting west of the village of Doncières when Captain Geoffroy, one of the heroes of Kufra, was killed while making a recce into a wood they expected to find deserted. The same incident saw Dubut, who had bluffed his way into the Italian fort of Gatroun in March 1942, very seriously wounded with three bullets in the head. These men were among Leclerc's best and longest serving officers. While Dubut fought for his life in the field hospital, Leclerc sat alone in his room at Château Gerbéviller. On the day of Geoffroy's funeral, Dubut succumbed to his injuries. Girard reflected in his journal, "What losses and of such quality! Perhaps, encouraged by their [the Germans'] flight they had underestimated the enemy, or they might have been surprised by a resistance which now seems to be stiffening. Alas they are always the most courageous."[37]

Death struck at random. The RBFM's chaplain, Père Sibille, visited the church at Mesnil, hoping it might be suitable for 2e DB services. As he opened a tin of C rations to share with the curate, a mortar shell exploded nearby, mortally wounding him. In the tradition of the White Fathers, he had been able to conduct a dignified service under almost any conditions from Africa to Normandy, and now it was someone else's turn to do the same for him.[38]

In the meantime, new men who joined the division after Paris were beginning to distinguish themselves. The young Ensign Gélinet, freshly gazetted into the RBFM and given a troop of Tank Destroyers in spite of his lack of experience, led a charge right into the centre of the village of Anglemont, the TD crewmen firing machine guns and throwing hand grenades from their open turrets. This so unnerved the Germans holding the village that they fell back. More TDs and Shermans from the 501e RCC joined in, destroying five Panther tanks.[39]

The 2e DB line from Vezouze to Rambervillers faced the Germans' Vosges fortifications, and General Hasso von Manteuffel placed anti-tank guns everywhere he thought Leclerc might attack. The division's next objective was Baccarat, with its crossings over the Meurthe, and Leclerc put Gribius to work on the plans. As at Dompaire, local intelligence proved fruitful. Twenty local *résistants* did splendid work finding out German troop displacements. For their protection if captured they were inducted into the 2e DB and given uniforms to prevent them from being regarded as spies and shot. The village priest of Domèvre in his black cassock kept the information flowing daily from his occupied parish.[40]

If parish priests could be partisan, a doctor's Hippocratic oath applied to everyone. Dr. Moretti, attached to the RBFM, had set up an aid station in a farm. No sooner had he and his team finished supper with the farmer and his family than a German shell took the top stories off the building. Shortly afterwards he was asked to deliver a baby in a cowshed. The speed of Allied advances and reasonable hope of liberation by the end of 1944 meant French peasants were often more willing to stay behind to look after livestock and property, and to assist the Allies.[41] There were no longer the endless processions of refugees dragging and pushing every type of over-laden cart as had been the case in 1940. Even so, there were enough de-serted houses for the 2e DB to requisition for their own use, though not everyone was lucky. Arthur Kaiser and the crew of *Bordelais II*, which now included Leclerc's second son, Hubert, found a house which still had furniture and warm bedding in which to take refuge from the autumn chill.

There were even some homemade preserves left in kitchen cupboards. Although the youngest, and with only a brief period of training, Hubert made himself indispensable to his crew by negotiating with the local populace for food, rabbits and chickens for their evening *popote*. Usually charm and simply being French was enough, or if not, the fact that his father was "*le Patron*" might be dropped into the conversation.[42]

Not all the French population behaved well. Pilfering of Allied fuel supplies became a serious handicap to frontline divisions, as country folk tried to get cars and trucks, laid up though the Occupation, going again. "The Americans are rich" was the thinking. They were—and they simply provided more petrol while the US Army tightened its security. Paul de Langlade later wrote bitterly about the behaviour of his fellow countrymen, but after four years of shortages, what else could be expected?[43]

Three visits by senior officers followed in quick succession through early October. First Haislip, then Patch, and lastly, on 11th October, the French Navy minister M. Jacquinot, accompanied by admirals Missoffe and Lemonier visited the 2e DB to inspect the shipless sailors of the Régiment Blindé des Fusiliers Marins. The RBFM paraded by a wood, the TDs still part covered in foliage, turret guns turned to nine o'clock. Their crews stood in fives, sporting the reinstated red lanyards looped through the left epaulettes of their US combat jackets, clipped with the 2e DB's divisional badge. Passing along the line, M. Jacquinot counted the white rings painted on gun barrels to mark a tank kill. The *Siroco* had nine, the *Mistral* six. In all they had accounted for 46 German tanks, including many Panthers and Mk IV Specials. Leclerc was relaxed, smiling and obviously very proud of what these men had accomplished for him and for themselves. These were not traitors, but simply men who, like the rest of the division, wanted their homeland free. The choice of whether to follow Vichy or de Gaulle had been made for them at flag rank. In any case, the French Navy's years of moral confusion caused by Vichy were well and truly over.[44]

With the elation of liberating Paris now seeming an age before, Girard found Leclerc once again concerned over France's standing in the world. The liberation saw more Anglo-Saxons in Paris than during the previous war, or indeed, at any time in its past. The capital had become the place every soldier in northwest Europe wanted to go on leave, with dance halls and variety shows springing up to cater to them. Once the first rush to purge collaborators was over and the Occupation's major players were consigned to the process of law, the old fissures of French politics, rich versus poor, bosses versus workers, were back on the agenda. Leclerc complained that the "old beards" were out again.

By contrast, the men of the 2e DB got on so well with each other that they gave both de Gaulle and Leclerc an overly idealistic idea of what could be done with post-war French politics. Leclerc's sons were serving in the ranks and making lifelong friends from different classes. When Commandant Witasse told his tanks to stop firing at a chateau because it belonged to his uncle, it was simply an amusing anecdote arousing no class rancour. Leclerc preferred being with his men to being among other Frenchmen, and when he was not with his division he liked *la chasse* best of all, and there were plenty of wild boar in the woods of Lorraine.

The division was a family to its members, especially the four-year men from Chad, but when they looked outwards, seeing the old barriers between Frenchmen rebuilt, they inevitably felt a sense of anti-climax. The *anciens* wondered what it had all been for, and whether it had been worth it. Some officers, such as Vézinet, would write later that they knew Britain and America could have liberated France without their help, but that was not the point. Over a million French soldiers were still prisoners in Germany, where they had been since *la chute*. Returning from a parade to award decorations to his sappers, Leclerc told Girard it was essential for Germans to see French soldiers on their soil, marching through their villages, and in any case, the real players now in the European war were no longer the Anglo-Saxons but the Russians.

De Gaulle was having a hard time re-establishing the French state amid acute shortages and destroyed communications. In the provinces, public order was often maintained by the FFI, for whom de Gaulle maintained a professional soldier's disgust. Brigandry existed in the rural southwest, and de Gaulle even offered Leclerc a post on the army's staff as a means of bringing him and his division back from the front to use them for maintaining law and order in France. Although keen for further advancement, Leclerc would have none of it. He would stay with his men, and the 2e DB would stay at the front, facing the Germans, until the end. But to reassure the Constable that no slight was intended, Leclerc visited Paris to explain his position. The 2e DB was a fighting division and he would not allow his original Free French to slip on any political banana skins. Leclerc suggested that such a role could be carried out by du Vigier's 1ère DB or Brosset's 1ère DMI (*divison motorisée d'infanterie*, Motorised Infantry Division) if de Gaulle needed regular forces for internal security. Leclerc knew that many senior French Army generals from the Pétain and Giraud eras regarded him as a gangster, which he rather enjoyed, but the inner turmoil of newly liberated France deeply affected him.

A few days later, Leclerc wrote to René Pleven saying he would leave the 2e DB and go into government only if it was absolutely necessary. Airing his thoughts to Girard as they sat in the handsome library of the Château of Gerbéviller, Leclerc said "You see, a decision like that cannot be taken lightly; on the other hand the great decisions need to be taken quickly or else it might be too late, as we have seen so often. Who knows? If the Russians attack, if the Americans cross the Rhine, if the Germans collapse and the war ends within a month, we might be able to go to Strasbourg. I think all the same that my duty lies with the government."[45] But this merely demonstrates how torn Leclerc was, and also how few people de Gaulle had at his disposal for high appointments both at the front and in France itself.

While the October hiatus continued, Leclerc sent a car for his wife and youngest daughters to come and stay with him at Gerbéviller. For a few brief days, Thérèse was a garrison wife again, and their two daughters endeared themselves to *les soldats de Papa*. This did not stop another blonde actress trying her luck with him. Marlene Dietrich wrote, "*Mon général*, I would be happy if you would allow me to see you and to tell you that my heart is with you and your troops. Marlene."[46] Gentlemen may prefer blondes, but Leclerc had married a brunette over twenty years before, and had his elder sons serving in his division. Although Leclerc had "that little touch of madness" that makes a good soldier, he was a good Catholic boy also and preferred that his men be so as well. And whatever the 2e DB had become, Leclerc himself remained very traditional. Dietrich subsequently romanced the US 82nd Airborne Division's General James Gavin.

Throughout his stay at the Château of Gerbéviller, the acting *châtelaine* was the late Marquis de Lambertye's daughter, the twenty-three-year-old Princess Gabrielle d'Arenberg, who ruled the *environs* with a rod of iron during her mother's absence. When she saw that the Spaniards of Putz's 3/RMT had raised the Red Flag on the balcony of the *mairie* which they had taken as their temporary HQ, Princess d'Arenberg pulled it down.

"By what right did you lower that flag?" protested Leclerc.

Unperturbed, Princess d'Arenberg coolly replied, "The Spanish Republicans are not a government."

"But they are excellent soldiers," Leclerc blasted. "They deserve their flag!"

"From now on," said the forthright young lady, "mind your own business!"

Leclerc could very easily have countermanded her, but it was just the sort of thing his father might have done at Belloy-Saint-Léonard, and like Thérèse, the princess had previously been forced to share her home with the Germans. The microcosm of the 2e DB had clashed with the world of his youth. Seeing both sides, he stayed assiduously out of the way when the princess entertained his officers to dinner and played card games in the evenings.[47] For his own needs, Leclerc had the ever-loyal Sergeant Loustalot, who traded US cigarettes and rations with the locals for fresh meat and vegetables, and always made sure Leclerc had a sitting room with a good fire and a tot of *eau de vie* of some kind to quaff when he came in. Writing to Ingold, Leclerc was far more interested in the local game: "Ah, I almost forgot to mention the very thing that would make you die of jealousy. I shot an old lone boar weighing 250 pounds!"[48]

If the month of inaction while Allied logistics found a new gear benefited the 2e DB, it also benefited von Manteuffel's men facing them. Above Rambervillers, two new Panzer brigades, the 111th and 106th, moved into the line and barred any advance by the US 49th Infantry and GT Guillebon. A new defensive system, their *Vor Vogessen Stellung*, had been hastily thrown together along the western foothills of the Vosges massif, stretching from Réchicourt-Blamont in the north to Badonviller-Senones further south. Through all this, the town of Baccarat with its world famous glass works still had to be taken.[49]

Through the preceding month the offices of Gribius and Repiton-Préneuf had been gathering intelligence about German displacements, which, even by 2e DB standards, was exceptional for quantity and accuracy.

As well as information from the local resistance, the 2e DB acquired additional intelligence from prisoners whose racial and national diversity testified to the exhaustion of German manpower. Repiton's staff found that east European prisoners press-ganged into Nazi service spoke happily over a cup of American coffee and a Camel cigarette. One Ukrainian deserter told them precise positions for over thirty machine-guns, information which was carefully passed to Colonel Crépin's artillery plotters.[50] They also discovered that Manteuffel expected an attack at any time, but was assuming his attackers would stick to the roads. The Germans had placed 88mm guns at crossroads in the villages of Azerailles to the north, Ogéviller to the northeast, and at a strongpoint in Hablainville. Manteuffel clearly expected an attack from the south, out of that belt of forest running from Rambervillers to Badonviller.

Instead, Leclerc decided to attack from the north, out of the Forêt de Mondon. This necessitated cutting paths through the woods, which would make noise, but the appalling weather provided an advantage. On the other hand, Leclerc worried over whether, once the tanks emerged from those woods, they would bog down in the mud. Leclerc arranged a little test in an especially waterlogged field. The Shermans coped.

Baccarat would be taken from the north after a feinting attack from the south. In the last days of October, GT Guillebon was switched from Rambervillers to the Forêt de Mondon, where it would be supported by GT Langlade. They made final preparations through the night of 31st October, and the attack commenced at 8.30am the following morning with a thunderous barrage. Sub-groups commanded by Massu, La Horie and Quillichini came storming out of the Forêt de Mondon across muddy fields to take German positions at Ogéviller and Azerailles from the rear. That achieved, they pushed on into Baccarat to take its bridge—and the famous glassworks—intact.

The operation was watched by Leclerc and Haislip from high ground to the west, with some officers sent over from de Lattre's First Army. German mines took a toll of the RMT infantry, but otherwise losses were mercifully light. German casualties were much worse, caused largely by the artillery barrage, which Captain Compagnon described as "Wagnerian." Leclerc's 2e DB made it look so easy that Baccarat has been called the *ballet héroïque*. If it was easy, it was the result of conscientious intelligence gathering and meticulous preparation by the *bureaux* of Paul Repiton-Préneuf and André Gribius.

Arriving at the glassworks, French officers were shown a set of crystal champagne glasses previously ordered by Reichsmarschal Goering. Leclerc's staff became their new owners and they were quickly filled. The director also had something awaiting delivery to Marshal Pétain, now under house arrest at Sigmaringen in Germany. A crystal *francisque* (fasces), the axe and rods that were once the symbol of power in ancient Rome, subsequently adopted by Mussolini and Vichy, had been made to adorn Pétain's gilded cage. Now this outsized glass trinket was offered to Leclerc.

"Look, Gribius," exclaimed Leclerc sarcastically. "The director's giving us a present that appears to be addressed faithfully to Marshal Pétain!"[51]

Leclerc then gave a short speech about patriotism and keeping faith with de Gaulle.

"It was on that day, I think," Gribius later wrote, "that I understood how much our country, so marked by opportunism and worries about survival, had lost that profound inner flame which engenders and maintains the greatest spirits."

Leclerc was disappointed that the success at Baccarat was not followed up. Had a US infantry division been at hand the breech could have been exploited, but it was a good local success. Dronne reached Vacqueville a few kilometres further east, its flames lighting the dark autumnal evening. In the meantime Leclerc moved his CP from Gerbéviller to Gélacourt, where the division stayed a fortnight while preparing and planning its next important task: Strasbourg.

CHAPTER TWELVE

THE LAST WINTER OF THE WAR

The provinces of Alsace and Lorraine had been claimed by both Germany and France for centuries, while for the most part their inhabitants believed they were French. Bismarck took them in 1870, and throughout Imperial Germany's existence they were under German sovereignty. After the Treaty of Versailles they reverted to France, an event that reaffirmed French patriotism against its powerful neighbour, and for which Leclerc's *promotion* at Saint-Cyr was called *Metz et Strasbourg*. These cities remained French for the next nineteen years until *la Chute* in 1940. Some Alsatians managed to get out and join the Free French, like Arthur Kaiser of the 12e RCA. Alsatians and Lorrainois were strongly represented among de Gaulle's followers. General Marie-Pierre Koenig was Alsatian, whereas Robert Schumann, a future prime minister, was Lorrainois. Men of military age who remained in the re-Germanised provinces were subject to Wehrmacht conscription, becoming the *malgré nous*—the "despite ourselves." As the capital of the region, Strasbourg had for many centuries mingled French culture with a certain Teutonic cosmopolitanism. The city once possessed a distinguished Jewish community. The family of Alfred Dreyfus, the officer falsely accused in the 1890s spying scandal, originally came from Strasbourg, though by 1944 most of Strasbourg's Jews had been swept away into concentration camps.

As the 2e DB pushed eastwards, the towns and villages took on a Germanic flavour. Since arriving in France, especially after Paris, Leclerc's successes were based on solid preparation, supported by good local intelligence enthusiastically offered. The Strasbourg operation had to be a success too. Leclerc ordered a relief model of the whole area sent from Paris and installed it in his CP at Baccarat. Again he set Gribius and Repiton-Préneuf to work uniting information from every source, including, as usual, *résistants* and interrogated prisoners. The autumn's losses had to be made good. In line with its élite status, the 2e DB now had its own replacement battalion at Saint-Germain-en-Laye directly under Leclerc's authority. This way of doing things was more British than French, and caused criticism from the general staff, but owing to his good relationship with War Minister Diethelm, Leclerc got his way. The recruits received a realistic training that facilitated their entry into the division.

When not engaged in planning operations or divisional business, Leclerc thought deeply about the problems of the French Army, the defeat in 1940, the Vichy years, and how the army should evolve from 1944 onwards. He despised the Vichy era, but he understood Pétain's moral authority as victor of Verdun, and knew that an army must be disciplined and obedient. However, his Jesuit upbringing taught him that the struggle between good and evil must always continue in a man's soul. Extrapolating from that idea, Leclerc also believed that the debate between mindless obedience and moral duty to country and the "general interest" should exist in an officer's mind at all times. Harking back to the débâcle of 1940, Leclerc felt that, had France's armed forces possessed more modern equipment and more evenly balanced airpower, the German invasion could have been halted, as it had been on the Marne in 1914. In this, he conveniently forgot that, during September 1914, the German effort was divided between France in the west and their eastern front, whereas in May 1940 France, assisted only by the small BEF, faced the full might of a very different German war machine with no other immediate threats to counter. These fervent and deeply patriotic, but not always realistic, views were shared with de Gaulle in a long, rambling letter sent in mid-November 1944.[1]

The divisional CP did not stay long at the hastily requisitioned Château de Gélacourt. The roof leaked, and officers working at plans day and night had to be reasonably dry. Even Leclerc was sleeping in a room where drips were caught by buckets. Luckily, pre-First World War German prepared-ness meant there was a Wilhelmine German barracks in Baccarat which they moved into. Gribius found the place, but Girard, as a sophisticated Parisian, found the decor lugubrious. Shortly after moving in, Leclerc sent Girard to Tailly to fetch Thérèse again, who was now, in the French custom, known as *la générale*. Then he gave both Girard and Captain Chambon a couple of days' leave. Girard returned to Paris to reintroduce himself to the Quai d'Orsay, where the French diplomatic service was rebuilding itself, while Chambon took a Jeep equipped with several jerrycans to see his mother in Cannes.[2]

In Paris, de Gaulle struggled to make the Allies observe traditional diplomatic courtesies to his provisional government, while Leclerc feared that the chance of liberating Strasbourg would escape him. Patton's Third Army was already in the Haguenau area northwest of the city. Leclerc vis-ited Haislip, taking the newly promoted Gribius with him. On arrival they heard that Haislip was ill and running a serious fever. Aware that Americans often regarded *Gaullistes* as nag-bags who were never satisfied, the French-men were sceptical. They need not have worried. Haislip was a Francophile. True, the fever was a white lie, but he was negotiating with Bradley and Eisenhower for the XV Corps to widen the breach around Haguenau to include Strasbourg. That particular American knew all about the Oath at Kufra and what Strasbourg meant to the Free French *anciens* from Chad. On 10th November, Leclerc was informed as soon as Haislip received the green light from SHAEF, although, as with Paris, the US staff coolly failed to mention Strasbourg except as a secondary objective.[3] The first orders for the Strasbourg operation were issued later that day. The 2e DB re-grouped in the Blette valley, while the front was held by the US 79th and 44th Infantry Divisions which now made up Haislip's XV Corps.

Several roads lead up into the Vosges massif but these become fewer as the crest chain is reached. The main road complexes traversing the wooded west slopes and giving access to the Alsace plain are Sarrebourg–Lutzel-bourg–Saverne in the north and the main road from St Die to Schirmeck further south. This left Haislip's XV Corps with little choice. The infantry would have to breach the Germans' *Vor Vogessen Stellung*, while Leclerc got the main weight of the 2e DB into the Saverne area and then made his bid for Strasbourg using the road complex north and west of the city.

Getting to Saverne would be an operation in itself. Leading the attack against the Vosges defences on 13th November, US infantry found it hard going, only taking a belt of land two kilometres wide in as many days. Any local advantages acquired were quickly blocked by the Germans. French armour, waiting to exploit a breach, found this very frustrating. Girard drove Leclerc through the autumn woods to observe American progress. Nearing the frontline a shell exploded, then another. "We have two choices," the young ADC told his *Patron*. "We can either wait or go on."

"Go on," replied Leclerc, as a third shell exploded.

Slithering along the muddy road, Girard glanced sideways at his boss. Leclerc was thoroughly enjoying himself. Past Ancerviller they paused in a copse within sight of the village of Halloville. American soldiers were lying uncomfortably in roadside ditches while further up they could see a couple of American TDs stopped in clear view of the enemy. Then an ambulance Jeep drove past them back downhill carrying wounded on awkwardly balanced stretchers.

Leclerc told Girard to stop the Jeep, and he walked to the edge of the wood to get his bearings from the terrain and the map. Recognising that there was no point in waiting for a breach to exploit, Leclerc decided that the 2e DB would have to look for its own. As he briefed Commandant Morel-Deville of the Spahis Marocain at their CP, four shells exploded nearby. Nothing unusual in that; it happened every couple of hours. Then another four explosions rattled the house door open.

"*Mon général*," said Morel-Deville, worried. "Don't you think it might be better to wait a while?" Leclerc demurred. He was determined to progress matters around US 79th Division's flanks and worried that the rain might turn to snow. He wanted to get the Vosges massif behind them before the weather and German resistance got any worse.[4]

The first breaches would be made by sub-groups Morel-Deville and La Horie. With a squadron of Spahis Greyhound armoured cars and a handful of 12e RCA Shermans, supported by a battery of six guns, Morel-Deville was tasked with inflicting a disastrous breach upon the *Vor Vogessen Stellung* and not to stop for anything. An expert at reconnaissance, Morel-Deville was accompanied by the brave curate of Domèvre, who had attached himself to the 2e DB after Baccarat. After skirting along the line they found a weakness at Halsviler. Meeting no resistance, they pushed on through until they reached the village of Nonhigny, then drove west to Parux, which opened up the route to Cirey-sur-Vezouze. From Cirey they fanned out in all directions.[5]

Germans situated behind their anti-tank guns at Badonviller were now in serious danger of having their flanks turned by Morel-Deville, and they left their dug-in positions despite facing a more immediate threat from sub-group La Horie to their front. As night fell, La Horie's men caught up with them, capturing 12 anti-tank guns and taking 200 prisoners. The following morning, sub-group La Horie pushed on to Bréménil to exploit their advantage, and German artillery opened up. La Horie took a piece of shrapnel in the neck and was rushed to the aid station set up in Badonviller, where he died soon afterwards. Of the 2e DB's notable losses that summer and autumn—which included Colonel Rémy's son, Corlu, Geoffroy, Mazieras and Dubut—it was the death of La Horie that affected Leclerc most deeply. He was at the divisional CP in Baccarat when he heard La Horie was wounded, and went to Badonviller straight away, arriving to find his old friend already laid out in the *mairie* under the village *Tricolore*. Along with Rouvillois, they had been contemporaries at Saint-Cyr and ridden each others' horses. Although taking different paths following *la chute*, their friendship was rekindled in 1943. Leclerc embraced his friend's corpse and said a few prayers and his *adieux*. Among other officers paying their respects, Gribius was also deeply affected.[6]

Neither La Horie's death nor other losses those muddy, cold and wet November days would be in vain. Unlike Baccarat, this time their progress was followed up. With the Vezouze crossings at Cirey-sur-Vezouze taken intact, the pack of the 2e DB's Shermans and Tank Destroyers was released behind the Germans' Vosges line, moving off swiftly in the directions of Bertambois and Lafrimbolle, while the US 79th Infantry Division seized Blamont.[7]

In fading light, Leclerc gave fresh orders to all GT and sub-group commanders. GT Dio would strike furthest north in the direction of Sarrebourg, Phalsbourg and Saverne, deceiving the Germans that the 2e DB was heading for the obvious Phalsbourg route through the Vosges. The real attack would be two pincers coming from little wooded mountain lanes north and, principally, south of Saverne. These southern lanes would be taken by GT Langlade, of which Massu's sub-group would have the main task of moving on Trois Fontaines, the crossroads at Rethal, Dabo and Marmoutier, while GT Guillebon stayed in reserve at Cirey-sur-Vezouze.

When Massu returned to his men it was dark. His sub-group would have to get going straight away. He called his officers around him—Rogier and Eggenspiller of the RMT, Lucien who commanded the sub-group's Spahi armoured cars, Captain de Vandieres of the 12e RCA, and Durville of the RBFM—and explained to them, while holding a flashlight over a map, what Leclerc wanted. Their task was to push up the mountainside roads west of the forest and head north from Saint Quirin to Dabo and Lutzelbourg, on routes that are narrow and which gave little room for manoeuvre. He was concerned that his right flank would never cease to be at risk of German counterattack from higher ground out of plentiful cover, but he knew it was better to bypass these mountain forests than fight through them. In the atrocious weather, speed was of the essence.

Leclerc stood by the roadside, stick in hand, watching sub-group Massu's halftracks and tanks pass their start-line at Cirey. "Go like brutes!" Leclerc shouted. Given the precarious nature of the route, the weather and the dark, they had no option but to use headlamps. A few kilometres on, they passed the frontier point where Germany presumed to separate Alsace-Lorraine from France. Forward positions were swept away, but then the Spahis were blocked by an anti-tank gun and fir tree trunks placed across the road. The few prisoners taken included *Gebirgsjagers*, mountain troops, distinguishable by their Edelweiss insignia and, as the operation bogged down, Massu quickly realised his infantry would have to dig out the opposition. A nearby farmer told them that the Germans had not laid mines for lack of time, which was a small blessing, but the French resigned themselves to a busy and dangerous night in rain and mud.

Casualties mounted, and included the Spahi Captain Lucien. Having received desperate reports, Gribius visited Massu's front to take stock of the German defences, and found treehouses and pill boxes manned by good mountain troops. Reporting back what he had seen, Leclerc was unmoved. "I understand his concerns," Leclerc said. "But tell Massu that he must continue. Without him there's nothing to play for. He must keep going at all costs."[8]

Sub-group Minjonnet also ran into trouble, being stopped at Niderhoff and Bertrambois. There were casualties among officers and men alike, including medical staff. The White Father's Père Nicholas moved among all, impervious to the bullets flying around him and miraculously untouched.

After a long, hard night Massu resorted to artillery, pounding the *Gebirgsjagers* in the winter dawn, then sent in tanks with infantry. German resistance was quashed, but the armoured cars and tanks of the Spahis and 12e RCA were still being held up by tree trunks laid across sunken roads which could only be removed manually. At last the sub-group broke through. "Now I can make the exploitation!" Massu radioed back to division. After the night's costly delays they moved fast, sometimes at 60km per hour, steaming ahead with all guns blazing into the chaos of German defeat. As the morning progressed they came upon a Wehrmacht artillery battery being pulled away by teams of half-starved horses. Lt. Sorret ordered his Jeep crews to loose off some Browning 0.3 Cal over their heads and the German gunners ran off, leaving their equipment and horses behind. In the next village, Captain Fonde told the inhabitants, whose farms had been ruthlessly exploited during the Occupation, to help themselves to the horses. A similar episode occurred as they entered Trois Fontaines.[9]

When Gribius retraced the previous night's route, his Jeep picking its way through a trail of dead soldiers, horses and abandoned kit, he could not find Massu's men. Here and there dazed Germans in cheap late-war uniforms were falling out of the woods, looking for someone to surrender to. US infantry were sent to gather them up. Then Gribius heard Browning machine guns and Sherman cannons in the distance. Driving on, he came across more dishevelled Germans hailing him, not to attack or harm him, but begging for directions out of Massu's inferno and for medical attention. Many German wounded were almost childlike. Catching up, Gribius discovered Massu's radio link had broken down. When Gribius reported the wounded men on the road, Massu replied that the Quakers and *Rochambelles* had more serious cases to deal with. The wounded Germans would have to wait, and Gribius knew many of them would not make it.[10]

Sub-group Minjonnet had also been busy, taking 14 German artillery pieces, of which eight were 88mms, and destroying three Panzer Mk IV Specials with the adroit use of RMT infantry in a flanking attack through a wood.[11] GT Dio now had orders to push as far north as possible and then turn east towards Saverne, even though Leclerc intended to take it from the south. GT Guillebon was ordered to reinforce the breach made by Massu, and drove on through the night of 20th–21st November with headlights full on. Leclerc wanted to get as many troops over the Vosges as possible to invest the Saverne road complex. His breach would be held open by the US 79th and 44th Infantry Divisions behind him.

Massu's advanced elements pushed on to the Rehthal road junction amid persis-tent drizzle. Lt. Riff was the sub-group's intelligence officer due to his command of German and knowledge of the area. The 2e DB's *alsaciens* were coming into their own. Riff had the good fortune to see a *kubelwagen* coming down a lane towards his halftrack. Realising their mistake the Germans attempted a u-turn, but a French halftrack haired after them and forced the *kubelwagen* into a ditch. Two officers were taken prisoner and interrogated. The 2e DB's German-speakers were also listening on Wehrmacht radio nets for information, noting down names and map references to assist Massu in formulating his plan for taking Dabo and the push to Saverne. Splitting off two mixed detachments led by Rogier and Eggenspiller, of infantry, Shermans and some of Durville's Tank Destroyers, Massu sent them off in the small hours. Leaving his HQ vehicles, Massu followed in a radio Jeep. The French troops reached Hazelbourg and found the Germans had not finished their defences. Road blocks were not ready, mined bridges were not blown, and the fort was not defended. Massu was thrilled. Rogier and Eggenspiller continued to Dabo, which they reached by noon after a small skirmish.[12] German unpreparedness was due to their expectation that the French main thrust would be from the northwest where Quillichini was making his feint at Phalsbourg. Quillichini was being blocked, as Leclerc knew would happen and intended that he should be.[13]

Guillebon caught up with Massu beyond Dabo. Rogier's men had emerged from the forest road to find themselves face-to-face with a German rearguard behind an 88mm gun, and more tree trunks across the road. Guillebon suggested an infantry attack from the woods. But, Massu, true to his name, sensed time would be saved by using a larger hammer: infantry, tanks and combat engineers. Two hours later, the column was breezing along again on ten kilometres of narrow road past beautiful pine saplings until the forest ended. Then they looked out over the Alsatian plain spread out below them in the distance in fading winter sunlight.[14] It's a beautiful view on such a day. In Paris the *alsaciens* in the 2e DB, such as Riff, Braun and Kaiser, had looked on as men like Gribius and Massu were reunited with their families. Now it was their turn to arrive home as liberators.

Quillichini's feint towards Phalsbourg also benefitted Rouvillois' 12e Cuirassiers. Rouvillois knew the area from garrison duty before the war. To find his way around the Phalsbourg defence system he went as far north as La Petite Pierre, where he had to wait for fresh supplies of petrol and to gather prisoners. After a costly skirmish at Schalbach where the casualties included 2nd Lt. Corap, Rouvillois emerged from the Vosges pine forest into Alsace the following day.[15] In the Vosges, Rouvillois's swift movement had so surprised the Germans that his force killed some 600, took 1,400 prisoners, and seized diverse supplies including hundreds of horses.[16] In the 2e DB's CP at Cirey, Leclerc was thrilled when he heard of Massu's and Rouvillois' progress. Walking into the Château's main salon, which they used as both office and dormitory, he collared Lt. Châtel and sent him over to Haislip, demanding US infantry to gather the prisoners. This was no time to be slowed down. At first Haislip was not keen; armoured commanders had a knack of borrowing another division's infantry to save their own from getting "chewed up," but Leclerc insisted they were strictly for gathering prisoners, so Haislip relented.[17]

On the 22nd, Leclerc ordered GT Langlade to take Saverne itself. Minjonnet would follow the eastern line of the Vosges forest northwards, while Massu swung out over the Alsatian plain to approach Saverne from the southeast. By 1pm, Minjonnet reached the main Phalsbourg-Saverne road and then turned back eastwards to surprise the German force that had been obstructing Quillichini from the rear. At 2pm, Massu linked up with Rouvillois at the crossroads of la Faisanderie. Saverne was enveloped and the Germans were scrabbling to get out. The population of the town knew liberation was near. When the 2e DB entered Saverne, tricolours fluttered from windows, and bottles of kirsch, schnapps and vin d'Alsace emerged from nowhere to be offered to French soldiers.[18] The language with which they were welcomed varied by age group. The very old, brought up before the Franco-Prussian War, learnt French at their mothers' knees; the middle-aged spoke Alsatian German; while the young of Arthur Kaiser's generation spoke French.

Now, supported by US 44th Infantry Division, Quillichini kept up the pressure on Phalsbourg. As Minjonnet pushed back westwards to link up with them, he captured a battery of six 88mm guns. German General Brusch saw he was encircled and surrendered with over 800 men. The French took him to Leclerc. Brusch was surprised to find the 2e DB's CP east of Saverne, in an empty, cold manor house at Birkenwald that had been shut up since 1940.[19] Leclerc and his staff had followed behind Massu through the trail of dead Germans, dumped equipment and unkempt columns of prisoners. Then there was news of another breakthrough in the Vosges, further south. Du Vigier had taken Belfort, regarded by the US press as a fine feat of arms.[20]

Leclerc wanted to go straight for Strasbourg while he had the momentum, to keep the Germans off balance. To do this he needed American agreement and the certainty of logistical backup. The US Seventh Army commander, General Patch, was not keen, but Haislip telephoned him saying, "We cannot take 'no' for an answer! Will you please confirm that it can be done?" This led to an altercation between the two Americans. Patch had become more cautious following his son's death in action. Haislip brought up the usual arguments about French feeling and Leclerc's Oath at Kufra, and Patch relented, allowing a French reconnaissance towards Strasbourg.

When they moved the divisional CP into the deserted manor at Birkenwald, Girard had set up a hurricane lamp and laid out the map on the dining table.

"A good success," said Girard about the Vosges operation. "We're going well."

"Yes," said Leclerc with a wry smile. "But there's no hesitation possible. If we're going to cut them right off we've got to get on with it!"[21]

Depending on which routes are taken, Strasbourg is thirty-five kilometres from Saverne. Intelligence was needed at once. Walking into the room taken by Repiton's *2e bureau*, Girard saw a captured German officer in a leather coat, looking dour and depressed among the tables and secretaries. He led the German into another room and attempted to interrogate him.

The German said he was a "simple colonel" who "hadn't even the time to know what was going on," and that they should wait for "the general they had captured at Saverne." Nice try, but Repiton-Préneuf appeared and soon established that the German was in fact the very same general Brusch captured earlier. Once the lights were turned on him, Girard saw the scarlet edging of his shoulder boards. Repiton did not get much more out of the German than the usual arrogant nonsense about racial superiority which the outcome of the war could not alter. General Brusch was kind enough to congratulate the 2e DB on the Baccarat operation, while nevertheless asserting that the Germans were doing well in Russia, a bizarre notion since, by the autumn of 1944, they had been pushed back into Poland.[22]

Leclerc could not wait while Repiton ground down Brusch's obfuscations. It would have been nice to know if the Germans had mined the bridge at Kehl, on the eastern side of Strasbourg, but it made little difference to his immediate reality. More news came in regarding du Vigier's 1ère DB. Mulhouse had been taken in a lightning operation, suggesting that the Germans did not have much left between the Vosges and the Rhine. It would be good for French prestige if another Alsatian city was liberated by French armour.[23] US XV Corps commander Haislip understood, and made it clear that speed and surprise were essential if Strasbourg was to be taken with minimal damage, but he advised Leclerc to be very careful.[24]

First, the gains of the previous two days had to be protected from German counterattack. The best intelligence for this was traditional reconnaissance. Quillichini's sub-group, now over the Vosges, would act as cover from the north, while Morel-Deville's Spahis set off southwards to report on German movements. Sub-group Minjonnet took over as reserve. This left five other sub-groups: those of Massu and Rouvillois, now under de Langlade; and Cantarel, Putz and Debray under de Guillebon. Their orders were to head for Strasbourg along whatever axis offered least resistance and break through. The radio codeword for Strasbourg would be "Iodine" and the 2e DB was the "Tissu." Once significant forces entered the city, the coded message would be *tissu est dans l'iode.* The operation would begin at 7am on 23rd November.[25]

Setting off before sunrise in incessant cold drizzle, they made good time. Massu took small country lanes in a southeasterly direction through Waldolwisheim, Duntzenheim, Gougenheim, Pfettisheim, and Pfulgriesheim, with Sorret, Rogier or Eggenspiller in the lead. In two and a half hours they had gone over twenty-five kilometres meeting no resistance. In the distance they could see Strasbourg Cathedral. Between them and the city was a line of old forts, renamed after French WWI generals like Foch and Pétain, to get past. Was this a line of German resistance?[26]

Massu's reconnaissance section bounded forward, followed by his 12e RCA Shermans. The lead tanks carried RMT men from 2nd Lt. Albert Jung's section. Jung was from Strasbourg, returning home. Then the Germans opened fire, and the lead group was hit badly, with Jung mortally wounded in the head. Eggenspiller was seriously wounded in the chest, while Sorret was hit in the leg but managed to report to Massu as he was being evacuated. The Germans were firing from a trench system behind a high embankment, and soon they opened fire from the forts as well. With his Shermans getting bogged down as they looked for routes to outflank, and casualties mounting up among the 2/RMT, Massu called in artillery to suppress the gunfire from the forts and embankments. The sub-group had the 2e DB's senior chaplain, Père Houchet, with them. Accompanied by a British Quaker stretcher-bearer called Fraser, Houchet flouted danger to tend the wounded. Fraser was killed beside him.[27]

Massu consulted with Langlade. With fields turned to bogs by the rain, there was not much they could do on the city's western approaches. Rouvillois and his 12e Cuirassiers, however, had better luck. In the previous engagements the glory tended to go to the 2e DB's other tank regiments, either Langlade's Chasseurs d'Afrique or Cantarel's 501e RCC. At Strasbourg, the Cuirassiers would be first. The 12e Cuir' took a northerly loop to approach from the little town of Brumath. Sweeping all before them, they reached the northern district of Schiltigheim and passed through the city's boundary at 9.30am. The lead tank was commanded by Captain Briot de la Crochais, nephew of the historical writer Jean de la Varende. Briot had spent the previous evening inspecting his men from the back of a thoroughbred horse he had found abandoned.

The people of Strasbourg and the German garrison simply could not believe it as Rouvillois' Shermans thundered along the cobbles, pulling up at junctions beside city trams. Phone calls from Saverne by German speakers from Repiton's *2e bureau* had spoofed General Vaterodt's staff into thinking there was still fighting there, so that reinforcements were sent into a trap. Now the 2e DB was in their midst.[28] Off duty German soldiers were walking the streets, and officers escorted their wives or sat at streetside cafés. Unless they put their hands up, the French gunned them down. With the war on their doorstep, the Strasbourgeois fled into their houses. Trams and carts were abandoned. Doors slammed shut. Suddenly the city seemed empty. Only the 2e DB and the Germans moved in it.

Leclerc set off to follow his division. Shortly after 10am a dispatch rider on a Gnome-Rhône motorcycle caught up with him bringing Rouvillois's message: "*Tissu est dans iode.*"

Leclerc gave a shriek of laughter, "Allez, on part!"[29]

When Massu heard Rouvillois was in the middle of Strasbourg, the costly attack on the western approaches could no longer be justified, and he retreated behind his artillery screen. From there he turned north to follow in behind Rouvillois via Berstett and Vendenheim. Lt. Riff led the sub-group through the lanes to the new axis of advance, accompanied in his Jeep by Henri de Hauteclocque, Leclerc's eldest son. "Faster, *mon lieutenant!*" said Henri.[30]

GT Guillebon approached the city from further south than Massu, finding itself checked by German anti-tank guns around Fort Kléber. They managed to turn this line but Guillebon's men still found plenty of Germans holding out in buildings on Strasbourg's south side. Of all the groups, Guillebon's would have the longest and hardest task.[31]

On his way into Strasbourg, Leclerc paused at Littenheim where he picked up a radio communiqué from de Lattre's First Army announcing that the 2e DB had seized Saverne and was 30 kilometres from Strasbourg, "struggling fast with the French First Army to seize the city."

Not only had Rouvillois been in the city for nearly three hours, but they were still benefitting from surprise[32] and Leclerc was furious with de Lattre's press office. He was also getting communiqués from his American masters going back on their decision of the previous evening. Having got wind of Leclerc's latest move to get ahead of other Allied armies, Eisenhower had countermanded Haislip.

Once again Leclerc told his liaison officers to misinform the Americans over 2e DB movements, just as he had over Guillebon's reconnaissance towards Paris.[33] It was too late for doubts. As he would write to his wife afterwards, he felt "Providence" leading him by the hand once again.[34] US generals Haislip and Devers came to see what was happening, threading their way through the rear echelons of the 2e DB. At a crossroads they came across Lt. Cristol.

"For the love of God, do you know where General Leclerc is?" asked one of the Americans.

"Certainly," replied Cristol graciously. "Here is the radio message that I have just received. The General is in Strasbourg."[35]

By 3pm, sub-group Massu was passing through Schiltigheim and on towards Place Haguenau. On the Rue de la Nuée-Bleu, Lt. Riff pointed out his birthplace to Henri de Hauteclocque. The sub-group parked up on the Place Broglie. Worried that the initial forces in Strasbourg were not strong enough to face a counterattack, Leclerc sent more tanks and troops from GT Dio which he had been holding in reserve. He also gave orders that his British Quaker stretcher-bearers, who wore British battledress with soup-plate helmets, take the wounded to as many different hospitals as possible to give the impression that there was a British contingent in the city as well![36]

As the first GT commander to enter Strasbourg, Langlade took control. He set up his CP at "Maison Rouge" and sent troops to take control of the University, Post Office and the Pont de la Bourse.[37] Gribius set up his operations room in the Kommandantur, from which garrison commander General Vaterodt and his adjutant, Major Vogel, had fled minutes earlier for the safety of Fort Ney. Walking into Vogel's office, Gribius found a cup of cold coffee still on the desk, which he drank.[38]

Rouvillois was still battling his way towards the Pont de Kehl area. In one of the few prescient actions carried out by the Germans that day, one of the three bridges had been blown. Langlade heard from the 12e Cuir' that Germans were holding out hard in the barracks on the east side, so he sent tanks and RMT infantry to lend a hand.[39] Among the 12e RCA Shermans was *Bordelais II*, driven by Arthur Kaiser, and its gunner was Leclerc's second son, Hubert. Busting onto a barrack square with *Augumois*, the two tanks found themselves coming under fire from high windows. Hubert put a high-explosive shell into any window showing movement, while Arthur Kaiser relished the destruction. The garrison of 250 Wehrmacht soldiers soon surrendered.[40]

The Pont de Kehl was the entrance to Germany from which the

abortive 1939 Saar offensive had kicked off, and there the Wehrmacht resisted stiffly. The 12e RCA lost five tanks, and the RMT several half-tracks. Among the casualties was Père Houchet, the senior chaplain, who was seriously wounded. The 2e DB would not be invading Germany yet.[41]

The 2e DB set up its HQ on the Kaiser Palast and normality returned to the centre of Strasbourg. The welcome the men received in Strasbourg was generous, but in late autumn's chill it was hardly the same as in Paris. Many Strasbourgeois would not be aware of their liberation until the following day and preferred to stay in their houses until certain. Accompanied by Girard, Leclerc visited Père Houchet, who was delirious and pale. As the division's senior chaplain since 1943, Houchet was deeply respected by the men. Leclerc was visibly upset seeing his faithful comrade dying. Houchet died during the night.[42]

Later that evening Leclerc wrote to René Pleven, with whom he had left London for West Africa in August 1940:

> My dear Friend,
>   A short note: today I entered Strasbourg in the midst of battle after a veritably heroic struggle lasting four days. Our men have been splendid.
>   This is the crowning moment! Now we can disappear. The task is complete.
>   I am tired but happy.
>   Our losses are slight but among them some good officers.
>   Warm regards
>   Leclerc[43]

From 6pm the *Tricolore* was flying from Strasbourg's cathedral spire. The oath made in Kufra's fort El Tag in March 1941 had been kept. At 9.30pm a French journalist, Max Corre, telephoned Girard to clarify which division had taken Strasbourg. German troops still fought in the city, which was also home to 15,000 German civilians, but Guillebon's men still pushed in from the south, taking control of one quarter after another. As in Paris, the telephone system still worked, and was used by both sides. Speaking fluent German, 2nd Lt Braun, a Strasbourgeois working in Repiton-

Préneuf's *2eme bureau*, built up a comprehensive picture of the Wehrmacht's local order of battle. He put the telephone service to good use, giving confusing and demoralising messages to any German stronghold he could get through to. Braun's supreme achievement that day was persuading four hundred Germans in Pfulgriesheim to march out of their stronghold behind their officers and surrender.[44]

The night of the 23rd–24th passed reasonably calmly, though German sappers were believed to be mining the remaining Kehl bridges. The following morning the Germans shelled the French-controlled part of the city, wrecking some buildings. Leclerc had set up his office in a sumptuous corner room of the Kommandantur. As usual Girard thought the room frightful, but nevertheless a table was laid for lunch near the fireplace where Leclerc, Repiton-Préneuf, Dio and he were to dine. When Dio arrived Leclerc said, "Well, here we are my old Dio. Now we can drop down dead!"[45] As they sat down, incoming artillery shells whistled and exploded nearby but not so close to cause alarm. The next moment the four men were rocked by a deafening explosion. The crystal chandelier crashed to the floor. Dust and smoke filled the room, obscuring everything as they sat in their chairs while the dust settled. As the air cleared they contemplated a spectacular scene of devastation. The room's lugubrious plasterwork was now rubble on the parquet, the windows were shattered, and the curtains were hanging in burning ribbons. Outside, vehicles were on fire. Dio got up first, clasping a hand to his neck.

"Dio, are you wounded?"

"No, no, *mon général*, it's nothing, nothing."

"What a dirty trick!" said Leclerc, chuckling.

Knowing the city layout, German artillery in the Kehl area had easily pinpointed Leclerc's HQ, so this was quickly moved to an old "brown house" that had once been an official Nazi Party office. Bagneux the specialist forager had found it, and the first thing the French did was to inspect the cellars.[46]

Suppressing German artillery now became a priority, and little by little this was achieved through the afternoon, though meanwhile some of the city's beautiful seventeenth-century buildings were reduced to rubble. At 4pm, Leclerc ordered de Langlade to seize Fort Ney on the north side, between Fauborg de Hoenheim and the village of Wantzenau. The German military governor of Strasbourg, General Vaterodt, had taken refuge there with about a thousand soldiers. Still in good humour after his lucky escape at lunchtime, Leclerc told Langlade, "Go, do it quickly, like you always do. Bring me General Vaterodt, and then as your reward you can go and see if your family recognise you and want to see you any more." Not having seen his family for over three years, Langlade appreciated the incentive.

With the end of the war in sight, taking Fort Ney without causing disproportionate casualties had to be avoided if possible. Fort Ney was modern enough to house powerful artillery, and sufficiently solid in concrete to withstand considerable punishment. However good Massu's infantry, taking a fort like that required something else. Langlade tried to think of useful precedents like the seizing of the Dutch fleet on the frozen Zuidersee by French cavalry during the 1790s, but that was not quite the same thing. First he requested support from the division's 155mm guns to supplement his Sherman-mounted 105s. Next, Langlade told Captain d'Alençon to present himself at Fort Ney and explain to the garrison the desperate plight awaiting them in the morning if they did not surrender.

Aspects of Paris repeated themselves. Vaterodt's envoy told d'Alençon that he could not surrender without some show of combat. Having already lost good men for Strasbourg, with the war nearing its end, this was not the kind of nonsense the French wanted to hear. D'Alençon raised the stakes, telling the Germans that if they did not surrender, US Flying Fortresses would be called in with 1,000lb bombs to reduce the fort to rubble. Still the Germans refused terms. Langlade had no option but to start making good his threat. With the benefit of good city plans, Crépin's artillery had fixed fire positions through the night and were zeroed in on Fort Ney. The first salvoes struck home and, as the smoke cleared, white flags appeared "Like lilies of the valley in spring."[47]

Yet, when d'Alençon and Braun entered the fort with two tanks to take Vaterodt's surrender, the German commander took two hours to make up his mind. Langlade waited outside the fort with a brace of Shermans and twenty men while nearly a hundred armed Germans waited behind the trees around him smiling and waving white handkerchiefs as though they did not care either way. To de Langlade it all seemed ridiculous. At last Vaterodt and his staff came out through the gate, calmly accompanied by d'Alençon and Braun. Vaterodt and Langlade saluted each other as Braun did the introductions in German.

"You could not know, *Monsieur*, how hard these moments are for an old soldier of irreproachable record," said Vaterodt.

"*Mon Général*," replied Langlade. "I understand you perfectly, particularly since from 1940 we have ourselves known the sad impressions which are now yours. But they must be even worse for you because they do not carry the hope of being reversed."

Braun acted as interpreter. Vaterodt requested that he might keep his staff with him along with their luggage, to which Langlade agreed. Langlade also allowed the German to keep his ceremonial dagger, but took as personal booty the pennant from Vaterodt's staff car. Triumphantly they drove back to Strasbourg, leaving d'Alençon to round up and disarm the prisoners. GT Langlade had taken Fort Ney without losing a single man.[48i]

Divisional funerals, including that of Père Houchet, had taken up much of Leclerc's day so it was late afternoon before he saw Vaterodt. For reasons of simple irony, Leclerc chose to receive Vaterodt in the wrecked room at the Kaiser Palast, which was once the dejected Teuton's office.[49] Although he was courteous to the defeated German, Leclerc could not resist rubbing it in and asked Vaterodt to what he attributed the Allied victory.

"Because you have the coffee and we do not," replied Vaterodt in an oblique reference to American plenty.[50]

Leclerc turned to Langlade. "Go, take some leave. I am giving you fifteen days. You've earned it."[51]

In five days the 2e DB had crossed the Vosges and liberated Strasbourg. The 2e DB inflicted severe losses on the enemy, killing over 2,000 and capturing over 12,500. They had destroyed or captured 16 Tiger and Panther tanks, 23 Mk IV Specials, 8 self-propelled guns, 800 half-tracks and over 150 guns including 88mms and 75mm Paks. German defences were thrown off balance in the whole area and the Strasbourg operation remains a model of manoeuvre and exploitation at Saint-Cyr and the École de Guerre to this day.[52]

On 26th November, a Sunday, the battle-scarred city prepared to celebrate its liberation. However, not only did the weather dampen people's spirits but German snipers and artillery were still making themselves felt. Irate at two of his soldiers being killed by snipers, Leclerc proclaimed that five German prisoners would be shot for every French soldier who lost his life due to either sniper fire or artillery directed by enemy spotters among the German portion of the city's population. As the *Tricolore* fluttered from the Cathedral spire, Leclerc and his staff were received by city notables, toasting liberation with vin d'Alsace served by girls in traditional costume. Leclerc was relaxed but, according to Girard, smiling in a way that seemed as if he dared not let himself go. Leclerc was pleased, but he knew what it had cost.

In the afternoon the 2e DB held a parade on the Place Kléber. Under the occupation the Germans had renamed it "Platz Karl-Roos." As the first to enter Strasbourg, Rouvillois' 12e Cuirassiers had the place of honour, their colour held up for all to see as a band jangled out *La Marseillaise*. *Tricolores* appeared from the windows and soon the Strasbourgeois were back on the streets again. Leclerc, dressed in formal khaki tunic, trousers with a general's dark stripes down the outside seams, and a képi with three stars, was one of the very few men in proper French uniform. Rouvillois was wearing US issue complete with canvas spat-style gaiters and Mk 1941 steel helmet. Leclerc saluted the parade while holding his cane like a sheathed sword, its task over. General de Gaulle paid a brief visit to the city and attended a Mass of Thanksgiving at the Cathedral. During his discussions with Leclerc he intimated that he wanted the 2e DB to join de Lattre's First Army, but the wish had yet to become an order.

A greater controversy was brewing that threatened to bring Leclerc and his division into disrepute. News of his threat to shoot five Germans if a French soldier fell victim to sniper fire reached the Wehrmacht high command, eliciting the response, "Several hundred thousand French prisoners of war and other French nationals are in Germany. If Leclerc and his commander, General de Gaulle, are considering initiating a round of reprisals contrary to international law, and using German prisoners of war as victims, they should know that the affair will not rest there, but that Germany will proceed with counter-reprisals most energetically." The Allied High Command responded in kind. Without disowning Leclerc or his statement, the Allies declared their adherence to the Geneva Convention, especially Article Two regarding the treatment of prisoners of war. Sixth Army Group went a little further, denouncing the French attitude. Reuters commented, "General Leclerc's proclamation is automatically cancelled."[53]

In any event, Leclerc's threat only referred to the duration of the 2e DB's stay in Strasbourg. His tanks were needed to meet up with de Lattre's First Army at Mulhouse. GT Dio was now forty kilometres away. But with orders not to cross the River Bruche, Boissieu's Stuarts stood idle as the Germans blew bridges. If the 2e DB had to remain longer in Strasbourg it was due to US Seventh Army's slowness in relieving them.[54]

The US 3rd Infantry Division relieved the 2e DB on 27th November. The following morning Leclerc left Strasbourg, heading south to link up with Jean de Lattre de Tassigny's First Army around the Colmar pocket. Discovering that General Devers had placed all forces in the Colmar sector under de Lattre, one of Leclerc's greatest fears was realised. Furious, he went to Paris to remonstrate with de Gaulle, but to no avail.

In the meantime Leclerc sent his new liaison officer, Jean Châtel, who now did the 2e DB's dirty work with the Americans, to meet de Lattre. After a Jeep ride down through the Vosges to de Lattre's HQ at Belfort, Châtel arrived cold and hungry, dressed somewhat spartanly in US combats. Patrician and paternal, de Lattre exclaimed, "The poor child needs warming up! Give him some turkey and champagne." For Châtel it was like stepping back in time to the pre-war French Army. France had finally disposed of monarchy in 1870, but its army had retained social divisions between officers and men more acutely than Britain's smartest regiments. De Lattre's staff were elegantly turned, out and his HQ was run in the old-fashioned way. Showing Châtel his map table, de Lattre explained the role he wanted the 2e DB to perform in the reduction of the Colmar pocket. De Lattre went on, "There must be no more of the 2e DB getting twice as many US cigarettes as First Army!" When Châtel reported back, Leclerc could not contain his anger. He decided to find another solution.[55]

Furthermore, as the French First Army reached the German frontier they were having a hard time compared to the first few weeks after landing in the south. Perhaps their fighting qualities had been overestimated, or perhaps German resistance was becoming more committed as the Allies reached German soil. There were five North African colonial divisions under de Lattre whose men were already losing confidence in the notion that France's liberation would ensure French concessions in post-war North Africa. The massacre at Sétif, which affected French North Africa as keenly as the Amritsar massacre affected British India, was less than six months in the future. De Gaulle was replacing experienced colonial troops with new ex-resistance units, such as Billotte's 10th (Paris) Infantry Division, which had entered service undertrained and armed only with captured German equipment, which inevitably caused resupply problems.[56]

Although he tortured his American superiors with his French, or rather specifically *Gaulliste* and "Kufran," agenda, Leclerc liked serving with characters like Wade Haislip. Haislip knew how to handle Leclerc in spite of his Gallic sensitivity, recognising that Leclerc was a pure blood that needed to be given his head from time to time. Whatever the Americans saw as Leclerc's faults, *vis-à-vis* obedience, he got things done. Leclerc had no confidence he would be able to achieve as much in de Lattre's army. In early December he wrote to both War Minister Diethelm and to de Gaulle, who was then engaged in the first visit to Russia by a French head of state since the liberation. In these letters, couriered by Repiton and Vézinet, Leclerc said that it would be better for French arms if their forces were represented in as many places as possible. He especially pointed out to de Gaulle the diplomatic advantages the "*Normandie-Niemen*" squadron of French pilots had provided in relations with Stalin. None of the other Western allies had sent men rather than supplies to Russia. Yet de Gaulle was also a traditionalist and took a dim view of his young friend refusing to be rejoined to the greater part of the French Army.[57]

For the time being, Leclerc concocted a fudge that would keep him under American auspices. He would consent to be under the orders of General Devers' US 6th Army Group, which consisted of General Alexander Patch's US Seventh Army and de Lattre's First French, but refuse to be attached to de Lattre. Before the transfer Leclerc spoke to Wade Haislip, "I want you to tell General Devers something from me. I, myself and every man in my division are volunteers. We do not have to fight and we do not want to fight, but we do so for the liberation and honour of France. But, if he ever attaches us to de Lattre de Tassigny, we will pack up and go home."

Haislip fully believed that Leclerc meant to do this if pushed too far.[58]

Such was Leclerc's determination to avoid serving under de Lattre that he would do anything to trip up the senior man. Using anecdotes provided by First Army personnel on leave, Leclerc suggested that de Lattre's command was too big anyway and too difficult to control, saying its men were a rabble from the colonies and the worst of the FFI who indulged in drum-head courts and summary executions, bringing fear to the French coun-tryside. He even called areas under de Lattre *centres contaminés,* "contam-inated areas," ostentatiously sending his own personnel to reassure the local people of any area he took over. In truth, Leclerc had put a very firm stamp on the 2e DB, and their conduct under the prevailing rules of war was ex-emplary, in spite of the threat made in Strasbourg. In his personal life and private tastes, Leclerc was a narrower, more disciplined and less complicated man than de Lattre. For some members of the 2e DB, especially those who had come from the former Vichy-controlled *Armée d'Afrique,* the quarrels between Leclerc and de Lattre seemed pointless. They believed that, what-ever de Lattre's failings, Leclerc was also to blame for the bitterness that developed. Paul de Langlade, though unswervingly loyal to Leclerc, would later write, "Always dominated by his desire to act quickly, he [Leclerc] lost patience, dipped his pen in vinegar and wrote to the person in question in such a way that all hope of success vanished from the arena." Coming from the *Armée d'Afrique,* "success" for Langlade was a unified French Army.[59]

The disagreements continued through the winter. Turning south to take control of a sector facing the Colmar salient, the 2e DB found their movement slowed by blown bridges over the Rhine's tributary rivers and canals. The troops tried to find crossing points but, after the speed of the Vosges campaign, the slow task of relocation in mud and frost sapped the spirits of Leclerc and his men alike.

The return to life of liberated villages offered some consolation. It was Advent, and the appearance of the *Tricolore* amid cold and snow made a big difference to men like Arthur Kaiser, for whom the frustration of the hold-up was made worse by his fears for France's political future. Christian Girard found memories of Fort Lamy flooding back like a golden era, whether it was commanding his first troop of armoured cars, the sight of Leclerc on a horse called Kufra, or papayas growing in his bungalow garden. Their thoughts also ran to the division's future once Germany was defeated. Leclerc believed that if Eisenhower allotted the French Army a sector to occupy that it would be the Rhineland area. And future wars? Leclerc believed machines would take over to an even greater extent.[60]

Local successes continued. On 30th November Quillichini's sub-group succeeded in capturing 300 Germans along with four tanks near Gerstheim. The following day Minjonnet found the Germans had evacuated Benfeld rather than face Leclerc's division, and had abandoned the Ill's west bank. The Colmar salient extended fifty kilometres into Alsace and, at its longest, it was seventy kilometres from north to south. However, from the thin sliver of land between the Rhine's west bank and the Ill, the Germans were still able to lob shells into the vicinity of the 2e DB's CP. "Very improper," Girard called it.[61]

Despite Leclerc lacerating de Lattre to anyone who would listen, in early December the 2e DB was placed under the command of Général de Monsabert's 2nd French Corps for the Colmar operation. Monsabert and his ADC lunched with Leclerc in his new CP at Erstein. Although Monsabert was correct and pleasant, there was a perceptible change in atmosphere. Girard "thought of Cambronne" but there was nothing a mere captain could do. Leclerc sent Repiton to Paris to try and prevent the transfer. The following day, accompanied by Girard, Leclerc visited GT Dio's sector. Walking into Dio's CP in an elegant villa, Leclerc called out and was greeted by the same Captain Briot who had led the 12e Cuirassiers into Strasbourg, this time wearing a smart dressing gown. Leclerc only allowed his officers to indulge in fripperies if they were diligent in their duties, and he grilled Briot about his troop dispositions in the event of a German attack on his front. Luckily Briot's answers showed he had things under control. Then they reminisced about Strasbourg, and Briot showed Leclerc some recently developed photographs. As they departed, Leclerc said to Girard, "That Briot, all the same, he's quite a chap!"[62]

Speaking to NCOs and other ranks, Leclerc found them all energized by the success of the Strasbourg operation. "One couldn't stop these chaps getting to Berlin," Leclerc remarked to his young aide. There was nothing like success to foster morale. On the other hand, before the Vosges and Strasbourg, Girard, whose writings are often the real barometer of the 2e DB's temperament, had commented on the tiredness of the *anciens* from Chad compared to the fresh inexperience of new arrivals. In eighteen months the division had grown fast and "founder members" often found themselves with men they had never met before. Original *Gaullistes* such as Girard had been reserve officers in the first place, but with the war almost over, wondered when they could recommence their original careers.

Leclerc's view was that they were part of the division's framework, a great effort was still expected, and they must do whatever de Gaulle said. Leclerc had little sympathy for the generation who reached early adulthood in the 1930s, who applauded both the Great War generation and de Gaulle, but would not follow them.[63]

On 7th December General Monsabert visited Leclerc again. Monsabert wanted the 2e DB to attack German positions simultaneously with an attack by *goumiers* from the southern Vosges Mountains. Leclerc, experienced in both mountain and armoured warfare, thought the plan bizarre and utterly lacking in speed and flair. The poor weather was largely to blame: there could be no surprise across waterlogged and frozen ground. Believing it would cost his division 300 men at a time when the end of the war was in sight, Leclerc thought this gave him the definitive argument to convince de Gaulle that the 2e DB should leave de Lattre's army.

The following day Leclerc visited General Haislip at US XV Corps HQ at Sarrebourg. Girard wrote that Leclerc was touched that so many US officers wore the 2e DB badge on their uniforms; even Haislip had one, and were all sorry to have lost Leclerc's men. But Haislip had other things on his mind than Leclerc's desire to leave de Lattre. The Germans had made a counterattack towards Sarrebourg and 130th Panzer Brigade had got within 6km of Haislip's HQ.

Reaching Paris two days later and hoping a personal meeting with de Gaulle would reverse the 2e DB's attachment to de Lattre's command, Leclerc found de Lattre had also been busy, claiming in newspapers that the 2e DB's swift seizure of Strasbourg was only made possible by the French First Army's activities further south. Leclerc also heard news from General Garbay, who had taken over command of the 1st DMI after Brosset was killed. The 1st DMI contained many of the original African members of *La Colonne Leclerc* from before the racist *blanchiment* demanded after the Anfa agreement. Garbay told Leclerc that he could not demand uniformity from his men over dress since they did not have enough clothes for their backs anyway. Before being transferred to de Larminat to contain the Atlantic pockets, the Americans had promised the 1st DMI new uniforms but they were delivered via Marseilles and taken by de Lattre's army. Combined with the stories of opulence in de Lattre's staff, such details sat ill with Leclerc. He met up with his old comrade, the former colonial gov-

ernor Masson, and found Masson's view of de Lattre equally uncompromising, "He is a s———, and more, he is a cretin."[64]

De Lattre's operation against the Germans' Colmar salient was becoming a sorry affair, as Leclerc had predicted. The First Army had been unable
to debouch against Sélestat and ran into trouble around Colmar. The 2e
DB had been asked to make a push in its own sector supported by the new
French Army's premier parachute battalion. The 1er RCP paratroops managed to seize a village, but at the cost of about 180 casualties. Gribius would
write, "My heart sank on hearing after the battle of Herbesheim that twenty
inexperienced young parachutists had fallen at our sides without us having
really adopted them as comrades in arms."[65] When visited by US Army
Group commander, General Devers, Leclerc explained the stark reality.
The Colmar salient needed infantry and a lot of artillery. It had already
cost the 2e DB more casualties than the operations from Badonviller to
Strasbourg. Devers, however, was not going to help Leclerc or de Lattre.
He had no infantry to spare from his own operation to puncture the
Siegfried Line, and in any case, he thought Colmar would fall of its own
accord if left as a salient.[66]

Leclerc visited Paris from 11th to 14th December in a final attempt to
cancel his division's attachment to de Lattre's army, only to walk slap into
the cut and thrust of post-liberation politics. His former adherence to
Action Française, the journal edited by Charles Maurras, who was now a
disgraced *collabo*, was becoming widely known and bandied about in leftist
circles. "Général de Hauteclocque de *l'Action Française*," Pierre Cot, former
minister of Leon Blum's pre-war government, called him following disclo-
sures that Leclerc had ordered a head count of Jewish members of the 2e
DB. In fact Leclerc was simply complying with a request from a rabbi.[67i]
And de Lattre? If Leclerc really could not tolerate him, the only other job
on offer was helping General de Larminat reduce the Atlantic pockets.
Leclerc did not wish to participate in those side operations, even though
he liked Edgard de Larminat as another uncompromising early *Gaulliste*.
He preferred the 2e DB to remain at the forefront of the Allied drive into
Germany.

On 16th December, 1944 Field Marshal Walter Model launched the Germans' Ardennes counteroffensive, sending the Americans retreating back

across southern Belgium. Panzer spearheads commanded by Hasso von Manteuffel made deep penetrations into the Allied front in a desperate bid to reach Antwerp and split the US and British armies. Wehrmacht and Waffen SS divisions attacked in areas held by inexperienced or tired US divisions. Of the US commanders on the spot, Leclerc's old Vth Corps commander from mid-August, Leonard Gerow, was among the first to recognise that the attack was "something big," while Bradley and Eisenhower hoped it was a spoiling attack aimed at halting Patton's pressure on the Saarland.[68] It was two days before SHAEF recognised the seriousness of what they faced and began plugging gaps by using resting airborne divisions to hold key junctions. In the meantime, US Third Army commander General George Patton, recognising the Belgian sector had become pre-eminent, sent three armoured divisions to assist Hodges' beleaguered US First Army.[69]

Eisenhower called a conference at Verdun, the scene of horrific French sacrifice during the first war. There the decision was taken that the German salient, or "Bulge" as the battle became known, represented a signal opportunity to take out the German Army in Western Europe. The Germans would be held on the right of the Meuse while Patton's army readied itself to wheel north in what would become an epic march, having as its focus the besieged US 101st Airborne Division at Bastogne.[70] But who would replace Patton's men in north Alsace and the Saar? The whole Allied line would have to redeploy men northwards. Devers' 6th Army group now had to take on the Saar front as well as Alsace. Eisenhower told him that if he felt pressed he should withdraw to the Vosges massif and hand newly liberated Strasbourg back to the Germans.

De Gaulle was horrified, and made it clear to the Americans that such an expediency was unacceptable to the French interest.[71] With this going on, Leclerc's displeasure at being attached to de Lattre was a minor consideration for de Gaulle. He told Langlade, who he received in Paris on 22nd December, that France's internal problems were his affair and that Leclerc would have to do as he was told. The 2e DB was still his favourite division, however, and he would stay with them for Christmas. When Devers called his army and divisional commanders to a conference, Leclerc hoped that the 2e DB would be chosen to join Patton's march into Belgium to rout the last German attack, and that the Americans would give him the kit and supplies they needed to take part.[72] This was not to be. The Americans had let the French have Paris and Strasbourg to themselves. Any glory attached to reversing American misfortunes in the Ardennes would go to US troops.[73]

De Gaulle's Christmas visit went off smoothly, though the freezing cold made parades exceedingly unpleasant. De Gaulle nevertheless stood immobile as stone before a march-past of Shermans from the 12e Cuirassiers. His cause had come a long way since June 18th 1940. The fact that Leclerc remained spiritually one of the Free French loners of those early days, spitting defiance at Vichy, lay at the root of the younger man's aversion to de Lattre's First Army. The truth also was that, unlike de Gaulle, Leclerc had had little news of his family until September 1944, he had never stopped fighting, and this was taking its toll. A note he put into de Gaulle's hands on Christmas Eve read,

> It is a little bitter to realise, after the proof given since 1940 of service and devotion to your cause, that you interpret my views and requests as fantasies motivated by self interest. In fact these views are also shared by my unit commanders and, I am quite certain, by my officers and even my men. I willingly consent to disappear but not in the direction of de Lattre, because this man will profit by any means he can to demolish my military reputation as soon as possible, which, thank Heavens, is still intact. This goal is indispensable to his ambitions and I have to be ready for it.

Folding the note, an exasperated de Gaulle told Leclerc, "This is exaggerated and unproductive."[74]

In fact, the 2e DB itself was proof that the French Army had moved on. Men such as Paul de Langlade, whom de Gaulle received in Paris only a few days earlier, were evidence of this. "I congratulate you, *mon général*." de Gaulle said, for Langlade had just received the stars of a *général de brigade*. Whatever disagreements happened between Leclerc and de Gaulle, his division was the nursery of many of the new generals in the French Army.[75] In forming his division Leclerc had been allowed to pick from the *Armée d'Afrique*'s best regiments to place alongside his Gaullist old timers. De Lattre's quarter of a million men were what was left over: colonial troops, former *résistants* and new recruits of diverse quality needing a leader who recognised that brutal frankness was not always preferable to sophistication and charm. De Lattre had also written to de Gaulle regarding the rift with Leclerc. Anxious to show himself the bigger man, de Lattre had been conciliatory.[76]

To confuse German artillery, in case they had known of de Gaulle's visit, Midnight Mass that Christmas Eve was brought forward to 1600 hrs. The congregation, made up of 2e DB personnel fresh out of the line, and specifically ordered not to tidy themselves first, entered Erstein's church to find candlelight and pitch darkness. The late afternoon dusk was further obscured by khaki blankets over the windows. Amid stringent security, the Mass began with Gregorian chants while photographers clicked away. Irritated by the flashes, Leclerc grabbed one of Boissieu's officers, Lt. Guibé, by the belt and told him to sort it out. There was, nevertheless, a radio commentator: "I am in a church in liberated Alsace to bring you the first Midnight Mass in the presence of General de Gaulle. I am surrounded by soldiers in combat uniform, covered in mud, who were, only a few hours ago, in the front line."[77]

Staying at the Villa Vogel, de Gaulle continued his discussion with Leclerc in the presence of his future son-in-law, Alain de Boissieu. "What would you do in his [de Lattre's] place?" de Gaulle asked. "If an ordinary divisional commander presumed to question your orders?"

Knowing he had enough credit with de Gaulle to get away with a lot, Leclerc replied cockily. "Yes, but me, I am intelligent!"[78]

De Gaulle, however, knew that Leclerc was too good an officer to be held back by this unfortunate personality clash, and he was already considering building a new army corps around the 2e DB with Leclerc as its commander.

The Battle of the Bulge continued through Christmas, and concern that Devers' 6th Army Group was overstretched meant that the evacuation of Strasbourg became a real possibility. De Lattre was ordered by Devers to withdraw from Alsace on 29th December. Since the order came in English, de Lattre did not understand at first that it was an *order* rather than a suggestion. After clarification, de Lattre was shocked and made provisions to protect Strasbourg even before de Gaulle asked him, sending three infantry divisions and the 1ere DB, now commanded by General Aimé Sudre. But owing to his army's displacements, de Lattre could only position them south of the city. Other generals, such as Patton, sensed the blow not only to French but Allied morale if Strasbourg fell back into German hands, or if there was any strategic retreat whatsoever from Alsace-Lorraine.[79] De Lattre's men swore to turn Strasbourg into another Stalingrad if the Germans came back.

With more pressing worries, General Devers was not going to waste time forcing Leclerc to like de Lattre. Any resort to using linguistic difficulties as an excuse plainly meant Leclerc should be with a French-speaking general, in spite of the fact that he had one of the US Army's most talented interpreters. Devers sent him back to Haislip's XV Corps, which Patch held in reserve to counter any German attack in Alsace. The divisional HQ moved from Erstein to Obernai. To some of the 2e DB, the withdrawal from the Colmar pocket, and failing to finish it off with de Lattre, was a disappointment.

The 2e DB was relieved by Garbay's 1ère DIM and, from the 31st December until 2nd January, they drove through ice and snow into the hills of the north Vosges. GT Langlade was the first to move from Sélestat to support the US 44th Infantry Division, with Massu's sub-group in the lead once again.

As feared, the Germans attacked towards the Vosges on the night of 2nd January, the picture being made more confusing by their use of abundant US kit and vehicles captured during the Battle of the Bulge. They took Gros-Rederching and seized the village of Achen. In the confusion, Massu wanted to wait until the following dawn before counterattacking, but Langlade insisted the counterattack go ahead that afternoon, and that Gros-Rechering be retaken before US reinforcements materialised. After a skilful outflanking manoeuvre, Shermans of the 12e RCA retook the small town from the north at 4.30pm. A few hours later about 40 American infantry turned up claiming to be the advance guard of more substantial forces. Yet something seemed strange. In the small hours of the morning, what appeared to be an American column arrived, led by a brand new Sherman in original green factory paint with head lamps blazing. This was odd; the Allies were managing to whitewash their vehicles at this time to camouflage them in the snow. The French opened fire. It was indeed a German *ruse de guerre*. Even so it was costly. Four 12e RCA Shermans were lost, Captain Langlois was captured by a German snatch patrol wearing US uniforms, and a well-liked troop commander from the 12e RCA, Roger Rives-Henrys, was killed by a bullet in the neck.[80]

The following morning Langlade ordered Massu to fall back to Dehlingen and Schmittwiller. Massu obeyed reluctantly while leaving a squadron of 12e RCA Sher-mans to support the Americans. Sub-group Minjonnet had also been attacked, but not as fiercely, and managed to hold onto Achen. During that day, GT Langlade restabilised the front, supported by US 44th Infantry Division, but the temperature was dropping, there was 40cm of snow on the ground, and the skies were grey as lead. The front settled down to a fortnight of static, frozen warfare. The Germans had brought in 2,000 mountain troops from Norway who were used to snow and operating at night. Though stretched along a 35km front between Bitche and Sarreguemines, they made enough trouble to bluff the Allies into believing their number was much greater.[81]

The costly Gros-Rechering affair and the loss of Lt. Rives-Henrys, who he had known for six years, affected André Gribius deeply. Ever since Langlade had joined his 12e RCA to the 2e DB, Gribius had been operations officer, a necessary job requiring disciplined and detailed thinking, which he was good at, but it did not entail the personal risks his comrades faced. With Rives-Henrys' death Gribius felt it was someone else's turn to take over the map table, and he asked Leclerc for a combat role. Reluctantly, Leclerc agreed. Gribius took over Minjonnet's sub-group, Minjonnet, "Père Mégot," went to the divisional staff, and forgiven *Vichysois* Lt. Col. Jean Lecomte became the new operations officer.[82]

Along with Gros-Rechering, the Germans had also retaken a number of villages from exhausted and ill-equipped divisions like the 1ère DMI—which the 2e DB considered its only Free French sister division.

"I am in the shit," General Garbay signaled Leclerc. "We have in front of us numerous modern German tanks. We have received eight ourselves but lack Tank Destroyers, the only weapon of any use against the *Boches* who are being reinforced every day. The II Corps has nothing to give me. I would apologise for seeming bleak but I fear the worst. If you can do something for Strasbourg and ourselves, hurry up." A few hours later

Leclerc heard that 772 original Gaullists from the 24e *bataillon de marche* of Garbay's division had been wiped out. Requesting Haislip's permission to go to Garbay's assitance, the answer was a firm "No." The available armour was to be kept in reserve.[83]

The German attack towards Strasbourg encircled an Algerian *tirailleur* battalion from General Guillaume's 3e DIA. The Germans, even at this stage of the war, were still excellent soldiers, and the force at Kilstett was an *ad hoc* formation made up of Volksturm, Hitler Jugend and a smattering of Waffen SS for backbone. With the Americans still prepared to abandon the city, Leclerc wrote to General Juin, "I do not need to emphasise the catastrophic moral effect that such a defeat would produce. Whatever pretexts are invoked, such a crime without fighting would be inexcusable. You can give us the order to get ourselves killed as soon as possible in the region of Haguenau and the plain of Alsace. We will carry it out even if it is contrary to American orders." Leclerc's liaison officer, Jacques Chambon, found General Guillaume close to tears; he knew his division could not hold on to Strasbourg unaided. "*Mon général*, hold on," said Chambon comfortingly. "You will soon receive support from sub-group Gribius. Then the whole of GT Langlade will re-inforce you."

Inconsolable, Guillaume replied, "You wait and see. They will accuse me of abandoning Alsace!"[84]

Ordered to push the Germans back over territory the 2e DB had taken without loss in November, sub-group Gribius lost five killed and several wounded from 2/RMT alone. Nevertheless, they took 300 prisoners and destroyed nine tanks. Leclerc signalled "Bravo Gribius!"[85]

At various moments during the war, the fact that he controlled large areas of territory was a trump card for de Gaulle. He told Eisenhower that if Strasbourg was not defended he would ban the Allies from using France's railways to supply their men. Churchill also insisted that Strasbourg must be held, and Patton went so far as to tell Eisenhower that, if Alsace-Lorraine were handed back to the Nazis, he would ask to be relieved of his command.[86]

De Lattre was duly authorised to send de Vernejoul's 5e DB into the city. The crisis was over.[87]

Looking at the coming year, Leclerc knew in his bones that the war would soon be over. The state of German prisoners made it clear that their manpower was exhausted. In letters to his sisters Yvonne and Colette he was bullish: "I don't think you will be invaded a second time."[88]

By mid-January, the Battle of the Bulge was well and truly over, and General Devers could re-juggle his priorities. On 17th January, somewhat bizarrely acting as liaison officer between his own divisional commanders, he visited the 2e DB HQ at Drulingen, accompanied by Lt. Colonel de Souzy, to inform Leclerc that he must leave Haislip's Corps once again and return to de Lattre to finish off the Colmar salient. Given reports of German defensive preparations, and the lack of up-to-date artillery among French divisions, this was not welcome news.[89] De Lattre's plan was to squeeze the salient from north and south. Though on a smaller scale, it was almost a template of the *Zitadelle* operation attempted by the Germans against the Red Army's salient at Kursk. Like the Russians, the Germans had also prepared in-depth defences, including blown bridges, flooded and frozen fields, dug-in tanks such as Jagdtigers and Jagdpanthers, machine-gun emplacements and plenty of snipers.

Beginning on 23rd January, Leclerc's role was to attack the northeasterly corner of the salient. For six days the 2e DB pushed south with GT Guillebon in the lead. Taking the town of Grussenheim cost GT Guillebon's infantry, the 3/ RMT, its battalion commander, the famous Commandant Putz, as well as several other good officers and men.[90] Guillebon's tanks, Cantarel's 501e RCC, also sustained heavy losses, including Lt. Michard, the troop commander whose tanks *Romilly, Montmirail* and *Champaubert* had followed Raymond Dronne into Paris on the evening of 24th August. Michard was just back from leave when a sniper shot him in the back of the head at Grussenheim. His crew, including Gaston Eve, carefully lifted him from his tank commander's chair and got him to an aid station, but he died the following day.[91]

At this stage in the war, when the endgame was so obvious, such losses seemed unjustifiable, especially from those who had given so much. The 2e DB had pushed a "finger" southwards between Colmar and the Ill, but, when Leclerc visited GT Guillebon and took stock of the attrition upon Cantarel's tankers and the 3/RMT, he concluded that there was little purpose in this operation if there were no infantry to hold the ground taken. The men of the 2e DB had no grudge against the French First Army, many of whom were friends, but when they could see their rank and file often went without adequate clothing while their pampered staff came up with unrealistic orders, conflicts and resentments were bound to arise. Supported by his officers, Leclerc confronted General de Monsabert and demanded two battalions of fresh infantry or else he would call off the attack. When Monsabert insisted that the operation continue, Leclerc said there were woodlands that needed clearing by infantry, and the 1e DMI were too exhausted for such a task. Still, Monsabert would not budge, and Leclerc lost his temper: "If I give an order and some of my officers tell me that it's nonsense, I stop, I think and then I change it."

"And the order I gave you is one of those?" asked Monsabert. Without waiting for Leclerc's reply the stocky, silver-haired Monsabert continued, "Write me then that you are refusing to attack!"

"If you like," said Leclerc. Vézinet concocted a wording, Girard typed it up and Leclerc signed it. But he wrote underneath, "Such an attack would need an American division as back-up."

"You're really boring me," said Monsabert. "All right, you go and ask the Army Group commander."

"That's precisely what I intend to do," said Leclerc.

In the end Leclerc got his way. The Americans did contribute infantry divisions to reduce the Colmar pocket. Furious, General de Lattre de Tassigny called his divisional commanders to a meeting at Molsheim on the evening of 1st February. There he had a private discussion with Leclerc, who was accompanied by Lecomte. Now things came to a head. Leclerc calmly explained his reasons for not carrying out Monsabert's orders and why he wanted to return to Haislip's US XV Corps. De Lattre, a theatrical man who liked showing his emotions, laid into Leclerc, accusing him of "knowingly building a legend," being "lucky" and "getting chances off the backs of others." He also accused Leclerc of "eccentricity," "bad comradeship," and "false pride," and blamed him for the losses to the 1ere RCP in December.

While the tirade went on Leclerc kept his cool while calmly interjecting remarks like "Utter nonsense."

De Lattre plunged on predictably. "During the course of this war you have had lots of chances like Paris and Strasbourg." He conveniently omitted to mention the chances Leclerc made for himself and for Free France in Equatorial Africa, Chad, Libya and Tunisia. De Lattre also plumbed the depths of pettiness. Once again the fact that the 2e DB obtained the American level of cigarette rations—while his French First Army had to content itself with black tobacco—was thrown up. And as for Leclerc's egotistical refusal to obey Monsabert's orders. . . .

In the end Leclerc exploded, his face reddened, and he banged his fist on the table. "I will serve under someone's orders but I will not serve under yours," he said vehemently. "If General de Gaulle insists that I stay with you then I will ask to be relieved of my command."

Then de Lattre tried a little dose of flattery but to no avail. De Lattre asked Lecomte to leave them while he spoke to Leclerc alone, but no one knows what was said between them.[92]

When they reappeared de Lattre was smiling. Leclerc left with Lecomte and Girard, and they heard Monsabert saying pointedly, "It's a pity General Leclerc can't stay for dinner."[93]

Luckily for Leclerc his view was understood in Paris. De Gaulle himself was concerned that US supplies were only reaching the French First Army in a most "restrained manner."[94] This could not help but effect combat capability. However, both de Lattre and Leclerc got their way to some extent. The US Army sent General Milburn's XXI Corps (3rd and 36th Infantry Divisions) to the Colmar salient and Leclerc took part with them in the final operation. On 2nd February elements of Jacques de Vernejoul's 5e DB, which was down to little more than thirty tanks, supported by the US 28th Infantry Division, succeeded in entering Colmar.[95]

On 3rd February, Leclerc found himself placed under General Milburn's US XXI Corps. He was ordered to push GT Langlade southwards along the west bank of the Rhine. Gribius's sub-group linked up with the 1ère DB at Fessenheim on 8th February, in spite of unfortunate friendly fire incidents with the Americans along the way. Friendly fire incidents between the French divisions were avoided because Gribius ordering his radiomen to listen in on frequencies used by the 1e DB. Surrounded, the last German forces in Alsace surrendered.[96] Leclerc wrote home, "We have pushed the *Boches* to the gates of France, with Henri and Hubert who are doing well."[97]

In Paris the disagreements between Leclerc and de Lattre were the talk of the *beau monde*. It was even said that Leclerc might be sent home by

Eisenhower. In another, less fissured army he might have been. But de
Gaulle could never allow such a fate to befall the best and longest serving
of Free France's combat generals. Instead, on 10th February, the First
French Army paraded for de Gaulle in Colmar. The following day, at
Monsabert's HQ, de Gaulle awarded Leclerc the highest order of Grand
Officer of the Légion d'Honneur, and eulogised the 2e DB for its role in
freeing France, while de Lattre looked on, a good deal less affable than
usual.[98]

CHAPTER THIRTEEN

A GOOD END TO A GOOD WAR

The Alsace campaign revealed the weaknesses not only of de Lattre's First Army but the French Army as a whole. They were ill-equipped in spite of the American re-armament programme, and unable to replace their dead and wounded with adequately trained men from the recently restarted recruitment cadres. Most of the French Army of 1940 was still behind barbed wire in Germany, while a majority of other Frenchmen of military age had been sent to Germany too, prisoners of the infamous *Service Travail Obligatoire.*

In liberated France, the ramshackle and sometimes dubious authority of the resistance took over much of the countryside. Members of the 2e DB on leave did not find "Old France" or the united, purposeful and essentially Christian "New France" hoped for by de Gaulle. Instead the Occupation left an embittered, vengeful cauldron, and Leclerc's men were often glad to return to their comrades. Leclerc had set up a divisional HQ in the requisitioned Pierre Cardin building in Paris, and also sought to deepen the community aspect of the 2e DB. Assisted by Florence Conrad, head of the Groupe Rochambeau, he set up a support service for his wounded veterans.

The main part of the 2e DB was now held in reserve with Wade Haislip's XV Corps, and having a well-earned rest in Lorraine. In recognition

of Haislip's helpful understanding of French priorities, de Gaulle's government awarded him the Légion d'Honneur, and it fell to Leclerc to decorate
his favourite American. Leclerc was pleased to be back with Haislip, but
another part of the new French Army had little access to the same degree
of American largesse. General Edgard de Larminat's *Armée de l'Ouest* stood
guard over the "Atlantic Pockets," where Germans still held the isolated
ports of Royan, La Rochelle, Lorient and Saint Nazaire. Larminat's army
wore uniforms made up from whatever was lying around provided it was
of a military-ish colour, and carrying captured or outdated weapons. Securing Channel ports like Le Havre and Cherbourg had been grim affairs,
so with the U-boat war largely over, the Allied Expeditionary Force had
bypassed these Atlantic ports, leaving them to wither on the vine, and life
within these "pockets" became increasingly squalid for both occupiers and
occupied alike. The German garrisons could only survive by barter and
haggling with farms lying within their perimeter. The formerly smart uniforms of the Wehrmacht and Kriegsmarine were patched and augmented
with civilian clothing, while vehicles ran low on petrol and spares. Nevertheless, they refused to surrender, held 125,000 French citizens hostage,
and prepared to hold out.

These pockets offered little threat, hence the Americans wanted to leave
them until the German capitulation. The largest and most useful port,
Bordeaux, had been liberated, but the Gironde estuary was closed to Allied
shipping by German forces in Royan. The *Armée de l'Ouest* was strong
enough to "hold" these port perimeters but not equipped to go on the
offensive. De Larminat begged the French high command for the assistance
of armoured troops and, in the first instance, the 1ère DB was considered.[1]

Leclerc had fresh orders to withdraw his division to Chateauroux, and
was expecting to form his new corps. He had already been promoted to
Lieutenant-General, with a fourth star added to his képi and shoulder
boards. It had been mooted that de Langalde would take over the 2e DB,
while Dio went to command an infantry division. Since Garbay's 1ère DFL
had been badly chewed up in Alsace, this would have to be a new division
raised from the resistance. Leclerc was enthusiastic, but, at the beginning
of March the plan was shelved. Barely able to conceal his disappointment,
Leclerc now worried that the 2e DB would be left out of the final campaign
in Germany.

He wrote to Colonel Bernard, "We are going to be at the party despite all obstacles. The final decision to send us back east has not been taken yet but it will be soon."

Leclerc was therefore horrified to discover that his men were not going east but to the Atlantic coast.[2] He deduced that Devers and de Lattre were behind this, and he remonstrated with de Gaulle and General Alphonse Juin. However, both felt Leclerc owed it to them to undertake this operation to wash away the bad blood created with de Lattre. *Gros Jean*, in spite of his Vichyite past, was going to be a little too important in the post-war French Army for de Gaulle to treat him cavalierly. On the other hand, Leclerc respected Larminat, another *Gauliste de première heure*, and the respect was mutual. On this occasion, however, Leclerc inclined to Eisenhower's view, that the Atlantic pockets would capitulate automatically once the war was over.[3] Unfortunately for Leclerc's 2e DB, Devers was now in a position where US 6th Army Group had more armour than could be used before the Rhine was crossed.

Leclerc's protests produced a compromise. The *Armée de l'Ouest*'s principal requirement was armour and artillery to breach Royan's defences, so only tanks from the 12e RCA and 12e Cuir' would go to Royan, along with the whole of the division's artillery and a company of engineers. These would be placed under General d'Anselme's Gironde Division of former *résistants*, supported by two further FFI brigades from Médoc and Oléron. The rest of the division would have a period of rest, "*farniente*" as Massu called it, in the department of the Indre.

Paul de Langlade was appointed to command the *groupe de marche,* but he was on leave at his home, also called Langlade, in the Loire, and owing to the breakdown of rural communications only discovered his appointment while driving through the wine-growing area of Pouilly and bumping into vehicles bearing divisional insignia. Astonished that the division was not where he left them, Langlade stopped a military policeman who said, "Ah, *mon général,* what luck to find you!"

Pressing on to Paris, he received the details of his new task from Leclerc at the new divisional HQ.[4] De Gaulle had placated Leclerc that Royan should only take a matter of days and would not prevent the 2e DB from finishing the war in Germany. Leclerc wanted it over quickly.[5]

Langlade set up his *groupe de marche*'s CP at the Chateau of Palluau, home of the Marquise de Veillard on the banks of the Indre, and established his office in a salon sumptuously decorated with Gobelin tapestries and *Louis Treize* furniture. Outside, the first spring since the Occupation ended was glorious with new promise as news reached the 2e DB that the Allies had crossed the Rhine and that de Lattre's troops had reached Karlsruhe.[6]

German Admiral Michaelis commanded Royan, and undoubtedly appreciated the significance of his position, controlling the mouth of the Gironde estuary. The town was protected by anti-tank ditches and a network of concrete strongpoints, and Michaelis, another *ganzharter*, was determined to hold out however hopeless the chance of victory. When food supplies ran low, his garrison made raids into liberated countryside, seized what they wanted and returned to Royan in a fashion reminiscent of English free companies during the Hundred Years War. Since their opponents were the ill-equipped *Armée de l'Ouest,* these forays represented little danger to Michaelis' men. While irritating to the French, these raids were small beer compared to the fighting enveloping the towns of western Germany.

Everyone in the 2e DB knew Royan and other Atlantic ports would fall by themselves in due course,[7] so why did this operation go ahead? The answer lies partly in the personality and fate of General Edgard de Larminat. One of the first and most senior Free French generals, he had, after August 1940, been a background figure in administrative and planning roles, and had not taken an active part in fighting. A man of great intelligence and biting wit, he was appointed to command a division in the French First Army, but de Lattre sacked him for being too political shortly after the Operation Dragoon landings in southern France. De Gaulle then appointed this most loyal officer to command the *Armée de l'Ouest*, which was fine on paper, but in reality little better than being appointed inspector of the Home Guard. Langlade wrote, "In short, he was bored to death."[8]

Perhaps a deeper reason for this unnecessary operation was the parlous state of French national pride, which would be the governing factor in French foreign affairs for the next thirteen years. The *Armée de l'Ouest* was desperate to be seen doing something. The French Navy also wanted an end to the Atlantic pockets. Under the US rearmament programme, port facilities at Brest and Cherbourg were being reconditioned, salvageable ships were raised from the bottom of Toulon harbour, and the navy's personnel was almost back to pre-1939 levels.[9] Waiting for the Germans to surrender the Atlantic pockets would not salve French pride nearly as much as rattling them out.

De Gaulle's government backed Larminat and also obtained the US 13th Heavy Artillery Brigade as well as the 2e DB's *groupe de marche*. Langlade wrote that he had never seen Leclerc so angry as when he explained the follies of the Royan operation. Leclerc had told de Gaulle that the operation was a *"coûteuse inutilité"*—a costly waste—of French lives at this late stage of the war, and even asked what the 2e DB had done wrong to deserve such a mission; but de Gaulle was adamant. Even if de Gaulle later wrote that Leclerc never disobeyed one of his orders, Langlade says that Leclerc visited Devers to ensure he reclaimed the 2e DB for operations in Germany through SHAEF as quickly as possible after Royan.[10]

Once it was clear that de Gaulle was determined to support Larminat over Royan, Leclerc went through the motions of obeying. Arriving in the Cognac area with his *groupe de marche* on 8th April, Langlade presented himself to Larminat. Leclerc himself refused to play any part in what he called a "masquerade." This attitude soon affected both Langlade and Dio, who inclined to be very selective over which orders they obeyed, and how the 12e RCA and 12e Cuir' were used. As far as the rest of the division was concerned, Leclerc was adamant that they would "fall in Germany if necessary but not in France and not in front of Royan!"[11]

Larminat knew that Leclerc was making plans for getting back into Germany, but believed the whole 2e DB was at his disposal. Leclerc soon put him right. After an awful tongue lashing from Leclerc, Larminat did not throw his authority about with those troops he did receive. Both he and General d'Anselme invited Langlade to lunch where they impressed him with their old world charm. Over the next three days Langlade took part in reconnaissance and fact-finding, while Royan's concrete defences were already being softened up by the re-equipped French Air Force.[12]

On 14th April, 1,200 US Flying Fortresses attacked the Germans concrete positions, their "bomb line" eliminating the bunkers and pill boxes the French were most worried about. However, when the attack was launched the infantry quickly became bogged down amid minefields and machine-gun nests. Even though German numbers were feeble, their sappers had made an environment in which only tanks could pass. On 15th April, tank groups led by Verdier and Gribius managed to reach the crossroads at La Tremblade before encountering heavy opposition from German artillery. With Langlade watching from the distance, Gribius got down from his tank, in full view of the enemy, to consult with Dorance, a junior officer he knew well. "Madness," thought Langlade as he prepared to scribble a message, but it was too late. Dorance was mortally injured in the neck by sniper fire, and seconds later Gribius was hit as if by a hammer blow on his right jaw and began spouting blood with each heartbeat. For a moment, he thought his carotid had been cut and his time had come, but Verdier, seeing Gribius' plight, held a dressing to the wound and bundled him into a Jeep. The perpetrator turned out later to have been a diehard German officer firing from the ruins of a blockhouse.[13]

Quickly hospitalised, Gribius was so heavily bandaged and sedated that he could barely see Langlade's silhouette, nor that of Père de Gevigney when they visited him. Leclerc came too, embracing his bandaged former operations officer without a word, but demonstrating by the gesture their comradeship. Gribius was too injured to return to his comrades before Germany capitulated. He got the action he craved after Roger Rives-Henry's death but it rapidly brought him a serious injury requiring several maxillo-facial operations, and left a deep scar over his right jaw for the rest of his life.[14]

In spite of these pointless French losses, the German forces in Royan were pushed into a steadily diminishing pocket. By the evening of 16th April, all the strongpoints had fallen except for the Saint-Palais area. The Adeline-Verdier column joined up with General Marchand's Oléron Brigade at Arvert, and Rouvillois' Cuirassiers reached the sea after subduing concrete fortifications manned by 1,000 German soldiers. The garrison commander, Admiral Michaelis, surrendered at dawn on 17th April, but would not order outposts still fighting to follow suit. Fortunately, by midmorning the remaining 800 soldiers surrendered, filing past Langlade with their officers and giving the Nazi salute. The *campagne aux huîtres* —"the oyster campaign" was over.[15]

While Langlade's *groupe de marche* supported de Larminat, the rest of the 2e DB, cantoned at Chatillon sur Indre, temporarily returned to the rhythms of garrison life. Citations for individual acts of bravery in Alsace had been confirmed, and Leclerc pinned a variety of medals—the *Croix de Guerre, Ordre de la Libération, Médaille Militaire* and *Croix de la Légion d'honneur,* or palm leaves and stars for mentions in dispatches—to the proud chests of their recipients. Massu was due for a palm on the ribbon of his *Croix de Guerre;* next came Lt. Podeur who had been with Leclerc since Chad. Next it was the turn of Leclerc's eldest son, Henri, to receive a *Croix de Guerre.* Moving along the line, Leclerc came to Henri. "Why this cross for my son? I don't agree."

"Excuse me, *mon Général,* but it really isn't your business," said Massu. "This soldier has been put up for a decoration on the recommendation of his Captain and myself. The fact that he is your son is beside the point."

Leclerc smiled wryly, as he often did at Massu's bits of cheek. Everyone present could tell Leclerc was very proud, and Henri de Hauteclocque's eyes sparkled with joy to be decorated by his father.

A few days later Leclerc wrote to Massu, "When my eldest son joined the division it was understandably my wish that he should be in good hands. I have not been disappointed, and I am counting on you to continue to turn him into what he must become." Leclerc continued this letter by writing chattily about divisional problems, as he often did with Chad veterans. "The last few weeks have been some of the hardest I have experienced since 1940. I have tried everything and have hit a wall. Général de Gaulle won't be moved from the idea that there is still plenty of time and that we will arrive in good time at the Rhine."[16]

Leclerc also vented his frustration at de Larminat in a letter written on 23rd April. He said the last couple of months had been among the "most painful" for him "from the military point of view," and that history would decide whether Germany or the Atlantic ports were primary objectives. Leclerc did not, however, blame Larminat for the unwanted detour which had seen a notable number of injuries and 364 killed, including some of his best officers. He blamed the French High Command for pointlessly putting his division in a place where they might miss the most important of European victories.[17]

Leclerc spent the days following the fall of Royan in Paris. When he asked army chief Alphonse Juin to be sent back to Germany, the old *pied noir*

told him the Americans would not like it. When Leclerc suggested going
in person to see Eisenhower's chief of staff, Bedell-Smith, Juin said "Oh,
no, no! Certainly not. Don't do that!" Leclerc realised at once that Bedell-
Smith was the very man to see. Unlike Juin, Leclerc had not been beaten
by the Americans during the *baroud d'honneur* in North Africa, so he was
not afraid of them.[18] Accompanied by Girard, he persuaded Bedell-Smith
to re-assign the 2e DB to General Patch's Seventh Army.

The Americans were over the Rhine and heading for the Danube.
Mainz, Frankfurt and Nuremburg were already in Allied hands. Redeploy-
ment of the 2e DB to Germany required a rail journey longer than from
Yorkshire to England's south coast, with all the logistics that went with it.
Lantenois' *4e bureau* surpassed themselves. The night before their departure, an immense feeling of pride swept through the division that their
general had won the argument and they would witness the *coup de grâce*.
The tanks were taken to Saint-Jean-d'Angély to be entrained, while
wheeled vehicles were driven back across liberated France, the Vosges, and
the Alsatian plain, until they found countryside freshly marked by war.
Once again Patton's US Third Army was in the lead. Yet the French were
pleased to hear that the Germans had not surrendered yet.[19] Leclerc and
Girard joined the division *en route*, leaving Paris in a ten-year-old car, so
poor were the French Army's internal services. They stopped off at Nancy
where Leclerc inspected the 3e Hussars before passing the night at the
Intendant's palace.[20]

Entering Germany meant a great deal to the RBFM's shipless sailors.
Raymond Maggiar saw ruined villages, "Well wrecked. Completely
wrecked. Nothing left. Someone had made quite a job of it. Everything
was upside down, the houses, the gardens, the countryside, and the
Germans, men and women, wandered among the wreckage with just that
look of misery that one wished to see. It was as if all the material destruction and human misery that had been experienced during eight months
of war on our own soil was crying out for vengeance, and at last we had
found satisfaction. But we wanted more than that. We remembered ourselves in 1940, and we wanted to see on German faces the look of the
vanquished."

Rolling through the Rhineland, the French saw what they wanted in
the scale of suffering: huge casualty clearing stations, liberated camps of

starving Russians waving red flags, immense material destruction and white flags at every village window.[21]

They crossed the Rhine at Mannheim and continued along roads filled with pathetic and ragged groups of the defeated, liberated and displaced. Among them were some of the million and a half French soldiers captured by the Wehrmacht in 1940, still wearing the khaki *vareuse* of the period, now walking home carrying small bundles of personal belongings wrapped in whatever material they could find. Like the Parisians in August 1944, they could not believe that men shouting at them from Shermans were French. There were other prisoners besides: Poles, Russians, Serbs, and Indians captured from the British in the desert.[22]

Leclerc sent Guillebon ahead with an advance guard to peg out the 2e DB's zone of action, and crossed the Rhine on 25th April accompanied by the ever-trusted Girard. "The General didn't say anything," Girard wrote. "He looked at the east bank of the river. He just wanted to get back to the front."

When they reached Heidelberg, General Jacob Devers confirmed Leclerc's reattachment to Patch's Seventh Army. They drove on to Patch's HQ at Kitzingen, where the countryside appeared less battle-scarred. Leclerc was pleased to bump into Wade Haislip. Although he was not returning to Haislip's XV Corps, Leclerc was happy to be back with the Americans. He rejoined Milburn's XXI Corps with whom the 2e DB finished the Alsace campaign, and Leclerc found Milburn both kind and charming.

On 28th April, they joined Guillebon's advance guard at Hall, and there Leclerc received the news from adjutant Weil that his father had died. It was hardly unexpected. Girard was with him by the roadside as they watched the 2e DB's tanks rolling by. Only a few remarks betrayed how much Leclerc was affected.[23]

The same day, Leclerc told his men that their conduct in Germany must be impeccable. There was to be no needless brutality, no pillaging, nor any inappropriate relations with the German population. They were to do honour to their uniforms, even though, and especially, because the collapse of the Third Reich had brought the French a chance to settle accounts.[24]

On 1st May, while the Russians were taking Berlin block by block, the

2e DB was strung out across 1,200 km of western Europe from Royan, where the last tanks were being loaded, to Augsburg, where de Guillebon's advance guard was acting as lead element for the US 12th Armoured Division. Ever since he began in Africa, Leclerc's primary goal had been to see the French Army take part in as much fighting as possible. Now Repiton-Préneuf told Leclerc that the division stood the best chance of taking part in the last actions if it managed to get back under Haislip's XV Corps. That same morning, Repiton was hospitalised after a collision with a recovery tank.

On that day, too, the Germans surrendered Munich. The only troops available to garrison the Bavarian capital were Haislip's, and the US 12th Armoured Division was called on to perform those garrison duties. This left Leclerc's 2e DB as the only armoured division capable of further advances in southern Germany.[25]

The following day, amid springtime snow, one of Guillebon's subgroups led by Sarazac, former *méhariste* from Chad, crossed the River Isar at Bad-Tolz, where the Waffen SS had their officer's training school. As GT Guillebon rumbled along the autobahn, the 501e RCC's Shermans passed an unending herd of German prisoners. Suddenly the crew of the tank *Douaumont* was hailed by a German soldier. He was the former commander of the Panther that Sergeant Bizien had rammed on the Place de la Concorde the previous August.

The fighting was not yet over when on April 30th Hitler shot himself. Deserted even by Goering and Himmler, Hitler had made Admiral Doenitz his successor. Near Munich, GT Langlade were among the first to hear of the Dachau concentration camp. If any of the 2e DB doubted the necessity of their four-year struggle, or that de Gaulle was the man France should choose, such doubts were expunged when they saw the camp. Leclerc sent Repiton-Préneuf with Châtel, Kaspereit and Girard's understudy, Guy de Valence, to visit Dachau and report back. They were horrified. At once Leclerc ordered the division's medical staff attend to French inmates and, after seeing the misery for himself, Leclerc was highly sceptical that local Germans had known nothing. He attended Mass at the church nearest the camp and then buttonholed the priest in front of the choir. Using his interpreter, though he spoke German perfectly well, Leclerc asked the priest how he could allow such horrors near his parish.

The priest swore by Almighty God he had no idea.

"You dare to tell me that you did not know? With all that smoke?"

The priest was visibly quaking as Leclerc turned away in disgust while muttering, "Unbelievable! Unbelievable!"[26]

Langlade would later write of his disbelief that so many Germans claimed ignorance of the concentration camps and the "Final Solution." The pretty young officer's wife in whose home Massu was billeted denied all knowledge until she was personally taken to Dachau, which was clearly marked with painted wooden signs of *gemutlich* jollity. Dachau was used for political prisoners rather than exterminating Jews, but there were gas chambers, execution pits, row upon row of unhygienic barrack huts, and piles of fly-blown corpses that had been gassed, shot or had died from disease or hunger. Of the French prisoners, Abbé Hénocque, formerly senior chaplain at Saint-Cyr, fell into Massu's arms, while former Gaullist resistance officer Edmond Michelet, arrested in 1943, showed him "the sights," and explained the camp's buildings and procedures with poignant dignity. The two hours Massu spent there coincided with one of the "tours" arranged on Patton's orders for German civilians so they could witness what Hitler had done in their name. Massu saw the young woman in whose house he was billeted, and how she had turned the palest white. He walked away profoundly disturbed, to pass through the delousing station all troops had to use before leaving the camp. The Americans prevented the inmates from leaving until their medical condition could be assessed, and the 2e DB's medical staff, the *Rochambelles* and the Quaker stretcher-bearers, were called in to assist.[27]

As Massu drove the German woman home, they passed a field where US soldiers had gathered German prisoners. "What about them?" the woman asked. "Do you think they aren't suffering as well?" In an instant Massu halted the car. Furious, he felt for his Colt automatic. Then, just as quickly, his mood passed.[28]

Leclerc was determined to see the 2e DB end its war on a high. On 4th May, he visited General Patch at Augsberg. Contradictory orders over the previous few days had exasperated him. He did not want his efforts to get the division back to the front in record time going for nothing. At US Seventh Army HQ, Leclerc heard that Patch had decided to send the 2e

DB and the US 3rd Infantry Division to Berchtesgaden and Salzburg. Leclerc was thrilled. The 2e DB would finish its war at Hitler's Alpine retreat, the Eagle's Nest.[29]

The Nazis had hoped to use Berchtesgaden as the centre of an Alpine redoubt from which to hold out after Berlin fell. How far the SS had the stomach for a last-ditch effort after Hitler's suicide remained to be seen. Their barracks had already been heavily bombed by the RAF. The Alpine homes of both Hitler and Goering remained largely intact, as were the rail-head and various storage depots which contained everything from weaponry to art treasures and liquor looted from all over Europe. Guillebon approached from the north and northwest, splitting his GT into three sub-groups commanded by Delpierre, Barboteux and the *méhariste* Sarazac. At the village of Inzell, Sarazac's men met with resistance from SS whom they outflanked in a classic and successful manoeuvre. There was only one French casualty, 2nd Lt. Mulsant being wounded. This skirmish was the 2e DB's last combat of the European war.[30]

GT Guillebon gathered in prisoners and continued its advance in tandem with the US 3rd Infantry Division, nicknamed the "Rock of the Marne" for its performance in France in 1918. They still came under sporadic fire, but most Germans they encountered now were sitting by the road, fully armed, waiting to surrender.

Bridges over small Alpine rivers such as the Paar had been blown and were repaired by US XXI Corps' engineers. It was at such crossing points that the keen sense of competition between the French and their US allies flared up. Leclerc arrived at a broken autobahn bridge between Munich and Berchtesgarden to find GT Guillebon held up in a traffic jam of US vehicles and a flood of prisoners going in the opposite direction.

"What's going on here," he asked de Guillebon.

"There's a hold up," replied de Guillebon. "The Americans won't let us pass because we would not be on their axis of advance."

"What?" fumed Leclerc. He spotted a group of US officers gathered around a stocky figure, presumably their divisional commander, and marched towards them, followed by Spahi Captain Châtel and Guy de Valence. Telling Valence to translate, Leclerc said, "Tell the general to let our group pass since we are part of the same army corps as his division, and that, since we do not have bridging equipment, it is proper for us to use that provided by US Army engineers."

The 3rd Infantry Division's General "Iron Mike" O'Daniel removed a glove to shake Leclerc's hand but was nevertheless uncooperative. "Tell your general," O'Daniel told Valence, "that I quite understand the significance of the moment. But, firstly, those are my sappers building that bridge and therefore it is my men who will cross first. Secondly, you are on my axis of advance and so you will pass when I wish."

Disgusted at this pointless piece of bloody-mindedness, especially as infantry and armour were meant to support each other, Leclerc told Valence to tell O'Daniel "That's because he knows there's no danger on the other side."

Like Girard, Valence was hoping to go into the diplomatic service, so he did not translate his general's words exactly, in spite of Leclerc's chivvying "You tell him, *hein?*"

O'Daniel was unmoved, so Leclerc returned to his Jeep and ordered Guillebon to "Push through!"[31]

GT Guillebon's vehicles infiltrated the jammed American columns, and the Americans had to let them use their bridge. They passed through Bad Reichenhall and reached the mountain town of Berchtesgaden to find it already occupied by the US 7th Infantry Regiment. The Americans had stopped there, whereas the objective of greatest interest a few hundred metres higher up, the Obersalzburg plateau, seemed to be ignored. Captain Touyeras of the 64e Artillerie passed them in the village and ordered his driver to speed up, devouring the four kilomètres to the Eagle's Nest, thereby becoming the first Allied soldiers to reach the famous complex of swanky summer residences from which Hitler had overseen Europe's nightmare.[32]

There is still some controversy over which unit actually reached the Eagle's Nest first, not helped by the fact that the Obersalzberg was a large complex. Furthermore, there were three divisions under US operational control operating in the area: the US 3rd Infantry Division, the French 2e DB and the US 101st Airborne Division, which had been acting as ordinary infantry since the Ardennes campaign. Among the units of the 101st Airborne Division was Colonel Robert Sink's 506th Parachute Infantry Regiment, one of whose nine companies was the famous "Easy Company."[+]

In fact, beyond the temporary bridge over the autobahn, where GT Guillebon had waited on the pleasure of the 3rd Infantry Division, the French
took a different route to the Obersalzberg, which enabled them to enter
the western side of the complex where they established control of the rail-
head with its warehouses. There they rescued treasures looted from France,
and enjoyed the luxuries of Goering's armoured train.

Christian Girard writes that the French and Americans reached Berchtesgaden at the same time, around 7pm, and that by the following morning
it was well and truly understood that elements of the 2e DB were first to
arrive at "the Berghof."[33] While the US 6th Army Group commander General Jacob Devers, under whom both de Lattre's and Patch's armies served,
is quoted by Henry Maule saying "The French 2nd Armoured certainly
got out in front there to Berchtesgaden. We sent the 101st Airborne in to
clear the place up, and the French already seemed to have made a good job
of clearing up the liquor!" Tony Triumpho, a US artillery officer attached
to the 2e DB, said, "We suddenly heard the goal was Berchtesgaden. We
made a dash for it, but when we got there we found a number of different
units, including Leclerc's French."[34] Each division liked to think it was first.

The following day, Leclerc walked among his men, especially his Chad old
timers, smiling and relaxed, thanking them for what they had done. From
the Berghof he surveyed his surroundings, as the Führer would have done.
It was a beautiful spot, an alpine valley of small villages among lush fields
and pine-covered hills, but the immediate vicinity was a chaos of craters
and damaged buildings left by Allied air raids. Leclerc and Girard walked
along the corridor of Hitler's chalet and came to the antechamber of the
grand salon that Frenchmen remembered from photographic news maga-
zines such as *L'Illustration* in the late 30s. Inside, through medieval-style
iron doors, they found the room burnt out and a large hole in the ceiling.
The floor was calcinated and there were the remains of large Bauhaus arm-
chairs. An elaborate landscape separated Hitler's mountain home from
Goering's house and a large crater had gouged the earth where the swimming pool had been. Shards of blue tiles lay all around. Further on, Girard
heard a voice. "If you're thirsty *mon capitaine*, the cellars are worth a visit!"
A French soldier appeared with a bottle of *Liebfraumilch*, bashed the top
off against a stone and handed it round.

On the first floor of Goering's villa, Leclerc and Girard found Chombard de Lauwe making himself comfortable at the Reichsmarschal's rubble-strewn desk, pretending to read a copy of *Mein Kampf* he had found. The window was blown, and the sight of a kestrel against the clear sky underscored the transitory nature of man's endeavours.[35] They found a door to the underground areas, and walked dark sinister corridors stuffed with wooden chests filled with every kind of object. There were small rooms for a dentist and a barber, bedrooms and offices, some with vainglorious photographs of Goering on the walls. In one room Girard swung open a cupboard door to find an enormous pair of long johns dangling from a hanger.

Outside, the men picked around the wreckage in silence. Someone had found a Dutch tricolour which has the same colours as the French, except that they go across not down, turned it around and draped it over a blackened balcony. Someone remarked that the ruined building resembled a charred dragon spewing striped toothpaste![36] Seeing one of his colonels behind the wheel of a lorry, Leclerc stopped him and discovered it was full of loot. Incensed, Leclerc ordered the contents distributed among the division, and that a system for handling loot be put in place whereby each article was stamped "2e DB." Parcels were organised for the divison's wounded at their hospitals in Paris. Leclerc was fond of fast cars, but somehow was not much tempted by those the 2e DB found at Berchtesgaden. He took a khaki Horch for his own use, and told Boissieu to send a magnificent Mercedes to de Gaulle. Later that crisp morning, Leclerc drank a toast with some of his officers: "And now we can start thinking like sunbathers."[37]

Perhaps there was some American jealousy. Girard recorded that, "American ill-humour wasn't slow to show itself," doubtless brought on by the sight of what the French called "vehicles *of retrieval.*" There followed an immediate order to depart, which had to be carried out by the following day. Since the 2e DB was dispersed over a large area, the order was not easily accomplished. When the division still had not moved by 7th May, a US staff officer arrived from XXI Corps HQ and demanded in a dry tone, "Haven't you received the order to move out?" Then he gave the French officers an outraged lecture on the pillage and devastations that were happening in the 2e DB's vicinity, citing US Army regulations.

Leclerc kept his cool to avoid a repetition of his behaviour towards Gerow's emissary in Paris. In spite of his captain's rank, Girard spoke up instead, to say that his house had been ransacked in France and his brother shot by the Germans. The Occupation had given French troops a different perspective on things German to the one the Americans may have had. Girard admits in his journal that he was really speaking more on behalf of his comrades. The liaison officer mellowed at this, saying he only spoke for the US 7th Army. He too perhaps did not want to finish on a disagreeable note.[38]

There can be little doubt that what the Americans saw as looting, the French saw as restitution for the wrongs done to their country under the occupation. "Easy" Company in the US 101st Airborne Division saw looting as "completely in accord with the practice of every conquering army since Alexander the Great's time,"[39] and so too did the 2e DB. Since 1940 the French had seen both sides of the looting question. Leclerc took the view that "reparations" deserved his support, and decided to delay the division's departure for a day while he appealed to US 7th Army for the means to make removals by road and rail. Captain Châtel departed with this mission at 7pm that evening. Later, d'Alençon produced a telegram from Guillebon asking if the staff of the 2e DB had heard that Eisenhower himself was coming to the Eagle's Nest the following day. They had not. In the small hours, Châtel arrived back from General Milburn with fresh orders that GT Guillebon was to leave the area by noon on 8th May at the latest. There would be no agreement to transport any vehicles loaded with "prize," and Milburn would be arriving to see them off himself![40]

Leclerc decided to make some concessions. Some of the 2e DB would move off towards the new assembly point at Ammersee while the rest, under Guillebon, stayed around Bad Reichenhall. As for lorries of "retrieved" goods, they stayed under guard at a military assembly point at Bad Reichenhall while the matter was referred to General de Gaulle.[41] The level of looting from France had in fact been immense. Twenty GMC lorries were loaded with nothing but cases of Champagne from the houses of Lanson and Bollinger! Then there were cultural artifacts such as wooden statues from churches dating from the first centuries of the Kingdom of France, tons of carpets from the Place Clichy, and world-class tapestries and paintings. The French officers and most of the 2e DB, being western

Europeans, usually had a better idea of what to look for than their American allies.[42] Sergeant Bernard de Nonancourt, whose family was connected to both the Lanson and Laurent-Perrier champagne houses, even recognised cases of champagne that he had witnessed the Germans requisition in 1940!

Milburn arrived at 10am accompanied by a large entourage. Leclerc met him with just his liaison officer, Châtel, Repiton-Préneuf, La Hitte, the one-armed Valence, Beurdeley and, of course, Girard. Milburn, visibly wound up, launched into Leclerc with a string of criticisms about the conduct of the 2e DB. Leclerc took it all courteously, inclining to sarcasm, but remained unshaken, disconcerting the Americans and making them apologetic. As for pillage, which was the main criticism levelled by the Americans, Leclerc replied that German pillage from France had been on an altogether different and monumental scale, and that the French were not so much pillaging as taking back a fraction of what had been taken from them, whereas the Americans were actually pillaging. Leclerc saved his best point for last, that US troops had even interrupted a church service in a nearby village to steal objects of value without any qualms of running riot in front of the outraged congregation. This information, garnered by Repiton's *2eme bureau*, seemed to disarm Milburn.[43]

After this exchange, Repiton departed in a Piper Cub to 7th Army HQ to obtain General Patch's permission for the 2e DB's "prize" lorries to depart for France. It was the only way to do it, as US MPs were stopping French vehicles and confiscating anything appearing to be booty. In the meantime, most of the 2e DB set off for its reassembly areas. Leclerc waited for Repiton's return, and Girard busied himself by getting Leclerc's new Horsch into running order.[44]

Paul de Langlade, normally a well-behaved guest of any country house which became his CP, found that a homily on good behaviour from a German châtelaine near Amersee took some swallowing after the ransacking of France by the Germans. He had her removed from her home and placed 300 metres up the drive in her own gatehouse. Leclerc managed to send him one of the three black Mercedes Benz sedans the 2e DB had found at Berchtesgaden, along with a grand portrait photo of the Führer himself.[45]

The same day that German General Alfred Jodl signed the document of unconditional surrender at Reims, a tragedy took place in French North Africa that would ensure the French Army barely had time to catch its breath before being plunged into its disastrous decolonisation wars.

If France was hobbling economically following its liberation, French North Africa was even worse off. During the Vichy years, a British blockade, only broken sporadically for specific materials after negotiations with the USA, had led to crippling shortages in the Maghreb colonies, especially of cotton needed for clothing, and everyday sundries normally taken for granted such as light bulbs and foodstuffs. Many Moslems believed that French military and cultural pre-eminence over them had been "washed away in the waters of Dunkirk" and the *débâcle* of 1940.

With the arrival of the Americans after Operation Torch in November 1942, the French spell over the Maghreb peoples was finally broken. France could not free itself without US help. Many *Armée d'Afrique* personnel put back into the field by General Giraud, and given US weapons under the Anfa programme, were North African Moslems fighting as much for their own liberation and the brave new world to come as for "Old France." In the towns and villages of Algeria, petty incidents of violence and disrespect towards the *colons* escalated through the last three years of the war, not helped by two bad harvests.

If the French mayor of Sétif was planning to celebrate the Allied victory, then the town's nationalist Moslems would also demonstrate for their own freedom. Some Europeans at a streetside café lost their nerve and a Moslem youth was mortally wounded by a shot in the stomach. Then all hell broke loose, with Moslems massacring Europeans wherever they could find them. Two other towns, Guelma and Kerrata, also broke down in murderous anarchy, with French petty officials being particularly sought out. It was only after five days of chaos that the French military, re-equipped with US weapons and aircraft, re-established control using methods that Graziani's Italians would have been proud of: summary executions, lynchings and massacres accounting for the deaths of thousands of Algerians. The French Army would not know a year of peace from that moment until they left Algeria in 1962.[46]

In the immediate aftermath of VE Day, the cleansing operation at Dachau was well underway and the camp now had an American commandant,

Colonel Joyce, whose job was to rehabilitate 30,000 walking skeletons. There had been 8,000 French inmates, of whom half survived. On 16th May, with the assistance of the 2e DB, six hundred of the least ill French prisoners were on their way home to France.[47]

Leclerc's HQ staff were billeted in a handsome villa at Bad Reichenall, guarded by Boissieu's protection squadron lest any of Skorzeny's SS commandos were operating in the area. Early one morning they were surprised at the arrival of an American truck. It disgorged a dozen Frenchmen who had been captured wearing Waffen SS uniforms. These were survivors of the *Charlemagne* division formed in the autumn of 1944 from former LVF and *miliciens* who dared not remain in post-liberation France. Nevertheless, they had fought desperately against the Red Army in Pomerania, and the survivors were sufficiently steadfast to fight on through the last act in Berlin. The guard squad took charge of them immediately, Staff-Sergeant Morgand lining them up in two ranks. Already separated from their weapons and helmets, they looked no different than any other German prisoners trudging to the POW cages in long columns, all wearing torn greatcoats and dishevelled field caps and carrying haversacks on their backs, but a short moment of conversation betrayed their origins.

While Frenchman of opposing sides eyed each other with reciprocal curiosity, an orderly was sent to inform Leclerc. Maybe, with the healing benefit of time, they would have been regarded as men who simply made the wrong choice, but if Leclerc regarded former Vichyites as traitors and turncoats, his attitude to Frenchmen in Waffen SS uniform, especially after seeing the liberation of Dachau, was predictably uncompromising.

When Leclerc appeared, cane in hand, accompanied by Valence, he walked along their ranks asking them their origins and why they had enlisted in the SS. Their viewpoints were anti-communism, longstanding adherence to the political right, once exemplified by *Action Francaise*, and pan-Europeanism. For the most part they seemed of good family.

"Aren't you ashamed to serve in this uniform?" Leclerc asked.

"You look very fine in an American one," replied one of the two officers.

Recoiling, Leclerc said, "Get rid of these [awful] people."

This command was taken as a condemnation to death by firing squad without trial. Leclerc returned to his office muttering that such men were the product of Vichy misleading the young. In the meantime the French

SS men were locked in the cellar of Leclerc's villa.[48] A chaplain from the White Fathers took their last confessions and held a communion for them, though one refused to participate. The communion was also attended by the officer commanding their firing squad.[49] The following day they were driven to a barracks taken over by the RMT and from there, in batches of four, were taken to a clearing in a wood near Kugelbach. Given their last rights by Père Maxime Gaume, to whom they handed letters to loved ones, they faced their executioners, old timers from the 4e Compagnie of the RMT. These original *Gaullistes* were struck by the proud bearing of the French Waffen SS, who were brave if nothing else, all refusing to be blind-folded. Their bodies were left where they fell until several days later when an American burial detail got to them.[50] A year after the war these executions probably would not have happened, but in the atmosphere of May 1945, when concentration camps were liberated and the full horror of Nazism opened to the world, such examples of summary justice were commonplace. The Americans had also summarily executed twelve guards at Dachau.

The 2e DB left the Berchtesgaden area under something of a cloud due to the looting issue, and regrouped around Diessen where Leclerc installed his HQ in another handsome villa. Improved messing facilities enabled him to welcome liberated officers such as Langlois de Bazillac back to the division in style, as well as giving some of the more notable French inmates of Dachau such as Père Michel Riquet and Edmond Michelet a taste of life outside the camp. The Americans had the place cordoned off due to the risk of a typhus epidemic, and the death rate was worse than before the liberation. Michelet told Leclerc that the remaining French inmates felt abandoned. The only visits were by strangers who seemed more curious than able to help. Leclerc assured Michelet that the division would do all it could. The following day Leclerc made a flying visit to Paris to put de Gaulle in the picture about the French still in Dachau. Then, on returning to Germany, Leclerc addressed the fittest of them on the camp square.[51]

"I have rarely been so moved as I am today, though my time in Germany has given me many occasions. We have struggled for the same cause, we have been through the same phases; each separated from France, without news of our loved ones. Suffering has been glorious for us, hard and humiliating for you. Your suffering in silence confers more merit than ours, which was alleviated by the excitement of battle. We will help you with the same *ardeur* as we have done for France."[52]

Yet Leclerc said this would take time, and the Dachau French groaned with disappointment. One inmate even threatened to break through the US cordon with weapons taken from the SS. Also, since the 2e DB was a fighting division, not a relief organisation, there was little more he could do. Dozens of his lorries were already committed to supplying food to the camp.[53]

"You are going to find a weakened France, divided by moral and political difficulties," Leclerc warned. "Will you work to rebuild it?"

At this the Dachau French cheered.

"Don't imagine that France is decaying. For four years I have been involved with Frenchmen of all types and from all regions. In battle they have shown an energy equal to their ancestors. Do not be embarrassed to be French. France is counting on you. She needs men matured by suffering; men who have fought."[54]

Leclerc gave a similar performance to other French prisoners at Dachau's satellite camp, Allach, where his speech was greeted with the *Marseillaise*. In the end it was de Lattre's First Army that got most of the French home from Dachau, but Leclerc's division was the first French unit involved in the camp's relief and they, once again, caught their nation's imagination.[55]

On 19th May General de Gaulle, accompanied by War Minister Diethelm, came to the airfield at Kloster-Lechfeld to salute a parade by the 2e DB. Over a thousand light tanks, Shermans, Tank Destroyers, Greyhound armoured cars and White halftracks, led by de Langlade in his own Sherman, the *Auvergne*, drove past a dais on which stood General de Gaulle and Leclerc. In pride of place was the Régiment de Marche du Tchad, *les fidèles*, who had followed these two remarkable men from the earliest days, along with the two original Gaullist armoured regiments, the Régiment de Marche des Spahis Marocains and the 501e RCC. The two regiments that Paul de Langlade brought to the 2e DB followed: the 12e Régiment des Chasseurs d'Afrique and the sister regiment formed from its surplus, the 12e Cuirassiers. Next came the artillery, engineers and the shipless sailors of Captain Maggiar's Régiment Blindée des Fusiliers Marins. In four years of campaigning, while one and a half million of the French Army of 1940 were behind German barbed wire, Leclerc and his men had never lost a battle. Furthermore, while the necessities of supply required them to wear British or American uniforms, never for a second did they dream of anything other than liberating their homeland, France. De Gaulle decorated Leclerc with the Grand Cross of the Légion d'Honneur.

At dinner afterwards de Gaulle teased Leclerc.

"Everyone knows that he never carries out the orders I give him, or, if he does sometimes, it turns out quite well. That's what happened in Africa. I told him to go to Chad and, understanding me well, he wanted to go to the Cameroons!"[56]

On 23rd May, the division began returning to France. General de Gaulle now had other tasks for Leclerc. The defeat of Nazi Germany and the imminent defeat of Japan in the Pacific did not mean that they could all go home. Leclerc would have to hand over the 2e DB to someone else. Paul de Langlade was already designated to command the new 3e DB, part of France's contribution to the military occupation of Germany, so, as one of the earliest *gaullistes*, Louis Dio took over the 2e DB. Leclerc still led the 2e DB in the victory parade in Paris which de Gaulle had called for the 18th June, the fifth anniversary of his first broadcast *appel* from London. De Lattre's First Army was certainly represented, but the 2e DB had pride of place. Leclerc arrived first at the Étoile in his command tank *Tailly*, drew to a halt and saluted the Unknown Soldier. Then, with the crowd cheering, he led his division down the Champs Élysées. Behind the 2e DB came Garbay's 1ère DFL, the remnants of Koenig's command at Bir Hakeim.[57]

On 22nd June, the division held a parade for itself at Fontainebleau to say its *adieu* to Leclerc, and for him to make his farewell speech which encapsulated much of his personal philosophy.

"Officers, NCOs and soldiers of the *Deuxième Division Blindée*! It is about a week since we gathered to think about our dead. It is also a few days since I had the honour to march at the head of you through the Paris that we liberated.

"Today, I have come to you to say 'good bye.'

"I am leaving the command of this division, but reassure yourselves that I am not leaving the spirit, and it is this spirit that I want to dwell on for a few moments before we part.

"The spirit which animated this division since its formation has been found in every aspect of its work, and in combat that spirit has been most important to the higher interests of France.

"Why, nearly two years ago, did we not hesitate to take into this Division men of the most varied origins and beliefs? Because we knew that France could only revive itself through a great union of all Frenchmen.

"Why did we demand and obtain the right to land in Normandy with the other Allied troops? Because we knew that it was indispensable that the Île-de-France, the heart of our country, should be liberated in part by French troops.

"Why did we march on Paris? Because the Division understood the moral importance for our country.

"Why did we all cross the Vosges and retake Strasbourg? Because it was necessary, to wipe away 1940, and for the French Army to return victoriously to Strasbourg.

"It wasn't just the desire to fight for its own sake or the love of glory at any price which guided us. It was yet again to seek in all circumstances the best for France.

"I am leaving you. But I am not removing the badge of our division from my uniform. I am keeping that. It will be my best medal. I ask you also to keep it. And when you feel your energy flagging think back to Kufra, Alençon, Paris and Strasbourg. Re-find your comrades and your leaders, and continue to nurture in this country the patriotism which was your own motivation."

After that parade, many of the 2e DB looked forward to civilian life and building the peace Leclerc spoke of. Under French laws of recruitment, the cessation of any threat to *la Patrie* meant they were entitled to do so. Arthur Kaiser returned to Mulhouse where he built up a large decorating and construction business and kept up with old comrades, including Hubert Leclerc, who became a distinguished businessman and forestry expert.

For others, serving their country had always been a career goal though not necessarily in military service. Christian Girard's ambition to become a diplomat had been delayed by the war. For many, military service remained their life, and the period of their careers with the 2e DB was the springboard to higher rank. The number of former officers of the division who went on to become generals or admirals during the decolonisation period is extraordinary by the standards of the English speaking world: Massu, Langlade, Vézinet, Compagnon, Gribius, Boissieu from the French Army; Raymond Maggiar and Philippe de Gaulle from the French Navy, to name but a few. General Charles de Gaulle's extraordinary character had opened the door for the Free French, but none of them would have enjoyed such success if it had not been for the exceptional military qualities and unfailing personal commitment of Philippe Leclerc.

CHAPTER FOURTEEN

INDOCHINE

Now that Germany was defeated, de Gaulle's next task was re-establishing France's rank in the world. Alongside Great Britain and the USA, France's status as a great power was largely defined by her ability to found and maintain an empire. Now de Gaulle believed if that empire had to be given up, it should be on terms as favourable and dignified to France as possible.

While considerably smaller than its British counterpart, France's empire had been the world's second largest, consisting of vast swathes of north, west and equatorial Africa, islands on every ocean, and its jewel, Indo-China, consisting of the modern countries of Vietnam, Laos and Cambodia. From the 1850s, the Second Empire of Napoleon III spread its tentacles around the globe, determined to acquire prizes as valuable as Great Britain's, and the coast of Tonkin, Annam and Cochin-China with its deltas of the Red River and the Mekong, beckoned temptingly. The Indo-Chinese, with their simple society of desperately poor peasants topped by a wealthy, immoveable mandarin class, were easy pickings. Within twenty years French pioneers had arrived to establish rubber plantations and grow silkworms which would provide the looms of Lyons with raw material.

Where French entrepreneurs saw opportunities, the French working classes saw oppressed brothers, and soon converted Asian intellectuals to socialism and Marxism. By the 1930s the working class movement in French Indo-China was well established and its leader was Nguyen Ai Quoc, otherwise known as Ho-Chi-Minh, a phrase which means "he who enlightens" or, in French, *lui qui éclaire.*

After the Japanese attack on Pearl Harbor in December 1941, Vichy shamefully allowed the Japanese safe passage through Indo-China to attack the British in Burma and Malaya. In exchange, the Japanese allowed the Vichy régime full authority over Indo-China's internal affairs, and civil unrest was put down by the Foreign Legion. On one occasion captured dissidents were tied to each other with wire threaded through the flesh of their hands. Political prisons such as the Pacific's "devil's island"—Poulo Condor—were bursting, and the firing squad and guillotine were used liberally.

French plantation owners and the colonial petite bourgeoisie tried to carry on as before. But seaborne traffic between Indo-China and the Métropole was reduced to a standstill and Indo-China's governor, Admiral Decoux, had to appoint more Indo-Chinese to senior positions. After so much humiliation, French authority disintegrated.[1]

Once France was fully back in the war, and the French Navy sent battleships like the *Richelieu* to join operations with the British Pacific Fleet, the Japanese ceased to regard Decoux's collaborationist enclave as useful. On 9th March 1945, as de Gaulle had long feared, the Japanese fell on the French in Indo-China, interning administrators and plantation owners and massacring anyone who offered resistance. Only a few thousand French troops from the garrison of Tonkin managed the trek northwards to China to be greeted frostily by Chiang Kai-Shek.

The Japanese then set up provincial Indo-Chinese governments. These were more independent than has often been credited, giving the Indo-Chinese a taste of self-rule they would not forget. Furthermore, Ho Chi Minh had been organising resistance throughout the war years, essential groundwork in his plan for a fully independent Indo-China. US war aims were anti-colonial too, so the French got as little sympathy from their powerful ally over Indo-China as they did in North Africa.[2]

De Gaulle's hopes had therefore been pre-empted. However much he may have known that the prevailing US-dominated trend in international politics was anti-colonial, de Gaulle was a proud man and not inclined to graciously wave good-bye to any French possessions that had been wrenched from him. He decided that Leclerc would lead an expeditionary corps to "liberate" Indo-China from the Japanese.[3]

Since the terrain of Indo-China offered little scope for armoured warfare, the 2e DB would not be sent, but when Leclerc asked the officers for a show of hands for a *groupe de marche*, Massu's arm went up by reflex and so did many others. Guillebon became involved, and so too did the divisional intelligence chief, Paul Repiton-Préneuf. Other troops came from the French 3rd and 9th Colonial Infantry Divisions; further colonial troops under General Blaizot came from Madagascar; and there were also the 6,000 French and Indo-Chinese who had followed General Alessandri to China in the spring.

A Corps HQ was set up on the Rue Francois Premier from which to carry out planning and administration.[4] Leclerc hoped that US assistance and appropriate equipment would be available under "Lend Lease." He certainly did not want a repeat of past uncertainties when his division enjoyed US plenty while fearing attachment to de Lattre's patchily equipped and uneven army.

Events conspired to overtake these concerns. From 15th to 25th July, 1945, leaders of the great powers met in the old Hohenzollern palace at Potsdam to discuss the future path of the war. In the absence of French troops, Indo-China would be cleared of Japanese by Chinese forces in the north and by British and Indian troops in the south, meeting at a new latitudinal dividing line, the 16th parallel. The US President Franklin D. Roosevelt was now dead and had been replaced by his vice president, Harry S. Truman. Truman had an ace up his sleeve for ending the Pacific war more quickly than anyone imagined. Nuclear tests in the Nevada desert had been successful, and two atomic bombs were on their way to the B-29 Superfortress base on Grand Tinian in the Marianna Islands.

In the meantime, the British chief of South East Asia Command, Admiral Lord Louis Mountbatten, had come to the conclusion that reconquering French Indo-China was vital to his strategy, and would be difficult without French local knowledge. He welcomed the notion of a *Corps Leger d'Intervention*. The Americans were not keen to support a

French return, but Mountbatten had argued strongly enough for General Blaizot to get his force from Madagascar to Ceylon by August. This was still not close enough, and the colossal sea distances meant Mountbatten had to use British Indian troops in Indo-China as a matter of urgency. General Gracey's 20th Indian Division, containing a strong contingent of highly disciplined Gurkhas, was on standby.[5]

Now Truman showed his hand. On the 6th and 9th August, the atomic bombs nick-named "Fat Man" and "Little Boy" were dropped from US Superfortresses on the Japanese cities of Hiroshima and Nagasaki. Japan heard the voice of Emperor Hirohito on the radio for the first time, asking his people to accept the "unthinkable."

At CEFEO's Paris HQ, Leclerc's staff had been mentally prepared for a long war in the Pacific and were taking long overdue leave when the news of Japan's capitulation came through. Leclerc's *Corps Leger d'Intervention* immediately lost its primary *raison d'être*. De Gaulle switched at once to his next priority: France's return to Indo-China. First, he appointed the sailor-priest Admiral Thierry d'Argenlieu as French High Commissioner to replace Admiral Decoux, who was languishing in an Indo-Chinese internment camp. Fiercely patriotic and combining great intelligence with religious asceticism, d'Argenlieu had already been Free French High Commissioner in the Pacific from 1941 until 1943. Leclerc was appointed Commander-in-Chief of French forces in the colony, though previously Leclerc had been senior to d'Argenlieu in the Free French hierarchy.

It would be several weeks before Leclerc or d'Argenlieu could get out to Indo-China. In the power vacuum caused by this hiatus, Ho Chi Minh saw the opportunity the sudden Japanese collapse afforded him. As with the Communists in Malaya, the Viet Minh had been the strongest and most organised of the anti-Japanese resistance movements and had no love for the French either. Thanks to Decoux's administration, they saw France as a fascist power that had collaborated with Japan. On 13th August a meeting of the Indo-Chinese Communist Party was called at Tan Trao, two days before the Japanese announced their surrender. On 19th August, Viet Minh resistance leader General Giap marched on Hanoi and took control of government buildings.

A Viet Minh delegation visited the Japanese-nominated puppet Emperor Bao Dai in the imperial city of Hué, suggesting politely that he should agree that a government should be formed under Ho Chi Minh. More interested in saving his life than his throne, Bao Dai agreed to abdicate on 25th August, becoming "Citizen Prince" Vinh Tuy. Ho Chi Minh even allowed him to become a government counsellor!

In the subsequent confusion, de Gaulle had to rely on his commissioner in the north, Jean Sainteny, a career colonial banker and administrator who had escaped from the Gestapo shortly before the liberation of Paris. Sainteny lost no time in making contact with Ho Chi Minh's new government. On 27th August he managed to meet General Giap, though unsurprisingly, the meeting was inconclusive since neither recognised the powers of the other. In Saigon, the capital of Cochin-China, the local Communist chief, Tran Van Giau, formed a regional government under the authority of Hanoi. Communist preparation was so deeply laid that Ho Chi Minh could announce his new republican government, with Giap as his Minister of the Interior, as early as the 29th of August.

Since returning from Germany, Leclerc had only spent ten days with his family. They were faced by the prospect of another prolonged parting, perhaps equally dangerous for Leclerc, and just as worrying for Thérèse , and their *adieus* felt immensely similar to their *adieus* at Les Vergnes in 1940. Thérèse subsequently told Leclerc's mother that his heart had been very full.

On 18th August, Admiral d'Argenlieu came to Le Bourget airport to see Leclerc off, more to stamp his authority on the matter than through any fellow feeling. Leclerc was accompanied on the Dakota aircraft by Colonel Lecomte and Captains Buis and Mus, the latter a peacetime professor at France's School of Oriental Studies who had been parachuted into Indo-China in February 1945 and only recently returned. Perched on an uncomfortable fold-down seat, Leclerc spent the flight reading the memoirs of Paul Doumer, governor of Indo-China in 1896, and talking to Paul Mus, from whom he learned that pro-French resistance were largely situated in Laos and the highlands.

On the same day, de Gaulle received a communiqué from Bao Dai warning him presciently that if France attempted a reintroduction of the old régime it "would not be obeyed. Each village will become a nest of resistance, each old friend an enemy, and your administrators and your colonists themselves will demand to escape from this suffocating atmosphere. The only means of safeguarding French interests and influence in Indo-China is, frankly, to recognise the independence of Vietnam."

It may be that de Gaulle did not read this plea from Bao Dai, or else that he took little notice of it. He was always a conviction politician, whereas Bao Dai, who had been educated in France, was an opportunist. In any case de Gaulle's simplistic belief at this time was that France must re-establish her rule over Indo-China as "the last phase of the Liberation."[6]

When his Dakota landed at Karachi to refuel, Leclerc found a telegram from de Gaulle waiting for him. He was appointed French signatory at the Japanese surrender planned to take place aboard the battleship *USS Missouri* in Tokyo Bay. Leclerc also heard that Admiral Mountbatten wanted to meet him in Ceylon. Landing at Kandy on 22nd August, Leclerc and Lecomte were met at the airfield by Mountbatten himself who put them in the picture as he drove a Jeep. "This is the situation. You've heard of the Potsdam agreement?"

"No," replied Leclerc, somewhat startled.

Neither de Gaulle nor Georges Bidault had seen fit to brief Leclerc over the recent accords, even though they had been decided over a fortnight before his departure from Paris—an unforgiveable oversight that smacked of both overconfidence and improvisation. Mountbatten had to explain to Leclerc that the disarmament of the Japanese in Indo-China would be carried out by the British in the south and the Chinese in the north. Though predisposed to mistrust an Englishman and a sailor, Leclerc appreciated Mountbatten's frankness and evident lack of illusions. Mountbatten was as good a friend as Leclerc was likely to find. "If you let the Chinese involve themselves in this matter, you won't get them out of it," was one of the royal sailor's pithier and more accurate remarks. As soon as he could, Leclerc wired de Gaulle, who was in the USA visiting President Truman. Mountbatten also told Leclerc, "If President Roosevelt was still alive you wouldn't be going back to Indo-China at all!"[7]

There had been a small French presence on Ceylon since the previous November. Leclerc was billeted in "The French Bungalow" while his staff were found lodgings at Mount School in the hills overlooking Kandy, all within easy distance of the British HQ at Peradeniya Botanical Gardens, among 145 acres full of bougainvillaea, mango trees and oriental floral wonders.

Several exchanges took place between Leclerc and the British theatre commander over the next few weeks. Mountbatten was surprised by the scope of French thinking. The British were already committed to provide landing craft and equipment to facilitate France's return to Indo-China. Then it turned out that the French 3ᵉ DIC would be leaving France without equipment, which they also expected from the British.[8] It seemed extraordinary to Mountbatten that a country which could barely arm itself should think of re-establishing colonial sovereignty while Great Britain, from comparatively speaking a much stronger position, had embraced the inevitability of giving her colonies their independence. During the next few weeks he often advised Leclerc to make a settlement and accept that times had changed. Each time the fiercely patriotic Frenchman replied obstinately "I have my orders." In any case, Mountbatten could see trouble ahead and hoped British forces would not get embroiled.[9]

On the flight from Kandy to Tokyo, Leclerc was accompanied by Repiton-Préneuf, Langlois de Bazillac, whose family had long been involved in Indo-China, and Paul Mus. They stopped off at Manila, one of the few capital cities in the Pacific war to have seen large scale street fighting, and could not help but be awed by the magnitude of the US war effort, and the abundant equipment which had been brought so far from America. A trip in a US Skymaster took them to Tokyo, where Leclerc met up with Soviet and Dutch officers as well as British and Americans. The most powerful among the victors, the USA and the Soviet Union, were anti-colonialist. Ironically, the British already knew they had to let their colonies go, whereas the least powerful, the French and the Dutch, seemed determined to hold on to the past.

General Douglas MacArthur personally welcomed Leclerc to the Allied breakfast party, and Leclerc congratulated him on the Pacific campaign. MacArthur, who had served in France during the first war, graciously declared that Leclerc had followed the examples of Joffre and Foch, and concluded by saying, "If you weren't with me the day would not be complete."[10]

Leclerc still wanted to keep the Chinese out of northern Indo-China, and hoped that the French troops who had retreated to Yunan the previous spring could be re-armed by the Americans. Geographically, Indo-China fell between the British and Chiang Kai-Shek. It was not part of MacArthur's remit. His chief of staff, US General Wedemeyer, was against the reassertion of French power in the region, and MacArthur himself did not want to get involved. Nevertheless, he allowed Leclerc to wire de Gaulle with the advice, "Bring troops, more troops, as many as you can."[11]

A motor launch took the delegates to the *USS Missouri,* which stood at anchor in Tokyo Bay surrounded by Allied warships. The five-star flags of both MacArthur and Admiral Chester Nimitz flew from her mast, alongside the US flag that flew from the Capitol on 7th December 1941. Commander Horace Bird, the ship's gunnery officer, called for silence as MacArthur and Nimitz came on deck. Cupping his hands round his mouth, Bird yelled "Attention all hands!" In the distance the destroyer *Lansdowne* could be seen drawing near with the Japanese delegation aboard. The chief of the Japanese imperial general staff, General Yoshijiro Umezu, climbed the gangway in khaki cotton cap, breeches and riding boots, accompanied by subordinates and Japanese diplomats dressed in top hats and morning coats.

With the Japanese delegation assembled, the *Missouri*'s tannoy system struck up the Star Spangled Banner. Then MacArthur stepped up to the microphone: "We are gathered here, representative of the warring powers, to conclude a solemn agreement whereby peace may be restored." MacArthur then spoke of the "earnest hope" that "a better world may emerge. . . . founded upon faith and understanding—a world dedicated to the dignity of man and the fulfilment of his most cherished wish—for freedom, tolerance and justice."[12]

The two copies of the surrender document, bound in leather for the Allies and in cotton for the Japanese, waited on the table. Shigemitsu, the Japanese Foreign Minister, hobbled forward, sat and looked at the document uncomprehendingly. "Sutherland, show him where to sign," MacArthur said crisply. Then came Umezu, who spurned the offer of a chair. Next came the Allied powers, the United States and British Commonwealth countries predominating. Leclerc, Repiton and Langlois, dressed similarly to the Americans except for their képis and insignia, stepped forward when MacArthur beckoned them. Leclerc sat down and signed for France while MacArthur looked on. When everyone had signed and the

Japanese were returning to their launch, a cloud of American aircraft appeared above, B-29 Superfortresses and dark blue-painted US Navy fighters and dive-bombers.

MacArthur returned to the microphone. "Today the guns are silent," he said. "A great tragedy has ended. A great victory has been won. The skies no longer rain death; the seas bear only commerce. Men everywhere walk upright in the sunlight. The entire world is quietly at peace. The holy mission has been completed. And in reporting this to you, the people, I speak for the thousands of silent lips, forever stilled among the jungles and beaches and in the deep waters of the Pacific which marked the way. . . . We have had our last chance. If we do not devise some greater and more equitable system, Armageddon will be at our door."

"The problem basically is theological," he continued, "and involves a spiritual recrudescence and improvement of human character that will synchronise with our almost matchless advances in science, art, literature and all material and cultural developments of the last two thousand years. To the Pacific basin has come the vista of a new, emancipated world. Today freedom is on the offensive. Democracy is on the march. Today, in Asia as well as in Europe, unshackled peoples are tasting the full sweetness of liberty, the relief from fear."[13]

Reflecting on MacArthur's advice earlier, but ignoring Mountbatten's, Leclerc informed Paris that the problem of France's return to Indo-China would be resolved "by the fastest possible arrival of an expeditionary corps putting French troops on the ground." To his friend René Pleven he wrote emphatically that "The problem of Indo-China is perfectly solvable if the French government decides to act instead of talk." His message to the new Foreign Minister, Georges Bidault, echoed this. "Thanks to the rhythm of Allied transport, we will not be in a state to react to the Chinese occupation for at least two or three months. — In my opinion there is not a moment to lose. The French government must act immediately."[14]

Although de Gaulle wrote in his memoirs that he sent "considerable forces" to Indo-China, in fact the numbers available that summer were far too parsimonious to have any hope of making a difference. General Sabattier, the French Army commander in Indo-China during the Decoux period, had estimated that 100,000 troops would be needed. By comparison, Leclerc's meagre 30,000 men would have to beg and borrow equipment from Great Britain and America even to get a foothold.[15]

Besides, the "unshackled peoples" of Indo-China were already "tasting the full sweetness of liberty." The French colonists and plantation owners were still in internment camps, and only a few Chinese troops had arrived to disarm the Japanese garrisons in the north who mostly had the good sense to stay in their barracks. Incidents between Japanese and Viet Minh armies were quickly defused,[16] but acts of revenge against the French for decades of oppression were inevitable. One of the grizzliest was the murder of Père Tricoire, who was lynched and stabbed before being lashed to a cross on the piazza outside Saigon Cathedral.[17]

The same morning that MacArthur took the Japanese surrender, the people of Hanoi were decorating their city with red bunting and their new red flag with a yellow star, celebrating their independent homeland. Banners were strung between buildings and lamp posts in Vietnamese, English, French, Chinese and Russian: "Viet Nam for the Vietnamese," "Down with French Colonialism," "Independence or death," "Support the provisional government," "Support President Ho Chi Minh!" Everyday life in the city came to a standstill as people converged on the former Place Puginier, which was now renamed Ba Dinh Square.[18]

Ho Chi Minh could be capable of Gandhi-like self-effacement. Wearing Western clothes he looked a little like the comedian Charlie Chaplin of early silent films. Compared to the self-indulgent lifestyle of former Emperor Bao Dai, this quality was part of the Viet Minh leader's charm, what made him come across as *un homme honnête*. Dressing in a high-collared light khaki suit and natural, latex-coloured rubber sandals, Ho Chi Minh was announced to the crowd by General Giap, now the Viet-namese Minister of the Interior. Then Ho gave a speech imbued with the spirit of the great libertarian revolutions of the late eighteenth century, the American War of Independence and the French Revolution. "All men are created equal! They are endowed by their creator with certain inalienable rights, among these are life, liberty and the pursuit of happiness.

"This immortal statement appeared in the Declaration of Independence of the United States of America in 1776. In a broader sense, it means: All the peoples on the earth are equal from birth, all the peoples have a right to live and to be happy and free.

"The Declaration of the Rights of Man and the Citizen, made at the time of the French Revolution, in 1791, also states: 'All men are born free and with equal rights, and must always remain free and have equal rights.'"

Ho Chi Minh then proceeded to draw the contrast between the best ideals of French patriots with the cruel realities of life under French colonial rule, its political prisons with their executions and tiger cages, its arrogance, its forced labour markets, and the life of poverty inflicted on the ordinary peasants. "Vietnam has the right to enjoy freedom and independence, and in fact has become a free and independent country. The entire Vietnamese people are determined to mobilize all their physical and mental strength, to sacrifice their lives and property in order to safeguard their freedom and independence."[19]

With General Giap, whose sister had been guillotined by the French, standing beside him, Ho Chi Minh engaged the crowd in a collective conversation. "My fellow countrymen, have you understood?" To which they roared back "Yes!"

In the sky above, a flight of twin-fuselaged US Lightning fighter planes roared ominously overhead.

Then the Vietnamese held services celebrating independence in both the city's Buddhist temples and its Catholic churches. Sensing the wave of change, the handful of French colonials in the crowd longed for a show of strength from the Métropole.[20]

As soon as he learnt of Ho Chi Minh's declaration of independence from Colonel Roos, the French attaché in Calcutta, before returning to Ceylon,[21] Leclerc repeated his earlier message, this time to his immediate superior, Admiral Thierry d'Argenlieu: "I am convinced that the outcome of this affair depends on the arrival as soon as possible of a well equipped expeditionary corps. None of the Allies are really going to help us reoccupy Indo-China. No senior commander wants to lend us aircraft or transport to use north of the 16th parallel without the order of his government."

Back at Mountbatten's base, Leclerc vented his frustration on Weil. He believed, correctly, that Paris was disinterested in the fate of Indo-China, even railing against de Gaulle for indulging himself in unfounded Anglophobia. "De Gaulle is an idiot," he told Weil, exasperated. "He is going to lose Indo-China just as he lost Syria." Mountbatten's posture consistently demonstrated that Great Britain's position regarding French colonies and mandates was far from predatory, whatever de Gaulle wished to believe. In fact, while he waited for troops and equipment, Leclerc found Mountbatten's generosity exasperatingly genial.

"Yes, no? Is it on?" the blue-blooded British admiral would ask, smiling serenely, while offering a pre-prandial snifter.

Leclerc declared bitterly, "Admiral, you have promised me your cooperation. All I can tell you is that if I fail in the task entrusted to me, of returning Indo-China to France, all Frenchmen will know the reasons."[22]

Admiral Thierry d'Argenlieu arrived in Kandy on 8th September. But without troops and transport, Indo-China's new French High Commissioner and Commander-in-Chief could only twiddle their thumbs and build on their already powerful personality clash. D'Argenlieu, the ascetic bachelor sailor-priest, versus Free France's most hands-on army commander and father of six. Tactfully, Mountbatten took Leclerc with him to receive Japanese Field Marshal Count Terauchi's surrender of Singapore.

Before leaving, Leclerc gave d'Argenlieu an aggressive and direct letter. Leclerc confessed himself puzzled by d'Argenlieu's appointment, especially as the sailor-priest had previously been his junior, whereas Leclerc had wielded political and military authority in French Equatorial Africa until January 1943. The CEFEO's slow arrival increased the problems it would face when it reached Indo-China, Leclerc explained, but insufficient French forces also meant the Viet Minh had been able to make "premature declarations before being able to grasp the reality of facts." Further, the French continued to be hamstrung without Allied cooperation, especially from the British who were not keen to risk lives over Indo-China. If confusion was to be avoided, Leclerc believed, it was necessary to place both civil and military power in the hands of one man—himself! Leclerc expounded his belief that it was only for reasons of interior politics that de Gaulle had appointed d'Argenlieu, in spite of the considerable service Leclerc had given in politically complex situations. Concluding, Leclerc gave d'Argenlieu three reasons for writing this insubordinate letter. First, he admired d'Argenlieu profoundly. Second, he was only interested in what was best for France. Third, many volunteers in the CEFEO were only coming out specifically to serve under him![23]

But what would sailor-priest, Louis de la Trinité, make of this blatant attempt to erode his prestige and authority? D'Argenlieu's reply was tactful in the extreme. Leclerc received it in Kandy on 11th September. D'Argenlieu reciprocated Leclerc's esteem and commended his handling of the Gabon crisis in October 1940. However, d'Argenlieu's orders came from General de Gaulle and he would obey them. The admiral would, however, allow Leclerc plenty of scope for initiative within his remit.[24]

In the meantime, the Chinese were preparing to send 180,000 men into northern Indo-China to disarm 60,000 Japanese, a venture that clearly had more to do with plunder than any agreement made at Potsdam. In the south the British were only sending 20,000 troops, mostly General Gracey's 20th Indian Division. On 5th September a British advance guard had landed at Saigon's Than San Nut aerodrome, followed by some Gurkhas a few days later. Owing to good relations with Mountbatten, a company of French troops from Colonel Rivier's 5e Colonial Infantry Regiment had been included. But 25,000 French nationals were hostages of the Viet-Minh or still languishing in the same internment camps that the Japanese had herded them into the previous March, and incidents between Vietnamese and French *colons* were escalating.[25]

Whatever Mountbatten's good intentions towards France, the warm welcome given to the Gurkhas by the indigenous population was a further smack in the face to French prestige. That French troops should appear clothed and equipped by the British did not help. It was as obvious to the Vietnamese as it had been to the people of French North Africa after the arrival of the Americans, that France could not reimpose her authority without assistance from other powers.

The 20th Indian Division's arrival in Saigon was calm, but the situation soon deteriorated. General Gracey had no alternative but to declare martial law, and had too few troops to enforce it. 1,000 French troops from the 11e Régiment d'Infanterie Coloniale had been interned by the Japanese in the prison of Brière de l'Isle. Gracey had them released and re-equipped. The 11e RIC promptly evicted all the Vietnamese from Saigon's public buildings. Six months incarceration on starvation rations is hardly balanced preparation for low-intensity operations, and some 11e RIC went on the rampage. Retaliation was swift in coming. Since mid-August, Tran Van Giau's south Vietnamese government had amnestied large numbers of civil prisoners from the jails, including many common criminals. Seeing the

11e RIC's atrocities as an affront to their new sovereignty, they massacred over a hundred French civilians in the French residential area of Héyraud. Another two hundred were taken hostage, never to be heard of again.[26]

British concerns at being sucked into French colonial problems grew, and Leclerc was becoming frantic. Gracey's men were doing their best, but there were not enough of them. The only other troops capable of policing duties were the defeated Japanese presently keeping to their camps. When British Field Marshal Slim arrived in Saigon to inspect Gracey's men, the newly released French Commissioner Cedile told him of the risks to French colonials due to inadequate policing. Slim's solution was practical, if not a little bizarre. He reminded the Japanese Field Marshal Terauchi of an occupying power's duty to maintain law and order, and an agreement was reached whereby Japanese soldiers augmented Gurkha patrols. While this was a temporary practical solution to prevent French *colons* from being murdered, it also demonstrated to the Vietnamese that occupying powers were very similar. When Gracey remarked that the new Labour Prime Minister, Clement Attlee, might not be pleased, Slim replied, "The minister has political responsibility, whereas I am responsible for the troops on the ground."

A few days later, Britain's Labour government made its feelings known. Intervention by Gracey's division against the "Annamites" after the Héyraud massacre was regarded as a most unwelcome development. At a meeting at Peredinya, which included Leclerc and Field Marshal Slim, Mountbatten declared his intention to sack Gracey. Leclerc was furious but Mountbatten was unswerving. "Gracey has exceeded his orders. I am going to send a telegram to London asking for his recall."

At once Leclerc spoke up, "Gracey couldn't have done anything else."

Slim agreed, "General Leclerc is right."

Mountbatten realised he had to support Gracey.[+] This enabled Colonel Cedille to negotiate a local truce with the south Vietnamese leader Tran Van Giau on 2nd October.

Mountbatten, however, remained concerned that French intentions in Indo-China were quite unrealistic. On 4th September, during an official conversation with Leclerc, Mountbatten said "I would say something officially to General Leclerc which I said to him in private yesterday. I advise you to make a clear declaration promising independence to Indo-China with *dominion* status."

"I have sent a cable to this effect to Admiral d'Argenlieu," replied Leclerc. "I know that the general [de Gaulle] wants to give autonomy to Indo-China."

"A declaration would have the effect of ending the struggle for independence since it would have been formally promised. It would also have an excellent effect on public opinion and in the United States," said Mountbatten.

"In France we don't have 'dominion status.' We say 'autonomy.'" replied Leclerc.[27]

Leclerc was in a difficult position. De Gaulle, to whom he owed his appointment—if not his whole career, had a separate vision from the British on how to mature France's empire towards independence, centred around the idea of a French Union. He thought the British attitude to France's empire was hypocritical and that the British were keen to undermine French imperial authority wherever they could, mid-1940s Syria being his favourite example. When Leclerc forwarded Mountbatten's suggestion to Paris, de Gaulle predictably rejected it, believing his own declaration of the previous March was good enough, and that any change would smack of a French climb-down which, he believed, would make things worse. "Besides," de Gaulle scoffed, "if France acceded to such ideas she would have no empire left." Great men make great mistakes. Amid France's internal problems, de Gaulle's grasp of the hopelessness of France's colonial ambitions in Indo-China was inevitably poor. He should have listened to his favourite general.

In his frustration Leclerc wrote to his sister Colette: "Here we are in the *merde* right up to our necks. Revolts and wars everywhere; against the English, the Dutch and, sadly, also against us. Waiting patiently like Sister Anne for my ships and soldiers, I get all the knocks from all the different factions, promising me on the Gospel to repay a hundredfold whatever I do. The situation worsens every day and has continued to do so for a month now. Still one goes on. I hope that our compatriots will not be murdered in the meantime."[28]

French troops were starting to arrive in greater numbers. The main party of the 5e Régiment d'Infanterie Coloniale, formed at Djidjelli in Algeria and transported to Ceylon in May, had been fully equipped by the British and landed in Saigon in early October, reinforcing Lt. Colonel

Rivier's advance guard.[29] For the British this meant their men would be relieved, and providing the French with uniforms and small arms was a small price to pay. Gracey's Gurkhas and Japanese were increasingly being drawn into the unpleasant cycle of attacks and reprisals such as burning villages. Mountbatten was correctly concerned that depriving peasants of all they possessed only fueled resentments and remonstrated with Gracey, "I was most distressed to see you had been burning down houses; in congested areas too." SEAC's Commander-in-Chief felt such '"unsavoury jobs" should be left to the French. Gracey remembered the newly released 11e RIC's rampage and its consequences, and replied that French soldiers did not "understand 'minimum violence' and would have burnt not twenty but two thousand huts."[30]

Leclerc, much to de Gaulle's consternation, had not yet set foot in Indo-China. Finally, on 1st October, he left Ceylon for Chandernagor with last orders from d'Argenlieu. The admiral told Leclerc not to take operations north of the 16th parallel where de Gaulle hoped diplomacy with the Chinese might be successful, and on no account to evacuate French colonials, whose presence justified the CEFEO's intervention. He also wanted a feasibility study for supplying the French community in the north from the sea.[31] The meeting ended with Leclerc believing d'Argenlieu was "honest and lets honest men get on with their work." D'Argenlieu remarked, "With General Leclerc relations have now been established on a basis of solid and reciprocal understanding. The old Free French camaraderie helps things."[32] In the autumn of 1945, both Leclerc and d'Argenlieu were consistent in as much as both shared an as yet unshaken desire to restore the French Empire to its pre-1940 state,

Viet Minh handling of the French was anything but consistent. When the Gaullist emissary Pierre Messmer parachuted into the north, he was captured by the Viet Minh and locked up. Jean Sainteny, on the other hand, had managed to live amid the Viet Minh's triumphalism that followed Ho's declaration of independence, in spite of his brass-necked occupation of Hanoi's Government Palace in the name of France on 22nd August. While Messmer languished in jail, Sainteny toughed out this role for six weeks, amid conflicting pressure from Americans, Chinese, Vietnamese and Japanese.

Japanese forces south of the 16th parallel were content to obey British orders. In the north, however, many who could not bear their Emperor's loss of deity and Japan's submission to western supremacy were slipping away, with their arms, to join the Viet Minh. Overall, the lives of 30,000 French *colons* were even more at risk.

On 5th October, Leclerc arrived in Indo-China for the first time. On landing at Saigon's rain-lashed Tan San Nhut aerodrome he was welcomed by Governor Jean Cedille and General Gracey. As they drove into Saigon in an old Pontiac, Leclerc was stupefied to see the number of armed Japanese soldiers presently under Gracey's orders.[33] Ten thousand French *colons* waited stoically in the pouring rain to welcome him. Whatever his private thoughts about French policy, surveying the rain-drenched *colons* who had been cut off from the Métropole for five years, terrorised by the Japanese *kempetai* and degraded by vengeful Viet Minh, Leclerc told them, "Have the minds of conquerors! The Indo-Chinese are influenced by pernicious propaganda. They are not your enemies. Tomorrow, they will retake their place in the French community." The *colons* cheered.[34]

The truce brokered by Colonel Cedille with Tran Van Giau on 2nd October foundered nine days later on French requests that the Viet Minh surrender French hostages taken during September. The following day, the Viet Minh murdered a British Indian officer and NCOs near Tan San Nhut. General Gracey was furious, telling Leclerc, "These Annamites! We've got to give them Hell!"

Whatever Gracey's previous views on the French understanding of "minimum violence," Leclerc's was now the voice of moderation. "If we do not, above all, establish a sense of our values, we won't gain anything. They must realise that we are not beaten. We must teach them a lesson and then we'll talk about it."[35]

French Indo-China consisted not only of modern-day Vietnam but Cambodia and Laos as well. Leclerc was forced to focus his actions on a very small scale, while still awaiting the arrival of the rest of the French Expeditionary Force. The Japanese had turned Cambodia into a police state under a puppet called Son Ngoc Thanh. Somehow the Japanese there had to be disarmed without driving Son Ngoc Thanh and his followers into the arms of the Viet Minh. Leclerc persuaded Gracey to fly in a detachment of British troops whose authority the Japanese accepted. On 15th October, Leclerc took off from Saigon and, an hour later, was in the

office of Lt. Colonel Murray in Phnom Penh. Then Leclerc invited Son
Ngoc Thanh to a meeting and suggested they take a little Jeep ride, just
Leclerc, Son Ngoc Thanh and the driver with no guard. Next Leclerc hus-
tled the unsuspecting Son Ngoc Thanh onto a Dakota which flew back to
Saigon where Leclerc immediately put the hapless ex-puppet in jail. Prince
Sihanouk of Cambodia subsequently signed an agreement with Admiral
d'Argenlieu to form an autonomous government within the French union.
In fact, this maneuovre kept Cambodia stable for several years until it
became embroiled in the larger Vietnamese conflict during the 1960s.[36]
Laos, being north of the 16th parallel, offered less scope for intervention
but, with Gracey's assistance, a detachment of French was sent to Paksé.

From 15th to 19th October, Jacques Massu's 2e DB *groupe de marche*
arrived. They had sailed in a small convoy consisting of the aircraft carrier
Béarn, the cruisers *Gloire* and *Suffren*, and a large-hulled cargo ship, the
Ville-de-Strasbourg. Infantry being higher priority in jungle warfare, the
RMT volunteers were grouped into a "4e bataillon," commanded by Ray-
mond Dronne and comprising four companies, the 13e, 14e, 15e and a
support company mounted in White halftracks. Massu also brought a
squadron of Spahis armoured cars under Lt. Duplay, and a company of
Stuart light tanks from the 501e RCC under Captains Compagnon and
Krebs. The *Groupement Massu* was supported by a company of engineers
and a medical unit, including drivers from the *Rochambelles*. *Méhariste*
Commandant de Sarazac was Massu's second in command.[37]

In Massu's words, undoubtedly written to counter the "para culture"
image that developed in the 1950s, these volunteers—who included both
the experienced, reluctant to return to the rhythms of peacetime, and the
inexperienced who joined the 2e DB late in the European war and who
still felt they had something to prove—"were not Praetorians." They simply
saw themselves as ordinary young men who wanted to help their compatriots in danger, uphold the laws of France, and preserve what their fore-
fathers had created.[38] They installed themselves at Camp Drouhet in the
Saigon suburb of Cholon, the original Chinese quarter, where the petty
bourgeoisie were hedging their bets with the Viet Minh and were keen to
see the French leave. Cantoning *Groupe Massu* in this area was a clear sign
the CEFEO was not going to be intimidated.[39]

Leclerc recognised that only a show of force would demonstrate whether or not France could re-establish control in Indo-China. The first task was to break the Viet Minh enclaves, "the crust of *salopards,*" that had grown up around Saigon. Assisted by Repiton-Préneuf, Leclerc briefed Massu. South of Saigon, the Viet Minh were active in the areas of Mytho and Cantho in the Mekong delta, an important rice growing area, where they destroyed bridges, blocked roads, carried out ambushes and conducted a campaign of intimidation and subversion. Mytho was the southern end of the Vietnam coastal railway, which stretched from north to south, and an essential supply port for Saigon. As a result, shortages were beginning to reduce living standards in Saigon, and an increasing number of refugee *colons* were arriving from the countryside.[40]

Massu's men were still coming ashore from the *Ville de Strasbourg* and *Suffren,* but the aircraft carrier *Béarn*'s draft was too deep for the river so it anchored at Cap Saint-Jacques. Its captain sent an advance guard upstream by launch which got so lost among the little delta tributaries that a Japanese officer, whose only second language was English, had to act as river pilot. The CEFEO included troops from eclectic sources such as marine parachutists and a company's worth of sailors from the *Richelieu,* then on secondment to the British Pacific Fleet.[41]

Aerial reconnaissance using an old Japanese fighter revealed as many as twenty-four Viet Minh roadblocks between Saigon and Mytho, a number Leclerc found so staggering that he accused the reconnaissance team of pessimism. Massu's forces set off at 4am the following morning, but only got a few kilometres down the road before reaching the first ditch. Working stripped to the waste in the intense heat, the sappers filled in and bridged first one ditch, then another and another. Eventually they ran out of wood and had to chop trees. Leclerc appeared alongside to encourage the men, but it was abundantly clear Mytho would not be "liberated" for a few more days. As the French slogged along the road, life in the rice paddies continued as normal. The Vietnamese peasants in traditional brown, black and grey clothing and wide straw hats toiled away, apparently indifferent to the tribulations of their occupiers.

The last obstacle before Mytho was the concrete bridge at Tân An, which had been blown up by a Vietnamese engineer educated in France. As the French repaired the bridge through the night, lit by truck headlamps, Viet Minh sharpshooters shot out the headlights and picked off French sappers. The following day progress was slow. But Commandant Ponchardier's marines had been quietly working their way towards Mytho along the delta rivers to attack the Viet Minh rear, and they achieved total surprise. Arriving in Mytho, Massu and Leclerc found Ponchardier smiling and relaxed. Even so, Leclerc was annoyed at the time lost. Massu and Dronne would have to do better.[42]

As if to make up for it, Go Cong was taken in only three days. On 29th October they took Vinh Long, then Cantho on the 30th, and Cai Rang in early November. This reassertion of French power also brought about the release of French prisoners of war from Japanese camps hitherto unreachable, including Admiral Decoux and his staff. Leclerc's attitude to these former *Vichysois* was as uncompromising as it had been in 1943 with the *Armée d'Afrique*. He reproached them for not having resisted the Japanese, and declared, "You have stained our honour!" Captain Jeandru, who had been taught by Leclerc at Saint-Cyr in 1931, found his former instructor's view somewhat simplistic. Jeandru had witnessed the three thousand Frenchmen killed when the Japanese attacked the previous March, and the subsequent death rate of seventy percent among those taken prisoner.[43]

On 30th October, Admiral d'Argenlieu arrived in Saigon from Chandernagor. His appeal to Viet Minh rebels for calm went unheeded, and the French Army continued its so-called "protection" of the ravaged population with further operations in Cochin China at Tây Ninh and Chon Thành. To accomplish this, the French relied upon an increasingly eclectic mix of army forces, veterans of the Legion and La Coloniale, volunteers from Paris, and pro-French or at least anti-Communist Chinese, Annamites and Eurasians. Their tactics were a new departure on the old theme of fixing the enemy position and then outflanking it with movements adapted to jungle and river terrain.[44]

Leclerc saw his task as "pacification" so everyday life could be resumed. Accordingly he said the Vietnamese should be respected for the loyalty they showed France in spite of *la Chute* and the Japanese occupation from March 1945. There was to be no indiscipline or pillaging. Villages were to be respected as if they were French villages.

Yet d'Argenlieu wrote to de Gaulle that Leclerc was seized with "the dream of 'reconquest'" and the winning of new laurels. D'Argenlieu had not quite understood Leclerc. The admiral's hopes of a French union to resist all forms of dictatorship in the post-war world could not have been established in Indo-China by goodwill alone. Its internal order had to be backed by force, and both men knew that. Ironically, as France slid towards war in Indo-China, Leclerc's views mellowed while d'Argenlieu's hardened. Both men were patriots, but d'Argenlieu was the idealist and Leclerc the realist. Like the British in Malaya, Leclerc wanted to win people's hearts and minds, and his discussions with his staff, Lecomte, Repiton-Préneuf, and Langlois de Bazillac, whose family had long been involved in Indo-China, resulted in a rich awareness of the nuances involved.[45]

Relieved of the Viet Minh noose choking its supply lines, Saigon recovered a vestige of normality. Following the French custom of renaming streets after a war, the smart Avenue MacMahon now became the Avenue Charles de Gaulle, and Leclerc took over the villa formerly used by Japanese Field Marshal Terauchi. The faithful Sergeant Loustalot got the house and garden back into order with the aid of twenty newly released prisoners and some furniture from Saigon's premier store, Pomone. Leclerc shared the villa with Langlois de Bazillac and Girard's replacement, the one-armed Guy de Valence. Peschaud, Mirambeau and Chaunac occupied an annex on the grounds. The whole complex was guarded by twenty-five men under Sergeant-Major Réal.[46]

Mealtimes were a chance to "switch off." Leclerc liked to dine with his aides, exchanging anecdotes either hilarious or moving, or gathering news from subordinates, and the tone was very much that of a cavalry mess. If he went into Saigon he either took an armoured car or was accompanied by a member of Réal's platoon armed with a submachine gun. Leclerc found some of the *colons* difficult to deal with, especially the "rubber colonels," owners of rubber plantations who had returned from Paris sporting the uniforms of officers with the five *galons* of a colonel. Repiton-Préneuf convinced him to make an effort with them. Notwithstanding his strong faith, Leclerc was dismissive of the Archbishop of Saigon, Monsignor Cassaigne. He limited the prelate to one dinner invitation, and when Cassaigne offered his hand for Leclerc to kiss, Leclerc said, "No, it is not Sunday." The Indo-Chinese aristocracy were entertained occasionally, and the memories of aides from this period clearly indicate that the atmosphere in Leclerc's villa was unsophisticated.

He missed Thérèse, and after so many years away from her and his home at Tailly he was becoming frayed. He often ended the evening alone in his room listening to classical music on the gramophone. Nor was Guy de Valence the same-calibre sounding board as Christian Girard. Valence came from Langlade's 12e RCA, and rather looked down on Leclerc for reading history instead of cutting-edge post-war French writers like Sartre and Camus. Leclerc's solace was in correspondence with his family, which had been barred to him during the Occupation. He often wrote to his sisters Yvonne and Colette, advising them to prepare their daughters for military service since he was convinced women would play a greater part in the wars of the future. Like many Catholic families, he and his sisters had so many children that he often forgot their names. When Vézinet's wife produced a daughter, Leclerc wrote back to him, "After all, a girl! It's not as bad as that!"[47]

Chiang Kai-Shek could not forget that Vichy French authorities in Indo-China had cooperated with the Japanese against him after *la Chute* in 1940, depriving him of supplies via Haiphong. He therefore regarded the resurgence of French power in the area with contempt. His Chinese Nationalist Army, which had arrived in northern Indo-China to disarm all Japanese north of the 16th parallel, was taking its time about it. This placed Ho Chi Minh in an awkward position. Although his supporter, Tran Van Giau, was pursuing a guerrilla war against the French in the south, it became clear to Ho that he needed French support to secure Chinese withdrawal in the north.

In Hanoi, Jean Sainteny was rather under the spell of Ho Chi Minh's personal simplicity and charm. Ho's experiences as a down-and-out scholar taking menial jobs on steamships, and in the restaurants of London and Paris, must have made endearing anecdotes. Sainteny developed a curious notion that Ho was somehow pro-French. In fact, Ho may have seemed that way at the time. Moscow was taking little interest in Indo-China, so he told Sainteny he was prepared to tolerate a prolonged French presence provided Paris accepted the eventual goal of Indo-Chinese independence.[48]

In the south, the Viet Minh were systematically burnt out of their villages by the French, and were unable to call upon help from the main Viet Minh army kept in reserve by General Giap in case he had to fight the Chinese in the north. Tran Van Giau decided to pull out his men, only leaving undercover cells throughout southern villages to fight another day. They trudged north in the guise of peasants, their weapons hidden in ox carts and barrows. Effectively, the south would remain separate until the North Vietnamese Army and Viet Cong smashed their way into Saigon in 1975.

In the north, Giap was developing a military infrastructure as yet unthinkable in the south. Ho Chi Minh was doing his best not to nettle the Nationalist Chinese, even pretending to abolish the Communist party, and ordered a fund-raising week in late summer to buy weapons from the Chinese Army. In fact, the 3,000 Japanese who joined the Viet Minh rather than return home included technicians and artificers capable of making faithful copies of any firearm.[49]

Pierre Messmer escaped from the Viet Minh and informed Leclerc that Giap's men were kings north of the 16th parallel and that their political outlook was more nihilist than Communist. Leclerc inclined to the simple view that Asians wanted Europeans out, and only force would change that. Leclerc wrote to d'Argenlieu that France would have to "reconquer" Indo-China, a word d'Argenlieu objected to.

"To reassure you," wrote Leclerc, "I would never have used the word other than in that letter and I ask you yourself never to use it. Nevertheless the fact is there. It makes more sense for us to retake the country foothold by foothold, to show above all our power to destroy resistance. It is our soldiers who, region by region, will re-establish French sovereignty."

At this stage Leclerc did not regard negotiation with the Viet Minh as an option. While de Gaulle remained in office, he retained faith in France having a consistent political will to re-establish its authority. "The final absurdity would be to regard Indo-China today as a country ready to govern itself, possessing an elite with which one could negotiate. If you go down this road, then all the embittered intellectuals of Indo-China, the Communists, especially escapees from Poulo-Condor, will wrong-foot our politicians into acting out of progress or sentimentality. And all under the kindly and interested eyes of Chinese generals or Anglo-Saxon capitalists imitating them."[50] A more typical regular army officer's outlook followed: "It was necessary to show world public opinion the brutality, total lack of humanity and civilisation of the bands who oppose us."[51] It took nearly two years for Leclerc to fully appreciate that the Vietnamese did not want their country occupied any more than he had wanted the Germans in France.

The Viet-Minh were not interested in being pressed into a French Empire. They did not care if France wanted to compete with the British or Americans, whom they regarded as just as bad. "You are a great big liar, Leclerc," said posters pasted to walls in Saigon. "You kill us for the smell of our blood! We will never forget it! Saigon is full of traitors and we will burn down the whole town. You Leclerc and your *Allies*, we will fight you to the end!"[52]

Leclerc still believed the Viet-Minh could be subjugated, and pressed for logistical and diplomatic preparations with the Chinese for a landing in the north. The French Army's man in Chungking was Lt. Colonel Robert Quillichini, formerly of the 2e DB, whom Leclerc knew and trusted, though he had little experience of Indo-China. Before leaving France, Leclerc had earmarked General Raoul Salan to take French troops back to the north, but he did not arrive until several months later. Subsequently one of the most controversial figures of the decolonisation era, in late 1945 Salan was widely regarded as politically neutral, not given to extremes but more in the de Lattre or former Vichy camp than the Gaullist portion of the army. But Salan was utterly committed to maintaining the French Empire, and Leclerc needed his oriental experience. Leclerc sent Salan to Hanoi to assist Sainteny with negotiations in preparation for French landings north of the 16th parallel. "The essential point of your mission is to prepare our return to Tonkin," Leclerc wrote Salan. "This return necessitates, if not the consent, then at least tolerance on the part of the Chinese. In conjunction with Sainteny you will prepare the ground as far as you can and keep me informed. The important thing to avoid is a war between France and China." Quillichini was then appointed by Leclerc to accompany Salan.[53]

Through December Sainteny negotiated with Ho Chi Minh. Ho preferred the idea of *autonomie* rather than full independence for the time being, provided that France applied the basic principle which de Gaulle had outlined at the Brazzaville Conference in January 1944. "There will be no progress that is real progress unless the people on their native soil profit by it morally and materially." He wanted this to apply to Indo-China as well as French Africa.

On 28 December 1945, d'Argenlieu wrote to de Gaulle that the Indo-Chinese had "tasted the dream of independence and there is no going back." The question for d'Argenlieu, however, was always how independence was to be granted, and the subsequent status of the countries making up Indo-China in the French Union. Ho Chi Minh's sphere of influence only covered Tonkin and Annam north of the 16th parallel, which was less than a quarter of French Indo-China's total land mass and excluded the rice basket of Cochin-China's Mekong delta. Nevertheless, without Cochin-China's rice the rest of the country would starve, and Ho Chi Minh knew that.

Often the "thinker" of the former Free French, in fact d'Argenlieu's plan for guiding the area towards independence did not involve Ho Chi Minh at all. This may seem strange now, and may have been in denial even then of the evidence of Ho Chi Minh's control and reach in Tonkin and north Annam, but, like many French conservatives, the priest-admiral gravitated to the idea of monarchy. His latest idea was the restoration of Prince Vinh San who, as a mere eight-year-old, first took the Annamite throne in 1907 as Emperor Duy Tan, only to be deposed by the French nine years later and exiled to the Indian Ocean Island of Réunion. Vinh San, however, had his own ideas, not least of which was that the three "key"—Tonkin, Annam and Cochin China—should be reunited under him as Vietnam. Following a meeting on 14th December, de Gaulle believed he could work with Vinh San. The Prince knew the dangers and was bravely determined, but death came to him quicker than anyone expected in an air crash over Africa as he returned to Réunion to inform his family of their new destiny. In one of his resurgent bouts of crackpot Anglophobia, de Gaulle even blamed the British Secret Service! "What bad luck France has," he muttered to Alain de Boissieu. "We have lost a master card for Indo-China!"[54]

In the meantime the Chinese were showing themselves to be utterly uninterested in any situation that might develop to France's advantage, so it seemed imperative to Leclerc that French troops be landed in Tonkin as soon as possible. On 14th January 1946, he wrote to de Gaulle from Saigon requesting that General Juin, now French chief of staff, visit Indo-China to see the situation for himself. Leclerc knew Juin had a good relationship with America's General George Marshall and could make the case for US support of French activities in Indo-China now that the Communist threat, and with it the Cold War, was beginning to become manifest. Leclerc was also concerned that the condition of those *colons* still in internment camps could only deteriorate if the matter was not resolved, though in fact Giap had taken care to offer them the minimum necessary protection during the weeks following Japan's collapse. Besides, Leclerc knew that if France accepted their deportation it would deprive the French Army of a pretext to reassert French sovereignty in Annam and Tonkin.[55]

However, the sudden turn of political events in Paris did not help France in Indo-China, and laid the pattern for inconsistent policymaking over the colony for the next eight years. At the end of January 1946, shortly after his daughter Elizabeth's wedding to Alain de Boissieu, de Gaulle resigned. In spite of his position being confirmed by full and free elections, he was exhausted by the previous six years, and pressures had been building up for months. Not only had the "old beards" of pre-war French politics hatched out in full, France needed large armed services but could not afford them, the economy was in tatters leading to the devaluation of the *Franc*, and the old defects of the Third Republic's constitution were resurfacing. On top of this, de Gaulle, great though he was, was also capable of enough vanity to imagine that if he resigned he would be coaxed back into office within a few months. In fact, he was out in the cold for thirteen years.

De Gaulle's replacement was the socialist Felix Gouin, a lawyer from Marseilles who had defended Leon Blum when Vichy attempted a show trial to discredit former members of the 1930s *Front Populaire* government. Although a gutsy advocate, Gouin was a more conciliatory character than de Gaulle. Indeed de Gaulle despised *le petit Gouin*. But the question now was: what policy would Gouin adopt for France in Indo-China?[56]

For all his determination that France should recover her *rang*, de Gaulle left no instructions on how the Indo-China policy should continue. Surprisingly perhaps, it was d'Argenlieu who was more deeply affected by this than Leclerc. The admiral returned to Paris for talks with the new government. Before his departure the sailor-priest instructed Leclerc on no account to use the word "independence" in talks with Ho Chi Minh. Ho had some warning of the likely French position via the American diplomat Kenneth Landon, and was immensely disappointed. At that time the

USA was itself granting independence to the Philippines.[57]

French talks with the Chinese progressed sufficiently to enable French troops to garrison those parts of the Sino-Vietnamese border used for gun-running, and Leclerc received the go-ahead for landings in Haiphong Bay in March. The French were due to relieve Chinese forces by March 31st, 1946, but Chiang Kai-Shek's army was short of cash and riven by petty warlords who wanted to drag out their departure until after the opium harvest in June. Finally, the French managed to get a departure agreement out of the Chinese at Chungking on 6th March.[58]

In early February, Salan advised Ho Chi Minh to cooperate with a French return. Ho, however, hated that idea and warned Salan that, while they loved the French, the Indo-Chinese would no longer live in slavery. Ho only agreed to a French return if the liberty of his people was accepted by the French government. At this point Leclerc began to show himself more realistic than d'Argenlieu. The admiral saw no reason for France to give concessions, but Leclerc and Salan saw in the concept of *autonomie* (carefully not mentioning the word "independence") an opportunity for the Viet Minh to keep face without eroding French prestige.[59]

At this time Ho Chi Minh still thought it necessary to retain French goodwill, certainly until the Chinese left, though he was undoubtedly being disingenuous.[60] On February 18th, Sainteny cabled Paris that he had persuaded Ho to abandon his demand for the word "independent" in any peace settlement, and agree to Vietnam's inclusion in the "French Union," provided Vietnam was allowed "self-government." Surely, thought Ho, the new French socialist government, committed to improving life for France's working classes, could not deny similar freedoms to colonial peasants? But while France's new government found its feet, political responsibility for Indo-China fell on the conservative shoulders of Admiral d'Argenlieu.[61]

Ho Chi Minh recognised that Sainteny, like so many European de-colonisers, expected to see the beginnings of Western-style democracy, with all groups in Vietnam involved in the settlement. Ho had no intention of going down that road. His brand of Communism was essentially Indo-Chinese, and he knew his people were not ready for Western-style democracy. He also knew that a showdown with the French was inevitable at some stage, so the Viet Minh government secretly prepared for war, with evacuations of children and elderly from Hanoi and the organisation of self-defence and home guard units.[62]

Jean Lacouture, a future foreign editor of *Le Monde*, was a correspondent in Hanoi at the time who knew his way around the Viet Minh leadership. He found the spectacle-wearing intellectual Tran Huy Lieu had little to discuss other than French "crimes." General Giap happily admitted that he would force France's hand if it came to a fight, and the indolent former emperor, Bao Dai, was utterly sceptical about an agreement with the French. Ho Chi Minh's own views were a strange mix of Gandhi-like peacability and belligerence. To French journalist Jean-Michel Hertrich, Ho said "France is a strange country. It is full of admirable ideas but when it goes travelling it does not export them." To P.M. Dessinges of *Résistance*, Ho remarked "We want to, we must, reach a private settlement. But mark my words, if we are forced to fight, we are determined to fight to the end."[63]

Ho Chi Minh's most extraordinary act that February before the French landings was to ask the former emperor Bao Dai, whom he had deposed the previous August, to resume power. Exhausted, Ho admitted to Bao Dai, "I don't know what to do. The situation is critical. I have well understood that the French will not treat with me. I have been unable to obtain the confidence of the Allies. The entire world finds me too 'red.'"

After a few hours consideration, Bao Dai decided to accept. But, even in that short time, Ho changed his mind, saying, "Please forget all that I told you this morning. . . . To return power to you now would be an act of treason on my part. I beg you to excuse this moment of weakness. I had planned to resign above all because of the opposition of nationalist parties to the accords we are preparing with the French."[64]

Returning from Paris to Saigon on 27th February, d'Argenlieu agreed to the deal Sainteny was trying to work out: a "British dominion"–style solution whereby Indo-China would have its own elected parliament, tax affairs and its own armed forces. D'Argenlieu insisted that Indo-China should remain under the "French Union" for the conduct of foreign affairs and, subject to referendum, should remain three separate countries.

Next, France agreed to relinquish its port concessions in Canton and Shanghai on the Chinese mainland, and the Sino-French accord was finalised.[65] Leclerc finally received a telegram from Paris saying that the French fleet could sail to Haiphong.

The CEFEO had spent February preparing for the Tonkin landings. The pacification of the south had been especially hard on vehicles, halftracks and tanks, none of which were new anymore. Massu had long waited for spare parts, including tank treads and tyres, to arrive from France. The show of force for Hanoi also included the Armée de l'Air's British-built Spitfires, and the biggest French amphibious fleet since Gallipoli was assembled under Admiral Auboyneau. At midday on 26th February, troop landing ships appeared at Cam Ranh Bay to take Leclerc's force on board.[66]

Leclerc sailed north on the cruiser *Émile Bertin*, while Massu's force boarded two LSTs and the cargo ships *C. Porché, Barfleur, Céphie, Bételgeuse* and *Espérance*. The warships and cargos sailed north separately, reuniting in the Gulf of Tonkin on 5th March. The next day, the fleet sailed up the Song Cua Cam estuary heading for Haiphong. The cruiser *Triomphant* led the way with the 9e DIC commander, General Valluy, aboard. Behind came Massu's LSTs. Cruising upriver, the Frenchmen admired the serenity of the northern Vietnamese coastline. Then, in spite of the Sino-French accords, the French convoy came under sustained machine-gun fire.

The open decks of warships offer little protection against raking machine-gun fire, and the LSTs, their decks loaded with vehicles and petrol, were particularly vulnerable. The French held their fire, watching little figures in green uniforms running amid the vegetation on the river banks. The efforts of General Salan and Colonel Quillichini in Chungking had gone for nothing, Leclerc's force had been fired on by the Chinese Army. While the wounded on the LSTs waited for the *Rochambelles* to reach them, their pitiful cries could be heard from the *Triomphant*. Smaller landing craft were easy targets, with men jumping overboard to save themselves, then needing pieces of wood thrown into the water to cling to until they could be pulled aboard a bigger boat.[67]

As they neared Haiphong's quayside the order was given to fire back at the Chinese. Warehouses were set alight, including an arms dump, but eventually white flags appeared. The Chinese were disconsolate at seeing their stores of loot go up in smoke. Colonel Gilles from Valluy's 9e DIC desperately waved a white flag at the quayside, hoping the Chinese would stop firing and talk. The Chinese commander, General Wang Lihuan, claimed not to know of any Sino-French agreements. Whatever was behind

the Chinese decision to open fire, it cost Leclerc's force thirty-two dead
and forty wounded, who were transferred to the *Béarn*.[68]

Leclerc was understandably furious, but he had known since the day
before that there could be trouble. On 5th March, wary of Viet Minh war
preparations, the Chinese government in Chungking had reneged on the
agreement. Hoping to block Chinese communications, agents controlled
by Repiton-Préneuf sabotaged Hanoi's central electricity supply, but to no
avail. Leclerc had been warned the previous evening that his fleet ought
not to land yet, but still had not expected that the Chinese would fire on
his men.[69]

Sensing the discord between the French and Chinese, Ho Chi Minh
spannered the works further by pressuring the French for more concessions
towards Vietnamese independence. Taking a lot on himself, Sainteny
agreed to a referendum in all three countries of Indo-China, but still excluded the word "independence." This was the atmosphere of uncertainty,
almost chaos, in which the French fleet had sailed up the Song Cua Cam
River to reoccupy Haiphong.

Even while the French and Chinese exchanged fire in Haiphong bay
that day, negotiations between Sainteny and Ho Chi Minh continued.
Sainteny now agreed to Vietnamese "self-government" within the French
Union if the Vietnamese agreed that 15,000 French troops should replace
the departing Chinese. After they signed, Ho Chi Minh told Sainteny, "I
am sorry, because fundamentally you have won the contest. You were well
aware that I wanted more than this. But I realise that I cannot have everything at once. My consolation is our friendship."[70]

That same day, General Giap met Leclerc in Haiphong to agree on cantonments for the incoming French forces. Jean Lacouture witnessed their
initial meeting and noticed a bemused expression on Leclerc's face when
Giap declared, "As a Viet-namese resistance fighter, I salute you as a great
French resistance fighter."

Leclerc replied, "Long live France and Vietnam within the French
Union!"

The Chinese Nationalist Army agreed to allow 5,000 French troops to
land on 8th March provided they kept to the western sector of Haiphong
town. Massu made his HQ in the old Shell offices. For ten days, the French
waited warily amid torrential rainstorms, mindful for their own safety,

ready to march on Hanoi as soon as they received the green light.[71] A few weeks earlier, the Viet Minh might have threatened that a French return to Hanoi would be cut to pieces, but the determination shown by Leclerc's force at Haiphong in the face of Chinese resistance unnerved the Chinese and the Vietnamese as well. However well organised Giap's fledgling Viet Minh army might have been in March 1946, it was not yet ready to take on the French. Giap knew this. In his first meetings with Leclerc he was so self-effacing and humble that Leclerc, now one of France's foremost soldiers, did not know what to make of him. Giap also saw, like Ho, that the Viets needed the French to see off the Chinese.

For the next few days, the Chinese packed up and headed for the border. Then, in the early morning of 18th March, Massu's *groupe de marche* set off for Hanoi, leaving a contingent at their base camp under Compagnon. They drove for 100km along a dusty road rutted with potholes, and eventually reached a Chinese roadblock where a nervous guard opened fire on the leading Jeep. Luckily there were no casualties. The Chinese wanted to control how many French vehicles entered Hanoi while they still could, but, at 11.30am, the French reached the long steel and concrete Pont Paul Doumer which crosses the Red River outside the city. Built in 1902 in a style similar to the Fourth Railway Bridge, and as long as the Champs Élysées, the bridge had two lanes with a railway track in the middle. The French had to take one lane, the left, which was sufficiently tight for any breakdown to cause a considerable hold-up. Getting the convoy across took all afternoon. Leclerc stood at the northern end with his walking stick as if he was on the road to Paris again.[72]

They had reached Hanoi, and in French eyes, the "last stage of the liberation" was complete. The irony was that the indigenous population regarded Leclerc and his men as returning occupiers. Only *les colons* were truly happy to see them. *Groupe Massu* paraded through Hanoi to the acclaim of that French expatriate community, who were thrilled to have the liberators of Paris come to their rescue. The Vietnamese looked on, wondering if they would ever be independent, and fearing the French were too strong for them.[73]

The ironies of this last "liberation" were not lost on Leclerc. He had not forgotten Mountbatten's wise words, even if he could not follow them. In the south he had gone in hard and it had been a success. Now he paused for thought. With only an infantry division and Massu's group split between Hanoi and Haiphong, Leclerc knew that if Giap recognised the extent of French vulnerability, and had the will to take them on, the CEFEO would be in serious trouble.

That afternoon the Vietnamese were content to behave impeccably, decorating Leclerc's vehicles with French and Vietnamese flags. Arriving at a reception in the Northern Palace, journalist Jean Lacouture watched Leclerc run up the steps of the residence to greet Ho Chi Minh, exclaiming in his deep voice, "Well, *Monsieur le Président*, so we meet as friends!" Considering that their backgrounds were poles apart, many observers, especially Jean Sainteny, found it surprising to see Leclerc's warmth when greeting such a well known Communist trouble maker. A few days later Ho remarked to French journalist, P.M. Dessinges, "Leclerc? He is a loyal, upright man—a *chic type*, as you say in French. If only one could always talk things over with men like that." As proof of his good will, Leclerc suggested that Viet Minh fighters should become part of his personal excort.[74]

The very same day, Ho Chi Minh sent former emperor Bao Dai to Chungking to request Chinese support for the Viet Minh against the French. And his interior minister told the Viet Minh rank and file, "Vietnam will revenge itself on France which has so long oppressed it. In two years time there will not be a single Frenchman left in Indo-China. For that we will make life impossible for them."[75]

Suspicious, but unaware of the power of the storm brewing, *Groupe Massu* and Valluy's 9e DIC found quarters in the Lycée du Protectorat and the Citadelle. *Colons* invited them for meals and parties, making the next few weeks an idyllic time. Leclerc inspected and saluted the Viet Minh guards at his villa as though they were his *anciens*, toasting their joint future whenever the opportunity presented itself.

Admiral d'Argenlieu, knowing that Ho Chi Minh's behaviour was less than frank, could not understand what Leclerc was up to. He thought Leclerc was behaving far too liberally and making over-generous, Munich-like concessions to Ho Chi Minh and Giap who, in their turn, were laughing. Perhaps d'Argenlieu was smarting that Leclerc was doing too much on his own without referring back to him. Both Leclerc and d'Argenlieu were authoritarian characters, but d'Argenlieu was more so. Plus, d'Argenlieu was a long way south and may have felt uncomfortably removed from the centre of political and military action. A conversation between d'Argenlieu and French journalist Philippe Devillers later that year suggests that the admiral thought it his duty to maintain stability until his true master, de Gaulle, returned to power![76] Either way, the ascetic admiral's worries were symptomatic of the inconsistencies that dogged French policy in Indo-China right through until 1954.

With the benefit of hindsight, Leclerc's soldierly *bonhomie* towards Ho and the Viet Minh, a gracious slide towards a looser relationship, had some wisdom to it. Perhaps that was the tack Mountbatten might have tried in a similar position, especially since the French government was showing little interest. In Paris the view of the French left, whether Socialist or Communist, was already "Not a man, not a gun, not a *sou* for the war of conquest in Indo-China." The left wing press even called them, "The *cagoulard* General Leclerc de Hauteclocque and the reactionary admiral and former priest, Thierry d'Argenlieu, are the missionaries of civilisation sent to the Annamite people."[77] For his part, Leclerc knew that without the political will to retain Indo-China, France was on a route to nothing.

Incensed that troops from France's élite armoured division seemed more interested in treating than fighting, d'Argenlieu indulged in a crude show of imperial force. He ordered a naval review of the French fleet in the Bay of Tonkin. Ho Chi Minh was invited aboard the *Émile-Bertin* to watch warship after warship steaming past.

At the reception afterwards in the *Émile-Bertin*'s ward room, General Raoul Salan witnessed the tail end of an angry exchange between d'Argenlieu and Leclerc, most of which had taken place behind closed doors. The admiral, white with anger, finished off by reminding Leclerc, "*Mon général*, here you are *my* military delegate!" Leclerc seemed to respond with an air of discourteousness. The phrase "an Indo-Chinese Munich" was in the air once again. Yet Salan, a future opponent of de Gaulle when he relinquished Algeria, and no anti-colonialist, had been in Hanoi throughout those days of March 1946 and neither saw nor heard anything from Leclerc that suggested appeasement, let alone "concession upon concession."[78]

Nor did d'Argenlieu's show of force impress Ho Chi Minh. Before Leclerc and Salan left the *Émile-Bertin*, Ho remarked to Salan, "If the admiral thinks I was cowed by his mighty fleet, he is wrong. Your dreadnoughts will never be able to sail up our rivers." A few days later Ho wrote to Chiang Kai-Shek again, this time begging for help in putting an end to French military parades![79]

The state of uncertainty over the future of Indo-China's different nations could not be left hanging, so a conference was proposed for mid-April at Dalat, a gracious little town which served as a French Simla to *les colons*. The French largely had freedom of movement in Cochin-China but clashes were still occurring. An arms depot near Leclerc's Saigon villa was blown up, with shrapnel even landing in his usual armchair, and a spate of murders and kidnappings of pro-French Vietnamese notables began, which lasted all summer. Yet, to Giap's dismay, d'Argenlieu refused to discuss Cochin-China with them at Dalat. It also became clear to the Vietnamese that the so-called "French Union" would be a federation in which Indo-China formed merely a part, and certainly not as a sovereign state. Ho Chi Minh and Giap returned to Hanoi disappointed, while saying euphemistically that "Both sides now understood each other better."

In fact, there was very little more to understand. Ho Chi Minh and Giap wanted the French completely out of their homeland while the French preferred not to go at all; but if they had to, they wanted to leave on the most favourable terms possible, keeping their prestige. Furthermore, the Viet Minh method of conducting warfare, reasonably courteous conversation from leaders while their underlings carried out campaigns of propaganda, intimidation and terror, both hidden and open, was wholly foreign to men like Leclerc and d'Argenlieu. There were no divisional manoeuvres to predict and no battle plans. In the pattern of low-intensity wars during the decolonisation era, action mostly happened at platoon or even section level. Generals merely read reports. Leclerc hated this. It was not his style. Consoling himself in correspondence, he wrote nostalgically to his sister Yvonne about their childhood at Belloy St Leonard, "which for us represented something like paradise." Indo-China was, he said, a country where "Chinese and Annamites never fight in the open." *La chasse*, which he normally loved, merely offered more disappointment. "The tiger, instead of taking the bait, prefers an indigenous peasant! I console myself with shooting a few antelopes." Yet there was some amusement. "I am looking forward to being decorated with the Order of a Million Elephants and a White Parasol by the King of Laos who my men saved from being massacred last week, along with the rest of his family. You see, sometimes we do good things."[80]

The last remark was a reaction to the French liberal press, which refused to accept that the CEFEO's role had any use at all. When *Le Monde* quoted Tran Van Giau saying that France returned to Indo-China thanks to the British, and that "Monsieur Leclerc'" only offered guns, Leclerc was both furious and disappointed. He was not a publicity seeker, but finding himself blamed for the policies of others, not least his immediate superior Admiral d'Argenlieu, hugely contributed to the rift between them.[81]

While d'Argenlieu's supporters replied by accusing Leclerc of favouring de-colonisation, a letter to his sister Colette belies this. "We continue the fierce struggle to save Indo-China for France. Militarily it's done, though one would not want to say the whole country is pacified, but more or less. Now the *salopards* are more and more committing individual acts of assassination and terrorism."[82]

Another set of talks, this time in Paris, was scheduled for June. Then another election loomed in France, and d'Argenlieu asked Ho Chi Minh to postpone his departure. Ho refused, insisting the date was kept.[83] "If mistakes are not committed in Paris, the thing is won," Leclerc wrote de Gaulle somewhat optimistically.

By the time the Viet Minh delegation reached Paris, President Gouin's Socialist government had been replaced by a conservative one led by Georges Bidault, which was more in favour of retaining the empire. Ho Chi Minh arrived in France while the new government was being formed, and stayed with relations of Jean Sainteny near Biarritz, only reaching Paris in late June. Still, Bidault's government was not ready to negotiate, and Ho had to wait at Sainteny's estate in Normandy. He killed time by visiting the invasion beaches, days he later claimed were among the happiest of his life.[84]

Unlike Leclerc and Sainteny, however, d'Argenlieu was not prepared to negotiate with Ho Chi Minh. In this he demonstrated a lack of practicality which lay at the root of his disagreements with Leclerc. After eight months in Indo-China, and in spite of intermittent bouts of malaria, Leclerc believed there was much to be positive about, and that the Viet Minh would lose their virulence if handled calmly in a non-doctrinaire way. But by April 1946, d'Argenlieu had had enough of both Leclerc and Raoul Salan, and asked Juin to recall them to France.

Leclerc was delighted at the prospect of going home, but he did not yet believe that France's position in Indo-China was untenable. All his complaints were directed at d'Argenlieu for being "an authoritarian who commands little . . . except perhaps after the battle." If d'Argenlieu thought Leclerc "ungovernable," Leclerc equally thought that d'Argenlieu failed to govern and was vainly egocentric. "I cannot remain because *mon amiral-évêque* picks a quarrel every time I don't genuflect when I see him," he wrote to his sister Colette.

Separately, both de Gaulle and Juin prevailed upon Leclerc to remain a few weeks longer in Indo-China. De Gaulle appealed to his patriotism, while Juin offered a fifth star which would be deferred until his return. Juin did not like politics interfering with the internal workings of the army. Writing back to de Gaulle, Leclerc said, "I only want one thing, to disappear home to my wife and children. If France becomes uninhabitable, then a governor's position in an African colony would have been my preference, as I told you last year. If, once again, one must throw oneself into great struggles, like in 1940, for the good of our country, then we will do it. In leaving France to join you, I swore to struggle all my life if necessary. That motivation has not changed."[85]

Leclerc wiled away the last few weeks of his Indo-China appointment by relaxing in the company of old comrades, Lecomte and Guillebon in particular, but also Crépin and Reption-Préneuf. They all recognised that, however distasteful, relations with the Viet Minh should be maintained. On 14th July, Bastille Day, 1946, he was finally ordered to return to France. After briefing his replacement, General Valluy,[86] Leclerc wrote a last letter to d'Argenlieu: "Our ideas on the methods and procedures of command are not identical, and it is better that I bow out. You know yourself that the good running of the service cannot suffer divergence of viewpoints. I would, however, say how much I admire the high overview with which you appreciate the French interest. In this, I am fully with you. You have decided to save Indo-China, I wish very much that you succeed and I will do all that I can to help you. Please accept, Admiral, my highest regards. Leclerc."[87]

What to do with him now? Thanks to the war, Leclerc's career had peaked early, and some were not keen on giving very senior positions to young generals. Juin and de Lattre already held the French Army's most senior positions. However, the *Armée d'Afrique* needed re-organising. With his fifth star and a newly awarded *Médaille Militaire* on his chest, Leclerc would take the role of Inspector General of forces in French North Africa, a position previously created for Marshal Lyautey.

On the morning of 19th July, accompanied by Mirambeau, Langlois de Bazillac, Peschaud, the one-armed Valence and faithful Sergeant Loustalot, Leclerc boarded a Dakota without regret. First stop was Calcutta where they were met by Christian Girard who, already re-embarked on his diplomatic career, was now acting as Vice Consul. Working in a two-day tour, the men flew to Agra to see the Taj Mahal before continuing via Karachi, Baghdad, Cairo and Athens. On 25th July Leclerc landed in Rome where he was received by Pope Pius XII in a private audience at the Vatican. The Pope questioned him about Indo-China, but Leclerc was unable to answer in any detail.

Deep within himself, Leclerc was exceedingly disappointed at the outcome of his appointment in Indo-China. He did not even bother to change out of his tropical kit before landing at Villacoublay, where he was greeted by Juin, Legentilhomme and his old friend Louis Dio. He just wanted to see Thérèse and his children. He refused to take a requisitioned apartment, and went instead to the Hotel Crillon. "My task in Indo-China is over," he told Raoul Salan. "I do not want to get mixed up in the talks in any way. I am staying on the sideline. Good luck and safe journey." it seems certain that Indo-China was causing him mood swings. Salan later wrote, "He was in despair at not having been listened to."[88]

At a press conference at the Naval Ministry, towards the end of the Fontainebleau conference, Leclerc lashed out at the journalists without even waiting for their questions. "I will tell you at once, we only dealt with military matters. The rest was not my affair. In France you say nothing about what really happens there. In October 1945 the situation was extremely tense, no doubt. Today life in Indo-China has revived, but you write that we're on the verge of a break down."

"But there are always incidents!" a journalist remarked.

"Yes," acknowledged Leclerc tersely, "from *salopards* who recognise neither France nor Viet Nam, often Japanese deserters."

He shrugged off further questions with "That's not my affair!"[89]

Ho Chi Minh was still in Paris. He had tried to see de Gaulle but the great man was conspicuously staying out of public life, repairing his estate at Colombey-les-Deux-Églises after its trashing by the Germans. Leclerc is reputed to have avoided Ho at this time, believing it would be improper for him to pursue any sort of personal agenda. Nevertheless, Ho was determined to see Leclerc. He decided to surprise him at the Hotel Continental, which had been taken over for offices while the renovation of Les Invalides were completed.

Ho wanted to avoid a situation whereby all talks with the French broke down, something that seemed increasingly likely with Admiral d'Argenlieu, and he hoped to use Leclerc as an intermediary. On the afternoon of 2nd August, Ho presented himself at the Continental without any form of pre-arrangement and confronted Leclerc. Receiving him courteously, Leclerc listened for a few moments to what Ho had to say, but there is no record of what he said in return. Nevertheless, he refused to involve himself further, even when a few days later Ho offered sympathies when Leclerc's eldest son Henri, serving with the *Groupe Massu*, was wounded in Tonkin. Nor did Leclerc appear at any receptions hosted by Ho Chi Minh.

Franco-Viet Minh relations deteriorated through the latter half of 1946, and there can be little doubt that the refusal of the two greatest Free Frenchmen, Leclerc and de Gaulle, to receive Ho and speak to him exacerbated the atmosphere of distrust that had developed between the Viet Minh and the old colonial power. Strictly speaking, de Gaulle and Leclerc would have been acting improperly if they had had unofficial dealings with Ho Chi Minh, but the uncertainties of French metropolitan politics at the time undoubtedly left the Viet Minh leadership without any sense of continuity over who to negotiate with.

For a few weeks Leclerc enjoyed the summer and family life. On 9th August he was best man at Langlois de Bazillac's wedding and then returned to Tailly the following day, a simple family pleasure denied him since 1939. He had almost completely missed the formative years of his younger children, and except for attending the second anniversary of the Liberation of Paris, he spent the rest of that summer at Tailly, deliberately oblivious of news from Indo-China.[90] Former members of the 2e DB staff came for weekends and he launched himself into the start of the shooting season, always important to any Hauteclocque. When Langlois returned from honeymoon he visited Tailly to find Leclerc relaxed and rejuvenated, and even putting on a little weight.[91]

The Fontainebleau talks resulted in an impasse for Ho Chi Minh. D'Argenlieu ploughed ahead with his federated Indo-China, beginning with Cochin-China while leaving Tonkin and northern Annam as a problem to be solved another day. D'Argenlieu also supported the French plantation owners of the high plateaux, a course of action which utterly underestimated Viet Minh determination.

In the face of Viet Minh resentment, the French built a customs house at Haiphong harbour to control Vietnamese trade. Ho Chi Minh protested, saying such a measure was in direct opposition to the *modus vivendi* agreed at Fontainebleau. The French replied that the very existence of a "French Union" implied the right to supervise trade.[92] The stage was set for a Boston Tea Party, but the commodity turned out to be petrol. When French harbour police searched a Chinese junk carrying motor fuel, a Vietnamese guard post intervened, firing shots at the French motor launch. Soon barricades were set up in the harbour and throughout Haiphong town.

The Franco-Vietnamese joint commission managed to damp things down sufficiently for some normality to return to the streets, though the barricades remained and Vietnamese had managed to infiltrate the French quarter. Concerned for French safety and prestige, General Valluy ordered Colonel Debes to reassert French authority and demolish the barricades, using a bulldozer if necessary. Inevitably the bulldozer was fired upon, leading Debes, known to loathe the Viets, to order the French quarter "purged" of all Vietnamese. Maddened further by the death of a French officer, Debes' men performed their task with considerable gusto.[93]

Officials in Hanoi and Saigon even managed to calm this down, but no sooner had the dust settled than General Valluy ordered Debes to remove all Vietnamese armed forces from Haiphong. Valluy, Leclerc's replacement, had hitherto been regarded as a "liberal," but General Louis Morliere, previously senior to Valluy, protested that these new orders Valluy had given to Colonel Debes would result in French garrisons being attacked throughout Tonkin. Valluy insisted, declaring that "the time has come to give a harsh lesson to those who have treacherously attacked us.

By every means at your disposal you must take control of Haiphong and bring the government and the Vietnamese army to repentance." Reinforced by this uncompromising attitude, Colonel Debes demanded Vietnamese withdrawal from Haiphong or he would open fire. The battleship *Suffren* waited in Haiphong Bay to offer support. When the Vietnamese ignored his ultimatum, Debes troops and the *Suffren* opened fire on Vietnamese sectors of Haiphong. Even by conservative French estimates, casualties amounted to a staggering 6,000![94] It is hard to imagine an action more calculated to harden resistance against a colonial power.

Ho Chi Minh's government now saw all agreements made with the French during 1946 as null and void. An attempt was made to revive the old trust that once existed between Ho and Jean Sainteny, but when Sainteny arrived in Saigon, Valluy placed him under house arrest for six days! When he eventually reached Hanoi, Sainteny found in Ho only the friendship of men, not of countries. The talking was finally over. Amid the growing catalogue of incidents, including a French paratrooper running amok in Hanoi's Rue Vermicelles killing ten local people, there was little to be said but sad good-byes. Although Ho had been glad to receive Sainteny, once again he was simultaneously ordering the evacuation of Vietnamese children.[95]

Called to advise on Indo-China, Leclerc saw that intransigence on the behalf of d'Argenlieu and hot-headedness by Valluy and his subordinates had created a situation that could only be controlled by stronger forces. In a fuller opinion prepared during early December, he advised that French troops were sufficient in Cochin-China and Annam but not in the north. He acknowledged that Ho Chi Minh was hostile to French interests, but at least they knew whom they were dealing with. Leclerc suggested that France should learn from the British in post-war Egypt. "The English negotiated and flattered, but would not give up the Suez Canal. It's the method we used six months ago in Tonkin. It's not for me to compare Ho Chi Minh to King Farouk, but what needs to be done is to manage and flatter without losing what's essential."[96]

That same month the internal politics of France changed again. The Fourth Republic was formed. Vincent Auriol became President and Leon Blum, former *Front Populaire* leader of the 1930s, became Prime Minister.

Leclerc was preparing for his first Christmas at home since 1938, but, on 2nd December, with all hell breaking loose in Indo-China, Leon Blum called him to the Matignon. Blum, Jewish and a great man of the French Left, impressed Leclerc with his patriotism. Blum wanted Leclerc to return to Indo-China at once as his representative and report back to him on the full situation. Before departing he contacted de Gaulle who refused to discuss the matter, not wishing to be thought of as exploiting the situation politically.[97] One can only imagine Thérèse's feelings when Leclerc told her he would be spending another Christmas away from home.

Since his North African appointment, Leclerc had been accorded a converted B-25 Mitchell bomber rather than a Dakota. The aircraft was faster and had greater range, but the removal of hefty bomb bay machinery between the wings and installation of a *couchette* in the tail altered the balance of the fuselage, making the aircraft potentially unstable. North American, the aircraft's manufacturer, recommended that a Mitchell converted to passenger use should not carry more than five passengers, excluding crew. Leclerc's Mitchell had more seats than that, but *Bouncing Betsy*, painted in French colours and renamed *Tailly II*, was Leclerc's pride and joy.

Leclerc left Villacoublay on Christmas Day, accompanied by Repiton, Vézinet, Mirambeau, Bonningues, Valence and Sergeant Loustalot.[98] After a brief stop in Cairo where they dined with the French ambassador, *Tailly II* took off late on Christmas evening, but had to turn back when the pilot found the artificial horizon indicator, essential for night flying, was not working properly. Landing again at Cairo's Heliopolis airfield, Leclerc was furious, ranting unreasonably, "You certainly can't trust French pilots!" and getting angrier still when Egyptian customs insisted on searching their baggage again.[99] Repaired, *Tailly II* reached Saigon in three days, landing at Tan Son Nhut on 28th December.

Hearing that Leclerc was back in Indo-China, Ho Chi Minh offered him a meeting. Leclerc was expecting to be joined shortly by the Colonial Minister Marius Moutet, and did not feel he could act alone. He did not handle the wait well, pacing his office and thumping the floor with his stick. "It is imperative that we go, it is imperative that we do not let this opportunity slip. Oh, if only Moutet were here. I cannot do anything without his approval."[100]

Frustrated at Leclerc's apparent refusal to negotiate, Ho Chi Minh went on Radio Vietnam. In an extraordinary speech, obviously addressed to Leclerc, Ho said "We want the independence and unity of Vietnam. We wanted to collaborate fraternally with your country. Just supposing that you can fight us for a while, you still have a problem, because if you are strong materially, we are strong morally with a firm will to struggle for our independence. These preliminary successes, far from adding to your glory as soldiers and your patriotic dignity, can only compromise them. I know that you are good, and just, as well as brave, you have fought the war, so now perhaps you can make a just and honourable peace suitable for our peoples. Whatever the situation that others have created, it is necessary to be friends. We have decided to remain in the French Union, and to cooperate loyally with France and respect her economic and cultural interests, but we have also decided to struggle for our independence and national unity.

> A just peace would avert this situation. France would gain nothing from a colonial war. General and dear friend, I speak to you with an open and bleeding heart, bleeding because it is profoundly distressing to me to see French and Vietnamese soldiers about to kill one another when our countries are destined to live as brothers. I send you my best wishes for the new year.[101]

The speech was picked up by French listening services, as Ho intended it should be.

In the last days of 1946, Leclerc consulted officials in Saigon, both French and Indo-Chinese, before departing for Hanoi where he spent New Year's Eve with Sainteny, who had been injured a few days earlier. Sainteny was still able to communicate with Ho Chi Minh, but the diplomat felt "obliged to recognise that those men who declared themselves ready for a close and friendly cooperation with France don't seem to have any other purpose than to evict us totally from Indo-China, and submit to the dictatorship of a falsely democratic party."[102] Coming from someone who believed in negotiating with Ho Chi Minh as much as any Frenchman could, such a remark from Sainteny demonstrated the depth of the crisis following the Haiphong incident.

On New Year's Day, Leclerc, followed by Valence, left the French residence via a back window to make impromptu visits to French officers and soldiers guarding their perimeter. In Hanoi's French enclave the atmosphere was strained due to hostage-taking by the Viet Minh before Christmas. Leclerc flew to Haiphong, with *Tailly II* hedge-hopping to avoid Viet Minh gunfire, to see his eldest son Henri who was still recovering from his wounded arm. Henri had been put up for a Légion d'Honneur, automatic once a soldier has seven citations including wounds. With other wounded to see, Leclerc could only spend a quarter of an hour with his son, but Sergeant Loustalot stayed a while longer. They continued their fact-finding tour to Nam-Dinh and the old imperial city of Hué. *Tailly II* had to fly so low that she clipped the top of a tree, the jolt throwing Loustalot about so badly that Leclerc feared he might be injured. Bullets rattled and punctured *Tailly II*'s aluminium skin as they landed at Tourane, where Leclerc inspected and encouraged the embattled garrison before returning to Saigon. Only after landing did they notice the full damage to the aircraft, including a broken aerial wire.[103]

On 6th January Leclerc finally managed to meet up with Moutet. Until then they had kept missing each other. Cochin-China now had an "autonomous" government headed by Dr. Le Van Hoach, who made little secret that he regarded his country's so-called *autonomie* as a French trick, especially since his residence was so much more modest than the *Palais de Cochinchine* occupied by Cedille's successor, Governor Tourel. Stupefied at this arrangement, Leclerc was also angry to hear from Crépin that French personnel had been indulging in gratuitous cruelty towards civilians. For this, Leclerc called for General Morlière to be sacked. This was not the fairest thing he could have done because Morlière was more moderate and conciliatory than General Valluy, but Morlière was that most detested thing for Leclerc: a former *Vichyste*, who had previously planned operations against him in Africa on the orders of the collaborationist Admiral Platon.[104]

Seeing the escalating hostilities in Tonkin and northern Annam, Marius Moutet regarded Ho Chi Minh's appeals for peace and brotherhood as entirely specious. Increasingly, the official French view became that Ho Chi Minh was either two-faced or else so many Viet Minh wanted war that his utterances were irrelevant. In any case, Viet Minh attacks on French positions were clearly long-planned, only awaiting a pretext. D'Argenlieu felt vindicated by events, telling journalists from *Paris Soir*, "From now on it is impossible for us to treat with Ho Chi Minh."[105]

Leclerc reported his military view that the encircled French garrisons had to be relieved as a matter of priority, but the CEFEO was acquitting itself well under the circumstances. General Valluy's actions had undoubtedly caused the "Haiphong incident," but he now showed himself competent at stabilising the situation. As events forced France towards hard-line military choices, and the Viet Minh resorted increasingly to terrorism to unite Annam against the French, MacArthur's warning that large numbers of troops would be needed to regain control in Indo-China hit home. Twenty-five thousand European troops were needed straightaway from an army already at full stretch. Leclerc observed the growing anti-French sentiment in the country when the French military did not have the means to deal with the crisis, and he saw the uncompromising attitude of some French officers and *colons* as ludicrous and insufferable. "There are too many people here who imagine that a bridge between France and Vietnam can be built on a mound of cadavers."

In the medium to long term, Leclerc's report prepared for Leon Blum could only advise a political solution. On the long flight back to Paris, he redrafted it before landing back at Villacoublay on January 12th.[106] Admiral d'Argenlieu, who blamed everything on Viet Minh terrorism, regarded a negotiated solution as a betrayal of those Indo-Chinese who simply wanted to live in peace within the French Union. Fifteen months earlier Leclerc might have agreed with him.

Impressed by Leclerc's analysis, Blum asked him to take over from d'Argenlieu. Allowed a few days to consider the proposal, Leclerc conferred with de Gaulle who was, of course, wielding considerable influence from the sidelines. De Gaulle advised Leclerc to refuse, saying that replacing d'Argenlieu would look like weakness at a time when there were already more than enough political changes. It was also becoming clear to de Gaulle that Indo-China was an ulcer, possibly one that he had exacerbated, that would end badly for France. He did not want Leclerc caught up in it. "Don't repeat the precedent of Lyautey's dismissal by Pétain," de Gaulle said. "It followed him all the rest of his life. Between two 'Companions of the Liberation' such an event would be awkward and far from easy to explain." De Gaulle continued in a paternal tone, "Leclerc, you are young. Keep your prestige intact. Keep your position for dealing with North Africa where problems are developing for us. In any case, who knows when France is going to need you?"[107]

However, Blum's government was not ready to take "no" for an answer. Even the Communist Maurice Thorez told Leclerc, "You must go to Indo-China, *mon général*. You are the only one who can pull us out of this shit." However Leclerc knew a socialist government would never provide the military means to hold Indo-China.[108] Furthermore, Pierre Messmer, now back in Paris, had seen enough internal government memoranda to know that French policy in Indo-China was a mess that could only lead to disaster. "A glorious general like you would be the ideal scapegoat," Messmer warned. Through February politicians continued to nag him. Even President Vincent Auriol had a go. Leclerc vacillated, but still refused. The American ambassador Jefferson Caffery, who had been in France since the Liberation, knew enough about de Gaulle's backseat driving to write for the State Department's benefit that Leclerc would do as de Gaulle told him.[109] Boissieu's memoirs show that Caffery was right.

Leclerc, however, did not leave his government in the lurch, and continued to advise: "One must not say that one will never negotiate with Ho Chi Minh. D'Argenlieu might say it, but not the French government." Leclerc regretted the admiral's hiving off Cochin-China as a separate state, denying the rest of the country the Mekong rice paddies. "Who holds Cochin-China holds Indo-China. If Tonkin has not got Cochin-China it dies of hunger. Ho Chi Minh knows that." Eventually a replacement for d'Argenlieu was found. Émile Bollaert, a Gaullist political heavyweight in the league of Moulin and Chaban-Delmas, got the job. Warning Bollaert that no more troops were available, Leclerc's parting advice was "Negotiate. Negotiate at all costs!"[110]

With that, Leclerc's involvement in French Indo-China ended.

CHAPTER FIFTEEN

BACK TO FRENCH NORTH AFRICA

For Leclerc, life back in France was both a disappointment and an anti-climax. With the Socialist government under pressure from the increasingly powerful Communist CGT, Leclerc was horrified at de Gaulle's apparent total abdication from French politics. "You prefer to wait," Leclerc wrote to him. "But other than yourself, there is only one solution, Communism." When de Gaulle took the opportunity of the Bruneval Raid's fifth anniversary to announce the formation of the new populist centre right grouping, *Rassemblement des Peuples Françcaises*, the RPF, Leclerc gave his full support. He thought, however, that de Gaulle's new stance did not go far enough and should appear as something more than a riposte to the left. Leclerc did not believe that the average Frenchmen cared much for the finer arguments over the new constitution which so vexed de Gaulle over the next eleven years. Instead, Leclerc told de Gaulle which issues he believed ought to be addressed: "The serious crisis of the Empire, the financial crisis, the crisis in the armed services, the international situation, and the extreme and unusual power of the CGT."[1]

Ever the patriot, Leclerc was always sorrowed to see Africa increasingly fall under the influence of the British and Americans, or else the Communist bloc. His socio-political views remained those of a continental European. Accompanied one evening by Valence and Duplay to the

Vélodrome d'Hiver, the cycling arena used for so many diverse purposes during the 1940s, from party rallies to rounding up Jews in 1942, or *collabos* in the wake of Liberation, Leclerc sat with his aides close to the track's edge as opposing teams from the USA and Europe played *roller-catch*, or roller skate relay-racing. Leclerc cheered for Europe at the top of his voice.

From his office in Paris he would saunter out during the lunch break to stroll along the Champs' Élysées or browse in the Left Bank's numerous antique shops. If it were a sunny day with many people about, he would invariably be recognised even if wearing a civilian suit. Sometimes the effusive thanks were too much and he would hide in his Horch.[2]

Nor was family life easy. His brother Guy, now head of the Hauteclocque family, found it difficult being in the shadow of his famously mettlesome younger brother and preferred to avoid contact. The broader cousinhood to whom Leclerc was related had often been *Vichysois*, and were well aware of his uncompromising stance since René de Tocqueville had visited 2e DB's HQ during the Normandy campaign only to be quickly shown the door. And, however deeply he and Thérèse loved each other, sharing six children, like so many married couples separated by wartime and different experiences, they had become strangers in some respects. Leclerc was frequently surprised at how "hands on" and practical his wife had necessarily become, even though his parting letter in 1940 advised her to garner plenty of ready cash, fat to preserve food, and to listen to the peasants!

"You should not be doing that," he exclaimed, catching her scrubbing a bath.

"Of course," replied Thérèse teasingly. "Even in a pearl necklace, I could do this."

Hint taken. It was time for wartime austerity to end. The dour general bought his wife some pearls.[3]

Leclerc had wanted the North African appointment since the European war ended. Pressures for independence were smouldering throughout French North Africa, but had not yet erupted into a full-scale war. Remembering how France's slow return to Indo-China was advantageous to rebel movements, Leclerc advised that prevention was better than cure.

Once again he demanded full authority over air and sea forces in the region as well as the army. In April he got it.

As with Indo-China, French North Africa suffered from a lack of interest in the Métropole. Forms of Communism were influential among the working classes, but usually linked to aspects of Islam. General Duval's swift punitive action following the Sétif incident might have squelched the possibility of rebellion in Algeria for a while, but in Morocco the threat to France was provided by the Sultan's nationalism and pan-Islamism. In High Commissioner Eirik Labonne, nominated by the Socialist government, Leclerc saw nothing but weakness.

"Certainly one must know how to evolve," he wrote to Leon Blum's replacement, Paul Ramadier, "but to evolve in weakness, in losing face in front of the Arabs, is to disappear." Besides, Leclerc believed with justification that many ordinary Moroccans preferred French rule to an Islamic monarchy, and that, with reforms in place, France could remain there.

Jean Lecomte's wartime *attentisme* was now long forgiven, and Leclerc used him as a sounding board to vent his patriotic sense of frustration. "We lost the campaign of 1940 because we had at the head of our armies highly intelligent men who lacked character. Are we ever to lose an advantageous position for such a reason?" With a sultan who was clearly selfish and hostile, the last thing Leclerc thought France needed was a weak High Commissioner like Labonne.

Leclerc began bringing in his team. André Gribius, now recovered from his facial injury, gave up an instructor's position at Saumur to return to his old chief, and Buis was called to Rabat straight from Saigon. Tanks were assembled for a show of force if necessary, and Lecomte did his best to alert French public opinion to the Moroccan problem by writing letters to *Le Monde* under a pseudonym. That was enough for Premier Georges Bidault to demand Labonne's recall in the Council of Ministers, and Marshal Juin took over as High Commissioner. Morocco remained French until 1956.[4]

Leclerc would have loved the Moroccan post himself. But, as a five star general at an age when most officers could hardly expect more than a colonelcy, he undoubtedly attracted jealousy, even hate. But the role of inspector of armed forces in French North Africa gave him a different type of scope. Nostalgic as well as patriotic, he took the opportunity to visit scenes of past triumphs. *Méhariste* Colonel de Sarazac was now governor of French-occupied southern Libya, and able to facilitate trips to places like Murzuk, where he saluted d'Ornano's grave, as well as Oum el Araneb, Traghen, and Sebha, where school children sang the *Marseillaise* for him.

Leclerc recognised that Algeria would become France's biggest problem. While he understood that any rebellion would be fuelled by the frustrated aspirations of ordinary Algerians who, having seen their young men fight and die for France in two world wars, now expected a similar standard of living, Leclerc's main concern was to have enough troops in place to squash it forcibly when it occurred.

The Métropole, however, had more pressing concerns. The first year of the Auriol presidency was beset with scandals from left and right. Following the imprisonment of Pétain, *épuration* (the purging of former *collabos*) was taking a deeper and more corrosive turn with arms caches and wanted traitors being discovered in convents and monasteries. Former Vichyites were far from apologetic, and the old Maurassian right wing of former *Action Française* supporters was still alive and kicking. De Gaulle was the target of their hatred, just as much as the Left, and rumours of assassination plots against him were widespread, even though he was out of power. For its part, the Communist press was ever anxious to link prominent Gaullists to the old French right, be it Koenig, de Larminat or Leclerc himself.[5]

Yet anyone who met Leclerc could tell he was not a natural politician and had no intention of becoming one. Although he sent officers in *mufti* to RPF meetings to report on the progress of de Gaulle's political brainchild, Leclerc was also acutely aware that he remained a government servant and was only able to see his former master privately.

Only in October, with the chill winter of 1947–48 already setting in, did Leclerc finally have a semblance of the homelife he last knew in 1938. The government apartment at 26 Avenue Kléber housed Thérèse, their four younger children, and his soldier servant, the faithful Sergeant Louis Loustalot, who refused demobilisation to stay with Leclerc.

Such fidelity was not unanimous, however; Guy de Valence, Girard's successor in May 1945, used his position to help friends get looted vehicles out of Germany. A trivial racket perhaps, but inappropriate under the circumstances. Leclerc flipped when he found out. "You should be working!" he shouted at Valence, while giving the young *aide* a tug on the ear as if he was a teenager. Believing such treatment beneath his dignity,

Valence insisted on being allowed to leave the army forthwith. Amazingly, Leclerc, supported by Colonels Vézinet and Fieschi, asked him to reconsider. The Bilko-like car-trading would be forgiven if Valence got on with his work, but Valence refused, determined to chuck two and a half years of loyal service over a trivial incident. To show bigness of heart, Leclerc even included the now-former aide in the first dinner party he gave at the Avenue Kléber apartment. Still no use. Would a nice little trip to Tamanrasset to see Père Foucauld's tomb tempt the sulking Valence? It would not. Ah, well. The one-armed Valence intended to return to civilian life in any event since a diplomatic career awaited him, and he would have been invalided out of the army anyway. It was sad for him, however, to depart on such a note. Yet in doing so, he possibly saved his life.[6]

If Valence had no premonition of disaster, the same cannot be said for his replacement. Robert Miron de L'Espinay was a Saint-Cyrien and career soldier, unlike his two predecessors, but with the necessary social polish and enough citations from Indo-China for his comrades not to resent him taking up this obviously privileged position. Even so, Miron did not see himself as an ADC or equerry type.

"I don't know if I am going to do this," Miron told Valence, whom he had visited to learn about the job.

"You have a wonderful opportunity," replied Valence. "Look at the amazing journey you'll have."[7]

The persuasion worked, perhaps because Miron de l'Espinay had his romantic side, often repeating that he wanted "to know a great love and die young." Maybe this verged on premonition; alternatively he may simply have seen too many operas.

There is no reason to say that Leclerc had any premonitions, or that any of his entourage thought him "marked by death" like, for instance, the Japanese Marshal Yamamoto shortly before US Lightnings shot him down into the Pacific.

Leclerc had entrusted both Girard and Langlois de Bazillac with important papers that would be needed in his memoirs. But given that Leclerc's role was of signal importance to France's recent history, that was fair enough. Girard had a strong academic background and had become a diplomat, while Langlois had been present throughout Leclerc's involvement in Indo-China.[8] A trip to Germany to visit the French Army of

Occupation's HQ at Baden-Baden was nothing unusual, nor, given France's need to celebrate those few wartime events in which she could take real pride, was Leclerc's arrival in Strasbourg on 23rd November for the third anniversary of the city's liberation.

At the apartment on Avenue Kléber, Leclerc affirmed from faithful Loustalot, "You won't abandon *Madame*, right?" But there may have been nothing in that either. Paris was a restless place at this time, and the process of national healing after the Occupation was clearly going to take more than three years. Only his youngest daughter, Bénédicte, said decades later, "He was especially gentle. We did not doubt that this was the last time we would see him, that there would be no more repeated, joyful ringing of the front door bell to say he was home from a trip or from *4 bis des Invalides*."[9]

Since the air crash that killed Leclerc occurred many years before black box recorders, little is known about events on the aircraft as it flew from Arzew to Colomb-Béchar. In view of North American's stipulations for converting Mitchell bombers to passenger use, it is clear that Leclerc's aircraft should not have been carrying so many passengers. On its own, however, this may not have been fatal. And if one is looking to the condition of the aircraft for an explanation, factors such as bullet damage sustained during Leclerc's last visit to Indo-China have to be taken into account. It must also be remembered that the artificial horizon meter had malfunctioned during the outward journey. Through both the war, and during her time as Leclerc's personal aircraft, *Bouncing Betsy–devenu–Tailly II* had taken quite a beating.

Yes, there was a sandstorm, but it seems quite clear that neither Leclerc nor his pilot, Francois Delluc, saw any reason to be phased by that. Subsequent inquiries indicate that there was no reason to believe that Leclerc's pilot lacked experience or competence.

De Gaulle realised early on that an assassination was unlikely, since the crash happened when *Tailly II* was already overdue at Colomb-Béchar. Even so, in the years since Leclerc's death, French conspiracy theorists have had hours of fun over the so-called "thirteenth body" believed to have been found at the crash site. Perhaps the additional body's existence can be attributed to the ramshackle nature of the forensic operation in Algeria in

the hours immediately following the crash. Modern DNA testing could go some way to laying this mystery to rest if the relations of the crash victims and the authorities agreed to exhumation.

No evidence was found of explosive among the wreckage of *Tailly II*. But successful time bombs capable of destroying aircraft in flight do not have to be large in order to ignite fuel tanks. The fact that Delluc was clearly trying to land *Tailly II* alongside the Mediterranean-Niger railway indicates that he knew his aircraft was in distress. Once again, it was accepted practice for aircraft in trouble over the desert to try and find either a road, track or railway beside which to make an emergency landing. Belly-landed aircraft are hard to find in the wilds of the Sahara, and can go undetected for years, sometimes forever.

Nevertheless, these realities aside, France's conspiracy theorists have had their say. Even the British Secret Service has been suspected of assassinating Leclerc, for a hodgepodge of reasons related to oil rights in the Fezzan, which remained under French mandate until the 1950s. Though how the deaths of Leclerc and the others on board *Tailly II* could assist either the British government, BP or any other British oil company, is hard to imagine. This idea has to be placed alongside other instances of "paranoid Anglophobia" which periodically afflict the French. Besides, the British admired Leclerc and, though he had frequently irritated Churchill to distraction, they invariably admired de Gaulle as well.

Undoubtedly, in the immediate post-war era, French society was deeply divided and embittered, especially those who suffered most under the Occupation or who had backed the wrong horse by being fervently *Vichysois* or outright *collabos*. Among those, perhaps the strongest motive for attempting an assassination can be found in veterans of the Waffen SS's *Division Charlemagne*, twelve of whose members were shot by the 2e DB during May 1945. Following French military law as revised in 1939, Leclerc would rightly have regarded the guilt of such men as indisputable. Yet in the chaos of the war's end, when the grey areas of patriotism and collaboration were thrown up at every *collabo*'s trial during the *épuration* period, even de Gaulle had to take a more merciful viewpoint.

One survivor of the *Division Charlemagne* was Christian de la Mazière, the son of a well-known aristocratic family from the Loire, and whose father served with de Gaulle on the French military mission to Poland

during the Russo-Polish War of the early 1920s. Having spent his youth as a *Camelot du Roi*, selling *Action Française* after Mass on Sundays, Christain de la Mazière was just the kind of French right-winger to whom collaborationist politics appealed. At the same time, his charm and frankness brought him many friends, even among the resistance, some of whom advised him, as late as August 1944, that it was not too late to change sides. With bizarrely honourable consistency, however, on the eve of liberation La Mazière departed France for Janowitz outside Prague, where the *Division Charlemagne* was being formed from ex-*Gardes Francs*, *Miliciens* and patrician idealists like himself. La Mazière would not have felt out of place. One of the division's senior officers was called Bassompierre, scion of a family that produced one of Henri de Navarre's marshals, while the divisional chaplain was the immensely grand Cardinal Jean Mayol de Luppé, former bishop of Aix-en-Provence, who always finished a Mass with "*Heil Hitler*." In early 1945 these misfits marched off to face the Red Army in Pomerania, where the division was decimated and scattered. The few who survived as an identifiable unit fought the Third Reich's last act to its conclusion in Berlin the following May.[10]

An agreement between the Soviets and de Gaulle's government required all French personnel to be repatriated. Captured by a Polish division of the Red Army, La Mazière was soon on his way home, luckily having long lost his SS uniform. As he was screened the truth came out, and he was imprisoned in Fresnes. Once the clearing jail for captured *résistants*, Fresnes was now full of *collabos*, including many blue-blooded, snobby, right-wing intellectuals who gave young La Mazière the job of running the prison library while he awaited his trial. Their attitude among themselves to having chosen *le mauvais camp*, "the wrong camp," was pretty fatalistic, with strong feelings of "win some, lose some," and *che sara sara*. Some undoubtedly expected to be shot. When La Mazière's turn came at the Palais de Justice he was infuriated that arguments of youthful immaturity were included in his defence, believing it undignified. That a family friend and veteran of de Lattre's First Army should tell the court, "Shoot him if you want to, but he will face the firing squad shouting *Vive la France*!" seemed infinitely preferable to La Mazière. He was sentenced to three years in jail, albeit released on Easter Monday 1948, amid a period of "national indignity," a new punishment that *gaullisme* had created for postwar France.[11]

By contrast with La Mazière's fate, and the affability and understanding shown him at his trial, with men who had liberated *la Patrie* speaking up to save his young life, Leclerc's mercilessness to those French Waffen SS men who fell into his hands on 6th May 1945 does seem extreme. In the late 1940s many such men would have been given the opportunity of redeeming themselves by serving in Indo-China. Even André Gribius helped his pre-war friend Roger Vincent, who also fought with the *Division Charlemagne*, back into French uniform during this period.[12] However, since Gribius spent May of 1945 recovering from the jaw wound sustained at Royan, unlike Leclerc, he would not have seen the human knackers' yard of Dachau shortly before.

Even if the enmity of *Division Charlemagne* veterans for the execution of twelve of their comrades supplies sufficient motive for blowing *Tailly II* out of the sky (along with its other eleven passengers, several of whom also had solid Free French careers behind them) there remains a problem. While the *Charlemagne* veterans had the motive they lacked both the means and the access. They simply could not have done it.

That leaves the Communists. For most Frenchmen they were the first suspects. Yet somehow they lack the intensity of motive of the *Charlemagne* veterans, and given the outpouring of national grief that followed Leclerc's death (eclipsing even grief over the high death toll of the Arras railway crash, itself attributed to sabotage), it is quite clear that Leclerc was a national hero whose appeal crossed both political and class divides.

There is no barometer for measuring the grief of nations when favourite public figures die. Men like Roosevelt, Gandhi and Churchill undoubtedly deserved noble admiration, while the sudden and comparatively youthful deaths of President Kennedy and Princess Diana have a different and somehow more intense effect on the public psyche. Without a doubt, Leclerc's death brought France to a standstill. (Though some might cynically argue that industrial action had brought her to a standstill already!) De Gaulle read the public mood correctly when he told his aide Claude Guy that the funeral arrangements would be "quite something."

Leclerc's early achievements in Africa alone undoubtedly outstrip those of Lawrence of Arabia. "Free France" would not have been the entity it was without him. Nor, given the parlous state of de Gaulle's credibility following his failure to take Dakar in September 1940, would he have been able to impose his vision of France if Leclerc had not secured him a land base in Chad and the Cameroons. Leclerc kept de Gaulle in the game, and de Gaulle recognised that.

It may even be true to say that if Leclerc had lived he would have been the greater man. When de Gaulle reassumed power in 1958 he was 67 years old, not an age at which many "out to grass" politicians would wish to restart their career. But his health was in reasonable order and he had given up the chainsmoking which had sustained him through the war. It was rumoured that Leclerc's death precipitated de Gaulle giving up his beloved cigarettes. A few years later his son-in-law, Alain de Boissieu, asked him if the two events were connected.

"Perfectly," de Gaulle replied. "The evening of Leclerc's death I had a terrible pain and I thought I had better manage my energies because Leclerc was no longer there to render important service to France should it be necessary. Therefore it seemed to me that I had better be fit enough to do it in his place."[13]

In 1952, when the Indo-China war was at its height, the French government created three Marshals from the war generation of senior officers: Jean de Lattre de Tassigny, who was dying of cancer; Alphonse Juin, the *pieds noir* who would outlive them all; and Philippe Leclerc de Hauteclocque, whose award was posthumous. The *baton* was received by the same Captain Duplay who had greeted Leclerc's sons at the 2e DB's Bois de Boulogne enlistment office following the liberation of Paris.

Two years later, in the valley of Dien Bien Phu, the French suffered the worst single defeat inflicted upon a Western power by an Oriental nation since 1945. The war in Indo-China cost France nearly 40,000 dead, including a whole generation of Saint-Cyriens; more men than the USA lost in Korea. The fatalities included Leclerc's eldest son, Henri, and de Lattre de Tassigny's only son, Bernard. It was to Leclerc's credit that he had the moral sense to know when a war should be fought and when it should not. But, given the greater depth of feeling among Algerian French compared to *les colons* of Indo-China, it is difficult to speculate what his attitude might have been to the "dirty war" ended by Algerian independence fifteen years after his death. By its methods of repression, which included torture, the French Army disgraced itself in Algeria. Tragically, one of the men Leclerc mentored, Jacques Massu, was involved in this (though this never prevented Massu from becoming head of the French Army in Germany, with whom de Gaulle sought refuge during the student summer of 1968). Another of Leclerc's associates, Raoul Salan, was one of the four generals who attempted a coup against de Gaulle. De Gaulle also knew when a war should not be fought. While it must be recognised that both de Gaulle and Leclerc were undoubtedly colonialists, they both undoubtedly knew that colonialism's days were numbered.

It has often been said that the personality cult among French officers contributed to excesses committed by the French Army in Algeria. Men like Massu, Salan and the famous paratrooper colonel Marcel Bigeard, could not have been created but for the defeat suffered by France in 1940 and the burning sense of injured national pride it engendered. The broken chain of command caused by that defeat, and subsequent confusion over whether to follow de Gaulle or Marshal Pétain, gave regimental colonels, ships' captains and colonial governors greater authority to choose one way or another. In 1940 most Frenchmen chose Pétain. In 1943 most Frenchmen who were able to choose opted for de Gaulle.

Would Leclerc have echoed de Gaulle in saying to French forces "obey me" when they were faced with the prospect of yet another humiliation and abandonment of their *harkis*? How can one tell? In dying young, Leclerc's reputation was saved from being tarnished by France's decolonisation wars, and most French towns, unless very small, have a street or square named after him. Of France's war generation, only diehard Vichyites and the handful of veterans from the *Division Charlemagne* spit at his memory. The majority of Frenchmen believe Leclerc's early death deprived France and her army of a wise, experienced head at a time she needed it most.

ACKNOWLEDGMENTS

Most writers would acknowledge that their first book was the hardest. Not only does a confidence barrier have to be broken but several steep learning curves also have to be climbed. One also has to overcome the cynicism of the doubtful who wonder if one even has the 'bottom' to see such a project through. In this I have been helped by the kind encouragement of friends and relations; my mother Bea Mortimer-Moore knew from the unpublished novels of my young adulthood that I could cover paper even if nothing came of it. Cousins including John Bate-Williams and Bertie Garforth-Bles never made anyting other than kind comments. Once there was a substantive manuscript, albeit in need of polishing, I was able to call in many other friends and relations who shared my enthusiasm for history including David Michel, Catherine Mansel-Lewis, Helena Drysdale, Olivia Inglefield, my late uncle, David Wharry (who read through some of the manuscript shortly before he died) and Lord Hotham whose home was used by Leclerc as his HQ for three months during the summer of 1944 and who waded through all 200,000 words of the first draft. Published authors whose kindness has been sustaining throughout include Professor Saul David (whose advice at Catherine Mansel-Lewis's dinner table that I should tranfer my questionable talents from novel writing to history can be blamed for much though in a nice way), Giles Macdonogh, my invalu-

461

able email friend who was always there with a useful snippet of experienced and genially offered wisdom, Antony Beevor who read the first draft and thought enough of it to use it as a source in his book, *D-Day*, and Martin Windrow for his complementary foreward to this biography. But mostly in this regard I must thank my cousin Mark Whitcombe (who has written six excellent books under the name Mark Bles) who gave me a month of his time going through the whole book with a red pen advising where and how it should be tidied up. In return for this I have so far only given Mark ten days helping lay out his olive plantation near Toulon. More to come Mark.

Once the manuscript was presentable I nervously made contact with members of Marshal Leclerc's family to find out which of them could not only read English but was also prepared to check through what I had done. I was put in touch with his grand-daughter, Madame Bénédicte Coste, daughter of Leclerc's eldest surviving son Hubert Leclerc de Hauteclocque, who checked through and kindly remarked that she had found *"rien de choquant."* What a relief that was.

At Casemate I would like to thank Steven Smith, Tara Lichterman and Simone Drinkwater for making the production process of my first book so pleasant, laced with that admirable American 'can do' spirit. Finding photographs turned out to be quite daunting. In this I was helped by Dr Christine Levisse-Touzé and Cécile Cousseau at the Mémorial du Maréchal Leclerc de Hauteclocque et de la Libération de Paris/Musée Jean Moulin Ville de Paris. At the Musée de l'Ordre de la Libération Vladimir Trouplin and Béatrice Parrain were also immensely kind, as was Madame Dominique Vincent at ECPAD. I also found a surprising number of useful pictures in the photograph archive of the Imperial War Museum, where Yvonne Oliver could not have been kinder and the excellent Ian Proctor made my visit a memorable day.

Finally I would like to thank my inestimable agent Robert Dudley for his boundless enthusiasm for the project from the start of his involvement right through to placement and now with the next project which is in production.

William Mortimer Moore

NOTES

PREFACE

[1] Notin, Jean-Christophe. *Leclerc.* Perrin 2005. Page 473.

[2] Ibid. Pages 475–76 and General Jean Compagnon, *Leclerc. Maréchal de France.* Flammarion 1994. Page 596.

[3] Martell, André. *Leclerc. Le soldat et le politique.* Albin Michel 1998. Page 478. & Beevor, Antony (with Artemis Cooper) *Paris after the Liberation.* Hamish Hamilton 1994. Page 367.

[4] Compagnon. Page 597. Most French biographies contain chunks of this speech.

[5] Martell. Page 479.

[6] Notin. Page 478.

[7] Generals Hugues Silvestre de Sacy and Jean-Louis Mourrut. *Du capitaine de Hauteclocque au Général Leclerc.* Éditions Complexe (Essays) 2000. Pages 436–37.

[8] Notin. Page 497.

[9] Ibid. Pages 479–81.

[10] Ibid.

[11] Ibid. Pages 481–82.

[12] Guy, Claude. *En écoutant de Gaulle.* Grasset 1996. Pages 360–61.

[13] Beevor. Page 367.

[14] Norwich, John Julius (Viscount). *The Duff Cooper Diaries.* Weidenfeld and Nicolson 2005. Page 287.

[15] Ibid. Page 300.

[16] Ibid. Page 453.

[17] Notin. Pages 483–84.

[18] Ibid.

[19] Guy. This exchange appears on page 363.

[20] Ibid. Page 364.

[21] Lacouture, Jean. *De Gaulle. The Ruler. 1944–1970*. Collins Harvill 1990. Pages 144–45.

[22] Notin. Page 484.

[23] Ibid. Page 485.

[24] Ibid. Page 486.

[25] Boissieu, General Alain de. *Pour servir le général*. Plon. 1990. Page 37.

[26] Notin. Page 487.

[27] Ibid. Pages 487–88.

[28] Ibid.

[29] Gribius, André. *Une Vie d'Officier*. Éditions France-Empire. 1971. Page 194.

[30] Beevor. Page 372 and Norwich, John Julius. *The Duff Cooper Diaries*. Weidenfeld 2005. Pages 453–54.

CHAPTER 1

[1] Compagnon, General Jean. *Leclerc, Maréchal de France*. Flammarion. 1994. Page 20 & Notin, Jean-Christophe. *Leclerc*. Perrin 2005. Page 11.

[2] Martel, André. *Leclerc. Le soldat el le politique*. Albin Michel. 1998. Page 30.

[3] Compagnon. Pages 18–19.

[4] Weber, Eugen. *Action Francaise*. Stanford University Press 1962. Pages 6–16.

[5] Tourtier-Bonazzi. Page 58.

[6] Fourcade, Olivier. (same essay collection as Tourtier-Bonazzi) Page 36.

[7] De Hauteclocque, Comtesse Adrien. *Souvenirs*. (same essay collection as Tourtier-Bonazzi.)

[8] Tourtier-Bonazzi. Page 57.

[9] Ibid. Page 59.

[10] Compagnon. Page 26.

[11] Ibid. Page 28. The school were taken in by the École de Saint Joseph.

[12] Compagnon. Page 26.

[13] Martel. Pages 41–42.

[14] Notin, Jean-Christophe. *Leclerc*. Perrin 2005. Page 15.

[15] Martell. Page 43.

[16] Notin. Pages 17–18. The Grand Montreuil had been the home of Louise of Savoy, wife of restored Bourbon Louis XVIII.

[17] See Hastings, Max. *Military Anecdotes*. Hastings includes the story of Maud'huy 'smartening up' a *poilu* as he was being marched to the firing squad for sleeping on guard.

[18] Ibid. Page 45.

[19] Notin, quoting letter to Colette. Pages 18–19.

[20] Ibid. Page 19 and Martell Page 45.

[21] Martel. Page 46.

[22] Ibid. Page 53.

[23] Ibid. Page 56.

[24] Notin. Pages 19–20.

[25] Martell. Page 57.

[26] Ibid. Page 58.

[27] Compagnon. Page 41.

[28] Ibid. Page 44.

[29] Tourtier-Bonazzi. Page 64.

[30] Notin. Page 23.

[31] Horne, Alistair. *The French Army and Politics.* Page -

[32] Notin. Page 23.

[33] Ibid. Page 24.

[34] Martel. Page 60.

[35] Clayton. Anthony. *France, Soldiers and Africa.* Brasseys 1988. Page 271.

[36] Notin. Page 26.

[37] Langlade, Paul de. *En Suivant Leclerc.* Au fil d'Ariane. 1964. Page 15.

[38] Clayton. Page 115.

[39] Ibid. Pages 291–94.C

[40] Notin. Page 27.

[41] Compagnon. Page 51.

[42] Clayton. Pages 85–119.

[43] Compagnon. Page 51.

[44] Clayton. Page 115.

[45] Compagnon. Page 55.

[46] Vézinet, General Adolphe. *Le Général Leclerc.* Éditions France Empire. 1997. Page 34.

[47] Martel. Page 69.

[48] Clayton. Page 217.

[49] Martel. Page 71.

[50] Compagnon. Page 68.

[51] Notin. Pages 31–32.

[52] Martel. Page 73.

[53] Compagnon. Page 71.

[54] Martel. Page 73.

[55] Compagnon. Page 73.

[56] Ibid. Page 75.

[57] Jackson, Julian. *France: The Dark Years.* Oxford University Press. 2000. Page 99.

[58] Tournier-Bournazzi, Chantal. Pages 70–71.

[59] Weber. Page 266.

[60] Tourtier-Bournazzi. Page 72.

[61] Ibid. Page 73.

[62] Ibid.

[63] Martel. Pages 82–83.

[64] Ibid. Page 83.

[65] Tournier-Bournazzi. Page 73.

[66] Martell. Pages 83–84.

[67] Compagnon. Page 86.

[68] Martell. Page 76.

[69] Compagnon. Page 91.

[70] Ibid. Page 93.

[71] Notin. Page 38.

CHAPTER 2

[1] Horne, Alistair. *To Lose a Battle*. Macmillan. 1969. Page 320.
[2] Compagnon. Page 117.
[3] Ibid Page 121.
[4] Maule, Henry. *Out of the Sand*. Odhams. 1966. Page 25.
[5] Martel. Page 103.
[6] Martel Page 103 and Compagnon. Page 123.
[7] Notin, Jean-Christophe. *Leclerc*. Perrin 2005. Page 48.
[8] Maule. Page 26.
[9] Lacouture, Jean. *De Gaulle the Rebel. 1890–1944*. Collins Harvill. 1990. Pages 233–34.
[10] Girard, Christian. *Journal de Guerre. 1939–1945*. L'Harmattan. Page 16.
[11] de Gaulle, Charles. *Memoires de Guerre*. Vol 1. 1st Page.
[12] Gildea, Robert. *Marianne in Chains*. Macmillan. 2002 Page 158.
[13] Gildea. Page 397.
[14] Notin. Page 53.
[15] Ibid. Page 52.
[16] Compagnon. Page 130.
[17] Compagnon. Page 132 & Vézinet, General Adolphe. *Le général Leclerc*. Éditions France-Empire 1997. Page 155.

CHAPTER 3

[1] Notin, Jean-Christophe. *Leclerc*. Perrin 2005. Page 58.
[2] *Chef d'escadrons* and *commandant* are the French equivalents of the rank "major." But *chef d'escadrons* is exclusively used in the cavalry or tanks.
[3] Notin. Page 59.
[4] Jean Lacouture. *De Gaulle: The Rebel*. Pages 271–72. Collins Harvill. 1990.
[5] De Gaulle, Charles. *Memoirs de Guerre. L'Appel*. Plon. 1954. Page 101.
[6] Corbonnois, Didier. *L'Odyssée de la Colonne Leclerc*. Histoires et Collections. 2003. Page 12.
[7] Notin. Page 60.
[8] General Jean Compagnon. *Leclerc*. Flammarion 1994. Page 138.
[9] Ibid. Page 141.
[10] Henry Maule. *Out of the Sand*. Odhams 1966. Page 96.
[11] Ibid. Pages 48–49.
[12] Ibid. Page 49.
[13] Compagnon. Page 143.
[14] Maule. Page 59.
[15] Compagnon. Page 145.
[16] Compagnon quoting Lt. Denise, Page 146.
[17] Maule, Page 60.
[18] Ibid, page 61.
[19] Lacouture, Page 273.
[20] Compagnon, Page 153.
[21] Notin. Page 82.
[22] Compagnon quoting Raymond Dronne, page 153.
[23] Notin. Page 84.

[24] Maule. Page 77.

[25] General Mangin, known as the 'butcher,' was an important general during the battle of Verdun 1916 and greatly admired by Leclerc.

[26] Compagnon, Page 156.

[27] André Martel. *Leclerc. Le Soldat et le politique.* Albin Michel 1998. Page 142.

[28] Martel, page 142.

[29] Compagnon, Page 173.

[30] Maule, Page 79.

[31] Lacouture, Page 281.

[32] Lacouture. Page 286.

[33] Ibid.

[34] Ibid.

[35] Ibid.

[36] Ibid.

[37] Lacouture. Page 287.

[38] Ibid.

[39] Ibid, Page 288.

CHAPTER 4

[1] Along with another expedition from the Congo led by Ensign Émile Gentil, after whom Port Gentil on the Gabon coast was named.

[2] Fergus Fleming, *The Sword and the Cross.*Granta 2002. Page 155.

[3] Ralph Bagnold. *Sand Wind and War.* University of Arizona, 1990. Page 133.

[4] Saul Kelly, *The Hunt for Zerzura: The Lost Oasis and the Desert War.* John Murray, 2002. Page 142.

[5] Bagnold. Page 87.

[6] Saul Kelly. Pages 74–75.

[7] General Jean Compagnon. *Leclerc. Maréchal de France.* Flammarion, 1994. Page 188.

[8] Ibid. Pages 188–89.

[9] Saul Kelly. Page 148.

[10] Massu describes d'Ornano as a swashbuckler who enlisted in the Spahis at 19, then transferred to the Coloniale infantry for four years after which he was commissioned. He spent the whole interwar period in Mauritania, Morocco and Tchad. Seven years older than Leclerc, he was a Corsican gentleman from a family that had given France two marshalls since the sixteenth century as well as a the famous Corsican Sampierro d'Ornano. General Massu, *Sept Ans avec Leclerc.* Plon 1974, revised Rocher 1997. Pages 14–15.

[11] Saul Kelly. Page 140.

[12] Massu. *Sept Ans avec Leclerc.* Page 12.

[13] Henry Maule. *Out of the Sand.* Odhams. 1966. Page 81.

[14] Christian Girard. *Journal de Guerre 1939–1945.* L'Harmattan. 2000, revised from 1975. Page 25, entry for 21st December 1940.

[15] Colonel Garbay's 'bataillon de marche' of Tchadiens would join General Marie Pierre Koenig's First Free French Brigade and serve at Bir Hakeim in June 1942.

[16] Compagnon. Page 203.

[17] Notin, Jean-Christophe. *Leclerc.* Perrin 2005. Page 108.

[18] Ibid. Pages 108–09.

[19] Ibid. Pages 109–10.

[20] Compagnon. Page 204.

[21] This is the real Count Laszlo de Almasy upon whom Michael Oondatje based his fictional character for *The English Patient.* That novel bears very little relation to historical truth, although it makes a pretty film, and should only be read for personal enjoyment—if at all.

[22] Saul Kelly. Pages 28–29.

[23] Ibid. Pages 151–52.

[24] W.B. Kennedy-Shaw. *Long Range Desert Group.* Collins. 1945. Revised Greenhills 1989. Page 55.

[25] M. Chrichton-Stuart. *Guards Patrol.* William Kimber, London, 1958. Page 32.

[26] Compagnon. Page 204.

[27] Ibid. Page 205.

[28] Massu. *Sept Ans avec Leclerc.* Page 20.

[29] Ibid. Page 21.

[30] Maule. Page 85.

[31] Massu. Page 22.

[32] Ibid. Page 23.

[33] Henry Maule. Page 87.

[34] Ibid. Page 26.

[35] Ibid. Page 27.

[36] Both Massu and Kelly cover this part. Massu, Page 29. Kelly. Page 154.

[37] Compagnon. Page 210.

[38] Notin. Page 110.

[39] Compagnon. Quoting Jean de Pange.

[40] Ibid. Page 211.

[41] Compagnon, quoting Jean de Pange. Page 212.

[42] Ibid. Page 213.

[43] Notin. Page 123. Quoting a note from Leclerc to de Gaulle 1/1/1940.

[44] Compagnon. Page 214.

[45] Maule. Page 91.

[46] This was in fact the thirty-one year old Marquess of Lansdowne, whose usual surname is Petty-Fitzmaurice. However the name Mercer Nairne comes into the family from a lesser barony they hold. *Burke's Peerage. 1938 GVI Coronation Edition.* Some English aristocrats used *nommes de guerre* as well in case of capture. The Germans tended to regard distinguished prisoners as *prominente* and lock them in Colditz.

[47] Maule Page 93.

[48] Ibid. Page 96.

[49] Notin. Page 119 and Didier Corbonnois's *L'Odyssée de la Colonne Leclerc* Histoires et Collections 2003. Pages 118–19. On 6th February 1960 a French Air Force Noratlas landed at Villacoublay bearing the recovered bodies of the crew.

[50] Corbonnois. Pages 31 and 54.

[51] Maule. Page 97.

[52] Compagnon. Page 217.

[53] Compagnon. Page 217. & André Martel. Page 160.

[54] André Martel. *Leclerc. Le soldat et le politique.* Albin Michel, 1998. Page 160.

[55] Notin. Page 122.

[56] Ibid.

[57] Notin. Page 123.

[58] Martel. Page 161. Compagnon. Page 220.

[59] Corbonnois. Page 58.

[60] Ibid.

[61] Notin. Page 123.

[62] Ibid. Page 124.

[63] Dronne, Raymond. *Leclerc et le Serment de Koufra.* Éditions du Temps. (J'ai Lu) 1965. Pages 12526.

[64] Compagnon. Page 222.

[65] Dronne. Page 127. & There are excellent photos of the fort at Kufra and the Free French in possession in Didier Corbonnois' *L'Odyssée de la Colonne Leclerc.* Histoires et Collections 2003. Pages 60–61.

[66] 'Askari' is a name often given to indigenous African troops during the colonial era.

[67] Breda machine guns were greatly prized by the Free French and LRDG when they could be captured with enough ammunition.

[68] Compagnon. Page 224.

[69] Martel. Page 164.

[70] Charles de Gaulle. *Memoires de Guerre.* Vol. 1. Chapter 'Londres.' Librairie Plon, 1954.

CHAPTER 5

[1] Notin, Jean Christophe. *Leclerc.* Perrin 2005. Pages 133–34.

[2] Ibid.

[3] Ralph A. Bagnold. *Sand, Wind and War.* University of Arizona. 1990. Bagnold says on pages 133-5 that there had been little rain for seventy years which meant meat was hard to come by. Nevertheless the Sarra tribesmen, once they knew Kufra's markets were open again, would drive 'fat tail' sheep two hundred miles across the desert with only one watering hole, presumably Sarra. Another problem was the currency, the franc coming from an axis occupied country, the lire from a vanquished enemy. Bagnold laid down an exchange rate in line with the Occupied Eenemy Territory Administration.

[4] John Bierman and Colin Smith. *Alamein. War without hate.* Penguin Viking. 2002. Page 42.

[5] Conceived as an act of support for the Greeks, the raid on Taranto was carried out by Fleet Air Arm Fairey Swordfish biplane torpedo bombers. Three Italian battleships were maimed or sunk. The Japanese were greatly impressed by the daring of this attack and it influenced their thinking in planning Pearl Harbour.

[6] Notin. Quoting letter from Lt. Mercer Nairne. Page 136.

[7] General Jean Compagnon. *Leclerc. Maréchal de France.* Flammarion. 1994. Pages 237–39.

[8] Massu, Geenral Jacques. *Sept Ans avec Leclerc.* Librairie Plon 1974. Revised Éditions Rocher 1997. Pages 37–38.

[9] Ibid. Pages 38–39.

[10] Ibid. Pages 39–40.

[11] Ibid. Page 40.

[12] Ibid. Page 41.

[13] This same General Henri Dentz had conducted the surrender of Paris as an 'open city' to the Wehrmacht during 'La Chute.'

[14] Christian Girard. *Journal de Guerre 1939–1945*. L'Harmattan 1975. Pages 27–28.

[15] Notin. Pages 137–38.

[16] Ibid. Quoting a letter from Mercer Nairne to General Spears.

[17] Ibid. Pages 138–39.

[18] Girard. Page 28.

[19] Henry Maule. *Out of the Sand*. Odhams 1966. Page 110.

[20] Massu. Page 42.

[21] Ibid.

[22] Notin. Page 140. Quoting a letter from Leclerc to Captain Hausherr.

[23] Ibid. Pages 140–41.

[24] Maule. Page 109.

[25] Notin. Pages 145–46. Quoting letters from Leclerc to Pauline Vanier and René Pleven.

[26] Ibid. Page 146.

[27] Ibid. Page 147.

[28] Ibid.

[29] Ibid. Page 148 and Compagnon. Page 249.

[30] Ibid.

[31] Compagnon. Page 249.

[32] Notin. Pages 149–50.

[33] For the exact specification of British military rum I am grateful to my cousin Major Mark Whitcombe formerly of the Royal Green Jackets and 22 SAS. It's just the sort of detail he would know!

[34] Compagnon. Page 248.

[35] Massu. Pages 49–50.

[36] Maule. Page 109.

[37] Compagnon. Pages 251–52.

[38] Ibid. Page 253.

[39] Girard. Page 28.

[40] Massu. Page 49.

[41] Ibid.

[42] Girard. Page 29.

[43] Corbonnois, Didier. *L'Odyssée de la Colonne Leclerc*. Histoires et Collections 2003. Pages 85–87. & Bierman and Smith. Page 136. Plus Notin Page 153.

[44] Compagnon. Page 254.

[45] Ibid, Page 257. & Massu, Page 51.

[46] Ibid.

[47] Ibid. Pages 258–59.

[48] Notin. Page 154.

[49] 'Général de brigade' equates to a 'Brigadier General' in the British Army. This must not be confused with a French *brigadier* which is a non commissioned officer in either artillery or cavalry of the French Army.

[50] Compagnon. Page 258.

[51] Massu. Page 52.

[52] Maule. Page 113.

[53] Corbonnois. Pages 75–76.

[54] Ibid. Page 79.

[55] Maule Page 113.

[56] It has to be said that the battered képi was an affectation in a similar vein to Monty's RTR beret, and probably went down well with La Coloniale. In his temporary role of governor general of the Cameroons Leclerc had access to the appropriate kit such as smart solar topees etc. Furthermore it is quite obvious from de Gaulle's impeccable turnout throughout his exile in Great Britain that London tailors were adept at making things for Free French officers.

[57] Massu. Page 53.

[58] Ibid. Pages 53–54.

[59] Ibid. Page 54.

[60] Massu. Page 55. Aspirant Lévy was captured by the Italians, who amputated his injured leg and sent him to Italy. Since he was of no further use as a soldier he was repatriated to the Free Zone.

[61] Compagnon. Page 260.

[62] Massu. Page 58.

[63] Ibid. Page 58.

[64] Compagnon. Page 261.

[65] Notin. Pages 158–67.

[66] Ibid. Page 169.

[67] Ibid. Pages 169–70.

[68] Vichy politicians such as Laval seriously desired a French re-entry into the war on the Axis side. Admiral Darlan who, like many in the French Navy was anti-British even before Mers el Kebir, even nurtured hopes of leading the French Navy against Great Britain. If these threats had materialised de Gaulle's position in Carlton Gardens would have become untenable.

[69] Jean Lacouture. *De Gaulle. The Rebel. 1890–1944.* Collins Harvill 1990. Pages 456–57. Refering to an article by Jacques de Guillebon.

[70] John Bierman and Colin Smith. Pages 173–74.

[71] Susan Travers. *Tomorrow to be Brave.* Bantam, 2000. Pages 214–38. Susan Travers was General Koenig's chauffeuse and mistress during 1941–42, and the only Englishwoman to be allowed to join the French Foreign Legion. Her account of the breakout from Bir Hakeim is truly gripping.

[72] Notin. Pages 175–77.

CHAPTER 6

[1] John Bierman & Colin Smith, *Alamein. War without Hate.* Penguin. Page 259.

[2] John Latimer. *Alamein.* P.239. Colonel Allesandri would later become a general and take part in the French decolonisation wars, particularly in Indo-China.

[3] After the fall of France many Air France pilots found themselves stuck in England or far out places like Brazil. Often too old for military duties, once de Gaulle managed to get American Lockheeds in exchange for allowing the US use of Pointe Noire airfield,

these pilots rallied to Free France and restarted the national airline.

[4] Christian Girard. *Journal de Guerre 1939–1945*. L'Harmattan 1975. Page 29–30.

[5] Compagnon. Page 284. The British 25-pounders would be used to subdue the fort at Oum-el-Araneb which had held out against the Fezzan raids of March 1942.

[6] Compagnon. Page 285.

[7] Perhaps named after Loire Atlantique town of Nantes because of the shooting by the Germans of 50 hostages there in 1941.

[8] The Desert Air Force's own complement of Hurricanes and Spitfires was being augmented by inferior early American marks such as Kittyhawks and Warhawks which were immensely vulnerable to skilled Me 109F pilots such as Lt. Jochen Marseilles.

[9] There was also an American liaison officer called Colonel Cunningham whose Francophilia was well known and excessive in the eyes of his American superiors. Compagnon. Page 285.

[10] Including Vézinet who went on to become a general.

[11] General Massu. *Sept Ans avec Leclerc*. Librairie Plon 1974, revised Édition Rocher 1997. Page 64.

[12] Ibid. Page 69.

[13] Admiral Darlan happened to be in Algiers to attend upon his son, Alain, stricken with polio. Darlan acted as Pétain's dauphin and commander in chief of all Vichy forces. R. Atkinson. *An Army at Dawn*. Little Brown, 2003. Pages 94-6.

[14] Ibid. Pages 158–59.

[15] Prince Amilakvari was a white Russian, greatly loved by his men who filed past his body after the battle. Susan Travers writes a lot about him in *Tomorrow to be Brave*. But this reference comes from John Bierman and Colin Smith's *Alamein*, Viking Penguin 2002. Page 284.

[16] Lacouture. Page 397.

[17] Notin, Jean-Christophe. *Leclerc*. Perrin 2005. Page 180.

[18] Compagnon. Pages 287–88.

[19] R. Atkinson. *An Army at Dawn*. Little Brown 2003. Pages 163–66.

[20] Compagnon. Pages 291–93.

[21] In 1940 Delange had taken part in the rallying of Brazzaville and the Congo. He had taken the 1e Bataillon de Marche from Tchad to Palestine for the Syrian operation. Massu. Page 70.

[22] Dr. Coupignies would later become a member of the French Senate.

[23] Massu. Page 71.

[24] Henry Maule. *Out of the Sand*. Odhams 1966. Page 133–34.

[25] Ibid. Page 134.

[26] "2e bureau" is the usual name for any French forces organisation involved with intelligence gathering. "3e Bureau" is operations. "4e Bureau" is logisitics.

[27] "Don't be such an idiot." Girard. Page 35.

[28] Ibid. Pages 35–36.

[29] Dronne, Raymond. *Le serment de Koufra*. Les Éditions du Temps. 1965. (J'ai lu edition – page 209.)

[30] Girard. Page 37.

[31] Notin. Page 185.

[32] Maule. Pages 136–37.

[33] Ibid. Page 139.

[34] Girard. Page 38.

[35] Ibid. Page 39.

[36] Henry Maule, Page 139 and Christian Girard Page 39. These are the best detailed accounts of the siege of Oum el-Araneb.

[37] Massu. Pages 75–76.

[38] Girard. Page 41.

[39] Compagnon. Page 295.

[40] Massu. Page 77.

[41] Fergus Fleming. *The Sword and the Cross.* Granta 2002. Pages 262 and 286.

[42] Massu. Pages 77–78.

[43] The Holocaust had not really got under way in north Africa; by the time of the Axis capitulation in Tunisia Obersturmbanfuhrer Walter Rauff had inflicted several months persecution on the Tunisian Jews. Gas chambers were in preparation on Tunisian soil, exploding the myth of Wehrmacht ignorance and non compliance with SS activities and also refuting the notion that the Afrika Korps, and Rommel in particular, were more chivalrous than other parts of the Wehrmacht. See *Verdict on Vichy* by Michael Curtis. Weidenfeld and Nicolson 2002. Pages 166–68.

[44] Massu. Page 79.

[45] Well known tailors in London.

[46] The equipage of a 25-pounder included an ammo trailer and a lorry derived tractor with cabin room for the whole gun crew.

[47] Henry Maule. Page 148.

[48] This quote comes from Nigel Hamilton's *Monty. Master of the Battlefield 1942–1944.* Hamish Hamilton 1983. A *mitrailleuse* is merely a machine gun. Five machine guns among a force of 3,500 is a very minor detail. It seems more likely that Leclerc would have meant *automitrailleuse* which is an armoured car.

[49] Girard. Page 44.

[50] Battledress consisted of a waist length tunic with two breast pockets and baggy trousers with large deep pockets gathered at the ankle with canvas gaiters. They came in brownish khaki, air force blue or navy blue depending on which service. The Canadian version was higher quality and copied by the French Army after the war.

[51] General Jean Compagnon says that the British gave Leclerc 2-pounders, whereas Henry Maule says they were given 6-pounders which were newer. The two pounder was outmoded by early 1943 and had largely been replaced in those British units expected to meet up to date German weaponry by the six pounder, which had been used to great effect by the Rifle Brigade in the Snipe engagement at Alamein. Leclerc's force were clearly not expected to take on Panzers. Maule also says that they were given a couple of Shermans at this stage (page 149) which seems highly unlikely.

[52] Girard. Pages 44–45 and Notin. Pages 191–92.

[53] Montgomery to Alanbrooke. Quoted in footnote by Bierman and Smith. Page 381.

[54] Girard. Page 47.

[55] Compagnon, quoting Raymond Dronne. Page 303.

[56] Girard. Page 47.

[57] Ibid. Page 45.

[58] Massu. Page 80.

[59] Girard. Page 48.

[60] Ibid. Pages 48–49.

[61] Bierman and Smith. Pages 375–76.

[62] Compagnon. Page 309.

[63] Ibid.

[64] Ibid.

[65] Ibid.

[66] Nigel Hamilton. *Monty. Master of the Battlefield. 1942–1944.* Hamish Hamilton, 1983. Page 182.

[67] Compagnon. Page 310.

[68] Christian Girard interviewed by Henry Maule for *Out of the Sand.* Odhams 1966. Page 154.

[69] Rick Atkinson. Page 427–29. & Laurie Barber (with John Tonkin-Covell) *Freyberg-Churchill's Salamander.* Hutchinson 1989. Pages 133–84.

[70] Maule. Page 156.

[71] Girard. Pages 55–56.

[72] Maule 160.

[73] Girard. 61.

[74] Ibid. Page 63.

[75] Maule. Pages 159–60.

[76] R. Atkinson. Page 527.

[77] Notin. Page 200.

CHAPTER 7

[1] Henry Maule. *Out of the Sand.* Odhams 1966. Page 161.

[2] Ibid.

[3] Lacouture brilliantly decribes these negotiations in Casablanca where Roosevelt calls Giraud the "groom" and de Gaulle the "snooty bride."

[4] Rick Atkinson. *An Army at Dawn.* Little Brown. 2003. Page 297.

[5] Girard. Christian. *Journal de Guerre. 1939–1945.* L'Harmattan. 2000. Page 75.

[6] Ibid. Page 75.

[7] Ibid.

[8] Ibid. Page 80.

[9] Ibid. Pages 80–81. This rant is written in prose by Girard, but its exuberance suggests that it was Leclerc speaking to his ADC and not the other way round.

[10] Admiral Muselier was one of de Gaulle's few early supporters from among the French Navy. However, he fell out of favour for inciting the Free French Navy to mutiny after a brush with British Intelligence.

[11] Girard. Pages 81–82.

[12] Massu. Page 87.

[13] Antony Clayton. *France, Soldiers and Africa.* Brasseys. 1988. Page 141.

[14] This was not strictly true. While Leclerc may not have been involved in the larger Gaullist versus Vichy battles such as Dakar or Syria, he had been involved in the small coups that rallied the colonies of French Equatorial Africa. Though du Vigier may not have realised this.

[15] Doubtless a reference to the controversy over *"spontanément mutés."*

[16] This exchange between du Vigier and Leclerc has been translated almost in its entirety by the author. It comes from pages 322–25 of General Compagnon's biography and was in its turn quoted from General Berthet, who was at the time attached to du Vigier's division.

[17] Paraphrased from a personal note by Leclerc himself. Fondation Leclerc. Compagnon. Page 325.

[18] French politician, influential in the founding of the Third Republic after the defeat of Napoleon III's Second Empire during the Franco-Prussian War of 1870–71. Gambetta escaped from Prussian-encircled Paris in a hot air balloon.

[19] Jean Lacouture. *De Gaulle. The Rebel. 1890–1944.* Collins Harvill. 1990. Pages 435–7.

[20] Chasseurs d'Afrique were recruited in the Metropole for colonial service, therefore they were mainly European. They originated as Zouaves a Cheval in the 1830s. Subsequently, through the mid-nineteenth century, Metropolitan cavalry regiments were converted, including a hussar regiment of which the future religious mystic Charles de Foucauld was a member. The Chasseurs d'Afrique's horses were Barbs, unimpressive to look at but surefooted for campaigning in mountainous areas of the Maghreb. Antony Clayton. *France, Soldiers and Africa.*

[21] The French equivalent of a rifle regiment.

[22] Leclerc, ever slow to put up the insignia of his promotion, didn't put the third star of a *général de division* on his képi or his bonnet de police until after the 2e DB landed in France on August 1st 1944!

[23] Paul de Langlade. *En Suivant Leclerc.* Au Fil d'Ariane. 1964. Pages 15–18.

[24] Ibid. Page 25.

[25] Ibid. Page 26.

[26] Ibid. Page 32.

[27] Notin, Jean-Christophe. *Leclerc.* Perrin 2005. Page 214. Quoting Guy de Valence.

[28] Girard. Page 89.

[29] Amdré Martel. *Leclerc. Le soldat et le politique.* Albin Michel. 1998. Page 233. Quoting General Giraud's book *Un seul but. La Victoire.* Julliard. 1949.

[30] There are two versions of this anecdote. One has Leclerc calling the Corps Franc d'Afrique "*crapules*" – "crooks." Another, quoted by Vézinet, has him calling them "*rouges*" – "reds."

[31] Massu. Pages 88-91. Massu does not give any reason for these grenade accidents or say whether they happened while training with French, British or American grenades.

[32] Girard. Page 98.

[33] Ibid. Page 99.

[34] Notin. Pages 217–18.

[35] Ibid. Page 208.

[36] Girard. Pages 97–101.

[37] Ibid. Page 102.

[38] Martel. Page 237.

[39] Leclerc and his staff discussed the divisional insignia one evening in the first command post at Temara. One suggestion was a small picture of the Arc de Triomphe de l'Etoile. Then Christian Girard suggested a simple white map of France which would symbolise both the diversity and unity of the Division. Girard. Page 108.

[40] This translates as "audacity is not unreasonable."

[41] The French translation of this Latin phrase is "Au danger, mon plaisir," which translates as "danger is my pleasure."

[42] Martel. Page 237.

[43] Fergus Fleming. *The Sword and the Cross.* Granta 2002. Page 141.

[44] The same Jean Compagnon who wrote one of the best of the many French biographies of Leclerc; an important source for the present work.

[45] Compagnon. Page 241. & Boissieu, Alain de. *Pour combattre avec de Gaulle.* Plon. 1981. 1999 Edn.

[46] Command of a battle group was strictly speaking a brigadier general's job. But since Leclerc was slow to put up his third star, out of deference to the army's traditional hierarchy, there were knock-on effects lower down.

[47] And his book shows this. Both de Langlade's and Massu's books are delightful reading for this very reason.

[48] Exact words of de Langlade: "un rassemblement de brebis belantes conduites par des patres semi séniles." Page 55.

[49] Arthur Kaiser. *Un artisan Alsacien dans la Division Leclerc.* éditions Muller. 2001. Pages 116–17.

[50] Compagnon. Page 339.

[51] Maule. Page 167. Maule is quoting Girard, who also has this incident in *Journal de Guerre*, though not told as strongly. Maule interviewed Girard in the early 1960s.

[52] Girard. Pages 104–07.

[53] Kaiser. Pages 117–18. Like Leclerc, de Langlade came from a conservative and Catholic background and this anecdote seems funnier in the post 1960s world.

[54] Boissieu, Alain de. *Pour combattre avec de Gaulle. Souvenirs 1940–1946.* Plon 1999 Edn. Page 213.

[55] Ibid. Page 214.

[56] Ibid. Pages 215–17. & Notin Page 227.

[57] Notin. Page 228. Quotation.

[58] Maule. Page 169.

[59] Vézy, Edith. *Gargamelle. Mon ambulance guerriere 2e DB.* l'Harmattan 1994. Pages 7–23.

[60] Jean-Marie Thomas. *Un Marin dans La 2e DB. "Mémoires d'un Plouerais."* Muller édition. 2000. Pages 50–65.

[61] Ibid. Page 76.

[62] Ibid. Pages 78–79.

[63] Martel. Page 248. Quoting Capitaine de frégate Raymond Maggiar, *Les fusiliers marins de Leclerc.* Pages 15–16.

CHAPTER 8

[1] Antony Clayton. *France, Soldiers and Africa.* Brasseys 1988. op cit.

[2] Antony Clayton. *Three Marshals of France. Leadership after Trauma.* Brasseys 1992. op cit.

[3] Massu, Jacques. *Sept ans avec Leclerc.* Librairie Plon 1974. Page 101.

[4] Christian Girard. *Journal de Guerre 1939-1945.* L'Harmattan. 2000. Pages 176-7.

[5] Compagnon, General Jean. *Leclerc. Maréchal de France.* Flammarion. Page 349.

[6] Girard. Page 177.

[7] Paul de Langlade. *En Suivant Leclerc.* Au Fil d'Ariane 1964. Pages 79–81.

[8] Compagnon. Page 350.

[9] Girard's italics, not mine. *"Helpful"* is a phrase that crops up in his diary to epitomise a particularly British character trait.

[10] Ibid. Page 185.

[11] Langlade. Pages 91–95.

[12] Henry Maule. *Out of the Sand.* Odhams 1966. Page 172.

[13] Arthur Kaiser. *Un artisan Alsacien dans la Division Leclerc.* Page 122.

[14] Maule. Page 172.

[15] Massu. Page 103.

[16] Girard. Page 187–88.

[17] Edith Vezy. *"Gargamelle." mon ambulance guerriere 2e DB.* L'Harmattan. 1994. Page 31.

[18] Massu. Page 106–07.

[19] Clostermann, Pierre. *The Big Show.* 2nd Edition. Weidenfeld and Nicolson. 2004. Pages 153–54.

[20] Girard. Page 197. "L'asceticisme du Général est effectivement terrible. Il n'a pas perdu sa jeunesse de caractere, mais ses manifestations en sont étouffées. Il a des moments de gaieté, et une gaieté juvénile, mais plus émouvante que détendante."

[21] Henry Frederick Hotham, 7th Baron Hotham was born in 1899. The Hothams date from the Norman era and, like the de Hauteclocques, used the 'de' prefix until the 15th Century. Lord Hotham's wife was descended from William Cecil, the 1st Lord Burghley, who was Queen Elizabeth I's closest adviser. *Burke's Peerage and Baronetage.* 1937 Coronation Edition and 2000 Edition.

[22] Notin, Jean-Christophe. *Leclerc.* Perrin 2005. Page 236.

[23] "Langlade lui a fait réserver deux chambres tres confortables dans un tres beau chateau des environs, appartenant a un Lord grincheux et hostile." Girard. Page 197.

[24] Kaiser. Pages 122–23.

[25] Girard. Page 199.

[26] Martel, André. *Leclerc. Le soldat et le politique.* Albin Michel 1998. Pages 254–55. Quoting Pere Fouquet.

[27] Hotham, Henry. (8th Lord Hotham.) Conversation with author. September 2004.

[28] Jean Lacouture. *De Gaulle. The Rebel. 1890–1944.* Collins Harvill 1990. Page 521.

[29] Ibid. Pages 525–26.

[30] Kaiser. Page 123.

[31] Letter from Leclerc to Pauline Vanier 12/6/1944. Also quoted by Notin; page 240.

[32] Maule. Page ?

[33] Boissieu, Alain de. *Pour combattre avec de Gaulle.* Plon. 1999 Edn. Page 230.

[34] Martel. Page 257.

[35] Jean-Marie Thomas. *Un Marin dans la 2e DB. "Mémoires d'un Plouerais.* Éditions Muller. 2000. Page 86.

[36] The 1st Polish Armoured Division was equipped on a largely British model with the personnel receiving British uniforms and side arms, British artillery, armoured cars, Bren carriers, tanks – including some "funnies" from short and discontinued production runs. But they also, like other British armoured divisions, had Sherman tanks, White halftracks and inevitably jeeps.

[37] Girard Page 222.

[38] Conversation between author and Lord Hotham 2004.

[39] Girard. Pages 226–27.

[40] Ibid. Page 228.

[41] For this verification I am grateful to Andrew who works in the gun room at Holland and Holland. They moved to 13 Bruton Street in 1960 and are now at 31 Bruton Street. Unfortunately he was unable to tell me of any new gun that might have been bought by Leclerc, having checked the ledgers from 1940–52. If Leclerc's purchase required attention to the safety catch it may well have been second-hand.

[42] Girard. Page 230.

[43] Ibid. Reading this episode of divisional discipline and personality clash in Girard's *Journal de Guerre* one is reminded of the film *Tunes of Glory* with Alec Guinness and John Mills. Though obviously Leclerc handles the matter far better than the John Mills character in the film.

[44] Ibid. Page 231.

[45] Compagnon. Page 364.

[46] Notin. Page 243.

[47] Compagnon. Page 364. Malaguti would never forgive Leclerc for denying him the opportunity to lead the armoured units in action that he had done so much to form. He nevertheless had a considerable career after the 2e DB, though more on the administrative side of soldiering.

[48] Notin. Page 242.

[49] Maggiar, Contre Amiral Raymond. *Les Fusiliers Marins de Leclerc. Une route difficile vers de Gaulle.* Éditions France Empire 1984. Page 158.

[50] John Keegan. *Six Armies in Normandy.* Jonathan Cape 1982. Page 305.

[51] Girard. Pages 234–35.

[52] Massu. Page 110.

[53] Girard. Page 234.

[54] Langlade. Page 120.

[55] Baigent, Michael and Richard Leigh. *Secret Germany. Claus von Stauffenberg and the Mystical Crusade Against Hitler.* Jonathan Cape. 1994. Pages 66–67.

[56] Girard. Page 237.

[57] Langlade. Page 121.

[58] Girard. Page 243.

[59] Edith Vézy. Pages 41-42.

[60] Kaiser. Pages 129–30.

[61] Girard. Page 244.

[62] Boissieu. Page 233.

CHAPTER 9

[1] Boissieu, Alain de. *Pour Combattre avec de Gaulle.* Plon. 1999 Edn. Page 233.

[2] Christian Girard. *Journal de Guerre 1939–1945.* L'Harmattan. Page 244.

[3] Girard. Page 245.

[4] Massu. *Sept Ans avec Leclerc.* Librairie Plon 1974. Revised Rocher 1997. Page 111–13.

[5] Massu. Page 114.

[6] Henry Maule. *Out of the Sand.* Odhams 1966. Page 181.

[7] Girard Page 246.

[8] Paul de Langlade. *En suivant Leclerc*. Au fil d'Ariane 1964. Page 128.

[9] Raymond Maggiar. *Les Fusiliers Marin de Leclerc. Une route dificile vers de Gaulle*. France Empire 1984. Pages 163–64.

[10] Notin, Jean-Christophe. *Leclerc*. Perrin 2005. Pages 247–48.

[11] Girard. Pages 249–50.

[12] Langlade. Page 129–30.

[13] Edith Vézy. *"Gargamelle" mon ambulance guerriere 2e DB*. L'Harmattan 1994. Pages 45-46.

[14] Girard. Page 248.

[15] Notin. Page 249.

[16] Ibid. Page 249.

[17] Ibid. Page 250.

[18] Neillands, Robin. *The Battle for Normandy. 1944*. Cassell 2003. Page 337.

[19] Langlade. Page 133.

[20] Langlade. Pages 134–35.

[21] Repiton-Préneuf, Paul. *2e DB La Campagne de France*. Imprimerie Nationale 1994. Original 1945. Page 3.

[22] Compagnon. Page 371. & Girard Page 250.

[23] Vézy, Edith. Pages 50–51.

[24] Boissieu. Page 235 & Antony Beevor, *D-Day*, Penguin 2009.

[25] Neillands. Pages 353–55.

[26] Compagnon. Pages 372–73.

[27] Ibid.

[28] Girard. Page 250.

[29] Massu. 120.

[30] Massu. Page 121. & Arthur Kaiser Page 135. The Sherman crewmen from the 12e Chasseurs d'Afrique were buried nearby at Ballon.

[31] Langlois commanded 6e Company of the RMT in Massu's 2e battalion in GT Langlade. Langlois features in the front row of the large photograph of 2e RMT officers taken in Yorkshire.

[32] Massu. Page 121.

[33] Boissieu. Page 236.

[34] Girard. Page 251.

[35] Boissieu. Page 236.

[36] Girard. Page 252.

[37] Ibid.

[38] Boissieu. Pages 237–38.

[39] The battleship *Strasbourg* escaped Admiral Somerville's attack on Mers-el-Kebir in 1940, fleeing to Toulon after a half-hearted pursuit by Fleet Air Arm Swordfishes. The *Jean Bart* fired upon the Americans during the farcical *baroud d'honneur*, ending up aground in Casablanca harbour for its pains until it could be repaired under the American re-armament programme.

[40] Maggiar. Pages 174–76.

[41] Compagnon. Page 375. de Boissieu Page 238 and Notin Page 252. There are several versions of this anecdote.

[42] Ibid. Page 376.

[43] Ibid. Page 376–77. & Massu Page 123. & Girard. Page 253.

[44] Ibid. Page 377.

[45] Massu. Page 124.

[46] Compagnon. Page 378. Historians of the US 5th Armoured Division have long blamed the 2e DB for their failure to reach Argentan. Nevertheless their mutual corps commander, General Haislip, bore no rancour towards Leclerc, maintaining absolute confidence in him throughout operations.

[47] Notin. Page 256.

[48] Maggiar. Pages 181–84.

[49] Hastings, Max. *Overlord.* Michael Joseph 1984. Page 340.

[50] Compagnon. Page 379 & Girard. Page 254.

[51] Girard. Page 255.

[52] Boissieu. Pages 242–43.

[53] Hastings. Page 353.

[54] Neillands, Robin. Page 357.

[55] Maule, Henry. *Out of the Sand.* Odhams 1966. Pages 190–91.

[56] Notin. Page 257.

[57] Girard. Page 257.

[58] Compagnon. Page 382.

[59] Ibid.

[60] The well loved General Maczek died in Edinburgh in 1994 aged 102. There is a museum for the Polish 1st Armoured Division at Breda in Holland.

[61] Kaiser, Arthur. Page 138–39.

[62] Girard. Page 261.

[63] Maule. Page 192.

[64] Collins, Larry and Dominique Lapierre. *Is Paris Burning?* Gollancz 1965. Page 80.

[65] Collins,& Lapierre. Pages 79–81.

[66] The old Plantagenet town renowned as home to the tapestry depicting the Norman Conquest of England from which all Anglo-French animosities in the mediaeval era derive.

[67] Fest, Joachim. *Plotting Hitler's Death.* Weidenfeld and Nicolson 1996. Pages 290–91.

[68] Collins, & Lapierre. Page 61.

[69] The Paris Police were involved in the *Grand Rafle* and *Velodrome d'Hiver* round-ups.

[70] Collins, & Lapierre. Page 78.

[71] Taittinger. *.....et Paris ne fut pas détruit.* Nouvelles Éditions Latines. 1956. Op cit. Also Eugen Weber, *Action Francaise* Stanford 1962 and Carmen Callil *Bad Faith* Jonathan Cape 2006.

[72] Collins & Lapierre. Pages 118–20.

[73] Girard. Page 261.

[74] Ibid.

[75] Ibid. Page 262.

[76] Collins & Lapierre. Pages 204–07.

[77] Girard. Page 264.

[78] Ibid.

[79] Ibid. Page 265.

[80] Ibid.

CHAPTER 10

[1] Collins and Lapierre. *Is Paris Burning?* Gollancz 1965. Page 142–43.

[2] Roger Borderon. *Rol-Tanguy.* Tallandier 2004. Pages 383–84.

[3] Collins and Lapierre. Page 173.

[4] Ibid. Page 183.

[5] Ibid. Pages 189–91.

[6] Ibid. Pages 202–03.

[7] Dansette, Adrien. *Histoire de la Libération de Paris.* Fayard 1946. Pages 240–41.

[8] This exchange is quoted and translated from Dansette. Another version is in Collins and Lapierre's book on pages 240–41.

[9] Collins and Lapierre. Page 241.

[10] Ibid. Pages 245–46.

[11] Ibid. Pages 262–63.

[12] Dansette. Pages 258–59.

[13] Collins and Lapierre. Page 266.

[14] Ibid. There is more about d'Orgeix in Christine Levisse-Touzé's *Paris 1944. Les Enjeux de la Libération.* Albin Michel 1994. Page 311.

[15] Dronne, Raymond. *La Libération de Paris.* Presses de la Cité 1970. Page 267.

[16] Gribius, André. *Une vie d'officier.* Éditions Grance-Empire 1971. Page 127.

[17] Compagnon, Jean. *Leclerc. Maréchal de France.* Flammarion 1994. Page 396–97.

[18] Dansette. Pages 260–61.

[19] Baker, Carlos. *Ernest Hemingway.* Charles Scribner and Sons. 1969. Page 629.

[20] Kaiser. *Un artisan Alsacien dans la Division Leclerc.* Pages 145–46.

[21] Dansette. Page 261.

[22] Lacouture, Jean. *De Gaulle. The Rebel 1890-1944.* Collins Harvill 1990. Page 568.

[23] Aron, Robert. *De Gaulle before Paris.* Putnam 1962. Pages 304–05.

[24] Ibid. It seems clear that de Gaulle ate before his meeting with Leclerc. No Frenchman would "dine" before 5pm.

[25] The plan drawn up by Gribius's 3eme bureau is reproduced in Compagnon's biography on Pages 400–01.

[26] This incident is famous and quoted in most French books on Leclerc or the Liberation of Paris.

[27] Dronne, Raymond. Page 269.

[28] Collins and Lapierre. Page 294.

[29] Langlade, Paul de. *En Suivant Leclerc.* Au fil d'Ariane 1964. Pages 196–97.

[30] Dansette. Page 266.

[31] Ibid.

[32] Dronne. Page 275.

[33] Notin, Jean-Christophe. *Leclerc.* Perrin 2005. Page 269.

[34] Dronne. Page 276.

[35] Notin. Page 270.

[36] Dronne. Page 277.

[37] Boissieu. Pages 251–52. Von Choltitz admitted receipt of Leclerc's message in captivity.

[38] Notin. Page 268.

[39] Dronne. Page 279 and Dansette Page 268.

[40] This exchange is well known and quoted by both Dansette and Dronne in their books. But Dronne's is better and more detailed, so I have relied on that. Dronne. Pages 280–81.

[41] Ibid.

[42] Ibid.

[43] Ibid. Page 282.

[44] Ibid. Page 283.

[45] Ibid. Page 284.

[46] Ibid.

[47] Ibid. Page 285.

[48] Notin. Page 271–72.

[49] Levisse-Touzé, Christine. *Les Enjeu de la Libération.* Albin Michel 1994. Pages 299–301.

[50] Ibid.

[51] Ibid. Page 301.

[52] Ibid. Pages 301–02.

[53] Compagnon. Page 406.

[54] Massu, Jacques. *Sept Ans avec Leclerc.* Plon 1974. Pages 141–43.

[55] Ibid. Page 143.

[56] Collins and Lapierre. Pages 394-395. & Maggiar, Raymond. *Les Fusiliers Marins de Leclerc.* Éditions France-Empire 1984. Pages 214–15.

[57] Collins and Lapierre. Page 396. That Panther stayed where it was for several days afterwards. General Sir David Fraser even mentions it in his memoir *War and Shadows*.

[58] Massu. Page 143.

[59] Ibid. Page 144.

[60] Kaiser. Page 149.

[61] Dronne. Pages 300–01.

[62] Ibid. Page 302.

[63] Ibid. Pages 303–04 & Collins and Lapierre, Pages 401–06.

[64] Dronne. Page 305.

[65] Dansette. Page 294.

[66] Ibid. Pages 296–98. & Notin. Pages 272–73.

[67] Notin. Page 273.

[68] Ibid. Page 274.

[69] Ibid.

[70] Ibid. Pages 274–75.

[71] Lacouture. Page 572. Quoting de Gaulle.

[72] Ibid.

[73] Ibid.

[74] de Gaulle. Philippe. *De Gaulle—Mon Pere.* Plon 2003. Pages 347–60.

[75] Notin. Page 275. Quoting an interview with Alain de Boissieu.

[76] Collins and Lapierre Pages 425–27. & Compagnon. Pages 408–09. & Lacouture Pages 572–73.

[77] Lacouture, quoting de Gaulle's Memoirs. Page 573.

[78] Girard. Page 271.

[79] Massu. Pages 147–48.

[80] Lacouture. Pages 574–75.

[81] Notin. Page 276.

[82] Ibid.

[83] Boissieu. Page 257.

[84] Ibid. Pages 257–58.

[85] This somewhat fruity version can be found in Arthur Kaiser's book on page 153. Since he is a close friend of Leclerc's eldest surviving son, Hubert, this anecdote is likely to be true. A slightly cleaned up version also exists in Paul de Langlade's *En Suivant Leclerc* on Page 226.

[86] Dansette. Page 320.

[87] Dronne. Page 319.

[88] Ibid. Page 321.

[89] Ibid. Page 322.

[90] Ibid.

[91] Gribius. Pages 139–40.

[92] Corbonnois, Didier. *L'Odyssée de la Colonne Leclerc.* Histoires et Collections. Page 31.

[93] Boissieu. Page 260.

[94] de Gaulle Philippe. Page s 352–53.

[95] Compagnon. Pages 414–15.

[96] Notin. Pages 279–80.

[97] Ibid. Pages 280–81.

[98] Ibid. Page 281.

[99] Ibid. Page 282.

[100] Ibid.

CHAPTER 11

[1] Hamilton, Nigel. *Monty. The Field Marshall. 1944–1976.* Hamish Hamilton 1986. Page 13. Quoting 21st Army Group War Diaries. War Office Records (WO 205/5B).

[2] Maule, Henry. *Out of the Sand.* Odhams 1966. Pages 227–28.

[3] Notin, Jean-Christophe. *Leclerc.* Perrin 2005. Page 282.

[4] Maule. Page 230.

[5] Boissieu, Alain de. *Pour combattre avec de Gaulle.* Plon 1981. Page 261.

[6] Wilmot, Chester. *The Struggle for Europe.* Collins 1952. Pages 536–37.

[7] Girard, Christian. *Journal de Guerre. 1939–1945.* L'Harmattan 2000. Pages 284–85.

[8] Maggiar, Raymond. *Les Fusiliers Marins de Leclerc.* Éditions France-Empire 1984. Pages 222–24. & Compagnon Page 426.

[9] Maggiar. Page 225.

[10] Langlade, Paul de. *En suivant Leclerc.* Au Fil d'Ariane 1964. Pages 238–40.

[11] Zaloga, Steven J. *Lorraine 1944.* Osprey 2000. Pages 54-59. & Maule Pages 234–35.

[12] Maggiar. Pages 227–28.

[13] Ibid.

[14] Langlade. Page 245.

[15] Langlade Page 246. & Girard Page 285.

[16] Maggiar. Pages 228-229. & Maule Page 235.

[17] Langlade. Page 247.

[18] Maggiar. Page 232.

[19] Gribius. *Une vie d'officier.* Éditions France-Empire 1971. Page 144. & Langlade. Page 248.

[20] Langlade 250.

[21] Luck, Hans von. *Panzer Commander. The Memoirs of Colonel Hans von Luck.* Cassell 1989. Page 217.

[22] Girard. Pages 285–86.

[23] Compagnon. Page 429.

[24] Ibid. Page 430 and Gribius Page 145.

[25] Notin. Page 285.

[26] Girard. Pages 287–88.

[27] Girard Page 289. & Maule, Page 236.

[28] Ibid.

[29] Compagnon. Page 431. Quoting Raymond Dronne.

[30] Maule. Page 237.

[31] Compagnon. Page 430.

[32] Girard. Page 291.

[33] Ibid.

[34] Girard. Pages 292–93.

[35] Girard. Page 296. Girard's memoirs is full of bits of "Franglais" such as *kidnappé* and *helpful* all printed in Italic.

[36] Ibid. Page 296.

[37] Ibid. Page 297.

[38] Maggiar. Pages 241–42.

[39] Maggiar. Pages 237–39.

[40] Gribius, André. *Une vie d'officier.* Éditions France-Empire 1971. Page 147–48.

[41] Maggiar. Page 240–41.

[42] Kaiser, Arthur. *Unn artisan Alsacien dans la division Leclerc.* Muller éditons 2001. Page 161.

[43] Langlade. Page 266.

[44] Maggiar. Page 244.

[45] Girard. Page 303.

[46] Girard. Page 302.

[47] Notin. Pages 287–88.

[48] Ibid. Page 289.

[49] Compagnon. Pages 440–41.

[50] Ibid. Page 443.

[51] Gribius. Page 150.

CHAPTER 12

[1] Compagnon, General Jean. *Leclerc. Maréchal de France.* Flammarion 1994. Pages 450–53.

[2] Girard, Christian. *Journal de Guerre. 1939–45.* L'Harmattan. 2000. Page 311. & Jean-Christophe Notin *Leclerc* Perrin 2005. Page 292.

[3] Gribius, André. *Une vie d'officier.* Éditions France-Empire 1971. Pages 152–53.

[4] Girard. Page 313.

[5] Gribius. Pages 154–55.

[6] Compagnon. Page 459. Girard. Pages 313–14. Gribius. Page 155.

[7] Compagnon. Page 461. and Gribius Page 155.

[8] Gribius. Page 157.

[9] Massu, Jacques. *Sept Ans avec Leclerc.* Rocher 1997. Pages 185–88.

[10] Gribius. Pages 157–59.

[11] Langlade, Paul de. *En Suivant Leclerc.* Au fil d'Ariane. 1964. Pages 304–05.

[12] Massu. Pages 192–93.

[13] Compagnon. Pages 462–63.

[14] Massu. Page 193.

[15] Compagnon. Page 462.

[16] Langlade. Page 308.

[17] Maule. Henry. *Out of the Sand.* Odhams 1966. Page 247.

[18] Compagnon. Page 463. & Massu. Pages 193–94.

[19] Gribius. Page 161.

[20] Girard. Page 316.

[21] Girard. Page 316.

[22] Girard. Page 317.

[23] Compagnon. Page 465.

[24] Maule. Page 249.

[25] Gribius. Page 162.

[26] Massu. Page 198.

[27] Massu. Pages 198–99.

[28] Maule. Page 253.

[29] Vézinet, Général. *Le général Leclerc.* France-Empire 1997. Page 168.

[30] Massu. Page 200.

[31] Compagnon. Pages 465–66.

[32] Girard. Page 318.

[33] Langlade. Page 317.

[34] Martel, André. *Leclerc. Le soldat et le politique.* Albin Michel 1998. Page 307.

[35] Langlade. Page 317.

[36] Maule. Page 258.

[37] Langlade. Page 324.

[38] Gribius. Page 164.

[39] Langlade. Page 324.

[40] Kaiser, Arthur. *Un artisan Alsacien dans la Division Leclerc.* Muller Éditons 2000. Pages 170–71.

[41] Compagnon. Page 466.

[42] Girard. Page 318.

[43] Compagnon quoting the actual letter. Page 466. Also Vézinet Page 168 and Martel Page 307.

[44] Langlade. Page 316.

[45] Maule. Page 256.

[46] Compagnon. Page 467. & Girard. Pages 318–19.

[47] Langlade. Pages 319–22.

[48] Ibid. Page 323.

[49] Girard. Pages 318–19.

[50] Maule. Page 258.

[51] Langlade. Page 323.

[52] Compagnon. Page 469.

[53] Notin. Pages 298–99.

[54] Ibid.

[55] Maule. Page 260.

[56] Vigneras, Marcel. *Re-arming the French*. Office of the Chief of Military History, United States Army. 1957. Pages 347 &353.

[57] Martel, André. Pages 317–19.

[58] Maule. Page 261.

[59] Langlade. Pages 334–35.

[60] Girard. Page 325–26.

[61] Ibid. Page 327.

[62] Ibid. Page 329.

[63] Ibid. Pages 329–30.

[64] Ibid. Pages 331–32.

[65] Gribius. Page170.

[66] Girard. Page 333.

[67] Notin. Page 303.

[68] Wilmot, Chester. *The Struggle for Europe*. Collins 1952. Page 583.

[69] Ibid. Page 588.

[70] Ibid. Page 589.

[71] Ibid.

[72] Girard. Page 334.

[73] Ibid. & Langlade Page 334. & Compagnon. Page 481.

[74] Notin. Pages 304–05.

[75] Langlade. Page 335.

[76] Notin. Pages 305–06.

[77] Ibid.

[78] Ibid.

[79] Lacouture, Jean. *De Gaulle. The Ruler: 1945–1970*. Collins Harvill. 1990. Pages 34–36.

[80] Massu. Pages 211–12.

[81] Ibid. Page 213.

[82] Gribius. Pages 171–72.

[83] Girard. Page 343. & Notin. Page 311.

[84] Notin. Pages 308–09.

[85] Gribius. Page 174. & Massu. Page 214.

[86] Lacouture, *De Gaulle–The Ruler. 1944–1970*. Harper Collins. 1991.

[87] Notin. Page 309.

[88] Ibid.

[89] Girard. Page 347.

[90] Compagnon. Pages 488–89. & Massu. Page 215.

[91] Maule. Pages 270–71.

[92] Compagnon. Pages 490–91. Compagnon quotes from papers given to him by Jean Lecomte describing this incident.

[93] Girard. Page 356.

[94] De Gaulle. *Mémoires de guerre: Le Salut.* Volumes Plon. Page 680.

[95] Compagnon. Page 491.

[96] Compagnon. Page 491 and Gribius. Page 175.

[97] Notin. Page 318.

[98] Ibid.

CHAPTER 13

[1] Compagnon, General Jean. *Leclerc, Maréchal de France.* Flammarion 1994. Pages 496–98. And Robert Gildea *Marianne in Chains.* Macmillan 2002. Pages 338–39 and 363–64.

[2] Notin, Jean-Christophe. *Leclerc.* Perrin 2005. Page 319.

[3] Compagnon. Pages 499-500.

[4] Langlade, Paul de. *En suivant Leclerc.* Au fil d'Ariane. 1964. Pages 375–78.

[5] Ibid. Page 378. & Notin Page 319.

[6] Langlade. Page 380.

[7] Ibid. Page 382.

[8] Ibid. Page 383.

[9] Vigneras, Marcel. *Rearming the French.* Office of the Chief of Military History. Department of the Army, Washington DC 1957. Page 378.

[10] Langlade. Pages 384–85.

[11] Ibid. Pages 386–87.

[12] Ibid. Page 388.

[13] Gribius, André. *Une vie d'officier.* Éditions France-Empire 1971. Pages 180–82. & Langlade Pages 390–92.

[14] Gribius. Pages 183–84.

[15] Langlade. Pages 393–94.

[16] Massu, Jacques. *Sept ans avec Leclerc.* Édtions du Rocher. 1997. Pages 217–18.

[17] Compagnon. Pages 501–02.

[18] Girard. Page 365.

[19] Maggiar, Raymond. *Les Fusiliers Marins de Leclerc.* Éditions France-Empire. 1984. Pages 343–44.

[20] Girard. Page 363 & Notin Pages 325–26.

[21] Maggiar. Pages 344–45.

[22] Ibid.

[23] Girard, Christian. *Journal de Guerre 1939–1945.* L'Harmattan. 2000. Pages 363–64.

[24] Ibid.

[25] Ibid. Page 365–66.

[26] Notin. Page 327.

[27] Massu. Page 219–20.

[28] Ibid.

[29] Girard. Pages 366–67.

[30] Compagnon. Page 505.

[31] Notin. Pages 327–28.

[32] Ibid. Page 329.

[33] Girard. Page 367.

[34] Maule, Henry. *Out of the Sand.* Odhams 1966. Page 277.

[35] Girard. Pages 367–68.

[36] Girard. Page 368.

[37] Maule. Page 278.

[38] Girard. Page 369.

[39] Ambrose, Stephen E. *Band of Brothers.* Simon and Schuster 1997. Page 261.

[40] Girard. Page 369.

[41] Ibid.

[42] Langlade. Pages 411–12.

[43] Girard. Page 369.

[44] Ibid. Page 370.

[45] Langlade. Page 414.

[46] Horne, Alastair. *A Savage War of Peace.* Macmillan 1977. Pages 23–28. See also Christine Levisse-Touzé *L'Afrique du Nord dans la Guerre.* Albin Michel 1998. Ch13 pages 344–54.

[47] Langlade. Page 418.

[48] Notin. Pages 330–31.

[49] Martel, André. *Leclerc. Le soldat et le politique.* Albin Michel 1998. Page 333. Reference to H. Rousso – *Pétain et la fin de la collaboration, Sigmaringen.* 1984. P 408 – and others.

[50] Notin. Pages 332–33.

[51] Ibid. Pages 334–35.

[52] Ibid.

[53] Ibid.

[54] Ibid. Page 336.

[55] Ibid.

[56] Ibid. Page 337.

[57] Martel. Page 336. Quoting Y Gras. Page 441.

CHAPTER 14

[1] Jennings.

[2] Lacouture. Pages 85–86.

[3] Compagnon. Page 509–10. & Lacouture. Page 86.

[4] Massu. Pages 223–25. & Compagnon. Pages 511–12.

[5] Ziegler, Philip. *Mountbatten.* Collins 1985. Pages 330–31.

[6] Compagnon. Page 518 & Lacouture Pages 86–87.

[7] Ibid. Page 519.

[8] Ibid.

[9] Ibid Page 520 and Ziegler Pages 330–33.

[10] Notin. Page 358.

[11] Ibid. Page 359.

[12] Manchester, William. *American Caesar. Douglas MacArthur. 1880–1964.* Hutchinson 1979. Pages 409–12.

[13] Ibid. Pages 413–14.

[14] Notin. Page 360.

[15] Manchester. Page 414. & Compagnon, Page 521.

[16] Duiker, William J. *Ho Chi Minh. A Life.* Theia Books. 2000. Pages 321–22.

[17] Notin. Page 360.

[18] Giap, Vo Nguyen. *Unforgettable Days.* Hanoi Foreign Languages Press 1975. Pages 25–26.

[19] Ibid.

[20] Duiker. Pages 323–24.

[21] Compagnon, General Jean. *Leclerc. Maréchal de France.* Flammarion 1994. Page 521.

[22] Notin, Jean-Christophe. *Leclerc.* Perrin 2005. Pages 361–62. Quoting Colonel Weil's souvenirs.

[23] This letter from Leclerc to d'Argenlieu is quoted in full by both Compagnon on pages 522–23 and by Massu in *Sept Ans avec Leclerc* Éditions Rocher 1997. Pages 230–32.

[24] Ibid. Page 524.

[25] Ibid. Page 525.

[26] Duiker, William J. *Ho Chi Minh. A Life.* Hyperion 2000. Pages 335–336. & Massu. Page 235. & Compagnon Page 526–27.

[27] Compagnon. Page 529. Quoting Jacques de Folin. *Indochine. 1940–1955.* Page 97.

[28] Notin. Page 367.

[29] Compagnon. Page 530.

[30] Ziegler, Philip. *Mountbatten. The Official Biography.* Collins 1985. Page 332.

[31] Compagnon. Page 530.

[32] Notin. Pages 367–68.

[33] Ibid. Pages 369–70.

[34] Massu. Page 235.

[35] Compagnon. Page 537.

[36] Martel, André. *Leclerc. Le Soldat et le Politique.* Albin Michel. 1998. Pages 383–85 & Massu Page 236. & Notin Pages 371–72.

[37] Massu. Pages 236–37.

[38] Ibid. Page 238.

[39] Ibid. Page 242.

[40] Ibid.

[41] Ibid. Page 244.

[42] Ibid. Page 245.

[43] Notin. Page 374.

[44] Ibid. Page 247.

[45] Compagnon. Page 543.

[46] Notin. Page 376.

[47] Ibid. Pages 377–78.

[48] Duiker. Pages 354–55.

[49] Macdonald. Peter. *Giap. The Victor in Vietnam.* Fourth Estate. 1993. Pages 69–70.

[50] Notin. Page 380.

[51] Ibid. Page 381.

[52] Ibid.

[53] Ibid.

[54] Lacouture, Jean. *De Gaulle: The Ruler. 1944–1970.* Harper Collins 1990. Pages 87–89. & Notin Page 383.

[55] Compagnon. Page 547.
[56] Duiker – Page 357. & Antony Beevor (with Artemis Cooper) *Paris after the Liberation*. Hamish Hamiilton 1994. Pages 269–70. & Julian Jackson *France. The Dark Years. 1940–1944*. OUP. Page 419.
[57] Duiker. Pages 356–57.
[58] Compagnon. Pages 551–52.
[59] Notin. Pages 387–88.
[60] Lacouture, Jean. *Ho Chi Minh*. Pelican Press 1968. Page 37.
[61] Duiker. Page 358.
[62] Ibid. Page 359.
[63] Lacouture. *Ho Chi Minh*. Pages 106–07.
[64] Duiker. Pages 359–60.
[65] Ibid.
[66] Ibid. & Compagnon. Page 553.
[67] Massu. Pages 268–70.
[68] Ibid.
[69] Compagnon. Pages 553–54. & Duiker. Page 362.
[70] Duiker. Page 363.
[71] Massu. Pages 270–71.
[72] Ibid.
[73] Duiker. Page 365.
[74] Lacouture. *Ho Chi Minh*. Pages 121–22.
[75] Notin. Page 399.
[76] Lacouture. *De Gaulle. The Ruler. 1945–1970*. Collins 1990. Pages 87-88.
[77] Notin. Page 400. Quoting a communist newspaper.
[78] Compagnon. Pages 562–63.
[79] Notin. Page 402.
[80] Ibid. Page 404.
[81] Ibid. Page 405.
[82] Ibid.
[83] Duiker. Pages 368–69.
[84] Ibid. Pages 370–72.
[85] Notin. Pages 406–08.
[86] Vézinet, General Adolphe. *Le général Leclerc*. Éditions France-Empire. 1997. Page 231.
[87] Martell. Pages 426–27.
[88] Ibid. 427–28.
[89] Notin. Page 417.
[90] Martell. Page 431.
[91] Notin. Page 420.
[92] Martell. 431–32. & Lacouture. *Ho Chi Minh*. Pages 140–41.
[93] Ibid. Page 142.
[94] Ibid. Page 144.
[95] Ibid. Pages 145–47.
[96] Notin. Pages 427–28.
[97] Ibid. Page 430.
[98] Compagnon. Pages 576–77.

[99] Notin. Page 432.

[100] Lacouture. *Ho Chi Minh.* Pages 154–55.

[101] Compagnon. Page 577.

[102] Notin. Page 433. Quoting a note by Sainteny.

[103] Compagnon. Page 578.

[104] Notin. Pages 434–35.

[105] Lacouture. *Ho Chi Minh.* Pages 155–56.

[106] Compagnon. Page 578–79. & Duiker. Pages 401–02.

[107] Martel. Pages 442–43.

[108] Ibid.

[109] Notin. Pages 445–47.

[110] Ibid. Pages 451–52 & Windrow, Martin. *The Last Valley.* Weidenfeld 2004. Page 86.

CHAPTER 15

[1] Notin, Jean Christophe. *Leclerc.* Perrin 2005. Pages 453–55.

[2] Ibid.

[3] Ibid. Page 470.

[4] Ibid. Pages 458–60.

[5] Ibid. Pages 462–64.

[6] Ibid. Pages 469–70.

[7] Ibid. Page 475.

[8] Ibid. Page 473.

[9] Madame Benedicte de Francqueville interviewed by Notin. Page 475.

[10] La Maziere, Christian de. *Le reveur casqué.* Éditions Robert Laffont. 1972.

[11] Ibid.

[12] Gribius, André. *Une vie d'officier.* Éditons France Empire. 1971. Page 151.

[13] Boissieu, Alain de. *Pour servir le Général. 1946–1970.* Plon. 1982 & 1990. Page 38.

BIBLIOGRAPHY

Ambrose, Stephen. *Eisenhower.* Simon and Schuster, 1990.

Ambrose, Stephen. *Band of Brothers.* Simon and Schuster, 1992.

Atkinson, Rick. *An Army at Dawn.* Little Brown, 2003.

Bagnold, Ralph A. *Sand, Wind and War.* University of Arizona Press, 1990.

Barber, Laurie & John Tonkin-Covell. *Freyberg. Churchill's Salamander.* Hutchinson, 1989.

Beevor, Antony & Artemis Cooper. *Paris after the Liberation.* Hamish Hamilton, 1994.

Beevor, Antony. *D-Day.* Penguin Viking, 2009.

Bierman, John & Collin Smith. *Alamein. War without Hate.* Penguin Viking, 2002.

de Boissieu, Général Alain. *Pour combattre avec de Gaulle.* Plon, 1991.

Bryant, Arthur. *The Turn of the Tide.* Collins, 1959

Bryant, Arthur. *Triumph in the West.* Collins, 1959.

Calvocoressi, Peter & Guy Wint. *Total War.* Allen Lane, 1972.

Cave-Brown, Antony. *Bodyguard of Lies.* W.H. Allen, 1976.

von Choltitz, General Dietrich. *de Sébastopol a Paris.* (German *Soldat unter Soldaten*) Éditons J'ai lu (Flammarion), 1964.

Clayton, Antony. *France, Soldiers and Africa.* Brasseys, 1988.

Clayton, Antony. *Three Marshals of France. Leadership after Trauma.* Brasseys, 1992.

Costello, John. *The Pacific War.* Collins, 1981.

Costello, John. *Love Sex and War.* Collins, 1985.

Compagnon, Général Jean. *Leclerc. Maréchal de France.* Flammarion, 1994.

Collins, Larry & Dominique Lapierre. *Is Paris Burning?* Victor Gollancz Ltd, 1965.

Cooper, Duff. *Old Men Forget.* Hart-Davis, 1953.

Corbonnois, Didier. *L'Odyssée de la Colonne Leclerc.* Histoire et Collections, 2003.

Curtis, Michael. *Verdict on Vichy.* Weidenfeld and Nicolson, 2002.

Dansette, Adrien. *Leclerc.* Flammarion, 1952.

Dansette, Adrien. *Histoire de la Libération de Paris.* Fayard, 1946.

De Gaulle, Charles. *Mémoires de Guerre. L'Appel.* Librairie Plon, 1954.

De Gaulle, Charles. *Memoires de Guerre, L'Unité.* Librairie Plon, 1956.

De Gaulle, Charles. *Mémoires de Guerre. Le Salut.* Librairie Plon, 1959.

De Gaulle, Philippe. *De Gaulle, mon pere.* Librairie Plon, 2003.

Dronne, Raymond. *Le Serment de Kufra.* Les Éditions du Temps, 1965.

Dronne, Raymond. *La Libération de Paris.* Presses de la Cité, 1970.

Duiker, William J. *Ho Chi Minh. A Life.* Hyperion/Theia, 2000.

Egremont, Max. *Under Two Flags. The Life of Major-General Sir Edward Spears.* Weidenfeld, 1997.

Fest, Joachim. *Plotting Hitler's Death.* Weidenfeld and Nicolson, 1996.

Fleming, Fergus. *The Sword and the Cross.* Granta, 2002.

Giap, Vo Nguyen. *The Military Art of People's War.* Monthly Review Press, New York, 1970.

Gilbert, Martin. *Winston S. Churchill. Volume VII. The Road to Victory.* William Heinemann Ltd, 1986.

Gildea, Robert. *Marianne in Chains.* Oxford University Press, 2002.

Gildea, Robert. *France Since 1945.* Oxford University Press, 1996.

Girard, Christian. *Journal de Guerre. 1939–1945.* L'Harmattan, 1975.

Gribius, André. *Une vie d'officer.* Éditions France-Empire, 1971.

Guy, Claude. *En écoutant de Gaulle.* Grasset, 1996.

Hamilton, Nigel. *Monty. Master of the Battlefield 1942–1944.* Hamish Hamilton, 1982.

Hamilton, Nigel. *Monty. The Field Marshall.* Hamish Hamilton, 1986.

Hastings, Max. *Armageddon.* Macmillan, 2004.

Hastings, Max. *Das Reich.* Michael Joseph Ltd, 1983.

Hastings, Max. *Overlord.* Michael Joseph Ltd, 1984.

Hastings, Max. *The Oxford Book of Military Anecdotes.* Oxford University Press, 1985.

Horne, Alistair. *The French Army and Politics. 1870-1970.* Macmillan, 1984.

Horne, Alistair. *Verdun. The Price of Glory.* Macmillan, 1962.

Horne, Alistair. *To Lose a Battle.* Macmillan, 1969.

Horne, Alistair. *A Savage War of Peace.* Macmillan, 1977.

Horne, Alistair. *Seven Ages of Paris.* Macmillan, 2002.

Jackson, Julian. *de Gaulle.* Haus Publishing, 2003.

Jackson, Julian. *France. The Dark Years. 1940–1944.* Oxford University Press, 2001.

Jennings, Eric T. *Vichy in the Tropics.* Stanford University Press, 2001.

Kaiser, Arthur. *Un artisan Alsacien dans la Division Leclerc.* Édition Muller, 2001.

Keegan, John. *Six Armies in Normandy.* Jonathan Cape, 1982.

Kelly, Saul. *The Hunt for Zerzura.* John Murray, 2002.

Kennedy Shaw, William B. *Long Range Desert Group.* Greenhill Books, 1945.

Lacouture, Jean. *De Gaulle. The Rebel. 1890–1944.* Collins Harvill, 1990.

Lacouture, Jean. *De Gaulle. The Ruler. 1944–1970.* Collins Harvill, 1990.

Lacouture, Jean. *Ho Chi Minh.* Pelican, 1968.

Langlade, Paul de. *En Suivant Leclerc.* Au Fil d'Ariane, 1964.

Latimer, John. *Alamein.* John Murray, 2002.

Levisse-Touzé, Christine. *Du capitaine de Hauteclocque au général Leclerc.* Éditions Complexe, 2000.

Levisse-Touzé, Christine. *L'Afrique du nord dans la guerre. 1939–1945.* Albin Michel, 1998.

Levisse-Touzé, Christine. *Les Enjeu de la Libération.* Albin Michel, 1994.

Luck, Hans von. *Panzer Commander.* Cassell. Original Edition Praeger, 1989.

Macdonald, Brigadier Peter. *Giap.* 4th Estate, 1993.

Massu, Général Jacques. *Sept Ans avec Leclerc.* Librairie Plon 1974.

Revised Éditions Rocher, 1997.

Massu, Suzanne. *Quand j'étais Rochambelle.* Grasset, 1969.

Martel, André. *Leclerc. Le Soldat et le politique.* Albin Michel, 1998.

Maule, Henry. *Out of the Sand.* Odhams, 1966.

Nadeau, Jean-Benoit & Julie Barlow. *Sixty Million Frenchmen Can't Be Wrong!* Robson Books, 2004.

Neillands, Robin. *The Battle of Normandy.* Cassell, 2002.

Notin, Jean-Christophe. *Leclerc.* Perrin, 2005.

O'Neil, Robert J. *General Giap. Politician and Strategist.* Cassell Australia, 1969

Ousby, Ian. *The Road to Verdun.* Jonathan Cape, 2002.

Ousby, Ian. *Occupation. The Ordeal of France. 1940–1944.* John Murray,. 1997.

Pakenham, Thomas. *The Scramble for Africa.* Weidenfeld and Nicolson, 1991.

Palin, Michael. *Sahara.* Weidenfeld and Nicolson, 2002.

Paxton. Robert. *Vichy France. 1940–1944.* Knopf, 1972.

Porch, Douglas. *Hitler's Mediterranean Gamble.* Weidenfeld and Nicolson, 2004.

Repiton-Préneuf, Paul. *2e DB. La Compagne de France.* Imprimerie Nationale, 1945.

Sainsbury, Keith. *The North African Landings.* Davis Poynter, 1976.

Schramm, Ritter Wilhelm von. *Conspiracy among Generals. (Der 20 Juli in Paris)* George Allen and Unwin, 1954.

Smith, Colin. *England's Last War Against France. Fighting Vichy.* Weidenfeld, 2009.

Shirer, William L. *The Rise and Fall of the Third Reich.* Secker and Warburg, 1959.

Shirer, William L. *Berlin Diary.* Hamish Hamilton, 1941.

Shulman, Milton. *Defeat in the West.* Greenwood Press. First Published 1947.

Slim, Field Marshall Viscount. *Defeat into Victory.* Cassell, 1956.

Summer, Ian & Francois Vauvillier. *The French Army 1939–45. (1)* Osprey Publishing, 1998.

Summer, Ian & Francois Vauvillier. *The French Army 1939–45. (2)* Osprey Publishing, 1998.

Taittinger, Pierre. . . . *et Paris ne fut pas détruit* Nouvelles Éditions Latines, 1956.

Thomas, Jean-Marie. *Un Marin de la 2e DB. "Mémoires d'un Plouerais."* Édition Muller, 2000.

Thornton, Willis. *The Liberation of Paris.* Hart-Davis, 1963.

Vigneras, Marcel. *Rearming the French.* Office of the Chief of Military History, United States Army, 1957.

Webster, Paul. *Pétain's Crime.* Macmillan, 1990.

Wilmot, Chester. *The Struggle for Europe.* Collins, 1952.

Windrow, Martin. *The Last Valley.* Weidenfeld and Nicolson, 2004.

Vézinet, Général A. *Le Général Leclerc de Hauteclocque, Maréchal de France.* Presses de la Cité, 1974.

Vézy, Edith. *"Gargamelle" mon ambulance guerriere 2e DB.* L'Harmattan, 1994.

Zaloga. Steven J. *Lorraine 1944. Patton Vs Manteuffel.* Osprey, 2000.

Ziegler, Philip. *Mountbatten.* Collins, 1985.

INDEX